UNDERSTANDING THE CITY

Studies in Urban and Social Change

Published by Blackwell in association with the *International Journal of Urban and Regional Research.* Series editors: Chris Pickvance, Margit Mayer and John Walton.

Published

Fragmented Societies
Enzo Mingione

Free Markets and Food Riots
John Walton and David Seddon

Post-Fordism
Ash Amin (ed.)

The People's Home? Social Rented Housing in Europe and America
Michael Harloe

Cities After Socialism: Urban and Regional Change and Conflict in Post-Socialist Societies
Gregory Andrusz, Michael Harloe, and Ivan Szelenyi (eds.)

Urban Poverty and the Underclass: A Reader
Enzo Mingione

Capital Culture: Gender at Work in the City
Linda McDowell

Contemporary Urban Japan: A Sociology of Consumption
John Clammer

Globalizing Cities: A New Spatial Order?
Peter Marcuse and Ronald van Kempen (eds.)

The Social Control of Cities? A Comparative Perspective
Sophie Body-Gendrot

Cinema and the City: Film and Urban Societies in a Global Context
Mark Shiel and Tony Fitzmaurice (eds.)

The New Chinese City: Globalization and Market Reform
John R. Logan (ed.)

Understanding the City: Contemporary and Future Perspectives
John Eade and Christopher Mele (eds.)

Forthcoming

European Cities in a Global Age: A Comparative Perspective
Alan Harding (ed.)

Urban South Africa
Alan Mabin and Susan Parnell

Urban Social Movements and the State
Margit Mayer

UNDERSTANDING THE CITY

CONTEMPORARY AND FUTURE PERSPECTIVES

Edited by
John Eade and
Christopher Mele

Blackwell
Publishers

Editorial Offices:
108 Cowley Road, Oxford OX4 1JF, UK
Tel: +44 (0)1865 791100
350 Main Street, Malden, MA 02148-5018, USA
Tel: +1 781 388 8250

First published 2002 by Blackwell Publishers Ltd

Library of Congress Cataloging-in-Publication Data has been applied for.

ISBN 0–631–22406–8 (hbk) 0–631–22407–6 (pbk)

A catalogue record for this title is available from the British Library.

Set in 10½ on 12 Baskerville MT
by SNP Best-set Typesetter Ltd., Hong Kong
Printed in Great Britain by TJ International, Padstow, Cornwall

For further information on
Blackwell Publishers, visit our website:
www.blackwellpublishers.co.uk

Contents

Illustrations

Tables

Contributors

Kay Anderson is Professor of Geography at Durham University. Her published work includes books and articles on race, place, and nation in Australia and Canada, such as *Vancouver's Chinatown: Racial Discourse in Global Times* (1991). She co-edited (with Fay Gale) *Inventing Places: Studies in Cultural Geography* (1992/1999) and, more recently, she has been writing about the nexus of culture/nature/colonialism.

Sophie Body-Gendrot is a Professor of Political Science and American Civilization at the Sorbonne in Paris and a CNRS researcher. Her research focuses on comparative public policies, urban unrest, ethnic and racial issues, and citizen participation. Among her books in English are *The Social Control of Cities? A Comparative Perspective* (2000), *The Urban Moment* (edited with R. Beauregard, 1999), and *Minorities in European Cities* (edited with M. Martiniello, 2000).

Bryana Britts was awarded an honors degree in Sociology at the University of California, Santa Cruz, where she teaches and researches urban social policy. Currently a postgraduate researcher at the Center for Global, International, and Regional Studies, she is conducting research on globalization, Islamic movements, civil society, and human rights. She plans to pursue a graduate degree in international public policy and human rights advocacy.

Kam Wing Chan is a Professor in Geography at the University of Washington. He received a Ph.D. from the University of Toronto. He is the author of *Cities with Invisible Walls* (1994) and has written extensively on China's urbanization, migration, the household registration system, labor market, and economic development. He has also served as a consultant to the Asian Development Bank, International Labor Office, World Bank, and the Chinese government.

John Eade is Professor of Sociology and Anthropology at Roehampton University of Surrey. He has undertaken research in Calcutta and, for the last twenty years, in the "East End" of London. He is the author of *The Politics of Community* (1989) and *Placing London* (2000). He also edited *Living the Global City* (1997) and co-edited (with Tim Allen) *Divided Europeans* (1999) and (with Michael Sallnow) *Contesting the Sacred* (1991). He is also a founder editor of *Journeys: The International Journal of Travel and Travel Writing* (Berghahn).

J. S. (Jerry) Eades is Professor of Asia Pacific Studies at the Ritusmeikan Asia Pacific University in Beppu, Japan, and Senior Honorary Research Fellow in the Anthropology Department of the University of Kent, where he formerly lectured. His early research concentrated on West Africa, migration, ethnicity, and the informal sector, but after teaching at the University of Tokyo from 1991 to 1994, his interests now extend to the Asia Pacific region, urbanization, the environment, and tourism. He is co-editor of the monograph series, *Japan in Transition* (SUNY Press), and *Asian Anthropologies* (Berghahn).

Ruth Fincher is Professor of Urban Planning and Adjunct Professor of Geography at the University of Melbourne. She received her Ph.D. from Clark University in Worcester, Massachusetts. Her research and writing about inequality and locational disadvantage and the politics of difference in cities are informed by feminist and political economic conceptualizations of institutions. Her recent work includes *Creating Unequal Futures? Rethinking Poverty, Inequality and Disadvantage* (co-edited with Peter Saunders, 2001), *Cities of Difference* (co-edited with Jane M. Jacobs, 1998), and *Australian Poverty Then and Now* (co-edited with John Nieuwenhuysen, 1998). She is currently conducting research on practices of ethnic differentiation in the residential construction industry, for a major project entitled "Building on Ethnicity."

Mark Gottdiener is Professor of Sociology and Adjunct Professor of Architecture and Planning at the University at Buffalo. His interests are in contemporary theory, semiotics, urbanism, and cultural studies. Among his many books are *The Social Production of Urban Space* (2nd edition), *The New Urban Sociology* (2nd edition with Ray Hutchison), *The Theming of America* (2nd edition), *Las Vegas: the Social Production of an All-American City* (with C. Collins and D. Dickens), and, as editor, *New Forms of Consumption*. His latest research is on the emerging social world of air travel and some of this work was recently published as *Living in the Air: Surviving the New Culture of Air Travel.*

Shlomo Hasson is Professor of Geography and Urban Planning at the Hebrew University of Jerusalem. He is the author of *Urban Social Movements in Jerusalem* (1993) and co-author of *Neighbourhood Organizations and the Welfare*

State (1994). He is currently writing on issues of divided cities, identity, culture, and urban morphology.

Michael Indergaard is Associate Professor of Sociology at St. John's University. He has published on economic restructuring and urban redevelopment in journals such as *Urban Affairs Review*, *Social Problems*, and *Research in Urban Sociology*.

Jane M. Jacobs is an Associate Professor in the School of Anthropology, Geography, and Environmental Studies at the University of Melbourne. She gained her Ph.D. from University College, London. She has published widely in the area of cultural geography, with special interests in the cultural politics of cities, contested heritage, and postcolonial spaces. She is the author of *Edge of Empire: Postcolonialism and the City* (1996), co-author (with Ken Gelder) of *Uncanny Australia: Sacredness and Identity in a Postcolonial Nation* (1988), and co-editor (with Ruth Fincher) of *Cities of Difference* (1998). She is currently writing a book on the cultural technologies of the globalized residential highrise.

Jan Lin is Associate Professor of Sociology at Occidental College in Los Angeles. He taught previously at Amherst College and the University of Houston. He is Principal Investigator on a three-year grant from the US Department of Housing and Urban Development to Occidental College for the Northeast Los Angeles Community Outreach Partnership Center. He is the author of *Reconstructing Chinatown: Ethnic Enclave, Global Change* (1998). He is currently engaged in research for a forthcoming book, tentatively titled: *Bright-Light Company Town: Redevelopment, Globalization, and Labor in Hollywood.*

Paul M. Lubeck is Professor of Sociology and Director of the Center for Global, International, and Regional Studies at the University of California, Santa Cruz. His first book, *Islam and Urban Labor in Northern Nigeria: The Making of a Muslim Working Class*, won the Herskovits Prize. Besides researching the potential of information technology as a regional development strategy in Southeast Asia, Mexico, and Africa, Lubeck directs a Carnegie Corporation-funded working group analyzing the impact of globalization and Islamic social movements on the capacity of national states to govern and sustain national identities.

Peter Marcuse is Professor of Urban Planning at Columbia University in New York City, where he teaches urban planning. He has also taught in the Union of South Africa and in both West and East Germany. He has written extensively on housing, urban development, and globalization. His most recent book, co-edited with Ronald van Kempen, is *Globalizing Cities: A New Spatial Order?* (1999). He is working on a book on the history of working-class housing in New York City.

Christopher Mele is Associate Professor of Sociology at the University at Buffalo. He is the author of *Selling the Lower East Side: Culture, Real Estate, and Resistance in New York City* (2000) and a number of articles on urban development and residential development in New York. He is currently completing a book-length study of regional development in southeastern North Carolina.

Leonard Nevarez is Assistant Professor of Sociology at Vassar College. He writes on corporate power and urban politics in the new economy, high-technology work and organizations, and the political economy of natural resource development. He is currently publishing a book on the local politics of "new economy" industry.

Chris Pickvance is Professor of Urban Studies at the University of Kent at Canterbury. His interests include urban theory, urban protest, locality, comparative analysis, and Central and Eastern Europe. He co-edited (with E. Preteceille) *State Restructuring and Local Power* (1991) and (with K. Lang-Pickvance and N. Manning) *Environmental and Housing Movements: Grassroots Experience in Hungary, Russia and Estonia* (1997). He is currently writing a book on local environmental policy implementation in Hungary.

Alexander J. Reichl is an Associate Professor of Political Science at Queens College of the City University of New York. He is the author of *Reconstructing Times Square: Politics and Culture in Urban Development* (1999), and he has published in the *Journal of Urban Affairs* and *Urban Affairs Review*. His current research examines the place of public housing in the changing social and physical landscape of US cities.

David M. Smith retired from his post as Professor of Geography at Queen Mary, University of London, in 2001. His research interests cover geographical perspectives on inequality, social justice, and morality, combining theory with case studies set in the United States, Eastern Europe, Israel, and South Africa. His books include *Geography and Social Justice* (1994), *Human Geography: A Welfare Approach* (1997), and *Moral Geographies: Ethics in a World of Difference* (2000). He lived and worked in South Africa for a year during the era of apartheid and has been a regular, recent visitor. In addition to publishing papers on South Africa he has edited two collections on urbanization and social change: *Living under Apartheid* (1982) and *The Apartheid City and Beyond* (1992).

Michael Peter Smith is Professor of Community Studies and Development at the University of California-Davis, and a Faculty Associate of the Center for California Studies at the University of California-Berkeley. He has published several influential books on cities, global migration, and urbanism, including *The City and Social Theory* (1979), *The Capitalist City* (1987), *City, State, and Market* (1988), *The Bubbling Cauldron* (1995), *Transnationalism from Below* (1998), and, most recently, *Transnational Urbanism* (2001). He is the editor in chief of the *Comparative Urban and Community Research* book series. His latest publication in this series is *City and Nation: Rethinking Place and Identity* (2001), co-edited with Thomas Bender. Smith is currently conducting a bi-national field research project, investigating a transnational community development initiative which links Mexican migrants from Napa, California, to economic and community development projects in their home town of Timbinal, Mexico.

Dorothy J. Solinger is Professor of Political Science in the School of Social Sciences at the University of California, Irvine. Her most recent book is *Contesting Citizenship in Urban China: Peasant Migrants, The State and the Logic of the Market* (1999). She is also co-editor of *States and Sovereignty in the Global Economy* (1999). She has also published *China's Transition from Socialism* (1993), a collection of essays about the reform of socialism in China's urban areas.

Smriti Srinivas received a Ph.D. in Sociology from the Delhi School of Economics, India, and worked at the Institute for Social and Economic Change, Bangalore, India from 1994 to 1997 as an Assistant Professor (Sociology). Between 1997 and 1998 she was attached as a Rockefeller Fellow to the International Center for Advanced Studies, New York University, and was a Mellon Fellow at the Department of Sociology, University of Maryland, College Park, in 1998–9. She is currently Assistant Professor, Division of Comparative Studies in the Humanities, Ohio State University. She is the author of *The Mouths of People, the Voice of God: Buddhists and Muslims in a Frontier Community of Ladakh* (1998), and *Landscapes of Urban Memory: The Sacred and the Civic in India's High-Tech City* (2001). Her research interests are in the study of cities and contemporary religious forms and practices.

Sophie Watson is Professor of Urban Cultures at the University of East London. She was formerly Professor in Policy Studies at the University of Bristol, and Professor of Urban and Regional Planning at Sydney. She wrote (with Peter Murphy) *Surface City: Sydney at the Millennium* (1997), and edited (with K. Gibson) *Metropolis Now* (1995) and *Postmodern Cities and Spaces* (1995), and (with Gary Bridge) *The Blackwell Companion to the City* (2001). She is currently working on public space and the multicultural city.

Series Editors' Preface

In the past three decades there have been dramatic changes in the fortunes of cities and regions, in beliefs about the role of markets and states in society, and in the theories used by social scientists to account for these changes. Many of the cities experiencing crisis in the 1970s have undergone revitalization while others have continued to decline. In Europe and North America new policies have introduced privatization on a broad scale at the expense of collective consumption, and the viability of the welfare state has been challenged. Eastern Europe has witnessed the collapse of state socialism and the uneven implementation of a globally driven market economy. Meanwhile, the less developed nations have suffered punishing austerity programs that divide a few newly industrializing countries from a great many cases of arrested and negative growth.

Social science theories have struggled to encompass these changes. The earlier social organizational and ecological paradigms were criticized by Marxian and Weberian theories, and these in turn have been disputed as all-embracing narratives. The certainties of the past, such as class theory, are gone and the future of urban and regional studies appears relatively open.

The aim of the series *Studies in Urban and Social Change* is to take forward this agenda of issues and theoretical debates. The series is committed to a number of aims but will not prejudge the development of the field. It encourages theoretical works and research monographs on cities and regions. It explores the spatial dimension of society, including the role of agency and of institutional contexts in shaping urban form. It addresses economic and political change from the household to the state. Cities and regions are understood within an international system, the features of which are revealed in comparative and historical analyses.

The series also serves the interests of university classroom and professional readers. It publishes topical accounts of important policy issues (e.g., global adjustment), reviews of debates (e.g., post-Fordism) and collections that explore various facets of major changes (e.g., cities after socialism or the new urban underclass). The series urges a synthesis of research and theory, teaching and practice. Engaging research monographs (e.g., on women and poverty in Mexico or urban culture in Japan) provide vivid teaching materials, just as policy-oriented studies (e.g., of social housing or urban planning) test and redirect theory. The city is analyzed from the top down (e.g., through the gendered culture of investment banks) and the bottom up (e.g., in challenging social movements). Taken together, the volumes in the series reflect the latest developments in urban and regional studies.

Subjects which fall within the scope of the series include: explanations for the rise and fall of cities and regions; economic restructuring and its spatial, class, and gender impact; race and identity; convergence and divergence of the "east" and "west" in social and institutional patterns; new divisions of labor and forms of social exclusion; urban and environmental movements; international migration and capital flows; politics of the urban poor in developing countries; cross-national comparisons of housing, planning, and development; debates on post-Fordism, the consumption sector, and the "new" urban poverty.

Studies in Urban and Social Change addresses an international and interdisciplinary audience of researchers, practitioners, students, and urban enthusiasts. Above all, it endeavors to reach the public with compelling accounts of contemporary society.

Editorial Committee
John Walton, Chair
Margit Mayer
Chris Pickvance

Preface

This volume is the product of a virtual community of scholars who were invited to contribute to a multidisciplinary analysis of (1) the directions that urban research has taken during the 1990s and (2) the avenues that may open up during the early part of the twenty-first century. The book provides a wide-ranging insight into recent debates where the widespread influence of political economy perspectives, as well as other, non-Marxist approaches, has been challenged by explorations of cultural processes and social difference. In particular, *Understanding the City: Contemporary and Future Perspectives* shows the degree to which a middle ground has emerged between political economy and cultural turn approaches.

We are grateful to the editors of the Blackwell *Studies in Urban and Social Change* series, especially Chris Pickvance and John Walton, for inviting us to produce this volume. They readily responded to our ideas and to the usual twists and turns involved in compiling a multi-authored work. Indeed, Chris Pickvance generously agreed to contribute a chapter on developments in Central and Eastern Europe. Sarah Falkus and Joanna Pyke at Blackwell also provided support and advice during the preparation of the volume. We thank Christina Weber and Joan A. Cabral, graduate students in sociology at the University of Buffalo, for their editing assistance. Last but not least, we should like to thank our colleagues for their forbearance and understanding. A special debt of gratitude is owed by John Eade to his wife, Caroline Egan-Strang, who understands well the obsessions of academics.

John Eade
Christopher Mele

Part I
Introduction

1
Understanding the City

John Eade and Christopher Mele

The beginning of the twenty-first century is an exciting time for those wanting to understand the city. There is a growing realization that the "cultural turn," through its emphasis on meaning, identity and the politics of difference, for example, provides the cutting edge of urban research. At the same time the cultural turn has contributed to the fragmentation of urban studies and has had little impact on traditional urban investigations. When culturalist analyses of cities have directly engaged with political economy or the older urban ecology approaches, they have usually sought to move beyond those perspectives. Here we resist this tendency and explore the dynamic interplay between the cultural turn and political economy. We want to contribute to closing this gap through explorations of a middle ground where the traditional concerns within urban studies – restructuring, globalization, North/South urbanization, for instance – may intersect with culturalist approaches. In *Understanding the City: Contemporary and Future Perspectives*, we aim to provide the first concerted effort at addressing this emergent middle ground.

What, then, does "understanding the city" entail? In our opinion it does *not* mean a descriptive survey of contemporary epistemological and theoretical approaches to the city. Furthermore, we do not want to place ourselves within a unified body (school or paradigm) of scholarship frozen in a particular moment of time or based exclusively upon a limited range (i.e., Western) of cases. We prefer to define "understanding" as an ongoing and continual transdisciplinary practice: an enterprise which is both an individual process of scholarly research and writing, *and* a collective dialogue with other people's work. This is an enterprise which corresponds to changes not only in the social world (globalization, migration, etc.) but also within the larger theoretical advances that derive from those changes and seek to comprehend (and change) them, such as feminist theory, postcolonialism, and poststructuralism.

In practical terms, understanding the city consists of multiple and modest endeavors aiming to reconcile the ways in which urban social processes (comprised of the cultural as well as the political and economic) are constituted at particular historical moments. At the same, this approach accepts that the reconciliation can never be fully comprehensive nor complete. It insists on an open scholarly awareness (recognition – but not necessarily full inclusion) of theoretical and empirical advances. It also calls for a conscious acknowledgment of the significance of structural forms of political economy and the indeterminacy of social and cultural processes to one's own work and to urban studies in general.

Perhaps most importantly, the perspective affirms that the initial issues of power, conflict, and social resistance in the urban context, which defined a paradigm shift three decades ago, remain critical. Those concerns are clearly political economic as well as cultural and social. The work of understanding the city is, therefore, not to fix and define, once and for all, the relationship between (or hierarchy among) the social, the cultural, and the political economic. Rather, it needs to problematize these connections in particular cities and time periods and continuously strive to develop new and innovative ways to comprehend their intersections.

The theoretical acknowledgment of the importance of signification and of the indeterminacy of the social to urban studies has, if anything, heightened the need for careful empirical work that produces situated knowledges (as opposed to static models or all-encompassing theories) about the city. While no single epistemology or related methodology appears comparatively better suited for understanding the city, the approaches taken by the contributors to *Understanding the City* identify a valuable set of prescriptions and precautions for urban studies. They examine the need for:

1 reconceptualizing scale beyond the simplified micro/macro (global–local) and, consequently, the city as a process as opposed to a fixed and defined object;
2 developing a more comprehensive conceptualization of agency as constitutive of race, class, ethnicity, sexuality, gender, and their intersections, as well as the dynamic and fluid nature of their formation;
3 integrating the analysis of rhetoric and urban discourses in the production of urban spaces and consequent struggles over representation, signification, and meanings of the city;
4 analyzing the important role played by memory and the imaginary as interpretive schema by which different social groups experience and know the city;
5 paying careful attention to everyday practices and experience to gauging the relevance of structural processes (and vice versa);
6 rejecting the conventional positivist inclination to devise models or exemplars based on a single case;
7 being wary of any simplistic adaptation of Western-based theories to study cities outside the West and affirming historical specificity and the

distinctiveness of cultural and ideological processes as relevant to the understanding of cities – non-Western and Western.

Yet before we proceed to a detailed introduction to the chapters comprising this volume, we want to develop our view of how we have come to this current, exciting, and emergent juncture in urban studies, where the city stands as a central subject of debate and research.

Symbols, Signs, and Discourse

The aftermath of the political and social upheavals of 1968 prompted a dramatic critique of urban studies in the West and hastened along a paradigmatic shift in the epistemologies, theories, and methods of studying the city. This shift crystallized over time as a considerable body of scholarship linked various aspects of cities and their historical and contemporary formations to capitalist political economic processes. Influenced by Karl Marx's writings (and, to varying degrees, by Max Weber's), post-1968 urban studies in the United States and Western Europe was committed to understanding processes of accumulation, including real estate speculation, investment, and disinvestment and the importance of state intervention in urban processes such as private development. The built environment of the city was a social construct subjected to dominant power relations, exploitation, and conflict always in play in capitalist social formations. Simultaneously, mounting a critique of mainstream urban studies (particularly, human ecology) and addressing social justice concerns, these structural approaches sought to disentangle the political and economic processes producing uneven development within, and between, cities and, for that reason, the debilitating effects upon the housing conditions, employment opportunities, and overall lifestyles of the urban poor and ethnic and racial minorities. Underlying most writings was a strong normative affirmation of the potential for emancipatory class politics or social movements.

Despite the intellectual legacy of such key figures as Georg Simmel and Walter Benjamin, whose writings on culture and the city are extensive and influential, the (re)emergence of and subsequent challenge from culturalist perspectives came relatively late to urban studies in comparison to other disciplines. Interestingly, the point of entry for most discussions of the centrality of cultural representation and signification to city life was through established concerns fundamental to critical political economy approaches. Following on the heels of David Harvey's influential work, *The Condition of Postmodernity* (1989), in which the interrelationship between cultural changes (postmodernism) and political economic changes (post-Fordism) are clearly articulated, urbanists in North America and Western Europe embarked on efforts to integrate analyses of cultural production and consumption into urban theories. Sharon Zukin's work in the 1990s, in particular, provided the theoretical armature and empirical foundation for the now-accepted claim of cultural signification as intrinsic to the economic structure of the modern city (Zukin 1991, 1995). Significant changes in capitalist accumulation – namely, the shift toward the production of services and spectacle – have placed the analysis of symbols and imagery to the fore of studies of urban development (see King 1996).

New "cultural" fields that have since been instituted in the academy include "tourism/leisure studies" and "consumption studies," but American urbanists have largely approached such studies in the context of political economic considerations. Mark Gottdiener, for example, has developed his notion of "theming" from European and American theories of semiotics and argues that the deployment of cultural forms as place themes is a development strategy in an era of increasing economic competition between cities (Gottdiener 1997). Recent work in a similar vein argues that prevailing discourses and representations about the city are intrinsic to the political economy of urban change, serving as key sources of legitimation and social control over processes such as community abandonment and redevelopment (Mele 2000; Reichl 1999).

Such approaches are evidence of considerable synthesis. As Kian Tajbakhsh notes, they nudge political economic approaches a significant step beyond the orthodoxy of Marxism, especially with respect to the theorization of culture (2001: 20–5). Within such work, the challenge has been to incorporate newer understandings of the symbolic and the cultural without doing away with the traditional focus on the state, class, and urban accumulation. Drawing on poststructuralist theories, it is increasingly apparent that the forms of discourse used to describe, analyze, and construct the city are central to social, cultural, political, and economic processes that produce the city and occur within it. Although material processes, such as the development of the urban built environment and the effects on urban employment, are not ignored, the analytical focus is shifted to the production and interpretation of their meanings. Tactics deployed within the real estate industry, including skillful use of language and the use of symbols to evoke particularly desirable themes, require textual and semiotic analyses. Yet the implications of these symbolic manipulations for material practices within the city are quite clear.

The embrace of the symbolic and discursive within urban studies has, as one would expect, moved beyond reference to political economic implications. The urban imaginary has become viewed as a constitutive element in the social production of the city. Within such conceptualizations, the built form of the city and the interpretive schemas of different social groups are in active engagement. Individuals and social groups make sense of and experience the places where they shop, socialize, and live, thereby shaping and being shaped by past, present, and future urban environments. These imaginings are as diverse and manifold as the social groups inhabiting the city. The ability of certain powerful urban stakeholders (e.g., planners, state bureaucrats, developers, and other city builders) to "realize" their notions of the city over others is not denied. Nonetheless, the focus upon the imaginary illuminates the multiplicity of experience and as such downplays any one notion of the city as defining or overly influencing all others. The imaginary, then, acts and is acted upon through the production of the city.

James Donald has problematized the relationship between the physical and the imaginary – between the vast arrays of city structures and their meaningful articulation in the everyday lives of city dwellers. He shifts toward the subjective experience of the city. Consciousness, memory, and processes of imagination rise to the fore of analysis. Consequently, his approach eschews a linear, causal connection between structure, experience, and action and embraces instead contingent and opaque relations. The city, as Donald writes, is understood as "a historically specific mode of seeing" (1999: 92), narrated and described and represented by different sets of actors with corresponding interests. These imaginings and other experiential processes have consequences for the type of social, economic, and cultural practices and structures that occur within the city and vice versa. Novels, cinema, and other mass media forms mediate these interrelationships between structure and experience.

The Indeterminacy of the Social

As explained earlier, urban studies' approaches in the critical political economy tradition have capably absorbed an analysis of cultural forms into a theory of social production of space. While clearly these approaches were concerned with the city as a force that shapes the everyday lives of urban dwellers, their main intent was to add much-needed complexity to an understanding of the structural forces that produce the city itself. An expansive notion of cultural processes – one that includes a broad range of identities and subjectivities in addition to class – was not a central epistemological concern but was viewed as a contemporary or postmodern condition emanating from materialist conditions (see Harvey 1989).

There were important and early efforts among urban theorists to account for new forms of social difference and identity within the political economic paradigm. Katznelson, in *Marxism and the City* (1993), sought to explain the emergence of new forms of group identities (ethnicity, race, territory) not by moving beyond Marxism but pushing and stretching the theoretical framework to include these new realities. Castells, particularly in *The City and the Grassroots* (1983), sought to incorporate new forms of social identities (other than class) by going even further and moving beyond conventional Marxist frameworks, through an emphasis on consumption processes and their role in the reproduction of labor.

The limitations of these approaches within political economy were laid bare in feminist theoretical advances, which questioned the emphasis placed on economic factors, especially by class-based theories. Among other things, feminist theories of difference have pointed toward the inadequacy of efforts to "capture" or fix the complexity of social life, to freeze various aspects of identity and subjectivity into categories, and the inability to allow for intersections, fluidity, and hybridity of social relations. Approaches wedded to a structuralist epistemology exclude subjective processes of becoming (what we are calling social indeterminacy) from understandings of the social and the cultural. Feminist theories draw our attention to the ways in which knowledge about the city and our study of that knowledge is created by discourses that reflect gendered power relations. The privileged representation of the city as site of, and for, capitalist reproduction is criticized as both narrow and excluding (see Deutsche 1991). Feminist critiques of the political economy of gentrification, for example, challenged the exclusive focus on the class relations in urban restructuring, arguing that it renders silent (and therefore insignificant) the powerful gender dimension inherent in the production and consumption of the city.

Along with feminist theory, postcolonial perspectives, which we address more fully in the following section, have questioned the normative assumptions implicit within political economy analysis and critiqued essentialized conceptions of class, race, gender, and sexuality. Their attention to the multiple and complex constitution of subjectivities seeks to challenge more conventional analyses of urban enclaves, "ghettoes," local communities, and the First World/Third World dichotomy. Work in this vein has called attention to the connections between social difference (defined both in its representational forms and in terms of subjectivity formation) and spatial practices. While retaining interest in the material consequences of these practices, these works tend to focus on revealing the larger power dynamics that the deployment of representations tap into, such as marginalization and exploitation. Cities, then, may be seen as the materialization of practices which are not simply political economic but also cultural. Likewise, spatial forms and the design of the built environment have considerable influence upon the constitution of social identities and subjectivities – the city as productive.

Postcolonialism, Transnationalism, and Globalization

Analytical interest in social difference and cultural heterogeneity has intensified as scholars whose work intersects or overlaps with postcolonial and transnational studies have turned their gaze to the study of the city. Postcolonial and transnational studies have had a profound influence upon contemporary urban studies, prompting a critical interrogation of many of the field's earlier theoretical assumptions. Postcolonialism and transnationalism represent a multiplicity of disciplinary focuses and related epistemologies and methodologies. Nonetheless, there are certain premises which these approaches share and which have a direct bearing on the study of the city. Both perspectives point toward the narrative of a privileged center infused in representations of the West and its relations to the "other" and the system of binaries that have historically categorized and essentialized subjects. Bhabha's *Nation and Narration* (1990), for example, dismantles and unmasks the constitution of the colonized world by the West – conceptions which define the Third World as unidimensional and naturally subordinate.

Such unmasking is part of a larger project of recognizing how given truths (nations, authorities, etc.) have been produced historically and how categories of social difference and identity have been accorded the appearance of stability and permanence. Both postcolonial and transnational studies call for analyses which destabilize (oversimplified) binaries and examine interstitial, in-between (borders) and overlapping (hybrid) spaces where subjectivities and identities are negotiated. Race, gender, sexuality, and class, for example, do not exist as discrete categories in isolation but come into being through conflict and negotiation with each other. Arjun Appadurai's ethnoscapes, mediascapes, technoscapes, financescapes, and ideoscapes, for example, constitute nonhierarchical realms of experience which reflect the complex everyday realities of tourists, refugees, exiles, and immigrants, among others (Appadurai 1990).

This focus on the terrain of intersubjectivity and experience has direct implications for urban analysis outside the political economy tradition. There has been considerable recent interest in the stranger as a primary feature of urban society, prompting scholars to return to the works of Georg Simmel. Simmel's work on the stranger is relevant to the analysis of diaspora and other indeterminacies of the global migrant experience – of mobility, shifting frames of reference, and not belonging. Recent discussions of postcolonialism raise the issue of the relevance of 1970s and 1980s Weberian analyses of British urban conflicts in the context of both race and ethnicity, for example (see Rex and Moore 1967; Rex and Tomlinson 1979), as well as non-Marxist empirical analyses of urban politics and policy.

The concern with identity, borders, and hybridity in postcolonial conditions has led some scholars to analyze the social and cultural dimensions of globalization. They have focused on so-called global cities, where they have placed less emphasis on the political economic dimensions of flows and more on the impact (and feedback) on social and cultural relations at the local level.

The effect is a greater understanding of how globalization is locally expressed – not as an unambiguous effect of structural processes of globalization but as experienced and understood by various social groups within the city. The potential for further synthesis here is promising, because such approaches concede the importance of political economic theories of globalization and yet embrace the indeterminacy of the social. Flows of information, capital, and people heighten the indeterminacy of social relations at the local level.

Structural processes, such as accumulation, which further material inequalities, are no less apparent, but the range of meanings attached to such processes and the experiences of them by different social groups resist simplistic categorization. Instead, meaning and experience at the local level are increasingly mediated by transnational and global processes, further compounding the complexity of social relations (community organizing and resistance, attachments to neighborhood, the construction of diasporic communities, etc.) within the city. Local, bounded physical spaces of neighborhoods are not necessarily the spatial referent for new forms of identity and the multiplicity of social identities. For transnational migrants, for example, notions of home and community are inclusive of multiple and often contradictory spaces and are fused from an array of imaginations, personal memories, and mediated representations.

So far this complex fusion has been explored by relatively few urban scholars. The rich empirical research on transnationalism, supported by national funding in both the United States and Britain, has largely taken the city as the background to discussion of social and cultural processes among migrant communities. Many studies of Britain's "ethnic minorities," for example, are still framed within an anthropological tradition which affirms the determining role of kinship and marriage regulations, related to religious practices, in sustaining communal bonds across national borders (see Ballard 1994; Werbner 1997; Shaw 2001).

The limitations of this approach have been exposed by Brah (1996), Anthias (1998), and Eade (2000), for example, as well as by an emerging cohort of urbanists (Alexander 1996; Sharma et al. 1996; Fortier 2000) who have been inspired by the work of Stuart Hall and Paul Gilroy, in particular. Critical work has also been developed by a group of scholars at Roehampton in the southwestern suburbs of the global city – London. Their blend of theoretical and empirical work was the basis for *Living the Global City* (Eade 1997), where they sought to locate global flows within the context of the social. M. P. Smith (2000 and chapter 6 in this volume) takes forward their emphasis on the social, while the work of Fincher and Jacobs (1998 and, with Anderson, chapter 2 in this volume) and Marcuse's critique of Castells (see chapter 7 below) also develop this area in quite different ways.

Toward Understanding the City

The more recent emphasis in critical social theory on identities and difference has problematized the assumption within political economy approaches that structural processes order – in ways both obvious and unambiguous – social relations and conditions within the contemporary city. Influenced by feminist and poststructuralist theories, the focus upon the construction of social difference demands an examination of the social world from varied perspectives of race, class, gender, sexuality, and other identifying social attachments in which social positions do not reflect a stable range of interests. There are always practices and related identities that exist outside the gaze of social structure, that exist "in the cracks that particular conjunctions open in the surveillance of proprietary powers" (de Certeau 1984: 37).

Recent work on the complex ways in which social difference, subjectivities, and identities are constituted and mediated problematize positivist-oriented efforts to demonstrate patterns of (structural) cause and (social) effect. The wide range of different subject positions within and among social groups who inhabit the city can never be bundled together as singular, all-inclusive categories that operate simply in relation to social structures. Following, it becomes necessary within an analysis of the city to map subjects (in short, to specify their formations and linkages to structural processes). These approaches suggest identities are terrains in which various social processes (in addition to economics) are imprinted (if temporarily) in complex, overlapping patterns (Fincher and Jacobs 1998; Featherstone and Lash 1999; Yon 2000).

In the problematizing of the constitution of subjectivity, the city – as site of multiple differences – becomes pivotal as the location where identities are constituted: the city transforms and is transformed by these processes. This, in turn, has led to newer and different meanings of the object of urban studies, the city itself. The city is conceived less as something found or simply "out there" and more as something constituted partially through representation and discourse and as a site of interlocking and conflicting meanings of cultural, political, and economic relations. The wholeness of the city (often presented uncomplicatedly in conventional urban studies, using geographic boundaries to demarcate and define) is viewed not only as a physical entity but also as a narrative device and as a plethora of signs and symbols infused with power relations. These newer approaches are less a critique of political economic modes of urban studies than a plea to move beyond them, to disentangle the processes of social experience and articulation from (the essentializing tendencies of) more materialist-oriented approaches.

About this Volume

This volume has been shaped around the theoretical and substantive interests of people from various disciplines, who are working on urban issues around the globe. We invited people who had not only already contributed to the intersection between culturalist and political economy approaches through edited volumes and single-authored work, for example, but also those who were beginning to examine the impact of these approaches within their area of urban research.

From the individual responses to our invitation a volume of six parts has emerged. After this Introduction, which comprises Part I, Part II brings together those who have mostly worked outside the confines of American urban sociology. Drawing on feminist perspectives, Anderson, Fincher, Jacobs, and Watson have made highly influential contributions to the development of cultural geography during the last twenty years. Issues of urban social justice in apartheid and post-apartheid South Africa have been a major theme of D. M. Smith's work, while Body-Gendrot has focused on urban violence in both the United States and Western Europe.

The opening chapter in Part II carefully explores the emergence of a middle ground between political economy and the cultural turn. The influence of the cultural turn on their approach is evident as Ruth Fincher, Jane M. Jacobs, and Kay Anderson begin by discussing the ways in which the "study of cities produces scripts of their coming into being, their logics and their inhabitants." Difference-directed rescriptings have "opened out important new questions that enhance our understandings of cities, implore us to pursue new trajectories of inquiry, and offer invigorated scope for constructing more just cities." These rescriptings reveal the limitations of three highly influential contemporary scripts – global city analyses, the "un-natural" city, and the "disorderly" city.

Yet their analysis of difference leads them toward, rather than away from, the concerns of political economy. They conclude that "difference perspectives protect against indifference to the subtle and diverse ways that injustice can be perpetuated" and provide the political means to uncover varied discriminations. These perspectives help "define new ways to be politically effective, as well as producing significant situated knowledges."

In chapter 3 Sophie Watson emphasizes the cultural turn's critique of early political economy approaches toward the public city. She examines the ways in which "the 'public' in all its various guises has been subject to a series of radical transformations during the last two decades." The attempt by Orthodox Jews in north London to establish an *eruv* is examined to support her argument that the "new approaches have opened up, or in some cases excavated, different terrains which extend the boundaries of what it means to construct a more fully democratic public realm." The case study reveals that "how to live difference in the city, especially when it is awkward to address rather than easy to celebrate the exotic, has to be a central focus of urban research and action over the following decades." Moreover, the power of symbolic space is revealed through a clash between the rational city of planning discourse and a symbolic city constructed through an ancient Jewish text. The cultural turn produces new understandings of the material inequalities and divisions highlighted by earlier political economy approaches. A more just city can be created through the new ways of thinking about the public city and public space.

The issues involved in creating a more just city are also investigated by David M. Smith. Focusing on the city and urbanization in apartheid and post-apartheid South Africa, he reviews the debate about social justice and the city during the last thirty years. He draws on such influential figures as Harvey, Rawls, Walzer, and Young, as well as making vivid use of his own experience and fieldnotes, to argue that "the challenge ahead is . . . not so much social scientific as ethical: to help devise a new theory of the good, incorporating inclusive material standards combined with an ethic of responsibility to the weak and vulnerable, persuasive enough to be a source of moral motivation as well as of social understanding. This would be progress in 'urban studies.'"

The theme of social justice is continued in chapter 5. Sophie Body-Gendrot considers changing views concerning urban violence from the perspective of the criminal justice system. She outlines the development of urban violence and its causes during the 1980s and 1990s through a comparison between French and American cities. She tracks the movement toward the contemporary "politicization of the crime issue" and the role played by "politicians, the media, and public opinion spokespersons [in taking] advantage of a global feeling of insecurity to pursue their own strategies." A new situation has emerged where elites are more willing to legitimate repressive policies than support preventive measures. This process is not globally uniform since it is shaped by local conditions across the United States and Europe. France and many other European countries subscribe to "social prevention" and reject policies articulated initially in America. Moreover, across Europe the symbolic unity of civic life is "often more valued than the expression of differences," and urban violence is seen as avoidable. She ends on a more upbeat note than David M. Smith, calling for a "new urban literature" which can tell us "the good news" – presumably, where our understanding of urban violence in America can draw on European traditions rather than the other way round.

In Part III we bring together three American urbanists who advance a critique of highly influential contemporary perspectives in order to propose future directions for research. Michael Peter Smith sets out an urban research agenda for the twenty-first century through a theorizing of the local and global. He challenges two approaches: (1) understanding locality as an embedded community where personal meanings, cultural values, and "traditional ways of life are enunciated and lived," and (2) where the global replaces the urban "as a metaphor for the central outside threat to the primary social ties binding communities." He questions both the structuralist "grand narratives of macro-social development" advanced by Harvey and Castells, for example, and the postmodern celebration of local ethnography, "partial truths," and the postcolonial subject.

Through a reimagination of the politics of everyday life, Smith moves toward "a transnationalized mode of ethnographic practice." Setting out the deficiencies of various perspectives, he argues for a careful analysis of "the intricacy involved in sorting out the social interactions and processes at multiple spatial scales that constitute the complex politics of place-making under contemporary conditions of transnational interconnectivity." Smith wants to move beyond not only the structuralist formulations of such leading urbanists as Harvey and Castells, but also the postmodern cultural studies and the study of the politics of everyday life. He advocates an analysis of "transnational urbanism" where the social is reintroduced and where the focus is on "power relations and meaning-making practices."

We then move to Peter Marcuse's critique of Castells's recent work on the "information age" which has had such a deep impact on the issues discussed by Michael Peter Smith. Marcuse argues that Castells has abandoned his neo-Marxist stance of the late 1960s and 1970s as he has been caught up in the contemporary enthusiasm for the study of the information age and globalization. Although he eagerly acknowledges Castells's vital contribution to urban studies over the last four decades, Marcuse regards his more recent publications as an implicit depoliticization where power and conflict disappear, classes play a subordinate role, and capitalism is ambiguously conflated with globalization. Powerful "groupings, actors and agents," shaping contemporary globalization, are replaced by a highly generalized "we" who can only hope to persuade "those in power" to respond to "our" interests. Castells remains committed to changing society but in ways which suppress the political. Marcuse's critique leaves us with a challenge – how to reformulate political economic perspectives in ways which embrace the ambiguous complexity of transnational linkages, global flows of capital, goods, information, and people, and local transformations where class solidarities decline in the face of fragmentary identity movements.

The cultural turn during the 1990s has been deeply influenced by geographers working at the University of California's Los Angeles campus. Ed Soja's publications have made a major contribution to postmodern investigations of space, while Soja's colleague, Michael Dear, has outlined an agenda for cultural geography's study of postmodern urban society in *The Postmodern*

Urban Condition (2000). There have been some moves toward a battle of the schools, with the Chicago School's approach toward the modern city being contrasted with its apparent successor – the LA School – and its study of Los Angeles as the archetypal, postmodern, "edge" city.

Mark Gottdiener seeks to cut the LA School down to size. In an impassioned critique, he challenges what he sees as the media hyping of particular LA academics. More generally, he questions the promotion of Los Angeles as "the exemplary suburban auto-era city" and the attempt to replace the Chicago School. Both moves fail to take into consideration the course of history. Suburbanization characterizes all American cities while the "Chicago School paradigm has been dead and buried for decades." The "new urban sociology," developed across the United States since the late 1970s, has directed attention away from the "bounded, centralized city that organizes its hinterland" toward multi-centered metropolitan regions where centralized cities are absorbed "in a matrix of increasingly personal, political, and business decisions." Indeed, some areas of the country have no centralized cities at all. Orange County, for example, is typical of areas which are "neither suburbs nor cities, yet they are fully urbanized." Hence, for Gottdiener, Las Vegas, rather than Los Angeles, exemplifies the multi-centered metropolitan region, as well as the decentered, postmodern cultural forces highlighted by Soja and Dear. Having said this, Gottdiener also claims that we must move beyond looking at particular cities as exemplary; rather, research needs to examine "the processes that have worked and reworked settlement space."

The contributors to Part II indicate the immense influence exercised by American urbanists upon research around the globe. The Chicago School and its later rivals have made a deep impact upon debates concerning urban structures and processes in Europe, the Pacific Rim, and the Middle East, for example. In Part IV we are able to follow these debates, as well as track research pursuing different directions, largely in response to particular historical, political, and ideological conditions. We want especially to draw attention to socialist and postcolonial perspectives, which resist American preoccupations and developmental models based on the assumption that – put crudely – "what America does today the rest of the world will do tomorrow."

Chris Pickvance's contribution to the "new urban sociology" has already been acknowledged by contributors to the previous sections. Here he reviews research undertaken in Central and Eastern Europe "as a context for theorizing about state socialism and post-socialism, and their associated urban patterns." During the 1970s state socialism and urban development became a central theme of international urban sociological debates while research focused on "the pattern of urban development, the allocation of housing, and urban spatial patterns."

International models of industrialization and modernization led to analyses of the degrees to which Central and Eastern European societies were underurbanized. A generic pattern was identified which was "directly attributable to state socialism in its forced growth phase" and which could be applied beyond the region to other state socialist societies and China in particular. Housing allocation was another major theme and a third research question focused on "whether there was a specifically socialist residential social pattern."

Since 1989 the combination of political and economic changes in Central and Eastern European has "provided a unique natural experiment." Rapid transformation challenged the explanatory capacities of social scientists. Pickvance contends that reliance on the "ubiquitous concept of 'transition' has concealed the fact that social science as a whole did not have ready a set of theories capable of understanding the process of macroscopic change" taking place across the region. Although theories of transition have provided limited explanatory purchase, "it remains to be seen" whether the application of "culturally based theories . . . will prove to have a parallel capacity for a comparative understanding of the questions they address."

In the next chapter in Part IV we move to China. Dorothy J. Solinger and Kam Wing Chan claim that urban research here "has not been driven by trends and fads in scholarship so much as it has been shaped by the nature of China itself as fashioned by the state (and later the market), and by the momentous shifts the nation has weathered because of political decisions." The study of Chinese urban processes by Western social scientists has been patchy. Economic geographers and planners have been more in evidence than anthropologists, for example, while cultural issues have only recently been examined. This situation is explained in terms of local exigencies where "three decades of fairly idiosyncratic socialist ideology and practices in China have made a big difference." The late arrival of cultural studies, for example, is partly "a function of the homogeneous nature of Chinese life, at least up until the early 1980s," and urban studies only emerged as a substantial subject during the 1980s and 1990s.

The trends reviewed by Solinger and Chan lead them to suggest two future directions for urban research in China. One locates the country along the same path trodden by "other industrializing, modernizing societies (such as Taiwan)," while the other suggests a much more bumpy journey characterized by conflict and serious social problems. Researchers will need to "develop theories that encompass and interrelate the new urban vitality, as citizens thrive on the new consumption, along with the various types of social breakdowns that accompany the evisceration of past and ruptured solidarities."

The contributors so far have written from the perspective of sociology, planning, criminology, and geography. J. S. Eades (not related to John Eade) introduces an anthropological approach in his survey of urban developments across East and Southeast Asia. He moves quickly from such well-established themes as the contrast between rural and urban society, aging, labor, education, and the family to more recent research, especially consumption, popular culture, and the environment. Analyses of how the global becomes local through consumption, personal choice, and the media have been complemented by research into the political economy of high-speed growth. The interweaving of consumption and the political economy can be seen most strikingly in the urban environment of eastern Asia.

The "rich empirical diversity in urban life," especially in Japan, leads Eades to explore changing theoretical interpretations and Castells's contribution in particular. His discussion of Castells's recent publications concerning the information age leads toward Gottdiener's earlier argument about American cities – "the more advanced, informational, and globalized a society becomes, the more the divisions between town and country become blurred, and the more the concept of what constitutes the city begins to disappear."

Understanding this process has encouraged researchers to work across academic boundaries and to ground analyses of urban culture more firmly in political economy processes than many contributors to the cultural turn would like. This deconstruction ensures that there is no such thing as the "Pacific Asian city," despite the similarities between what has been occurring in Japan and other cities across the region. Looking to the future, Eades suggests that globalization, however defined, has moved researchers toward new subjects and methodologies. The analysis of cultural processes, such as consumption, will go hand in hand with the exploration of the urban environment, leading toward a multi-faceted activism promoted through cyberspace and cybercultures.

In Part V we explore the ways in which the processes outlined in the previous sections operate within different urban contexts. We begin with Smriti Srinivas's chapter on the Indian city of Bangalore, which lies at the heart of the country's "Silicon Valley." She wants to build on "subaltern histories of the sociological discipline" so that she can advance beyond political economy and culturalist approaches. Since Indian urban sociology has been seriously hampered by the disconnection between sociology and history, Srinivas wants to analyze "discourses of return, 'quest' stories that tie institutional and personal biographies together" in the context of five models of the city. These narratives are related to the "creation of new metropolitan fringes" which occupy sites "abundant with spatial and ritual memories." Discourses of return use the languages of a "sacred quest" which are explored through a case study of the Sai Baba cult and three religious sites on the fringes of Bangalore. Through a mnemonics of space and an analysis of embodied memory, Srinivas reveals "a reorientation within the city, recovering spatially peripheral tracts and older axes of the city from a zone of urban amnesia, and also using contemporaneous axes and institutional sites in other patterns of meaning." In the process she seeks to reveal the lacunae in models of the city and stage "other possibilities of the urban tied to the inner, affective, cultural, and spiritual worlds of the subject of the metropolis."

History is also the focus of Shlomo Hasson's investigation of urban morphology, culture, and power. In the context of Jerusalem he examines the relationship between different cultures and landscapes, the relationship between cultures, and the relationship between landscapes over time. Through a discussion of "urban morphology and design, cultural landscapes, political relationships between landscapes, and the factors that shape these relationships," Hasson shows how the city's landscape embodies three main cultures shaped by (1) religion, (2) nationalism and modernity, and (3) national conflict, consumerism, and globalism.

The premodern, early, and late modern periods in Jerusalem's history refer to specific morphologies of the city which are, in turn, related to religion, the nation-state, and a more recent consumerist society. Roads, residential areas, land-use patterns, public and private space, and the city's outskirts are shaped by these different forces, leading Hasson to ask how the three cities of Jerusalem relate to one another today. Responses to this question take two forms – a dominant, closed-hegemonic discourse and a subordinate, open-dialogical discourse. The dominance wielded by the closed-hegemonic discourse is explained in terms of three power systems (political, economic, and cultural), but Hasson also explores the resistance strategies adopted by Arab residents and the factional divisions among their Jewish neighbors.

In this struggle the religious premodern city and the nationalist early modern city are dominated by the late modern, outer city. This dominance offers "the potential to reduce tensions and create a city that is less clannish, fanatical, less steeped in ceaseless conflict." At the same time Hasson urges decision-makers to appreciate Jerusalem's other cities and their unity "which lends the city its unique character and image." Urban development depends, therefore, upon understanding and respecting each city's "rules and resources, which crystallized during the course of history."

The final chapter in Part V examines Muslim cities in the Middle East and elsewhere in the context of civil society, social movements, and globalization. Paul Lubeck and Bryana Britts consider the future of the Muslim city where "Muslim discourses and civil society groups coalesce to launch a diverse stream of urban social movements united in their opposition to what they view as an illegitimate and failed postcolonial order." They outline the historical emergence of Islamism or political Islam – a "modern urban movement empowered by a profound discursive shift" across society which challenges the postcolonial nation-state weakened by "neo-liberal global restructuring." This shift is analyzed within the context of political economic structural factors, the Iranian revolution, the development of Islamism in Egypt, "the contradictory positions expressed by women representing themselves in urban public space," as well as "the novel discursive practices of Muslim feminist groups."

The future of Muslim cities will, therefore, be deeply influenced by Islamism because "globalization, state withdrawal, and rising urban inequality create a social milieu ideally suited for the efflorescence of Islamist civil society groups." Islamists' observance of democratic practices once they have acquired power will depend on how far their interests are included by existing regimes. Urban theorists and policy-makers need to engage in dialogue with Islamist movements "and include them in their policy and planning agendas."

In Part VI we focus on three American cities (New York, Las Vegas, and Los Angeles), as well as South California's Silicon Valley. As the other chapters have shown, any discussion of a particular city has to account for both its unique characteristics and the commonalities it shares with other cities. Furthermore, transnational and global processes ensure that the issues investigated are not necessarily bounded by specific administrative and political structures of the city, region, or nation-state.

Consequently, when Michael Indergaard comes to explore new media circuits of innovation, speculation, and urban development in New York, the urban locality is the site for a cyberspatial transformation where the global interweaves with the local. He raises a question already examined more theoretically by the contributors to Part I, in particular: "Can a just and coherent city emerge amidst a swirl of financial, cultural, and technological forces?" Indergaard shares the view of others in this volume – a critical urban theory needs to answer this question by confronting "the problem of reconciling material and cultural analyses." New centers of power will be required to control and explain the relationship between real and virtual business spaces. We must rethink the assumption that "financial flows are divorced from, and antagonistic to, culture and social relations" and explore the ways in which "Silicon Alley has served as an institutional nexus for weaving together circuits and a matrix of power for making relationships, identities, and spaces."

Lower Manhattan illustrates how entrepreneurs have sought to eliminate boundaries between virtual and real worlds. They have broken New York's traditional role as a supplier of venture capital to other parts of the country by organizing district circuits through social networks. Rather than global capital flows shaping local fortunes, Silicon Alley actors were able to connect "the dot.com segment to the bull market." New media stock options and images formed a currency which led to a real estate boom in Manhattan which threatened to displace "not just individual firms but entire sectors" in the older economy – a threat alleviated by the Spring 2000 crash. However, images of Silicon Alley are employed by real estate developers as the focus shifts to the Times Square area.

Venture capitalists and real estate developers have "mobilized power through their ability to create and link circuits, and convert 'currencies.'" As for the question of social justice, imagined cyberspace has played a key role "in transforming real space and in creating new forms of inequality." City government has encouraged this process through supporting a "development that is neither inclusive nor sustainable" and a strategy which promotes the "hypergrowth of a new monoculture in the short term, but depletes the city's rich milieu."

The relationship between cultural processes and political economy is also the principal theme of Alexander J. Reichl's study of sex, political economy, and public space. He locates the cultural turn within "a long tradition of drawing on the urban landscape as a blueprint to the circuitry of power." Culture does not simply provide "ideological support for the capitalist order" but plays a crucial role in producing economic wealth. However, more clarity is required concerning "how new cultural forms of urban development might serve as an instrument of political power." Recent political developments in the United States make it even more important to understand "the impact of spatial practices on democratic political life."

Reichl pursues this argument through an empirical study of "sex-related adult entertainment" in Las Vegas and New York. Sexual practices promise new insights into the relationship between culture and urban political economy because they are a contested terrain. A prominent feature of this contestation in both cities is the institutional "desire to control public space." This conflict is expressed through different political strategies in the two cities: "Adult entertainment circulated differently into the symbolic representations of each city, reinforcing the seductive appeal of Las Vegas and the perceptions of disorder and decline in New York."

Reichl concludes his chapter by linking his empirical analysis to theories concerning the political value of public space. This space should be understood as a "forum for open political expression" where sex-related businesses, for example, should be governed by standards concerning the use of that space. Reliance should be placed on local political action rather than zoning laws. Democratic, First Amendment public space "presupposes nothing about who should be present or what they should be 'saying'; but it does presuppose a limited degree of corporate or state control, such as that exercised by the casinos of Las Vegas or the public–private authorities in charge of Times Square. Above all, a valuable public space must be a place of possibility."

Leonard Nevarez also wants to engage the poststructural (cultural) turn through his training as an urban political economist. He focuses on reassessing corporate elites in the light of two developments: (1) the challenge presented by sociospatial and poststructural perspectives to assumptions concerning urban elites and (2) "recent changes in corporate organization associated with the new economy." Nevarez pursues his reassessment through a discussion of how the elite concept has been used since the 1960s. The recent collapse of cohesive urban elites with the expansion of rootless capital and its management has led scholars to question "whether urban agency, urban politics, and, implicitly, urban elites matter any more." Yet although poststructuralist critiques appear to "undermine the theoretical value of the urban elite concept as constructed by urban political economy," they also create a theoretical space where urban elites as objects, not subjects, of representation can be investigated. The role of new economy executives can still be analyzed through an analytical framework which "infuses the urban political economy problematic of urban elites with the poststructural focus on local meaning."

Empirically, the chapter rests on a study of new economy executives, business leaders, and political activists in Santa Monica, Santa Barbara, and San Luis Obispo. The executives can be described as ambiguous and inarticulate urban elites "because their local interests are illegible to themselves and to others." A new structural mechanism has emerged – "the capacities of labor markets to organize production and capital investment in new economy sectors" – which "gives elite workers a political economic stake in the quality of life district different from the conventional corporate interest in 'pro-business' social relations." Because these workers are unaware of this mechanism, a crisis has emerged in the representation of their local interests to both themselves and others, ensuring that their political future is unclear.

We remain in California for the last chapter by Jan Lin. He investigates the relationship between mass culture, symbolic sites, and urban redevelopment in Hollywood. Like others in this volume, Lin draws on the "new urban sociology," especially the critical cultural perspective shaped by Sharon Zukin and Mark Gottdiener, in particular, and its examination of "how metropolitan fortunes under postindustrialism are increasingly derived from the fabrication of thematic sites and symbols." Hollywood provides Lin with an analytical window through which he can "augment our understanding of Los Angeles as a world city, while contributing to our theoretical and empirical understanding of the connections between globalization, consumption, and urban sociology."

An outline of the historical development of Hollywood as a machine of mass cultural production leads to a discussion of dream palaces, mass spectacle, and urban iconography. Recent redevelopment schemes center around the proposal to build a $388 million complex at the intersection of Hollywood Boulevard and Highland Avenue, which would greatly encourage tourism. The proposal was challenged by local residents and businesses on environmental grounds, as well as by those who "drew attention to the host of social problems besetting the low-income population of Hollywood."

Bibliography

Alexander, C. 1996: *The Art of Being Black.* Oxford: Clarendon Press.
Anthias, F. 1998: Evaluating "diaspora": beyond ethnicity? *Sociology* 32 (3): 557–80.
Appadurai, A. 1990: Disjuncture and difference in the global cultural economy. In M. Featherstone (ed.), *Global Culture: Nationalism, Globalization and Modernity*. London: Sage.
Ballard, R. (ed.) 1994: *Desh Pardesh: The South Asian Presence in Britain.* London: Hurst.
Bhabha, H. (ed.) 1990: *Nation and Narration.* New York: Routledge.
Brah, A. 1996: *Cartographies of Diaspora: Contesting Identities.* London and New York: Routledge.
Castells, M. 1983: *The City and the Grassroots.* Berkeley: University of California Press.
Dear, M. 2000: *The Postmodern Urban Condition.* Oxford and Malden, MA: Blackwell.
De Certeau, M. 1984: *The Practice of Everyday Life.* Berkeley: University of California Press.
Deutsche, R. 1991: Boys' town. *Environment and Planning D: Society and Space* 9: 5–30.
Donald, J. 1999: *Imagining the Modern City*. London: Athlone Press.
Eade, J. (ed.) 1997: *Living the Global City: Globalization as Local Process.* London and New York: Routledge.
——2000: *Placing London: From Imperial Capital to Global City*. New York and Oxford: Berghahn Books.
——and Mele, C. 1998: Global margins: the Lower East Side of New York and the East End of London. *Rising East* 3 (1): 52–73.
Featherstone, M. and Lash, S. 1999: Introduction. In M. Featherstone and S. Lash (eds.), *Spaces of Culture: City, Nation, World.* London: Sage.
Fincher, R. and Jacobs, J. M. (eds.) 1998: *Cities of Difference.* New York and London: Guilford Press.
Fortier, A.-M. 2000: *Migrant Belongings: Memory, Space, Identity*. Oxford and New York: Berg.
Gottdiener, M. 1997: *The Theming of America: Dreams, Visions, and Commercial Spaces.* Westview Press.
Harvey, D. 1989: *The Condition of Postmodernity*. Oxford: Blackwell.
Katznelson, I. 1993: *Marxism and the City*. Oxford: Oxford University Press.
King, A. D. 1996: Introduction: cities, texts, and paradigms. In A. D. King (ed.), *Re-Presenting the City: Ethnicity, Capital, and Culture in the Twenty-first-century Metropolis.* New York: New York University Press, 1–22.
Massey, D. 1994: *Space, Place, and Gender*. Cambridge: Polity Press.
Mele, C. 2000: *Selling the Lower East Side: Culture, Real Estate, and Resistance in New York City*. Minneapolis: University of Minnesota Press.
Reichl, A. J. 1999: *Reconstructing Times Square: Politics and Culture in Urban Development.* Lawrence: University Press of Kansas.

Rex, J. and Moore, R. 1967: *Race, Community and Conflict*. London: Oxford University Press.

—— and Tomlinson, S. 1979: *Colonial Immigrants in a British City: A Class Analysis*. London: Routledge and Kegan Paul.

Sharma, S. et al. (eds.) 1996: *Dis-Orienting Rhythms: The Politics of the New Asian Dance Music*. London and New Jersey: Zed Press.

Shaw, A. 2001: Kinship, cultural preference and immigration: consanguineous marriage among the Pakistanis. *Journal of the Royal Anthropological Institute* 7 (2): 315–34.

Smith, M. P. 2000: *Transnational Urbanism: Locating Globalization*. Oxford and Malden, MA: Blackwell.

Tajbakhsh, K. 2001: *The Promise of the City: Space, Identity, and Politics in Contemporary Social Thought*. Berkeley: University of California Press.

Werbner, P. 1997: Essentialising essentialism, essentialising silence: ambivalence and multiplicity in the constructions of racism and ethnicity. In P. Werbner and T. Modood (eds.), *Debating Cultural Hybridity: Multi-cultural Identities and the Politics of Antiracism*. London and New Jersey: Zed Books.

Yon, D. 2000: *Elusive Culture: Schooling, Race and Identity in Global Times*. Albany, NY: SUNY Press.

Zukin, S. 1991: *Landscapes of Power: From Detroit to Disney World*. Berkeley: University of California Press.

—— 1995: *The Cultures of Cities*. Oxford: Blackwell.

Part II
A Middle Ground? Difference, Social Justice, and the City

2
Rescripting Cities with Difference

Ruth Fincher, Jane M. Jacobs, and Kay Anderson

The study of cities produces scripts of their coming into being, their logics, and their inhabitants. These urban explanations are at the same time positioned narratives that work to legitimate or naturalize particular interpretations of urban events, calling for the collection of data in certain ways to bolster this understanding. The interdiscipline of urban studies has hosted an array of these scripts. They have coexisted, influencing each other and yet retaining their standpoints. Our use of the term "script" in this chapter refers, then, to the ways in which cities are subject to certain explanatory modes that bring different aspects of urbanism and urbanization into view at the expense of other cities, other lives, and other processes.

For example, in the 1970s and 1980s, political economy perspectives on the city provided a broad and sophisticated framework for many in urban studies, who used it to form persuasive analyses of power and class, and to establish norms about what was progressive and regressive in urban change. In the 1990s, by contrast, urban studies came under the influence of various theories of difference emanating from feminist and postcolonial perspectives and queer theory. As Tony King (1996: 2) notes, explanations of urbanism and urbanization that had become the "privileged territory" of certain subsets of social science now share that terrain with a range of urban commentaries constituted by way of quite different categories of knowledge and disciplinary concerns. To this diversification of explanatory perspectives is added the distinctive scripts produced by "different genders, ethnicities, ideologies, races, classes, sexual orientations, nationalities." These brought into view the "cultural logics" of urbanism and new sensitivity to the axes of difference that contribute to disadvantage. More challengingly, they "read" the city not in terms of explanatory processes but in terms of surface effects, turning the city into a "text," a semiotic space shaped by struggles over meaning and signification. Within what is itself a diverse set of rescriptings, it is not surprising that some urbanists have viewed theories of difference as destabilizing the progressive certainties and the reforming intent of urban studies grounded in a radical political economy. Yet this cacophony of difference-directed rescriptings has also opened out important new questions that enhance our understandings of cities, implore us to pursue new trajectories of inquiry, and offer invigorated scope for constructing more just cities. The ways in which theories of difference have contributed to bringing these other city scripts into view is the specific focus of this chapter.

Situated Scripts

All explanatory representations of cities, despite claims about their universal applicability, are in fact always situated knowledges. This contradiction is nowhere more clearly expressed than in the case of the Chicago School of urban sociologists. Often treated as a universal spatial typology of the city, their famous concentric circle model was constructed from very specific field studies of a particular place and time. Specifically, their models of racialized "ghetto" formation and stages of "invasion" and "succession" drew upon Chicago in the 1920s. This was a time when African Americans and others were migrating in great numbers to the northern and eastern cities of the United States, a migration understood to be causing "disturbances" to the healthy "metabolism" of the city (Duncan 1996: 257). On the one hand, the model was an attempt to account objectively and scientifically for the logic of change in cities. But, on the other, it was produced from anxieties about urban disorder and dysfunction, those anxieties resulting from specific new experiences of cohabiting with racialized difference. In this sense, the model had embedded in it a set of normative ideas about proper urban living and appropriate (i.e., manageable) urban subjectivities (Jacobs and Fincher 1998: 6). So a historically and geographically specific moral stance in relation to urban life – and one "generated inductively" from detailed observations of the "laboratory" called Chicago – was presumed to apply to "any town or city" (Burgess [1925] 1967: 50, quoted in Duncan 1996: 257). This is a classic example of what Rob Shields (1996: 229) described as the way such representations (and especially those valorized by the authority of science) come to "replace or stand in for the city." As he (and the Chicago model) so graphically reminds us, such representations can become "treacherous metaphors, summarizing the complexity of the city in an elegant model."

The universal claims of the Chicago model are an easy target for challengers. Not least, the "truth claims" of such abstracted models challenge our commonsense notion of how applicable they really might be to other cities. There is a more recent example of this type of synecdoche, whereby the experiences of one place are expected to stand for the experiences of all cities. Nowhere is such a bold claim more apparent than in the emergence of the "Los Angeles School" (Dear 2000: 10). It is certain that there is a large body of scholarship on the patterns of growth, urban forms, lifestyle choices, economic restructurings, technological innovations, and social conditions of Los Angeles and its surrounds. By volume of output alone, it is quite reasonable for scholars of LA urbanism to claim for their city and their scripts a "paradigmatic" status (Soja 1989: 221). The claim that this is the city within which all contemporary urban logics are embodied was greatly advanced when the renowned urban commentator, Mike Davis, put pen to paper in the 1990s and doodled his own LA version of the Chicago concentric circle model. In redrawing the Chicago model with LA's condition of "fear," much of what that model stood for was challenged, albeit not for the first time.

If Davis's model was intended to query the applicability of the Burgess one, then it did so very belatedly, arriving after decades of critical research and alternate model-making. Davis's rescripting of the Chicago model was probably a simple borrowing of an existing urban model of iconographic status. The effects of that borrowing, and the epistemological aspirations it stood for, are evidenced in the kind of claims made by contemporary scholars of LA. Although few have offered an alternate schematic model, Dear's "Keno capitalism" model (2000: 157–8) being an exception, many claim that the processes evidenced in LA are symptomatic of urbanisms worldwide. All this claim-making is made in and through the logics of postmodernism, such that the will to script a "paradigmatic city" sits, albeit uncomfortably, alongside a political and theoretical commitment to heterodoxies of all kinds.

One of the problems that claimants of the LA School have had with predecessors like the "Chicago model" is the way in which they cast the conditions of cities like Los Angeles as quirky "exceptions" to a set of urbanistic "rules" derived from elsewhere (Dear 2000: 10). Yet it is true that all urban scripts are, in various ways, the products of "exceptional" circumstances. The LA School is a case in point. It is itself an outcome of a peculiar convergence of urban conditions, scholars, funding opportunities, and theoretical traditions. Of course, not all urban scripts or their script-makers seek to, or can, claim such authority, nor can they rely on such conducive conditions. Not least, the formation of both academic and pragmatic urban studies scripts is often influenced by structures of governance that may encourage or discourage certain forms of knowledge about cities.

The urban rescriptings of particular interest to us in this chapter present a "difference perspective," delivered by way of a variety of theoretical openings, for example, feminism, queer theory, poststructuralism, and postcolonialism. Framed by a "difference perspective," explanations of urban processes and city lives have proceeded with a careful sensitivity to diversity of experiences and subtle differentials of power. In part, this rescripting has brought into view certain category groups whose experiences of and circumstances within cities had previously been relegated to the margins, or construed only in terms of deviations from standardized norms or generalized patterns. Furthermore, through this rescripting new questions have been raised of many of the mainstream concerns of urban studies such as processes of urbanization, and the distribution of services and amenity. Under the influence of difference perspectives, cities that were previously understood in terms of undifferentiated (often global) processes or undifferentiating (hegemonic) logics came to be populated with an ever more differentiated set of urban inhabitants, each living in a world in which power relations were more complexly and contingently configured.

In the two sections of this chapter to follow, we consider, first, theoretical debates being played out now, in attempts to evaluate the usefulness of difference-directed perspectives. We then discuss some benefits of difference-influenced thinking about the urban, by evaluating three influential scripts about cities. These are: globalization and the world city, the city as an entity set apart from nature, and the city as disorderly and in need of social cohesion. The three scripts we have elected to interrogate in this chapter may seem unlikely in terms of the many issues and processes that preoccupy contemporary urbanists. Yet respectively they each reveal important lines of narrative inclusion and exclusion: first, which cities come to be seen (or are privileged) in our explanatory models and which are rendered invisible (marginalized); second, what is brought into view, and what is left out of view by our urban narratives; and third, what conditions are judged acceptable by them and what unacceptable.

Difference in Urban Analysis – Theoretical Takes

An interest in difference has helped to write new or amended scripts for urban studies. Not least, it has been a significant part of what Ed Soja (1996: 193) refers to as a "new terrain of critical urban studies." This new terrain appeared not simply because of some epistemological imperative. Cities have changed as have the forces that structure them and the lives lived in them. As Soja notes:

> To continue to approach the postmodern metropolis with the same analytic frameworks and confident epistemologies that were applied to understand the capitalist city in the 1970s is now highly unlikely to provide the same powerful insights. Recognizing this, the new critical urban studies has itself become radically expanded in scope, involving in the study of urbanism not just the . . . political economy . . . that dominated radical modernist approaches but a much wider range of disciplines and critical perspectives. (1996: 193)

Susan Fainstein, reflecting upon differing explanatory paradigms for the urban, tackles the transformation in urban explanations from the other direction. In her view the contribution of poststructuralist theory to urban studies has been "in its recognition of diverse bases of social affiliation and multiple roots of oppression" (Fainstein 1996: 26). Significantly, she notes that this viewpoint results in what she describes, somewhat skeptically, as "a veneration of diversity."

There are those who would see difference-sensitive rescriptings as entirely beneficial to the development of the interdisciplinary field of urban studies. Not least, they have usefully complicated our knowledge of cities. And certainly one might imagine that those whose lives and circumstances were previously unrecognized or misrecognized by urban explanations would be beneficiaries of this new scholarship. The work of Saskia Sassen on the "global city" is exemplary in this regard. Sassen has used difference perspectives to elaborate the logics by which world cities function. Her investigation of the "analytic borderlands" (Sassen 1996: 185) has brought into view gendered and racialized "presences that are not represented" in the dominant "facts and narratives about the economy of the city" (1996: 183). Sectors, firms, and workers, whose role in the economy of world cities had been overlooked or devalorized, have been revealed as she asks (1996: 184): "How do we construct a narrative about the city, and particularly the economy of the city, that includes rather than evicts?" Her work reminds us of lives and cultures evicted from the corporate image-making of cities.

It is important not to assume any necessary relationship between difference and poststructuralist explanations. Sassen, of course, has used difference as a thread by which to elaborate a political economy of the world city. Other urbanists, often those identified as poststructuralist, may use difference as a way of entering into a more cultural explanatory frame. Fainstein (1996: 27), in questioning the political potential of poststructuralist approaches to the city, argues that in this scripting "culture rather than economics becomes the root of political identity." Fainstein's account concludes that the political ambition of poststructuralist urbanisms is to eradicate "social subordination" and to facilitate what she refers to as "the free expression of group difference" (1996: 28). This is, she notes, a political model entirely consistent with liberal pluralism which gives rise only to a "weak . . . largely oppositional" political expression (1996: 29).

Fainstein's critique reiterates the radical skepticism emerging from scholars who are in principle sympathetic to the political and intellectual intentions of theories of difference, but concerned about perceived limits or risks to this perspective. These critiques focus primarily on the way in which certain difference perspectives have replaced a politics of claims-making based on redistribution with one based on recognition. That is, a materially linked politics of equity seems to have lost ground to a politics of identity, and just at the moment when, as Fraser puts it, "an aggressively expanding capitalism is radically exacerbating economic inequality" (2000: 108; and see Harvey 1996).

In almost all cases this skepticism is influenced by a clear set of assumptions that difference perspectives lead to an overemphasis on identity politics.

So, for example, explanatory scripts concerning themselves with inequity or urbanization or social polarization might be assumed to have been replaced by seemingly less analytical, and presumably less political, descriptions of the machinations of subject formation, or the violence of certain processes of subjection (of people or places), or the strategies certain identifiable groups use to reclaim their sense of complete and rightful selfhood. This kind of "radical skepticism" about difference scripts sees them as disturbing political economy – compromising its politics and the clean links of these politics to the Marxist theorization of capitalist social relations as based on class.

Nancy Fraser, although "disturbed" by the consequences of the new "grammar" of difference scripts, seeks a reconciliation between the politics of recognition she sees as emerging from difference-based perspectives that use a variety of group attributes to cement identities for political strategy, and the politics of redistribution deriving from solidly class-based perspectives. Such reconciliation is necessary, she says, because of the disadvantaging outcomes that can attend moves to replace redistribution with recognition in political practice (Fraser 2000: 108). She argues that issues to do with identity and recognition (what she also glosses as the "identity model" or "culture") are in fact meaningful associates of redistribution, often "deeply imbricated with economic inequality" (2000: 109). The explicit value of Fraser's critique of the "identity model" of difference is that it reminds us that the costs of being misrecognized or "disesteemed" are not simply compromising of one's ("healthy") sense of oneself or what she refers to, somewhat disparagingly, as "cultural harm" (2000: 109, 110). Misrecognition can fundamentally structure a person's material circumstances. For example, institutional judgments can work to "misrecognize" individuals by considering them of lesser status, so reducing their capacity for full social participation. Much of contemporary urban studies that is fueled by an interest in difference reveals the roots of institutionalized regimes of difference in capitalist social relations.

In her case against recognition or the "identity model," Fraser's work converges with one of the significant strands in Iris Marion Young's argument about a politics of difference. Like Fraser, Young seeks to bring a recognition politics (read "culture") back in touch with a redistributive politics (read "political economy"). Not least, Young's model is of particular interest to us because it comes from thinking through the matter of justice and difference in the context of the urban condition. In doing so Young rejects a schema of reform based simply on recognition. She questions the value and necessity, for just outcomes, of radically different but co-present subjects becoming "transparent" to each other. Not least, she implies that such processes of recognition, while seemingly acknowledging difference, are often based on an assimilationist fantasy of community. In this sense Young is very serious about accepting that cities are constituted out of both "seen and unseen strangers" (Young 1990: 237) and that justice cannot simply await, nor can it simply be effected by, a state of transparency produced by a process of "proper" recognition. She does not indulge the utopian fantasy that recognition needs to be based on mutual transparency or a kind of face-to-face intimacy that the intensity and scale of city life have long been unable to sustain.

Of course utopian models of how highly differentiated urban populations might coexist frequently differ from actual lives lived together. As is discussed below, difference is often so difficult to negotiate that the response is willful separation, a geography of exclusion. Scholarship on gated communities, for example, has shown that new urban sociospatialities arise from an admixture of an intensified class differentiation (social polarization) and an anxious sensitivity on the part of the middle classes to the disturbances and threats various others are presumed to produce. Such geographies of fear are often supplemented by another, more complex stance in relation to urban diversity. In those political conditions where there is a recognition of difference and provisions for those who are unfairly differentiated – we might think here of the self-consciously multicultural city – a number of aberrant reactions can arise. On the one hand, resentments can develop among those whose privilege has suddenly had to give way to the special interests of minorities. This can lead to new expressions of resentment and the development of what Neil Smith (1996) has termed the revanchist city. On the other hand, Merrifield (1996: 204) has suggested that political models that "celebrate otherness" can be subverted by a "dialectical twist" through which an "openness to unassimilated difference" (to use Young's terms) spirals off toward a proliferation of exclusive or separatist claims.

In this apparently free market of claims-making, questions arise: who adjudicates the more important differences among the many differences being claimed, and, on the basis of what moral or political terrain are such adjudications being made? In short, who manages the city of difference? Recent work on self-consciously multicultural states, for example, has suggested that this structure for inclusion does not always displace the power of those who are seen to be without "ethnicity," that is, those who are "white" and who remain in charge of the purpose and fortunes of multicultural policy (Hage 1998; Povinelli 1998). Indeed, such inclusionary models often operate as structures to stabilize certain normative notions of what difference should be and how it should be expressed.

Three Contemporary Scripts about Cities

Differentiating the global city

Urban studies has long invested in globally scoped explanations of urbanization and universally applicable models of urban form. Wallerstein's world systems theory and its legacy of theories of globalization is foundational, particularly its designation of cities as of First or Third Worlds, North or South. These theories absorbed cities across the globe into an integrated developmental narrative. In this narrative, cities come to be known for their place in a global urban hierarchy produced by one single force that has spatially differentiated outcomes. Cities are centered and empowered, or marginalized and dominated.

Within this integrated script of urbanization certain cities and urban conditions presented a quandary. Those cities not fitting the processes and trajectories diagnosed in this explanation – usually "Third World Cities" or cities of the "South" – became cities that, quite literally, did not "make sense." Scholarship on cities of the South or the Third World City attempted to detail such differences and provide logical alternative models. We might take as an example that proposed by Terry McGee (1967, 1989, 1991) to account for the morphology and socioeconomic development of Southeast Asian cities. His now famous *desakota* model proposed that the Southeast Asian urban system was a unique mix of *kota* (town) and *desa* (village or country), in which rural and urban lifestyles and economies integrated in ways not seen in First World Cities. McGee was suggesting that in Southeast Asia the city followed a distinctive trajectory of urbanization, incommensurate with that found in the First World.

Such conceptually useful (or empirically real) deviations have not managed to dislodge the hold of integrated, globally scoped explanations of urbanization. Rather than losing ground to the suggestive evidence of these different urbanization logics, a globally broad explanation of urbanization has been invigorated by the newly felt intensities of globalization. For example, Rimmer and Dick (1998) have recently suggested that urban geographies of Southeast Asian cities need to move "beyond" the idea of the Third World City. They criticize explanations like that of *desakota* for being too differentiated and for having "shut out First World elements." In their words, "globalisation has made the paradigm of the Third World City obsolete in south-east Asia" (1998: 2304). Rimmer and Dick even go so far as to suggest that the identification of an explicitly "South-east Asian" urban logic is "orientalist" (1998: 2314). It is perhaps here that we see the kind of "dialectical twist" that Merrifield implied could be associated with theoretical and political stances seeking to admit difference. In this post-orientalist adjudication of how to script the Southeast Asian city, it is simply not possible to stand outside the West. To claim difference is apparently to activate an essentialist (area studies) stereotype, to deny difference is to assume integration into what Rimmer and Dick refer to as "a single urban discourse" (1998: 2303). This double bind is most suggestive of the dangerously integrative power of current scripts about the process of urbanization.

To illustrate the need to abandon highly differentiated, area-specific scripts for Southeast Asian cities, Rimmer and Dick refer to the appearance of gated residential communities in Jakarta. In following this strategy they build on a wide body of scholarship charting the appearance of the gated community throughout cities of varying sizes and locations. The role of the gated community in recent scripts of globalization and urbanization may well be an example of what Amin and Graham (1997: 416) refer to as the "problem of synecdoche" – the "methodological dangers of overgeneralizing from one or a few examples or overemphasizing particular spaces, senses of time and partial representations within the city."

There is now a vast scholarship on gated communities in cities of the First and Third World, cities of the North and of the South, and cities in the West and the East. As McLaughlin and Muncie (1999: 117) note: "[i]n an ever-increasing number of global contexts, the middle and upper classes in cities are opting . . . to live, shop, and work in privately guarded, security conscious, fortified enclaves." The gated community, no matter its location and no matter its circumstance, acts as artifactual evidence not simply of globalization, but of globalization's peculiar urbanistic outcomes. In the case of the gated communities of Jakarta, Rimmer and Dick (1998: 2309) suggest that although the "debates and literatures" on US and Southeast Asian gated communities are separate, "in reality many issues are the same."

The way in which gated communities are scripted in current urban literature is a useful example of the complex and uneven ways in which theories of difference have percolated through to our understandings of urban processes. On the one hand, much of the analysis of gated communities is premised on recognizing and theorizing the kinds of fears and antagonisms that a lived experience of radical difference in urban settings can produce. Yet the gated community that is the outcome of this condition of hyperdifferentiation lends itself well to globally broad explanations that reduce everything to the same. As Teresa Caldeira (1999: 83) argues, in the context of São Paulo, "the proliferation of fortified enclaves has created a new model of spatial segregation . . . in many cities around the world." Indeed, for Caldeira (1999: 83, 84), the story of gated communities in São Paulo offers a "caricature" of "a pattern of segregation that is widespread in cities throughout the world." Here we glimpse a mirror image of the claims made for Los Angeles: São Paulo as the "paradigmatic" city.

If we are alert to the very peculiar ways in which specific cities come to be connected to aspects of the global economy, then the apparent evidence of sameness can be approached differently, in a way that sees difference in that sameness. For example, detailed ethnographic accounts of gated communities, like that offered by Caldeira, also suggest certain processes that are not so readily encompassed into a globally scripted model of hyperdifferentiation.

As Caldeira (1999: 90) notes, the dream of fortified separation sought by the middle classes in São Paulo is utterly dependent upon maintaining relations with their servants, the very people they disdain. There is an obvious resonance between Caldeira's account and that given by Sassen of the "underbelly" of the finance sectors of global cities. And certainly, similar observations about connections and dependencies have been noted about other examples of urban hyperseparation, such as the divided cities of South Africa.

Globalization provides us with repeated instances in which some thing or some process manifests itself again and again in different times and places. As we make out scripts of urban spaces we have theoretical, representational, and political choices as to how we interpret and script those instances of sameness. In short, there are different ways of receiving what appears as repetition. And how that repetition is received and which theoretical stance it comes to serve is no small matter, for it is itself a response to representational imperatives such as (say) assembling more proof of global convergence.

Nowhere is the link between repetition and sameness more entangled than in commonsense understanding of globalization-as-homogenization – and a phenomenon like the gated community readily serves such scripts. Recent scholarship has contributed to dismantling such interpretations of globalization. Yet for all this work, there remains a tendency to assume that globalization works against difference. Globalization may intensify certain kinds of social polarization, it may cleverly market local specificities, and it may even excite new kinds of resistant differentiations. But such difference is then construed skeptically as simply coming into being in and through globalization's single and inexorable purpose. In this way the globally scoped scripts of urbanization enact their own misrecognitions, assimilating both repeated instances and expressions of difference to the same.

The "unnatural" city

Among the most enduring of city scripts in urban studies scholarship and policy has been the narrative placement of the space of the urban outside, or beyond, the natural world. In simple terms, the city has been portrayed as an unnatural artifact that has lifted itself "out" of nature. Here we witness the reiteration of a broader opposition in Western philosophical thought between the spheres of the sociocultural and the natural, a separation that has itself relied on the longstanding dichotomy between the human and nonhuman. The city, in somehow gathering together all the attributes of the human world, long since acquired an essential character and separate positioning from nature.

A number of scholars have attempted to disrupt the naive depiction of city and nature as worlds apart. Particularly notable have been the efforts of geographers working in the fields of critical cultural theory (e.g., Hinchliffe 1999; Pile 1999); those inspired by historical materialism such as David Harvey (1996); and, from an altogether different direction, those seeking to advance a more "animal-centered" urban studies (especially Wolch, West, and Gaines 1995; but also Philo and Wilbert 2000). Of these efforts, a brief review of Hinchliffe's intervention will be undertaken before proceeding to address the implications of conventional scripts for conceiving (or not) of difference in the city, and in particular for depicting racialized city spaces.

One of the subsets of the broader polarity in Western thought between culture and nature has been the simplified spatial mapping that opposes the "rural" and the "urban." Recently, however, Hinchliffe (1999) has sought to disrupt this cherished binary, including its premise of the city as an exclusively social and cultural achievement. His strategy has been to expose the two major narratives that have displaced a sense of nature from the Western city. Building on his outline we can observe, first, a persistent "civilization" tale, that is, a storyline that plots the "progressive settlement" of humans into habitats protected from an apparently untamed wilderness beyond. Here the "natural" is depicted as an essence which humanity has heroically managed to hold outside the city boundaries. If nature does enter the city, it is seen as doing so in proudly civilized enclosures that celebrate nature's domestication at the hands of humans (for example, as parks, gardens, zoos, flower and agricultural shows). Although having its narrative roots in the Greco-Roman model of the "polis" (see Owens 1991), this concept of the city as the idealized unit of human realization sharpened under the regimes of colonialism and modernity from the fifteenth century. From that time, Europe extended its empires into (what were thought of as) the wild and savage spaces of the New World, so justifying a quite specific form of "civilizing" mission.

In the second, more negative scripting of the city, people's alienation from nature – far from being read as a measure of mastery and triumph – has been taken as an indicator of humanity's decay and degeneration. Nostalgia for things rural is the driving rhetorical device in this tale. It is perhaps no surprise therefore that this urban story gained its coherence during the changing patterns of capitalist development associated with Western Europe's industrial revolution (Williams 1973). The poverty, squalor, disease, violence, and vice that accompanied those transformations were thought to find their grim culmination in the space of the city. The city thus came to stand for all the social ills that accompanied humanity's separation from the benign spaces of rural nature. In Victorian England, for example, middle-class attention came to fix on "Darkest London," where degenerate forms of life and livelihood were thought not only to exist, but multiply (see Pick 1989). Clearly the meanings surrounding the twin spaces of city and country in the anti-urban tale differ radically from those driving the civilizational tale, but as Hinchliffe observes, there is the shared premise of a neat separation between the territories of "cultural" (city) and "natural" (country).

Many accounts of urban life today replay the narrative contradictions of, on the one hand, the city's proud monumentalism and, on the other, its monstrously depraved underbelly. This is most apparent in fiction, film, and artistic renderings that juxtapose the city's spectacle, energy, freedom, and cosmopolitanism with its pathology, anonymity, and latent underlife (Robson 1994; see also Drewe 1997). The savage undercurrents of city life certainly register as menacing in portraits, including newspaper reports, of inner-city riots and other "uprisings." The twin narratives have also traveled without much critical notice into academic accounts of cities, including those in the writings of twentieth-century theorists of urban culture and personality such as Louis Wirth, Sigmund Freud, Georg Simmel, and Robert Park.

Since that time, the field of urban studies has remained rather slow to transcend the characterizations of urbanism outlined above. The field has been noticeably reticent in engaging with recent debates about nature's sociality that collapse the nature/society divide from a range of critical perspectives (see Braun and Castree 1998). A conspicuous minority of scholars have, as mentioned earlier, broken this silence in working across the divide of society and nature underpinning our received models of the urban, noting for example that cities are physically built out of the materials of humanly transformed nature (Cronon 1991; Pile 1999). In the words of David Harvey (1996: 186), "[t]here is nothing unnatural about New York city," just as for Callicott (1994: 64) "Chicago is no less a phenomenon of nature than is the Great Barrier Reef." Nonetheless, work remains to be done in (1) critically excavating existing scripts of cities for the misplaced characterizations of urbanism described earlier, and (2) offering revisionings that transcend the false binaries buried within them. And while there is wide scope in this task for pluralizing our understanding of a range of urban social natures, which "allow in" more mixed collections of species to the ethical frame of city life than are currently accepted, the remainder of this section is devoted to just one such recasting: of racialized scriptings of urbanism through the lens of culture/nature critique. In many such scriptings, especially in the United States, we find that the urban anti-tale has been a central device for figuring the counterpoint ghettoized spaces of the proudly "civilized" metropolis. That is, narrative couplings of whiteness/civilization, and blackness/degeneracy, replay some stale tales of urbanism itself – tales which defy the reality of the heterogeneous lifeworlds of the city.

Few spaces of the contemporary Western city have been as thickly accreted with representational layers as the racialized slum or "ghetto." The segregated enclaves of black and other nonwhite Americans have attracted perhaps the most (dis)repute (Davis 1990: ch. 4). But so too has the apparently incongruous presence of indigenous people in Australian and Canadian cities – people presumed to more properly belong in the open and "remnant" spaces of "nature" – who have attracted pernicious targeting (Anderson 1993; Gale 1972; Peters 1996). In the US context, at least since Robert Park (1924) first observed that steep social distance gradients operated between blacks and whites in northern cities, the Jewish and, later on, black ghetto has succumbed to the simplified vocabularies of modernity's anti-urban tale. Still in widespread circulation today, these are languages of lawlessness, barbarity, drunkenness, vice addiction, and violence – of a menacing wildness symptomatic of the apparent loss of moral cohesion in the movement from rural to urban.

Far from inhering in the living space of the ghetto, however, such characterizations owe more than has been acknowledged to specific urban scriptings, and their practical force and effect. We see traces of these scripts, both in the depiction of the urban spaces in which nature's barbarism has been apparently civilized and purified – the proudly monumental spaces of the idealized white metropolis – as well as the narrativized spaces of the ghetto where residents have apparently lost or failed to acquire a moral cloak of "civility" or rational self-government. It follows that the violence and depravity of the black American inner city from which there has been widespread "white flight" to distant gated suburbs are only ever conceived of as an inversion of civil order (Ross 1994; and see pp. 35–6 of this chapter). The point to be made here is that so long as the city is itself enmeshed in oversimplified narrations – ones that draw on a false ontological fixing of the cultural and the natural – racialized difference is made to enter the city in only ever "uninvited," pathologized ways. Mixed mappings of whiteness and blackness are not envisaged. The ghetto never escapes its defining images of degeneracy and decay. As Fraser (2000) might say, this is as much a matter of inequitable practice and policy as it is of textualization and scripting.

The "disorderly city"

Another narrative about cities takes up the longstanding idea that they are sites of disorder, places where strangers appear on waves of migration, seeking new lives but somehow not fitting in with accepted mores and practices. The urban condition has always evoked narratives of social disorder, not least because urban life brings diverse groups of people together in unique concentrations and configurations. To talk of the city is necessarily to talk of difference and diversity. The authors of a recent Open University text dwell on matters of movement, disorder, heterogeneity, and unsettlement, as well as settlement, as the proper subject matter for the study of the contemporary urban condition. McDowell (1999) refers at length to Richard Sennett's accounts of the emergence in the nineteenth-century European city of public and private spaces – the public the domain of strangers and the private the domain of regulated and regulatable domesticity. We noted earlier the importance of Young's questioning of whether a just urbanity consists of subjects in cities, in their diversity, relating to each other, or whether cities can justly mix both "seen and unseen strangers" (Young 1990: 237). Accepting that strangers will coexist in the city, Young resists a finding that a failure of universal, face-to-face intimacy in the city is to be regretted.

Scripting the city as disorderly seems on the face of it to be taking into account diversity, accepting difference, avoiding universalizing accounts of the appropriate urban citizen. But of course in the very idea of disorder is a yearning for order. And in their attempts to impose order on disorder, institutions set up categories of difference, rewarding those falling within some categories and disadvantaging those outside them. In a well-known example, modernist urban planning, segmenting and controlling diverse activities and population groups spatially as part of its search for progress and improvement, sought to reduce urban disorder. Dear (2000: 93, citing Christine Boyer) discusses how, a century ago, American land-use planning discourse had appeared, emphasizing unity, control, and expert skills: "this new disciplinary order had as its goal the use of surplus capital for civilizing and socializing purposes. It required state intervention, a revised municipal politics, and the production of a category of experts."

Investigating urban planning, within institutional frameworks, for public spaces in Australian cities, Iveson (2000) shows how the recognition of particular groups' claims over public space is simultaneously an act of material redistribution. Here he follows Fraser (2000). He argues for the actions of planners in fixing certain identities to public spaces, via top-down visions for those places that are frequently enacted in urban design, to be revealed for the political statements they are. They cement perceived order on perceived disorder. Clearly, the norms of order and disorder require close analytical scrutiny.

There is another, more contemporary example of institutions' use of ideas of order and disorder to establish a regime of difference, and then to criticize those deemed different within it. A concern with the spatial regulation of urban dwellers continues to be expressed in European writings about social cohesion. This writing describes policy interest amongst European governments in disciplining, or reducing the spatial segregation of, those of "different" ethnicities (entwined with particular social and economic circumstances) in cities. These "strangers" are often recent, and not-so-recent, immigrants, their "strangeness" the product of their deviance from national, taken-for-granted, institutionally assisted, ethnic norms, and of the narrowness of policy expectations about them. Narratives emphasizing the need to control the disorderly urban persist, then, in such contexts. Kearns and Forrest examine the meaning of the term social cohesion in its contemporary European use, and the suggestions it makes for urban governance at the spatial scales of the interurban, the city as region, and the neighborhood. Discipline, control of the disorderly and assimilation, the search for "common values" and "social solidarity," "territorial belonging" and "identity" are key words in their critique of the cohesion concept (Kearns and Forrest 2000: 996).

As with the modernist urban planning example, there are positive aspects to the ordering being sought here, as well as apparently negative ones associated with the suppression of diversity. In the modernist planning case, the public health benefits of improvements to sanitation in built environments cannot be denied. In the contemporary European example of the management goal of social cohesion, few would disagree with the aim of reducing disparities in wealth. The assertion of norms, and their definition, is always political and contested.

Kearns and Forrest are almost silent on the question of how ethnic differences amongst city dwellers and the presence of immigrants in cities contribute to policy stances in favor of social cohesion. They do conclude their paper, however, by remarking that "[a]s cities have become more globally embedded and as city life and civic culture have become more hybridized and multicultural . . . [there has been] . . . increasing policy preoccupation with social cohesion" (2000: 1014). Other analysts of European urbanism pay more attention to worries about ethnicity and ethnic segregation in cities, as a cause of loudly expressed desires for more social cohesion and less social exclusion (see Musterd and Ostendorf 1998; Andersson 1999). Diken (1998) theorizes this phenomenon skillfully, examining the circumstances of Turkish immigrants to Aarhus in Denmark and the urban planning responses to their presence. The institutions of urban planning are rendered the more fixated with order, he finds, because of their intersection with the politics of immigration in this context. The politics of immigration, resting as it does on a discourse of "us" (Danes) and "them" (Turks – the strangers), cannot cope with ambivalence and hybridity in the identities of immigrants (Diken 1998: 129). In its intersection with this immigration politics, urban planning in Aarhus walls off the immigrants into separated public housing estates, and then identifies as a problem their very spatial and cultural separation. Thus, Diken (quoting Sennett and Bauman) finds the immigrant spaces of Aarhus become places subject to a strong but indifferent institutional gaze, rather than places whose stranger-residents are "touched" by intercultural communication. The sociospatial stratification of the population in the city becomes a "war on strangers" (Diken 1998: 130–2), the resulting walled communities exhibiting a multiculturalism without intercultural connection.

Diken's analysis, made from what we would term broadly a difference perspective, calls into question the narratives of social cohesion so prevalent in contemporary urban studies and policy. Whose narratives are these, and do they admit the stranger, or at least the possessors of hybrid identities, to the city they envisage? In another context, Australian metropolises, long the destination for immigrants from very many source countries, are rarely scripted for their ethnic sociospatial segregation in this way. Perhaps this is because those suburbs or public housing estates built to shelter the labor forces of now-departed manufacturing rarely were totally occupied by one immigrant birthplace group, or, if they were, were occupied by those perceived to be of assimilable (British) ethnicity (see Peel 1995). Perhaps there is a legacy here of a national self-definition of multicultural diversity – of multicultural diversity being accepted as itself a form of social cohesion. This view of the nation has long had bipartisan political support in the parliament (if not everywhere in the population, and despite the analysis of Hage [1998] that what exists is white multiculturalism, a framework to console white worriers and to aid the preservation of their hegemony). Perhaps the silence about immigrants' concentrations in Australian cities is because the degree of their spatial segregation is really very small (see Burnley et al. 1997: ch. 3). Suffice it to say that when an interpretation is presented of Australian urban populations being disadvantaged by spatial concentrations of particular ethnic groups, it receives very little academic or public attention – although the spatial concentration of low-income groups entrapped in certain suburbs is receiving some scrutiny.

As we have argued, it is important to note the relationship to institutional practices of this contemporary desire for social cohesion, for the replacement of (some) disorder with (some) order in the cities of some nations. Not only do institutions respond to diversity; in fact they create and problematize difference, seeing it and then responding to the fruits of their own gaze, as Diken (1998) describes. In this vein, Fraser (2000: 114–15) depicts institutions as the "makers" of diversity. That is what institutions do – they differentiate and adjudicate. The importance of the link between difference-influenced perspectives of the urban, and the analytical search for the means by which differences are embedded in time and place, cannot be overemphasized. We seek to find "located politics of difference," that is, the exercise of power in the forming of differentiation, rather than merely noting and celebrating expressions of diversity in urban environments (Jacobs and Fincher 1998: 2). Seeking the situated politics of difference encourages an interest in a range of institutions as rule-setters and power wielders. It acknowledges that institutions' practices affect urban lives, and can draw in a range of urban dwellers and producers of urban form as complicit in the ongoing, often micro-exercise of power. This means institutions may not be taken for granted as black boxes that precede diverse and differentiated outcomes "on the ground," in the "local." Rather, institutions are themselves engaged players "on the ground," and certain urban dwellers are complicit with particular institutions as they live their lives according to the dictates of, or benefiting from, institutional practices.

Nowhere, perhaps, has the guiding hand of institutions in cities, as they contribute to the imposition of an urban order, been documented in more detail than in research on gentrification, conducted since the 1980s in urban studies. Gentrification has become one of the favored objects of study of critical urban scriptings of new sociospatial arrangements in cities, and research about it has often been inspired by questions about differentiations. Usually, the relevant institutional power has been expressed as benefiting richer rather than poorer people: the located politics of difference has been shown to marginalize the underresourced. In Neil Smith's ongoing scrutiny of gentrification (Smith 1996), the transformation of declined American inner-city spaces was charted early on in rent models, and later in terms of struggles between the wealthy and the homeless. In all forms of Smith's account, gentrification has been viewed as guided by institutions acting in certain class interests. Banks, national government departments with their schemes of aiding certain mortgage purchases rather than others, city planning departments – the policies and practices of these organizations have supported some and disadvantaged others. But emphasis on the class-selective actions of public and private institutions does not exhaust the scripts of gentrification. A pathbreaking article by Rose (1984) demonstrated how professional working women, not always wealthy, benefited from gentrification and used institutionally sponsored changes in inner-city housing and services. In an equally influential account, Mitchell (1993) revealed institutions' use of the national policy of multiculturalism in Canada to justify preferential treatment for investors from Hong Kong in the real estate of inner Vancouver, which was contested locally on economic and ethnic lines. Research over many years on gentrification shows the engagement of institutions in ethnically differentiating politics in the urban built environment, as well as in class-differentiating ones. While the gated community has become a feature of focus in discussions of globalization and the apparent uniform order it is imposing on cities worldwide, gentrification has over an even longer period been a phenomenon of focus in urban studies, the redistribution of resources it results in noted alongside the identities of its protagonists.

In practice, and in particular contexts, some forms of differentiation are more pronounced than others, and some forms of difference produced by institutional and others' actions are more "respectable" than others. A case of the sharply differentiated topographies of "difference" in central Sydney clarifies this point. Apparently not all differences are equal before the institutions of political and economic power, with some local formations of difference attracting commercialization and sponsorship, and other enclaves exclusion and neglect (Anderson 1998). The area around Dixon Street known as "Chinatown" has since the 1970s figured prominently in City of Sydney plans for district beautification and heritage definition. The area's legibility as a site of Oriental difference has been fanatically etched on the landscape through the efforts of city planners and politicians, as well as Chinatown merchants of Chinese, Vietnamese, and Thai origin. Most recently, one witnesses the updating of the Oriental facades added in the 1970s with features using Feng-shui design (including a "Heaven and Earth" Lantern at the Little Hay and Dixon Street corner) that are expected to appeal to today's difference-discerning tourists (City of Sydney 1998).

By contrast, the area of Aboriginal settlement in nearby Redfern has experienced a more troubled relationship with all arms and agencies of the state, including the department of the federal government committed to Aboriginal self-determination. Since its official designation as a site of Aboriginal housing in the early 1970s, Redfern's diverse and by no means united residents endured the hostility of non-Aboriginal locals and police, lurid stereotyping by the media, and recurring rounds of redevelopment of their increasingly blighted terrace houses. Most recently, in the wake of Olympics-led boosterism and soaring inner-city property prices, the contested block of housing was demolished and the remaining tenants dispersed with the blessing of certain Aboriginal interests (*Sydney Morning Herald* 2000). Hardly "celebrated" for its contribution to cosmopolitan Sydney, then, this local case, when set alongside that of Chinatown, reminds us that the entrenched institutional structures of colonial capitalism (analyzed so comprehensively by Yeoh [1996] for Singapore) are as alive in structuring the urban fabric and experience as the postmodern city's appetite for "playful pastiche."

Claims that cities are disorderly usually precede managerialist statements desiring the imposition of order. This is despite the long theoretical tradition in which the diversity of city dwellers, and the capacity of strangers to be positioned in the midst of this diversity, has been discussed and lauded. Difference-influenced scripts reveal the tension between accepting diversity in theory, and boxing and suppressing diversity in practice.

Conclusion

We have talked in this chapter of "scripts" about cities and the urban, referring to the ways cities are subject to certain explanatory modes that highlight different aspects of urbanism and urbanization at the expense of others. In the scripts on which we have dwelled to provide examples, there are clear traces of past rationalities – that the Chicago School is so often an object of critique, for example, is testament to its ongoing presence in our narratives about city lives. Though our particular interest has been to trace the amendments made in longstanding urban scripts by perspectives on difference, it is very clear that the concerns of political economy for social justice influence the very form of those newer difference-based perspectives on the city.

Scripts about difference continue on with narratives about cities, then, rather than always and everywhere producing new ones. And an emphasis on difference and the creation of diversity in cities does not erase the partiality and situatedness of the knowledge we produce about the urban. But perspectives developed from thinking about difference shed light on biases in longstanding urban narratives and explanations. They highlight the tendency of urban research to focus on favorite examples. Writings about the global city privilege certain cities as exemplars, and have nothing to say about most others. Most of urban studies is silent about social nature in cities, and continues the long tradition of positioning the urban outside the natural world. Reifying the urban as such also has secondary implications for scriptings of racialized and other axes of difference. Policy scripts make narrow judgments about the unacceptable existence of diversity in urban contexts, so that the strangers of certain migrant streams can be isolated and shunned, institutionally. Using perspectives influenced by thinking about difference exposes such tendencies.

Some urbanists have viewed theories of difference as destabilizing the progressive certainties and the reforming intent of urban studies grounded in a radical political economy. We conclude, instead, that difference perspectives protect against indifference to the subtle and diverse ways that injustice can be perpetuated. That is what they protect against – rather than protecting/preventing us from constructing generalizable similarities and uniformities that can be used for political purposes. The protection afforded by difference perspectives is political – and there can be progressive norms that result. Racisms, sexisms, or heteronormativities are exposed. Class issues, long the prerogative of political economy, are exposed too, as they cohere with other differentiating identity attributes.

When arguments occur in urban studies about the benefits of difference-oriented perspectives, it can be argued in fact that these perspectives help define new ways to be politically effective and inclusive, as well as producing significant situated knowledges.

Bibliography

Amin, A. and Graham, S. 1997: The ordinary city. *Transactions of the Institute of British Geographers NS* 22: 411–29.

Anderson, K. 1993: Place narratives and the origins of Sydney's Aboriginal settlement, 1972–73. *Journal of Historical Geography* 19 (3): 314–35.

Anderson, K. 1998: Beyond a cultural politics of race polarity. In R. Fincher and J. M. Jacobs (eds.), *Cities of Difference*. New York and London: Guilford Press, 201–25.

Andersson, R. 1999: "Divided cities" as a policy-based notion in Sweden. *Housing Studies* 14 (5): 601–24.
Braun, B. and Castree, N. 1998: *Remaking Nature: Nature at the Millennium.* London: Routledge.
Burgess, E. W. [1925] 1967: The growth of the city: an introduction to a research project. In R. E. Park and E. W. Burgess (eds.), *The City.* Chicago: Chicago University Press, 47–62.
Burnley, I. et al. 1997: *Immigration and Australian Cities.* Sydney: Federation Press.
Caldeira, T. P. R. 1999: Fortified enclaves: the new urban segregation. In S. Low (ed.), *Theorizing the City: The New Urban Anthropology Reader.* New Brunswick, NJ and London: Rutgers University Press.
Callicott, J. B. 1994: The role of technology in the evolving concept of nature. In F. Ferre and P. Hartel (eds.), *Ethics and Environmental Policy: Theory Meets Practice.* London: University of Georgia Press, 54–69.
City of Sydney 1998: *Haymarket Upgrade*, loose flier.
Cronon, W. 1991: *Nature's Metropolis: Chicago and the Great West.* New York and London: W. W. Norton.
Davis, M. 1990: *City of Quartz: Excavating the Future in Los Angeles.* London: Verso.
Dear, M. 2000: *The Postmodern Urban Condition.* Oxford and Malden, MA: Blackwell.
Diken, B. 1998: *Strangers, Ambivalence and Social Theory.* Aldershot: Ashgate.
Drewe, R. (ed.) 1997: *The Penguin Book of the City.* London: Penguin.
Duncan, J. S. 1996: Me(trope)olis: or Hayden White among the urbanists. In A. D. King (ed.), *Re-presenting the City: Ethnicity, Capital and Culture in the Twenty-first-century Metropolis.* Basingstoke and London: Macmillan, 253–68.
Fainstein, S. 1996: Justice, politics and the creation of urban space. In A. Merrifield and E. Swyngedouw (eds.), *The Urbanization of Injustice.* London: Lawrence and Wishart, 18–44.
Fraser, N. 2000: Rethinking recognition. *New Left Review* 3: 107–20.
Gale, F. 1972: *Urban Aborigines.* Canberra: Australian National University Press.
Hage, G. 1998: *White Nation: Fantasies of White Supremacy in a Multicultural Society.* Sydney: Pluto Press.
Harvey, D. 1996: *Justice, Nature and the Geography of Difference.* Oxford: Blackwell.
Hinchliffe, S. 1999: Cities and natures: intimate strangers. In J. Allen et al. (eds.), *Unsettling Cities: Movement/Settlement.* London: Routledge, 137–80.
Iveson, K. 2000: Beyond designer diversity: planners, public space and a critical politics of difference. *Urban Policy and Research* 18 (2): 219–38.
Jacobs, J. M. and Fincher, R. 1998: Introduction. In R. Fincher and J. M. Jacobs (eds.), *Cities of Difference.* New York and London: Guilford Press, 1–25.
Kearns, A. and Forrest, R. 2000: Social cohesion and multilevel urban governance. *Urban Studies* 37 (5–6): 995–1017.
King, A. D. 1996: Introduction: cities, texts and paradigms. In A. D. King (ed.), *Re-presenting the City: Ethnicity, Capital and Culture in the Twenty-first-century Metropolis.* Basingstoke and London: Macmillan, 1–22.
Low, S. 1996: The anthropology of cities: imagining and theorising the city. *Annual Review of Anthropology* 25: 383–409.

McDowell, L. 1999: City life and difference: negotiating diversity. In J. Allen et al. (eds.), *Unsettling Cities*. London: Routledge, 96–135.

McGee, T. R. 1967: *The Southeast Asian City: A Social Geography of the Primate Cities of Southeast Asia*. London: G. Bell.

—— 1989: Urbanisasi or kotadesai? Evolving urban patterns of urbanization in Asia. In F. J. Costa et al. (eds.), *Urbanization in Asia*. Honolulu: University of Hawaii Press, 93–108.

—— 1991: The emergence of *desakota* regions in Asia: expanding a hypothesis. In N. Ginsburg, B. Koppel, and T. R. McGee (eds.), *The Extended Metropolis: Settlement Transition in Asia*. Honolulu: University of Hawaii Press, 3–25.

McLaughlin, E. and Muncie, J. 1999: Walled cities: surveillance, regulation and segregation. In S. Pile et al. (eds.), *Unruly Cities? Order/Disorder*. London and New York: Routledge, in association with the Open University, 110–48.

Merrifield, A. 1996: Social justice and communities of difference: a snapshot from Liverpool. In A. Merrifield and E. Swyngedouw (eds.), *The Urbanization of Injustice*. London: Lawrence and Wishart, 200–22.

Mitchell, K. 1993: Multiculturalism, or the united colors of capitalism? *Antipode* 25: 263–94.

Musterd, S. and Ostendorf, O. (eds.) 1998: *Urban Segregation and the Welfare State*. London and New York: Routledge.

Owens, E. 1991: *The City in the Greek and Roman World*. London: Routledge.

Park, R. 1924: The concept of social distance: as applied to the study of racial attitudes and racial relations. *Journal of Applied Sociology* 8: 339–44.

Peel, M. 1995: *Good Times, Hard Times: The Past and the Future in Elizabeth*. Melbourne: Melbourne University Press.

Peters, E. 1996: "Urban" and "Aboriginal": an impossible contradiction. In J. Caulfield and L. Peake (eds.), *Critical Perspectives on Canadian Urbanism*. Toronto: University of Toronto Press, 47–62.

Philo, C. and Wilbert, C. (eds.) 2000: *Animal Spaces, Beastly Places*. London: Routledge.

Pick, D. 1989: *Faces of Degeneration: A European Disorder, c. 1848–1918*. Cambridge: Cambridge University Press.

Pile, S. 1999: What is a city? In D. Massey et al. (eds.), *City Worlds*. London: Routledge, 3–52.

Povinelli, E. A. 1998: The state of shame: Australian multiculturalism and the crisis of indigenous citizenship. *Critical Inquiry* 24: 575–61.

Rimmer, P. and Dick, H. 1998: Beyond the Third World City: The new urban geography in South-east Asia. *Urban Studies* 35 (12): 2303–21.

Robinson, J. 1999: Divisive cities: power and segregation in cities. In S. Pile et al. (eds.), *Unruly Cities? Order/Disorder*. London and New York: Routledge, in association with the Open University, 149–201.

Robson, B. 1994: No city, no civilisation. *Transactions, Institute of British Geographers NS* 19 (2): 131–41.

Rose, D. 1984: Rethinking gentrification: beyond the uneven development of Marxist urban theory. *Environment and Planning D: Society and Space* 2: 47–74.

Ross, A. 1994: *The Chicago Gangster Theory of Urban Life*. London: Verso.

Sassen, S. 1996: Analytic borderlands: race, gender and representation in the New City. In A. D. King (ed.), *Re-presenting the City: Ethnicity, Capital and Culture in the Twenty-first-century Metropolis*. Basingstoke and London: Macmillan, 183–202.

Shields, R. 1996: A guide to urban representation and what to do about it: alternative traditions of urban theory. In A. D. King (ed.), *Re-presenting the City: Ethnicity, Capital and Culture in the Twenty-first-century Metropolis*. Basingstoke and London: Macmillan, 227–53.

Smith, N. 1996: *The New Urban Frontier: Gentrification and the Revanchist City*. London and New York: Routledge.

Soja, E. W. 1989: *Postmodern Geographies*. New York: Verso.

—— 1996: Margin/Alia: social justice and the new cultural politics. In A. Merrifield and E. Swyngedouw (eds.), *The Urbanization of Injustice*. London: Lawrence and Wishart, 180–99.

Sydney Morning Herald 2000: There goes the neighbourhood. October 14, p. 33.

Williams, R. 1973: *The City and the Country*. London: Chatto and Windus.

Wolch, J., West, K., and Gaines, T. 1995: Trans-species urban theory. *Environment and Planning D: Society and Space* 13 (6): 735–60.

Yeoh, B. 1996: *Contesting Space: Power Relations and the Urban Built Environment in Colonial Singapore*. Oxford: Oxford University Press.

Young, I. M. 1990: *Justice and the Politics of Difference*. Princeton, NJ: Princeton University Press.

3
The Public City

Sophie Watson

This chapter charts shifts in notions of the public city, be it in the form of public resources, public space, or public sphere. Using feminist work and an ethnographic study of Orthodox Jews in North London as two lenses through which this complicated and complex terrain can be focused, I argue that the idea of the "public" in its various guises has been subject to a series of radical transformations over the last two decades. Partly this is a result of a markedly different political climate, and partly this results from new theoretical paradigms, which have disrupted or dismantled earlier ways of thinking.

I shall pursue a number of themes here. First, I shall look at the early political economy approaches to the public city, here conceived as the welfare state, which dominated so much of urban analysis from the 1970s to the early/mid-1980s. The next part of the chapter considers some of the ways that this dominance has been challenged, and how my own work has been influenced by, and in small measure contributed to, these shifts. The second section of the chapter considers new writings within urban analyses on the public city as public realm/public sphere, which have emerged as a result of the cultural turn. The argument here is not that political economy no longer has anything to offer us in understanding the public arenas of the city. Rather, it is to argue that the new approaches have opened up, or in some cases excavated, different terrains which extend the boundaries of what it means to construct a more fully democratic public realm. The final part of the chapter addresses the question of difference in the city in the context of claims by members of the Orthodox Jewish community for an *eruv* in Barnet, North London.

Political economy analysis counterposed the public city as a space of collective consumption where resources could be shared and services provided, in opposition to the capitalist city where provision of goods and services was linked to private capital and the pursuit of profit. In this formulation the public sector offered the potential for a more egalitarian city, while the pursuit of capital and private goods was seen to be inevitably implicated in the exploitation of one class by another. The public was thus celebrated as a space where working-class needs could be met and where gains in the form of public housing or public services were won or wrested from the capitalist system. This notion, however, was by no means unambiguous, and indeed was fiercely contested within different political economy approaches. Some political economists saw the welfare state (or public sector) as produced by class conflict and necessary to the success of capitalism since it kept workers (relatively) happy and mitigated against dissatisfaction with the system and potential revolt. Others saw the welfare state as a genuine gain won by workers in their struggles with capitalists (Ginsburg 1979; Gough 1979), while for some theorists the welfare state within capitalist societies was paradoxical; as Claus Offe put it, "while capitalism cannot coexist with, neither can it exist without, the welfare state" (1984: 153).

For feminists the welfare state was even more contradictory and ambiguous. Early feminist theory, drawing on Marxism or radical feminist notions of patriarchy, conceptualized the state as patriarchal and capitalist and as operating as some kind of unity, albeit a complex and contradictory one. In this model the state existed as a set of coherent and even homogeneous interests, based on underlying economic or sexual relations that existed outside the state and were directly represented or embodied in it. Though there was a diversity of positions and theory (Wilson 1977; McIntosh 1981; Williams 1989), there was a strong consensus around arguments that articulated the ways in which the welfare state within capitalism embedded women in patriarchal family relations, where women consistently were responsible for domestic labor and dependants, and were marginalized or excluded from a secure or well-paid position in the labor market.

Thus the patriarchal capitalist state was seen to work not just in the interests of capitalists but in the interests of men also. The lack of certain public services such as childcare or a public city that worked for women, such as public transport oriented to the complex journeys of women's daily lives rather than to the needs of commuters from the suburbs to the central city, illustrates the point. While public services were seen as potentially emancipatory and necessary for women to be independent of men and able to enter the public realm, women were thought to have little power in the public realm also. Men, so the story went, usually had the power to control and allocate resources and these resources themselves were often male defined and conceived. To take housing as an example (Matrix 1984; Watson and Austerberry 1986; Watson 1988), single women were shown to have less access to accommodation than single men, while fewer women were housing officers and managers in the public sector, lenders or landlords in the private sector, or architects, builders, or developers on the production side. Thus even where women did gain access to secure and affordable housing, feminists argued that it did not necessarily meet their needs. In this early formulation needs were seen to be given and knowable in advance and relatively (though not entirely) undifferentiated by race or sexuality.

Though in its welfare role the state was seen to have something to offer, in the early days it was resisted and embraced at the same time (London Edinburgh Weekend Return Group 1979). Feminist suspicion of the state was particularly strong in Britain, in contrast to the United States, Scandinavia, Australia, and Canada, where more benign or liberal feminist versions of the state saw its potential as a space of reform, equality legislation, and provider of resources (Watson 1989). Thus attempts to work within the arenas of the state were regarded with suspicion and were likely to be seen as indicative of co-option. Instead, *In and Against the State* (LEWRG 1979) exhorts people to build a culture of opposition. As the public city in Britain came under increasing attack in the 1980s, these early critiques left feminists defending resources and services which there had been little opportunity to change or influence.

Such arguments were increasingly criticized as poststructuralist critiques on the one hand, and, in Britain, black and Asian women on the other, disrupted and questioned these rather monolithic ways of seeing the world. From the perspective of race, gains made by women in the public sphere were exposed as far more ambiguous for minority women, since the welfare state was shown to be much less benign in its treatment of nonwhite women (Bhavnani and Coulson 1986; Williams 1989). The work of Foucault, in particular, opened up new ways of thinking which challenged the earlier Marxist paradigms and in particular the notion of power as possessed by the few – be it the bourgeoisie or some patriarchal section thereof. In this earlier formulation, for equality and emancipation to be won, workers, women, and other minorities had to wrest some of this power for themselves. Instead power came to be seen as exercised rather than possessed, and networked and capillary rather than fixed. Adopting a more fluid notion of power as residing in all social relations opened up the possibility of a multiplicity of forms of resistance. As Brown (1992: 28–31) reflected in relation to the United States, as the state's masculinism became more pervasive and potent it also became more diffuse, multiple, and contradictory, and thus potentially deconstructible. My own work (1989; Pringle and Watson 1989, 1992, 1996) on the state was part of this trajectory.

Of relevance here was our focus on a politics of interests (Pringle and Watson 1992, 1996) to disrupt and challenge the more traditional formulations of the state and of need. Laclau and Mouffe's (1985) work was also important in facilitating a break with essentialist conceptions of the state and social structure in its rejection of totalizing theories of society. While not denying that a real world exists, they indicated that the distinction between discursive and nondiscursive is unnecessary. If we look carefully at "nondiscursive" complexes, we will find that they are always given meaning through discursive practices. We thus suggested that rather than seeing the state as a unified structure, it would be more useful to see it as a set of arenas, which were a byproduct of political struggles. At the same time, seeing interests as discursively constructed and constituted in interactions within and between the arenas of the state, rather than as fixed and defined in advance, avoided the traps associated with seeing the state as a fixed entity. This move was made possible by the "critique of a category of unified subject which open(ed) the way to a recognition of a plurality of antagonisms constituted on the basis of different subject positions" (Pringle and Watson 1992: 67). Thus interests could be seen as created through different languages and discourses where different possibilities for change could emerge.

There are parallels here with Fraser's notion of multiple publics or subaltern counter-publics (Fraser 1990). In her argument the differences between groups constitute distinct public realms rather than a singular public realm which, in her thinking, is organized around a concern with the balance between a politics of representation and a politics of recognition. Exclusive public realms (what she calls subaltern counter-publics) might enable the disempowered to gain recognition. Following the logic of this argument, the ambiguous nature of urban space for different groups, produced in different places and spaces of power, makes the notion of a singular public realm or public space that suits everyone highly problematic.

A second strand that can be identified is work on the private/public dichotomy. Again, there is a plethora of debates and developments that could be charted here. In summary, though, over the last two or more decades the old binary of public–private has been increasingly dismantled and the old analytic divisions between public and private have become more fluid and differentiated. City spaces are thus less easily defined as either public or private, while the recognition of less visible practices in the city has changed the boundaries of public and private spaces. Feminist critiques have played a crucial role in this conceptual shift. Reflecting on my own early work on homelessness (published in 1986 but conceived two or three years earlier in the heyday of political economy) in the context of this chapter, I was struck by two things. On the one hand, my Marxist-feminist – or political economy – sympathies at that time led to an interpretation of my research findings on homeless single women as showing that women were homeless as a result primarily of a patriarchal capitalist housing system which marginalized women's housing needs. Indeed, this intellectual sympathy obscured some of the other possibly relevant issues of a woman's psychic state, criminal record, drugs use, and so on, since these, I argued, endorsed earlier models of homelessness which blamed the victim.

At the same time, the research gestured toward, and even opened up some space for, the subsequently more culturally influenced approaches to the problem. It also strongly challenged the notion of public–private boundaries and questions of public visibility. Women's homelessness was hidden, I argued, precisely because the "home" contained different meanings for women, and so also did homelessness, which took different forms from the more public nature of men's homelessness. What was missing, though, was any address to questions of embodiment, transgression, performativity, and subjectivity which would be at the center of any similar study that I might undertake now.

Thus, when I came to write recently on this question, on the basis of secondary material (Watson 1999), I found that recent research had identified psychological factors and a history of abuse and violence as important as the more structural issues (Brotchie n.d.; Tomas and Dittmar 1995; Passaro 1996; Cowan 1997). Of interest to me also was how homeless women subjects were constructed and in particular how they are seen as embodied subjects. Drawing on the work of Wright (1997), who makes the point that "people living on the street are not just neutral bodies, but subjugated bodies and resisting bodies moving through, sitting, lying down, and sleeping in, the social-physical spaces of the city, a negative trope for surrounding housed society" (1997: 58), I suggested that:

> homeless women's bodies can be seen to represent a challenge to the feminine body, the mother or wife located in the home, cooking in the kitchen, going about her daily domestic tasks. In a sense she comes to be the feared "other," held up as a counterpoint to happy "normal" life. As such the homeless woman serves to keep housed women in their place, by her presence she becomes a reminder to all women of what they might become if they step out of line. By sleeping on the street wrapped in a blanket, by bringing her bed into the street as it were, she is also starkly disrupting the public/private boundary on which much planning regulation is based. What we see in a graphic way is the private seeping into the public in disruptive and threatening ways. Where women in a society signify caring, nurturing, cleanliness, well kept, groomed and maintained bodies, the homeless woman's body comes to be seen as all the more grotesque. (1999: 96)

I suggested further that how homeless bodies are constructed offers an illustration of the way in which negative symbolic representations can serve yet further to marginalize the already marginalized. This represents a rather different trope to that which framed my earlier work. Having said that, however, is not to suggest, as a response to my most recent paper on this topic (Ravetz 2000) argued, that I would no longer see women's homelessness as centrally a product of a housing system oriented toward profit and favoring those with high incomes (who may also often be white men); simply, it is to introduce further nuances to the argument.

Theoretical shifts have played a crucial role in thinking about the state and public provision. An equally important force for change has been the political and economic climate of the 1980s and 1990s, particularly during the Thatcher and Reagan administrations. During this period the new right agenda that emerged managed to shift irrevocably the terms of the debate such that notions of the public became increasingly tainted with notions of rigid bureaucracy, red tape, inefficiency, lack of flexibility, poor responsiveness, wastage, poor design and innovation, and so on. The success of this position subverted the idea that comprehensive public provision in the city might be beneficial, let alone possible or even desirable. As the grip of new right thinking and policy lost its hold, having wreaked havoc with large areas of public provision – particularly in Britain – such as public housing, new ideas have arisen which advocate a more mixed economy, diverse forms of provision, and links between private and public initiatives. This represents a new kind of politics – in Britain characterized by New Labour's "third way," which looks for a private–public mix. According to Jessop (2000: 171–85), what we see is the shift from a "Keynesian welfare national state" to a "Schumpeterian workfare post-national regime." This, he suggests, represents a greater subordination of social policy to economic imperatives. These political shifts have spawned innovative debates in the academic arena (see Lewis et al. 2000) which raise new dimensions to welfare such as those presented by the body, emotions, and time, and argue for an expansion of the boundaries of social policy to include more complex understandings of the subjects of welfare practice. However, the public city as a space of extensive, democratic, and equitable public provision seems a long way off.

A final strand of work on the public city that warrants attention here is urbanists' work on public space over the last decade or more, which is broadly developed also within a political economy framework. Many studies have drawn attention to the ways in which urban space has increasingly been privatized or savagely withdrawn, particularly in the downtown areas, to serve the interests of the growing middle classes and to sanitize the streets for the tourist gaze. Here we find cogent accounts of the decline of the public space and public realm (Zukin 1991; Sorkin 1992; Mitchell 1995). In non-Western cities street traders, hawkers, and the homeless are purged from the streets to make way for a certain sort of public life that serves the interests of the wealthy and the "formal" economy. This goes for Western cities as well. At the extremes the privatization of public space has been exposed as fortress-like and militaristic as private interests exert literal or symbolic violence on those urban dwellers whose presence unsettles economic interests. There are rolltop benches to prevent rough sleeping in Los Angeles (Davis 1990) to militaristic sweeps of city streets in Yogyakarta to clean up the street children (Beazley 2000). Hitherto open and uncontrolled public spaces of the city, sites of unpredictable encounter, have been revealed as subject to controls and surveillance or as reconstructed into semi-privatized spaces as the enclosed atrium replaces the courtyard and the shopping mall replaces the street. Other urbanists have explored how the power of private capital to thematize and commodify these spaces as sites of consumption has further degraded the opportunity for idling, casual mutual performance and display, and chance engagement (Sorkin 1992).

Public Space – Public Realm

With the cultural turn in urban theory there has been a move away from a focus on the distribution of public resources as materially defined to a more fluid and complex understanding of the public realm as defined by notions of the symbolic, the imaginary, performance, and theatricality. Though political economy approaches tended to ignore these realms, a long tradition of writing on the city and on public space from modernist to psychoanalytic writers had preceded the rather drier period of Marxist and neo-Marxist analysis which wrote out the more subtle understandings of subjectivity. Thus, for example, Virginia Woolf powerfully interwove the inner thoughts and musings of her characters with the spaces of the city through which they moved. In a late draft of "The Years" (Woolf 1998: appendix; see Johnson 2000), we find Eleanor in London looking at a big shop that was being pulled down:

> a line of scaffolding zigzagged across the sky. There was something violent and crazy in the crooked lines. It seemed to her, as she looked up, that there was something violent and crazy in the whole world tonight. It was tumbling and falling, pitching forward to disaster. The crazy lines of the scaffolding, the jagged outline of the broken wall, the bestial shouts of the young men, made her feel that there was no order, no purpose in the world, but all was tumbling to ruin beneath a perfectly indifferent polished moon. (1998: 401)

As Johnson concludes in her discussion of Joyce, Woolf, and the city:

> Both Joyce and Woolf repeatedly and insistently returned to site their novels in the urban space of the Modern City. For both, the sedimented layers of history lay behind and beneath and upon the surfaces of Dublin and London. For both, the meaning of the lives of those who lived therein were produced within and by means of those very material cities. For both . . . these cities were insistently themselves and persistently something other. (2000: 211)

Literary and psychoanalytic theorists have known this for a long time. But what has changed is that urban analysts in the last ten to fifteen years have become interested in these ways of seeing and have drawn on a diversity of philosophical, literary, and psychoanalytic texts to understand the city.

Thus Pile in his book *Body and the City* (1996) mapped the borderlands between psychoanalytic and geographical imaginations producing a different understanding of urban space. In a more recent chapter (2000) Pile develops these ideas further, drawing parallels between cities and dreams which, he suggests, though apparently random, have "an inner meaning, an inner rule, a perspective, a discourse" (2000: 76). Like others (e.g., Vidler 1992; Gilloch 1996; Cohen 2000; Keith 2000) he draws on the writings of Walter Benjamin and Sigmund Freud to reimagine the city in less material ways. In particular, Freud's writing on the uncanny – the *unheimlich* – drew attention to the way in which ghosts or figures from the past can reemerge in the familiar spaces of the city and unsettle us, while Walter Benjamin's writings allude to the phantasmagoric, fantastical, surreal, and illusory facets of the city and the city as "text and emblem" (Keith 2000: 414).

Another strand of urban writings sees the public realm as a space of everyday life, performativity, and play. Here, the writings of de Certeau (1984) and Lefebvre (1991) have been particularly influential. In Lefebvre the idea of rhythmanalysis can reveal the daily rhythms that organize everyday life in the city, while in de Certeau we follow the notion of the poetics of walking in the city to discover those things that urban analysis in its conventional sense has failed to alert us to:

> The ordinary practitioners of the city live "down below," below the thresholds at which visibility begins. They walk – an elementary form of this experience of the city; they are walkers, *Wandersmanner*, whose bodies follow the thicks and thins of an urban "text" they write without being able to read it . . . The networks of these moving, intersecting writings compose a manifold story that has neither author nor spectator, shaped by fragments of trajectories and alterations of spaces: in relation to representations, it remains daily and indefinitely other. (de Certeau 1984: 93)

Rossiter and Gibson (2000) explore this idea through analyzing an experiment in Melbourne by a group of performance artists, who sealed themselves in isolation in a shop window for sixteen days as they conducted their daily routines in full view of the public. In order partly to expose the increased technological surveillance of life in the city, the "experiment turned the disciplinary power of panopticon vision into a game. The Urban Dream Capsule transformed a common tactic of the urban marginalized – occupation and performance – into an acceptable art form" (Rossiter and Gibson 2000: 442).

Through a different route of intellectual enquiry Sennett also arrives at his own version of performativity in the public realm. For him the crucial question is how to revivify the public realm. Starting with *The Fall of Public Man*

(1974), Sennett's concern is to reverse what he sees as the decline of the public sphere and a retreat into the private domain. In part he attributes this to the monofunctional and bland spaces of the city and the savage destruction of public space by private interests and capital. To reverse this trend and to build a city where difference can thrive, Sennett proposes the idea of the *teatro mundi* – an idea of public life where there are spaces conducive to role playing. In these spaces which are multifunctional and disordered, people are provoked to notice others who are different, to react to them and to encounter strangers. This, according to Sennett (1974: 385), creates more vivacity in public spaces and enhances public life.

Difference in the City and the Making of Symbolic Space

In the last part of this chapter I want to suggest two things. First, that taking difference seriously in the city can be uncomfortable and difficult. This proposition represents a departure from an earlier notion that race, gender, class, and other divisions could at some level be resolved. Instead it is to suggest that urban research and politics need to address the "others" with whom we are at the very least uncomfortable, and at most, toward whom we feel antagonism. So much of the celebration of difference in the city has obscured relations of power. It has also shied away from confronting how, for example, to deal with groups like the far right or those whose cultural practices and values differ from our own in unpalatable ways. Or to raise an even more difficult question, what does it mean to encounter strangers in the city when these strangers are out to do us in? That said, I shy away from the idea of interviewing the young white men who killed Stephen Lawrence in Southeast London, and who have been responsible for countless other instances of racial and sexual harassment.

The second point, and there is now already a considerable body of work in this field, is to argue for attention to be paid to the symbolic realm of public spaces and how these are imbued with power (Keith and Pile 1993; Zukin 1995; Cohen 2000). This terrain was a significant lacuna in the political economy project.

These two concerns have led me into a small study of the conflicts that have arisen in a borough of North London – Barnet – over the attempts by one section of the Orthodox Jewish community to construct an *eruv* (to be defined shortly). My interest arose precisely because this was a minority claim which has sparked considerable hostility both from middle-class professionals in the locality and Jewish socialists of my acquaintance. Given both these groups often express support for spatial claims by minority and ethnic groups in the city, I was interested to find out whence this hostility arose. This work is in progress. In the meantime I have discovered other published work on this issue (see Cooper 1996; Valins 2000), but for my purposes here I am drawing on my own interviews and assembled council documents.

According to the Boston *eruv* website:

> The purpose of an *eruv* is to integrate a number of private and public properties into one larger private domain. Consequently, individuals within the *eruv* district are then permitted to move objects across what was before the erection of the *eruv* a public private domain boundary. Thus, one may carry from one's home to the sidewalk, and then, for example, to someone else's home.

Or, according to the definition of the Public Works Committee of Barnet council, June 30, 1992:

> An *eruv* is a zone which makes public areas "private" in nature to the followers of the Orthodox Jewish faith. Without an *eruv* they are prohibited from carrying anything in public, i.e., outside their homes on the Sabbath, this requirement extending to keys, handkerchiefs, medicine and the pushing of babies in prams.

In the absence of an *eruv* traditional Jews are prevented by the laws of the Talmud from carrying anything outside the home on the Sabbath. This restriction impacts particularly on women with young children, the disabled, the frail elderly who need sticks, and so on. From the Orthodox Jewish point of view, the *eruv* is a rational solution to a problem. It is a very complex and intricate concept defined also in a further volume of the Talmud. Though in contemporary Western thought, particularly following feminist critique, the public–private distinction is recognized as highly symbolic, problematic, and even pernicious, in the Talmud the distinction is taken as literal and thus a literal solution is found. Thus the public is redefined as domestic by virtue of a new physical boundary. By building a perimeter or demarcating space, for the purposes of the Sabbath, that area becomes defined as a private domain or as one community and permits those people who need to carry, to reach a synagogue on the Sabbath, and to meet with friends in neighborhood zones and to share a festive meal together to do so. In the Barnet case those benefiting, were the *eruv* to be constructed, are estimated to be ten thousand people. A number of Orthodox Jewish women I interviewed were particularly keen on the *eruv*, since for them it meant the considerable diminishment of the isolation they experienced as mothers of small children.

There are over 150 *eruvin* in other cities of the world, including in the United States, Canada, South Africa, Europe, and Australia. What interests me is the extent of particular resistance to the concept in this case. The application for planning permission for the *eruv* was first lodged by the United Synagogue in 1992. What is being sought is the permission to put up poles to be connected by fish wire in thirty-seven locations in the borough. These are required to join up any gap where the perimeter is breached by a highway or other feature. The rest of the boundary is constituted by existing structures such as a railway, road, or rows of houses. The proposed poles are of metal or timber, in line with lighting or telegraph poles, and as such are intended to blend in with the existing streetscape.

The application was refused by the Town Planning and Research Committee in October 1993 on the grounds that the poles and wires would be visually intrusive and detrimental to the character and appearance of the street scene. As a result of an appeal by the *Eruv* Committee, the Ministry of the Environment carried out an inquiry. The Inspector's report, which claimed that the issue was one of poles and wire, and not the concept of the *eruv*, recommended planning permission should be granted on the grounds that there was no substantial basis for objection. Nearly a decade later the *eruv* has still not been constructed as a result of different objections raised whenever planning permission has been requested for any specific location. In the words of one rabbi interviewed:

> it looks like it will run and run. When each pole requires site inspection and approval by the five utilities and the council, and if one objects and asks for the pole to be moved five feet to the left, with the result that the process starts all over again, then it is easy to see how this could go on for ever.

At the same time reams of objections have been lodged by local residents' associations. What is interesting is that many of these groups include large numbers of non-Orthodox Jewish people, as well as another section of the Orthodox Jewish community who object to the *eruv* on religious grounds. As the superintendent of Hampstead Heath (a corner of which is encompassed within the *eruv* boundary) explained, "[t]his is the single most divisive issue that the Jewish community has ever seen."

The objections from the council were articulated either in a rational discourse of the impediment the poles would cause to other users or in a discourse of aesthetics. There was no doubt in the minds of some of the protagonists whom I interviewed that these masked a level of racism. As several explained, there are countless poles in the street, many of which have been put up since 1992, such as for cable television or parking, which do not raise the same objections and which likewise serve only a section of the community. The objections from the local residents' associations, of which there were many, were also framed within apparently rational claims but likewise seemed to mask forms of racism and hostility. Indeed, some were little short of ludicrous:

> Location 4, Lyndale Avenue, NW2:
> "encourage fouling by dogs"

"threat to security and encourage burglaries"
"blot on landscape and would reduce value of our property"
"post would flout our rationalist and humanist convictions"

Location 25, Watford Way:
"Sunnyhill Park is an area where young birds nest and any loss through the young flying into the wire would be disastrous"

Location 13, Wildwood Road, NW1:
"attract graffiti and vandalism"
"detrimental to health"
"hazard to wildlife"

Location 08C, Hermitage Lane, NW2:
"posts will add to the already numerous problems for the old, blind and small children"
"the reduction in visibility of oncoming traffic caused by the pole"
"raise house prices in the area"

Various Jewish people whom I interviewed, who would define themselves as socialists, were particularly hostile to the *eruv* on the grounds it would make a spectacle of the community and open them to abuse and hostility. Here the argument is that while the *eruv* is simply symbolic, the symbolism is the very point – symbols have power, power to define boundaries of segregation and exclusion. They see the Orthodox Jews as making spectacles of themselves and raising visibility, thereby mobilizing racism in the non-Jewish community. Other Jewish people in the area concurred with this view:

Location 2, Farm Avenue, NW2:
"Sister survived Auschwitz and we are worried of her reaction when confronted with these posts and wires"
"as Jewish refugees we arrived in England from Hitler's Europe. Every time we leave our house we will be reminded of concentration camps and the division of areas for Jews and Non-Jews"

Location 4, Lyndale Avenue, NW2:
"creation of a Ghetto"
"will create racial tension and anti-Semitism"
"do not wish to encourage trouble from any religious group"

Location 05A, Sunnyside, NW2:
"would encourage segregation and a ghetto mentality, and may result in the National Front targeting the area"

The symbolic nature of the *eruv* is thus central. For members of the council, the significance of the *eruv* was hard to grasp or take seriously. In response to this the Orthodox Jews claimed that "if the *eruv* has no meaning for you, what are the foundations for any objection, given the marginal impact and material impacts of its construction?" What we have is one system of meaning clashing with another and two rational legal frameworks – one premodern which derives its authority from God, and one post-Enlightenment which derives its authority from "man." Yet by denying its construction the opposers also are acknowledging its symbolic and social significance – its potential to mobilize spaces of inclusion and exclusion – even if in different terms, while to submit to the construction of the *eruv* is implicitly to submit to a different system of rationality, to give it some credibility and recognize its relevance.

There are many interesting arguments to be made about the *eruv*, but for my purposes here, there are several points that I want to draw out. First, on the question of difference. What this case study raises is the problem of multiculturalism in Britain. As Hall (2001) argues, there are many different multiculturalisms – conservative, liberal, pluralist, commercial, corporate, critical – each of which has its problems. Multiculturalism is a highly contested term, but what is clear is that we live in a multicultural society where difference in the city has to be negotiated and confronted, and a new multicultural political logic has to be identified: "such a strategy would . . . effect a radical reconfiguration of the particular and the universal, of liberty and equality with difference" (Hall 2001). This is no easy task, as Hage, writing in the context of Australia, suggests (1998: 53); those national subjects who are born to the dominant culture, who "accumulate the national capital in the form of the dominant linguistic, physical and cultural dispositions," aspire to the fantasy of an imagined space – the "White Nation" – in which they can legitimately control and spatially manage others.

As this case study shows, tolerance to, and acceptance of, "the other," multicultural policies, and the various strategies for inclusion are all predicated on the assumption of legitimate power and control. The following objection from a local residents' group illustrates the assumed dominance of an English subject position only too well:

> It seems unfortunate that the committed local interests involved were not informed at an early stage that the law of the highway embodies fundamental English ideas about the liberty of the subject. It speaks of "the rights of the public," "all of her Majesty's subjects," "the public generally" . . . The Rabbinic legal concepts of the *eruv* are out of keeping with the laws of England, which in the case of the basic law affecting the public highway, derive from time immemorial. As a matter of law those members of the public, who have sensed that their legal and democratic rights are threatened by the pursuit of this scheme, are right. (Barnet Town Planning and Research Committee minutes, October 27, 1993: 114)

If we start from the basis that negotiations need to recognize and confront power relations, then where a community is itself divided on how to represent itself and its cultural practices, these negotiations are likely to be even more complex and fraught. Putting aside the lack of support from within the Orthodox Jewish community, which Valins (2000: 583) suggests partly derives from the difficulties of applying ancient concepts to a contemporary urban conurbation, and partly from fear of the social consequences of easing Sabbath restrictions, the more widespread hostility from non-Orthodox Jews warrants some explanation. The views expressed seemed either to focus on the problem of Jewish people constructed as spectacle, or on the anticipated abuse and violence that would arise from increased visibility. Certainly, the *eruv*, as Valins puts it (2000: 582), "normalises orthodox Jews to come out as 'ordinary' citizens. Yet the essential otherness of the orthodox Jew remains. The *eruv*'s danger is it allows such 'otherness' public expression." Or, it could be argued, that for assimilated and secular Jews "the *eruv* proposal publicly identified, and produced, them as alien in ways that jeopardized their place within the cultural hierarchy" (Cooper 1996: 538). Given that assimilation has meant conforming to dominant Anglo-Christian norms, this is undoubtedly the case.

What is clear here is that the different subject positions within this potentially differentiated and marginalized group are not easily resolved in any one solution. Nevertheless, how to live difference in the city, especially when it is awkward to address rather than easy to celebrate or exotic, has to be a central focus of urban research and action over following decades. The second conclusion to be drawn from this case study is the power of symbolic space. Here in Barnet we see a clash between the rational city, as mobilized in planning discourses, and the symbolic city, as mobilized in an ancient religious text. These two systems of meaning are apparently incommensurable, yet space in the city can be read in a multitude of ways and produces an infinite set of meanings. Exploring these will provide another fruitful path for future urban research.

In conclusion, then, this chapter set out to show that though political economy approaches highlighted and continue to highlight important material inequities and divisions in the city, inequities that still need to be tackled and addressed, the new literatures of difference and the cultural turn in urban studies have produced understandings which extend these earlier approaches in new and exciting ways. Here I have argued that in order to build (and rebuild) a public realm or public city where different needs can be expressed and met, where new meanings can be articulated, and where marginalized and excluded populations can find a voice or space in the city and have access to the resources they need, different ways of thinking about the public city and public space need to be found and woven into the more established demands for social justice and equity. These would combine insights both from political economy and from cultural approaches to urban studies in stimulating and productive ways.

Bibliography

Barrett, M. and Phillips, A. (eds.) 1992: *Destabilising Theory*. Cambridge: Polity Press.

Beazley, H. 2000: Streetboys in Yogyakarta: social and spatial exclusion in the public spaces of the city. In G. Bridge and S. Watson (eds.), *A Companion to the City*. Oxford: Blackwell, 472–88.

Bhavnani, K. and Coulson, M. 1986: Transforming socialist feminism: the challenge of racism. *Feminist Review* 23.

Bridge, G. and Watson, S. (eds.) 2000: *A Companion to the City*. Oxford: Blackwell.

Brotchie, J. n.d.: *No Place like Home*. Brighton: Brighton and Hove Women's Homelessness Project.

Brown, W. 1992: Finding the man in the state. *Feminist Studies* 18 (1): 7–34.

Cohen, P. 2000: From the other side of the tracks: dual cities, third spaces and the urban uncanny in contemporary discourses of race and class. In G. Bridge and S. Watson (eds.), *A Companion to the City*. Oxford: Blackwell, 316–30.

Cooper, D. 1996: Talmudic territory? Space, law and modernist discourse. *Journal of Law and Society* 23 (4): 529–48.

Cowan, D. 1997: *Homelessness: The (In)Appropriate Applicant*. Aldershot: Ashgate.

Davis, M. 1990: *City of Quartz: Excavating the Future in Los Angeles*. London: Verso.

De Certeau, M. 1984: *The Practice of Everyday Life*. Trans. S. Rendell. Berkeley: University of California Press.

Fraser, N. 1990: Rethinking the public sphere: a contribution to the critique of actually existing democracy. *Social Text* 25: 56–80.

Gilloch, G. 1996: *Myth and Metropolis: Walter Benjamin and the City*. Cambridge: Polity Press.

Ginsburg, N. 1979: *Class, Capital and Social Policy*. London: Macmillan.

Gough, I. 1979: *The Political Economy of the Welfare State*. London: Macmillan.

Hage, G. 1998: *White Nation*. Sydney: Pluto Press.

Hall, S. 2001: The multicultural question. In B. Hesse (ed.), *Un/Settled Multiculturalisms*. London: Zed Books.

Jessop, B. 2000: From the KWNS to the SWPR. In G. Lewis et al. (eds.), *Rethinking Social Policy*. London: Sage.

Johnson, J. 2000: Literary geography: Joyce, Woolf and the city. *City* 4 (2): 199–214.

Keith, M. 2000: Walter Benjamin, urban studies and the narratives of city life. In G. Bridge and S. Watson (eds.), *A Companion to the City*. Oxford: Blackwell, 410–29.

—— and Pile, S. (eds.) 1993: *Place and the Politics of Identity*. London: Routledge.

Laclau, E. and Mouffe, C. 1985: *Hegemony and Socialist Strategy*. London: Verso.

Lefebvre, H. 1991: *The Production of Space*. Oxford: Blackwell.

Lewis, G. et al. (eds.) 2000: *Rethinking Social Policy*. London: Sage.

London Edinburgh Weekend Return Group (LEWRG) 1979: *In and Against the State*. London: Pluto Press.

McIntosh, M. 1981: Feminism and social policy. *Critical Social Policy* 1 (1): 32–43.
Matrix, 1984: *Making Space: Women and the Man Made Environment*. London: Pluto Press.
Mitchell, D. 1995: The end of public space? People's Park, definitions of the public and democracy. *Annals of the Association of American Geographers* 85: 108–33.
Offe, C. 1984: *Contradictions of the Welfare State*. London: Hutchinson.
Passaro, J. 1996: *The Unequal Homeless: Men on the Streets, Women in their Place*. London: Routledge.
Pateman, C. 1988: *The Sexual Contract*. Cambridge: Polity Press.
Pile, S. 1996: *The Body and the City*. London: Routledge.
——2000: Sleepwalking in the modern city: Walter Benjamin and Sigmund Freud in the world of dreams. In G. Bridge and S. Watson (eds.), *A Companion to the City*. Oxford: Blackwell, 75–86.
Pringle, R. and Watson, S. 1989: Fathers, brothers, mates: the fraternal state in Australia. In S. Watson (ed.), *Playing the State: Australian Feminist Interventions*. London: Verso.
——and ——1992: Women's interests and the post-structuralist state. In M. Barrett and A. Phillips (eds.), *Destabilising Theory*. Cambridge: Polity Press, 64–80.
——and ——1996: Feminist theory and the state: needs, rights and interests. In B. Sullivan and G. Whitehouse (eds.), *Gender, Politics and Citizenship in the 1990s*. Sydney: University of New South Wales Press.
Ravetz, A. 2000: A response. *City* 4 (1): 105–6.
Rossiter, B. and Gibson, K. 2000: A Melbourne chronicle. In G. Bridge and S. Watson (eds.), *A Companion to the City*. Oxford: Blackwell, 437–47.
Sennett, R. 1974: *The Fall of Public Man*. New York: W. W. Norton.
——2000: Reflections on the public realm. In G. Bridge and S. Watson (eds.), *A Companion to the City*. Oxford: Blackwell, 380–7.
Simmel, G. 1903a: The metropolis and mental life. In *Metropolis: Centre and Symbol of our Times*. Ed. P. Kasinitz. Macmillan: Basingstoke, 30–45.
——1903b: On spatial projections of social forms. *Zeitschrift für Sozialwissenschaft* 6: 287–302.
——1903c: Soziologie des Raumes Jahrbruch für Gesetzgebung. *Verwaltung und Volkswirtschaft* 27: 27–71.
Sorkin, M. 1992: *Variations on a Theme Park: The New American City and the End of Public Space*. New York: Hill and Wong.
Tomas, A. and Dittmar, H. 1995: The experience of homeless women: an exploration of housing histories and the meaning of home. *Housing Studies* 10 (4): 493–17.
Valins, O. 2000: Institutionalised religion: sacred texts and Jewish spatial practice. *Geoforum* 31: 575–86.
Vidler, A. 1992: *The Architectural Uncanny: Essays in the Modern Unhomely*. Cambridge, MA: MIT Press.
Watson, S. 1988: *Accommodating Inequality*. Sydney: Allen and Unwin.
——(ed.) 1989: *Playing the State: Australian Feminist Interventions*. London: Verso.
——1999: A home is where the heart is: engendering notions of homelessness. In P. Kennett and A. Marsh (eds.), *Homelessness: Exploring the New Terrain*. Bristol: Policy Press.
——and Austerberry, H. 1986: *Housing and Homelessness: A Feminist Perspective*. London: Routledge.

Williams, F. 1989: *Social Policy: A Critical Introduction*. Cambridge: Polity Press.
Wilson, E. 1977: *Women and the Welfare State*. London: Tavistock.
Woolf, V. 1998: *The London Years*. London: Penguin.
Wright, T. 1997: *Out of Place: Homeless Mobilisations, Subcities, and Contested Landscapes*. Albany, NY: State University of New York Press.
Zukin, S. 1991: *Landscapes of Power*. Oxford: Blackwell.
—— 1995: *The Culture of Cities*. Oxford: Blackwell.

4
Social Justice and the South African City

David M. Smith

These restless broken streets where definitions fail – the houses the outhouses of white suburbs, two-windows-one-door, multiplied in institutional rows; the hovels with tin lean-tos sheltering huge old American cars blowzy with gadgets; the fancy suburban burglar bars on mean windows of tiny cabins; the roaming children, wolverine dogs, hobbled donkeys, fat naked babies, vagabond chickens and drunks weaving, old men staring, authoritative women shouting, boys in rags, tarts in finery, the smell of offal cooking, the neat patches of mealies between shebeen yards stinking of beer and urine, the litter of twice-discarded possessions, first thrown out by the white man and then picked over by the black – is this conglomerate urban or rural? No electricity in the houses, a telephone an almost impossible luxury: is this a suburb or a strange kind of junk yard? The enormous back yard of the white city, where categories and functions lose their ordination and logic. Gordimer (1979)

Introduction

When I edited a collection of papers on urbanization and social change in South Africa two decades ago (Smith 1982), I used the quotation above as an epigraph. Nadine Gordimer eloquently and perceptively evoked the landscape of the African or black "township," a settlement form devised in colonial times, multiplied under apartheid, and modified by the material necessity of those forced to live there. As she was writing, the institutional rows of the

The research on which this chapter is based has been supported by the Human Sciences Research Council (South Africa), the Central Research Fund and Hayter Fund (University of London), the British Council, and the Leverhulme Trust. I am particularly grateful to Brij Maharaj and colleagues in the Department of Geography, University of Durban-Westville, for their assistance on visits from 1996 to 1999. Earlier visits were facilitated by the Universities of Cape Town, Natal, and the Witwatersrand. Thanks to Gustav Visser, Rob Higham, and Priscilla Cunnan for commenting on the chapter in draft, and also to the latter for permission to draw on her research.

archetype of such places, Soweto on the edge of Johannesburg, were being infiltrated by spontaneous accretions, from backyard shacks to the shantytown which enveloped what the planners had left as open space for a golf course. Neat land-use zoning was yielding to the spontaneous reaction of the victims of that special form of racial discrimination and injustice that characterized apartheid.

Informal "squatter" settlements were also consolidating and spreading elsewhere, most extensively around Durban, as growing numbers of black people sought a precarious perch close to the economic opportunities provided by the city. It was the survival of the famous Crossroads near Cape Town in the middle of the 1970s, against the threat of the bulldozers which the authorities had customarily used to impose their spatial order, that gave these places some semblance of security, and eventually permanence. In the process, those who saw them as part of the solution to black urbanization rather than part of the problem, in the spirit of the increasingly permissive attitude to informal settlement elsewhere in the underdeveloped world, inadvertently invited further challenges to the grand design of apartheid society.

The notion of "the city" and of "urbanization" took on both practical and mythological significance under apartheid. Those large and densely settled areas which resembled Western European and American cities were thought of and designated by those who ruled as "white." A major imperative of state planning practice was to maintain this myth, in the face of the reality of large numbers of black residents required to supply the mines, factories, and municipal services with labor. Hence the policy of "influx control," which attempted to restrict further black rural-to-urban migration. This involved the invention of black mini-states ("homelands" or "Bantustans") based on tribal affiliation, where the African people were supposed to reside and indulge their political rights – even if actually living in the "white" cities. That some townships adjoining the city of Durban, for example, could be deemed part of what was supposed to be (or become) an independent black state further consolidated the official geographical imagination. Meanwhile, the people themselves created their own geographies, although not in conditions of their choosing, as they brought their customs from the countryside to the townships and shack settlements.

Questions of definition – whether these places were "urban" or "rural," "city" or otherwise – were thus of more than purely academic interest. They formed the basis of the apartheid state's spatial politics of divide and rule, by means of which a minority of the population could maintain the myth of a white nation, with its own territorial integrity, through the power literally to externalize the black franchise. They also facilitated the special South African version of exploitation, under which substantial parts of the cost of production and reproduction of labor could be avoided by the use of migrants or commuters from neighboring states – real or imaginary. They helped to sustain the myth that it was somehow possible for the "white" Republic of South Africa to have ready access to cheap black labor, without conceding the vote and other rights of citizenship. This required the virtual separation of the capacity to labor from other aspects of its human embodiment: the fundamental contradiction on which apartheid eventually foundered.

A discourse of the urban thus helped the apartheid regime to put the black population in its place – for a while. However, popular struggle for material existence led to the ever more conspicuous erosion of the supposed distinction between the "white" city and "black" somewhere else. It was the inevitability of large-scale black "urbanization" which eventually challenged the power of the state to maintain social control and minority rule. And the architects of apartheid had themselves to blame, trying to create and maintain the myth of spatial forms so discordant with reality. Nadine Gordimer saw this clearly, in a passage in which she resolves her earlier categorical confusion, to conclude with remarkable prescience: "a 'place'; a position whose contradictions those who impose them don't see, and from which will come a resolution they haven't provided for" (Gordimer 1979: 150–1).

Social Justice (and the City?)

The last annual meeting of the Association of American Geographers that I attended before leaving the United States for a year in South Africa was held in Boston in 1972. The highlight was David Harvey's paper entitled "Social justice and spatial systems," specifying the conditions which would have to be fulfilled for a just distribution justly arrived at. First, the distribution of income (or command over society's scarce resources) should be such that the needs of the population within each territory are met, resources are allocated to maximize interterritorial multiplier effects, and extra resources are allocated to help overcome special difficulties stemming from the physical and social environment. Second, the distributive mechanisms should be such that the prospects of the least advantaged territory are as great as possible (Harvey 1973: 116–17).

Harvey's first set of principles introduced territorial distribution, spatial structure, and environment into a discourse of social justice hitherto devoid of geographical content. The second, prioritizing the prospects of the least advantaged, reflected a central principle of the theory of justice expounded by John Rawls (1971). Harvey soon shifted his focus to the more specific scale of the city and its mechanisms of redistribution grounded in the class relations of capitalism, as he abandoned liberalism for Marxism. But it was the spaceless Rawlsian world which was to be the context for mainstream debates on social justice for most of the succeeding two decades.

Rawls argued that there is no case at the most basic level of justification for anything except equality in the distribution of the "social primary goods" of liberty and opportunity, income and wealth, and the bases of self-respect. However, some degree of inequality may be permitted. After prioritizing an equal right to the most extensive possible liberties, along with equal opportunities, Rawls's difference principle required social and economic inequalities to be arranged so that they are to the greatest benefit of the least advantaged. This is the resolution persons are supposed to arrive at by viewing society from behind a "veil of ignorance" as to their actual position within it, imagining the possibility that they could be among the worst off. Even if the morally arbitrary good fortune of natural assets or social circumstances is taken to undermine the credit for most if not all individual achievement, the difference principle is a defensible concession to the fact that inequality could be to the advantage of the poor.

What became known as the argument from arbitrariness, or luck egalitarianism, featured prominently in subsequent work on social justice. A crucial problem was how to define the limits of individual responsibility, leading to proposals for just outcomes to be ambition-sensitive but not endowment-sensitive, and for equalizing human capabilities or resources rather than welfare (Smith 2000a: 2–4). The debate rumbles on into the new millennium, in an argument for giving priority to improving the well-being of those who are badly off and not substantially responsible for their own condition (Arneson 2000), in reply to a critique of luck egalitarianism which stresses the importance of social relationships (Anderson 1999).

As the 1970s proceeded, serious challenges to liberal egalitarianism emerged (Kymlicka 1990; Smith 1994). The most potent was from Marxism, which was suspicious of the very idea of social justice under capitalism, but not entirely clear about what would follow the revolution. Distribution according to need should eventually prevail under communism, but in the transitional society some residual "bourgeois right" to the value produced would be recognized. It took a contemporary moral reading of Marx to show that distributional principles similar to those of Rawls might be deduced, but with economic and social security given priority over liberty (Peffer 1990). Thus, everyone's physical integrity should be respected and everyone should be guaranteed a minimum level of material well-being, including those basic needs that must be met in order to remain a normal functioning human being. Only then does Rawls's maximum system of equal basic liberties apply.

Another challenge came from communitarianism. Michael Walzer (1983) argued that the meaning of goods subject to distribution could vary with social and cultural context, requiring different distributional principles in different spheres. Michael Sandel (1982) saw social justice as merely a remedial virtue, coming into play only when communal understandings of entitlement had broken down. The relational nature of social justice has also been stressed by feminists hostile to the impersonal rights and rules of mainstream (some say masculinist) perspectives. The most searching challenge from feminism has been the ethic of care, initially proposed by Carol Gilligan (1982), which prioritizes responsibility to particular persons in need. Tensions between the modern ideals of universality and impartiality and the parochial tendencies of both communitarianism and the ethic of care raise the issue of how far beneficence should be extended, to distant "others" who also happen to be different (Smith 1998).

By the middle of the 1980s, various critiques of established theories of social justice had begun to coalesce in a preoccupation with difference. A politics of difference emerged, challenging ways in which people may be treated unfairly on grounds of disability, ethnicity, gender, postcolonial status, sexual orientation, and the like. Some saw the demands of these different others as group identity replacing class interests: "Cultural domination supplants exploitation as the fundamental injustice. And cultural recognition displaces socioeconomic redistribution as the remedy for injustice and the goal of political struggle" (Fraser 1995: 68). But others responded that the material effects of political economy are inextricably bound to culture (e.g., Young 1997). While the process of domination and oppression was recognized to be complex and multifaceted, the focus of debates on social justice shifted in the direction of culture.

The exposition of the politics of difference by Iris Marion Young (1990) was notable for its attention to the city. She proposed a normative ideal of city life, manifest not in liberalism's atomized individuals or in some idealized community but in a society of groups open to unassimilated others. The aim would be social differentiation without exclusion, and the expression of varied lifestyles. Cities involve the being together of strangers; finding affinity with some should not lead to denial of a place for others. Social justice thus involves "equality among groups who recognize and affirm one another in their specificity" (Young 1990: 248). Such a perspective resonated with the emerging spirit of multiculturalism and toleration of "alternative" ways of living.

Claims that cultural or lifestyle recognition are matters of justice challenge the restrictive scope of the distributional paradigm, which Young so vigorously criticized. But such claims are often means to more material ends, associated with economic and social equality. Thus, "the impulse to include difference is driven by a conviction that one's identity as the member of a race, sex or linguistic culture should not disadvantage one in social life" (Sypnowich 1993: 106). A fear that recognition of increasingly complex identities, after the fashion of some postmodern accounts, could lead to a view in which there is nothing but diversity has brought calls to limit the scope of morally relevant differences.

The focus on difference has broadened the scope of social justice, and drawn attention to the disadvantage of specific groups. But in the process there has been an erosion of the sense of human sameness, or close similarity, on which the case for egalitarianism rests. When I suggested this in the draft of an earlier publication, a referee accused me of failing to acknowledge that the recognition of politically salient forms of difference may have helped to counter the oppressive aspects of a universalizing modernism. I responded that the struggles for black civil rights in the United States as well as against apartheid in South Africa were more a case of the universalist notion of equal moral worth countering particular social constructions of difference (Smith 1998: 36–7). There is a growing movement to revisit some arguments for equality grounded in essential characteristics of human being, which have been subdued by preoccupation with difference (Smith 2000b).

What do the past three decades amount to, in terms of progress in understanding social justice in urban studies? The first point is that, apart from Harvey (1973) and Young (1990), very little theoretical work has been explicitly directed at the city, despite a return of social justice to the agenda of geography (e.g., Smith 1994; Harvey 1996). A second point is that, rather than observing a major paradigm shift or a process of steady incremental change, the emergence of diversity in the form of competing theories best describes the experience, reflecting a changing intellectual climate manifest in postmodern hostility to a dominant metanarrative. There has also been growing awareness that any theory of social justice is itself underpinned by a theory of the good (Smith 1997); as Michael Walzer (1994: 24) has remarked, "we are distributing lives of a certain sort, and what counts as justice in distribution depends on what that 'sort' is." In addition, issues of social justice have increasingly been raised in the field of development studies, while the notion of environmental justice has also broadened the scope of normative discourse (Smith 2000c: chs. 8 and 9).

Despite all this, some common features continue to characterize theories of social justice. One is a concern with the distribution of means of human well-being, though there are differences as to the crucial means (e.g., primary goods, capabilities, opportunities, basic needs). The second is a concern with equality, though there are differences as to the crucial dimension (e.g., race, gender). The third is a concern with the structure of society and its institutions, though there are differences as to the crucial aspect of social identity and relations (e.g., class, culture, citizenship). A final feature is that thin, general theories continue to require contextual thickening if they are to reach normative conclusions sensitive to actual manifestations of injustice.

The discussion now moves on to explore some of these aspects of change and continuity in theorizing about social justice, in the unique and demanding setting of South Africa. In so doing, I follow the editors' invitation to personalize my account, not in the role of community activist adopted by some students of urban affairs, but as a geographer whose work relies on field experience as well as on abstraction. This perspective might help to underline the interdependence of theory and practice in the ongoing pursuit of the meaning of social justice in particular contexts.

South Africa under Apartheid

> Cape Town: August 6, 1989. Day set aside for fieldwork. Advised not to visit black townships, but able to renew acquaintance with Crossroads (pumping out after heavy rain), and to see the amalgam of shacks, site-and-service schemes and formal housing making up Khayelitsha as it sprawls out to the south-eastern edge of the Cape Flats. This further reinforces the impression gained elsewhere, of a widening disparity in black housing. As the state relies increasingly on private provision, the (few) well-to-do can buy attractive homes while the rest are increasingly forced into self-built shacks. Then to Mitchells Plain, a large town for the so-called "Coloured" people, where most businesses are closed as part of the anti-election protest, and where barriers of burning tires eventually discourage further fieldwork. Back to the UCT [University of Cape Town] campus, where by late afternoon a dozen or so fires could be seen down in the Cape Flats. About 20 deaths were reported there that night. (Author's field diary, general election day, *The Times Higher Educational Supplement*, October 20, 1989)

Whatever theory may suggest, there can be few more persuasive indications of social injustice than people taking to the streets and setting fires. Such was increasingly the South African experience, as the country approached the last general election before the ruling National Party released Nelson Mandela from prison in February 1990. Large proportions of the Colored and Indian populations had rejected the dubious dispensation of the vote for their own segregated house in the national parliament, which still had no place for an African majority unimpressed by such constitutional "reforms." As graffiti appeared associating freedom with an AK47 rifle, the writing was on the wall for the apartheid regime.

With respect to theory, liberal egalitarianism was well suited to the ideology of the internal opposition to apartheid. Race is an unchosen identity, in particular when the official categories of "black" or "African," "Colored," "Indian," and "white" were imposed on people by legislation (the Population Registration Act). Like other accidents of birth, race should carry no moral credit or penalty. Insofar as justice is manifest in people getting what they deserve, race should have no bearing on living standards. The fact that it did was shown by vast racial inequalities in economic and social indicators, underlining the degree of white privilege and of African disadvantage (Smith 1990: 6–9). It followed that social justice meant "racial equality."

In practice, however, pursuit of racial equality was focused very much on the repeal of discriminatory legislation. The objective of removing such barriers to individual advancement often failed to recognize that, to equalize opportunities in anything other than a formal sense, positive discrimination in favor of the hitherto disadvantaged population groups would be required. Merely to equalize resource inputs by race group, in the form of per capita expenditure on social services, would be inadequate. However, while equalization of outcomes, or living standards, might have been the ultimate objective, it was seldom argued explicitly. In any event, this conception of racial equality was bound to take many years: projecting trends at the end of the apartheid era into the future suggested that it would be half a century before racial shares of income matched those of population (Smith 1999: 160–1). There were also other dimensions of inequality to consider, notably gender, and an increasing socioeconomic stratification of the African population.

Under the strict censorship which prevailed in the apartheid era, voices other than the mainly white liberal opposition tended to be silenced. This included the liberation movement in exile, represented by the African National Congress (ANC), with its commitment to the revolutionary overthrow of apartheid and its replacement by a socialist society. The works of Marx were as hard to find as the novel *Black Beauty* or *Playboy* magazine, and structural interpretations of inequality were seldom heard. There were nevertheless some important contributions to the understanding of South Africa's distinctive form of labor exploitation (e.g., Wolpe 1972). South African reality also prompted some refinements of the crude class analysis of Marxism, recognizing possible conflict among fractions of capital as well as the role of racism.

Insofar as a progressive politics of difference might have operated under apartheid, it was discouraged by the nonracial stance of the internal opposition. Black consciousness movements were as threatening to white liberals as to the apartheid state. But there was, of course, much racial and tribal consciousness in action, not only white chauvinism and strong Afrikaner identity as God's chosen people to civilize this part of a dark continent, but also the tribal affiliation among Africans perpetuated and officially encouraged by the homeland policy.

How did "the city" and "the urban" figure under apartheid? Some of the indications in the introduction to this chapter may be elaborated further to explain the spatial structure that characterized apartheid society. Three levels of racial discrimination were customarily recognized (Smith 1990). At the macro scale was the subdivision of the country into ten black or African homelands (four of which achieved formal "independence" from the Republic of South Africa), leaving the remaining 87 percent of the land for the whites along with the Colored and Indian populations. The next level was segregation of residential space within towns and cities, under the Group Areas Act. Finally, there was the "petty apartheid" manifest in segregation of public space and facilities, from beaches to buses, imposed by the Reservation of Separate Amenities Act. The grand design at the macro scale served to preserve white political power where it mattered, in the metropolitan areas and white farmlands, and to facilitate the supply of cheap and disenfranchised black labor. Residential segregation and petty apartheid regulated the inevitable encounters among strangers within the cities, where racial "integrity" was most at risk to the mixing of blood and to the cultural homogenization associated with urbanization.

It was within the cities that racial friction was most likely, and most feared by the whites. As "unrest" increased, from the Soweto uprising of 1976 through the 1980s, it was in the cities that the authorities were faced with mounting problems of social control. And as organized opposition to apartheid built up, it was issues of particular significance in the cities, especially desegregation of public facilities and the abolition of residential group areas, which tended to attract the greatest attention and support. It was terminologically as well as strategically significant that the response of big business to the Soweto riot was to set up the Urban Foundation, to promote improvement in black housing and other conditions. This organization tended to dominate the urban development discourse in the declining years of apartheid, consolidating the role of the state as facilitator of private initiatives rather than as housing producer for the poor.

The perception of South Africa as a city versus countryside or core/periphery spatial structure was encouraged by the adoption of prevailing models from Anglo-American geography and development studies (Fair 1982). It was convenient to simplify matters in this way for expository purposes (Smith 1990: 35, 74), especially for audiences unaware of the spatiality of apartheid. What passed for state urban and regional development policy sought to normalize the South African situation, through strategies of industrial decentralization and urbanization control similar to those adopted in many other countries, as a cover for trying to keep blacks out of the cities. The unreality of conventional categories was no more clearly demonstrated than by the emergence of so-called "frontier commuters," traveling daily from residence in a "black homeland" to workplace in a "white city." This was a refinement of the migrant labor system, which served the same function of ensuring the availability of black labor within the metropolis but transferring the cost of its service infrastructure as well as its franchise across a supposed international frontier.

As suggested in the introduction, it was the impossibility of maintaining the geographical myths required by apartheid which, as much as anything, led the Nationalist government to seek its rapprochement with the ANC at the beginning of the 1990s. It was the contradictions built into apartheid's legacy of Nadine Gordimer's restless broken streets where definitions fail that generated the resolution those who imposed them had not provided for. Its origins were not in "the city," "the urban," or "the rural," but in the entire dysfunctional as well as unjust spatial structure, and its underlying exploitative as well as racist political economy.

Social Justice after Apartheid

Durban: September 10, 1994. Staying in a block of holiday flats on the sea front. This was the family home for some months more than twenty years ago, and part of my research strategy (if this is not putting it too grandly) is repeated visits to the same place to observe who is doing what, where, and with whom. The stretch of Marine Parade and its beach, which I can see from my balcony, once protected white space, is now integrated. African occupation is increasingly confident, young men gently gyrating to music from radios as they try to make a few Rand directing car parking. Then, suddenly, peace is shattered by a big white man picking a fight with an African, knocking him to the ground, and kicking him senseless. Another African remonstrates, and I can hear the white man's fist hit his jaw from my eighth floor. The thug picks his second victim up effortlessly, and dumps him on the prone figure of the first. There are enough Africans gathered around to challenge the white man, but the prudence of historical experience, as well as fear, seems to constrain them. He walks away. Sleep interrupted at 4.00am by a solo drummer somewhere below, a group dancing to the beat in the half-light of dawn, untroubled by the white menace. (Author's field diary)

Bloemfontein: September 16–17, 1994. Start the day with a visit to the base of the statue to apartheid architect Hendrik Verwoerd, toppled last week rather like Lenin in Soviet cities. Then visit to informal settlements in the city before driving fifty kms to Botshabelo: one of the most distressing monuments to apartheid urban planning. Laid out as a new town for blacks suitably distanced from the white city, it now houses 250,000, many of them in self-built shacks. Visit employment generation project where people are making building blocks, and such things as candles, furniture and toys by recycling materials found locally. The formal job prospects here are limited and uninviting: foreign firms pay R1.5 [approximately 25¢] an hour, at which rate a day's wages would just buy a hamburger at the Thaba 'Nchu Sun resort built for white holidaymakers nearby. Dinner with the Provincial Minister of Housing (former freedom fighter with a spell in prison to his credit), who says that upgrading Botshabelo is one of his first priorities. Others question the wisdom of investing further in this remote location. ... Time to reflect on the deep divisions between whites and blacks, rich and poor, built into South Africa's settlement patterns, and sure to survive the end of apartheid by decades. (Author's field diary)

At the end of the 1980s, I gave a seminar at the University of Cape Town on "the post-apartheid city." I surprised my audience by telling them to look around, it was already there, in outline if not in detail (Smith 1992a). The formerly separate facilities had largely been integrated already, and the so-called "graying" process had been eroding residential segregation well before the repeal of group areas legislation. As to the broader, racialized patterns of differentiated socioeconomic status reflected in housing quality, it was hard to see this changing very much: those blacks who could afford to move into white neighborhoods would be few, even if they preferred this to their own version of the American "gilded ghetto," and it was fanciful to think of even the poorest whites moving into black townships. The vast swathes of shack settlement were obviously there to stay, so unlikely was it that a post-apartheid government with so many other priorities would be able to replace them with formal housing. Much of this was captured by David Simon (1989), in his revision of the classic portrayal of the apartheid city by Ron Davies (1981). More radical visions, like the expropriation of large white-owned homes and their redistribution to blacks in dire need, were receding as quickly as the socialist regimes of Eastern Europe were entering their terminal stage.

Nevertheless, the end of apartheid raised great expectations of redistribution as a means toward social justice (e.g., Smith 1992b, 1995). The ANC assumed power and produced a major strategy document, *The Reconstruction and Development Programme*, or RDP (ANC 1994), which quickly became government policy (Republic of South Africa 1994). The RDP placed primary emphasis on the satisfaction of basic human needs – for jobs, land, housing, water, electricity, telecommunications, transport, a clean and healthy environment, nutrition, healthcare and social welfare – in terms largely familiar to the international development discourse of the times. There was a Rawlsian ring to the commitment "to improve the quality of life of all South Africans, and in particular the most poor and marginalized" (ANC 1994: 15).

However, the RDP was shortlived. In 1996 it was effectively replaced by a macro-economic strategy dubbed "growth, employment and redistribution," or GEAR (RSA 1996). The new emphasis on reduced state spending, investment incentives, wage restraint, labor market flexibility, and privatization strongly resembled the neoliberal development strategy promoted elsewhere by the World Bank and International Monetary Fund's structural adjustment programs. It is heavily reliant on the expectation of a substantial trickle-down effect from the enhanced economic growth thought to be encouraged by capital-friendly policies. While its supporters see GEAR as a realistic response to globalizing market competition, its critics point to the limited benefits generated for the mass of the poor (Marais 1998).

The post-apartheid government has overseen the construction of 750,000 new houses, 400,000 electricity connections, and over 5 million water connections. Yet the housing deficit is still estimated to be 3 million, and 6 million people have no access to basic water services (Hassen 2000: 14). Almost 7.5 million live in squatter settlements or backyard shacks – approaching one in five of all South Africans (Jones and Datta 2000: 393). While poverty remains severe in the countryside, it is in the metropolitan areas that unmet needs are most concentrated. Asking why it has been so hard for municipalities to address the apartheid backlog of services, Patrick Bond (2000: 19) argues that virtually all state policies are excessively neoliberal: "too market oriented, stingy, insensitive to poverty, incapable of integrating gender and environmental concerns, unsympathetic to problems associated with public health and worsening geographical segregation." He points to the hegemony of official mainstream analysis and public policy reflecting market-oriented ideology, promoting class-based apartheid. Hence the reassertion in some quarters of a Rawlsian conception of justice: "The allocation of resources should reflect that the least advantaged have benefited and that an overwhelming share of resources has been allocated to the lowest income group" (Hassen 2000: 16).

What of the challenges to mainstream conceptions of justice, as applied to post-apartheid South Africa? While apartheid itself represented a perverse politics of difference, there has subsequently been a conscious effort to make a virtue of population diversity, reflected in the notion of a "Rainbow Nation." "New" South African citizenship is supposed to transcend ethnicity and race, while still recognizing and respecting difference. However, ensuring democratic representation of population groups, as well as positive discrimination in favor of those previously disadvantaged, involves perpetuating the racial categories of apartheid. And alongside inclusive aspirations is a more exclusive search for perspectives grounded in Africa and Africanism, manifest in an "African Renaissance" involving "new ways of thinking and feeling about Africa, its history, and its economic, social and political status . . . an invitation to reinvent ourselves and what we do, how we do it and who benefits from it" (Ntuli 1998: 7).

An important element in resurrecting African values is the notion of *ubuntu*. This refers to the significance of group solidarity, with its emphasis on membership of a community where individualism is harmonized with social responsibility, characteristic of traditional African society. Augustine Shutte (1993) has argued that this provides an alternative philosophical perspective to both liberal individualism and socialist collectivism (what in other political contexts might be described as a "third way"). Some see links between the premodern African communitarianism and the contemporary ethic of care, and between an "Afrocentric" morality and the relational ethics associated with feminism (Smith 1999: 169). Some even envisage this combination providing a challenge to the consolidation of neoliberal values.

But at present it is hard to see any alternative ethics dislodging the individualistic materialism of contemporary South Africa. For blacks as well as whites, the good life remains symbolized by the spacious single-family suburban home, with its extensive well-manicured garden, behind increasingly robust defenses against the theft of its contents. If there is any moral and political leverage to be found, it is more likely to be in the Western liberal tradition, with its stress on rights of citizenship, than in a return to premodern ethics, far less to some idealized tribal community. The Bill of Rights incorporated into the 1996 Constitution includes a generous array of socioeconomic rights: access to housing, healthcare, water, social security, and an environment not harmful to health and well-being. Turning these rights into reality would go a long way toward relieving the misery endured by millions of post-apartheid South Africans.

There is no great mystery about the origins of dire poverty and gross inequality in South Africa. The particular local combinations of class exploitation and cultural domination need little further theoretical or empirical elaboration. What is required for social justice is also quite clear in theory (if not in the minds of many South Africans): a process of equalization involving redistribution in favor of the worst off, narrowing gaps arising from morally irrelevant accidents of birth and subsequent circumstances, very much in the spirit of John Rawls. Something of the mutuality associated with *ubuntu* and an ethic of care might even be found in Rawls, as is suggested by some sympathetic feminist readings which point to the role of empathy and concern for others implicit in his principles of justice (e.g., Okin 1989: 247–8). One interpretation of the veil of ignorance behind which we are to approve social arrangements, highlighted by Stuart Corbridge (1993: 464), is that it invites us to think ourselves into the place of others, and to imagine what it would be like to be among the worst off. It invites relatively privileged South Africans to ask what social arrangements they would endorse, if under present circumstances they might find themselves living in a township or shack settlement.

However, social justice as equalization cannot be envisaged as bringing up the mass of the poor to the material living standards of the well-to-do minority, for this is both economically unattainable and environmentally unsustainable. The satisfaction of everyone's basic needs, everywhere, entails more equal sharing of the means of a more modest conception of the good life. If we are distributing lives of a certain sort, as Michael Walzer reminds us, this sort must surely be capable of extension to everyone. The challenge ahead is thus not so much social scientific as ethical: to help devise a new theory of the good, incorporating inclusive material living standards combined with an ethic of responsibility to the weak and vulnerable, persuasive enough to be a source of moral motivation as well as of social understanding. This would be progress in "urban studies."

Epilogue

Every year Durban hosts a major surfing competition. Bronzed and bleached-haired beauties strut their stuff on daunting waves, and in hotel bars when the sun goes down. This is a very white event. Over the years, I can recall hardly any participants whose skin was naturally brown: even if tempted onto the surf in the apartheid era, they would not have been able to cross the segregated "white" beach. But blacks do not entirely miss out: many enjoy the spectacle and accompanying excitement. There are also business opportunities, especially for the hundreds of African women selling "native" craftware and other souvenirs on the pavements of Marine Parade: exotic others positioned for the tourist gaze in what was once resolutely white space. The women spend most of their waking hours here. Many have young children; some are breastfeeding. When the last potential customers have gone, the women leave for long journeys home to their township or shack settlement. Most are better housed than their counterparts at the railway station, where the women share crude shelters constructed on the pavements themselves. That they make a "living" demonstrates some kind of trickle down. Meanwhile, well-heeled locals join the holidaymakers in bars and restaurants, to start the trickle. The beggar in the doorway tries to divert a few coins. Men in suits and power-dressed women exchange business-speak at the glitzy convention center adjoining the Hilton nearby. I conclude with other voices, from the street:

> "When you are sleeping they come to rape you. . . . We changed places when it's sleeping time, so they don't know who is the young one and who is the old lady. But they still came. Some people came to help us and told us to buy whistles. If we shout, sometimes the others can't hear because the big noise from cars and buses. We sleep holding our whistles or sometimes it is on a string round your neck. When you hear someone you just blow very hard. All the women get up and we hit him as hard as we can."
>
> "I can sit here for days eating bread and drinking only water. This cement is cold and this wind from the sea is cold, it makes my bones pain. I am here early in the morning till late at night, you can't tell when these whites will buy. This life is bad, sometimes I can sit here the whole day and no one buys. It can make you sick."
>
> "You see that lady, sometimes she screams, she is not right in her head, can't take this life. Now we look after her, we give her what we eat but she will die if the police don't take her away, get knocked maybe ... it's too late, her head is damaged, finished." (Mavis, Thandi, and Maria, Durban street traders, conversations with Priscilla Cunnan, 1998–9)

I wonder how many holidaymakers and conventioneers imagine themselves in the place of these others, and ask how lives of this sort can be justified.

Bibliography

ANC 1994: *The Reconstruction and Development Programme.* Johannesburg: African National Congress.

Anderson, E. S. 1999: What is the point of equality? *Ethics* 109: 289–337.

Arneson, R. J. 2000: Luck egalitarianism and prioritisation. *Ethics* 110: 339–49.

Bond, P. 2000: Infrastructure delivery: class apartheid. *Indicator South Africa* 17 (3): 18–21.

Corbridge, S. 1993: Marxism, modernities, and moralities: development praxis and the claims of distant strangers. *Environment and Planning D: Society and Space* 11: 449–72.

Davies, R. J. 1981: The spatial formation of the South African city. *GeoJournal*, suppl. 2: 59–72.

Fair, T. J. D. 1982: *South Africa: Spatial Frameworks for Development.* Cape Town: Juta.

Fraser, N. 1995: From redistribution to recognition? Dilemmas of justice in a "post-socialist" age. *New Left Review* 212: 68–93.

Gilligan, C. 1982: *In a Different Voice: Psychological Theory and Women's Development.* Cambridge, MA: Harvard University Press.

Gordimer, N. 1979: *Burger's Daughter.* London: Jonathan Cape.

Harvey, D. 1973: *Social Justice and the City.* London: Edward Arnold.

—— 1996: *Justice, Nature and the Geography of Difference.* Oxford: Blackwell.

Hassen, E.-K. 2000: Are bricks and mortar enough? Infrastructure delivery. *Indicator South Africa* 17 (3): 13–17.

Jones, G. A. and Datta, K. 2000: Enabling markets to work? Housing policy in the "new" South Africa. *International Planning Studies* 5: 393–416.

Kymlicka, W. 1990: *Contemporary Political Philosophy: An Introduction.* Oxford: Clarendon Press.

Marais, H. 1998: *South Africa: Limits to Change: The Political Economy of Transition.* London and New York: Zed Books.

Ntuli, P. P. 1998: Who's afraid of the African Renaissance? *Indicator South Africa* 15 (2): 15–18.

Okin, S. M. 1989: Reason and feeling in thinking about justice. *Ethics* 99: 229–49.

Peffer, R. G. 1990: *Marxism, Morality, and Social Justice.* Princeton, NJ: Princeton University Press.

Rawls, J. 1971: *A Theory of Justice.* Cambridge, MA: Harvard University Press.

Republic of South Africa (RSA) 1994: *White Paper on Reconstruction and Development: Government's Strategy for Fundamental Transformation.* Pretoria.

—— 1996: *Growth, Employment and Redistribution: A Macroeconomic Strategy.* Pretoria.

Sandel, M. 1982: *Liberalism and the Limits of Justice.* Cambridge: Cambridge University Press.

Shutte, A. 1993: *Philosophy for Africa.* Rondebosch: University of Cape Town Press.

Simon, D. 1989: Crisis and change in South Africa: implications for the apartheid city. *Transactions of the Institute of British Geographers* 14: 189–206.

Smith, D. M. (ed.) 1982: *Living under Apartheid: Aspects of Urbanization and Social Change in South Africa.* London: George Allen and Unwin.

—— 1990: *Apartheid in South Africa*, 3rd ed. Cambridge: Cambridge University Press.

—— 1992a: Conclusion. In D. M. Smith (ed.), *The Apartheid City and Beyond: Urbanization and Social Change in South Africa.* London: Routledge, 314–17.
—— 1992b: Redistribution after apartheid: who gets what where in the new South Africa. *Area* 24: 350–8.
—— 1994: *Geography and Social Justice.* Oxford: Blackwell.
—— 1995: Redistribution and social justice after apartheid. In A. Lemon (ed.), *The Geography of Change in South Africa.* Chichester: Wiley, 45–64.
—— 1997: Back to the good life: towards an enlarged conception of social justice. *Environment and Planning D: Society and Space* 15: 19–35.
—— 1998: How far should we care? On the spatial scope of beneficence. *Progress in Human Geography* 22: 15–38.
—— 1999: Social justice and the ethics of development in post-apartheid South Africa. *Ethics, Place and Environment* 2: 157–77.
—— 2000a: Moral progress in human geography: transcending the place of good fortune. *Progress in Human Geography* 24: 1–18.
—— 2000b: Social justice revisited. *Environment and Planning A* 32: 1149–62.
—— 2000c: *Moral Geographies: Ethics in a World of Difference.* Edinburgh: Edinburgh University Press.
Sypnowich, C. 1993: Some disquiet about "difference." *Praxis International* 13: 99–112.
Walzer, M. 1983: *Spheres of Justice: A Defence of Pluralism and Equality.* Oxford: Blackwell.
—— 1994: *Thick and Thin: Moral Argument at Home and Abroad.* Notre Dame and London: University of Notre Dame Press.
Wolpe, H. 1972: Capitalism and cheap labour-power in South Africa: from segregation to apartheid. *Economy and Society* 1: 425–56.
Young, I. M. 1990: *Justice and the Politics of Difference.* Princeton, NJ: Princeton University Press.
—— 1997: Unruly categories: a critique of Nancy Fraser's dual systems theory. *New Left Review* 222: 147–60.

5

The Dangerous Others: Changing Views on Urban Risks and Violence in France and the United States

Sophie Body-Gendrot

A few years ago, when I was called by the French Republic to serve as a jury member in Paris, I went through a major life experience. It seems that most of my current research concerning notions of crime definition, social justice, and institutional responses to urban dilemmas has been shaped by this experience. Before it, I was just a political scientist with a deep suspicion of institutions. If I used the word "police," I would frequently associate it with "abuse" and the word "justice" with "denial of." In France, jury members – sitting with the judge – not only decide on the offender's guilt and on possible mitigating circumstances but they also have to decide on the sentencing as well (fortunately, the death penalty was abolished after 1981). The experience lasts two weeks on average, during which several cases are judged by the popular jury. The twelve selected jury members suspend their current occupations during that time so that they can commit themselves to this very important task. When cases are examined over several days, the jury members learn every possible detail about the offenders' lives, their offenses, and the accompanying circumstances. The accused and their geographical, social, and cultural environments become very familiar.

What occurred then is that in the three cases I was called upon to judge, the other jury members and I felt a profound understanding/empathy with the motivations that had triggered the offenders into behaving the way they did. We could have felt the same emotions as those experienced by the accused when they committed their offenses. These feelings were universal (humiliation, jealousy, a moment of madness, anger). We could have been the offenders if other circumstances had not "protected" us from a path of violence. We were not judging here Mafiosi or hardcore criminals, but neither were we judging angels. The moment we grasped the ambiguity of the motivations and the ambivalence of the violent actor who was also a victim, it was increasingly difficult to "judge," that is, to send a message to the victims and to society according to classifications we might not have necessarily chosen, had we had the choice.

The second lesson, I think, came from the observation that the law enforcers' attitudes under such circumstances had been exceptional, at least in the cases I examined. I had to revise my opinions. The policemen, who could have pulled the trigger when in danger, did not. They resisted provocation, checked their emotions, and controlled the escalation process. The judge and his assistants remained extraordinarily self-controlled, pushing the jurors to the limits of their logic and convictions in order to restrain potential attitudes of negative populism. This was a great lesson in democracy: citizens acting collectively to produce the best possible decision despite their own diversity, doubts, and contradictions; institutions respectful of the law and of the "people's voice."

This experience of criminal justice, however, also revealed that all the offenders we judged at this session belonged to the poor (two out of three came from immigrant backgrounds). They all lived at the margins of the city, that is, where problems concentrate and accumulate, while being judged by a more or less "middle-class," employed, and white jury living at the center. Their crimes were those of the poor – those that are committed in a heavily handicapped social environment where preventive or adjustment measures are blatantly lacking. For instance, one of the offenders, the youngest of all, had been socialized for many years by an older brother who had taught him how to survive in a problematic neighborhood, with no adult presence (no father and a continuously absent mother, a traveling saleswoman).

The nature of the dilemma between the ethics of conviction and the ethics of responsibility felt by us, the members of the jury, during that time is similar to the one we may feel as researchers of urban violence, now that we know much more than we did twenty years ago. We have become more modest; we have discarded the grand narratives and their binary interpretations and integrated the complexity of processes. We feel compassion for the poor as structural victims of society's indifference and of double standards. We require more social justice and yet we admit that these offenders are violent actors, that they hurt other poor, frequently in their own neighborhood, and that victims are entitled to demand retribution. It becomes more and more difficult to sustain a simplistic view of "us" and "them" on issues of law and order. Complexity, fragmentation, uncertainty, the questioning of former norms, the emergence of new ones accompany the postmodern urban discourse.

In this chapter, I intend to show how the definition of urban violence and its potential causes has evolved in the last two decades. Radical rethinking has marked the evolution of research. The institutional control developed in American and French cities has also changed, yet in opposite directions. The global trend of negative populism in the United States is being softened, here and there, locally, by welfarist measures, while the policies of social welfare in France have evolved toward more rigorous policies on crime control, the local enforcers hesitating between options which might prove divisive for the community and often preferring the status quo. What is the new profile of pluralism concerning actors, circumstances, and anti-crime policies? We lack conceptual tools at this stage to describe the overlapping of structures, the blurring of boundaries, the complex games of actors ending up in policies, but we may grasp that the purpose of this lack of clarity is not innocent.

The Evolution of Research: Redefining Urban Violence and its Potential Causes

Crime is what society decides it to be. The "dangerous classes" are defined arbitrarily by institutions in the same recurrent way as in the past. Labels were then given to the "unmeltable," the "scum," on one hand, and to ghettos, skid rows, and shantytowns on the other. The poor and the destitute have always been reproached for their irresponsible behavior and there is little difference in the way these pariahs were pointed out formerly and the way marginalized and socially excluded populations are stigmatized today. Old processes continue to operate. The past is transformed, it is not obliterated. The claim that "postmodern cities" have displaced old or modern cities is not convincing. "Novelty is always a rhetorical move and history ever-present" (Beauregard and Haila 2000: 23). Classifications represent stakes within the fragmented, stake-competing state apparatus and they may change according to economic cycles.

In the 1960s, the American nation was alarmed by violence rending cities apart. After the Kerner Commission addressed the nation moving apart into two unequal societies, President L. B. Johnson appointed an eighteen-month commission (later labeled the Violence Commission) to address the causes and prevention of violence under the chairmanship of Milton Eisenhower, the President of Johns Hopkins University. Most of the commission's analysis and recommendations today are ignored. Yet they are worth remembering (Body-Gendrot 2002). Currently a shift has occurred in the United States toward concern about crime in cities rather than about urban violence. But are the two concepts equivalent? What link is there between the Oklahoma bombing, a mugging on Main Street, the Los Angeles riots, the Columbine massacre, or ethnic confrontations in Crown Heights? The link is provided by journalists and politicians, who use the same terms – urban violence, urban crime, riots, disorders, disturbances, unrest, urban danger, rebellion, confrontation, lawlessness, delinquency, and many more – to characterize such events.

The use of similar terms makes all things look alike. Commentators do not seem to be aware that by failing to define clearly such words as violence and crime, they include within the same category phenomena which are distinct in extent and nature. Most people associate violence with physical injuries and possibly death, whereas crime, with the legal classification differentiating types of offenses, often refers to offenses against goods. Using one term rather than another already gives a subjective and sometimes abusive interpretation of events (Body-Gendrot 2000). Lexicological research on elusive terms encompassing different philosophical, sociological, and ethical meanings cannot be avoided.

Take violence, for example. Everyone knows what violence is from birth. There is an aspect of "vital force" in the term derived from the Latin *vis*. Violence becomes a problem when it is not channeled or socialized. Violence is in fact less a concept than "a set of situations all connected one to another, even if their intensity and forms cannot be compared." Most of them refer to behaviors, the goal or effect of which is to hurt the Other's body (integrity, affects, mind, goods) and territory (Héritier 1999). Violence denies everyone's aspiration to inviolability, protection, dignity, justice and this explains why it is such an "existential" threat. Moreover, if violence is associated with the urban, there is a collective and philosophical element implied, referring to a failure of the social cohesiveness which the city, in its political sense, is supposed to generate. In France, the debate on urban violence involves the entire society, a society which is smaller and more socially integrated than in the United States. The type of societal debate, which was reflected in the report of the Violence Commission, has disappeared in the United States. There the use of the legal term – "crime" – externalizes the issue; it connects it to "dangerous classes" in specific places, to an underclass (i.e., black) which is not part of "us." It exonerates society from its responsibilities and its guilt.

Hotspots versus Violent Youths: The Theoretical Debate

Linkages between social inequality and crime have been subjected to speculation since the early days of criminology. It is necessary at this point to outline the evolution of the theoretical debate related to the correlation of the structural causes of inequality versus individual responsibilities leading to violence and crime in large cities (Hagan and Peterson 1995: 55).

Criminogenic places in American cities?

The early and influential theory of Clifford Shaw and Henry McKay (1942) on social disorganization integrated Park's and Burgess's ecological theory of cities (1925) by focusing on neighborhood characteristics associated with high rates of delinquency. In *Juvenile Delinquency and Urban Areas* (1942), they suggest that some places are more criminogenic than others. They acknowledge contagion effects, the seductions of crime, and the attractions of vice. Shaw and McKay worked on maps of delinquency in Chicago that they analyzed over time (between 1900 and 1930). Three structural factors – low economic status associated with poverty, racial or ethnic heterogeneity, and residential instability – were seen as consistent predictors of delinquency. The authors anticipated that such places would not be easily improved. There was a lack of community-based social control – an absence contributing to crime. They claimed that these problems were intergenerationally transmitted in criminogenic neighborhoods, so that the spatial clustering of social problems persisted in the same areas over time.

This is an important claim because it is clear that high rates of delinquency do persist in hotspots over the years, regardless of changes in immigrant and minority populations. Consequently, processes of transmission of delinquent socialization in certain areas are more likely to explain delinquency than categories. Instead of racially stereotyping dangerous classes, Shaw and McKay demonstrate that black neighborhoods (there were 4 percent of blacks in Chicago in 1920) are not a homogeneous category, neither are young black males. Variations in crime rates correspond to heterogeneous black neighborhoods. In some areas, the residents exert less control over unsupervised teenagers and the social agencies are inefficient; they are outsiders who do not understand the residents. Newcomers produce delinquency. The transition from a rural life to the complexity of urban life adds to the teenagers' destructuration. Delinquency can then be interpreted as a mode of adaptation to confront problems of rapid mutation in a city like Chicago. Yet after families move to a second place of residence, the rates of delinquency generally diminish. Mobility tends to solve such problems. Smith and McKay conclude that black neighborhoods with stabilized families experience lesser rates of crime.

One of the best syntheses on the topic of criminogenic places has been written by criminologist Robert Sampson and sociologist W. J. Wilson (1995). In continuity with the research of the Chicago School, they emphasize the importance of space and of neighborhood effects. Crime remains attached to certain places regardless of what populations experience them, they say. Hotspots, unsafe housing projects and streets, interstitial zones are well known to the police. Location does matter. The place stigmatizes the residents, who become ashamed to give their address as they know it will criminalize them in the eyes of the police and in the search for a job, for relationships, and for any entry outside the area. Research in various countries shows this finding to be true (Harrison 1983; Bourdieu et al. 1993). According to Jargowsky (1996), who studied the patterns of thousands of ghettos and barrios, the more a poor neighborhood is surrounded by other spatial areas of poverty, the harder it will be for this neighborhood to lift itself out of poverty and its correlates. This is all the more true when spatial segregation is increased by global trends.

Criminogenic places in French cities?

In France, research on "urban violence" has also been constructed via criminogenic places. From the 1950s to the 1970s, large public housing projects were built rapidly and cheaply in the banlieues to accommodate population growth and alleviate the pressure on city centers. Some 10 million housing units were thus built, most frequently – but not always – at the periphery of cities. Among other things, research emphasized the fact that the problems with these urban spaces were both environmental (the first oil shock after 1973 was said to have prevented the development of adequate public transportation, of social amenities, and of commercial facilities) and political (a change in policies at the end of the 1970s encouraged housing ownership over the improvement of public housing units). Many tenants, members of a mobile middle class, moved out. The public management filled the vacant units with low-income immigrant families.

Unlike the social differentiation caused by American race relations, French people moved out because access to the individual home was tempting and not just because immigrant families moved in. The arrival of immigrant families occurred later when restrictive immigration policies prevented guest workers from traveling back and forth, thus accelerating family reunification and settlement (de Rudder 1992). A difficult mixing of cultures and the threat of downward mobility for white working-class families were then exacerbated by the stigma attached to these areas and the rapid decay of the buildings (Body-Gendrot 1993). Labor leaders and lower-middle-class executives, who had acted as role models, now deserted these places. The widespread vandalism of buildings and of public amenities may be interpreted as a protest by residents against the way the public housing projects were designed for the poor, furthering their social stigmatization. Conversely, it can be interpreted as their response to the state intervention that placed all public housing residents into nearly identical mortar and concrete boxes, denying them the right to design how they wanted to live (Bachmann and Le Guennec 1996).

Race, ethnicity, and crime in American cities

Other researchers choose to emphasize the impact of people more than of places on urban disorders. Marginalization or social exclusion are elusive concepts (Silver 1993). In the 1970s, Carol Stack's ethnographic research revealed that people in ghettoized areas were bifocal subjects. They knew how the other half lived, but to survive daily in their environment they had to stretch their values and develop a schizoid approach. In this respect, "marginal" populations are highly integrated. Their disintegration is seen as problematic only from the normative perspective of outsiders who ignore the marginals' diversity, resistance, adaptation, and plurality. The extent of their integration is always shaped by the dominant categories which require marginals to imagine urban change and utopian schemes. When they fail to do so, they are harshly judged and their behavior interpreted as a consequence of a "culture of poverty" (Elias and Scotson 1965; Lewis 1966; Stack 1975).

In the United States, urban crime is mostly perceived by these researchers as a problem of young, disadvantaged, jobless, minority males. "While inequality promotes violence, racial inequalities are especially productive of violence because of feelings of resentment," observes criminologist John Hagan (Hagan and Peterson 1995: 22). In the 1970s and 1980s, the literature also frequently reported on ethnic and racial conflicts over local turf, public jobs and housing, resources and power. This is less the case now, for three reasons. Many upwardly mobile ethnic groups left the ghettoized areas for the suburbs (currently, the historic ghetto of Chicago has lost half its population since the 1970s) – moving out being a solution to conflicts. The politics of identities has replaced the vision of a common world to be shared. Finally, during the Reagan years, the "underclass" has been essentialized as a black street culture with which very few groups would identify (Murray 1984; Mead 1986; Aponte 1990). Yet some researchers question this aspect of the discourse. While there is an interrelationship in American research among serious, violent offending, race, and slum areas, ethnic differences also attract attention (Mann 1993: 97; Marshall 1997: 15). The questioning of data based on arrest records frequently betrays police bias (Hagan and Peterson 1995). More recently, victimization surveys and self-reported crime studies have shown how inconclusive patterns of racial differences can be.

As for youth subcultures produced by certain urban territories, it appears that they are competing with modes of socialization which are in crisis. For Doreen Massey, spatiality is always and everywhere full of power, because it is constituted out of social relations (1997: 114). Identities and spatialities are established in and through relations of dominance and subordination. Such elements interact with all the variables already mentioned. The neighborhood must be seen as a unit, submitted, reacting, resisting, or yielding to both internal and external forces.

In New York, Jeff Fagan and Donna Wilkinson recently engaged in research to reconstruct the stages and the transactions within gun events among inner-city adolescent males (sixteen- to twenty-four-year-olds) in East New York, Brooklyn, and the South Bronx, neighborhoods which experienced a gun epidemic between 1985 and 1992. They listen to the youths' narratives at length, including those out of jail or in emergency rooms. They also try to understand how their "scripted" behaviors sustain violence, as well as the context of "situated transactions" in which disputes are settled, with or without guns (Fagan and Wilkinson 1998). Among other factors, they analyze the importance of bystanders, drinking, and drugs. As confirmed by French fieldwork, patterns and functions of adolescent violence are linked by achieving and maintaining status, "respect," and identity; acquiring material goods as a source of status; exerting coercion, domination, and power; experiencing pleasure; managing conflict; expressing an oppositional culture, etc. But instead of reifying the actors of violence, Fagan and Wilkinson point out that their interactionist approach also requires an analysis of events, of "the person-event" and "person-place" and "person-context" shaping event outcomes.

Ethnicity and crime in French cities

Until very recently, research in France carefully avoided associating delinquent youth, race, and ethnicity. Produced by social scientists who were influenced by their work on the labor movement, the analyses of the 1980s attempted to see in riotous or delinquent youths the future actors of urban social movements. Riotous youth became visible to public opinion via the media after disorders occurred in the public housing projects on the periphery of Lyon. The lack of understanding of actions, which conveyed no political message, produced the label "galley slaves" to describe the boredom, idleness, social exclusion, and poverty experienced by these youths who consumed the culture of affluent society and yet felt hampered in their access to it (Dubet et al. 1987). The growth of urban disorders, the races with stolen cars around the housing projects, the clashes between youths and the police, the burning of public buildings did not retain the researchers' attention at the time. Researchers were more concerned with analyzing a latent social movement in the anti-racist marches which mobilized other, as well as sometimes the same, youths (Jazouli 1986).

Due to the scathing anti-immigrant discourse of the extreme right in France, left-wing social scientists were eager to demonstrate that social assimilation through school and public welfare policies operated for immigrants (Taguieff 1991; Tribalat 1991). The taboo against the term "race" prevented researchers from linking discrimination, colonial history, frustration, and urban violence. The emphasis put upon inequalities hitting the unskilled working class did not refer to the specific problems of male immigrant youths, who felt humiliated by their fathers' fate in France and who were now using their "voice" to avoid the same fate. The Republican model of integration was hardly questioned at the time and the actors of urban violence not defined according to their race or ethnicity. Apart from very few ethnographic studies (Begag 1990; Roy 1990), there was a glaring absence of coverage of ethnic clashes among young people. Where there was discussion the clashes were described as territorial conflicts.

It is in the 1990s that the tone of research changed. As in the case of the jury members I described above, more French researchers began to fluctuate between their empathy for the delinquent youths and their revolts, on the one hand, and a concern for their victims, on the other. Even so, the delinquents generated more fascination than their victims. Juvenile delinquency was depicted as initiated by groups of adolescents who were attempting to forge collective identities and search for boundaries in a world which adults had deserted. A new development, initiated by juvenile court judges and educators, refers to a "delinquency of exclusion" among youths, frequently of immigrant background, who grew up in these disqualified areas, without guidance, in a normative blur, and with an identity disorder (Salas 1997). The major problem for these youths today "is less one of social control than of social exclusion, less an issue of regulation than of how to learn to live without norms, less an appeal to freedom than to disenfranchisement, less a resistance to social pressure than an acceptance of a vacuum" (Garapon 1996: 121). Delinquency and urban violence today, it was argued, reveal this identity disorder. If delinquency is usually linked to a denial of contemporary social order and to socialization problems, violence is also a sort of language which has yet to be understood.

Violence may be interpreted as a way of constructing new and more dangerous rites, or to return the violence which others and, more generally, society has inflicted on them and their families. The difficulty for social research comes from the clash between sociology and law. The ethics of conviction leads to young people being perceived as structural victims (as in the case of the jury members described above). Yet offenders hurt those who threaten the self-contained world that they attempt to construct outside of laws and community rules. Moreover, an extreme fluidity in the youths' motivations and actions forbids any reification. Physicians note the growth in the number of juveniles either in the emergency room or in custody for violating public order. They are two sides of the same coin: they are both actors and victims.

Writing about France, American researcher Pamela Irving Jackson seeks to link ethnicity, high unemployment, and crime. She notes that "for the *étranger* population nationally, the rate of unemployment in 1990 was over 19.5%." She continues:

> Those who took French citizenship – 3% of the population – had a slightly lower rate of 14.3%. France's overall unemployment rate of 11% underscored the unemployment problem of the North African groups, especially where their population was the greatest. . . . Overall, it is apparent, then, that official crime

> rates in France are the highest in those *départements* with the largest official counts of *étrangers*... it does help to explain French perceptions of trouble in those locations with the largest minority populations. (1997: 137, 139)

She then draws a parallel with US transitional areas in which poor, unemployed minorities and immigrants have been found to have the highest crime rates:

> not only because their social disorganization destabilizes conventional normative structures, allowing deviant norms to prevail, but also because those outside of these areas recognize that these are places where residents are less likely to initiate contact with the police to report drug sales or other criminal behavior. (1997: 140)

What is interesting here is that in research (as distinct from politics), only an outsider would be bold enough to link unemployment, ethnicity, and crime in France so openly. Most French researchers have made their own the official diktats forbidding a distinctive recognition of "minorities" and those who did not were violently criticized as communitarians or saboteurs of the French Republic (Wieviorka 2000: 13). There are almost no Foundations funding independent research on the theme of ethnicity. This orientation explains why no statistics track second generations referred to by Irving Jackson as "the North African groups." Once citizenship is obtained through a mix of *jus soli* and *jus sanguinis*, nothing legally distinguishes the former alien from the old-stock French. For state officials, these minorities do not constitute *a priori* ethnics or communities. They are either French or foreigners (Body-Gendrot 1993). It is very likely that the construction of the European Union will force France to adjust its singular stance. New developments in research on discrimination, which are replacing the debate on social integration, point to such changes.

Business Cycles, Polarization, and Urban Threats

According to the theory of relative deprivation, higher crime rates are experienced in cities and neighborhoods where low-income communities live in close proximity to high-income ones. This is precisely the configuration of global cities. "The concentration of wealth and poverty in the same geographical area is more exacerbated in the American city," Sullivan observes, "and it constitutes the precondition of street crime in the city" (1991: 225). Seeing others' wealth and possessions, the delinquents may be motivated by a "predatory" delinquency because of emotional frustration, latent animosities, and opportunities (Sampson 1985: 8; Brantingham and Brantingham

1980). According to the sociologist Richard Block, who studies Chicago neighborhoods, the proximity of poor and wealthy families may account for 56 percent of the variance in homicide rates and almost 40 percent of the variance in robbery and assault rates (1997: 52–5). But if low-status youth living in high-status areas commit more crimes than those living segregated in poor areas, does not this seem to justify practices of segregation and a rationalization for gated communities?

In France, research has also focused on the deep economic transformations which produced massive marginalization during the last twenty years. The former social question was relabeled the "urban question," the city mirroring societal changes (Donzelot 1991). As social inequalities increased, vertical integration collapsed with the "end of work" and the gap between the "ins" and the "outs" widened (Touraine 1991). The urban crisis was analyzed through the interaction between the global and structural forces, on one hand, and the local sphere and business cycles on the other. Urban areas, integrated by the functioning of the Fordist system, were left behind by the new economy. They constitute a historical and exceptional example of motionlessness. According to Catherine Bidou-Zachariasen (1997), such Fordist residential space was too "functionally" designed at the start to allow an efficient matrix to confront social and economic mutations. Social "anomy" explains the high rate of unemployment of these areas and the lack of resource mobilizations from the residents, except those involved in the underground economy. Yet such broad generalization calls for empirical testing.

According to conventional representations, at the individual level unemployment opens indeed a potential pathway to a criminal career. At the collective level, it allows institutions to create meaningful, status-loaded categories which resonate with police officers, welfare workers, judges, and others sorting out deviants and shaping the moral order. Yet theory linking polarized cities and crime in relation to unemployment is inconclusive at this point and far too deterministic. "The same problems that plague time series analyses of wages, interest rates, and unemployment plague time series analyses of crime," Freeman observes. "Differences in years covered or in the model chosen or in the particular measures used affect results substantively. The safest conclusion is that the time series are not a robust way to determine the job market–crime link" (Freeman 1995: 8). The 1960s were affluent, yet crime was rising in US cities. May 1968 erupted at a time of high consumption in French cities. Today juvenile delinquency remains high in prosperous Denmark, whereas Spain, with a 20 percent rate of unemployment, has not experienced high levels of delinquency. Other factors have to be included in the analysis, such as urbanization, family structures, the circulation of weapons, social integration/stigmatization of socially excluded categories, societal responses to household hardships, institutional priorities in terms of prevention and repression measures, and the consent of their clienteles to such measures. So far, explanations in terms of places and people continue to develop side by side. As for the impact of outer forces which formerly called for grand narratives, the connection between business cycles, polarization, and urban threats currently remains a riddle for social sciences. Here researchers are more cautious about coming to any conclusions.

Radical Rethinking: The Evolution of Policies of Social Control in Cities

Do national policies matter?

The instantaneous knowledge of violence and crime in the inner cities – and less frequently in the rest of the city – forces public authorities to react. Tensions affecting any point of the urban space in middle-size European countries spread like a shock wave across these societies. The effects of urban disorders are, however, more diffuse in federal countries where transmissions are as much horizontal (from one land or state or county to the other) as they are vertical. When trying to evaluate how cities use their resources to respond to urban threats and when dealing with the local *per se*, where the meaning of spatial scale is involved, researchers confront theoretical pitfalls. If they argue that the city mediates, that is, resists, adapts, acquiesces to outer forces, is it some quality of scale that enables the local to "filter" forces emanating from other spatial scales or "a reference to the frictional interaction of actors with different geographic reaches" (Beauregard 1995: 238)? National politics trickle down by creating moods and expectations among anxious city dwellers. Yet what matters just as much, it seems, are the local arrangements – the governance and the social engineering taking place at the city level. The various forms of control exerted across Western cities may explain why they remain on the whole pacified, compared with other arrangements in more volatile contexts. People and institutions have invested dearly in the city. It is my assumption – confirmed by interviews in cities – that it is not in the interest of any mayor, police commissioner, judge, community, or church leader, or the business community, to allow antagonistic relations to grow between various social components of the city which make up, one way or another, their clienteles. People identify with their neighborhoods and business owners commit to locations for other than purely economic reasons. The value of their investments depends on the continuity of relationships (Beauregard and Haila 2000: 36). Do we not observe mayors attempting to slow down the exodus of the middle and working classes by making the neighborhoods safe through upgrading education and playing down criminalization? Even though their stakes may be different, many actors in the city seem to share the same goals.

How do cities use national policies of prevention and safety in the United States and in France and respond to their constituents' anxious questions? Or are national policies imposed upon them without their consent? France represents one extreme in terms of policies of social prevention, the United States the other in terms of repression. These two countries and their cities differentiate themselves in the responses they have constructed to deal with urban threats.

The evolution of control in American cities

Despite major transformations, continuities appear more important than discontinuities in the history of punishment in the United States. The ideology of the past contains a hidden agenda for the present, as ideas take different forms and institutions adapt to changing sensibilities and socioeconomic circumstances. Nobody would understand the success of the current repressive policies without being aware of the progressive lack of legitimacy of the "therapeutic" approach that had preceded them (Garland 2001: ch. 2). The approach was popular during the time of the Violence Commission, that is, when a structural analysis of the violence plaguing society made the United States and Europe quite close to one another. Yet, as crime kept increasing in inner cities during the 1970s and 1980s (the same evolution also occurred in France and in the UK) and as an American "underclass" was seen as threatening for the well-being of the middle classes, public opinion expressed signs of concern and "compassion fatigue." An influential article with the title, "What works?," questioned the whole therapeutic approach and concluded that in fact nothing worked, a point of view which had a colossal impact on penology as well as on criminal justice policies (Martison 1974). The experts' discourse had criticized so much the efficiency of the system in combating the fear of crime that people had come to regard it as dysfunctional. Very soon, funds for rehabilitation programs were cut and the managerial model that prevails today came into force and added one more layer to the already hypertrophied system of crime control (Austin and Krisberg 1981; Cohen 1985).

It is interesting to observe that, instead of being represented by a blindfolded woman, holding a set of scales in her hand, Justice came more and more to be symbolized by a funnel. In 1976, another criminologist, Andrew von Hirsch, claimed that punishment depended on the type and seriousness of the crime rather than on the delinquent's capacity to be reincorporated in the mainstream. From the 1970s onwards, the collapse of the inner-city economy and increased legal and political demands for accountability produced a new construct, the managerial model with performance parameters displacing the goal of normalization (Simon 1993: 9). The means of control in this narrative are as revealing as their ends and intentions.

Pressures for efficiency, productivity, and rational control emanate not only from managers, experts, and technocrats, but also from cost-conscious and vote-conscious politicians together with counter-cultural and ecology-conscious groups and critics of bigness, waste, formalism, and irrationality (Heydebrandt 1979: 32, 52). With the management of cases, the assessing and reassessing of risks and needs, the developing and updating of action plans, the securing of controls and the provision of services, the individual offender is lost from view. The computer dictates when to have reports done and it sets the priorities (Simon 1993: 131). The search for new grounds for credibility is generated by public anxiety about criminal violence and the lack of confidence in professionals.

A limited toolkit and a plurality of actors

The new American modes of local governance involve nonprofit organizations, private firms, and civil society in a "co-production of safety." Unlike many European countries, the United States has no cabinet official in charge of a national crime policy. Experiments are introduced randomly by states and cities through the financial support of the federal government and the states (the cities being their "creatures"). Some states (and consequently cities) refuse to send a person to jail for a small quantity of drugs, while others impose a strict sentence. Some states choose to have the death penalty and enforce it, others have it but do not use it, while others ban it. New modes of thinking about the legitimacy and efficiency of norms emerge almost everywhere. It would be difficult in the fifty states in charge of law and order not to find a spectacular innovation, risky yet meant to lessen the endemic violence and the fear it creates, even though one might also find the same kind of innovation rejected elsewhere. As Alexis de Tocqueville remarked a long time ago, local autonomy and culture and the voters' choices to which institutions are accountable make up the American participatory democracy – despite or because of globalization (Body-Gendrot 2002). It is therefore quite difficult for a researcher on US cities to make any broad generalization. One should rather imagine the quilted urban American territory as a toolkit, where some tools attract attention.

In a majority of states, "get tough" politics on crime and drugs has animated law and order policies for at least a generation. The national sphere has an impact on cities when it launches a major war on drugs supported by a large consensus and when it withholds money from the states unless they accept repressive policies favored by a conservative Congress. The interference of the federal state in the issue of crime produces the "federalization" of a traditional local issue.

National lawmakers have decided to impose mandatory sentencing, that is, set sentences for particular types of offenses, thus depriving local judges from leverage on certain types of crimes, mainly related to substance abuse. Because crime repression is politically so rewarding, all kinds of political actors try to benefit from it. "The debate over crime and drugs has become less important for the possibilities of concrete public action than for its breadth as a contested terrain on which battles over power and principle rage," Diana Gordon notes (1994: 5). Republicans and Democrats vie in Congress and with the White House and with governors to get hold of the crime issue.

There is no space here to go into details, but the most recent legislation – the 1994 Anti-Crime Act – was designed to send a message to the public that crime was being taken care of at the higher levels, both by Congress and the President. The issue of sanctions shows clearly how a conservative Congress imposes its wishes on the local sphere via federal funds. For example, a bill offered $1.5 billion in 1997 to states meeting new standards of harshness in their treatment of young offenders. Violent juvenile delinquents have to be tried in adult courts, unless the state attorney-general finds that "public interest" is better served by trial in a juvenile court (Lewis 1997). Since 1992, forty-five states changed their laws to try juvenile delinquents over fourteen (over ten in Vermont and in Kansas) as adults. Conversely, local attitudes may influence federal agents according to the states, as shown by the diversity of decisions relative to the death penalty by federal prosecutors. States may also influence one another, as demonstrated by the "three strikes" laws. These movements – top down, bottom up, horizontal – impact on cities.

Local initiatives

Given these parameters, American cities try various approaches, according to who is in charge, following what types of elections, on what type of platform, with what finances, and in what culture. Everyone has heard of the successes and failures of the zero-tolerance approach in New York (Body-Gendrot 2001). The experiment led by Boston into the reduction of homicides among gangs illustrates both the success and the limits of modes of governance involving all kinds of actors in charge of law and order under the leadership of a local police team. The problem, defined as a priority, was eventually solved and deterrence perceived as efficient. Toughness, coherence, cohesion, and a continuous contact between the youths and motivated institutional partners (the police and probation agents circulating together in the same cars to ensure that the contract the youths had passed with them was respected) proved successful. Since the beginning of the experimentation three years ago, homicide rates among the gangs fell by two-thirds in Boston (Kennedy 1998). The symbolic weight of the approach is not to be denied: institutions demonstrated that they had the capacity to handle a problem seemingly beyond control. Lowell (Massachusetts) and Minneapolis (Minnesota) also registered spectacular murder declines among gangs after conducting similar initiatives.

However, the limits come, first of all, from the fact that such approaches can only last a limited period of time in a circumscribed space, due to the colossal resources and amount of will required. Philosophically, they also raise the question of a logic that opposes force with force and imposes a paramilitary management of spaces and bodies, without looking for the causes of violent behavior. The police cling to a behaviorist discourse. The violent environment in which the gangs move is the only language they are able to understand. One cannot help thinking about the remark of a community activist who, while acknowledging that the youths are no saints, thought that any policy grounded on arrests was problematic because "in one fell swoop the police showed how easy it was to wipe out a sizeable part of the young lifeblood in (a) neighborhood." The gang members could have represented a positive youth force in the community if some preventive effort had been made earlier (DeLeon-Granados 2000: 45; Body-Gendrot 2001).

Other cities and other neighborhoods try diversified, multidimensional, penal welfarist measures. Drug courts, for instance, in-between therapeutic injunction and punishment have now been adopted by 150 cities in thirty-eight states. In San Diego the police orientation, "safety and care," characterizes a very different approach from the "zero-tolerance" one and has met with statistical success and an approval of local public opinion. The severity and the range of safety problems differ, of course, in San Diego, New York, or Baltimore. But after rejecting a repressive approach San Francisco saw its number of arrested delinquents fall by two-thirds between 1996 and 1999. Clearly, each city can find its own ways to combat delinquency.

The evolution of control in French cities

Since the beginning of the 1980s, France has often been cited abroad as having initiated a model of social prevention which is meant to deter youths from delinquency. For a long time, national elites have refused to associate urban disorders with urban dysfunctions in the working-class/immigrant neighborhoods, where a lot of public housing is concentrated, for fear of officially stigmatizing them. Selective help brought to such neighborhoods, under the auspices of urban policies (*la politique de la ville*), operated as a form of territorial affirmative action.

Elites at the top thought that social programs in problematic territories would bring back excluded populations into the social mainstream. People were perceived as less responsible for disruptive actions than the dysfunctional sites in which they lived. Solidarity was the key word used by social democratic elites during the 1980s to fight class segregation and social marginalization. Urban and social programs meant to improve the standards of living in these neighborhoods were thought to be efficient enough to combat urban delinquency. This structural analysis is very different from the crime prevention policies developed at that time in the United States and the UK.

We cannot relate here in detail the various stages of this policy (Body-Gendrot 2001: ch. 4). What is of interest to us is that this policy of social prevention (*politique de la ville*) was structured by urban riots in the banlieues and in other problematic urban neighborhoods, without anyone acknowledging this factor until late in the 1990s and without any attempt at creating partnerships between the local actors of social prevention and the law enforcers. Indeed, law enforcement officers were perceived as obscure evils by Left militants, including mayors. Consequently, the representatives of the national police were not very involved in the local commissions that dealt with the prevention of delinquency (Bonnemaison 1982). They limited their role to the sharing of statistics, while national magistrates, at the local level, tried to retain their control over decision-making by not participating in the new modes of governance. The disconnection between those engaged in social prevention and repression in France was striking.

The second novelty comes from the weight given to the local sphere. However, in France this was not an achievement by local institutions but the result of a decision from the central state aiming at more efficiency. A hypertrophy of prevention policies marked the 1980s, each mayor fighting to have his/her share of the national bounty (i.e., subsidies and staff). Such prevention policies did not express any awareness of the macro-mutations affecting cities in terms of segregation, racism, crime, disenfranchisement, and (global) complexity. Locally, actions were never targeted sufficiently, goals and practices were not tightly articulated, and minor tools were used to address the major traumas caused by a high rate of unemployment and deep cultural transformations in sensitive areas.

The evolution from policies of social prevention to policies of safety occurred after the Left came back to power in 1997. Better communication at the European level also forced France to harmonize its policies with neighboring countries, despite the fact that safety remains a sovereign function *per se*. Electoral concerns also affected the anxieties of mayors versus public opinion. Urban safety appeared as their number two priority after employment. French mayors who, at the beginning of the 1980s, would never have used the word "repression" were now requiring more police resources, more sanctions, more local control. Some mayors from diverse political backgrounds passed repressive measures, forbidding aggressive panhandling or imposing curfews. Such local ordinances were censored by the state council, the higher administrative court in France, as a threat to civil liberties. Most mayors observed the status quo. However, they were rarely overtly punitive and populist, as though they could not measure the impact of such rhetoric and measures upon their constituents. The will to preserve the "social link" and to avoid playing one component of the local population against another seemed the safer course. It would explain the reluctance to negatively label people according to their race or ethnicity, even if they were well-known drug dealers. People were identified according to the micro-territory where they lived, which was quite enough to stigmatize them.

At the national level, it was decided in 1998 that the police and the gendarmes would be redeployed to "sensitive" urban neighborhoods to combat the prevailing fear of crime. This decision of fairness was, however, fiercely opposed by the police and gendarme unions and by the mayors of rural communities eager to keep their police stations, despite the low rate of crime. The police corporation, in particular, showed its capacity to resist pressures and demands. Neither the growth of delinquency (a 50 percent increase since 1990; see Bousquet 1998) nor the threat of urban disorders (Bui-Trong 2000) shook it. The powerlessness of the state confronted by the determination of organized groups was obvious. The only way to enforce reform was to hire new police adjuncts and to launch community policing and partnerships as a way of restoring the image of the police among the public. This approach was part of a wider reorientation by the national state in terms of territorialization: the state pursued policies it was unable to enforce nationally with tools more suitable to a complex and multicultural society. It was not a retreat, a "hollowing out" of the state, but a continuation of former policies through other means.

One of the publicized policy approaches, showing that the state had perceived the city dwellers' concerns, focused on "local contracts of safety," usually signed by the *préfet* representing the state, the mayor, and the local prosecutor. The four hundred contracts, already signed, challenge the imposition of uniform rules all over the country. Formerly, policing was done along the same lines in Marseille and in Lyon, in Neuilly and in St Denis, according to demographic statistics. The new contracts admit variety in the mode of operation and in the diversification of resources. After evaluating local needs in terms of safety, the participants ideally involve themselves in new schemes which are meant to produce more pacified cities.

No one knows whether the former actors of social prevention (*politique de la ville*) will enforce the contract and whether the state will keep to its promises (more police, more resources, more subsidies, etc.). No one knows either if insecurity will decrease in cities. Currently, new agencies in charge of security and of mediation have been hired on a massive scale at the local level to supervise public spaces, schools, buses and railway stations, public housing, and so on. Such jobs are frequently held by immigrant youths from problematic neighborhoods who rarely hold a diploma. Their economic future is uncertain. The cooperation with the police and even with young police adjuncts, socialized in the same housing projects, has not proved successful (Body-Gendrot and Duprez 2001). As the state attempts to "steer" more and "row" less, it authorizes, licenses, audits, and inspects the doing of others. Processes of control and verification allow those who "steer" to monitor and correct the activities of those who "row." Similar processes are observed in Britain as well as in France (Crawford 2001).

Other reforms have focused on the functioning of the criminal justice system. Widely criticized for being too slow, opaque, and costly, the unfairness of the system for the victims of urban violence was blatant. New structures – the Houses of Justice and Law – have attempted to create a parallel criminal justice system, closer to the problematic neighborhoods, processing cases rapidly, using mediation as a possible way of reconciliation between the offender and the victim. Not all judges are convinced by this approach, which requires them to act more as referees than judges. Moreover, only seventy "community courts" of this type are in operation and the current lack of staff and resources hampers their operations.

Another innovation involves the local treatment of delinquency by the criminal justice system (*groupes locaux de traitement de la délinquance*). As in the American cases already mentioned, priority is given to problem solving during a limited time in a circumscribed area. Then once the diagnosis is made, all the institutional partners work together under the authority of the prosecutor to attempt to eradicate the delinquency plaguing the neighborhood. This approach is fairly successful but the required resource mobilization, coherence, and leadership make it quite exceptional.

Currently, social scientists lack conceptual tools to draw conclusions from these developments. No one will deny that for the last few decades, pragmatic solutions adjusted to local contexts differentiate cities and that, in this respect, international convergences have appeared. Yet by managing risks seen as coming from a minority of youths in problematic spaces, do authorities respond as well to the larger demands for protection emanating both from low-income residents and street-level agents and from the middle classes? Do they come forward with a meaning given both to the new forms of violence and to the solutions that have been concocted?

Conclusion: An Elusive Complexity

The current politicization of the crime issue draws its success from complex processes. Social restructuring and rising crime rates allow politicians, the media, and public opinion spokespersons to take advantage of a global feeling of insecurity to pursue their own strategies. This manipulation is facilitated by a widespread perception of potential victimization (supported by the continuous flows of violent images) rather than by the witnessing of offenses. What is new is that elites, whose world was insulated from crime and who bought social peace through welfare policies (a phenomenon more developed in Europe), are now assailed by their constituents' pressures and influenced by their own perceptions of insecurity. They are, therefore, more eager to give legitimacy to repressive policies, an easier choice than social prevention. Indeed, the discourse on crime involves the construction of a set of narratives which allows the kept, the keepers, and the public to believe in the ability to control (Simon 1993: 9). Yet as ideological constructions, these narratives are full of contradictions and paradoxes.

An interactive process

Stuart Scheingold warns us to be cautious in our judgment of politicians' behavior. He admits that:

> national politicians . . . have strong incentives to politicize street crime. For them, it provides a unifying theme and thus a valence issue. While victimization is experienced differentially according to class, race, gender, and geography, the threat it poses to property and person evokes comparable fears throughout the society. National and gubernatorial political leaders can, therefore, deploy the fear of crime to unify the public against the criminal. (1984: 3, 179)

Yet, Scheingold is quick to add that:

> it is an interactive process combining elements of responsiveness with elements of manipulation. Politicians do not so much "expropriate our consciousness" as take advantage of punitive predispositions about crime that are rooted in American culture. The public engages and disengages from the politicization process for reasons that have at least as much to do with the place of crime in the culture as with the impact of criminal victimization in our lives. (1984: 54)

In other words, politicization is a reciprocal process, with political leaders taking the initiative as much as responding to the public. But politicization has only an indirect and unpredictable impact on policy. Power games begin long before demands surface and debates take place.

Is there a pilot?

Besides taking account of interactive processes, another difficulty for researchers is to find out who is in charge of policies. A multiplicity of public, private, and nonprofit community actors at diverse levels is currently involved in the crime issue. (The same is true of welfare measures, which still remain abundant in cities, as social programs provide jobs to the middle class.) In the case of France, elected officials at different levels frequently appear as political entrepreneurs setting in motion so-called public interest operations with diversified partners and, thereby, revealing new modes of governance over regulation issues. Territorial problems force them to work together on imagined spaces, *à la carte,* beyond conventional institutional boundaries. If the problem extends beyond the community level, supra- or extra-institutional mediators will smooth the connections, recreating the capacity for action and the need to reach agreement. These collective actors, at the edge of economic, social, or law and order spheres, construct themselves according to the problems to be solved. The same complexity is revealed in a federal country like the United States, where the concept of governance involving all kinds of actors blurs the boundaries between the public and the private spheres.

What is the right level to intervene?

On the issue of city governance, the pyramidal shape of power does not fairly account for what is going on, nor does a structure which piles up jurisdictions on top of one another. The trend is toward regional forms of governance made of bits and pieces, the interests of which are to define goals and avoid parochial rivalries. On such a complex topic as urban safety, redefinitions and arbitrations cannot be avoided. The articulation of different modes of regulation resurrects a capacity for action, provided each party remains committed to playing its part – an elusive expectation.

In this new environment, the territory plays a role in its own formulations, articulations, or disembeddedness. Processes allow relations among various actors to be adjusted, whether they are integrated or marginalized in the dominant system of decision-making. The articulation of scales, however, does not guarantee the coordination of stakeholders. The scale of a "local" common good, of a neighborhood versus a city or a region, may diverge radically. The heterogeneity of the demands from the periphery and the prevailing disorders reveal the contradictions at the center. The current orientation fosters a proliferation of networks and a fragmentation of decision-making, which is interpreted as a failure in terms of pace, lack of transparency, and cost. Disaggregated partnerships give the impression of institutionalizing the rites of distrust and of creating negative dynamics. The role of the state is either reaffirmed or occulted, depending on the context (Garland 2001). "Authority comes from the top, trust from the bottom," the

French Revolutionary Abbé Emmanuel-Joseph Sieyès used to say. Currently, there is neither one nor the other.

In sum, what do we learn from this evolution both in terms of research and of urban politics? Each country, according to its traditions, history, and values, chooses different ways of categorizing, excluding, criminalizing, punishing, managing, and integrating. On the whole, the European choices are not American in terms of the death penalty, self-defense, the sanction of juvenile delinquents, the choice of massive incarceration, the rights of the majority versus those of the delinquents, and so on. Except for British policies, which display forms of punitive populism, and for isolated regions in other countries, France and (generally) other European countries still speak strongly against zero tolerance, communitarianism, and binary rhetorics and support social prevention (Robert and van Outrive 1999; Duprez and Hebberecht 2001). However, no one can assert that locally, more punitive policies will not prevail if conservative coalitions win the elections.

The historical idea of what a city is still carries a powerful political meaning for Europeans, however (Paquot, Body-Gendrot, and Lussault 2000). Symbolic unity – *unum ex pares* – displayed in the use of public spaces and in shared festivities is often more valued than the expression of differences. The term "citizenship" has powerful connotations and is very attractive to upwardly mobile second and third generations. The point here is not to choose between group and identity loyalties, on the one hand, and universal definitions which threaten to dissolve or change these loyalties, on the other. For cities, the multidimensional challenge of the coming times entails the construction of a coexistence and an active pluralism, which contrasts with an indifferent relativism or an equivalence of differences.

In European urban thinking, there is also a refusal to see urban violence as unavoidable. Let us remember that, in the past, cities brought protection to their residents, in contrast with the fear that reigned in the hinterland. During the twentieth century, gun culture has been disapproved of and conflict, debate, and a general "civilizing process" are seen as the democratic way to put an end to impulsive "acting out." Realistic utopias continually emerge to present the city as a "good" surprise with its overflowing vitality, its constant innovations, and its crises in the "search for solutions." The civic cultures of cities, their philanthropic or activist traditions, their repertoires of surveillance are tools used to combat "social fragmentation," racism, and the negative consequences of rapid change. It is said that the current era is confused and complex and this is obviously so. Yet a new urban literature is needed to tell us about the good news. To each generation of cities there corresponds a new imagination of the world, offering innovative responses to continuous challenges.

Bibliography

Aponte, R. 1990: Definitions of the underclass: a critical analysis. In H. Gans (ed.), *Sociology in America*. Newbury, CA: Sage, 117–37.

Austin, J. and Krisberg B. 1981: Wider, stronger and different nets: the dialectics of criminal justice reform. *Journal of Research on Crime and Delinquency* 18/1 (January): 165–96.

Bachmann, C. and Le Guennec, N. 1996: *Violences urbaines*. Paris: Albin Michel.

Beauregard, R. 1995: Theorizing the global–local connection. In P. Knox and P. Taylor (eds.), *World Cities in a World System*. Cambridge: Cambridge University Press, 232–48.

——and Haila, A. 2000: The unavoidable continuities of the city. In P. Marcuse and R. van Kempen (eds.), *Globalizing Cities: A New Spatial Order*. Oxford: Blackwell, 22–36.

Begag, A. 1990: La révolte des lascars contre l'oubli à Vaulx en Velin. *Les Annales de la recherche urbaine* 49: 114–21.

Bidou-Zachariasen, C. 1997: La prise en compte de "l'effet de territoire" dans l'analyse des quartiers urbains. *Revue française de sociologie* 38 (1): 97–117.

Block, R. 1997: Risky places in Chicago and in the Bronx: robbery in the environments of Rapid Transit Stations. Working paper.

Body-Gendrot, S. 1993: *Ville et violence*. Paris: Presses universitaires de France.

——2000: *The Social Control of Cities? A Comparative Perspective*. Oxford: Blackwell.

——2001: *Villes: la fin de la violence?* Paris: Presses de Sciences-Po.

——2002: An outsider's understanding of American violence: Tocqueville revisited. In L. Curtis (ed.), *Violence in America: Then and Now*. Boulder, CO: Rowman and Littlefield.

——and Duprez, D. 2001: Les politiques de sécurité et de prévention dans les années 1990 en France. In D. Duprez and P. Hebberecht (eds.), *Les Politiques de sécurité et de prévention dans les années 1990 en Europe. Déviance et société* 4.

Bonnemaison, G. 1982: *Face à la délinquance: prévention, répression, solidarité*. Paris: La documentation française.

Bourdieu, P. et al. 1993: *La Misère du monde*. Paris: Le Seuil.

Bousquet, R. (ed.) 1998: *Nouveaux Risques, nouveaux enjeux*. Paris: L'Harmattan.

Brantingham, P. and Brantingham, P. 1980: Crime, occupation and economic specialization. In D. Georges-Abeyie and K. Harries (eds.), *Crime: A Special Perspective*. New York: Columbia University Press.

Bui-Trong, L. 2000: *Violences urbaines*. Paris: Bayard Editions.

Cohen, S. 1985: *Visions of Social Control*. Cambridge: Polity Press.

Crawford, A. 2001: The growth of crime prevention in France as contrasted with the English experience: some thoughts on the politics of insecurity. In G. Hughes et al. (eds.), *New Directions in Crime Prevention and Community Safety*. Milton Keynes: Open University Press, forthcoming.

De Rudder, V. 1992: Immigrant housing and integration in French cities. In D. Horowitz and G. Noiriel (eds.), *Immigration in Two Countries: French and American Experiences*. New York: New York University Press, 247–67.

DeLeon-Granados, W. 2000: *Travels through Crime and Place*. Boston: Northeastern University Press.

Donzelot, J. 1991: Le déplacement de la question sociale. In J. Donzelot (ed.), *Face à l'exclusion, le modèle français*. Paris: Editions Esprit, 5–11.

Dubet, F. et al. 1987: *La Galère: jeunes en survie*. Paris: Fayard.

Duprez, D. and Hebberecht P. (eds.) 2001: *Les Politiques de sécurité et de prévention dans les années 1990 en Europe. Déviance et société* 4.

Elias, N. and Scotson J. L. 1965: *The Established and the Outsiders*. Newbury, CA: Sage.

Fagan, J. and Wilkinson, D. 1998: Situational contexts and functions of adolescent violence. In D. Elliott and B. Hamburg (eds.), *Violence in American Schools*. Cambridge: Cambridge University Press.

Freeman, R. 1995: The labor market. In J. Q. Wilson and J. Persilia (eds.), *Crime*. San Francisco: ICS Press, ch. 8.

Garapon, A. 1996: *Le Gardien des promesses*. Paris: Odile Jacob.

Garland, D. 2001: *The Culture of Control: Crime and Social Order in Contemporary Society*. Chicago: University of Chicago Press.

Gordon, D. 1994: *The Return of Dangerous Classes*. New York: Norton.

Hagan, J. and Peterson, R. (eds.) 1995: *Crime and Inequality*. Stanford, CA: Stanford University Press.

Harrison, P. 1983: *Inside the Inner City*. London: Penguin.

Hebberecht, P. and Sack, F. (eds.) 1997: *La Prévention de la délinquance en Europe*. Paris: L'Harmattan.

Héritier, F. 1999: *De la Violence*. Paris: Odile Jacob.

Heydebrandt, W. 1979: The technocratic administration of justice. *Research in Law and Sociology* 2: 29–42.

Hirsch, A. von 1976: *Doing Justice: The Choice of Punishments*. New York: Basic Books.

Irving Jackson, P. 1997: Minorities, crime and criminal justice in France. In I. Marshall (ed.), *Minorities, Migrants and Crime*. Thousand Oaks, CA: Sage, 130–47.

Jargowsky, P. 1996: *Poverty and Place: Ghettos, Barrios and the American City*. New York: Russell Sage Foundation.

Jazouli, A. 1986: *L'Action collective des jeunes maghrébins de France*. Paris: L'Harmattan.

Kennedy, D. 1998: Pulling levers: getting deterrence right. *National Institute of Justice Journal* (July): 2–8.

Lewis, A. 1997: More juveniles charged as adults. *New York Times*, May 19.

Lewis, O. 1966: The culture of poverty. *Scientific American* 215: 19–25.

Mann, C. R. 1993: *Unequal Justice: A Question of Color*. Bloomington: Indiana University Press.

Marshall, I. H. 1997: Introduction. In I. Marshall (ed.), *Minorities, Migrants and Crime*. Thousand Oaks, CA: Sage.

Martison, R. 1974: What works? Questions and answers about prison reforms. *Public Interest* 35: 25–54.

Massey, D. 1997: Space/power, identity/difference: tensions in the city. In A. Merrifield and E. Swyngedouw (eds.), *The Urbanization of Injustice*. New York: New York University Press, 100–16.

Mead, L. 1986: *Beyond Entitlement: The Social Obligations of Citizenship*. New York: Free Press.

Murray, C. 1984: *Losing Ground: American Social Policy, 1950–1980.* New York: Basic Books.
Paquot, T., Body-Gendrot, S., and Lussault, M. (eds.) 2000: *La Ville et l'urbain: l'état des savoirs.* Paris: La Découverte.
Park, R. and Burgess, E. (eds.) 1925: *The City: Suggestions for Investigation of Human Behavior in the Urban Environment.* Chicago, IL: Chicago University Press.
Robert, P. and van Outrive, L. 1999: *Crime et justice en Europe: évaluations et recommandations.* Paris: L'Harmattan.
Roy, O. 1990: Dreux: de l'immigration au groupe ethnique. *Esprit* (February): 5–10.
Salas, D. 1997: Mineurs: une justice à refonder. *Informations sociales* 62: 84–92.
Sampson R. 1985: Neighborhood and crime: the structural determinants of personal victimization. *Journal of Research on Crime and Delinquency* 22 (1): 7–40.
——and Wilson, W. J. 1995: Towards a theory of race, crime and urban inequality. In J. Hagan and R. Peterson (eds.), *Crime and Inequality.* Stanford, CA: Stanford University Press, 285–313.
Scheingold, S. 1984: *The Politics of Law and Order.* New York: Longman.
——1991: *The Politics of Street Crime.* Philadelphia: Temple University Press.
Shaw, C. and McKay, R. 1942: *Juvenile Delinquency and Urban Areas.* Chicago: Chicago University Press.
Silver, H. 1993: National conceptions of the new urban poverty: social structural change in Britain, France and the U.S. *International Journal of Urban and Regional Research* 17 (3): 185–203.
Simon, J. 1993: *Poor Discipline.* Chicago: Chicago University Press.
Stack, C. 1975: *All Our Kin: Strategies for Survival in a Black Community.* New York: Harper and Row.
Sullivan, M. 1991: Crime and the social fabric. In J. Mollenkopf and M. Castells (eds.), *Dual City: Restructuring New York.* New York: Russell Sage Foundation, 225–43.
Taguieff, P.-A. (ed.) 1991: *Face au racisme.* Paris: La Découverte.
Touraine, A. 1991: Face à l'exclusion. In J. Donzelot (ed.), *Citoyenneté et urbanité.* Paris: Editions Esprit, 165–73.
Tribalat, M. (ed.) 1991: *Cent ans d'immigration: étrangers d'hier, Français d'aujourd'hui.* Paris: INED/Presses universitaires de France.
Wieviorka, M. 2000: *La Différence.* Paris: Baland.
Zimring, S. and Hawkins, G. 1996: *Crime is not the Problem: Lethal Violence in America.* New York: Oxford University Press.

Part III
The Global and Local, the Information Age, and American Metropolitan Development

6
Power in Place: Retheorizing the Local and the Global

Michael Peter Smith

Two dominant themes have informed the construction of the "local" in the discourse on the global–local interplay in urban studies. The local has been frequently represented as the cultural space of embedded communities and, inversely, as an inexorable space of collective resistance to disruptive processes of globalization. In writings ranging from classical urban sociology to contemporary discourses on globalization and place, the "locality" has been used to signify an embedded community. "Community" in turn is represented as a static, bounded, cultural space of being where personal meanings are produced, cohesive cultural values are articulated, and traditional ways of life are enunciated and lived. In classical urban sociological thought the "urban" served as a surrogate for the rational instrumentalism of the capitalist market and the bureaucratization of the lifeworld – the transformation of *Gemeinschaft*-like social relations into the mediated impersonal ties of a *Gesellschaft*-like urban society. In the contemporary period the "urban" has been replaced by the "global" as a metaphor for the central outside threat to the primary social ties binding local communities. "Globalization" has been represented as a new form of capitalist (post)modernity, a process inherently antagonistic to the sustainability of local forms of social organization and meaning-making.

I begin this chapter by arguing that the schemata used by urban structuralists such as David Harvey and Manuel Castells to conceptualize the global–local connection reify the theoretical terms in this dialectic, privileging (while marginalizing) the local as the place of culture or "community," while marking the global as the dynamic economic space of capital and infor-

This chapter is based on revised materials drawn from my book, *Transnational Urbanism: Locating Globalization* (M. P. Smith 2001). Empirical and ethnographic evidence supporting the arguments advanced here can be found in greater detail and depth in my book. I wish to thank Rene Francisco Poitevin for his helpful comments on this revision.

mation flows. I go on to argue that, ironically, key conceptualizations informing ethnographic practice in postmodern cultural studies and even the conceptualization of "everyday resistance" informing the politics of everyday life problematic in urban studies also rely upon a binary dichotomization of the global versus the local.

In the remainder of this chapter I further disrupt this binary by showing the myriad ways in which social networks and practices that are transnational in scope and scale are constituted by their interrelations with, and thus their groundedness inside, the local. I then ask what constraints have been placed on urban theory and research by the persistence of this dichotomous way of thinking and what can be done, both epistemologically and methodologically, to overcome these constraints. The aim is to frame a more dynamic conception of locality, one more likely to capture the connections linking people and places to the complex and spatially dispersed transnational communication circuits now intimately affecting the ways in which everyday urban life is experienced and lived. Writing from a social constructionist standpoint, I recommend that the sociological imagination be enriched by an engagement with a multi-sited mode of ethnographic research that is historically contextualized and recognizes the importance of everyday practices without romanticizing the local or losing sight of the structures of power/knowledge created by human practice.

The Confines of the Local in Urban Structuralism

The representation of the local as a once firmly situated cultural space of community-based social organization now rendered unstable by the global dynamism of capitalist (post)modernity is well captured in the following excerpt from David Harvey's *The Condition of Postmodernity* (1989: 238–9, emphasis added):

> Movements of opposition to the disruptions of home, community, territory, and nation by the restless flow of capital are legion. . . . Yet all such movements, no matter how well articulated their aims, run up against a seemingly immovable paradox. . . . [T]he movements have to confront the question of value and its expression as well as the necessary organization of space and time appropriate to their own reproduction. In so doing, they necessarily open themselves to the dissolving power of money as well as to the shifting definitions of space and time arrived at through the dynamics of capital circulation. Capital, in short, continues to dominate, and it does so in part through superior command over space and time. The "othernesses" and "regional resistances" that postmodernist politics emphasize can flourish in a particular place. But they are all too often subject to the power of capital over the co-ordination of universal fragmented space, and the march of capitalism's global historical time *that lies outside*

> *the purview of any particular one of them.* . . . Part of the insecurity which bedevils capitalism as a social formation arises out of this instability in the spatial and temporal principles around which social life might be organized (let alone ritualized in the manner of traditional societies). During phases of maximal change, the spatial and temporal bases for reproduction of the social order are subject to the severest disruption.

In this narration of the waning power of local cultural formations in the face of capitalist globalization the author of social change is never in doubt. Capital's superior global command over resources to reorganize time and space is opposed to the disorientation of defensive "local" social movements representing the interests of home, community, place, region, and even nation. The latter are represented as static forms of social organization, efforts to organize social life around "being" rather than "becoming." Defensive place-based movements are represented as cultural totalities expressing entirely place-bound identities in a world in which the dynamic flows of globalization exist entirely outside their purview. Oppositional movements representing "locality" may win some battles in what Harvey terms "postmodern politics." But they confront a restless adversary, whose processes of accumulation thrive on constantly disrupting the spatial and temporal arrangements upon which stable forms of local social organization might be constructed. Thus, in this grand narrative, in the final analysis, "capital" is the only agent of social change. Capitalist economic dynamics continue to dominate localities whose specific histories are relegated to the dustbin, rendering them fit only for periodic bouts of reactionary politics. As for the role of people in this grand narrative, we never know who lives, works, acts, and dies in Harvey's urban spaces since people are seldom represented as anything other than nostalgic romantics or cultural dupes.

Manuel Castells is another urban theorist who has represented the local as a political space of social movements defending threatened cultural and political meanings placed under siege by global economic and technological restructuring. At first glance his view of locality appears to be different from Harvey's theorization. In Castells's work, late modernity is represented as an informational mode of development, a "space of flows" which accelerates global financial and informational linkages, converts places into spaces, and threatens to dominate local processes of cultural meaning. While the space of flows is a global space of economic and technological power, the space of cultural meaning and experience remains local (Castells 1984). The global networks of wealth and power accumulate and exchange information instantaneously as a central source of institutional power. This boundary-penetrating process disrupts the sovereignty of the nation-state and threatens to marginalize the lifeworlds of local cultural "tribes." As Castells (1984: 236) expresses this argument:

> On the one hand the space of power is being transformed into flows. On the other hand, the space of meaning is being reduced to microterritories of new tribal communities. In between cities and societies disappear. Information tends to be dissociated from communication. Power is being separated from political representation. And production is increasingly separated from consumption, with both processes being piecemealed in a series of spatially distinct operations whose unity is only recomposed by a hidden abstract logic. The horizon of such a historical tendency is the destruction of human experience, therefore of communication, and therefore of society.

Following from this logic is a structuralist dialectic of domination and resistance. Global domination produces local resistance. Resistance to globalization is tied not to the agency of specific actors confronting unique historical conjunctures but to the very structural dynamic of the technological revolution which threatens to render the local "tribes" irrelevant to the new informational world that has come into being. In his view the nation-state is disintegrating as a space of internalized identity formation. Rather, two modes of identity formation are said to give rise to different types of communal resistance to globalization – "project identities" and "resistance identities" (1997: 11). The former are viewed as encompassing such bases of social identity as religious fundamentalism and ethnic nationalism. It is the structural connection of vastly different cultural formations as "bypassed" cultural spaces, forged in the context of disintegrating national civil societies, that allows Castells (1997) to lump together social movements as diverse as the Zapatistas in Mexico, the militia and patriot movements in the United States, and the Aum Shinrikyo cult in Japan, treating them as functionally equivalent "social movements against the new global order," despite their historical differences in goals, ideologies, national and local contexts, and specific histories.

Castells's analysis of local "resistance identities" is also framed by using a structural logic that leaves little room for localized processes of identity formation which might emerge out of social practices not only of resistance but also of appropriation or accommodation to, or even modification of, various aspects of globalization or transnationalism. Nor does he consider the possibility that a multiplicity of local identities might be selectively internalized by variously positioned local social actors operating in the context of historically variable local and national civil societies experiencing processes of globalization or transnationalism. Instead, he inscribes the "local" dimension of urban social movements as precisely something that produces meaning entirely against the dynamics of global processes. This is well captured in Castells's *The Power of Identity* (1997: 61). According to Castells, by the 1980s urban social movements were becoming:

> critical sources of resistance to the one sided logic of capitalism, statism, and informationalism. This was . . . because the failure of proactive movements

> [e.g., political parties and organized labor] . . . to counter economic exploitation, cultural domination, and political oppression had left people with no other choice than either to surrender or to react on the basis of the most immediate source of self-recognition and autonomous organization: their locality. Thus, so emerged the paradox of increasingly local politics in a world structured by increasingly global processes. There was production of meaning and identity: my neighborhood, my community, my city, my school, my tree, my river, my beach, my chapel, my peace, my environment. . . . Suddenly defenseless against a global whirlwind, people stuck to themselves: whatever they had, and whatever they were, became their identity.

This passage is somewhat different in tone from the passage by David Harvey quoted above. Yet in one key respect Harvey and Castells converge – namely, both represent the local as a cultural space of communal understandings, a space where meaning is produced entirely outside the global flows of money, power, and information. People in these narrow social worlds make sense of their world and form their political identities in a culturally bounded microterritory, the locality. These local cultural meanings, in turn, are represented as generating identities inherently oppositional to the global restructuring of society and space. For both, then, "place" is understood as the site of cohesive community formations existing outside the logic of globalization. While Harvey and Castells differ in their assessments of whether globalization will annihilate or defensively energize these community formations, they both maintain a systemic disjunction between local and global social processes.

The Limits of the Postmodern Turn to the Local

In seeking to displace the reliance of social theory on grand narratives of macro-social development, such as those of Harvey and Castells, some social theorists embracing the label "postmodern" have turned to what Foucault (1977) has termed the "essentially local character of criticism." In my view, despite their rhetorical gestures in the direction of the desirability of grounded fieldwork, some proponents of this turn to the local have posited an equally grand theory of local knowledge which privileges the ethnographic conversation as the only reliable route to personal knowledge, and personal knowledge as the only reliable measure of the "partial truths" about the workings of the world. This is the case, for instance, when postmodern anthropologist Stephen Tyler (1987: 171) asserts, with totalistic rhetorical flourish, that "discourse is the maker of this world, not its mirror."

The image that first comes to mind in this move, which some might regard as "postcolonial," is the "travel writing" found in colonial anthropology which relied upon the discourse of thick ethnographic "description" to fix, construct, and hence master colonized objects. It vividly detailed the habits, customs, speech acts, and bodily practices of conquered peoples in order to comprehensively "know," and hence implicitly control, the colonial subject. Ironically, however, the simple inversion of this hierarchy has often been the case in the postmodern cultural turn in urban ethnography in which the "thick description" of ethnographic narrative is relied upon to romanticize "the postcolonial subject" as embodied in the everyday practices of such socially constructed "communities" as urban taggers, street gangs, or various insurgent social movements.

When the discourse on postmodern ethnography first emerged in the late 1980s, a variety of new ethnographic practices were valorized as ways of overcoming the white, Western male "colonial" positionality of ethnographic research and anthropological writing. Advocates of "postmodern" ethnography sought to develop experimental research methods that would create a narrative space for the "postcolonial" subject. (For alternative views of postcolonial studies that would likely reject this way to give voice to postcolonial subjects as "Eurocentric" see Spivak 1988; Dirlik 1990.) Some working within this postmodern ethnographic genre sought to develop more effective ways to directly involve the cultural subjects of ethnographic research in the process of signification and the production of meaning. The aim of this move was to give "voice" to the postcolonial subject's view of the world. Anthropologist Stephen Tyler (1986: 122–40), for example, termed postmodern ethnography a form of "cooperative story making," a kind of "vision quest" on the part of the researcher to recover and evocatively communicate to the reader a "local narrative" about the lifeworld of the subject, a story produced by mutual dialogue rather than imposed by the authorial scripts of anthropologists and other "writers of culture." Tyler's aim was to produce a "cooperatively evolved text" in which neither subject, nor author, nor reader, no one, in fact, has the exclusive right of "synoptic transcendence" (Tyler 1986: 126, 129).

In these respects, Tyler romanticized the process of "intersubjective dialogue." The "penetrating" ethnographic encounter became a kind of grand narrative in its own right – one which enshrined and mystified the ethnographic conversation as a "deep" discovery of partial truths through an interpsychic process of "transference" and a transcendental process of "polyvocality" (see Tyler 1987: chs. 5–7). This strain of postmodern ethnography thus tried to have it both ways – while making no pretense to objective truth, indeed while denouncing such claims to scientificity as pretentious, the approach suggested by Tyler nonetheless tended to consecrate the postcolonial subject, as adduced by the ethnographer, thereby making this subject's voice into the measure of all things. In so doing this strain of postmodern ethnography displaced old master narratives of capitalism's structural logic that denied the agency of ordinary people with a new master narrative in which populist local voices "from below" were released from bondage by the skillful ethnographer and became decontextualized kings and queens of the world. In seeking to transcend the intellectual limits of structural-functional metanarratives this move unduly romanticized the "local narrative" produced by sensitive fieldworkers "on the ground" as a sure route to the partial truths of postcolonial subjectivity.

Rethinking the Ethnographic Turn

Must the ethnographic imagination be reduced to the pursuit of idiosyncratic *petit* narratives which then become ventriloquized voices of postcolonial resistance? This is not necessarily the case. Another strain of postmodern ethnography first suggested by George Marcus and Michael Fischer (1986) sought to refocus ethnographic inquiry amidst global sociocultural, political, and economic restructuring upon what they called the power–domination–accommodation–resistance motif. This motif, by situating the constitution of subjectivity within the context of rapidly changing sociospatial boundaries, provided an intelligible starting point for understanding the complex dynamics by which new subject positions can be seen to emerge in and through, for and against, such presumably "global" phenomena as urban sociospatial restructuring, transnational migration and grassroots activism, new state formation, and the bubbling cauldron of ethnic and racial conflict currently being stirred up by symbolic politics in transnational cities throughout the world.

Marcus and Fischer thus early on provided urban theorists with a useful opening for moving beyond the limits of the binary categories of global versus local, structure versus agency, and modern versus postmodern historical epochs in the formation of consciousness and social practice. They called their project "anthropology as cultural critique." In their characterization of contemporary "global conditions," they envisioned a world still full of cultural differences but in which most, if not all, "cultural worlds" had come into contact and communication "on the ground." They sought to unearth the hybrid or recombinant possibilities of contemporary life by studying the ways that in daily life people in various life situations accommodated to or resisted the cultural worlds colluding and colliding in their own time and place. They stressed various modes of "local" accommodation or resistance to "global conditions" as one strategy for mapping actual cultural change "from below" in a world that seemed to some an increasingly homogenized world of global modernity "from above." Apart from calling for a study of the hybridity emerging from intercultural contact and communication, however, their specification of "global conditions" remained somewhat limited.

On the ground, however, there has been over a decade of richly textured transnational ethnographic story-telling undertaken since Marcus and Fischer first issued their call for anthropology as cultural critique. Throughout the 1990s, numerous multi-locational practitioners of a transnational form of ethnographic fieldwork produced a body of research uniquely sensitive to the social construction of contextuality as well as identity (e.g., Rouse 1991; Kearney 1995; Schein 1998). These new modes of ethnographic inquiry successfully asked quite big questions of little people and obtained very intriguing results. For example, by asking transnational migrants involved in circular migration networks to first construct their understanding of the opportunities and constraints they faced in the world(s) in which they lived, and then to talk about the ways in which they appropriated, accommodated to, or resisted the forms of power and domination, opportunity and constraint that they experienced as they traversed political and cultural borders, this mode of ethnographic practice opened up a discursive space for contextually situated ethnographic narratives that captured the emergent character of transnational social practices.

Drawing on this growing body of transnational field research two anthropological theorists, Akhil Gupta and James Ferguson (1997a: 42–4), have called into question the spatialized understanding of cultural difference informing Marcus and Fischer's early writings of postmodern ethnography. Marcus and Fischer, to be sure, usefully prompt us to inquire into the global contextuality of local ethnographic narratives. Yet their own view of that global context still remains very much a framework in which different and distinct entities called "cultural worlds" now collide with each other more frequently in myriad ways. The main difference wrought by globalization in the "cultural critique" view is that "different societies," including "our own" and "other" societies, now provide us with critical tools for generating "critical questions from one society to probe the other" (1986: 112–77; this point of view is extensively critiqued in Gupta and Ferguson 1997a: 42–3).

As Gupta and Ferguson point out, this view of globalization as necessarily entailing intercultural learning, whether intentionally or not, ends up parsing out cultural difference in spatially quite familiar ways, neatly inscribing a world consisting of unproblematized territorial "homes" and "abroads." Marcus and Fischer fail to problematize the internal coherence of both the here and the there, which the findings of transnational ethnography clearly suggests is necessary (see Smith and Guarnizo 1998 and Smith 2001 for a synthesis of the central findings of transnational ethnographic fieldwork). Marcus and Fischer's view is one in which contact and communication take place between "societies" and "across cultures" rather than within and between transnationally linked localities, each containing historically specific difference-generating relations of power and meaning. Critiquing Marcus and Fischer's construction of "global context," Gupta and Ferguson propose a more fruitful alternative. Their interest lies "less in establishing a dialogical relation between geographically distinct societies than in exploring the process of production of difference in a world of culturally, socially, and economically interconnected and interdependent spaces" (Gupta and Ferguson 1997a: 43). This shortcoming of the anthropology as "cultural critique" perspective suggests that there may well be an unavoidable tendency for even ethnographically sensitive social researchers to read new meanings into the discourse on globalization derived from their own imaginations rather than from the constructions of their subjects.

But is the alternative of simply listening closely to and "recording" ordinary people's characterizations of globalization enough to explain the links they may have to a changing structural context? In my view there is also a clear danger inherent in the postmodern ethnographic effort to assume a subject position of tentativeness, if not authorial passivity, in "recording" the pure, authentic voice of the "marginal" and the "different." Cultural voices are historically contingent, not timelessly pure. The temptation to capture the essence of a "local voice," inscribing it as a heroic individual or collective challenge to the oppressive forces of global modernity, precisely mirrors the problem of idealizing the "other culture" as a radically strange entity which characterized colonial discourse.

My version of social constructionist urban analysis is at home with the view of cultural practice as adaptive, inventive, and multivalent. It thus rejects the view that "cultures" are closed local systems or singular wholes that can be penetrated by the simple ethnographic act of "being there" as much as it questions the view of "the global" as a single modernist/capitalist social space that can be captured only by a pure act of political economic theoreticism. By my reading it is necessary to question all abstractions that tend to ignore the historically specific conditions of cultural production as these become localized, interrelated, and mutually constitutive in particular places at particular times.

Transnational Networks and the Localization of Power/Knowledge

From the social constructionist perspective from which I speak, understanding the building blocks of social relations should not simply shift our attention from macropolitics to a micropolitics discernible by ethnographic transference, and then valorize the latter, as if the two were distinct and irreducible binary opposites. Nor are social relations of power and meaning deducible from purely macro-structural logics or mechanisms. Rather, we need to shift our attention to modes of inquiry capable of understanding and describing the material and discursive social practices whereby networks of power and meaning constructed at every point from the most "local" to the most "global" are formed, related to each other, and transformed. Since human agency operates at multiple spatial scales, and is not restricted to "local" territorial or sociocultural formations, the very concept of the "urban" thus requires reconceptualization as a social space that is a pregnant meeting ground for the interplay of diverse localizing practices of regional, national, transnational, and even global scale actors, as these wider networks of meaning, power, and social practice come into contact with more purely locally configured networks, practices, meanings, and identities.

This way of envisioning the process of localization thus locates "globalization" in the realm of social practice and situates the global–local interplay in historically specific milieus. It extends the meaning of the global–local nexus to encompass not just the social actions of "global capitalists" interacting with "local communities" but of the far more complex interplay of cultural, economic, political, and religious networks that operate at local, translocal, and transnational social scales but which intersect in particular places at particular times. Closer study of this interplay will, in my view, enable urban researchers to explain the formation of new "subject positions" (Laclau and Mouffe 1985) and give due attention to the multiple patterns of accommodation and resistance to dominant power relations and discursive spaces, particularly the patterns of dominance entailed in the current discourse on "globalization" itself.

My view of "culture" as a fluid and dynamic set of understandings produced by discursive and material practices is not restricted to the understandings developed in closed and self-contained local communities. The circuits of communication and everyday practice in which people are implicated are resources as well as limits. People's everyday lives are sites of criss-crossing communication circuits, many of which transcend the boundaries of local social and political life. They constitute sometimes separate, sometimes overlapping, and sometimes competing terrains for the contestation as well as the reproduction of cultural meanings, for resistance as well as accommodation to dominant modes of power and ideology. My emphasis upon the social construction of social relations through acts of accommodation and resistance to prevalent modes of domination has significant implications for urban research. We need a new way of conceptualizing the locality as the place where localized struggles and alternative discourses on the meanings of "global conditions" are played out. This effort brings to the forefront of urban research the fact that "globalization" is a historical construct, not an inevitable economic force operating behind people's backs independently of their actual material and discursive practices. It requires examining at close range but in rich contextual detail the specific historical and contemporary conditions by which "global conditions" are made meaningful in particular places at particular times. Cities thus may be usefully conceptualized as local sites of cultural appropriation, accommodation, and resistance to "global conditions" as experienced, interpreted, and understood in the everyday lives of ordinary people and mediated by the social networks in which they are implicated.

In considerable measure, as a result of the growing transnational interconnectivity among localities, the "local" itself has become transnationalized as transnational modes of communication, streams of migration, and forms of economic and social intercourse continuously displace and relocate the spaces of cultural production. The rapid sociocultural transformation of localities by the accelerated flows of transnational migration has thus significantly modified the social relations of "community" that had grounded traditional ethnographies in more or less convergent social spaces of cultural production and place. These growing disjunctures require us to develop new modes of urban research and refine old methods of social inquiry to better fit the new spaces of cultural production and reproduction in these times of growing transnational interconnectivity.

For these reasons, I argue, the cultural turn in urban studies to the realm of the politics of everyday life requires a move toward a transnationalized mode of ethnographic practice. The goal of this methodological turn is to gain insight into how articulatory practices are actively inserted in the particular locales of everyday life and how these articulations, in turn, empower or disempower their audiences (Grossberg 1988: 169). The social imaginary necessary to discern the significance of urban social relations under conditions of contemporary transnationalism requires a kind of historically contextualized, multi-sited ethnography that can make coherent sense of our times and give concrete meaning to the notion of "global interdependence."

Reimagining the Politics of Everyday Life

Urban researchers interested in the social production of the practices of everyday life have often conflated the local level of analysis with the politics of everyday life. In so doing, they follow in the footsteps of the leading French urban theorists of "everyday life" such as Henri Lefebvre (1971, 1991) and Michel de Certeau (1984), particularly the latter. In so doing they also provide yet another instantiation of theoretical process of legitimating local spaces of resistance to modernity in its various forms – capitalism, statism, and technological development. For Lefebvre and de Certeau, for example, ordinary people in their everyday life activities appropriate and use urban space in ways that challenge the abstract urban spaces constituted by capital and the state. Lefebvre (1971, 1991) uses this motif in situationist fashion to legitimate a transformational politics of direct action to secure for all urban residents a "right to the city." De Certeau's (1984) imaginary uses the rhetoric of everyday life to paint a picture of the evasive child-like spatial practices by which people escape the synoptic gaze of urban planners and "inhabit the street" in ways that slip through the disciplinary boundaries of the urban spatial plans enacted by central planners. Despite their differences, these urban theorists of the everyday share with Castells the tendency to equate "the local" with an oppositional space of individual and collective resistance to more global structures of domination.

In *The Practice of Everyday Life* (1984) de Certeau identifies some of the myriad ways that social space is produced and maintained by discursive and material practices. In his view the very meaning of "the city" is intimately tied to the politics of representation. Discursive practices, accessible to ethnographic observation, construct alternative images and boundaries of urban space by weaving alternative tapestries out of any city's "isolatable and interconnected properties" (de Certeau 1984: 94). However, one of the foremost critical problems facing ethnographic accounts of "local" everyday life under today's circumstances of growing translocal interconnectivity is that "everyday life" is not a fixed object of investigation, a readily discernible set of practices that can be easily located and subjected to empirical observation and cognitive mapping. In my view, at the current transnational moment "the politics of everyday life" needs to be opened up more widely as a social and political imaginary. The "everyday" needs to be freed from its association with purely local phenomena. In transnational cities people's everyday urban experiences are affected by a wide variety of phenomena, practices, and criss-crossing networks which defy easy boundary setting. Multiple levels of analysis and social practice now inform the urban politics of everyday life throughout the world.

In his discussion of what he terms the "transversal" politics of everyday life David Campbell (1996) has clearly expressed this multiplicity:

> Likewise, neither is "everyday life" a synonym for the local level, for in it global interconnections, local resistances, transterritorial flows, state politics, regional dilemmas, identity formations and so on are always already present. Everyday life is thus a transversal site of contestations rather than a fixed level of analysis. It is transversal . . . because the conflicts manifested there not only transverse all boundaries: they are about these boundaries, their erasure or inscription, and the identity formations to which they give rise.

Consider the following example of emergent transnational urban practices and identities. Sociologists Martin Albrow, John Eade, Jörg Dürrschmidt, and Neil Washbourne (1997: 20–36) have written insightfully on the social construction of the boundaries of imagined community in British Muslim neighborhoods in cities throughout the United Kingdom. Rather than viewing religious fundamentalism as a local expression of belonging and identity framed against economic globalization, as in the work of Barber (1995) and

Castells (1997), these scholars connect the rhetorics of belonging found in various local British Muslim enclaves to a wider social construction of Islamic community (*umma*) transmitted by transnational religious and cultural networks. Everyday life in the Muslim neighborhoods is infused with knowledge and meanings produced in these transnational networks and encountered in the local neighborhoods on a daily basis. The social construction of belonging to a transnational Islamic community is produced and transmitted through a transnational network of social and technological linkages including religious ceremonies, telephone conversations, television and radio programs, newspaper accounts, videos, and music. As these scholars conclude, in everyday visits to relatives and friends, in interactions at work, and in other neighborhood forms of community involvement, local Muslims employ this transnational network, which is physically absent but hardly spiritually distant, to socially construct their "locality." In this construction Islam is viewed not as a purely local or "tribal" reaction to the globalization of capitalism but as a transnational cultural formation, as much involved in the transnationalization of information, cultural exchange, and network formation as are the networks of financial transactions that comprise what we now regard as the globalization of capital.

In short, everyday life is neither a fixed spatial scale nor a guaranteed site of local resistance to more global modes of domination, whether capitalist or otherwise. Rather, in today's transnational times our everyday lifeworld is one in which "competing discourses and interpretations of reality are already folded into the reality we are seeking to grasp" (Campbell 1996: 23). Grasping this sort of reality now requires us to develop a transnational imaginary and to fashion perceptual tools capable of making sense of the new identities emerging from this politics of representation and boundary setting.

In the late 1980s, in the context of the locality studies debate in British urban geography, Andrew Sayer (1989: 253–76) wrote an important, and to my mind underconsidered essay, "The 'New' Regional Geography and Problems of Narrative," which helps move this search for a new urban research imaginary forward. There Sayer advanced the argument that social structures are context dependent and are thus produced and reproduced within specific historical and geographical (time-space) contexts. Sayer made a strong case for a narrative approach to urban studies that situates agency, that is, the social actor, in historically particular time-space settings, particularly the setting of the locality, and recognizes these settings "as constitutive rather than as passive" (1989: 255). Contextualizing his own move, Sayer explained that the so-called "empirical turn" from structural Marxist social theory in urban studies was driven by the widening gap between class-based theories of consciousness and the resurgence of neoconservative and neoliberal thinking among ordinary citizens and workers in the 1980s. It was fueled as well by growing sociospatial unevenness in conditions of everyday urban life.

Sayer praised the turn to locality studies for seeking to grasp the everyday life experiences of ordinary people in terms of concrete social practices rather than in abstract terms. To his credit, Sayer was one of the first urban theorists to call for a close articulation of the then dominant political economy approach to urban studies with emergent debates in sociology and anthropology on postmodern ethnography. He advocated a methodological marriage of political economy and ethnography, because, in his view, ethnography was capable of shedding light on "preexisting cognitive and cultural materials" (1989: 256) not available through political economic analysis. This move produced a convergence of one stream of radical urban geography with an emerging trend among qualitative researchers toward a contextualized ethnographic practice premised on a desired unification of ethnography and political economy (for a coherent defense of this approach in anthropology see Marcus and Fischer 1986; for an excellent recent example of one such successful marriage see Gregory 1998).

In my view, however, this marriage of methodological approaches is desirable for reasons other than those suggested by Sayer. As I have tried to show above, it is simplistic to assume that ethnography is a sure-footed, transparent empirical tool for mapping "preexisting cognitive and cultural materials" onto an otherwise abstract political economic terrain. Cultural materials, like political economic arrangements, are constantly being produced, reproduced, or transformed by human practice rather than standing outside the realm of practical life as pre-given generators of meaning and social action. Accordingly, it is necessary to historicize both political economy and ethnography. Once this is accomplished the two approaches to urban studies can be used in tandem to enrich our sociological imaginations by helping us to make sense of highly fluid social processes affecting particular places at particular times. This combination of historicized methods of social inquiry forces to our attention contingent questions of agency and meaning-making. It can help us to sort out the trajectories of the criss-crossing networks of spatially dispersed social relations of co-presence through which social action in a transnational context is now filtered and informed.

Transnationalism and the Politics of Place-making

In an effort to unbind the conceptualization of "place" from the conflation of locality and community, critical urban geographer Doreen Massey has advanced an imaginative response to the question of the interplay of the global and the local. Massey's view of place is decisively fluid. On the one hand, her critique of David Harvey's conception of "time-space compression" warns against the tendency to view the implosion of time and space that Harvey terms the condition of postmodernity as equally accessible to all.

In her view different individuals and social groups are differently positioned *vis-à-vis* the flows and interconnections that constitute the "globalization" of capital and culture (Massey 1993: 61). On the other hand, these flows and interconnections intersect in particular places at particular times, giving each place its own unique dynamism and making it possible for us to envision a "global" or "progressive" sense of place.

Theoretically, Massey depicts localities as acquiring their particularity not from some long internalized history or sedimented character but from the specific interactions and articulations of contemporary "social relations, social processes, experiences, and understandings" that come together in situations of co-presence, "but where a large portion of those relations . . . are constructed on a far larger scale than what we happen to define for that moment as the place itself" (1993: 66) When understood as articulated moments among criss-crossing networks of social relations and understandings (1993: 67), places do not possess singular but multiple and contested identities. Placemaking is shaped by conflict, difference, and social negotiation among differently situated, and at times antagonistically related, social actors, some of whose networks are locally bound, others whose social relations and understandings span entire regions and transcend national boundaries. Massey, in short, provides key theoretical ingredients for conceptualizing the transnational interconnectivity I seek to locate in this chapter. Massey's approach would trace the trajectories of both residents' and nonresidents' routes through a place as well as identifying "their favourite haunts within it, the connections they make (physically, or by phone or post, or in memory and imagination) between here and the rest of the world" (1993: 65). This is a good way to grasp the fluidity, diversity, and multiplicity of any place and the ways in which social relations affecting that place are stretched out over space and memory (i.e., time). It is also a good way to avoid an essentialist construction of localities as closed communities, as ontological "insides," constructed against a societal or global "outside" by tracing connections between the locality and what Arjun Appadurai (1991) has called the "global ethnoscape."

Gupta and Ferguson (1997a, 1997b) have offered another clear-headed critique of the scholarly conflation of place and culture that is germane to my effort to contextualize emergent transnational social relations and to situate them in the field of urban studies. Gupta and Ferguson point out that representations of localities as cohesive community formations fail to recognize and deal with a variety of boundary-penetrating social actors and processes now very much a part of the transnational world in which we live. Left out of such localized communitarian narratives are the border dwellers who live along border zones separating localities, regions, and nation-states. These social actors engage with actors and networks based on the other side of juridical borders in processes of intercultural borrowing and lending which anthropologists now call "transculturation" (for useful studies of this process see Herzog 1990; Martinez 1994). The "locality as community" problematic is equally inattentive to the sociocultural and political implications of the growing number of border crossers – i.e., migrants, exiles, refugees, and diasporas – who now orchestrate their lives by creating situations of co-presence that link social networks across vast geographical distances across the globe. Such border-penetrating processes go a long way toward helping explain, though they by no means exhaust, the difference-generating relations of power that constitute cultural and political identity and difference within localities defined as both political jurisdictions and as sociocultural spaces.

Gupta and Ferguson have identified three dimensions of cultural production that are complicating efforts to view localities in communitarian terms and thus to ground ethnographic practice and urban research locally in a transnational world. The first of these is the growing interdependence (economic, sociocultural, and informational) across linked spaces that belies notions of discrete, autonomous local cultures. Second, the emergence of wider discourses and practices of postcolonial politics (abetted, in my view, by the globalization of mass media) is producing a variety of hybrid cultures, even in geographically remote localities and nations, that problematize the very notion of "authentic cultural traditions" even as social analysts seek to inscribe and preserve them. Finally, the boundary-penetrating processes now characterizing our transnational world have facilitated the social construction of "communities in the making" as imagined spaces, often occupying the same geographical locale. These imaginings of communal identity necessarily entail processes of inclusion and exclusion, i.e., processes which create "otherness." For example, the social construction of the constitutive outside, or "other," is very much part of the ethnic and racial relations that have erupted antagonistically in the past decade in transnational cities throughout the world (see, for example, Smith and Tarallo 1995).

The culturally and politically constructed character of such racial antagonisms and their relation to power and place has been well captured by Gupta and Ferguson (1997b: 17). Identity and alterity, they explain, are produced:

> simultaneously as the formation of "locality" and "community." "Community" . . . is premised on various forms of exclusion and construction of otherness. . . . With respect to locality as well, at issue is not simply that one is located in a certain place, but that the particular place is set apart from and opposed to other places. The "global" relations that we have argued are constitutive of localities are therefore centrally involved in the production of "local" identities too.

Viewing locality (like ethnicity and nationality) as complex, contingent, and contested outcomes of political and historical processes rather than as timeless essences also challenges the theoretical framing of "locality" as an inexorable space of resistance to globalization. Instead of opposing autonomous local cultures, be they tribes, militias, urban formations, or regions (*à la* Castells or Benjamin Barber 1995), to the economic domination of global capital, the homogenizing movement of cultural globalization, or the hegemonizing seductions of global consumerism, Gupta and Ferguson recommend paying close attention to the ways in which dominant global cultural forms may be appropriated and used or even significantly transformed "in the midst of the field of power relations that links localities to a wider world" (1997b: 5).

Germane to this larger question, are several more particular ones:

- How are perceptions of locality and community discursively constructed in different time-space configurations?
- How are the understandings springing from these perceptions internalized and lived?
- What role in producing politically salient differences within localities is played by the cultural, political, and economic connections localities have with worlds "outside" their borders that configure their interdependence?
- What roles do the global and local mass media play in framing the understandings and practices within socially constructed communities and their constitutive fields of otherness? (On the latter two questions see Smith and Feagin 1995; Thompson 1995; Cvetkovic and Kellner 1997; Gupta and Ferguson 1997b; Kellner 1997.)

Having raised these questions I would further suggest that we leave open to sociological and historical investigation the character of the contextualizing sociospatial interdependence in which particular localities are enmeshed at particular times. Specifically, I agree with Gupta and Ferguson that it is possible for local interventions to "significantly transform" dominant cultural forms. I would therefore leave open the question of whether or not the crisscrossing relations of power that come together on the ground in localities must necessarily be understood hierarchically. When Gupta and Ferguson turn from the question of the patterning of power relations across space to the issue of the social construction of space as place, they acknowledge the contingency of power relations. The open-ended questions they raise in response to this issue are, in my view, as germane to questions of the spatial distribution of power as they are to issues of identity and place-making. These questions are: "With meaning-making understood as a practice, how are spatial meanings established? Who has the power to make places of spaces? Who contests this? What is at stake?" (Gupta and Ferguson 1997a: 40).

It is precisely questions such as these that can move urban researchers interested in the social construction of locality beyond essentialist assumptions about the equivalence of locality and culture. For example, research on the politics of urban heritage has produced a spate of studies on "the making of place" by a wide variety of political actors, including local neighborhood groups, government officials, and business interests as well as wider networks of social practice such as architectural activists, historic preservationists, and global developers. In particular places these actors collude and collide in contests over the cultural meanings of place (see, for example, Watson 1991; Bird 1993). Sociologically, historically, and ethnographically grounded case studies bring into focus the issue of the politics of representation, thereby modifying a discourse on globalization and community that has been dominated by agency-less narratives of urban and regional change that tend to exclude noncapitalist actors and their representations of space and place from consideration.

In an insightful essay, "Mapping Meanings: A Cultural Critique of Locality Studies," Peter Jackson (1991: 215–28) considers the complex politics of place-making found in a series of detailed case studies of historic preservation. Jackson's study (1991: 225) nicely illustrates how the turn to the analysis of culture by leading urban political economists like Harvey and Zukin (1991) has been partial, naively modernist, and even essentialist. It is a projection of "authenticity" onto a putatively disappearing historical past for the purpose of denouncing the role of capitalism in the historical present. Jackson suggests that the "heritage debate" is better understood as raising questions about the politics of representation rather than posing a stark choice between "genuine preservation" and "misappropriation" of an actually existing "authentic" urban past. "Rather than simply showing how capital 'uses' culture in an instrumental way," he concludes, abundant case study evidence demonstrates that:

> such a crude argument has to be modified in light of the contingencies of each particular situation. Which groups were involved and how were their interests articulated? How did the changing legislative and fiscal environment make certain forms of investment more attractive than others? What coalitions between different interest groups were sought and achieved, and with what effects? Clearly, one cannot divorce the "cultural" aspects of reinvestment or preservation from the apparently "political" and "economic" dimensions . . . but neither can the political economy of urban and regional change be understood without a more fully developed understanding of its cultural politics. (Jackson 1991: 225)

In short, economic processes like investment, disinvestment, and reinvestment in "place" are unavoidably culturally coded. Likewise the cultural processes of representation take place in and change their material contexts, including the built environment of cities. We, as analysts, are thus unavoidably involved in interpretive reconstructions of who produces and who consumes particular images of place and space, and with what effects. The study of these processes from the vantage point of the politics of representation enables urban researchers to move beyond a reified and unitary view of "actors" like "capital" to a historicized analysis of precisely "whose past is being perceived, how it is being represented, and whose interests are being served by such unavoidably selective readings"(Jackson 1991: 220; see also Jackson 1992). In sum, any local community's historical past is a historically contested rather than a timelessly embedded social phenomenon.

Moreover, the contested politics of representation applies not only to any locality's historical past but to the shaping of its present and the formation of its alternative future(s). This brings to the forefront the vexing question of just what makes a place a place like no other place. Phrased differently, what about a place persists and what changes over time? And this is precisely what power struggles over "place-making" are all about, namely, who changes what in alternative representations of any place's present and future, and how do these changes selectively appropriate or reject particular elements of any place's historical past?

Bringing the Social Back In

In this chapter I have sought to move urban studies beyond naturalistic constructions of "locality" which view the local as an inherently defensive community formation. I have tried to show that even the most material elements of any locality are subject to diverse readings and given different symbolic significance by differently situated social groups and their corresponding discursive networks. The result is a highly politicized social space where representations of place are constructed and contested. I have argued that the prevailing structuralist schemata used to conceptualize the global–local connection by leading urban theorists such as Harvey and Castells has tended to reify the terms in this dialectic. In so doing they have reproduced a totalizing binary framework in which the global is equated with the abstract, universal, and dynamic (i.e., "capital"), while the local is invested with concreteness, particularity, and threatened stability (i.e., "community"). Such a discourse of capital versus community treats the global *a priori* as an oppressive social force while constructing localities in more positive, albeit more static if not anemic, terms (see Cvetkovic and Kellner 1997).

Ironically, key conceptualizations informing ethnographic practice in postmodern cultural studies and even the conceptualization of "everyday resistance" informing the politics of everyday life problematic in urban studies also rely upon binary dichotomizations of global power versus local culture which overlook the ways in which transnational social networks and practices are constituted by their interrelations with, and thus their groundedness inside, the local. The theoretical frames of reference critiqued in this chapter tend to ignore the considerable interplay of spatial scales and discursive practices to be found in any locality. They elide or underestimate the intricacy involved in sorting out the social interactions and processes at multiple spatial scales that constitute the complex politics of place-making under contemporary conditions of transnational interconnectivity.

To overcome the conceptual confinement of the global–local dichotomy and restimulate the sociological imagination, I recommend the further refinement of a multi-sited, translocal mode of transnational ethnographic practice, inflected with the domination–accommodation–resistance motif, and combined with a historicized approach to political economic and social relations. This recombinant method of social inquiry can be used to make sense of the power relations and meaning-making practices I have elsewhere termed "transnational urbanism" (Smith 2001). The social spaces through which social actors move and within which they operate to give meaning to "place" are crucial and increasingly translocal and multi-scaled, thus making translocal ethnography and carefully historicized political economic and social research both necessary and possible. A fusion of these heretofore distinct, if not opposed, approaches to urban studies is a good way to bring "the social" back into urban theory and research, where it belongs.

Bibliography

Albrow, M., Eade, J., Dürrschmidt, J., and Washbourne, N. 1997: The impact of globalization on sociological concepts: community, culture and milieu. In J. Eade (ed.), *Living the Global City: Globalization as Local Process*. New York and London: Routledge, 20–36.

Appadurai, A. 1991: Global ethnoscapes: notes and queries for a transnational anthropology. In R. G. Fox (ed.), *Recapturing Anthropology: Working in the Present*. Santa Fe: School of American Research Press, 191–210.

Barber, B. R. 1995: *Jihad vs. McWorld*. New York: Times Books.

Bird, J. 1993: Dystopia on the Thames. In J. Bird et al. (eds.), *Mapping the Futures: Local Cultures, Global Change*. London and New York: Routledge, 120–35.

Campbell, D. 1996: Political processes, transversal politics, and the anarchical world. In M. J. Shapiro and R. Alker Hayward (eds.), *Challenging Boundaries*. Minneapolis: University of Minnesota Press, 7–31.

Castells, M. 1984: Space and society: managing the new historical relationships. In M. P. Smith (ed.), *Cities in Transformation*. Beverly Hills and London: Sage, 235–60.

—— 1997: *The Power of Identity*. Oxford: Blackwell.

Cvetkovic, A. and Kellner, D. (eds.) 1997: *Articulating the Global and the Local: Globalization and Cultural Studies*. Boulder, CO and Oxford: Westview Press.

De Certeau, M. 1984: *The Practice of Everyday Life*. Berkeley: University of California Press.

Dirlik, A. 1990: Culturalism as hegemonic ideology and liberating practice. In A. JanMohamed and D. Lloyd (eds.), *The Nature and Context of Minority Discourse*. New York and Oxford: Oxford University Press, 394–431.

Foucault, M. 1977: *Power/Knowledge*. Ed. C. Gordon. New York: Pantheon Books.

Gregory, S. 1998: *Black Corona: Race and the Politics of Place in an Urban Community*. Princeton, NJ: Princeton University Press.

Grossberg, L. 1988: Putting the pop back in postmodernism. In A. Ross (ed.), *Universal Abandon? The Politics of Postmodernism*. Minneapolis: University of Minnesota Press, 166–90.

Gupta, A. and Ferguson, J. 1997a: Beyond "culture": space, identity, and the politics of difference. In A. Gupta and J. Ferguson (eds.), *Culture, Power and Place*. Durham, NC and London: Duke University Press, 33–51.

—— 1997b: Culture, power, and place: ethnography at the end of an era. In A. Gupta and J. Ferguson (eds.), *Culture, Power and Place*. Durham, NC and London: Duke University Press, 3–29.

Harvey, D. 1989: *The Condition of Postmodernity*. Oxford: Blackwell.

Herzog, L. A. 1990: *Where North Meets South: Cities, Space, and Politics on the U.S.–Mexico Border*. Austin: Center for Mexican American Studies, University of Texas.

Jackson, P. 1991: Mapping meanings: a cultural critique of locality studies. *Environment and Planning A* 23: 215–28.

—— 1992: *Maps of Meaning*. London and New York: Routledge.

Kearney, M. 1995: The effects of transnational culture, economy, and migration on Mixtec identity in Oaxacalifornia. In M. P. Smith and J. R. Feagin (eds.), *The Bubbling Cauldron: Race, Ethnicity, and the Urban Crisis*. Minneapolis: University of Minnesota Press, 226–43.

Kellner, D. 1997: *Media Culture*. London and New York: Routledge.

Laclau, E. and Mouffe, C. 1985: *Hegemony and Socialist Strategy*. London and New York: Verso.

Lefebvre, H. 1971: *Everyday Life in the Modern World*. New York: Harper and Row.

—— 1991: *The Production of Space*. Oxford: Blackwell.

Marcus, G. E. and Fischer, M. M. J. 1986: *Anthropology as Cultural Critique: An Experimental Moment in the Human Sciences*. Chicago and London: University of Chicago Press.

Martinez, O. J. 1994: *Border People: Life and Society in the U.S. Mexico Borderlands*. Tucson and London: University of Arizona Press.

Massey, D. 1993: Power-geometry and a progressive sense of place. In J. Bird et al. (eds.), *Mapping the Futures: Local Cultures, Global Change*. New York and London: Routledge, 59–69.

Rouse, R. 1991: Mexican migration and the social space of postmodernism. *Diaspora* 1 (1): 8–23.

Sayer, A. 1989: The "new" regional geography and problems of narrative. *Society and Space* 7: 253–76.

Schein, L. 1998: Forged transnationality and oppositional cosmopolitanism. In M. P. Smith and L. E. Guarnizo (eds.), *Transnationalism from Below*. New Brunswick, NJ: Transaction, 291–313.

Smith, M. P. 2001: *Transnational Urbanism: Locating Globalization*. Oxford and Malden, MA: Blackwell.

—— and Feagin, J. R. 1995: Putting race in its place. In M. P. Smith and J. R. Feagin (eds.), *The Bubbling Cauldron: Race, Ethnicity, and the Urban Crisis*. Minneapolis: University of Minnesota Press, 3–27.

—— and Guarnizo, L. E. (eds.) 1998: *Transnationalism from Below*. New Brunswick, NJ: Transaction.

—— and Tarallo, B. 1995: Who are the "good guys"? The social construction of the Vietnamese "other." In M. P. Smith and J. R. Feagin (eds.), *The Bubbling Cauldron: Race, Ethnicity, and the Urban Crisis*. Minneapolis: University of Minnesota Press, 50–76.

Spivak, G. 1988: Can the subaltern speak? In C. Nelson and L. Grossberg (eds.), *Marxism and the Interpretation of Culture*. Urbana and Chicago: University of Illinois Press, 271–313.

Thompson, J. B. 1995: *The Media and Modernity: A Social Theory of the Media*. Stanford, CA: Stanford University Press.

Tyler, S. A. 1986: Postmodern ethnography: from document of the occult to occult document. In J. Clifford and G. Marcus (eds.), *Writing Culture: The Politics and Poetics of Ethnography*. Berkeley and Los Angeles: University of California Press, 122–40.

—— 1987: *The Unspeakable*. Madison: University of Wisconsin Press.

Watson, S. 1991: Gilding the smokestacks: the new symbolic representations of deindustrialized regions. *Environment and Planning D: Society and Space* 9: 59–70.

Zukin, S. 1991: *Landscapes of Power*. Berkeley and Los Angeles: University of California Press.

7

Depoliticizing Globalization: From Neo-Marxism to the Network Society of Manuel Castells[1]

Peter Marcuse

The Evolution of Urban Studies

A new wind began to blow through urban studies in the late 1960s,[2] a critical wind, discontent with existing conditions in cities, attempting to chart new directions in their analysis and envisioning some radically different alternatives which it hoped directly to influence. It came from a number of directions, attached to several names: Manuel Castells and a French group of researchers, quickly picked up in England by Chris Pickvance and others under the name of the new urban sociology; in geography, provoked by David Harvey and *Social Justice and the City* (1973); in philosophy, with the concern for space and its "production," about which Henri Lefebvre wrote. It built on a heritage of Marxism, but with a strong neo-Marxist, sometimes even neo-Weberian, slant. It gave prominence to classes, to conflicts over urban issues ("collective consumption"), to economics but in the form of political economics, to the role of the state as a vehicle for both power and administration.[3] "Urban" was often simply defined as the locus of specific types of conflicts, centering around issues of collective consumption (Castells [1972] 1977).[4]

These developments were directly related to what was actually going on in countries around the world in the period. Perhaps the two critical events were the Paris uprisings of May 1968, with their parallels in many other countries, and the civil rights movement in the United States. In both cases urban discontent played a major role, both as immediate cause and long-term symptom of a deeper distress. The hopes of the immediate post-World War II period, in which the defeat of fascism was anticipated to usher in a period of universal democracy, freedom, and prosperity, seemed, despite the veneer of growth, to be disappointed, the democracy shallow and limited, the prosperity excluding many, the freedom not producing the just society that ought to be its product. There had been extensive protests around urban issues in the immediate postwar period, dealing with displacement through urban renewal, with inadequate housing, with suburban sprawl, and generally with persisting poverty and inequality. A minority of writers and researchers in urban studies had called attention to these issues,[5] while the field as a whole continued with the equanimity and supposed objectivity of the past. But in the late 1960s protests jelled in the form of what has become known as the "new social movements," and these formed the impetus for the new turn in urban social science.

Politics was deeply involved both in the movements in the cities and in their reflection in urban studies. The mass protests in Europe saw themselves as radical, indeed revolutionary; in Germany, Red Rudi Dutschke spoke of the "long march through the institutions" of bourgeois democracy, the French street protests and strikes were almost anarchist in their orientation, the civil rights movement in the United States questioned whether what they wanted was admission to the existing society or a quite new society, and the anti-Vietnam war movement had explicit political targets. Politics, in both the immediate and more abstract sense, was central in the new intellectual movements also. The leaders of the French group were either members of the Communist Party in France or close to it; in the United States, the links between urban criticism and the New Left were visible everywhere, with neo-Marxist analysis the analytic foundation of the urban-oriented New Left. They differed from older orthodox Marxisms in seeing social movements taking the place of the working class as the leaders of basic social transformation,[6] but they agreed with much of the Marxist analysis and saw conflict as an inherent component of progress, and were eager to join in it. The new turn in urban studies was explicitly political.

Things have changed. By 1983 Chris Pickvance, one of the English pioneers in studying the new urban movements, was writing: "The study of urban movements has a problem: urban movements have ceased to exist."[7] Indeed, despite the controversy that surrounds the fate of urban movements, much was indeed quite different from what had been anticipated even fifteen years earlier. Margaret Thatcher's Conservative government took office in the UK in 1979, Ronald Reagan's in the United States the next year; the tide turned against the welfare state, and with it against the progressive urban policies that the new urban movements had advocated and the new urban studies writers had endorsed, expanded, and justified. Resistance of course continued, with movements as disparate as the environmental movement, the women's movement, and identity politics, including ethnic, "racial," and gay/lesbian rights, becoming major factors, but the urban was not central to them.

"Globalization" is the term that has often been used to describe the set of events that produced this turnaround. The term deserves more careful definition than it is usually accorded. For our purposes, the following definition is used:

Globalization is a combination of
1 *advances in technology, particularly in communications and transportation, with*
2 *increased international mobility of persons and capital and exchange of goods,*
3 *centralization of control and increase of power by dominant business groups vis-à-vis labor and the forces of resistance, using this technology and mobility, resulting in a*
4 *commodification of goods, services, and cultural production and practices on a global scale to maximize financial return.*

Globalization is a dominant phenomenon of the years after the early 1970s. It is not a brand new phenomenon but a further development of trends and forces at work for centuries, yet it is a development so remarkably rapid in its pace and in its geographic spread as to deserve attention as a separate phenomenon. It represents a significant shift in power, not only of capital *vis-à-vis* labor but also of the political forces allied with capital against those that formed the basis for the social movements which had inspired so many with so much hope in the 1960s.

With the actuality of globalization came its ideological justification, in an increasingly dominant paradigm of urban analysis that accepted globalization not only as reality but as the only reality, and a desirable one. Its policy orientation, as far as urban issues were concerned, was in the direction of facilitating and rationalizing the competition among cities to produce greater and more sensible growth in the whole city system as each looked to its own comparative advantage and settled into its accepted place in the inevitable hierarchical order of cities. Social problems resulting from the apotheosis of the market were acknowledged but were considered short term and unavoidable, perhaps to be dealt with by some sort of safety net. Thus the leaders of the forces and institutions of globalization, meeting in Davos, Switzerland at the "World Economic Forum" in January 2001, quite peacefully accepted the existence of a counter-"World Social Forum" at Porto Alegre, Brazil with the welcome: "you deal with the social problems, we'll deal with the economic problems."[8] And thus book titles such as "globalization and its discontents" can imply that globalization is a dominant process from which some unfortunately did not benefit, rather than a contested process in which winners' gains were directly connected to losers' suffering.[9] "Globalization and its victors and vanquished" would give a quite different impression.

So what has been the impact of these developments on the newly developed urban analysis? It is now some two score years since the new wind in urban studies began to blow. What has happened to its strength under the impact of globalization, and in what direction is it going today? In general, three different currents, often intermingling, can be discerned. One turns pragmatic, sees the revolutionary visions of the earlier period as presently irrelevant, and focuses with integrity on current reform: publicly supported housing, environmental protection, social inclusiveness, amelioration of inequality, through achievable redistribution and anti-discrimination. A second continues the critical approach, sometimes retaining its comprehensive societal edge, in other cases focusing on narrow spheres of urban activity. It continues to apply the earlier critique, sometimes with, sometimes without, specific reference to its relationship to earlier neo-Marxist work. The newest element here, and perhaps intellectually the most pathbreaking, goes in the direction of cultural studies and cultural criticism, examining in particular the meaning and impact of commodification in its spread through everyday life and culture. (Fredric Jameson and Nancy Fraser are among many in this tradition.) There is often a disconnection in this current between analysis and day-to-day political reality, not from any desire to withdraw from direct engagement but because the link between theory and practice has become attenuated and is barely visible in the overwhelming presence of the dominant powers.

The third current has meshed much more closely with immediate events on the ground (and in the air and the ether – more on this later) in cities around the world today. It is a ghostly Marxism, one in which echoes of Marxist analysis can be still be vaguely discerned but retreating from any radical political content, both in its analysis and its prescription, backing off from the earlier urban social and political critique and instead moving forward enthusiastically into the description of a hi-tech society it sees as the overwhelming event of the present period, conflated with a loosely defined discussion of globalization. It ends up, I shall argue, as not simply a depoliticized but an anti-political analysis of urban conditions, and thus contributes to an effectively conservative posture on those larger issues the new urban movements of the 1960s had so aggressively tackled. It is implicitly conservative even though on individual issues it retains the flavor of progressive criticism. It thus ends up supporting the superficial social democratic "third way" rhetoric now dominant in governing circles in the UK, Germany, and other countries.

The Information Age and the Network Society in Manuel Castells's Trilogy

I shall use the evolution of Manuel Castells's published work as a central representative of this current, centering around an examination of his three-volume *magnum opus, The Information Age: The Rise of the Network Society* (1996), *The Power of Identity* (1997a), and *The End of Millennium* (1998). Anthony

Giddens is today perhaps the best-known representative of the ideological position that results from it.[10]

Any critical evaluation of Manuel Castells's work must begin with a straightforward acknowledgment: Castells's contribution to urban sociology and to the examination of the processes of globalization is absolutely central for our period. He has initiated and/or contributed to every major theme in the current discussions in these fields; all future discussions must take into account his seminal work. Since what follows is deeply critical of the direction in which it now seems to me to be going, I want to start with an acknowledgment of the extent of his contribution and his direct influence on my own thinking in these areas, both of which have been great. It should also be clear that, for better or for worse (and sometimes both!), Castells's evolution from Marxism to his present form of analysis and worldview is not unconscious or lacking in self-reflection; he himself has addressed this directly on many occasions. Castells has clearly abjured his more radical past analysis as inappropriate to the changing configuration of events since the 1960s.[11] The question posed here is whether, in this process of open learning and adjustment of perspective that Castells has undertaken, an implicit process of depoliticization has occurred, so that the conclusions to be drawn from his present stance constitute a retreat from those that might be drawn from a hard analysis of the actual changing developments he is studying.

In rejecting his earlier neo-Marxist and structural analysis of urban issues Castells seeks a more nuanced, less economistic, explanation for events, one which takes technological change and cultural/social movements more into account. Yet his earlier structural approach survives, and sometimes is among those solid contributions which his new three volumes make. For instance, the distinction between "mode of production" and "mode of development" which he makes early in volume 1 (1996: 14) is parallel to the classic Marxist distinction between "relations of production" and "forces of production"[12] (although Marx is not cited for the conceptualization). Similarly, the distinction he makes in volume 2 between legitimating, resisting, and project identities (more on this below) contains strong echoes of the earlier discussions initiated by Andre Gorz between reformist and revolutionary projects, although Gorz is never cited.[13]

Castells's evolution is indeed reflected in the evolution of his book titles: selectively, starting with *The Urban Question: A Marxist Approach* ([1972] 1977) and *The Economic Crisis and American Society* (1976) to *City, Class, and Power* (1978), to *The City and the Grassroots: A Cross-cultural Approach* (1983), in which he first abjures his earlier structuralist neo-Marxist analyses, to the edited *High Technology, Space, and Society* (1985), to *The Informational City: Information Technology, Economic Restructuring, and the Urban–Regional Process* (1989), *Technopoles of the World: The Making of Twenty-first-century Industrial Complexes* (1994), to *The Collapse of Soviet Communism: A View from the Information Society* (1995), to the most recent three volumes. The movement from Marxist concepts, issues of class and oppositional political and social movements to a preoccupation with technological developments and their multiple manifestations is quite clear. The earlier political discussions of class and opposition do not drop out but become subordinated to a focus on the ineluctable march of technological progress.

The Rise of the Network Society is the title of the first volume of Castells's trilogy, and it similarly betrays the shift of focus from substantive characteristics of social relationships to a more superficial characterization. Networks reappear throughout Castells's recent work as a defining characteristic of the Information Age. Yet networks are simply forms of organization, and forms that have existed since time immemorial: kinship networks, religious networks, old boy networks, and so on.[14] If it is a form of organization that has increased in recent times, to make it the center of the analysis is substituting form for content, a particular organizational form for a particular distribution of power. Whether the growing use of networks reflects a centralization or a decentralization of power would seem a critical question to examine; the focus on the form rather than its use does not lead in that direction. To the contrary; power appears to be becoming less, rather than more, concentrated: "as the process of globalization progresses, organizational forms evolve from *multi-national enterprises to international networks* . . . the globalization of competition dissolves the large corporation" (1996: 192, 193, italics in the original).

Castells's style makes criticism of his underlying direction difficult, because the rich tapestry he presents has threads that go in almost every direction. For any one particular quote, one can generally find another, apparently contradictory, quote elsewhere. Everything that should be said is said somewhere or other in the three volumes – but so is its opposite. The evidence that is adduced to prove one point often contradicts a point made elsewhere. While reality is itself often contradictory, the "trilogy aims to understand the system,"[15] and the direction the work takes overall is clear.

Castells's work is at the same time a provocative extension of some of the new urban studies/political economic approaches of the 1970s that Castells himself helped stimulate, and an erosion of their critical thrust. It makes prevalent processes (e.g., globalization) actor-less, agent-less, inexorable. It can be used to support the pabulum in Giddens's radio lectures,[16] to current third way "social democracy," to global cities worship. Although it retains a rhetorical obeisance to "social movements," it can support the kind of "competitive city" prescriptions that Borja and others (including sometimes Castells) are promoting around the world, and that Michael Porter sells nationally. It undermines even the attempt to think about utopias, in direct contrast to the utopian thinking that inspired much of his work originally. It empties the concepts of political economy of their critical value, and can serve to feed discussions of globalization suitable for "world leaders" from Davos to Hong Kong to Berlin to Moscow.

That the policy conclusions to be drawn from this recent work are in sharp contrast to those flowing from his earlier approaches does not of itself impugn the validity of the analysis. In fact, on many immediate policy issues Castells's positions remain as critical, as socially sensitive, as concerned with issues of justice and equity, as ever. Yet the implications of his analysis lead in other directions. That does not in itself undermine them, but it does give reason to look at the analysis very closely and see what is happening to it. Given such a look, the analysis, it is here contended, turns out to be inadequate for its subject.

The Depoliticization of Globalization in Castells

It is precisely the shift of focus away from the nature of, and the relationships among, social groups that marks Castells's trajectory. It is a move that suppresses the political, in the broad sense of the dynamic between the exercise of power and the resistance to it, and moves toward a determinism that undermines the relevance of political action. Power and conflicts over power disappear from view;[17] classes, when they appear, have a very subordinate role. Capitalism is conflated with globalization, but in an ambiguous and ahistorical fashion; technology, the media, demographic changes, the state appear as homogeneous, autonomous entities, actors themselves, behind whom actual actors are not to be seen. It is a classic case of reification, making the relations among human beings appear as a relationship among things, the relationships of social and economic position appear as relationships to or against technology, to or against the ascendance of "information." In place of the tensions, the contradictions, the conflicts among human actors and groups as the motor of change, there is a march of technology, of organizational forms, of their own accord, inexorably, globally. Human actors only react to these developments (some benefit from them, but not much attention is paid to them, and they are not seen as more than passive participants in the march). The critique of globalization implicit and often explicit in the books concludes with an appeal to "us" to understand, communicate, become aware, together; any drawing of policy conclusions or indications for action is deliberately rejected. The discussion becomes depoliticized, both in its analysis and in its stance toward prescription: in Castells's words, "the power of flows takes precedence over the flows of power" (Castells 1996: 469).[18]

To be clear: by "depoliticized" I do not mean that Castells, or any other author, has an obligation to draw political conclusions and/or present political prescriptions as part of his or her work, although it may be desirable that more extend their work in these directions than now do. I mean rather that the political content present in the world Castells is analyzing is suppressed, played down, becomes incidental, in contrast to its role in reality. I take the political to be centered on relations of power among social actors; these play at best a secondary role in Castells's analysis, where they appear at all. The criticism is not that Castells fails to introduce a political analysis into the material he examines, but that he does not adequately deal with the content that is in fact in his material; not that he should politicize material that is nonpolitical, but that he has depoliticized material that is itself heavily political.

The problem is symbolized and encapsulated by the very title of Castells's *magnum opus*: *The Information Age*. What is central in the analysis is a technical development (and a somewhat mystified one at that – see further below, on just what "information" means), not a social one. It makes the tools of production, rather than the relations of production, the characteristic of the age: thus the sequence might be: Stone Age, Bronze Age, Iron Age, Steam Age, Information Age,[19] rather than Imperial Age, Feudal Age, Capitalist Age, Imperialist Age, Fordist Age, followed perhaps by various attempts at a further definition: Neo-Imperialist, Post-Fordist. The point is not the accuracy of any of these classification schemes, but what it is that is at the center of them, what is taken as the indicative classificatory criterion. Even in traditional sociology and traditional economics, and certainly in Marx, it is the relations among and characteristics of groups within each society that are its defining characteristics. Not here.

The depoliticization of what would be, underneath it all, a sharp analysis of events can be traced in a number of areas. The language used systematically undermines the substance of the analysis and robs it of a political force it might otherwise have. A few examples highlight the issues here raised.

The eradication of human agency

A key aspect of depoliticization is to make everything that happens anonymous, actor-less. It is not merely the old agency versus structure argument within Marxism, for in those discussions both sides always assume that structure refers to the pattern of relations among actors, among classes, and the issues involve scale, proportion, relative weight, scope of human agency within structure. With Castells, agency vanishes, actors disappear from sight. Both the language and the content of what he writes lead in this direction.

Castells does at times deal with the question of agency: "who are the capitalists?" he asks (1996: 473). He points out that there is no simple answer, that they are a "colorful array" (1996: 473) of characters, and seems to open the door to a deeper discussion of class composition in advanced industrial societies and their global linkages.[20] But then he proceeds: "above a diversity of human-flesh capitalists and capitalist groups there is a faceless collective capitalist, *made up of financial flows operated by electronic networks*" (1996: 474, italics added). Important points do need to be made here as to the autonomy of individual capitalists, the difference between a conspiracy and a class, how power is exercised, and so on. But the discussion does not go in this direction. Instead, the conclusion is the flat statement that "there is not . . . such a thing as a global capitalist class." Rather, "capitalist classes are . . . appendixes to a mighty whirlwind" (1996: 474). "Who are the owners, who the producers, who the managers, and who the servants, becomes increasingly blurred" (1998: 475). Maybe to Castells, but not to the majority of the world's peoples, I would guess. This is depoliticization with a vengeance: not power relations, but a "mighty whirlwind governs our actions. . . . Power . . . is no longer concentrated in institutions (the state), organizations (capitalist firms), or symbolic controllers (corporate media, churches). It is diffused in global networks of wealth, power, information, and images. . . . *The new power lies in the codes of information and in the images of representation around which societies organize their institutions. . . . The sites of this power are people's minds*" (1997a: 359, italics in original).[21] If power should be challenged, then, the entity responsible is the "society" which does the organizing; it does no good to criticize the state, or firms, or the media. The "realpolitik" of domination, to which Castells also refers elsewhere, is not the issue.

The excluded without the excluders

In general there is much detail on those who are excluded, but not on those who exclude them. The process of exclusion is faceless, a world-historical process at the "end of millennium," not one for which any single group or class can be held accountable. In the substantial discussion of the exclusion of "the majority of the African population in the newest international division of labor," Castells concludes "that *structural irrelevance* (from the systems point of view) is a more threatening condition than dependency" (1996: 135);[22] "a considerable number of humans . . . are irrelevant . . . from the perspective of the system's logic" (1998: 364).[23] Irrelevance is from "the systems" point of view, not from the point of view of those who can make no profit from the lives of the excluded. Some are excluded, but no one does the excluding. Actors disappear entirely in the blanket laid down by the language of sweeping phrases: "social forms and processes induced by the current process of historical change" (1996: 376). (And one might raise the question of whether the excluded are really excluded from the system, or whether they are in fact quite useful for it but simply excluded from its benefits . . .)

In the conclusion to the third volume, Castells deals most explicitly with the question of who is responsible to the new informational/global economy.

"The rule is still production for the sake of profit, and for the private appropriation of profit, on the basis of property rights – which is of the essence of capitalism. But . . . [w]ho are the capitalists?" (1998: 362). The discussion then begins with a logical description: a "first level" which "concerns *the holders of property rights*" (1998: 362, italics in the original). The "second level . . . refers to *the managerial class*" (1998: 362, italics in the original). But here the reference to class ends; we get no closer than this to the flesh and blood of real actors. For "the third level . . . [has to do with] the nature of *global financial markets. Global financial markets, and their networks of management, are the actual collective capitalist . . . global financial networks are the nerve center of informational capitalism*" (1998: 362, italics in the original). So, in the end, the capitalists are not a "who" but a market; not those networking, but the network itself.[24]

The passive voice

Castells uses the passive voice constantly, where an active grammar would raise the question of exactly who is responsible, or, if simple agency is not adequate to explain structural patterns, what forces, what relationships of power, what institutions or practices are involved and should be held accountable. The problem occurs from the opening to the closing of the three volumes. In the first chapter, "global networks of instrumental exchanges selectively switch on and off individuals, groups, regions, and even countries, according to their relevance in fulfilling the goals processed in the network, in a relentless flow of strategic decisions . . . **Our societies are increasingly structured around a bipolar opposition between the Net and the Self**" (1996: 3, bold face in the original). "The" Net (capitalized?) and "the" Self (capitalized?). Just what does that mean? Networks among some groups are indeed in opposition to the self-development of other groups; there is "opposition" in the patterns Castells describes, but not conflict. In fact, it is not "global networks of instrumental exchanges" but networks of specific corporations, power blocs, states that "switch on and off" very specific individuals, groups, regions, and countries – and not any random individuals, countries, etc., all characterized by their concern with the "Self," but poor and working people, Third World countries, women.

In the last chapter, the passive voice continues to color the discussion the transformations the three volumes describe. "*Relations of* production have been transformed"(1998: 361, italics in the original; the italicized phrase harks back to Marx). "[L]abor is redefined in its role as produced, and sharply differentiated according to workers' characteristics," and "generic labor is assigned a given task" (1998: 361). "[C]apital is as transformed as labor is in this new economy" (1998: 362), just as Castells elsewhere gives ample evidence of who benefits and who is hurt. But the presentation shifts the focus away from any person's or group's responsibility and on to the tools, the instruments, the "networks of instrumental exchanges" used by some to achieve their results at the cost of others.[25]

The imputation of agency to things

This is, in a sense, the mirror image of the disappearance of real actors from view: processes and relationships become reified, become actors themselves, autonomously, independently of human agency. Real actors disappear, and things become actors.

Technology becomes an independent actor, an autonomous force. We read sentences like: "technology has transformed the political role of the media" (1997a: 319). Not that political actors have taken advantage of technological developments to use media in a new role; the technology itself achieves the transformation.[26] The new "techno-economic paradigm . . . is based primarily on . . . cheap inputs of information" (1998: 60–1).[27] The role of the media is indeed analyzed perceptively, even with an undertone of moral condemnation, but, since technology is to blame, there is no suggestion that calls for different ownership or control of the media would make a difference. The kind of media analysis undertaken by writers such as Herbert Gans, Noam Chomsky, or Douglas Kellner is not mentioned.

The opposite view is also to be found in Castells, with the contradictions unresolved. For instance, elsewhere Castells explicitly abjures technological determinism; he could hardly have said it more bluntly: "The Information Technology Revolution DID NOT create the network society" (1997b: 7, capitalization in the original). Yet, as is frequently the case, the language of the discussion constantly contradicts the broad theoretical statement. Technology is an independent process, independent both of economics and culture (1998: 356). At the same time, "Information technology bec[omes] the indispensable tool for the effective implementation of processes of socio-economic restructuring" (1998: 356–7). The ambivalence as to the explanatory role of technology *vis-à-vis* socioeconomic restructuring runs throughout the discussion. For any analysis of the politics of the developments he describes, clarity on that issue would seem vital, since if it is "technology that transforms," little can be done about it, absent Luddite initiatives, but if socioeconomic forces are involved, they can indeed be addressed, and with them the uses to which technology is put.

Globalization as "actor," all-powerful

It is treated as an entity, an active force; indeed, if the whirlwind has a name, it is globalization. Yet the precise meaning of globalization remains fuzzy. In volume 1 it appears primarily as a globalization of the economy, coupled necessarily with "informationalism," as a "historical discontinuity" from the past (1996: 66–7). In volume 2 its sweep is broader, and it assumes cultural and social forms as well. The issue of its newness "does not concern my inquiry" (1997a: 244, n. 4).[28] Yet we read that "globalization . . . dissolves the autonomy of institutions, organizations, and communication systems" (1997a: 66). If that is the case, just what globalization is, whether it is a new phenomenon or not, becomes critical, despite Castells's claim to the contrary. The picture suggests that not specific actors, not multinational corporations overriding national boundaries, not capital moving without effective restraint to and from wherever it wishes are at work, but the anonymous process of globalization. If globalization is not new, then we might well ask whether it is not capitalism as such, perhaps simply in a further advanced form, which is responsible for the developments Castells accurately describes. And if it is indeed capitalism, then capitalists might also bear some responsibility, and the political content of the conceptualization becomes clear. With the shift of focus to globalization, that political content disappears.[29]

Nowhere is there an intimation that globalization is a process that can be altered or stopped, that really existing globalization is not the only form globalization might take. Globalization is presented as whirlwind (1997a: 61), sweeping everything in its path.

Conflict is bypassed or suppressed[30]

The second volume, titled *The Power of Identity*, focuses on social movements, which are defined "as being: purposive collective actions whose outcome, in victory as in defeat, transforms the values and institutions of society" (1997a: 3). The implication here is that conflict, victory or defeat, is the essence of what social movements are about, with those who support and represent the "values and institutions of society" as their clear antagonists. Conflict might thus be expected to be a critical element in the discussion of social movements, now discussed under the rubric of "identity." But in what follows "social actors . . . excluded from . . . the individualization of identity . . . in the global networks of power and wealth" are not engaged in conflict with those who have excluded them (nameless; see below), but rather these social actors are engaged in a search "for the construction of meaning." Their organizations, social movements, are not movements defined by conflict with those who have deprived them of meaning (and, presumably, of key material resources for living a decent life – the term "exploitation" does not feature in any of the three volumes). They are "cultural communes," "organized around a specific set of values . . . marked by specific codes of self-identification" (1997a: 65). As elsewhere, Castells has it both ways.

In the end, there need not be conflict; ultimately, the solution is for "all urban [*sic*] agents [to develop] a city project which impregnates civic culture and manages to achieve broad consensus" (Borja and Castells 1997: 121). The earlier centrality of conflict has given way to the anticipation of consensus.

Identity (social movements) becomes a reactive phenomenon

What identities react to, and indeed the definition of identity, is unclear. A formal definition is provided: "I mean by identity the process by which an actor . . . constructs meaning primarily of the basis of a given cultural attribute . . . to the exclusion of a broader reference to other social structures" (1996: 22). Why an identity thus constructed cannot also have reference to other social structures is uncertain, and indeed in many examples in volume 2 they clearly do, for example, the feminist movement or the civil rights movement. And within a few pages fundamentalism, clearly taken as an identity movement, is put forward as a reaction to the exclusion of large segments of societies (1996: 25), presumably a "reference to other social structures." And why is a working-class identity not an identity? And to what are "identities" reacting? In one place it is to "the logic of apparatuses and markets" (1996: 23), in other words, to social circumstances; in other places it is to globalization (1998: 1, 2); in others, to "excluders" (1997a: 9, unnamed, but elsewhere "the exclusion from modernity," 1997a: 20); in another, to "the crisis of patriarchalism" (1997a: 25); in still another, to "the unpredictability of the unknown" (1997a: 61). Granted that identities are indeed very diverse, in what sense can then one use the category as a meaningful single concept?

And yet, in the discussion, the functional differences among identities in the end disappear; all identities are treated as reactions, and reactions against generalized processes. Enemies do not appear; processes operate without operators or subjects. Although there is detailed and perceptive discussion of resistance movements in volume 2, the resistance is not against any one or any group in particular:

> Religious fundamentalism, cultural nationalism, territorial communes are . . . defensive reactions. Reactions against three fundamental threats . . . Reaction against globalization . . . Reaction against networking and flexibility . . . And reaction against the crisis of the patriarchal family . . . When the world becomes too large to be controlled . . . When networks dissolve time and space . . . when the patriarchal sustainment of personality breaks down . . . [people react.] (1997a: 65)

The reaction is not by people to other people doing things to them, but to faceless processes. True enough, people often do not see who is doing what to whom, and the descriptions Castells provides are often graphic and trenchant. But then is it not precisely the obligation of analysis to clarify who and what is involved, and are not formulations like those above in fact concealing what is happening, disarming more targeted resistance? In presenting identity movements as against faceless and actor-less processes, the movements themselves become similarly "soft"; they are not defined by their own interests, their own capacities, their own understandings, but only by that "process" which they are up against.

In fact, Castells also includes a much more analytic and political discussion of identities, differentiating between legitimizing identities, those which are introduced by dominant institutions and reinforce domination, resistance identities, those generated by the dominated to creates trenches of resistance, and project identities, those seeking to redefine positions in society and the transformation of the overall social structure (1997a: 8ff., 355ff.). It is a useful categorization, harking back to the discussions of the 1960s as to the nature of social movements and their radical or system-maintaining roles. But it is a tool not then consistently carried forward in a discussion in which religious fundamentalism, the Zapatistas, the Patriot Movement in the United States, Japan's Aum Shinrikyo, the environmental movement, the women's movement, and the Lesbian and Gay Liberation movements are more or less given equal treatment under the uniform heading of "identity" movements.

Are there in fact any "project identities"? John Friedmann (2000) points out that the category of "project identity" into which Castells puts movements that "seek the transformation of overall social structure" (1997a: 8) is empty. Castells is a little ambiguous on the issue; at one point, he suggests that project identities may be involved in efforts at liberating women "through the realization of women's identity," or in movements, "under the guidance of God's law, be it Allah or Jesus" (1997a: 10). At another point he says that from "cultural communes" "new subjects . . . may emerge, thus constructing new meaning around *project identity*" (1997a: 66, italics in the original). And in the concluding chapter of the volume entitled *The Power of Identity*, he speaks merely of "project identities potentially emerging from these spaces [of resistance]" (1997a: 359).[31] Identity, social movements built around identity, are not then today agents of political action; identity is not very powerful, according to Castells, despite the book's title.

The independence of key phenomena

This is a part of the picture. At various times and places, Castells suggests the connections among the various phenomena he includes together under the various umbrella terms that frequently appear: the "information age," the "network society," the "global era." While these phenomena are discussed separately in the three volumes, Castells brings them together in a summary article: "The Information Technology Revolution . . . The restructuring of capitalism . . . The cultural social movements." And he is explicit about the connection: "The network society . . . resulted from the historical convergence of [these] three **independent** processes, from whose interaction emerged the network society" (Castells 1997b: 7, bold face in the original). The language is slippery: are they independent if they interact? To what extent does their interaction determine their nature and direction? Is the "historical convergence" just an accident? The detailed discussion of each suggests that they are indeed independent forces, each with an independent shape. Technological development, appearing independent, moves by its own laws, outside of political control, and social movements are not presented as efforts to control, redirect, or prevent the restructuring of capitalism. That a coherent set of actors is involved in each of the three phenomena drops out of sight. The evidence that "capitalist restructuring" molded the direction, extent, and nature of technological change, coming into conflict with, exacerbating, and highlighting cultural and social movements, is not taken up.

"The depoliticization of space" (1997a: 359)

This is a somewhat unexpected aspect of Castells's presentation. Castells has made a major contribution to the contemporary discussion of space in his evocation of the duality of the space of places and the space of flows (1996: ch. 6); the terms have become an accepted part of the social science vocabulary. The space of places refers to that space to which some people are bound: perhaps unskilled workers, those without the means or the legal status for mobility, those to whom a particular location, city, territory, is a fundamental part of their identity, those who are tied to a particular space/place. The space of flows, by contrast, is used by those with unrestricted mobility and is the space in which capital moves, in which high-level financial transactions occur, in which decisions are made and control exercised, the space which the dominant networks of the advanced network society occupy. There is real meat here: the worlds of those who are location-bound and those with unrestricted mobility, both in their personal lives and in their transactions, are two different worlds; although, as Michael Peter Smith points out in his contribution to this volume, to set the two up as a binary opposition hardly reflects their complex and overlapping nature: the users of the "space of flows" are also place-bound in many aspects of their activities, and many denizens of the "space of places" frequently move large distances and across borders, in increasingly frequent transnational patterns.

Is it useful to convert the differences between these two worlds into a difference originating in/characterized by their use of space, rather than looking at the differences in the use of space as the outcome of differences in wealth, power, resources? Is the space of flows in any meaningful way really a space, or is it not rather a freedom from spatial constraints? Is the space of places really not also made up of flows as well as localities?[32] What needs analysis, for political evaluation, is the extent to which those who use the "space of flows," the dominant groups in the global society, are or are not free of locational bounds.[33] The difference between the occupants of the space of places and the users of the space of flows is a class difference, reflected in their relationship to space, reinforced but not created by it.[34] Examining differences in the use of space without examining the differences in class, power, and wealth which produce those spatial differences is stripping social science analysis of its political relevance: depoliticization.[35]

Worse, space itself becomes an actor, affirmatively displacing real persons and interests: "Function and power . . . are organized in the space of flows . . . the structural domination of its logic . . . alters the meaning and dynamic of places . . . a structural schizophrenia between two spatial logics . . . threatens to break down communication channels . . . a horizon of networked, ahistorical space of flows, aiming at imposing its logic over scattered, segmented places. . . . Unless cultural *and physical bridges* are deliberately built between these two forms of space, we may be heading toward life in parallel universes whose times cannot meet" (1996: 428, italics in original). The logic of space becomes the cause, not the consequence, of social change. Just how do you build a "*physical*" bridge to a space of flows? An interesting conceptualization, with which Castells does not play; perhaps just an errant use of words. In any case, the insight has moved from a potentially striking and politically meaningful one into a play of metaphors,[36] in which it is the "logic of space" that needs to be dealt with, not the relations among people using space. It hardly helps to get a grip on industrial relations in a global age to be told that "the very notion of industrial location [has been transformed] from factory sites to manufacturing flows . . . [by] the logic of information technology manufacturing [and] the new spatial logic" (1996: 393).[37]

Playing with time

As with the treatment of space, this is insightful and provocative in Castells's handling, but depoliticized; he fails to pursue his real insight to its logical conclusion. He points out, and illustrates, the differences in the "time-boundedness" of different actors and activities. To some extent the differentiation parallels longstanding Marxist and classical economists' distinction between those paid hourly wages and those on longer-term salary bases or making profit without regard to time spent, a distinction that then feeds into definitions of class and class relations. Castells deepens the differentiation: it is not just between those paid hourly and those paid in other ways, but between those for whom time itself is an important factor in determining the way their lives are lived and those independent of it, living in "timeless time" (1996: ch. 7). Time is thus a constraint on some much more than on others; it "means" different things to different people. Fine. But to different classes? No, the analysis does not go in that direction; it rather plays with the catchy phrase "timeless time" as characteristic of a type of person and activity, jet-setters, instant communicators and instant manipulators of capital, and instant and constant (time-independent) exercise of control. The truth is that some control the time of others but are free to determine their own time, while the time of others is controlled despite their will. Just as with "space of flows," the metaphor reflects a real truth, but the emphasis on the metaphor conceals the very real class differentiation it in fact only reflects.[38] "Selected functions and individuals" do not "transcend time" (1996: 467); they simply have the power to control their own use of time, and that of others.

The autonomy of the state

This is a complex subject. The intellectual and political tradition from which Castells comes had a central concern with the role of the state. Marx's classic formulation of the state as the "executive committee of the ruling class" was widely seen not as wrong but as incomplete. To explain contemporary developments, Castells's close friend Nicos Poulantzas produced a complex analysis of the subject that was at the heart of the intellectual ferment in which Castells first worked. But Castells opens his chapter on the state with a repudiation of Poulantzas's description as no longer applicable (1997a: 242).[39] Little of the earlier rich discussion survives, except as an echo. Instead, the state becomes an actor: "the state's effort to restore legitimacy," "the state's attempt to reassert its power" (1997a: 243). And there are sweeping statements such as "the nation-state . . . seems to be losing its power, although, and this is essential, *not its influence*" (1997a: 243). Or elsewhere: "the state does not disappear. It transforms itself. This transformation is induced not only by globalization, but by structural changes in the work process, and in the relationship between knowledge and power" (Carnoy and Castells 2001: 6). There are outside pressures, but the state itself acts to transform itself.

What does that mean? Castells never returns to the formulation, but at the end of the chapter says that "in the 1990s, nation-states have been transformed from sovereign subjects into strategic actors" (1997a: 307). It is a muddled discussion. One possible interpretation might be that the nation-state remains important in the development of technology and in the support of "its" multinationals. Indeed, Castells emphasizes both points in various contexts in all three volumes. But why is that not a continuing source of power? The "nation-state" is used as a synonym for "state" in the global era, but the distinction between nation and state is never explored in the analysis;

the capacity of the nation-state "is decisively undermined by globalization" but not by any specific actions of any specific actors, even though as a result multinationals can operate freely disregarding national borders. The nation-state has a "commitment to provide social benefits" (1997a: 254), although why that commitment should exist is not clear. There is a "destabilization of national states" through the globalization of crime (1997a: 259) and a "crisis of legitimacy" that is equally applicable to the Mexican and the United States state, although both countries seem remarkably stable in almost every regard. Such an interpretation simply avoids the question of what the state is. Throw-away lines like "states are the expression of societies, not of economies" (1996: 102) do nothing to help. Furthermore, Castells describes the state's activities as if it was or had been an independent, autonomous actor (1997a: 261)[40] – precisely the conception that has been so systematically questioned in critical sociology over the last century and more. Yet there is also, in passing, the comment that "each nation-state continues to act on behalf of its own interests, or [*sic*] of the interests of constituencies it values most" (1997a: 266). That latter comment might be the beginning of a discussion of where power in and over states actually lies, a discussion opening up the political questions that are so little regarded in the books. But it is not a comment that is pursued. And its very formulation is already misleading: the question is posed as who "the state" autonomously values, the state as actor, the constituency as passive beneficiary, rather than as what active "constituencies" control or put pressure on the state. Remarkably, little of the current discussion about the state "losing control" ever specifies who is winning control.[41]

And so we end with what appears a most ambiguous comment in the post-Seattle world: "the International Monetary Fund experts do not act under the guidance of governments . . . but as self-righteous surgeons skillfully removing the remnants of political controls over market forces" (1997a: 269). Of course, the International Monetary Fund and its related international bodies are deeply concerned with regulating, using the political power of governments and international transactions, and are critically dependent on governments for all of their activities – and particularly the one most powerful government in a one-superpower world. And in so doing they hardly act as independent experts or surgeons but are directly serving identifiable and very specific interests. Their actions are the subject of heated political discussion in countries around the world. Yet any discussion of those politics, however, is avoided.

Conclusion: The Subtleties of Language

The concluding paragraph, at the end of three volumes of dense discussion, illustrates exactly the ultimate failure of the analysis to be of help in remedying the difficulties it documents. The language is worth examining in detail. It begins in what seems to be an activist mode: "there is nothing that cannot be changed by conscious, purposive social action, provided with information, and supported by legitimacy."

"Provided with information" can be, but need not be, an ambiguous phrase: grassroots opposition to various governmental or corporate acts is often branded as "ill-informed," "if they only understood"; but certainly the better informed the forces of change, the better (at least up to a point, beyond which further information may not be needed). "Supported by legitimacy"? An ambiguous term: legitimacy in whose eyes? In any event, we read on to see whose action it is that is being called for.

> If people are informed, active, and communicate throughout the world; if business assumes its social responsibility; if the media become the messengers, rather than the message; if political actors react against cynicism, and restore belief in democracy; if culture is reconstructed from experience; if humankind feels the solidarity of the species throughout the globe; if we assert intergenerational solidarity by living in harmony with nature; if we depart for the exploration of our inner self, having made peace among ourselves. If all this is made possible by our informed, conscious, shared decision, while there is still time, maybe then we may, at last, be able to live and let live, love and be loved.

Well! Certainly nothing can be said against the sentiments, and throughout Castells leaves no doubt as to which side he is on, as to where his own values lie (although he also inserts a curious digression on the neutrality of the social sciences; see further below). But what is being asked for here? Who are to be the agents of the changes that can be made? "People," "business," "the media," "political actors," someone (the passive voice is used) reconstructing culture, "humankind," and "we." It is a jumble of categories, some so general as to be useless ("people," "humankind"), some in fact responsible for many of the problems needing change ("business," "the media"), and some devoid of any specific referent ("we").

With Castells, it is the language of the presentation as well as, and sometimes even more than, the substance that depoliticizes. The lack of specific referents for key formulations is in fact a major indicator of the extent of that depoliticization that is taking place, the removal of specific groupings, actors, agents, who in reality are the players in the globalized world, in favor of generalized terms such as "we." Who are the "we" that are to "make peace among ourselves" (it takes more than one party to make peace; who are the parties?). Castells quotes, with apparent approval, Petra Kelly's statement, "*We* must learn to think and act from our hearts" (1997a: 127, italics added) in the context of a discussion of "*the creation of a new identity, a biological identity, a culture of the human species*" (1997a: 126, italics in original). At some point, indeed, "we" do all have the same interest in the continuation of the species, but that argument is hardly likely to persuade either side in the unpeaceful, politically divided world in which we live to make peace today, nor does it help to define the useful terms of such a peace. Perhaps the implication is that if those responsible for all the conditions that are so eloquently presented as needing change only realize their "biological identity," all will be solved. If that is indeed the implication, it is a profoundly disempowering one. It means not that political conflict, nor the resolution of clashes of interest, nor the empowering of the disempowered are required, but rather a focus on the persuasion of those in power. Such a point of view, which is in fact that of many parts of the environmental movement and many religious faiths, may be quite valid, but it requires substantial evidence and argument; nothing elsewhere in Castells provides such support.[42]

Prescription: What is to be Done?

The avoidance of any real discussion of the potentials or possible avenues of change is deliberate. Castells titles the penultimate section of his last chapter "What is to be Done," an obvious echo of Lenin but with a very different result. He opens with: "Each time an intellectual has tried to answer this question, and seriously implement the answer, catastrophe has ensued."

The statement is reminiscent of Karl Popper's classic argument, that it is big ideas and holistic theories, not the lust for power or profit, nor imperialism or unemployment, nor nationalism or bigotry, that cause mass violence in the world.[43] Is Castells's implication that there is nothing to be done? Castells does not want to say that. He considers "social action and political projects to be essential in the betterment of a society that clearly needs change" (1998: 379). "In this sense . . . by raising some questions and providing empirical and theoretical elements to treat them . . . I am not, and I do not want to be, a neutral, detached observer of the human drama" (1998: 379).

But then he explicitly objects to "trying to frame political practice in accordance with social theory" (what, then, does "if people are informed" in the earlier quote mean?). Then come the astonishing statements:

> Theory and research . . . should be considered as a means for understanding our world, and should be judged exclusively on their accuracy, rigor, and relevance [*sic*]. How these tools are used, and for what purpose, should be the exclusive prerogative of social actors themselves.

And thus an explicit rejection of Marx's call for philosophers to go from interpreting the world to trying to change it, which the language echoes: "in the twenty-first century, [Castells says,] it is time for them to interpret it differently" (1998: 379).

But this effort at being nonpolitical distorts what is in fact political in the effort at "accuracy and rigor"; the loophole Castells provides himself by adding the word "relevance," which might be taken as "relevant to action for change," is not in fact used. Castells may not wish to draw conclusions as to political practice from his own analysis, but such conclusions are implicit in it. The analysis bypasses agency and reifies social relations. Its impact, whether its author wishes it or not, is political: to depoliticize.

And this is, to my mind, the central weakness of Castells's analysis, the intellectual rationale for his – and not only his – movement away from the political stance of an earlier day. The problems of injustice, lack of democracy, domination and exploitation, with which Castells was and is still concerned, remain. I do not mean to imply that his values have changed or are any less concerned with issues of social justice than they once were. The "society . . . clearly needs change." But the "social actors" who alone have the "prerogative" to bring about such change have disappeared. The proletariat is dead.[44] The social movements that might have been its successor as an agent of change are gone. The "identity movements" that have replaced them are fragmented, of ambiguous impact, not capable (yet?) of producing real change. "The disjunction between . . . two spatial logics . . . shifts the core economic, symbolic, and political processes away from the realm where . . . political control can be exercised" (1997a: 124). Nothing is to be done.[45]

In the end, the message is both analytically depoliticized and politically disempowering. Castells's analysis, which had played such an important role in producing the new wind in urban studies, has passed on, leaving only its echoes blowing in provocative but ultimately frustrating circles.

Notes

1 In the discussion of the work of Manuel Castells, which I see as remarkably fertile in the history of attempts to understand the underlying trends of our times, I have benefited from a number of reviews of his work, including Watson (1998), Tilly (1998), Friedmann (2000), Waterman (1999), and Bender (2000). I have also benefited substantially from the sharp perceptions of the students in the Ph.D. Colloquium in the Urban Planning program at Columbia University (and of Professor Tom Vietorisz, with whom I co-taught it) in the course of our discussions there of the three volumes, including both their agreements and their disagreements with some of the conclusions presented in this chapter.

2 For an account of mainstream sociological attention to urban issues before this period see van Kempen and Marcuse (2001). By and large, prior mainstream approaches stressed individual preferences functioning through the market as the key forces shaping the uses of urban space. Critical approaches focused on macro-structural elements, with urban phenomena as their simple side effects.

3 Among the classics in the field should be mentioned: Lefebvre (1968), Castells ([1972] 1977), Harvey (1973), and O'Connor (1973). Pickvance (1976) first brought the French neo-Marxist literature to English-speaking attention.

4 For an explicit discussion, see Katznelson (1984, 1992).

5 Among the noteworthy examples: Gans (1962), Duhl (1963), and especially Fried (1963: 151–71). See also essays collected in Wilson (1966).

6 Thus Gorz (1982).

7 Paper for conference at the University of Paris X, October 10–12, 1983, 1. For a fuller and more nuanced statement of Pickvance's views, see Pickvance (1985).

8 A summary of the course of the somewhat chaotic simultaneous telecast of exchanges between participants of the two meetings on their last day. Many in Davos of course have a quite sophisticated understanding of the social problems globalization has caused, but their willingness to confront them does not extend to questioning their own right to exercise that power that has produced the problems.

9 The phrase has been used as a book title by three different authors in recent years: Burbach (1997), Sassen (1998), and McBride and Wiseman (2000). The phrase has the unfortunate (and no doubt unintended) overtones of a psychological problem: discontent is a state of mind (harking back of course to Freud's *Civilization and its Discontents*). Each of the volumes gives evidence of the real suffering caused by globalization.

10 Giddens's endorsement is printed on the back cover of the third volume of *The Information Age*.

11 See particularly the discussion at p. 298 of *The City and the Grassroots*, in which he describes his first major published work as "a fiasco." Chris Pickvance drew my attention to the comment.

12 In fact, "relationships of production" is the phrase used in the conclusion to *The Information Age* (Castells 1998: 361).

13 See Gorz ([1964] 1968: 7ff.).

14 In one odd paragraph discussing "organizational trajectories in the restructuring of capitalism" (1996: 152), Castells says "organization changes interacted with the diffusion of information technology but by and large were independent, and in general preceded the diffusion of information technologies" (1997a: 153, and see 1996: 168). But he also says "the network enterprise [is] the organizational form of the informational/global economy" (1996: 171), and, overwhelmingly, the "information age" and "the network society" are treated as virtual synonyms.

15 The wording is that of Peter Hall, Castells's sometime collaborator, quoted on the back cover of the final volume.

16 Published as Giddens (2000). My own critique of Giddens's recent popular writing is in process.

17 Power does not indeed disappear from the reality, it becomes "inscribed . . . in the cultural codes through which people and institutions represent life and make decisions, including political decisions" (1998: 367). But conflicts about power are not therefore political conflicts; to the contrary, "*Cultural battles are the power battles of the Information Age*" (1998: 368, italics in original).

18 As with so many of Castells's elegant phrases, the immediate words might be taken in a different meaning from their obvious one: here, it might be that Castells wishes to allude to the manner in which the new society of "flows" dominates even those who hold power within it. But that point is not raised in his text; he speaks specifically of "networking logic" as a "social determination of a higher level than that of the specific social interests expressed through the networks": network logics determine what happens, not social interests. This is what I mean by depoliticization.

19 Indeed, Castells garbles the taxonomy he suggests, which separates "modes of production (capitalism, statism) and modes of development (industrialism, informationalism)" (1996: 14), when he says that "capitalism is oriented towards profit-maximization" (1996: 16), but "industrialism is oriented towards economic growth" (1996: 17), which most would consider an attribute of the drive for accumulation, a characteristic of capitalism rather than industrialism.

20 Indeed, there is a large literature on the topic, ranging from the early Giddens to Erik Olin Wright and beyond, but that work is not cited. See the reader edited by Patrick Joyce (1995).

21 In the perhaps less careful language of a lecture, Castells's departure from any conception of power as political or economic is flat: "Knowledge generation and information processing are the sources of value and power in the Information Age" ("The culture of cities in the Information Age"; lecture at conference on "The Frontiers of the Mind in the Twenty-first Century," Library of Congress, June 17, 1999).

22 What does "structural irrelevance" mean? "Most primary commodities are useless or low priced, markets are too narrow, investment too risky, labor not skilled enough, communication and telecommunication infrastructure clearly inadequate, politics too unpredictable, and government bureaucracies inefficiently corrupt" (1996: 135). That is apparently not part of earlier or continuing dependency.

23 Castells has repeated similar formulations elsewhere: "the global economy is at the same time extraordinarily inclusive of what is valued in the networks of business interaction, and highly exclusive of what is of little or no interest in a given time and space" (2000: 53).

24 There is indeed an important issue involved in these formulations: that the real actors, the real capitalists, are themselves not free agents, acting as they please, but subject to the constraints of markets and networks – people are free to act, but under conditions not of their own choosing. It is an important dialectic, and one which may underlie Castells's approach, but it does not relieve actors of responsibility for the choices they do make, and in any event is not explored in the text.

25 "[C]apital is globalised" is the formulation in a more recent essay, again a passive with no actor as subject, in a paragraph describing the process of globalization well without ever mentioning who runs or benefits from that process. Adding later "we [*sic*] have created an Automaton, at the core of our economies. . . . Random movements rather than economic calculations seem to be the primary forces shaping market trends. So the random Automaton thrives, simultaneously

inducing growth and wealth and triggering disinvestment and crisis" (Castells 2000: 53, 56, 59).

26 As is so often the case, multiple quite different formulations are found: elsewhere Castells speaks of "two relatively autonomous trends: the development of new information technologies . . . [and the use of] the power of technology to serve the technology of power" (1996: 52). (Why not just "to serve power?") Granting information technology the power of an actor runs throughout much of Castells's writings; see, for instance, Castells (2000: 62).

27 Quoted with approval from Christopher Freeman. See also Castells (1996: 65).

28 See also Castells (1998: 356, n. 1), which ends with the odd thought: "if nothing is new under the sun, why bother to try to investigate, think, write, and read about it?" One might think of a few reasons.

29 In a later article with Martin Carnoy, Castells (although it is jointly written, so attribution is not certain) continues the confusion: on the one hand, the article contains many formulations such as: "globalization and information technology is transforming work" (Carnoy and Castells 2001: 7), "Globalization limits the sovereignty of the state . . . it redefines the social boundaries of the state." Thus globalization as an actor. The use of the passive voice is recurrent: "values and norms are in the process of being globalized" (p. 9), "workers are now being successfully disaggregated from class identity" (p. 8), and so on. The main theme is that "the locus of the relation between power and knowledge has moved out of the nation state" (p. 1), that "power over knowledge in the global economy is moving out of the control of the national state" (p. 11) (on its own?), but where control now lies is never stated. In the "chain of decision making" in the "new form of the state," corporations never appear (p. 14). On the other hand, the article also says that "without decisive state intervention, globalization could not have taken place" (p. 5), that "the G-7 group . . . takes major decisions in managing the global economy" (p. 13), and finally that "*vis-à-vis* dominant classes (that is the collective capitalist), class domination is ensured by managing and spreading globalization" (p. 15). The dominant language is that of globalization as itself an actor, of external developments in technology determining basic changes in social structure; but the echo of the earlier political economy approach is there too.

30 Flat statements as to what is not in Castells are always dangerous, because in fact he says, in one place or another, almost everything, whether consistent with or contradictory to other statements. Many conflicts are thus in fact described in the course of Castells's account of identities. But conflict is never elucidated as a source of change in the larger theoretical discussions.

31 But one looks in vain for any discussion of the conditions under which such potential may be realized, as Margit Mayer pointed out to me.

32 Michael Peter Smith, referring back to Doreen Massey's discussions, makes this point eloquently in Smith (2001: ch. 5).

33 This is a key question to which Saskia Sassen has devoted a good portion of her recent research. The issue is as to the necessities of spatial base for global activities: to what extent do all "flows" have to come down somewhere, and to what extent must the processing of what flows be done in very specific spatial locations with very specific physical requirements?

34 Certainly the elite occupy (live in, take vacations in, enjoy) the spaces of places also, and certainly some oppositional movements, even some of the excluded, use the space of flows, e.g., the Internet, to communicate, build solidarity, organize resistance (the World Social Forum in Porto Alegre in January 2001 could not have taken place without the use of the Internet). That does not change the relationship between the elite and the excluded, nor their dominant position in the flows/spaces duality. Their constitution precedes, not depends on, their use of places and flows.

35 Later Castells goes further and drops whatever potential linkage the space of flows had to relationships of power: "the space of flows, which started as the space of power and dominant functions, is extending its realm to the whole diversity of human activity" (lecture at conference on "The Frontiers of the Mind in the Twenty-first Century," Library of Congress, June 17, 1999). The point is important but then becomes quite nonpolitical. Yet later in the same lecture power reappears in the local/global duality: "The culture of cities in the Information Age brings together local identity and global networks to restore the interaction between power and experience."

36 Castells indeed undercuts some of the power of his own metaphor when he speaks of the "three layers of material supports that, together, *constitute* the space of flows" (1996: 412, italics added). They are: electronic impulses, nodes and hubs, and the segregated spaces of the elite. These might more plausibly be discussed as the place-based aspects – limits – on the space of flows. Both the looseness of the language and the deconcretization of the ideas result in statements like "Belleville [a Parisian working-class *quartier*] is . . . a place, while I am afraid I look more like a flow" (1996: 423). Castells may consider his own charming corporeal personality a flow, but the financiers, managers, and politicians who dominate decision-making in the real world are not adequately described as simply "flows." It is sometimes hard to separate problems of facile, often imaginative and catchy, writing from problems of content in the three volumes.

37 The full paragraph reads: "And as the logic of information technology manufacturing trickles down from the producers of information technology devices to the users of such devices in the whole realm of manufacturing, so the new spatial logic expands, creating a multiplicity of global industrial networks whose intersections and exclusions transform the very notion of industrial location from factory sites to manufacturing flows."

38 In fact, in passing Castells directly vitiates the substantive political content of his analysis when he applies his conception to "two groups: high-level professionals and unskilled service workers" (1996: 441). While he acknowledges that the two groups work longer hours for different reasons, putting them into the same box would be misleading in an analysis that focuses on who controls their own time and that of others, and whose time is controlled by others.

39 In a later article, Castells argues in detail that "in the twenty years since Poulantzas' untimely death, much has changed" (Carnoy and Castells 2001).

40 Elsewhere, Castells says that "nation-states have been transformed from sovereign subjects into strategic actors" (1997a: 307). It is hardly self-evident that states were ever "sovereign subjects"; the literature to the contrary is enormous.

41 See, for instance, Carnoy and Castells (2001: 11): "Knowledge formation and power over knowledge in the global economy is moving out of the control of the nation state . . . The nation state is also losing control over the educational system." Elsewhere, the authors take a quite different approach: "The Network State resulted from the outcomes of social struggles" (p. 15), and the "collective capitalist" reappears, only to be defined as "represented by global financial markets" (p. 16). There is a tension between concepts here begging for exploration.

42 The language is worth quoting at length: "The ecological approach to life, to the economy, and to the institutions of society emphasizes the holistic character of all forms of matter, and of all information processing. Thus, the more we know, the more we sense the possibilities of our technology, and the more we realize the gigantic, dangerous gap between our enhanced productive capacities, and our primitive, unconscious, and ultimately destructive social organization. This is the objective thread that weaves the growing connectedness of social revolts, local and global, defensive and offensive, issue-oriented and value-oriented, emerging in and around the environmental movement. This is not to say that a new international of good-willing, generous citizens has emerged. Yet. As shown in this volume, old and new cleavages of class, gender, ethnicity, religion, and territoriality are at work in dividing and subdividing issues, conflicts, and projects. But this is to say that embryonic connections between grassroots movements and symbol-oriented mobilizations on behalf of environmental justice bear the mark of alternative projects. These projects hint at superseding the exhausted social movements of industrial society, to resume, under historically appropriate forms, the old dialectics between domination and resistance, between realpolitik and utopia, between cynicism and hope." The fulcrum of change here seems to be "the more we know"; knowledge itself will produce change, and presumably overcome "old and new cleavages of class, gender, ethnicity." Yet it will also lead to a resumption of "the old dialectics between domination and resistance." An effort to have it both ways? And note the "we."

43 See the detailed refutation in Herbert Marcuse (1972).

44 There is a curious passage in which Castells says he speaks in the Marxian tradition and divides "producers" (presumably meaning workers) into "knowledge generators and information processors," who are valuable, and generic labor, which is not. The generic workers need the knowledge producers, but not vice versa, and thus "class solidarity" is gradually dissolved. Yet, "in one sense, nothing has changed *vis-à-vis* classic capitalism: . . . their employers . . . appropriate a share of informational producers' work" (word order slightly changed). But: "we can hardly consider that there is a class contradiction between these networks of highly individualized producers and the collective capitalist of global financial networks" (1998: 365). Why is not quite clear.

45 To be sure, there is ground for pessimism, and both analysis and politics must be grounded in reality, even if that reality is bleak. But at the very least the analysis must make clear who in that reality is doing what to whom, and what the lines of conflict are. Compare David Harvey's treatment of many of the same themes in Harvey (2000), particularly Parts 3 and 4, dealing with "the utopian moment" and "the plurality of alternatives."

Bibliography

Bender, T. 2000: Describing the world at the end of the millennium. *Harvard Design Magazine* (Winter/Spring): 68–71.

Borja, J. and Castells, M. 1997: *Local and Global.* London: Earthscan.

Burbach, R. 1997: *Globalization and its Discontents: The Rise of Postmodern Socialisms.* London and Chicago: Pluto Press.

Carnoy, M. and Castells, M. 2001: Globalization, the knowledge society, and the network state: Poulantzas at the millennium. *Global Networks* 1 (1): 1–18.

Castells, M. [1972] 1977: *The Urban Question: A Marxist Approach.* Cambridge, MA: MIT Press.

——1996: *The Information Age.* Volume 1: *The Rise of the Network Society.* Oxford: Blackwell.

——1997a: *The Information Age.* Volume 2: *The Power of Identity.* Oxford: Blackwell.

——1997b: An introduction to the information age. *Cities*: 6–16.

——1998: *The Information Age.* Volume 3: *End of Millennium.* Oxford: Blackwell.

——2000: Information technology and global capitalism. In W. Hutton and A. Giddens (eds.), *On the Edge: Living with Global Capitalism.* London: Jonathan Cape, 52–74.

Duhl, L. J. (ed.) 1963: *The Urban Condition: People and Policy in the Metropolis.* New York: Basic Books.

Fried, M. 1963: Grieving for a lost home: psychological costs of relocation. In L. J. Duhl (ed.), *The Urban Condition: People and Policy in the Metropolis.* New York: Basic Books, 151–71.

Friedmann, J. 2000: Reading Castells: *Zeitdiagnose* and social theory. *Environment and Planning D: Society and Space* 18: 111–20.

Gans, H. J. 1962: *The Urban Villagers: Group and Class in the Life of Italian-Americans.* Glencoe, IL: Free Press.

Giddens, A. 2000: *Runaway World: How Globalization is Reshaping Our Lives.* New York: Routledge.

Gorz, A. [1964] 1968: *Strategy for Labor: A Radical Proposal.* Boston: Beacon Press.

——1982: *Farewell to the Proletariat* [*Adieu au Prolétariat*]. London: Pluto Press.

Harvey, D. 1973: *Social Justice and the City.* Baltimore: Johns Hopkins University Press.

——2000: *The Spaces of Hope.* Berkeley: University of California Press.

Joyce, P. 1995: *Class.* Oxford: Oxford University Press.

Katznelson, I. 1984: *City Trenches: Urban Politics and the Patterning of Class in the United States.* New York: Pantheon.

——1992: *Marxism and the City.* Oxford: Clarendon Press.

Lefebvre, H. 1968: *Le Droit à la ville.* Paris: Editions Anthropos.

McBride, S. K. and Wiseman, J. R. 2000: *Globalization and its Discontents.* New York: St. Martin's Press.

Marcuse, H. 1972: Karl Popper and the problem of historical laws. Reprinted in *Studies in Critical Philosophy.* Boston: Beacon Press, 191–208.

O'Connor, J. 1973: *The Fiscal Crisis of the State.* New York: St. Martin's Press.

Pickvance, C. G. (ed.) 1976: *Urban Sociology: Critical Essays.* London: Tavistock.

—— 1985: The rise and fall of urban movements and the role of comparative analysis. *Environment and Planning D: Society and Space* 3: 31–53.

Sassen, S. 1998: *Globalization and its Discontents*. New York: New Press.

Smith, M. P. 2001: *Transnational Urbanism: Locating Globalization*. Oxford: Blackwell.

Tilly, C. 1998: Review. *American Journal of Sociology* 103 (6): 1730–2.

van Kempen, R. and Marcuse, P. 2001: The academic formulations: explanations of the partitioned city. In P. Marcuse and R. van Kempen (eds.), *Of States and Cities: The Partitioning of Urban Space*. Oxford: Oxford University Press, 35–58.

Waterman, P. 1999: The brave new world of Manuel Castells: what on earth (or in the ether) is going on? *Development and Change* 30: 357–80.

Watson, S. 1998: New orders, disorders and creative chaos: the information age and the network society. *Policy and Politics* 26 (2): 227–33.

Wilson, J. Q. 1966: *Urban Renewal, The Record and the Controversy*. Cambridge, MA: MIT Press.

8

Urban Analysis as Merchandising: The "LA School" and the Understanding of Metropolitan Development

Mark Gottdiener

If the *Chronicle of Higher Education* ran a story regarding a group of academics who claimed the moon was made of green cheese, no doubt there would be some responses that it could print from other academics both pro and con. It might even get a letter or two stating that someone was helped by the article because they hadn't really thought about that issue before. The *Chronicle* could then pat itself on the back and believe that it had done a genuine service in the interests of science. When it, in fact, printed the article by D. W. Miller on the so-called "LA School" (2000), it actually acted as if it had raised the issue of the moon and green cheese. The premise of the LA School, that somehow Los Angeles is uniquely positioned as the exemplar of contemporary urban studies, is as ridiculously false as anything Dr. Seuss may have said about the lunar landscape.

In Peter Wollen's (1993) analysis of consumer society he notes how commodity-oriented capitalism thrives by raiding the past and converting other people's ideas and culture into products that are then marketed as "new." The LA School has adopted this strategy for what seems like shameless self-promotion at the expense of scholarship. Perhaps this phenomenon is now part of the more general effect of social positioning for spectacular rewards and notoriety brought on by globalization. Surely, academics permit almost any kind of behavior, short of plagiarism, by their colleagues. But we can rightly wonder why the LA School seems so desperate for media hype while sacrificing the cumulative project of urban science in its transparent attempt at intellectual elitism.

There are many things wrong with the assertion by Michael Dear that there is an "LA School," including the systematic way urbanists elsewhere are excluded by their media-oriented hype, but the worst is his consistent refusal to cite previous work that would clearly challenge the very premise of his argument. In brief, what is disturbing about the "intellectual amnesia" on the part of the new crop of geographers in Los Angeles is their limited contribution to the understanding of contemporary development patterns and processes. Before discussing the latter, which is my interest, it is necessary to briefly address the former because of its potentially negative effects on urban studies.

The "LA School" as a Form of Logocentric Ideology

The geographers living in Los Angeles who hype the "LA School" have fashioned an exclusionary ideology that pyramids work on metropolitan regionalism into a hierarchy, placing themselves at the top. This discourse, which hides a rampant elitism, logocentrically valorizes a select group at the expense of others through exclusionary techniques that are then promoted in popular venues, like the press, which cannot be easily challenged by fellow academics. The discursive hierarchy is created by valorizing a particular place rather than specific ideas critical to an understanding of contemporary urban patterns. The fact that the true intellectual pursuit of the latter proves false the claim of the former is completely obscured. The LA School ideology has the following components. It excludes other well-respected, practicing urbanists within the same geographical area; it objectifies physical location at the expense of social processes and forces; it treats history as simply descriptive; it excludes pertinent and important approaches in other disciplines.

The exclusion of other urbanists

The notorious "New Urban Studies" article (Miller 2000) begins with a description of Michael J. Dear as he rides a helicopter "2,000 feet up" in order to map the "ever-changing topography" of the "Los Angeles" region. Apparently, Dear prefers to make this graphic and spectacular claim to the media rather than calling the Department of Geography at the University of California, Riverside. The latter is a campus lying below the flight path of Dear's helicopter about 50 miles east of LA. There are first-rate geographers on that campus who, no doubt, have acquired some appreciation for the spatial or "topographic" arrangements in their own backyard and who can report on them with ease. In fact, not too far from the Riverside campus is the location of the firm that developed the Geographical Information Systems (GIS) software which is used by every serious urbanist, apparently except Dear, interested in tracking the "ever-changing topography" of developing areas around the globe. They also have both a phone number and useful software.

Second, LA School hypsters exclude from their group well-respected urbanists, such as Eric Monkkonen and Ivan Light, who are both professors at UCLA. Small wonder, then, if they can ignore people just down the hall from where they work, that they have also excluded, in their media drive to promote themselves, serious urban scholars working on other campuses in the area. I was a professor, for example, from 1977 to 1994 at UC Riverside. Spencer Olin, a distinguished professor of urban history, works at UC Irvine and co-edited the important book, *Postsuburban California* (1988), a book, by the way, that does significantly more to explain contemporary regional patterns of growth than anything ever written by the LA Schoolers. It is also worth pointing out that, not that far from Los Angeles, the campus of UC at Santa Barbara has several well-known urbanists, and that Harvey Molotch, the co-originator of the influential Growth Machine perspective, for example, worked there for decades. All of these "other" urbanists, and many more, are simply excluded from the self-promoting group of which Michael Dear is the most vocal media representative.

The Ideological Objectification and Valorization of Physical Location

Essential to LA Schoolers like Dear and Soja is the claim that the vast developing area east of Los Angeles city limits be included conceptually in their discursive referent – the "Los Angeles area." However, this is simply an ideological construction. In truth, the Southern California region around Los Angeles comprises three metropolitan statistical areas (MSAs) – LA/Long Beach, Riverside/San Bernardino, and Orange County. The area to the east, the one which Michael Dear is fond of flying over in his "rented helicopter" (Miller 2000), is designated by the United States Census as the Riverside/San Bernardino MSA. Recently the census has consolidated these into one massive superurban category, called a consolidated metropolitan statistical area (CMSA). In 1995 there were thirteen of these regions identified in the United States, with the New York area the most populous. It is precisely the emergence of these sprawling, developing, urbanizing regions outside the more commonly recognized and historical central cities, like Los Angeles, that contributes to the need for new concepts and theories of urban growth. In the United States, very few cities have been able, like Houston, Texas, to annex their hinterland, making regional development for most places a highly fragmented affair with contending political jurisdictions and spatial competition increasingly characteristic of this arrangement.

What makes the new spatial patterns compelling to understand and analyze scientifically is precisely the regional, multi-centered character of development that overshadows in importance the influence of any particular city. By conflating the three different MSAs comprising the region in and around Los Angeles/San Pedro/Hollywood/Beverly Hills/Compton/Burbank/Pasadena/Glendale/Anaheim/Irvine/San Bernardino/Fontana/

Riverside/Marino Valley/Palm Springs/Banning, etc., into their discursive construction called "Los Angeles," the LA Schoolers obscure in the worst possible way the very phenomenon they seek to study.

Clearly, the LA Schoolers, by attempting to valorize Los Angeles as the exemplar of contemporary growth, simply pyramid themselves into position at the top of the academic hierarchy by justification of location alone. Their "LA area" is a convenient fiction and the prime quality of their importance is not their individual work on the matter of sprawling development, but simply the address of their campus office.

Can it even be claimed that Los Angeles is illustrative par excellence of contemporary urbanism? In reality, has urban studies up until the present been anchored by the objectification of 1930s Chicago as the exemplar, and has the field now, thanks to Michael Dear and Edward Soja, been superseded by the example of 1990s Los Angeles? Is urban studies today bedrocked on a foundation that uses a single city as its exemplary model for its concepts? These are precisely the core assertions, the essential claims, of the LA School. Serious scholars view their field in precisely the opposite way. It is not the objectification of a city as an ideal case but the painstaking study of societal processes and their sociospatial effects on settlement space everywhere that defines the field.

Contemporary urbanism seeks to study the forces and agents that produce new spatial forms (Harvey 1973; Castells [1972] 1977; Lefebvre 1992; Gottdiener [1985] 1994). No single city can possibly encapsulate all the complex nuances of present-day metropolitan growth. The LA School seeks to make its location the primary referent for this study, but understanding contemporary urbanism requires a referent of an entirely different kind. What unifies the quest of urban scholars is not our commonality with any particular city, but our common interest in understanding the powerful social forces arising from the economic, cultural, spatial, and political dimensions of social behavior that shape and reshape local areas around the world.

Downplaying History

Scholars ignore history at their peril. Los Angeles is touted as the exemplary suburban, auto-era city. The automobile, in particular, is viewed as the generator of current spatial patterns, especially the sprawl of regional growth. The history of Los Angeles is not only quite different but is instrumental to an understanding of contemporary spatial processes in the CMSA. One hundred years ago, prior to the mass production of cars, the area in and around Los Angeles already had an extensive regional public transportation infrastructure based on rail and electrified trolleys (see Crump 1962;

Gottdiener [1985] 1994). Most significantly, it was the network of trolleys, which in the early 1900s extended from San Pedro harbor, the westernmost part of Los Angeles, to Lake Arrowhead in the San Bernardino mountains, high above the expanding region, that provided the infrastructure for real estate development. Much later, many of the automobile routes simply paved over these tracks and followed them to create the present-day system of freeways (Gottdiener 1994: 69). Evidence from other metropolitan areas also supports the view that suburbanization is a phenomenon characteristic of every city and that the highly centralized, bounded city that was the model for the Chicago School and is the convenient strawman for the LA School simply never existed (see, for example, Warner 1962; Walker 1981; Jackson 1985). Processes of real estate development, capital flows, factions of capital, returns to capital, local politics, decentralization, recentralization, agglomeration, and dispersal are the key topics requiring study by the new urban approach (see Castells [1972] 1977; Harvey 1985a, 1985b; Kling, Olin, and Poster 1991; Lefebvre 1992; Gottdiener and Hutchison 1999).

The LA School claims to be replacing the Chicago School as an influential brain's trust. It forgets history; this time, the history of its own field. The Chicago School paradigm has been dead and buried for decades. Any serious urban scholar can tell you that it even took fatally ill shortly after Burgess published his famous "concentric zone" model of city growth. In this light, the claim by Michael Dear and his significant others to be replacing the Chicago School seems more like a call to recast *Night of the Living Dead.* Consider the following observation:

> The urbanization theory of the early Chicago School began to receive a critical response in the 1930s (Davie 1937; Hoyt 1933; Alihan 1938; Gettys 1940; Harris and Ullman 1945; Firey 1945; Form 1954). Contentiousness over theoretical assertions surfaced during this time, especially over the Chicago School's reluctance to recognize the important role which cultural values played in the determination of locational decisions and its reliance on economic competition as paramount in social interaction. In addition, however, Alihan raised another issue, namely, that taken as a whole, ecologists used the term "community" to specify both an empirical reality and an abstract unit of ecological organization (1938). In this way, the Chicago School confused the "real" with its "theoretical" object of analysis and which, as its critics maintained, was misguided even as an ideal type (Hoyt 1933; Harris and Ullman 1945). (Gottdiener 1985: 34)

If Milla Alihan were alive today, she would make the very same criticism of the LA School. No "real" city can also serve as an "ideal" type that totally exemplifies core social processes. Those that claim otherwise confuse theory with analysis, a fallacy that nineteenth-century social scholars, such as Max Weber, already conditioned academics to avoid.

Is Geography, and the LA School Geography in Particular, the Only Insightful Discipline Studying Contemporary Urbanism?

Michael Dear and his friends work hard to exclude mention of the work of urbanists in other disciplines and obscure the importance of their contributions, which, in many cases, were made significantly before the LA School hyped the value of its own importance. Miller titles his *Chronicle of Higher Education* piece "The New Urban Studies." More than twenty years ago, sociologists were articulating the conceptual framework for the "New Urban Sociology." There has even been a multi-edition urban textbook in print for almost a decade on this subject which specifically advances ideas about new urban forms (Gottdiener 1994; Gottdiener and Hutchison 1999). Sociologists spoke a decade ago of a paradigm shift in urbanism away from the ideas of the early Chicago School, the later Chicago School, and the human ecologists toward an approach centered on analyzing and understanding the new social forces and processes structuring metropolitan regions (Gottdiener and Feagin 1988). One of the true founders of the new approach, Manuel Castells, is a sociologist, as was the seminal thinker Henri Lefebvre, whose ideas have inspired an entire generation to consider urbanism in precisely this new light (Lefebvre 1992). Political science also has many practitioners who subscribe to the new ideas and have done so for decades. Finally, there are even some new urban geographers who do not live in Los Angeles. Surprisingly, a few of them have also managed to publish important work with insights from their experience with other cities that are helpful to the new urban approach (see, for example, the work of David Harvey).

What Can Be Learned from the Critique of "LA School" Hype?

Academics would prefer not to be harsh with their colleagues. After all, the key activity characterizing our profession is the serious advancement of knowledge. However, in the wake of the *Chronicle*'s article and the obvious arrogant hype that it seeks to pass off in place of respectable scholarship, it was necessary to dissect the phenomenon more systematically. But what can be learned from this critique?

There is, in fact, a strong need to get away from the old vocabularies describing forms of urbanization. There is also a need to outline the factors that are critical to an understanding of the new sociospatial forms. Finally, there are important theoretical issues for urban analysis that are raised once we acknowledge the current limitations of thinking about sociospatial forms and processes. Curiously, the economic, political, cultural, and spatial aspects of contemporary growth processes have already been studied with considerable effect and insight by academics that do not live in Los Angeles.

Understanding the New Spatial Form

Writings about contemporary urban processes remain city-based. The use of the city focus for urbanization is a fallacy. Yet, almost without pause, publishers persist in producing book after book using the "city" as the referent for organized and constructed settlement space. We hear about the "postmodern city," the "culture of cities," "edge cities," "global cities," and the like. For some time now, I have argued against this discourse and its referent. The bounded, centralized city that organizes its hinterland, as the Chicago School sociologists, geographers, urban economists, and so-called "postmodern" interpreters all believe to be the correct model of space, simply no longer exists (Gottdiener [1985] 1994). Contemporary urbanization is characterized by the general process of deconcentration – a ubiquitous leveling of both population and societal activities across space that has produced intranational and intraregional fragmentation. Reformation of the new spatial form, the multi-centered metropolitan region, is characterized by the operation of two distinct sociospatial forces: decentralization and recentralization. Before the latter two can be understood within the context of contemporary urbanization, it is necessary to describe the massive scale of deconcentration and its effects, because the processes are all interrelated – each one has both developed and, in turn, contributed to the conditions of development of the others.

Deconcentration

After World War II America's population was concentrated in the Northeast and the Midwest. After the 1980 census, just thirty years later, the population had deconcentrated in a massive shift to the south and west, a region known as the "Sunbelt." Growth in the Sunbelt was both substantial and rapid. Entire industries relocated there, not just people. And this trend continues. New York dropped from the number one slot as the country's most populous state in 1980, to be replaced by California. Now Texas has a larger population and New York is ranked third. Of the ten most populous cities in 1994, three – Houston, Dallas, and San Antonio – were in Texas, two – Los Angeles and San Diego – were in California, and one – Phoenix – was in Arizona (Gottdiener and Hutchison 1999: 4). In short, it is the Sunbelt that dominates urban life today, despite the persisting health of places like New York City and Chicago.

Now trends show that deconcentration continues even within the Sunbelt. Between 1990 and 1994, Los Angeles lost over 1 percent of its population and Dallas was growing slowly. Places like El Paso, Texas, and Las Vegas, Nevada, became boom towns, the latter largely because of flight from LA. Manufacturing and office work also dispersed (Gottdiener and Hutchison 1999: ch. 5; Gottdiener et al. 1999).

Deconcentration has a second component; the shift to the suburbs. Not confined to any particular part of the nation, this post-1950s phenomenon took place within every metropolitan area. By the 1970 census more people in the United States were living outside the major central cities than within them. In 1994–5 New York City had a population of slightly over 7 million but its metropolitan region contained over 18 million people, that is to say, more than a multiple of two. The region of Los Angeles was larger in population by almost a multiple of five than the city itself. Chicago's central city population declined slightly between 1990 and 1994 but its metropolitan area population increased by over 4 percent. The metro areas with the most rapid growth during that same period were Dallas-Fort Worth (10.2 percent), Atlanta (16 percent), and Phoenix (14.5 percent). But even classic "Rustbelt" cities like Detroit, which lost over 15 percent of its central city population between 1980 and 1994, possessed metro areas that gained population, rising 1.8 percent between 1990 and 1994 (Gottdiener and Hutchison 1999: ch. 1).

With suburbanization dominating growth patterns so completely it seems odd that urbanists persist in focusing their thoughts on the city. More significantly, suburban areas have themselves changed and matured so that the simplistic city/suburb dichotomy no longer has relevance today (Kling et al. 1991). As in the case of the Sunbelt shift, movement outside the central city involves economic as well as demographic components. Factories, banking, retailing, and other consumer services dispersed throughout metropolitan regions after the 1950s (Gottdiener [1985] 1994). Nor can it be said that these dramatic shifts were the consequence of globalization alone, as some currently contend. More complex, more domestically sourced, and more structural or institutional in form, the forces that brought about the deconcentration of both the economy and the population to the Sunbelt and the suburbs have their basis in fundamental processes of our society (Gottdiener [1985] 1994), which I shall discuss in more detail subsequently. These include the features of analysis emphasized by what has come to be called the "new urban sociology," namely, the central role of institutional factors, such as the actions of the federal government in channeling resources and transferring value across space, structural changes that provided new incentives such as depreciation laws for factory buildings, real estate development and speculation, wage differentials and the varying institutional impact of unions across space, the powerful role of sign value and symbolic factors in affecting growth, deindustrialization and the dominance of the global economic level, and the rising affluence of the general population (see Gottdiener [1985] 1994; Gottdiener and Hutchison 1999).

Taken together these new forces and factors have produced a pattern of growth that supersedes the central city and its organizing powers. There is a new form of settlement space. I call it the multi-centered region and it has replaced the central city as the referent for growth.

Characteristics of the Multi-centered Metropolitan Region

The new form of settlement space has not eliminated the classic central city but has only absorbed it in a matrix of increasingly personal, political, and business decisions that has assumed a regional shape. At the same time, every part of this deconcentrated mix has become more functionally specialized since the 1970s, so that, in particular, the historical central city has itself undergone profound change. Furthermore, it is precisely because of the action in space of population and business dispersal, that is, the process of deconcentration, that the new functional specialization of spatial nodes and areas became necessary within expanding metropolitan regions. Consequently the decentralization of both population and societal activities – economic, political, and cultural – and their recentralization in new centers within expanding regions are both functionally related to the more global pattern of deconcentration. Much of the power of the central city prior to the 1960s was its role as the location for manufacturing, office services, finance, retailing, and residential living. Now these same activities are dispersed in a massive regional array. Central cities have become, in turn, more specialized, especially with the loss of their manufacturing base. Now they focus on tourism, finance, business services, information, and the provision of housing for the more affluent segments of the population, most of which do not have children. In some cases, however, types of manufacturing, such as textile and clothing production, which involve low-wage immigrant labor, persist in the central areas of cities despite these counter-trends.

The key characteristic of the new spatial form is that the historical central city no longer organizes growth in the hinterland. In fact, as an extreme example, there are a number of multi-centered metropolitan regions across the country that have no single, large central city at all. These areas are neither suburbs nor cities, yet they are fully urbanized in the developmental sense. Perhaps the best example is Orange County, California (Kling et al. 1991). It had a population of close to 2 million in 1980 but the largest city it contained, Anaheim – the home of Disneyland – had only 219,311 residents in that same year, i.e., about one tenth of the county population. This county, which became an MSA in its own right, is a net employer with an economic base that imported workers from outside the area and which had an employment to residence ratio in 1980 of 0.84, a figure that is larger than many central cities. The county comprises several functionally specialized nodes, like Irvine, which are connected by highways and which provide services and retailing through strip-zoned streets and agglomerations like malls and shopping centers. Although this pattern of development seems to some observers as quite suburban in form, Orange County is not a suburb of Los Angeles. It is an entirely separate area that is culturally, economically, socially, and, of course, politically independent. In sum, Orange County, more so than Los Angeles, exemplifies the new form of settlement space that is, in fact, also characteristic of expanding, massive areas like those containing our older, central cities – the multi-centered metropolitan region.

In 1980 there were at least twenty other areas like Orange County in the United States which were fully urbanized and yet contained no large, central city (Gottdiener and Kephart 1991: *passim*). Eight of these places were in the Sunbelt, but the others, like Fairfield County, Connecticut, were in the region known as the "Rustbelt." Despite having populations that varied from a low of 503,173 (Monmouth County, New Jersey) to a high of 1,932,709 for Orange County in 1980, only one of these areas (Hillsborough County, Florida – the region of Tampa/St. Petersberg) contained a city with more than 20 percent of the total county population. A classic suburb in the outmoded central city model of urbanism would have a very low employment to residence ratio because most of the people living there would be working outside the area. Its "bedroom community" status would be indicated by an employment to residence ratio of well under 50 percent. In our 1980 sample, this ratio varied from a low of 0.54 (Fairfax County, VA) to a high of 0.99 (Montgomery County, PA), a very impressive range that indicates the urbanized and independent quality of these sprawling regions which has undoubtedly been fortified over the last two decades.

Multi-centered regional growth is the spatial pattern characterizing all development in the United States, even those areas that include our largest cities, as indicated above. People no longer need the benefit of living near highly centralized places of employment, retailing, social or business services. Due to the reliance on automobile transportation, people today routinely drive to work, to shop, to obtain needed services, to visit institutions of education or medicine, and to participate in recreational activities. Owing to the functional specialization of multi-centered areas, they visit nodes spread out across an expanding spatial array. Yet, because of the reliance on the car and the expansive nature of the new spatial form, developers have taken advantage of the need for agglomeration and created new centers that offer a variety of economic, social, or cultural opportunities. Perhaps shopping malls are the best example. They draw customers mainly because of the presence of large, so-called "anchor" department stores, but they contain scores, if not hundreds, of smaller shops that also hope to attract consumer dollars. These shops pay rent to the owners of malls and support their concentrated way of doing business. In other cases, counties themselves may provide businesses with special zones that offer reduced taxes, proper transportation infrastructure, and restricted land uses, such as office or industrial parks. These highly specialized nodes are also spread out within the regional mix of the multi-centered region.

Clearly, the dominance of this sprawling growth pattern also results in many problems that can be directly attributed to the use of space. Traffic congestion, such as the serious gridlock conditions in and around Atlanta, Georgia, is just one example. I shall address these matters below, but it is also important to note that none of these emergent concerns that also make up the new urban research agenda is particularly unique in any sense to Los Angeles.

A Typical Multi-centered Region

The LA Schoolers, in their effort to validate their own address, have things backwards. Understanding contemporary urbanism requires us to distance ourselves from any one place and, instead, to appreciate the abstract settlement patterns of the new spatial form. We do need an ideal type, but, as the simplest understanding of that theoretical concept dictates, there is no actually existing place that can be tendered as the model. Instead, all areas should be compared with the tendencies and patterns abstracted as the ideal.

A typical multi-centered region has the following features:

1 There is one (or more) historical central city that once dominated the region but does so no longer.
2 There is a massive, sprawling array of residential developments that mix high- and low-density dwellings and separate centers for retailing, manufacturing, office work, wholesaling, shipping, leisure and cultural activities located throughout the region.
3 These multi-centers vary in scale of development from, for example, immense regional shopping malls, sometimes called "Gallerias", to strip development along shopping streets. Historical centers retain daytime density but have become functionally specialized according to differentiation within the regional array. Cultural and leisure activities have their own centers, such as sports stadiums, concert venues, golf courses, and recreational areas, each varying in their capacity to draw customers.
4 Political jurisdictions produce their own mini-centers of government within the region. Governance itself is fragmented. While in the past local politicians were once capable of commanding prestige and national attention, now even "big city" mayors have lost their national clout. Current political jurisdictions compete with each other for regional resources,

while no single elected official commands a hierarchy of influence powerful enough to command national attention in the delivery of votes. Local politics in the multi-centered region is trivialized and petty, with the county, state, and federal levels acquiring increasingly more power at the expense of the city and other incorporated areas.

5 The aggregated regional array of cities, suburbs, strip-zoned vectors, specialized centers, leisure areas, and dispersed institutional buildings is connected everywhere by expanding networks of automobile-oriented modes of transportation. The multi-centered region is a place of highways, gas stations, feeder roads, connector roads, expressways, service roads, and strip-zoned streets. Access in and out of this baffling, networked array is provided by regional airports that increasingly have taken over the economic functions and the importance of the large, central city (Gottdiener 2001).

Understanding the Sociospatial Forces of Multi-centered Development

Perhaps the most frustrating aspect of the LA Schoolers' discourse is its failure to supply analytical depth. They describe but do not go beyond extolling the virtues of their own location as a place that exemplifies the new urban trends. Their superficiality is a direct consequence of their intentions. By purposely ignoring other urbanists they also ignore what other urbanists do and what they have been doing during the same period in our recent past, namely, studying and researching the forces that are molding and changing our metro regions. Their writings cannot help us understand multi-centered regional life because they do not analyze its underlying dynamics.

The sociospatial forces producing and reproducing the new form of settlement space are well understood (see the summary in Gottdiener and Hutchison 1999: 18) and have been researched by writers from Europe and Latin America as well as the United States. An excellent source of information about these contributors is the membership and activities of the International Sociological Association's Research Committee 21. The factors studied are not simply static categories but frame active research agendas as scholars relate spatial patterns, on the one hand, to the logic of capital, on the other, while also paying attention to empirical facts on the ground in different but related ways. Among the most important forces associated with the understanding of new sociospatial patterns and processes are the following:

1 The role of the interventionist state in the transfer of value and the subsidization of growth – the institutional component of development.

2 The role of capital logic, especially with regard to the development of real estate as a second circuit of capital.
3 The role of location and space as a part of socioeconomic relations.
4 The role of culture and symbols in the development process.
5 The structuration and effects of uneven development, especially as it relates to persisting inequalities in class, race, ethnicity, age, and gender.

It is essential to ignore this formidable research agenda and the incredibly diverse set of writers working in the "new urban" tradition in order for the LA School hypsters to succeed in valorizing their work. However, among urbanists, the above approach is so well known, having been actively refined for several decades, that it is not even necessary to discuss these aspects, but refer to the literature (for a good review, see Harvey 1988; Feagin 1988; Gottdiener and Hutchison 1999; Gottdiener et al. 1999). Instead of reviewing these factors, I shall isolate a few aspects in order to demonstrate the logocentric bias of the LA School discourse and the fallacy of using Los Angeles as an exemplar of twenty-first-century urbanism.

The Multi-centered Form and the Interventionist State

It is often argued that metropolitan regions are a product of capital. Some writers, such as Harvey (1982, 1985a, 1985b, 1996) or Smith (1996) consider this factor exclusively as the determining force. Most of the LA School geographers follow suit (see the work of Scott, Storper, for example). Such economism is wrong. For this reason I like to begin discussions about the causes of contemporary urban development by focusing on the actions of the state, which are not always taken in the service of capital and which are too often overlooked by writers who proclaim "new" modes of production and "new" economic structures as explaining contemporary patterns.

Los Angeles would be only one of several heavily populated southwest areas if it were not for World War II. Because of our fight against Japan, immense resources were committed to the West Coast and the Los Angeles area was a main beneficiary in California because of its excellent rail connections and harbor. Precisely because of the war effort, Los Angeles became a key manufacturing city in the United States. Aerospace, shipbuilding, military hardware manufacturing, and transportation industries grew up there. The government transferred billions of dollars in value to underpin this infrastructure. The scale of this spending activity was unprecedented. An entire steel industry was built from scratch in Fontana, California, outside of San Bernardino, for example, because of this effort. Yet, World War II military spending was just the beginning of government largess. Dollar amounts during the 1940s were dwarfed by spending because of the "Asian" wars that followed – Korea and Vietnam. By the 1970s Los Angeles, in particular, was the direct beneficiary of thirty years of colossal military spending that created a high-technology infrastructure of industries employing highly trained professionals who lived affluent lifestyles. During the period of rapid expansion following the Vietnam War buildup in the 1960s, it seemed like Los Angeles and Orange County military contractors hired entire graduating classes of engineering schools, fueling not only the general trend of deconcentration but also a specific brain drain from the East Coast.

Often overlooked, the transfer of value by the federal government during the successive wars against Asian countries – Japan, Korea [China], Vietnam – is the key factor in Sunbelt growth, because it helped grease the wheels of population and economic deconcentration for decades. State spending aided the economies of Houston, Texas (shipbuilding and shipping), Tampa-St. Petersberg and Pensacola in Florida (defense spending, military bases, and training facilities), Las Vegas, Nevada (military bases, manufacturing), Los Alamos, New Mexico (atomic energy), and along the entire coast of California. Just as significantly, the federal government continues to provide these areas with large sums of money, which represents a transfer of value from other regions of the country because it continues to support active bases for all military branches. If the successful development of the Los Angeles/Riverside/San Diego region, that is, Southern California, seems like a miracle to some, let me remind readers that this place is the location of major military bases with multi-billion dollar annual spending like Camp Pendleton (Marine Corps), Miramar Naval Air Station, the US Naval Air Station on Coronado, March Air Force Base, Norton Air Force Base, Twenty Nine Palms Marine Corps Base, the Long Beach Naval Shipyard, El Toro Marine Air Corps Base, along with many other smaller facilities and other federally supported agencies such as the Jet Propulsion Laboratory near Pasadena.

More familiar ways that the federal government has helped subsidize multi-centered regional growth as the new form of settlement space include the highly critical homeowner tax subsidy, which single-handedly created a mass market for family homes in suburbia, and the national system of defense highways, the Interstate Highway System, which opened up the hinterland of the United States to construction and development of all kinds. These and other spending programs and the transfer of value they represent helped provide the foundation for the settlement patterns we see today in the United States through the spending of billions of dollars. Although private sector business was certainly the means through which much of this spending translated into goods for society, even today we know that military spending is not capitalism but a particular form of state-supported development. The immense outlays of military spending are the means by which geopolitical and regional governmental influence meshes with the perceived needs of a world power guided by elected officials who are tied to special interests working for personal gain. Government spending is not just a branch of capital, as writers like Harvey persist in implying. It is a separate means by which both individuals and companies can become wealthy.

The Role of Real Estate in the Production of the Multi-centered Metropolitan Region

Driving from Santa Monica pier on the westernmost boundary of the Southern California region directly east on Interstate 10, housing developments begin to peter out after Redlands because of the sudden rise in elevation as the crumpled land zone of the San Andreas and its lesser faults tilts the earth, making it difficult to build. That drive is a distance of over 70 miles. But it is absurd to imply, as does the LA School, that this sprawling region of an automobile-oriented settlement space is prototypical as Los Angeles. East Coast regions were there first. How convenient it is for LA hypsters to ignore reference to Jean Gottmann. He wrote his classic, *Megalopolis: The Urbanized Northeastern Region of the United States*, back in 1961 when Los Angeles was mired in Oakie corruption and Zoot Suit riots. All the important ideas, lessons, and implications for future research were already evident in Gottmann's work when he looked at the East Coast from Philadelphia to Boston, a distance of hundreds of miles.

The LA School prefers to take the west-to-east gaze when it valorizes its work. Following the forgotten Gottmann, however, it is equally illuminating to view urbanization from Tijuana, Mexico, in the south all the up through San Diego and its military/education/tourism-based economy, continuing north across the Los Angeles/San Bernardino/Riverside region to the complex of oil/military/education/tourism/agriculture-based economic activities represented by Ventura and Santa Barbara counties. As mentioned above, that south-to-north vector is also Southern California. It is even a more illustrative model of multi-centered space than the west-to-east axis emanating out of Los Angeles.

Multi-centered growth depends on the continual creation of real estate deals, investment in land, political maneuverings to create or change zoning, the selling of single-family housing that eschews larger conceptions of community, bribes, graft, and greed, all of which were discussed in Mike Davis's important book on Los Angeles, *City of Quartz* (1990). But Davis was neither the first person to call this pattern of settlement space production to our attention, nor is the LA case particularly exemplary of this process. The issue raised by the discovery of the second circuit of capital as a central research concern is not which city or area is more illustrative of these shenanigans, but how this process works itself out in place after developing place across the country and from the earliest suburban developments (Gottdiener 1977; Jackson 1985) to the present (Feagin 1983; Fishman 1987; Frug 1997). By attempting to validate the opposite emphasis, in order to valorize the work of a select group located in a particular place, the LA Schoolers miss the most significant research implication of contemporary real estate development patterns. Quite literally, the important theory of Henri Lefebvre and its refinement by subsequent writers on the ubiquitous use of real estate as a means to acquire profits, which is studied seriously by scholars from Singapore to Seattle, from Hollywood to Helsinki, from New York to São Paulo, and from London to Moscow, seems to pass over the heads of these LA School avatars.

The Role of Space in the Production of the Multi-centered Region

A decentered space, which is no longer structured by forces dominating from the center, is a region that is subjected to locational competition in all its aspects. Within the multi-centered region space is important because there is locational competition and no single place is inherently valorized. In the past people would automatically travel "downtown" to the department stores of the central city in order to pursue retail shopping. Now people no longer view downtown as a magnet. They have their choice of immense retail shopping malls that are scattered around the expanding region and each of these constitutes a separate center, a destination that needs to attract people in order for it to remain economically viable. Competition across space, the dilemma of spatial distance between customer and retailer, is the very essence of profit-making within the multi-centered region. Even as malls have worked hard to succeed by becoming destinations, they now face the added competition from Internet sellers who have annihilated space completely. Shopping in the multi-centered region is about space – its transcendence, its valorization as a unique location, and, today, its eradication through electronic means.

Is LA the exemplar of this process? What could have possessed the LA Schoolers to make this claim? To be sure, Jameson (1984) encountered the "hyperspace" of postmodernism at the Bonaventure Hotel in "downtown" Los Angeles, and this inspired his classic article. But this visit was the result of meetings held by the Modern Language Association in that particular place. He could have encountered the same kind of experience had he checked into Portman's San Francisco Hyatt, which, in its own way, is even more illustrative of the hyperspatial sublime that turned Jameson on.

In Chicago, Montreal, Toronto, São Paulo, Minneapolis, and Kuala Lumpur, for example, a visitor can find the same kind of disorienting postmodernism produced by the built environment. The issue, again, is not what is so prototypical of Los Angeles in this regard, but what is so essential to contemporary economies that they have redefined space – the space of shopping, tourism, leisure, banking, and entertainment – so that the classic elements of modernism simply no longer exist or are even viewed as necessary by capital as a means of organizing and signifying social activities?

Multi-centeredness and Multiculturalism

Both Dear and Soja emphasize the point that Los Angeles represents a new spatial and institutional array produced by immigrant groups who are different than those who have shaped other, especially older, cities. They ignore work elsewhere that demonstrates the same pattern existing in places like New York City and Chicago. Korean grocers, East Indian newspaper shops, and Arab-run convenience stores are increasingly the markers of inner-city business throughout the United States. Nomadology practice provides the empirical evidence to question the LA School premise through examples from abroad as well. I have been driven by Iraqi cab drivers in both Stockholm and Manhattan, served by Italian waiters in both London and São Paulo, and bought convenience store goods or pizza from businesses owned by East Indians, Jamaicans, Iranians, Koreans, Nigerians, and Russians in entrepot cities from Toronto to Helsinki.

Soja (2000) reaches to say something profound by selectively focusing on Los Angeles-based research regarding the political and cultural implications of the new immigration. His points are lost on readers who know about literature reporting research in other places. The issue of governance and multiculturalism has been treated by Green and Wilson (1992), Kasinitz (1992), and Sleeper (1990), among many others, for the case of New York. Miami is covered by Portes and Stepick (1993) and Abrahamson (1996); San Francisco by Loo (1991).

A number of studies have also highlighted the settlement of suburbia by new immigrants as a means of countering the conception that all new arrivals settle first in the inner city (Horton 1992; Fong 1994; Gottdiener and Hutchison 1999). Finally, the claim that inequality is no longer correlated to ethnicity by Soja (2000: 289) as being something new and exemplified by the Los Angeles case seems odd when other literature on the new immigration is examined and placed in a global context (see Appadurai 1996; Gottdiener and Hutchison 1999).

In short, as with other aspects of the claim to exemplariness and distinction made by the LA School hypsters, an informed reading of recent research highlights new processes relating multiculturalism to sociospatial effects within metropolitan areas, rather than the putative uniqueness of the Los Angeles experience alone.

The Role of Culture/Symbols in the Production of the Built Environment

Quite obviously, as an urban scholar I have taken the claims of the LA School personally. But I have many reasons for doing so. Perhaps the one most current is the way LA Schoolers write about a new, "postmodern" city as exemplified by Los Angeles. Their city-centric discourse aside, can there be anything more exemplary of postmodernism in this regard than Las Vegas (Gottdiener et al. 1999)? Based as it is on the casino-gambling economy, Las Vegas is nothing if not the true exemplar of the particular cultural forces that LA Schoolers have in mind. As Venturi, Brown, and Izenour (1972) taught us many years ago, we learn from Las Vegas, not LA. Significantly, however, Las Vegas is a multi-centered region, not a city. Most of the people live and most of the action takes place outside the downtown city boundaries. The famous Las Vegas Strip, overwhelmingly the most popular destination for tourists, is not located within the city limits. It is in the multi-centered region known as Clark County. The Las Vegas lived space of housing development, encompassing almost 2 million permanent residents, spreads west to the mountains (Summerhill), south (Spring Valley), north (North Las Vegas), and east (Green Valley and Henderson). It is the fastest-growing area in the United States. The region is beset by multicultural waves of new immigrants. It receives from five to six thousand new residents a month, although a thousand or more also leave. It gets over 35 million tourists a year. And almost every job, every dollar earned, is based on casino gambling – an economic activity that produces no product and no value.

Is the attempt to valorize Los Angeles by the very "postmodern" LA Schoolers just a desperate act in the face of new landscapes like Las Vegas, Nevada, and Orlando, Florida? Maybe not. But ignoring first-rate and finely grained case studies of these "other" areas (Zukin 1991; Gottdiener et al. 1999) is no way to advance their argument.

Cultural signs are important to an understanding of multi-centered regions because the spatial competition, which is at its core, is dependent on symbols. This is especially true for retailing and consumerism. Consumption today is fueled by media images and effected by themed environments, which are the new consumer spaces of our society (Zukin 1995; Gottdiener 1997, 2000). Franchising structures the delivery of services (Ritzer 1999). Our environment is increasingly themed and McDonaldized. This fact is as evident anywhere in the United States as it is in Los Angeles. Is LA particularly exemplary of this trend? Hardly. By focusing instead on the process, as I have repeatedly suggested, we discover that it is theming and franchising which provide a crucial dimension to the organization of the new form of settlement space. Ironically, it is this same theming and franchising that also annihilates the uniqueness of place. The same firms – selling hamburgers, ethnic foods, clothing, furniture, jewelry, loans, cars, and cold cream – can be found in large malls or along commercially zoned strips everywhere in the country. One place, any place, has begun to look just like any other place in the nation. As Ritzer (1999) points out, this process of McDonaldization has recently been extended to the delivery of social services like healthcare and education. Presciently observed by Edward Relph almost thirty years ago (1976), we struggle in the new multi-centered environment to orient ourselves between Place and Placelessness, among the built structures that are the same everywhere, like McDonald's fast-food outlets or the scary familiarity of mall shops, and those elements within our daily purview that are not only signifiers of locality and uniqueness but to which we have grown attached as a marker of our own existence in space. Los Angeles is neither the earliest version of this existential struggle – "there is no there, there" was how Gertrude Stein described Oakland – nor particularly exemplary of its many dimensions.

Beyond LA Hype

The Chicago School's urban theory has been dead since the 1930s. An "LA School" exists in the mind of only a few geographers. But the "new urban" approach has been around for over two decades and counts political scientists, sociologists, geographers, and others among its adherents. Despite the ongoing research, the urban field remains weak and the LA School approach is a strong indicator, because it is so confused about its real object of analysis. Some of these problems about identifying empirical and theoretical objects of analysis for a uniquely "urban" science were already discussed in a penetrating and insightful way in the early work of Manuel Castells ([1972] 1977; see also Pickvance 1977). Yet we still lack a consensually understood real object of analysis that can ground contemporary work. Much research by urbanists today persists in being bound up by the "city" as the object of analysis. While "region" is a useful counter-term, broadening the city-based approach in the right conceptual direction, it is much too amorphous. I believe my term, the multi-centered metropolitan region, is both specific enough and conceptually accurate enough to qualify as the new object of analysis that urban science now needs.

Of course, it is always possible to continue to talk about "the city," and, indeed, with its new, more specialized functional array, bounded areas like the City of London, Manhattan, The Loop of Chicago, the Market Street section of San Francisco, downtown Minneapolis, and Burbank, Hollywood, West Los Angeles, and the "downtown" section of Los Angeles within the LA region, are all important in their own right as places to observe urban processes. However, the argument above pleads for a view that places structurational processes first. No actually existing city is the exemplar of the new social forces remaking settlement space because, as the most basic understanding of such theoretical arguments claims, an object cannot be both actually existing and an ideal type. Even to pose this question, as the LA School has done, reveals a basic, fundamental ignorance of the real issues facing urban analysis today. Significantly more critical is the advancement by urbanists everywhere of our understanding of the processes that have worked and reworked settlement space by increasing its scale, fragmenting its communities and nodal points of interaction; by decentralizing its businesses and then recentralizing them in new, functionally specialized nodes; by perfecting a cultural array of themes that organizes business through franchising, centralized malls and decentralized strip zones; by fragmenting populations according to class, race, ethnicity, and even age; by producing uneven development and reproducing social inequalities across the generations; and, finally, by making it increasingly difficult for society to deal adequately with problems related to environmental quality, equality, governance, the quality of community life, the issue of social mobility, public transportation, and civic culture. In the forthcoming productions of urbanists everywhere, I look forward to substantial contributions to this research agenda.

Bibliography

Abrahamson, M. 1996: *Urban Enclaves: Identity and Place in America.* New York: St. Martin's Press.

Alihan, M. 1938: *Social Ecology.* New York: Columbia University Press.

Appadurai, A. 1996: *Modernity at Large.* Minneapolis: University of Minnesota Press.

Castells, M. [1972] 1977: *The Urban Question: A Marxist Approach.* Cambridge, MA: MIT Press.

Crump, S. 1962: *Ride the Big Red Cars: How Trolleys Helped Build Southern California.* Los Angeles, CA: Crest Publications.

Davie, M. 1937: The pattern of urban growth. In G. Murdock (ed.), *Studies in the Science of Society.* New Haven, CT: Yale University Press.

Davis, M. 1990: *City of Quartz: Excavating the Future in Los Angeles.* London: Verso.

Feagin, J. R. 1983: *The Urban Real Estate Game.* Englewood Cliffs, NJ: Prentice-Hall.

—— 1988: *Houston: The Free Enterprise City.* New Brunswick, NJ: Rutgers University Press.

Firey, W. 1945: *Land Use in Central Boston.* Cambridge, MA: Harvard University Press.

Fishman, R. 1987: *Bourgeois Utopias: The Rise and Fall of Suburbia.* New York: Basic Books.

Fong, T. 1994: *The First Suburban Chinatown.* Philadelphia, PA: Temple University Press.

Form, W. 1954: The place of social structure in the determination of land use. *Social Forces* 32: 317–23.

Frug, G. 1997: New urbanism or new suburbanism. *Harvard Design Magazine* (Winter/Spring): 54.

Gettys, W. 1940: Human ecology and social theory. *Social Forces* 18: 469–76.

Gottdiener, M. 1977: *Planned Sprawl: Public and Private Interests in Suburbia*. Beverly Hills, CA: Sage.

—— [1985] 1994: *The Social Production of Urban Space*, 2nd ed. Austin, TX: University of Texas Press.

—— 1997: *The Theming of America*. Boulder, CO: Westview.

—— 2000: *New Forms of Consumption: Consumers, Culture and Commodification*. Lanham, MD: Rowman and Littlefield.

—— 2001: *Life in the Air: Surviving the New Culture of Air Travel*. Lanham, MD: Rowman and Littlefield.

—— and Feagin, J. R. 1988: The paradigm shift in urban sociology. *Urban Affairs Quarterly* 24: 163–87.

—— and Hutchison, R. [1994] 1999: *The New Urban Sociology*, 2nd ed. New York: McGraw-Hill.

—— and Kephart, G. 1991: The multi-centered metropolitan region: a comparative analysis. In R. Kling et al., *Postsuburban California*. Berkeley, CA: University of California Press, 31–54.

—— et al. 1999: *Las Vegas: The Social Production of an All-American City*. Oxford: Blackwell.

Gottmann, J. 1961: *Megalopolis: The Urbanized Northeastern Region of the United States*. Cambridge, MA: MIT Press.

Green, C. and Wilson, B. 1992: *The Struggle for Black Empowerment in New York City*. New York: McGraw-Hill.

Harris, C. and Ullman E. 1945: The nature of cities. *Annals of the Academy of Political and Social Science* 242: 7–17.

Harvey, D. 1973: *Social Justice and the City*. Baltimore, MD: Johns Hopkins University Press.

—— 1982: The urban process under capitalism. In M. Dear and A. Scott (eds.), *Urbanization and Urban Planning in Capitalist Society*. New York: Methuen, 91–122.

—— 1985a: *The Urbanization of Capital*. Baltimore, MD: Johns Hopkins University Press.

—— 1985b: *Consciousness and the Urban Experience*. Baltimore, MD: Johns Hopkins University Press.

—— 1988: *The Condition of Postmodernity*. Oxford: Blackwell.

—— 1996: Social justice, postmodernism and the city. In S. Fainstein and S. Campbell (eds.), *Readings in Urban Theory*. Oxford: Blackwell, 415–35.

Horton, J. 1992: The politics of diversity in Monterey Park, California. In L. Lamphere (ed.), *Structuring Diversity*. Chicago: University of Chicago Press.

Hoyt, H. 1933: *One Hundred Years of Land Values in Chicago*. Chicago: University of Chicago Press.

Jackson, K. 1985: *Crab Grass Frontier: The Suburbanization of the US*. New York: Oxford University Press.

Jameson, F. 1984: Postmodernism, or the cultural logic of late capitalism. *New Left Review* 146: 53–92.

Kasinitz, P. 1992: *Caribbean New York: Black Immigrants and the Politics of Race.* Ithaca, NY: Cornell University Press.
Kling, R., Olin, S., and Poster, M. 1991: *Postsuburban California: The Transformation of Orange County Since WWII.* Berkeley, CA: University of California Press.
Lefebvre, H. 1992: *The Production of Space.* Oxford: Blackwell.
Loo, C. 1991: *Chinatown.* New York: Praeger.
Miller, D. W. 2000. The new urban studies. *Chronicle of Higher Education*, August 18.
Pickvance, C. (ed.) 1977: *Urban Sociology: Critical Essays.* New York: St. Martin's Press.
Portes, A. and Stepick, A. 1993: *City on the Edge.* Berkeley, CA: University of California Press.
Relph, E. 1976: *Place and Placelessness.* Harmondsworth: Penguin.
Ritzer, G. 1999: *McDonaldization.* Newbury Park, CA: Pine Forge.
Sleeper, J. 1990: *The Closest of Strangers.* New York: W. W. Norton.
Smith, N. 1996: Gentrification, the frontier, and the restructuring of urban space. In S. Fainstein and S. Campbell (eds.), *Readings in Urban Theory.* Oxford: Blackwell, 338–58.
Soja, E. 2000: *Postmetropolis: Critical Studies of Cities and Regions.* Oxford: Blackwell.
Venturi, R., Brown, S., and Izenour, S. 1972: *Learning From Las Vegas.* Cambridge, MA: MIT Press.
Walker, R. 1981: A theory of suburbanization. In M. Dear and A. Scott (eds.), *Urbanization and Urban Planning in Capitalist Society.* New York: Methuen.
Warner, S. B. 1962: *Streetcar Suburbs.* Cambridge, MA: Harvard University Press.
Wollen, P. 1993: *Raiding the Ice Box.* London: Verso.
Zukin, S. 1991: *Landscapes of Power.* Berkeley, CA: University of California Press.
—— 1995: *The Cultures of Cities.* Oxford: Blackwell.

Part IV
Urban Research in Particular Regions of the Globe

9

State Socialism, Post-socialism and their Urban Patterns: Theorizing the Central and Eastern European Experience

Chris Pickvance

This chapter will look at Central and Eastern Europe as a context for theorizing about state socialism and post-socialism, and their associated urban patterns. In particular it will ask whether there are state socialist patterns of urban development and urban spatial structure, and how we are to understand post-socialist patterns of development.

The study of urban processes in Central and Eastern Europe has had a perhaps unexpectedly significant impact on urban studies. This has been so at two periods: in the state socialist period and the post-socialist period. I shall argue that, paradoxically, social science and urban studies have proved more able to make sense of the former period than the latter. We consider the two periods in turn.

The State Socialist Period

In 1972 Castells argued that "whereas the theory of the capitalist mode of production has been elaborated, at least in part (especially as far as its economic sphere is concerned) by Marx, in *Capital*, the theory of the socialist mode of production exists only in an embryonic state" (1972: 90). Hence, he argued, the term "socialist" lacked analytical power. Following this one might have expected that what came to be termed "state socialist"[1] societies would be neglected by sociologists. In fact they were the object of considerable attention, both empirical and theoretical, among sociologists in the region, and it was the social networks linking these sociologists to those in the West that resulted in the debate about state socialist societal and urban development becoming central to international debates in urban sociology. (Amiot's [1986] account of the development of urban sociology in France devotes a whole chapter to this contribution.)

The empirical issues in this debate were the pattern of urban development, the allocation of housing, and urban spatial patterns. Underlying them were the theoretical issues of the role of the state and the nature of state socialism. I will explore how each of these issues was analyzed and how this affected the theoretical development of urban sociology.

First, a word is necessary about the family resemblance among state socialist societies. Writers on state socialist societies approach them using a theoretical model of state socialism which has the following structural features:

- an economy in which all units are state-owned;
- central planning of these units;
- a polity in which the Communist Party has a monopolistic position;
- an integration of party and state structures into an intertwined whole. (Kornai 1992)[2]

Deviations between the model and reality (such as, in different cases, the existence of significant private ownership in agriculture, in small-scale industrial and service provision, or in housing; loosened forms of economic planning; or the toleration of political dissent and citizen organizations) are then explained as due to:

- the complexity of the real world compared with the abstraction of any model;
- the successive phases of development of state socialism, which bring with them different policy priorities. The phases of state socialist development may or may not be seen as necessary phases, i.e., involving unilinear evolution. For example, forced or accelerated industrialization is generally identified as the priority after the Communist Party's assumption of power; and central economic planning could be expected to undergo some loosening as its weaknesses become apparent;
- the admixture of non-state socialist forms due to the "legacy" of pre-socialist forms and/or to the emergence (and authorities' tolerance) of capitalist forms during state socialism.

We now examine in turn writing on underurbanization, housing distribution, and spatial structure.

Underurbanization as the state socialist form of urban development

Before examining interpretations of state socialist urban development a brief digression is necessary on theories of urbanization in the Third World. Early writers on Third World urbanization treated the path of Western economic development as a model to be followed by all other societies and "modernization theory" sought to identify the various conditions which had been present in Western industrialization in order that newly industrializing countries could follow in their footsteps. Among the conditions of successful "take-off" was a proportionate relation between industrialization and urbanization (Reissman 1964). In other words, it was argued that there should be a positive relationship between industrialization (the proportion of the working population employed in manufacturing) and urbanization (the proportion of the population living in urban areas). This could be expressed as a straight diagonal line on a graph of these two variables and represented the path taken by Western countries as they industrialized. Significant deviation from this path was seen as inimical to successful industrialization.

Davis and Golden (1954) introduced the term "overurbanization" to describe the position of any country that deviated from this line in the direction of having a higher level of urbanization than was warranted by its level of industrialization, a situation to be avoided if at all possible. The assumptions behind the concept of overurbanization, and the concept itself, were challenged by Sovani (1964) on both theoretical and empirical grounds, but this did not stop the concept gaining acceptance. Sovani pointed out that "on the other side of the regression line there would be cases of 'underurbanization'" (1964: 115) but did not cite any examples.

This gap was filled in 1974 when Konrad and Szelenyi identified underurbanization as the characteristic pattern of state socialist societies.[3] They argued that the level of urbanization in such societies was less than was typical of Western societies at the same level of economic development.[4] This statistical observation was the point of departure for some very interesting analyses of urbanization in the state socialist world in which economists were as prominent as sociologists.[5]

Economists gave an economic interpretation of the statistical fact of underurbanization in Central and Eastern Europe by linking it with the investment priorities characteristic of (at least one phase of) state socialism. They argued that these societies had gone through a "forced growth" phase with high levels of investment and low levels of consumption, and that in order to industrialize as fast as possible they had concentrated their investment in manufacturing industry, and especially in heavy industry, in line with the Marxist idea that nonmaterial products such as services did not form part of national output (Kornai 1992: ch. 9). The corollary of this was that there was underinvestment in "infrastructure." This term has always been defined broadly but has been measured in different ways. Measures of the level of transport, communications, housing, health, and education provision per capita in 1974 showed Eastern European countries below the trend line for all countries (Ehrlich and Szilagyi 1980; Csizmadia, Ehrlich, and Partos 1984).

To make sense of these investment and underurbanization patterns compared with market economies at the same economic level, Ofer (1976, 1977) put forward the hypothesis that they were due to an implicit state socialist policy of "economizing on urbanization." By this he meant that in order to maximize investment in industry the associated costs of infrastructure were held down. This was done by (1) restricting expenditure on infrastructure and services per urban resident; (2) keeping down the ratio of nonproductive to productive urban workers (e.g., by encouraging high rates of female participation in the labor force); and (3) restricting the number of rural to urban migrants (partly because infrastructure costs in rural areas were much lower). Ofer, however, also pointed out that there was a pattern of underurbanization in pre-socialist Eastern Europe and that state socialist policy was facilitated by this.[6]

Sociologists also emphasized underurbanization but drew attention to its social effects. The first of these was that the urban housing stock was insufficient to house those employed in urban areas. This was despite the fact that state housebuilding was concentrated in the cities at the expense of the rural areas, reflecting the ideology in the 1950s–1970s that state housing investment should primarily support industrial growth. The result was a serious urban housing shortage. Young couples had to live as "concealed households" with their parents before they could acquire a place of their own. The typical wait for a state flat in the 1980s ranged from three to four years in East Germany to fifteen to thirty years in Poland (Kornai 1992: 234). And finally, the housing shortage also encouraged overcrowding and subletting.

The second effect of underurbanization was the growth of commuting from rural areas. This was a "solution" for those who could not get urban housing. Research showed that they were poor, unlike Western commuters, most of whom choose to commute. In rural areas infrastructure was worse than in the cities, so these commuters experienced a double disadvantage (Konrad and Szelenyi 1974). Some have argued that these commuters were not as badly off as suggested since rural dwellings were often larger and had a garden that could be cultivated or enjoyed, and because the person commuting had some access to urban facilities (Wiles 1974).

Third, the underurbanization policy required a control system to prevent rural residents moving to urban areas. This operated via a requirement to have a registered place of residence. The corresponding document or "internal passport" gave people a right of residence in a particular place and in principle gave the authorities control of the location of the population. In practice it was far from fully effective (French 1995: 99–100). In particular, enterprises were motivated to evade the registration system in order to secure labor owing to the shortage of labor and the penalties they faced for nonfulfillment of production quotas. Fictitious marriages were another such response. Similarly, individuals could evade control by living at places other than those where they were registered. In other words, the paper control required extensive checking to back it up which would have been very labor intensive. Thus, urban residence became a privilege since it meant access to better housing and other infrastructures as well as more job opportunities.

In sum, a distinctive pattern of urbanization, underurbanization, was identified as a feature of state socialist societies in Eastern Europe and was linked theoretically to the nature of the state socialist system, particularly in its "forced growth" phase, and to its requirement to "economize on urbanization."[7]

A further development of this argument was made by Murray and Szelenyi (1984), who identified four distinct phases of urbanization in the socialist world: deurbanization and zero-urban growth phases (in Asian socialist countries only), underurbanization, and "socialist intensive urbanization." Although they use the term "phase," they do not imply a unilinear evolution in which all state socialist societies go through all phases. As far as Eastern Europe is concerned, their main contribution is to identify the "socialist intensive urbanization" phase in which, in contrast to the underurbanization phase, industrial employment stops rising as a share and starts to decline and infrastructure investment increases. This is exemplified by Hungary from the late 1960s. This raises an interesting question of interpretation. One possibility is to say that socialist intensive urbanization occurs when state socialism has moved out of the forced growth stage and gives greater priority to consumption and services, in which case it is a step on the way to what Murray and Szelenyi call "fully developed socialism." Another possibility they consider is that it is a step toward capitalism, in favor of which they note that it coincides with a period in which a private economic sector based on small-scale activity was allowed to develop and became a significant source of personal income. This in turn allowed people to save and build houses, thus contributing to infrastructure investment. On balance they reject this interpretation.

In sum, the study of state socialist urbanization has led to a widening of existing studies of urbanization and industrialization and the identification of a generic pattern directly attributable to state socialism in its forced growth phase. The power of this analysis is shown by the way it has been used to reinterpret Chinese urbanization between the late 1950s (the end of Soviet influence) and 1979 (the start of the reform period). For a long time this period was interpreted as showing a "Chinese road to socialism" inspired by Mao Zedong. Chan's (1994) analysis, however, makes clear that there was a vast gap between Mao's statements and the continuous emphasis on industrialization based on heavy industry throughout this period, which even reached a peak at the very time (1958–62) that the Great Leap Forward was announced, based on small-scale rural industrialization (Chan 1994: 61).[8] Chan shows that Chinese urbanization and economic development can largely be understood in terms of the "economizing on urbanization" model familiar from Eastern Europe.

A final point about the work on state socialist urbanization is that, apart from the writing which accepted a Chinese road to socialism just mentioned, it did not give weight to cultural differences. The approach used was rigorously political economic. Ideological statements by the regimes were not given any special explanatory value but were tested against empirical evidence as far as this was possible.

State socialist housing allocation

A second major theme in writing on Eastern Europe was the distribution of housing. Left critics of welfare capitalism were interested in the performance of states in state socialist societies but treated them as representing only one version of socialism rather than what could ideally happen under a socialist system. In state socialist societies, on the other hand, the prevailing ideology stressed that unemployment and poverty had been abolished and that housing had been taken out of the market and was available at very low rents. But there was no empirical research to explore such claims until a pathbreaking 1968 housing study conducted by Szelenyi in Hungary. The design of Szelenyi's study was simple: a survey of residents in two provincial cities to establish what social groups lived in what housing. This study provided a chance to see how state socialism worked in practice and extended the debate about the role of the state to state socialist societies. In addition, it used the concepts such as "housing class" and "redistribution" familiar in UK urban research.

Weberian writers, such as Pahl (1975), had generalized from the notion of access to housing controlled by gatekeepers to the idea of "urban resources" controlled by "urban managers" and had argued that their decisions could either exacerbate, reproduce, or reduce income inequalities, or, in another language, have regressive, reproductive, or redistributive effects. For Pahl, urban managers were the "independent variable" in urban resource allocation and their decisions would reflect their professional values. Marxist writers, on the other hand, rejected this model, insisting that the idea of resource blurred the distinction between private and state sectors, and that the role of state officials was not independent but determined by the broader role of the capitalist state. In particular the balance between redistributive and regressive allocation would depend on the changing state of class relations.

The concept of "housing class" was introduced by Rex and Moore (1967) to refer to combinations of housing tenure categories, house types, and locations within two ranking systems (private and state). It was opposed by other Weberians for misunderstanding Weber's distinction between class and status

Table 9.1 The housing situation of different occupational groups in two provincial cities in Hungary in 1968 (row percentages)

Occupation	*% with per capita income over 1,200 forints*	*% tenants of state flats*	*% in best state flats*	*% in worst state flats*	*% owners*
High bureaucrat	71	59	48	10	34
Clerical	40	54	46	5	35
Skilled manual	33	40	25	12	49
Unskilled manual	18	36	23	12	52

Source: Szelenyi (1983: tables 2.3, 2.5, 2.11).

group, and by Marxists for its use of the word class outside the work sphere and for suggesting that housing classes might be the base of significant conflict.

To apply the housing class concept, Szelenyi's study identified three main categories of urban housing: state-owned housing (built and financed by the state, or prewar housing which had been nationalized); cooperative housing built using state loans to individuals; and private housing built using a mixture of state loans to individuals and private savings. However, the question of how to measure housing quality to establish a hierarchy of housing-class situations proved a difficult one to resolve. Since rents were low and were based on floor space, but not on quality, location (centrality), or age, they were not a good guide to differences in quality. Instead, to measure quality differences, Szelenyi used the degree of state subsidy embodied in the dwelling. This was equated with the gap between the rent paid and the economic cost of construction, or the interest rate subsidy in the case of houses built with loans. However, it was an imperfect measure of quality or use value. For example, a flat with a good location but built pre-1900 or a spacious prewar owner-occupied house with no subsidy would show up as less subsidized and thus of lower quality than a modern but perhaps peripherally located flat which was costly to build. Nevertheless, the study was an attempt to tackle a hitherto unstudied phenomenon, housing differentiation under state socialism.

Some of the results are shown in table 9.1. This table shows the income differentiation of four occupational groups (column 2) and for each group the proportion in different types of housing (columns 3–6). The striking result is that high bureaucrats were more likely to be state tenants and to occupy the best state flats (measured as explained) than unskilled manual workers, while the latter were more likely to live in owner-occupied housing.

Szelenyi describes this as a regressive pattern of distribution, since those with most income are gaining most (in terms of subsidy) from housing allocation, and those with the lowest incomes are gaining least. He considers three explanations for this: (1) that it is accidental; (2) that it is due to official corruption; and (3) that it is a systematic result of state socialism. He argues that the evidence is too systematic for the result to be accidental and that officials had previously operated fairly. He concludes that it is a product of a state socialist system facing an enormous shortage (as described earlier) and having to find an additional criterion by which to allocate housing. This was "social merit," which translated into priority for people doing "important" jobs. The fact that workplaces could influence housing allocation (and indeed, in many countries owned large shares of the housing stock) facilitated this influence. Councils were more likely to allocate according to need. Szelenyi's analysis was thus closely related to the UK work at the same time and this led to many exchanges between urban sociologists in Eastern and Western Europe. These centered, for example, on whether differences in the working of housing allocation were due to differences in economic level (as Pahl argued) or to differences in socioeconomic system (as Szelenyi argued).

Based on this work but also drawing on similar findings elsewhere in Eastern Europe, Szelenyi (1978) developed a theoretical conception of the state socialist system as distributing resources in an inherently regressive way. The structural bias in this direction he attributed to the power of a new social category (party and state officials, and enterprise managers), who channeled state resources to their own advantage.[9]

This provoked a debate in Hungary and elsewhere about the accuracy and/or inevitability of this pattern. (Interestingly, Szelenyi's equation of housing quality with subsidy level was challenged by Hegedus and Tosics [1983] but not turned into a major line of criticism.) Other Hungarian researchers pointed out that the 1970s reforms of state housing opened the sector up to poorer households (Tosics 1987). However, Szelenyi (1987) replied that (1) this was only so because of a large expansion of housebuilding and (2) subsidized loans were now available in the private sector, which would help better-off groups.

In fact, Szelenyi argued that the better off had four advantages over time: the initial allocation of better-quality state flats, the greater possibility of moving into the private sector using a subsidized grant, the possibility of cashing in the value of their tenancy when they made this move and "sold" their tenancy on the informal market, or, if they remained in the state sector, the chance of privatizing their flat – see below. The result was that throughout the 1970s and 1980s the better-off groups became spread across the best housing in both state and private sectors.

Writers on welfare policy more generally challenged Szelenyi and argued that social security payments did not show the pattern he was suggesting, but he countered by arguing that in a lot of services (access to the best schools, medical care, etc.) a regressive pattern could be found. Both sides in this debate made valid points, but the lack of systematic data on access to services meant that the debate was never finally resolved. However, the question of whether a debate about trends in Hungary was a debate about the character of state socialism was left aside. Like China today, Hungary in the 1980s was politically socialist but in economic terms the private sector had grown to a significant size.

Finally, the debate about housing stratification raised a provocative question for comparative method. Did the fact that housing distribution seemed to be status-based in Central and Eastern Europe as well as in the "West" show that differences in socioeconomic system were irrelevant and that a status-based housing distribution followed from some common feature of the societies concerned, for example, the fact that they were industrial? In answering this question using comparative method as conventionally practiced, the answer would have to be yes, since common effects must have common causes. But it is clear that this methodological assumption is too strong and excludes a frequent occurrence, namely, that similar features are produced by different causal processes in different societies. This led to the introduction of an additional form of comparative analysis based on the idea of plural causation (see Pickvance 1986, 2001a).

In this debate urban sociology transcended the narrow topic of housing allocation to raise major issues about the character of state intervention and resource distribution in different types of society. In this way it came close to central macrosociological debates and made major contributions to the theories of the state then being developed.

Residential social segregation

A third body of writing concerned the question of whether there was a specifically state socialist residential social pattern. The reason for thinking that there might be is that under state socialism all economic enterprises are in principle state-owned, as are housing and land. In theory, therefore, the party-state could pursue social objectives through its planning and building powers without obstruction from private owners, and without having to think of land costs. This could lead to a more balanced pattern of regional economic development, and a pattern of urban land use which avoided the marked residential social segregation found in capitalist societies. For reasons of space this section does not cover aspects of land use beyond residential patterns (on which, see French and Hamilton 1979; French 1995; Smith 1996).

French and Hamilton have written that "everywhere, social segregation in the socialist city is absent or very greatly diminished, although in each city there is a tendency for some social segregation by apartment building to be found" (1979: 16). But is this the case? We will consider in turn evidence and explanations.

Although there are problems in comparing studies which measure residential social segregation,[10] a number of general conclusions can be safely drawn. The studies of Budapest by Ladanyi (1989), Moscow by French (1995), Prague by Mateju, Vecernik, and Jerabek (1979), and Warsaw by Dangschat (1987) find that:

- there was residential segregation in the state socialist period but its level was lower in the 1950s–1970s than in the interwar pre-socialist period (Prague, Budapest);
- there were different degrees of segregation among social groups, which follow a U-shaped curve. In Budapest and Warsaw the most highly educated groups were most segregated, the intermediate groups were least segregated, and the lowest-educated groups were more segregated than the latter but not as much as the former;[11]
- levels of segregation declined between 1970 and 1980 (Budapest, Prague);
- there is also some suggestion that segregation is by block or building scheme in Warsaw and Moscow;
- there is evidence of sectoral patterns of social segregation in Moscow (Smith 1994: 193–202).

How do these findings relate to the quotation from French and Hamilton? Actual patterns of residential segregation depend on:

- How party-states dealt with the existing housing stock when they assumed power, and, in particular, whether a private housing sector was allowed to continue, and if so, under what conditions.
- How extensive war damage and the need for reconstruction were.
- What volume and types of new housing were built, where, and of what quality. For example, some inner-city private redevelopment could lead to reduced social segregation.
- What the respective roles of workplaces (such as state enterprises and administrations) and local governments were in building and allocation.
- What demolition occurred and where.
- What encouragement was given to new building by the private sector.
- How far households could move through informal processes, thus changing initial patterns of housing distribution.

There is no space to explore all these points. Only the third and fourth points, which are probably most closely linked to the nature of state socialism, and the last, which relates to how households cope with the housing situation they face, will be discussed.

Housebuilding and residential social segregation. Within state socialist societies resources for housebuilding could be channeled to ministries and state enterprises or to councils.[12] The former channel had priority as part of the pursuit of rapid industrialization. The housing funds allocated to workplaces were used to help them house and maintain their own workforces. They did not have to pursue wider social goals through housing, as did councils. Beyond housing they built preschool facilities to help recruit female workers and also equipped the neighborhood with facilities, giving rise to interneighborhood differences in quality of schools, social facilities, and so on.

This explains how block and neighborhood-based differentiation could occur as ministries and enterprises used land allocated to them to build a series of blocks for their workers, irrespective of what was happening on neighboring land. As Shomina writes:

> Soviet cities cannot be divided into [areas] on the basis of income levels or ethnic composition. However the boundaries of districts associated with well-off factories can be distinguished quite clearly: these [areas] are set apart by their attractive modern buildings, by the presence of diverse cultural facilities, shops, child-care centres and so on, while in districts linked to poor enterprises the housing needs repair and cultural facilities may be entirely lacking. (1992: 226)

The most systematic evidence of this type of segregation emerges from a Chinese study, where the same financing pattern operated, which found that the facilities in a neighborhood depended on the status of the enterprise or administrative body that funded it and that this was the driving force in residential social segregation (Logan and Bian 1993). In other words, where people lived and what neighborhood facilities they had depended on their workplace and not on their occupation.

This pattern of what may be called "enterprise-driven residential social segregation" is most likely to occur in societies where most funding for housing is channeled via the workplace. The USSR probably ranked highest in this respect, since even in 1980 three-quarters of all state sector urban housing was owned by enterprises, administrations, and other workplaces, while only a quarter was owned by local councils (Andrusz 1984).[13] These proportions had changed little over decades, despite official encouragement of a transfer of housing to councils. In other state socialist societies, state administrations and enterprises had a smaller share of the housing stock than in the USSR so enterprise-driven residential social segregation should have been less marked. Unfortunately, no systematic studies appear to have been published in English with this question in mind.[14] Nevertheless, one can see here an ideal-typical state socialist city-building strategy, led by the needs of state enterprises and administrations, even if its incidence was variable between countries.

Household movement and residential social segregation. A second influence on residential social segregation is less linked to the state socialist system itself and more to how people respond to the opportunities and constraints it creates. The image of housing allocation, whether by councils, administrations, or state enterprises, is that, once allocated a flat, households remained in it. In fact, this was not the case and residential movement took place because tenants had strong rights and could exchange the right to occupy flats even without reference to the owning body. Tenants could even sell this right on an unofficial market to someone who was not a state tenant (for example, as part of a move into private housing) (French 1995; Douglas 1997). A household with spare income and little space could pay another household which had more space but preferred a cash payment to exchange flats. This means that tenants' preferences would be reflected in such moves. This is relevant to residential segregation since such moves would allow income to become more prominent as a factor in residential distribution. How this translates into residential segregation is more complex.

If we start from the idea that since land markets did not exist, land had no value, then location would not be an element in building costs or in rent levels (which in any case were highly subsidized). However, if tenants give importance to location then this may be one of the characteristics of housing which are implicitly traded in intertenant exchanges.[15] Whether this leads to greater residential segregation depends on whether locational preferences follow some convergent pattern (such as greater preference for more central locations) or whether they are divergent and favor no particular zone. It follows that where exchanges allow people with higher incomes to express their preferences, and where those preferences follow a systematic locational pattern, greater residential social segregation will result.

To summarize, we have presented what fragmentary evidence exists on residential social segregation in state socialist cities, but have not attempted to compare levels with cities in advanced capitalist societies. We have argued that although there was a potential for a radically lower level of residential social segregation to emerge, this was not (or was only partially) achieved in practice due to (1) the role of state enterprises and administrations, which were allowed to develop neighborhoods for their employees, creating a distinctive pattern of enterprise-driven residential social segregation, and (2) residential mobility processes among tenants making use of their rights to dispose of the right to occupy a flat or by exchanges.

We conclude that the key to understanding actual patterns of residential social segregation is not the underlying political ideologies but the power structures that emerged as much in spite of these ideologies as because of them. It was the power position of state enterprises within the nominally centrally planned system, and the mobility of households within a system of administrative allocation of housing, that were some of the proximate causes of the segregation patterns we described.

We can also speculate that there is a tendency for enterprises to lose some of their power in resource allocation *vis-à-vis* councils in the second "intensive growth" phase of socialist urbanization, and that when this happens it leads to a shift away from the ideal-typical enterprise-driven pattern of residential social segregation as well as away from the regressive distribution of housing described earlier.

Post-socialism

The period after 1989 in Central and Eastern Europe has provided a unique natural experiment. Unlike the "democratic transitions" in Southern Europe and Latin America, Central and Eastern Europe have seen change in the economic as well as the political sphere. The precise nature and extent of this change is a matter of debate and certainly varies between countries – compare, for example, the images of "capitalism without capitalists" in Central Europe and "capitalists without capitalism" in Russia (Eyal, Szelenyi, and Townsley 1998: 5).

Among other things, these changes provided a test of the ability of social science to make sense of dramatic change. Political scientists were able to deploy elite-centered theories of "democratic transition and consolidation" based on Latin American and Southern European experience (Linz and Stepan 1996). Economists were less well equipped and were more likely to see radical economic change as possible in a short timespan since the "collapse" of state socialism was conceived as having left a "vacuum," which meant there would be no obstacles to the creation of new institutions. For them the nature of the destination of transition, namely, a combination of multi-party democracy and capitalism, was not in doubt. Sociologists, on the other hand, were also weakly equipped and have relied on Bourdieu's analysis of the forms of capital and their reproduction which, in other places, has been criticized as one-sided and static.

In my view the ubiquitous concept of "transition" has concealed the fact that social science as a whole did not have ready a set of theories capable of understanding the process of macroscopic change of the sort witnessed in the region after 1989. The term transition emphasized the points of departure and destination rather than change itself. The implications are that (1) the destination is markedly different from the point of departure, (2) the period involved is a temporary one, and (3) once the destination is reached the pace of change slows down to a "normal" level. "Transition" was thus a temporary label to be applied until these societies had safely reached the harbor of a familiar societal type.

In general sociologists were more skeptical than economists about the direction and speed of change and emphasized the multiplicity of possible destinations. They used the transition concept but rejected the image of a vacuum and instead stressed the role of "legacies" from the old system in the construction of new systems. These legacies could take various forms: patterns of distribution of economic and social capital (e.g., economic resources and social network links), patterns of values, and patterns of behavior (e.g., lack of entrepreneurialism). This thinking was elaborated into the grandiosely named path dependency theory, whose advocates strenuously denied that it meant no more than that the past influenced the present or that "timing mattered."

To illustrate two approaches that emphasize the destination and the point of origin, respectively, one can contrast Nee's theory of market transition with Stark's recombinant theory.

For Nee (1989), in an economy in which market rather than state coordination is dominant, bureaucrats have less power to allocate resources, and industrial and agricultural workers have more power. This results in workers' wage levels rising relative to those of bureaucrats, and greater opportunities for social mobility which allow the poor to become entrepreneurs. For him, therefore, the analytical focus is on changes in household incomes and occupational positions and his expectation is that in both respects quite rapid changes will follow.

Stark (1996), on the other hand, emphasizes the continuities in stratification and power structures between state socialist and post-socialist societies. He sees change as due to the recombination and redeployment of existing resources. He expects those with economic, social, and political capital to be able to reuse these resources to ensure they do well in post-socialism. Stark is equally interested in institutional change, where his theory leads him to suspect that new forms conceal old structures. For example, he cites cases of state enterprises that reorganize and issue shares but where further probing reveals patterns of cross-ownership and ownership by friendly banks that seem designed to resist change.

In my view Stark's approach is as partial as that of Nee. Restricting our conception of change to the recombination of existing resources seems as limited as viewing past patterns as being irrelevant to the direction of change.

Fortunately there is now some empirical evidence on emerging patterns in post-socialist societies from a large-scale study which tracks the fortunes of members of the former state socialist elite after 1989. In a study carried out in the Czech Republic, Hungary, and Poland in 1993, Eyal et al. found that those who were part of the elite in 1988 underwent "massive downward mobility" (1998: 117). Only half retained positions of authority, while only 4 to 6 percent became entrepreneurs and 15 to 19 percent took early retirement. The political elite did worst and the economic and cultural elites did best relatively – 25 percent of the economic elite became entrepreneurs. Eyal et al. conclude that "the successful conversion of communist political capital into post-communist economic capital has been the exception rather than the rule among former *nomenklatura* members in all three countries" and that "[t]he big winners in the transition have been members of the technocratic fraction of the old ruling estate. This group shares the benefits of the transition with former dissident intellectuals who have moved in large numbers into top positions in politics, state administration and culture" (1998: 123–4, 132). A related study based on samples of the whole population found that "self-recruitment" (i.e., ownership of a business in 1988) was more likely to lead to ownership of a business in 1993 than former *nomenklatura* position (Domanski 2000: 98–9).

Turning to the urban implications of post-socialism, we will focus on housing privatization and analyze it within this framework of winners and losers from "transition."[16]

As was indicated earlier, urban housing distribution under state socialism showed a typical pattern of inequalities in which households with higher incomes obtained the best state flats (measured in subsidy terms) and were most able to benefit from loans for private housing. An immediate consequence of the post-1989 changes was that both Western policy advisers and many local politicians identified the extent of state ownership of housing as the main housing problem (Struyk 1996). They saw state ownership as intrinsically less efficient than private ownership and regarded the low or negligible rent levels as discouraging authorities' spending on maintenance and preventing a market in housing from developing. Privatization was expected to bring the ownership pattern of urban housing into line with that in the United States, raise rents to a market level, encourage market actors, and eventually to tackle other problems such as the shortage of supply and the level of disrepair.

In practice there was variation between Russia, where private housing was poorly developed in urban areas, and Hungary and Bulgaria, where it was highly developed. But the policy of privatizing state-owned housing was new.[17] Differing familiarity with the notion of a housing market affected the speed of response to the possibility of privatization. Tenants in Moscow, for example, felt some security living in a flat with negligible rents, where the state was responsible for repairs and where the flat could be passed on to a child registered as living there. Ownership was initially seen as involving new liabilities (for repairs, for the common parts of the building, for possible future taxes on owners).

The conditions of privatization varied from free of charge privatization, where tenants became owners on simple application, to paying privatization, where a payment was made based on the value of the flat with a sitting tenant and usually with some discount to reflect the state of repair of the dwelling. There were obstacles to privatization in certain cases, for example, in those blocks where restitution claims were pending, and in blocks where the council had plans to redevelop them for retail, office, or high-rent accommodation. In such cases protest groups could form among the excluded (Pickvance 1996).

Interestingly, in Moscow the privatization of housing was slow to start but caught on very quickly, whereas in Budapest with its long familiarity with markets it grew more steadily. The crucial factors in Moscow were the development of an open market in second-hand flats, which made people aware of the monetary value of a flat, and the hyperinflation of 1992, which meant that all rouble savings were wiped out and people saw that a flat could be an asset that kept its value (Pickvance 1994).

Bearing in mind the variable quality of state flats, it is interesting to examine which households were first to privatize them. A study in Budapest showed that the 18 percent of tenants who had privatized their flats by January 1992 were most likely to be in better-quality flats as measured by space and condition of the flat and building (Bodnar 1996). However, interestingly, while education had a direct effect on privatization, income did not, though it did show an indirect effect via quality. In other words, those in the sector who had higher incomes were living in the better-quality flats (for the reasons set out earlier) and these were the most likely to be privatized, but income had no effect additional to this. The study also showed that the districts of Budapest with the highest house values had the highest levels of privatization of state flats. The implication of this is that, as in the UK, remaining state flats will be of poorer than average quality and will be in residualized estates.

In Moscow a parallel study showed that pensioners and those with the highest prestige occupations (who were living in the best-quality and best-located housing) were most likely to be among the first households to privatize their flats (Daniell and Struyk 1994). The authors also found that anxiety about future rents and passing on the tenancy and the desire to be safe from eviction were important motivators. In social terms it can be concluded that those in the best state flats have been able to preserve their position, while those in the worst flats have chosen not to privatize them. In other words, housing privatization has reproduced the status quo, helping those in the best situations to maintain them.

It would be rash to generalize from this to say that all those well provided with assets under state socialism have maintained their position. As the Eyal et al. study showed, assets varied in their convertibility: political capital was much less convertible than economic and cultural capital. Housing as an asset is distinctive in that (1) it (generally) keeps its value whereas other assets may not, and (2) privatization is a closed process in which only the tenant has the right to take part, whereas investment of economic capital in business is more open to competition and the vagaries of the market.

Conclusion

To summarize, it can be seen that work on Central and Eastern Europe has occupied an important place in urban sociology. It has allowed theories developed in the "West" to be applied and their scope tested, and has sparked innovative interpretations and methodological questions. In addition theories developed within the region have shown the limitations of Western interpretations. On the other hand, as the discussion of post-socialism above has shown, "theories of transition" have proved disappointing. These debates among scholars inside and outside the region have occurred within a common theoretical framework, that of political economy broadly understood, and overall demonstrate its fertility in understanding certain types of question. It remains to be seen whether culturally based theories, when they are turned toward Central and Eastern Europe, will prove to have a parallel capacity for a comparative understanding of the questions they address.

Notes

1 Throughout this chapter the term state socialist is used to refer to the "actually existing" forms of socialism in Central and Eastern Europe up to 1989.

2 The notable omission from this list is any reference to socialist ideological claims about social welfare and class differentiation. These are treated as hypotheses for research rather than as a guide to actual achievements.

3 Some writers take a different view. Thus Enyedi says that "East Central European socialist countries replicated stages of a more generally applicable global process of urban development" (1996: 102). However, he ignores completely their distinctive pattern of underurbanization.

4 For some data see Preston (1988). His graph of industrialization and urbanization between 1950 and 1970 for twenty-one groups of countries shows "Eastern Europe" and USSR as being on the underurbanization side of the trend line and as becoming increasingly so by 1970.

5 Another theme in writing on state socialist urbanization concerns the anti-urban ideologies found among the leaderships of socialist states, which are traced to Marx and Engels's writings on the need to transcend the urban–rural division found in capitalism. However, attempts to explain actual patterns of urbanization in terms of the strength of anti-urban (and pro-urban) ideologies among the leadership have been notably unsuccessful. These ideologies appear to have been

slogans used in mobilizing political support within factions of the ruling elite rather than indicators of changing policy directions. For a devastating critique of the extensive body of writing on Chinese urbanization that relied on leadership proclamations rather than evidence on economic and population trends, see Chan (1994).

6 He also notes that East Germany and Czechoslovakia had the most developed pre-socialist economies and the least subsequent underurbanization, which supports his hypothesis (Ofer 1977: 289).

7 It is interesting that the convergent work of Konrad and Szelenyi, and Ofer, appeared in English at the same time (at conferences in 1972). However, Ofer and Szelenyi have confirmed to me that it was developed independently.

8 The only gap in Chan's analysis is that his data are not broken down in terms of the urban or rural location of investment.

9 To counter this outcome he suggested introducing market processes, believing that even if these reproduced inequalities, as market processes normally do, the outcome would be less regressive than allocation by state officials. Interestingly, housing reforms in 1971 did this to some extent.

10 The Index of Segregation of a group measures the proportion of that group that would have to move to other areas for its spatial distribution to match that of the whole population. So the closer the value of this index is to 100, the more segregated the group concerned. Unfortunately, this measure is very sensitive to spatial scale. This is shown by Ladanyi (1989), who shows that the Index of Segregation in 1980 in Budapest for college-educated workers changed from 23.2 to 28.3 to 33.6 as one moved from districts (with a population of about 100,000) to census tracts (4,000) to enumeration districts (200). It is therefore difficult to compare studies that use different sizes of unit. The conclusions presented here avoid this problem by being phrased in general terms.

11 The conclusion about Budapest is based on my interpretation of Ladanyi's data rather than his own, which denies that there is a U-shaped curve.

12 Self-built and private housing is ignored here.

13 In China in 1981 the comparable figure for the 225 officially defined cities was 65 percent (based on Wang and Murie 1999: 106).

14 We have presented enterprise-driven residential social segregation as creating internally homogeneous neighborhoods. In practice there is nothing to rule out some internal differentiation too, for example, so that better-paid workers get better housing even within, say, a well-provided neighborhood. In "new towns" built to house workers within a single enterprise such differentiation existed.

15 In fact, our own research on Moscow and Budapest in 1993 (admittedly after state socialism) showed that location was a far higher consideration for residents in Budapest than in Moscow, for whom the most important characteristics were basic ones such as not sharing with a parent and dwelling size; see Pickvance (2001b).

16 For a wider discussion of urban spatial change see Kovacs (1994) and Sykora (1998).

17 In Hungary it had existed as a possibility since 1969 but was subject to so many constraints as to be insignificant.

Bibliography

Amiot, M. 1986: *Contre l'Etat, les sociologues*. Paris: Editions de l'EHESS.

Andrusz, G. D. 1984: *Housing and Urban Development in the USSR*. London: Macmillan.

Bodnar, J. 1996: "He that hath to him shall be given": housing privatization in Budapest after state socialism. *International Journal of Urban and Regional Research* 20: 616–36.

Castells, M. 1972: *La Question urbaine*. Paris: Maspero.

Chan, K. W. 1994: *Cities with Invisible Walls*. Hong Kong: Oxford University Press.

Csizmadia, M., Ehrlich, E., and Partos, G. 1984: The effects of recession on infrastructure. *Acta Oeconomica* 32: 317–42.

Dangschat, J. 1987: Sociospatial disparities in a "socialist" city: the case of Warsaw at the end of the 1970s. *International Journal of Urban and Regional Research* 11: 37–59.

Daniell, J. and Struyk, R. 1994: Housing privatization in Moscow: who privatizes and why. *International Journal of Urban and Regional Research* 18: 510–25.

Davis, K. and Golden, H. 1954: Urbanization and the development of pre-industrial areas. *Economic Development and Cultural Change* 3: 6–26.

Domanski, H. 2000: *On the Verge of Convergence*. Budapest: CEU Press.

Douglas, M. J. 1997: *A Change of System: Housing System Transformation and Neighbourhood Change in Budapest*. Urban Research Centre: Utrecht University.

Ehrlich, E. and Szilagyi, G. 1980: International comparison of the Hungarian infrastructure 1960–1974. *Acta Oeconomica* 24: 57–80.

Enyedi, D. 1996: Urbanization under socialism. In G. D. Andrusz et al. (eds.), *Cities after Socialism*. Oxford: Blackwell.

Eyal, G., Szelenyi, I., and Townsley, E. 1998: *Making Capitalism without Capitalists*. London: Verso.

French, R. A. 1995: *Plans, Pragmatism and People: The Legacy of Soviet Planning for Today's Cities*. London: UCL Press.

French, R. A. and Hamilton, F. E. I. 1979: Is there a socialist city? In R. A. French and F. E. I. Hamilton (eds.), *The Socialist City*. Chichester: Wiley, 1–22.

Hegedus, J. and Tosics, I. 1983: Housing classes and housing policy: some changes in the Budapest housing market. *International Journal of Urban and Regional Research* 1: 206–26.

Konrad, G. and Szelenyi, I. 1974: Social conflicts of underurbanization. In A. A. Brown et al. (eds.), *Urban and Social Economics in Market and Planned Economies*. Westport and London: Praeger, Vol. 1, 206–26. (Published in Hungarian in 1971; reprinted in M. Harloe (ed.), *Captive Cities*. Chichester: Wiley, 1977).

Kornai, J. 1992: *The Socialist System*. Oxford: Oxford University Press.

Kovacs, Z. 1994: A city at the crossroads: social and economic change in Budapest. *Urban Studies* 31: 1081–96.

Ladanyi, J. 1989: Changing patterns of residential segregation. *International Journal of Urban and Regional Research* 13: 555–70.

Linz, J. and Stepan, A. 1996: *Problems of Democratic Transition and Consolidation*. Baltimore: Johns Hopkins University Press.

Logan, J. and Bian, Y. 1993: Inequalities in access and community resources in a Chinese city. *Social Forces* 72: 555–76.

Mateju, P., Vecernik, J., and Jerabek, H. 1979: Social structure, spatial structure and problems of urban research: the example of Prague. *International Journal of Urban and Regional Research* 3: 181–201.

Murray, P. and Szelenyi, I. 1984: The city in the transition to socialism. *International Journal of Urban and Regional Research* 8: 90–107.

Nee, V. 1989: A theory of market transition: from redistribution to markets in state socialism. *American Sociological Review* 54: 663–81.

Ofer, G. 1976: Industrial structure, urbanization and the growth strategy of socialist countries. *Quarterly Journal of Economics* 90: 219–44.

—— 1977: Economizing on urbanization in socialist countries. In A. A. Brown et al. (eds.), *Internal Migration*. London: Academic Press, 277–303.

Pahl, R. E. 1975: *Whose City?* 2nd ed. Harmondsworth: Penguin.

Pickvance, C. G. 1986: Comparative analysis and assumptions about causality. *International Journal of Urban and Regional Research* 10: 162–84.

—— 1994: Housing privatization and housing protest in the transition from state socialism: a comparative study of Budapest and Moscow. *International Journal of Urban and Regional Research* 18: 433–50.

—— 1996: Environmental and housing movements in cities after socialism: the cases of Budapest and Moscow. In G. D. Andrusz et al. (eds.), *Cities after Socialism*. Oxford: Blackwell, 236–67.

—— 2001a: Four varieties of comparative analysis. *Journal of Housing and the Built Environment* 16: 7–28.

—— 2001b: Inaction, individual action and collective action as responses to housing dissatisfaction: a comparative study of Budapest and Moscow. *Research on Social Movements, Conflict and Change* 23: 179–206.

Preston, S. H. 1988: Urban growth in developing countries: a demographic reappraisal. In J. Gugler (ed.), *The Urbanization of the Third World*. Oxford: Oxford University Press, 11–31.

Reissman, L. 1964: *The Urban Process*. Glencoe, IL: Free Press.

Rex, J. and Moore, R. S. 1967: *Race, Community and Conflict*. Oxford: Oxford University Press.

Shomina, E. S. 1992: Enterprises and the urban environment in the USSR. *International Journal of Urban and Regional Research* 16: 222–33.

Smith, D. M. 1994: *Geography and Social Justice*. Oxford: Blackwell.

—— 1996: The socialist city. In G. D. Andrusz et al. (eds.), *Cities after Socialism*. Oxford: Blackwell, 70–99.

Sovani, N. V. 1964: The analysis of "over-urbanization." *Economic Development and Cultural Change* 12: 113–22.

Stark, D. 1996: Recombinant property in East European capitalism: organizational innovation in Hungary. In D. Stark and G. Grabher (eds.), *Legacies, Linkages and Localities: The Social Embeddedness of the Economic Transformation in Central and Eastern Europe*. Oxford: Oxford University Press, 35–69.

Struyk, R. (ed.) 1996: *Economic Restructuring of the Former Soviet Bloc: The Case of Housing*. Aldershot: Avebury.

Sykora, L. 1998: Commercial property development in Budapest, Prague and Warsaw. In G. Enyedi (ed.), *Social Change and Urban Restructuring in Central Europe*. Budapest: Akademiai Kiado, 109–36.

Szelenyi, I. 1978: Social inequalities in state socialist redistributive economies. *International Journal of Comparative Sociology* 19: 63–87.

—— 1983: *Urban Inequalities under State Socialism.* Oxford: Oxford University Press.

—— 1987: Housing inequalities and occupational segregation in state socialist cities. *International Journal of Urban and Regional Research* 11: 1–8.

—— 1996: Cities under socialism – and after. In G. D. Andrusz et al. (eds.), *Cities after Socialism.* Oxford: Blackwell, 286–317.

Tosics, I. 1987: Privatization in housing policy: the case of the Western countries and that of Hungary. *International Journal of Urban and Regional Research* 11: 61–77.

Wang, Y. P. and Murie, A. S. 1999: *Housing Policy and Practice in China.* London: Macmillan.

Wiles, P. J. D. 1974: Comments on chapter 10. In A. A. Brown et al. (eds.), *Urban and Social Economics in Market and Planned Economies.* Westport and London: Praeger, Vol. 1, 258–63.

10
The China Difference: City Studies Under Socialism and Beyond

Dorothy J. Solinger and Kam Wing Chan

Chinese cities since socialism's emergence in 1949 have been more or less the creature of the state's designs: more so, surely, in the decades when the doctrinal dicta of the state truly held sway (up through 1978), less so as that other great organizing principle, the market, came progressively to entrench itself in urban space. As a consequence, urban research on China has not been driven by trends and fads in scholarship so much as it has been shaped by the nature of China itself, as fashioned by the state (and later the market), and by the momentous shifts the nation has weathered because of political decisions. City studies have also been the product of changing data sources and much improved access for researchers as state controls receded as a function of the state's economic policies in the 1980s and 1990s. Thus, given the obstacles posed by China's version of socialism, by its adherence to a Marxist political economy framework for understanding the world, and by the lack of transparency of its internal affairs right up until quite lately, the China urban studies field has been little affected by scholarly fashion, but much influenced by Chinese politics and state policy.

The Impact of Politics

During the first three decades of the People's Republic, a number of factors affected research on cities (and, in fact, research of any sort about China). In the first place, a phenomenally well-organized Communist Party rather quickly imposed an overarching dominance and stultifying uniformity upon culture, manifestations of gender, social categories, economic life, and even food (through rationing in the cities and through control of what was planted in the villages) and clothing. Daily life in cities for ordinary people was determined by life within the *danwei* (or work unit), with work patterns, housing, and mobility relatively undifferentiated throughout much of urban society. Moreover, outsiders could only sense regional variation among cities through careful inspection of the choice of wording in local leaders' official speeches. These various circumstances meant that, while this regime lasted, there was no space for studies of cultural outputs as creative products of the populace, since for much of the time little or no scope for originality existed.

Furthermore, omnipresent surveillance – if often enforced by co-workers and neighbors, not by the police – ensured tight control over revelations of aberrant or even personal feelings and behaviors to outsiders (or even to insiders, in the severest periods). Except during the Cultural Revolution (1966–76), official documentary materials virtually never fell even into Chinese citizens' hands, and even the chief newspapers were not available for purchase on the street by anyone, but were simply distributed by the government to all work units and neighborhoods. All forms of news media were heavily censored and strictly homogeneous, bearing only messages approved by the highest levels of the Party. Besides, Americans could not even visit the country until the 1970s. Statistical data, moreover, were for the most part kept secret; those which were published were often suspect at the time and later found to be misleading. So research sources and methods were seriously compromised. These facets of the regime made work on the politics and society of the time a mix of reading between the lines, consultations with refugees in Hong Kong, and varying degrees of pure guesswork. Only for short times in the mid-1950s (the Hundred Flowers movement), a year or so in the early 1960s, and during the late 1960s did ordinary people have a chance to speak their minds. But even then, there was much use of ellipsis and euphemism.

Once the post-Mao leadership wrenched Chinese society in a totally new direction after 1978, it wantonly overrode with increasing boldness all the values Mao Zedong had held sacred (collectivism, anti-materialism, anti-consumerism, egalitarianism, anti-elitism, to name some of the most central ones). In order to stimulate productivity and satisfy long-pent-up urges among the populace for a life of more commodities and leisure, the Party decentralized much of the decision-making and financial powers it had long monopolized, activated the marketplace, and initiated global economic involvement.

The opening of the country, in a bid to bring China up to par internationally – intellectually, economically, and technologically – allowed for the entry of foreign teachers and businesspeople, who, of course, carried in their wake new lifestyles, new ideas, and novel values. Interchange with outsiders loosened up access, making interviews and survey research by foreigners possible by the mid- and late 1980s; such exchanges, plus the upgrading of the quality and accessibility of Chinese data, led to a vastly heightened accuracy of research materials.

Meanwhile, society itself underwent a startling conversion, as diversity, consumerism, enhanced personal autonomy, and cultural creativity began to appear with growing force. But though the state markedly lessened its hold, even into the early 1990s anthropologist Mayfair Yang's fieldwork was shadowed by ongoing political sensitivity, a "culture of fear," the "politicization of daily life," and a "large realm of secrecy" (Yang 1994: 15–25). Thus, an uneasy blend of consumption and policing still marked the end of the century and continued to cause Western researchers to work with a healthy dose of caution, even as their sources opened up and their subjects for legitimate examination multiplied (Mackerras 1998: 22).

Western Literature: Disciplinary Approaches

For the reasons of governmental policy and the unreliability and unavailability of source material noted above, in the past, practitioners of certain disciplines – such as economic geography – found it more possible to pursue their craft (albeit with inferior data) than did others – such as anthropologists. Scholars with explicitly cultural interests never really bothered to explore the Chinese metropolis until recently. Urban anthropology, too, is a field that only appeared in China at the very end of the 1980s (Guldin and Southall 1993: 3).

Indeed, of the more than thirty books examined in preparation for writing this chapter, about a third (ten) were written or edited by geographers and urban planners, only six by political economists and political scientists, six by sociologists, six by anthropologists, and just three by cultural studies scholars. One conference volume has such a range of disciplines represented among its contributors that it cannot be classified as belonging to any one discipline (Davis et al. 1995).

Books by anthropologists on the city began to be published only in 1993 and none of the three volumes by cultural studies scholars covered in our survey was published before the mid- to late 1990s.[1] Moreover, it is fair to say that, although the work of sociologists and political scientists goes back to the 1960s, the quality, depth, and accuracy of their early research unavoidably suffered from the limited sources upon which they were compelled to base their analyses and their absolutely total lack of access to the place.[2]

Comparisons can lend these observations concrete form. For instance, there are vast differences between two volumes of urban sociology on China, one relying on data from the 1970s and the other using material from the late 1980s and early 1990s (Whyte and Parish 1984; Tang and Parish 2000), in terms of the nature of their sources as well as their findings, despite the very similar content they share (family, employment, education, interpersonal relations, quality of life). For, whereas the scholars in the first used interviews with *émigrés* living in Hong Kong who were asked to recall the circumstances of their neighbors, those in the second volume were fortunate enough to gain access to semi-annual urban social surveys undertaken over a five-year period. And while the former had as themes the weight of bureaucracy upon daily lives and the widespread equality and economic security existing before 1980 – if marred by political pressure – that then obtained in cities, the latter delved into the ongoing social, cultural, and political liberalizations that accompanied the economic transformation of the 1980s and 1990s from a planned to a market society, as well as the difficulties and complications of this shift.

Another contrast is between the volume edited by John Wilson Lewis, published in 1971, and the collection edited by Deborah Davis, Richard Kraus, Barry Naughton, and Elizabeth Perry that came out in 1995. Both compilations aim to comprehend notable features of the cities of their day, but, as Lewis quite humbly notes in his introduction: "It is a sad commentary on our times that none of the authors represented in this volume has actually set foot in a city in Communist China." He goes on to acknowledge the necessity of working with "data that blur distinctions" and the "many gaps in our coverage"; he also laments that, "we have not always escaped the biases found in the published record" (Lewis 1971: vi–vii).

The 1995 jointly edited volume, on the other hand, contains the output of scholars all of whose chapters relied on actual fieldwork within China, once Chinese leaders opened their society. By then, massive alterations marked the object of their study, as compared even with a decade or so before. These researchers were able to address such disparate topics as changing urban form in the era of reform, the new regulatory state at the county level, filmmaking, the suddenly popular martial arts, and avant-garde art, perhaps in part in recognition of the turn to culture in scholarship of the 1990s about other places. But this changed approach probably came about even more in response to the radically transformed nature of city life in China itself at that point.

For a third comparison, two books about the same city, Guangzhou, researched some two decades apart, evince huge disparity in the mode of conducting research from the 1960s to the 1980s. The first relies on conversations with former residents who left China for Hong Kong before the late 1960s and on old issues of the city's official newspaper; its author even concedes that the primary sources on which he relied "do not meet high standards of objectivity" (Vogel 1968: viii). And the second, founded on fieldwork and interviews conducted on the spot in the late 1980s and in 1991, was blessed with sponsorship by the provincial social science academy and excellent personal relationships with local cadres working in resident committees. Besides, this second project was enhanced by the author's familiarity with contemporaneous television programs and her perusal of an array of official and nonofficial daily papers, in addition to local yearbooks and records, all of which had become open, if one had the right "connections" (Vogel 1968; Ikels 1996, respectively).

Vogel's study is more a political history than a work of sociology, despite his disciplinary training, as it traces in some depth the intricacies and machinations of the Party's grapplings with the remaking of Chinese society through a series of campaigns from 1949 through the late 1960s. Ikels, by contrast, is able to use her skills as an anthropologist to the full by the late 1980s, given her contacts and the new openness of China. She depicts living standards, leisure activities, and family and household activities and relationships, demonstrating in great detail how economic reforms were altering the material circumstances and general well-being of urban residents at that time.

Other pairs of books illustrate a separate point. True, later studies yielded more accurate and culturally relevant information, gleaned from research at a far closer range. But this was so because the political environment within China had been grossly altered and not because of any international trends in scholarship. Nor did all scholars of Chinese urbanism in the 1990s suddenly succumb to vogues *au courant* among those studying other places. Though Mayfair Yang's 1994 anthropological treatment of social networks, culture and power, modernity and the state is replete with Foucauldian influences (Yang 1994), Kam Wing Chan's work of geography of the same year looks at such comparatively traditional topics as migration and urbanization, policy and population growth, investment patterns and services. And while the late 1990s saw the appearance of Dorothy Solinger's configurative, largely qualitative examination of peasant migrants in large cities, which concerns itself with themes such as community, citizenship, and identity, her political science colleague Tianjian Shi's survey-research-based work on political participation in Beijing (1997) had no cultural leanings at all.

Another political scientist, Jae Ho Chung, in 1999 produced an edited, quintessentially political economic collection of essays on pairs of cities in China, emphasizing the impact of their endowments (location, history), their administrative arrangements, the policy treatment they received from the central government, and their leaders' strategies as decisive factors in their economic development. The next year, sociologist Deborah Davis published an edited work on the new consumerism in Chinese cities, which, while containing cultural themes, in the main eschewed cultural analysis. All of these works consider the enormous metamorphosis that marketization and enhanced personal local autonomy have meant for the cities and the actors they describe. At the same time, while Davis's and Solinger's publications discuss culturist issues and do have a bit of overlap with the concerns of cultural theorists who study other places, in style they are probably more akin to the more political economic approach found in the Chung and Shi studies.

The point is that three decades of fairly idiosyncratic socialist ideology and practices in China have made a big difference. Beliefs and behaviors instilled by the Communist Party radically differentiated urban studies projects in the Chinese case from those done on other societies. We proceed to look more closely at the evolution of each of the five principal disciplinary approaches to work on urban China over four decades, bearing in mind that many individual pieces of scholarship have had not simply a disciplinary but often an interdisciplinary bent as well.

Geography and Urban Planning

Geographers and urban planners could ply their trade without needing the same level of access to people as did researchers in other disciplines, and some of their findings could be reached without on-site observation. Thus, despite problems with insufficient or sometimes inadequate data, their work progressed throughout the reign of socialism. Some of their topics of study – the historical development of cities and of industrialization; governmental policies on cities; urban planning and development trends; and state decisions on housing, industrial location, and rank-size relationships among cities – could be explored and estimated even before good access became available (Ma and Hanten 1981; Kirkby 1985; Sit 1985).

Nonetheless, with better connections to Chinese geographers living in China – indeed, volumes such as Sit (1985) grew out of conferences in which Chinese geographers participated – to geography departments in universities, and to research institutes as the 1980s wore on, Western scholars began to feel more and more certain about their data and their findings. So, whereas Sit's personal visits to departments of geography in the early 1980s could not yield more than "piecemeal information" (in lieu of the systematic and comprehensive data that would have been desirable), by the middle of the next decade he was able to write a book on Beijing drawing upon unpublished documents, reports, and working papers (1995). Conference volumes from this late 1980s/early 1990s period were able to address small towns, land utilization, patterns of resource flows between urban and rural areas, and shortages of infrastructure and services with some accuracy (Kwok et al. 1990). One more study about geographical subjects, which came out in 1987, offered statistical data on housing, transportation, and migration (Kojima 1987). Also, following Kirkby's (1985) initial work on reinterpreting Chinese urbanization strategy, nine years later, Chan (1994) provided a systematic and theoretical treatment of the "Chinese urban model" based on more reliable urban population and economic data. While the approaches of these two works are different, they have established the relationship between China's industrialization strategy and rural–urban segmentation. Their work has shattered the once-dominant myth of Chinese pro-rural development in Western literature.

Moreover, a project on China's coastal cities that began in 1984, involving collaboration with institutes of geography at the Chinese Academy of Science and elsewhere, was able to include information on port and industrial facilities, satellite towns, population density, the status of infrastructure, land usage, and spread effects of urbanization in thirteen coastal cities, despite continuing deficiencies in the level of information then available (Yeung and Hu 1992). Yeung's work in organizing thematic papers led to a relatively comprehensive volume on China's largest city, Shanghai (Yeung and Sung 1996). By the second half of the 1990s, China's linkage with the World Bank enabled two World Bank researchers to publish a reasonable account of the dynamics of urban growth in Shanghai, Tianjin, and Guangzhou (Yusuf and Wu 1997). Their volume included data on the impact of economic reform policies upon the structure and infrastructure in cities, the cities' financial arrangements with the central government, their resource endowments, levels of technology, and the capital flows to which each was a party.

But even up to century's end, some China geographers remained faithful to the Marxian political economy approach, which has always had a strong influence in the urban studies field (see Harloe et al. 1998). In particular, Tang's (1994) and Wu's (1997) articles in the *IJURR* follow this tradition as they applied its concepts and vocabulary to study the role of capital in Chinese urban land development and urban economic restructuring. While about two decades ago, articles on China in the same journal adhered to the Chinese socialist model under Mao (e.g., Basso 1980), Tang's and Wu's have come to a more nuanced understanding of Chinese socialist urban complexities. As Tang noted with some amazement:

> It is widely believed among the social critics in the capitalist countries that once land is nationalized, all sorts of urban land development problems will disappear. One of the shocking findings of this paper is that although a socialist form of land ownership is important, it cannot eliminate the problems. (Tang 1994: 412)

Thus, as time passed and China became more open, geographers and urban planners took advantage of the increasing availability of data and the progress that had been made in the collection of more sophisticated data to pursue essentially the same topics they had studied in the past, but to study them better.

Political Science

Political scientists were at work attempting to understand Chinese urbanism already in the 1960s. As noted above, the first product of their efforts was the conference volume edited by John Wilson Lewis that came out in 1971. Though half the essays in the book were composed by scholars from other fields, five political scientists wrote, respectively, on issues such as law and order, cadre recruitment and mobility, trade union worker cultivation, commerce and education, and the Cultural Revolution in Shanghai. Their sources were usually documentary, though a few had spoken with refugees in Hong Kong, and their findings necessarily entailed a great deal of creativity in trying to piece together bits of not always reliable material.

Two other books from that early period were on individual cities, Kenneth Lieberthal's on Tianjin (1980) and Lynn White's on Shanghai (1978). Both authors were able to interview (in Hong Kong) former residents of their cities, and both had access to reams of local newspapers (both official and non-official), radio broadcasts, governmental policy statements and organizational files, Chinese journals, and translation series. These were ambitious books, Lieberthal's tracing the impact of interpersonal relations (*guanxi*) on the Party's conduct of mass mobilization and organizational control; White's showing the various incentives that local political cadres utilized to "guide" young people into following career routes devised by the Party. But despite the ingenuity of their methodologies and conclusions, White had to admit that his "most reliable sources were official ones" (White 1978: 5). Given the level of rhetoric and propaganda in such sources, this was a sorry claim.

In the 1990s, regardless of cultural studies' incursion into the social sciences in other fields, political scientists who worked on Chinese cities retained the concerns of their predecessors: they were still interested in political participation and the political dimensions of daily life (Shi 1997), larger concerns over order in the cities and the workings of bureaucracy among officialdom (Solinger 1999), and policy-making (Chung 1999). But, as noted above, their ability to rely on survey research (Shi), interviews with officials and migrants (Solinger), and a vast multitude of local documentary sources plus talks with urban politicians and sometimes even political gossip (Chung) both enriched and helped to substantiate their claims.

Sociology

Like political scientists, sociologists did not alter their research subjects or even their perspectives over the years so much as they simply availed themselves of better sources and better access, as China opened up to foreigners and became progressively less authoritarian. As already discussed, Whyte and Parish produced the first genuinely sociological study of Chinese cities (if we discount Vogel's more politically oriented history of Guangzhou), though their research mainly drew upon materials from and the reminiscences of ex-residents of only two provinces (Guangdong, Guangxi). In accord with the nature of China at the time, their foci were the bureaucratization and equality that stamped existence in cities then, as they essayed to capture the ways in which cities were organized and the nature of social relationships within them in a work they characterized as "collecting urban ethnographies, but at a distance" (Whyte and Parish 1984: 5).

The field had to wait another twenty years for further tomes in this discipline to appear. Two came in quick succession, Cecelia Chan's on welfare delivery in urban neighborhoods (Chan 1993), and Yanjie Bian's study of work and inequality (Bian 1994). The first was made possible by the generous cooperation of local cadres, who gave the author information on policy and introductions to officials in the street offices. This assistance permitted Chan to challenge the previously all-pervasive rhetoric of the superiority of socialism, as well as some myths about neighborhood care that had infected even the work of such careful and objective scholars as Whyte and Parish. Chan was also able to assess the actual extent of service provision and the changes that economic reform were making to welfare planning. Her work rested on opinion surveys of citizens and in-depth interviews on the spot, neither of which Whyte and Parish had been able to conduct.

By the 1980s and 1990s, the possibility of doing systematic social surveys in Chinese cities had opened up many opportunities for mainstream empirical sociologists, armed with statistical packages, to test Western-based sociological hypotheses in China. This is exemplified by the work of Logan and his former students on urban housing (e.g., Logan, Bian, and Bian 1999). In an earlier piece, Bian's key data came from a 1988 representative sample of 1,000 adults in Tianjin and from official statistics and in-depth interviews in 1983–5 in that city, as well as from 1988–92 talks with Chinese *immigrés* in the United States. He was able to use analyses of his material to reach conclusions about the impact of work organizations on social stratification in the cities, and to demonstrate how these organizations determined the often unequal distribution of resources and opportunities for urban workers. He gleaned a great deal of information on job mobility patterns, work compensation and benefits at different units, political life, and housing. Although many of these topics had been covered in Andrew Walder's 1986 book on networks and power relations in factories, Walder was forced to rely just on the accounts of refugees living in Hong Kong in 1979—80 when he conducted his research, who could only recount from memory their experiences of the early and mid-1970s.[3]

The last two works by sociologists appeared in the year 2000, one effectively an updating of Parish's earlier socioethnography with Whyte (Tang and Parish 2000), and the other Deborah Davis's edited volume on consumerism. As explained earlier, the two ethnographies of cities shared many concerns, and their chapters' objects of study are often identical: they address the same issues of urban life, from family behavior to political organization and social relations to patterns of employment. But superior data sources and fundamental alterations in the nature of China by the 1990s altered the content considerably. While the first grounded its analysis in assessing the realization (and difficulties therein) of socialist ideals, the second confronted the redefinitions of the bond between the state and the individual in the wake of economic transformation, and explicitly compared the pros and cons of socialist versus market societies.

Davis's work is the outcome of over a dozen carefully crafted investigations of activities now prevalent among the newly well-to-do who have profited from the economic reforms in Chinese cities. These behaviors include buying wedding dresses, taking vacations, eating at McDonald's, dancing, feasting, and bowling. As in Davis et al.'s 1995 conference volume, this one too – despite its cultural topics – is written to describe contemporary consumption more than to subscribe to cultural theories. Again we see that the concerns of sociologists – just as those of geographers and political scientists – remained more or less constant over the decades, shifting only to encompass corresponding changes in the nature of Chinese society once markets reemerged after 1980, and to take advantage of the presence of new opportunities for researchers.

Anthropology

Urban anthropology was unknown within China until Gregory Guldin and Aidan Southall chaired a meeting in Beijing in December 1989 and invited some native anthropologists to contribute (Guldin and Southall 1993). Before the country opened up, Western anthropologists had to resign themselves to working in either Hong Kong or Taiwan, as there was absolutely no possibility for doing fieldwork on the mainland. Even when Western anthropologists began to examine China in the 1980s, they turned to the countryside at first.

Only in the mid- and late 1980s did a few of them switch their attention to city life, and four ethnographies resulted, the first two seeing the light of day in 1993. Ole Bruun's 1987–91 fieldwork in Chengdu, Sichuan, examined the social context of the private business that began to flourish in the economic reform period, and he treated conventional themes in political anthropology, such as local community interaction, bureaucratic power, and household strategies.

The other 1993 work is by William R. Jankowiak, on the city of Huhhot in Inner Mongolia. Though Jankowiak did his work in a minority "autonomous" region, he draws no distinctions between the culture of the minority Hui people and that of the majority (80 percent in this city) Han Chinese, and indeed, he finds little difference between them. Jankowiak takes up the usual topics of cultural anthropologists, including kinship and family, social hierarchy, sexuality and cosmology, funerary rites, folk beliefs and behaviors, and thus his book displays no particular awareness of the advent of cultural studies. The book by Charlotte Ikels – another typical ethnography – was already noted earlier (Ikels 1996).

Only Mayfair Yang's 1994 study of *guanxi*, based on her fieldwork between 1981 and 1985 in Beijing (with follow-ups in the early 1990s), takes on topics such as a "modern technique and telos of power," writes from a stance of self-reflexivity, and tackles the *problématique* of "culture" as a concept (Yang 1994: 31–45). Though her observations and her data about social interactions and relationships are the stuff of traditional sociocultural anthropology, she interprets them in light of current cultural theories, unlike any other social scientist working on Chinese cities today.

Cultural Studies

While the great majority of works by Westerners on Chinese cities have thus remained quite conventional in cast, still, cultural studies did come to China urban studies, but not until the mid-1990s. Its tardy arrival is in part a function of the largely homogeneous nature of Chinese city life at least up until the mid-1980s, which may well have discouraged research aiming at exploring diversity of any sort. As Mayfair Yang explained, under the rule of Mao Zedong, there was a "tendency to erase gender difference"; the state also exercised hegemony over all manner of classifications and administrative categories (Yang 1994: 44).

Among the books we label cultural studies, two concern popular culture and the city as imagined in literary and film texts, respectively, and both were published in the mid-1990s (Zha 1995; Zhang 1996). The former was written by a scholar who lived in China until 1981 and could build her ideas – on Beijing intellectuals' moods and ethos, the new politics of culture and commercialism, and the emerging cosmopolitanism and consumerism of the big city – on her trust and talks with old friends and their acquaintances. Her subjects include television soap opera, urban planning, filmmaking, the mass media, pornography, and sexual politics. The latter work takes as its theme psychic experiences of the city, as configured in the imagination of writers in modern China, and focuses on topics such as space, time, and gender in the country's two most modern cities, Beijing and Shanghai.

There is also Michael Dutton's collage of urban street scenes and the kinds of behaviors one might find on them today in his 1998 book, *Streetlife China*. In it he consciously adapts the mode of Walter Benjamin, who, he notes, "wanted to 'write' using snip-bits of work stolen from the pens of others" (Dutton 1998: xii). His bits include material from his own interviews, translated clips from newspapers, fragments of Chinese journal articles, segments of Chinese books, excerpts from Chinese literature, and governmental regulations on matters that tend to appear on the streets – including prostitution, beggars, wanderers, architecture, and ordinary city slang among them. His iconoclastic perspective smacks of novel angles on what, for China, are largely 1990s' phenomena.

So, for the most part, cultural studies have so far become the realm only of those who work specifically on culture, but not of the social scientists who study Chinese cities. But this was not because social scientists studying the People's Republic of China (hereafter, PRC) in its earlier years followed a fad of political economy in deference to (or in sympathy with) trends in urban studies elsewhere. Instead, scholars of China's urban areas spent their energies first struggling to make sense of propagandistic documents and faulty and insufficient data, and attempting to use refugee interviews to understand China. Later, such scholars were bent upon capturing the complexity of a country undergoing massive transformation. As the leadership and the market worked in tandem to pry away the veil of secrecy and uniformity that had obscured and even obliterated the customs and the choices of the populace before 1980 or so, scholars progressively found their subject more and more palpable, more genuine, and also more comprehensible and coherent. This new reality became what they wished to depict, and it was this that drove their researches.

Urban Studies in the PRC

Urban studies has evolved to become a substantial focus of research in the PRC only in the last two decades (Yeung and Zhou 1991; Chan 1994). This late start reflects not so much the data and source material constraints that faced China researchers working in the West and in Hong Kong. It was, instead, more the result of policy and paradigm shifts that came about as China opened its door to the world, and as PRC scholars looked outside the country for new ideas, theories, and methods of social science research. At the beginning phase in the early 1980s, scholars in the "urban studies" field in the PRC were few, concentrated in geography and urban planning, and narrowly preoccupied with a set of issues directly related to China's population and regional policies and national development strategy. However, by the end of the twentieth century, urban researchers in the PRC had become a sizeable group spread over several disciplines and engaged in a variety of topics, in some ways similar to those pursued by their colleagues in the West.

Geography,[4] with its pragmatic and empiricist orientation to urban issues, was the first major discipline to devote a significant amount of energy to urban topics in the country, while many other social science disciplines (such as sociology) were still in the process of being reestablished as or were focusing on other more pivotal issues.[5] Reflecting many of the policy and urban planning concerns of the state at that time, geographers with an urban interest did research mainly on urban definitions, urbanization trends, and urban development policies. In the early 1980s geographers started to look outside China, through some limited comparative work, and began to notice some special features of Chinese urban development and/or to question its "irregularities" (such as Wu 1981; Zhou 1982; Yao and Wu 1982; see also papers in Yeung and Zhou 1988).

Urban research by geographers started to gain visibility around the mid-1980s in China. A count of the articles on urban geography in major geographic and urban planning journals in the PRC yielded an annual output of thirty-four articles in 1986 and thirty-nine articles in 1987, compared with only two in 1980 and ten in 1981 (Gu 1999), in addition to several books (such as Xu et al. 1987). While focus on urbanization and related policies remained strong, urban systems and urban spatial structure also became major areas of study in Chinese geography/planning publications. In the 1990s Chinese geographers continued to broaden their interests. By the year 2000, they had added a number of notable subfields – including migration, urban environment, and urban social geography – to the field of urban geography. These changes have broken the past domination of economic perspectives in this field. Still, urban research in China by geographers and planners remains heavily empirical and descriptive.

Outside geography and planning, other disciplines have treated urban research mostly as a marginal pursuit. Though in lesser quantity, economists, demographers, and sociologists also debated national, macro issues of urbanization strategy (see, e.g., Fei 1984; Liu 1990). However, this does not mean that there is a dearth of interesting and provocative works. Mirroring trends in urban studies in the West, these studies have often taken an interdisciplinary tilt. For example, in economics, Gu Shengzu's (1993) work on China's development strategy and urbanization policies in many ways echoed Chan's (1990, 1994) research in the West. The popularity of new institutional economics among young economists in China in the 1990s led to a number of systematic economic works on such topics as institutional change and urbanization (Liu 1999) and urban labor markets and institutions (Cai 1998). Increasingly, as PRC scholars of urban society developed their work, they also turned their attention to more micro-level, and more contentious, issues of urban society and politics. This appears in a number of works on urban income distribution, stratification, poverty, and social welfare by economists (such as Guan 1999; Zhao et al. 1999), and studies done within the general area of the rapidly expanding "community studies" subfield in sociology (see Wang 2000). The sociologists explore urban social issues, such as the power transformation of the work-unit system, urban governance, civil society, changing social structure, occupational mobility, migrant networks in cities, and "working girls" (female migrant labor) in urban areas (some of the recent examples are Xiang 1998; Li and Li 1999; Tang and Feng 2000). The spurt of rural–urban geographical mobility in China over the last two decades has also generated volumes of migration studies in China. Many of these are conducted by demographers, whose primary concerns are often with measuring the migration (a very complex subject in itself) and examining policy issues. These migration studies often touch upon questions about the socioeconomic impacts of migrants on cities.

Unlike their Western colleagues studying urban China, whose work is often significantly shaped, if not dictated, by the accessibility of information, research in the PRC is often driven by policy concerns and the availability of government funding on particular topics at a given time. This situation, no doubt, continues to reflect the strong influence of the government pon academic work in China, and the constraints faced by researchers there. Urban studies in China is still in the formative stage, but there is rapid development, especially in sociology. What Yeung and Zhou (1991) noted about human geography in China ten years ago is by and large still true today, and can be generalized to urban studies as well. For various reasons, pragmatism and the neglect of theoretical and methodological explorations and innovations still prevail in social science studies. In theory and methodology, the gaps between the scholarly literature in the PRC and that in the West are still quite large. However, this does not mean that one can ignore Chinese urban scholarship; rather, one could make just the opposite argument. Given the immense size of the Chinese urban populace, and the rapid pace with which it is changing, eventually, the PRC scholars, many of whom are quickly absorbing outside knowledge, will become the core researchers in investigating, understanding, and theorizing their own society.

The Future

What are the implications for future research on Chinese cities in the West, given the motivations and situational factors that have brought it to its present juncture? One approach to such speculation is to look at the most recent scholarship and then extrapolate potential directions from it. If we follow this route, we might conclude, with Tang and Parish (2000), that China is marching along the same path that other industrializing, modernizing societies (such as Taiwan) have taken in the late twentieth century, and that, to chart a future course, we need only to look at any other society presently at later stages along the same trajectory. In some ways the concerns of the Davis (2000) volume speak, if only very implicitly, to the same image. For, as she cogently concludes her introduction:

> Whether or not the millions of apolitical market transactions have realigned institutional power and authority, the multiplicity of horizontal ties and the increased invisibility and privacy of personal life have already created a society for which the past conventions of the authoritarian rule appear ill-suited. Eating a Big Mac will not bring down a dictator, but it can send a million daily messages that old ways have changed. (Davis 2000: 22)

The work of other authors, however, presages a very different prospect. Another recent edited volume on conflict and contention in Chinese society discovers dissension and opposition at nearly every turn (Perry and Selden 2000). Solinger's and Dutton's studies highlight marginality and hint at possibilities of resistance in the time to come. They also indicate that there are serious social issues to be resolved in the cities – such as coping with masses of in-migrating but out-caste peasants there, and confronting and addressing criminality and poverty of various derivations – before Tang and Parish's smooth progress toward liberal outcomes can be achieved. Given these discrepant outlooks, probably in order best to conceptualize the city in the offing researchers will need to develop theories that encompass and interrelate both the new urban vitality, as citizens thrive on the new consumption, along with the various types of social breakdowns that are accompanying the evisceration of past and ruptured solidarities.

Notes

1 See the bibliography. We also include some journal articles to cover areas not reflected in the books.

2 There have also been a couple dozen articles published with cities as their theme over the past three decades. Their topics and approaches are pretty much identical with those of the books surveyed in this chapter: job allocation and mobility, housing, stratification, educational attainment, gender, inequality, the family, labor markets, marriage, urbanization, social networks, income distribution, power, and mate choice. Those who have contributed to this literature include Yanjie Bian, Montgomery Broaded, Deborah Davis, Yok-shiu Lee, Nan Lin, John Logan, Margaret Maurer-Fazio, Dwight Perkins, Danching Ruan, Andrew Walder, David Wank, Martin Whyte, and Xueguang Zhou. An excellent bibliography can be found in Tang and Parish (2000).

3 Whereas Walder's concern was with politics within the typical state-owned factory, Bian's is with stratification of workers city-wide.

4 Economic geography and urban planning in the PRC are fairly intermingled. Economic geography is the most dominant subfield of geography in China.

5 Economists in the early 1980s were preoccupied with issues such as price, productive forces, and the role of the market.

Bibliography

Basso, F. M. 1980: Urbanization, deurbanization and class struggle in China 1949–69. *International Journal of Urban and Regional Research* 4: 485–502.

Bian, Y. 1994: *Work and Inequality in Urban China.* Albany: State University of New York Press.

Bruun, O. 1993: *Business and Bureaucracy in a Chinese City: An Ethnography of Private Business Households in Contemporary China.* Berkeley: University of California, Institute of East Asian Studies.

Cai, F. 1998: The transformation of employment structure in a dual labor market. *Zhongguo Shehui Kexue* 20 (3): 4–14.

Chan, C. L. W. 1993: *The Myth of Neighbourhood Mutual Help: The Contemporary Chinese Community-based Welfare System in Guangzhou.* Hong Kong: Hong Kong University Press.

Chan, K. W. 1990: Shi fenxi shehuizhuyi guojia chengshihua de tedian (An analysis of the features of urbanization in socialist countries). *Zhongguo Renkou Kexue* (*Population Science of China*) 21: 6–12, 53.

—— 1994: *Cities with Invisible Walls: Reinterpreting Urbanization in Post-1949 China.* Hong Kong: Oxford University Press.

Chung, J. H. (ed.) 1999: *Cities in China: Recipes for Economic Development in the Reform Era.* London: Routledge.

Davis, D. S. (ed.) 2000: *The Consumer Revolution in Urban China.* Berkeley: University of California Press.

——, Kraus, R., Naughton, B., and Perry, E. (eds.) 1995: *Urban Spaces in Contemporary China: The Potential for Autonomy and Community in Post-Mao China.* Cambridge: Cambridge University Press.

Dutton, M. 1998: *Streetlife China.* Cambridge: Cambridge University Press.

Fei, X. 1984: Xiao chengzhen da wenti (Small towns, a big issue). *Liaowang* (*Outlook*), January 16–30, Nos. 2–5.

Gu, C. 1999: Development of urban geography in China since 1978. *Scientia Geographica Sinica* 19 (4): 320–31.

Gu, S. 1993: *Feinonghua ji chengzhenhua lilun yu shijian* (*The Theory and Practice of Non-agriculturalization and Urbanization*). Wuhan: Wuhan daxue chubanshe.

Guan, X. 1999: *Zhongguo chengshi pingkun wenti yanjiu* (*Research on Urban Poverty in China*). Changsha: Hunan renmin chubanshe.

Guldin, G. E. (ed.) 1992: *Urbanizing China.* New York: Greenwood Press.

—— and Southall, A. (eds.) 1993: *Urban Anthropology in China.* Leiden: E. J. Brill.

Harloe, M. et al. 1998: IJURR: looking back twenty-one years later. *International Journal of Urban and Regional Research* 22 (1): i–iv.

Ikels, C. 1996: *The Return of the God of Wealth: The Transition to a Market Economy in Urban China.* Stanford, CA: Stanford University Press.

Jankowiak, W. R. 1993: *Sex, Death, and Hierarchy in a Chinese City: An Anthropological Account.* New York: Columbia University Press.

Kirkby, R. J. R. 1985: *Urbanisation in China: Town and Country in a Developing Economy, 1949–2000 A.D.* London: Croom Helm.

Kojima, R. 1987: *Urbanization and Urban Problems in China.* Tokyo: Institute of Developing Economies.
Kwok, R. Y., Parish, W. L., and Yeh, A. G., with Xu, X. (eds.) 1990: *Chinese Urban Reform: What Model Now?* Armonk, NY: M. E. Sharpe.
Lewis, J. W. (ed.) 1971: *The City in Communist China.* Stanford, CA: Stanford University Press.
Li, H. and Li, L. 1999: Resource and exchange: the dependency structure in work-unit organization in China. *Shehuixue yanjiu* 4: 44–63.
Lieberthal, K. G. 1980: *Revolution and Tradition in Tientsin, 1949–1952.* Stanford, CA: Stanford University Press.
Liu, C. 1999: *Zhongguo chengshihua de zhidu anpai yu chuanxin* (*Institutional Arrangements and Innovations in Urbanization in China*). Wuhan: Wuhan University Press.
Liu, Z. et al. 1990: *Woguo yanhai diqu xiaochengzheng jingji fazhan he renkou qianyi* (*Economic Development and Population Migration in Small Towns in the Coastal Region in China*). Beijing: Zhongguo zhanwan chubanshe.
Logan, J., Bian, Y., and Bian, F. 1999: Housing inequality in urban China in the 1990s. *International Journal of Urban and Regional Research* 23 (1): 7–25.
Ma, L. J. C. and Hanten, E. W. (eds.) 1981: *Urban Development in Modern China.* Boulder, CO: Westview.
Mackerras, C. 1998: History and culture. In B. Hook (ed.), *Beijing and Tianjin: Towards a Millennial Megapolis.* Hong Kong: Oxford University Press, 1–30.
Perry, E. J. and Selden, M. (eds.) 2000: *Chinese Society: Change, Conflict and Resistance.* London: Routledge.
Shi, T. 1997: *Political Participation in Beijing.* Cambridge, MA: Harvard University Press.
Sit, V. F. S. (ed.) 1985: *Chinese Cities: The Growth of the Metropolis since 1949.* Oxford: Oxford University Press.
—— 1995: *Beijing: The Nature and Planning of a Chinese Capital City.* Chichester: Wiley.
Solinger, D. J. 1999: *Contesting Citizenship in Urban China: Peasant Migrants, the State and the Logic of the Market.* Berkeley: University of California Press.
Tang, C. and Feng, X. 2000: The differentiation of migrant peasants in "Henan Village." *Shehuixue yanjiu* 4: 72–85.
Tang, W. S. 1994: Urban land development under socialism: China between 1949 and 1977. *International Journal of Urban and Regional Research* 18 (3): 392–415.
—— and Parish, W. L. 2000: *Chinese Urban Life under Reform.* Cambridge: Cambridge University Press.
Vogel, E. 1968: *Canton under Communism: Programs and Politics in a Provincial Capital, 1949–1968.* Cambridge, MA: Harvard University Press.
Walder, A. G. 1986: *Communist Neo-traditionalism: Work and Authority in Chinese Industry.* Berkeley: University of California Press.
Wang, Y. 2000: Urban development studies: retrospect and prospect. *Shehuixue yanjiu* 1: 65–75.
White, L. T. 1978: *Careers in Shanghai: The Social Guidance of Personal Energies in a Developing Chinese City, 1949–1966.* Berkeley: University of California Press.
Whyte, M. K. and Parish, W. L. 1984: *Urban Life in Contemporary China.* Chicago: University of Chicago Press.

Wu, F. 1997: Urban restructuring in China's emerging market economy: towards a framework for analysis. *International Journal of Urban and Regional Research* 21 (4): 640–63.

Wu, Y. 1981: Guanyu woguo chengzhen renkou laodong goucheng de chubu yanjiu (A preliminary study of the labor structure of city and town population in China). *Dili xuebao* (Acta Geographica Sinica) 36 (2): 121–33.

Xiang, B. 1998: What is a community? A study of floating population settlements in Beijing. *Shehuixue yanjiu* 6: 54–73.

Xu, X. et al. 1987: *Zhongguo xiaoshizhen de fazhan* (*The Development of Small Cities and Towns in China*). Guangzhou: Zhongshan daxue chubanshe.

Yang, M. M. 1994: *Gifts, Favors, and Banquets: The Art of Social Relationships in China.* Ithaca, NY: Cornell University Press.

Yao, S. and Wu, C. 1982: Woguo nongcun renkou chengshihua de yichong teshu xingshi – shilun woguo de yinong yicong renkou (A special form of urbanization of rural population in China: a comment on the population of both peasants and workers). *Dili xuebao* (*Acta Geographica Sinica*) 37 (2): 155–62.

Yeung, Y. and Hu, X. (eds.) 1992: *China's Coastal Cities: Catalysts for Modernization.* Honolulu: University of Hawaii Press.

—— and Sung, Y. (eds.) 1996: *Shanghai: Transformation and Modernization under China's Open Policy.* Hong Kong: Chinese University Press.

—— and Zhou, Y. (eds.) 1988: Urbanization in China: an inside-out perspective (II). *Chinese Sociology and Anthropology* 21 (2).

—— and Zhou, Y. 1991: Human geography in China: evolution, rejuvenation and prospect. *Progress in Human Geography* 15 (4): 373–94.

Yusuf, S. and Wu, W. 1997: *The Dynamics of Urban Growth in Three Chinese Cities.* Oxford: Oxford University Press.

Zha, J. 1995: *China Pop: How Soap Operas, Tabloids, and Bestsellers are Transforming a Culture.* New York: New Press.

Zhang, Y. 1996: *The City in Modern Chinese Literature and Film: Configurations of Space, Time, and Gender.* Stanford, CA: Stanford University Press.

Zhao, R. et al. 1999: *Zhongguo jumin shourou fenpei zaiyanjiu* (*A Re-study ofIncome Distribution of Chinese Residents*). Beijing: Zhongguo caizheng jingji chubanshe.

Zhou, Y. 1982: Chengshihua yu guomin shengchan zongzhi guanxi de guiluxing tantao (An exploration of the relationship between urbanization and the gross domestic product). *Renkou yu jingji* (*Population and Economy*) 1: 28–33.

11
Economic Miracles and Megacities: The Japanese Model and Urbanization in East and Southeast Asia

J. S. Eades

In considering the state of play in urban studies in general, and urban anthropology in particular, at the start of the twenty-first century, the Pacific Asia region, comprising East and Southeast Asia, occupies a special position. It is here that economic growth was most rapid during the last half of the twentieth century (Chan 1993; Thompson 1998; Tipton 1998), so that it is here that social groups, cultures, and lifestyles have probably changed most rapidly from a global perspective. These changes have also been reflected in research on the region, both in its burgeoning megacities and elsewhere. Within this region, Japan occupies a central position for a number of reasons. First, it was the first economy to experience an economic "miracle" after World War II, blazing a trail which has been followed by most of the other countries in the region: the "little tigers" or "dragon economies" of Hong Kong, Korea, Singapore, and Taiwan, and, more recently, those of Thailand, Malaysia, and the coastal regions of mainland China. Second, it has been Japanese capital and investment and the offshoring of Japanese production which has largely underwritten these second- and third-generation economic miracles. Third, even though Japan has been prevented by its constitution and historical baggage derived from the colonial and wartime periods from exercising political or moral leadership in the region, it has exerted a degree of cultural hegemony, due not least to the various high-tech consumer goods and gizmos which its economic ascendancy has produced. This may be changing, of course – Hong Kong, Singapore, and even Taiwan and Korea have advanced so far that they have their own new technologies and cultural agendas, but at the same time the increasing speed of circulation of the "new middle classes" throughout the region means a degree of cultural homogenization, for which Japan provided many of the initial models.

In this brief review, therefore, I will begin with an analysis of the changing nature of urban studies within Japan. I then trace the ways in which the

Japanese urban experience is being replicated in the other societies of the region, and the implications of this for the future development of urban studies as a discipline.

From the 1980s to the 1990s in Japanese Urban Ethnography

Luckily for would-be reviewers of the mass of ethnographic research on Japan published in the postwar period, there are two excellent benchmarks in the form of essays written by Kelly in the early 1990s, reviewing much of the work that had been done up to the end of the 1980s (Kelly 1991, 1993). I have surveyed the general literature on Japan following on from his 1991 paper elsewhere (Eades 2000), so here I will concentrate on the urban literature, which he discussed more specifically in his article on metropolitan Japan in 1993. The subtitle of this article, "ideologies, institutions and everyday life," aptly summarizes much of the content. Both the statistical and ethnographic evidence on postwar Japan can be read in ways that support two rather divergent pictures of what was happening in Japanese society: both homogenization (typified by the growing army of salarymen) on the one hand, and enduring social differences (typified by accounts of the persistence of traditional institutions) on the other. The contradictions between these two models he explores at three different levels: ideological processes, including discourses of culture and class and the changing lifecycle in an increasingly childless and aging society; institutional patterns, including work, school, and the family; and, bringing these together, individual lifeways, in the form of personal histories.

Certainly many of the topics which he highlights are still important in Japanese urban research. The contrast between "rural" tradition and contemporary urban life, as exemplified in the *furusato* or home-town nostalgia boom in popular culture and advertising, has provided a central focus for research in anthropology (Ivy 1995: 103–8; Graburn 1998: 199), rather in the same way as the study of class has for the sociologists. The aging society, now perhaps seen more acutely as a major problem, is perhaps even more pervasive as a topic than it was ten years ago, permeating discussions of topics ranging from rural depopulation (Traphagen 2000) to housing (Brown 1996) and the provision of welfare (Campbell 1992; Freed 1993; Formanek and Linhart 1997). Studies of work have continued, though probably the focus within anthropology has been away from the large corporations (still an important object of scrutiny by economic historians and management scientists) toward smaller, more traditional companies and enterprises (Kondo 1990; Roberson 1998). Given the depth of the economic recession since 1991, it is not surprising that casual labor, foreign workers, the unemployed, and the homeless have also become prominent in the literature (Fowler 1996; Stevens 1997; Gill 2000, 2001). Education is another continuing topic, though the focus has probably shifted away from basic documentation of the system to the efforts of the state at reform, even if the reform agenda itself is highly contested (McVeigh 1997, 1998, 2000; Rohlen and LeTendre 1998). The diminishing birthrate and the aging society provide the backdrop here as well, as educational institutions such as universities face the problems of competing for a decreasing pool of young people and marketing their products to new social groups of *shakaijin* (students with social experience, i.e., mature students). The focus of studies of the family has probably shifted even more dramatically, with a growing number of studies of gender, sexuality, and alternative lifestyles (Allison 1994; Frühstück 1998; Lunsing 1998).

Along with these well-established areas of research, there are others that have expanded and flourished during the 1990s, including consumption, popular culture, and the environment.

Consumption

Much of the best work on Japan during the 1990s was carried out by anthropologists, under the influence of scholars such as Appadurai (1990), Clifford (1992), and Hannerz (1992).

The *leitmotif* in much of this work is that of cultures on the move, with processes such as "creolization" (Hannerz 1987) and "McDonaldization" becoming the rule rather than the exception. One of the most important sources of work in this area is the ConsumAsiaN series published by Curzon and Hawaii and edited by Brian Moeran and Lisa Skov. This has now produced volumes on such varied subjects as gender (Skov and Moeran 1995), advertising (Moeran 1996; McCreery 2000), popular culture (Treat 1996), weddings (Goldstein-Gidoni 1997; see also Edwards 1989), department stores (MacPherson 1998), and Japanese *manga* or comic books (Allison 1996; Kinsella 2000). Outside the series there have been a number of other studies of major cultural forms such as *pachinko* (pinball) (Manzenreiter 1998) and *karaoke* (Mitsui and Hosokawa 1998), in addition to a number of edited volumes on popular culture and leisure in general. An attempt at theoretical generalization in this area is the book by Clammer (1997).

Clammer sees consumption as a tool for revealing cultural patterns and economic organization, given that much of Japanese social life revolves around it. Consumption is gendered – most if it is in the hands of women – and is also linked to age and social stratification. Indeed, Clammer argues that in this largely homogeneous society social groups are increasingly differentiated by consumption practices, cutting across the traditional bonds of kinship and neighborhood. Social change, he argues, is led by consumers, and especially by women. Shopping is approached mainly in terms of choice, and many of the goods consumed are imported – the internationalization of consumption in action. Popular taste is greatly influenced by the popular magazines, which provide an enormous amount of information on what people should consume, and when and how they should consume it. Thus the global is made local through consumption, and it is all driven by personal choice and the media.

To complement this kind of analysis it is also worth looking at the work of the political economists and economic historians. Consumption preferences and personal choice are not only dependent on the individual choices of consumers, but also on the producers of consumer goods and the choices they present to the consumers. Consumers cannot necessarily consume what they want: they can only choose between the goods on offer in the retail market. Nor can they necessarily live or work where they want to: they can only move to where they can find jobs and houses, and this also depends on entrepreneurs (often the same entrepreneurs that run the department stores). In the case of Japan, the main underlying factor has been the massive flow of capital and people away from the smaller towns and villages toward the major growth poles: the Tokyo, Osaka, Nagoya, and Fukuoka regions (Fujita and Hill 1993; Karan and Stapleton 1997). More specifically, a major constraint on choice has been the development of the infrastructure, particularly railway networks both within and between cities. The most important intercity train is the *Tôkaidô-Sanyô Shinkansen*, which runs from Tokyo in the east to Fukuoka in the west. The rapidity and frequency of these trains (trains from Tokyo to Osaka run at roughly six-minute intervals throughout the day) have had an enormous effect on people's perceptions of space and decisions as to where they live and work. The line connects together nine of the twelve major cities in Japan: Tokyo, Yokohama, Nagoya, Kyoto, Osaka, Kobe, Hiroshima, Kitakyushu, and Fukuoka, all with over a million inhabitants. The zone through which the line runs is now nearly entirely urbanized, a near-continuous cluster of cities sometimes dubbed the "Tôkaidô megalopolis," with a staggering 70 million inhabitants or more. It is often quicker to get between major cities than between different points in the same cities, so that locations near *shinkansen* stations are at a premium for businesses. Since it began in the 1960s, the *shinkansen* service has radically altered the shape of urban development in Japan and helped its concentration into this single linear zone.

The major intercity lines interface in turn with the urban rail networks, and these are particularly closely linked with other forms of consumption, given that railway companies are often also involved in retailing and hotel developments. The most spectacular example in terms of scale, but not an untypical one in terms of the mix of related enterprises, is that of the Seibu-Saison group of enterprises run by the Tsutsumi brothers Seiji and Yoshiaki, two of the richest men in the country and perhaps the most influential of all in terms of their influence on consumption by the rest of the Japanese population (Havens 1994; Downer 1995). The family business was started by their father, Yasujiro, a politician and entrepreneur who began with real estate development in the now fashionable resort town of Karuizawa. Hotels and leisure complexes are still a major part of the Tsutsumi empire, as are railways in Tokyo and department stores throughout the country. These enterprises are linked and integrated. The Seibu railway makes its way to Tokorozawa, home of the Seibu baseball team through real estate developed by Seibu enterprises. At various points on the line are department stores, also run by Seibu. In Karuizawa the landscape is dotted with Seibu villas, and the Seibu bus and taxi services can also take you to shop in the main department store, which just happens to be Seibu. So are most of the leisure facilities, including the skating rink and bowling alleys. This is also true in Hikone where I used to live and which is close to Yasujiro's birthplace in Shiga prefecture. The Seibu presence here is also highly visible: Tsutsumi enterprises run the buses, the taxis, the boats on the lake, the local private railway, and the largest hotel in town. Consumption choices, in other words, are not the result of the hidden hand of the market but are shaped by leaders of fashion and taste, among whom Tsutsumi Seiji with his department stores and Tsutsumi Yoshiaki with his resorts and hotels are among the most influential. It is from what they, and entrepreneurs like them, choose to provide that the consumers have to choose. The title of Havens's study, *Architects of Affluence*, sums it all up. But Japanese retailing, like Japanese *karaoke*, golf, cartoons, and comic books, has also been internationalized. Most of the major cities in Asia also boast their local versions of the Japanese department stores. In Tianjin in 1995 the local Isetan department store had become something of a minor tourist attraction, with children riding the escalators and their parents gazing at the latest Japanese gear, made inaccessible only by the Japanese price tags.

The point of all this is that the political economy of high-speed growth and the expansion of consumption are linked, not simply because people become wealthier and can therefore consume more, but because the capitalist companies that are causing the economic growth are also selling goods that have to be consumed. This applies most spectacularly to the automobile and leisure industries throughout the region, with implications for the environment.

Pollution and social movements in Japan

Where consumption and the political economy intersect most dramatically in the cities of Eastern Asia is in relation to the environment. In leading the pack in high-speed growth during the 1950s Japan also became the regional leader in another less fortunate way, in terms of pollution and damage to the environment. For a long time this was ignored – the times were too good and the economic growth too fast, and people were prepared to put up with the pollution that went along with rapidly rising standards of living. But by the 1970s it was clear that something had to be done: the sea and the lakes were dying, along with much of the vegetation around them, the rivers were covered in concrete, and the shorelines of the bays near the major cities were lined with heavy industrial sites (Smith 1978: 8–10). Mysterious new diseases, some of them named after the places where they were first identified, such as Minamata disease and Yokaiichi asthma, also began to appear, resulting in long-drawn-out court cases by local residents once the causes were traced to pollution from local industry (McKean 1981) Luckily the economy was still buoyant, and the government spent huge sums of money over the next few years trying to mitigate and reverse the damage that had been done (Nakamura 1999). But money still poured into construction projects, thanks to the cozy relations between the state and the construction industry (Tabb 1995: 172–3; McCormack 1996: 25–77; Woodall 1996), upgrading the road network, building tunnels, and – above all – constructing dams, to the extent that there is hardly a river in Japan which has not been dammed at some point or another, whatever the costs or environmental consequences (McCormack 1996: 44–8).

One of the solutions was to offshore many of the most polluting forms of production to other parts of the region. Japanese firms started to relocate their plants, to Taiwan, Korea, China, Malaysia, and Thailand, cutting down the levels of pollution at home but increasing those abroad. The government moved away from policies of rapid development to the pursuit of the leisure society (McCormack 1996: 78–112) – even though it meant that the large construction firms which had been constructing heavy industry during the period of high-speed growth were still in business, though now constructing golf courses and leisure resorts.

Even these seemingly more innocuous forms of development are not without their problems. Building resorts still means more concrete and less natural shoreline. Building golf courses means cutting down trees and constructing greens that require considerable application of fertilizers, weed-killers, and other chemicals, and these in turn find their way into the water courses and pollute the rivers. Golf courses and dams are among the main targets of the environmental movements throughout the country at the present time.

Two other results of the country's increasing wealth have been the increasing number of cars on the road, and the increasing quantities of garbage. Because it retained a comprehensive railway network, Japan has probably the best and most efficient system of public transport in the world, especially in and around Tokyo and the other large cities (Cervero 1998: 118–20). There are serious drawbacks to driving, including the relatively high cost of petrol (by American standards, if not by British), the crowded roads, the enormously expensive motorway tolls, and the difficulties of finding anywhere to park. Even so, the ratio of road to rail travel has gradually risen, so that by the mid-1980s the Japanese were, statistically at least, a nation of road users.

The problem of garbage has also been simmering away in the popular consciousness for a long time but has taken on a new urgency recently. Japan has a major problem because of the density of the population and the lack of suitable alternative ways of getting rid of the stuff. Greater Tokyo actually produces a lot less garbage than Greater New York, even though the populations are similar in size, but the available methods of disposal are basically the same: burning, burying, and recycling (Eades 1998). Much of the garbage has been buried in landfill sites as part of the programs of land reclamation, particularly in Tokyo Bay during the period of the bubble economy when these schemes could be justified partly by the high price of land, but many of the sites are now full and public opinion is in favor of retaining what little of the natural shoreline is left. There is recycling of "unburnable" garbage of various types, including metals, plastics, and *sodai gomi* ("large garbage," in the form of unwanted household furnishings and equipment), but there are limits to what this can achieve. That leaves incineration. Japan has been a world leader in this technology, but recent research has turned up alarming evidence of high concentrations of dioxins in and around garbage disposal facilities throughout the country. There are reports of hundreds of residents in locations where new garbage disposal facilities have been set up suddenly suffering from mysterious diseases, which of course they quickly come to associate with the facilities. In parts of Tokyo which have been subject to dumping for years there is also a long tradition of citizen activism in relation to garbage problems (Eades 1998: 98–102), and this has been spreading to other areas in recent years (Vosse 2000; Waley 2000).

The results have been increasing levels of citizen dissatisfaction and protest, and many schemes have had to be abandoned or moved as a result. Contrary to conventional analyses of Japanese citizens as relatively quiescent and willing to go along with the guidance of government, there is growing evidence of widespread dissatisfaction with the damage to the environment, and some well-documented cases of local activism. In relation to waste disposal, there is the case of Oita prefecture which has been well documented by Broadbent, where protests over landfill sites date back to the 1970s (Broadbent 1998). The other classic case in the literature, also dating back to the 1970s, is the construction of the Tokyo International Airport at Narita to the northeast of the city. This became a *cause célèbre* for political activists: twenty years after the construction of the original airport small groups of farmers who refuse to sell their land continue to block the planned construction of additional runways (Apter and Sawa 1984). There are also considerable local protests at the construction of other new airports, such as Kobe in

Kansai, which is near two other underused airports (Osaka and Kansai), and at Hino in Shiga prefecture, which is relatively close to Nagoya.

The Implications for Urban Theory

This rich empirical diversity in urban life raises a common question in urban studies: what are the theoretical threads, if any, which can be used to tie it all together? Since the industrial revolution, the nature of cities has changed so rapidly that theoretical paradigms are hardly able to catch up with the reality. The assumptions of the 1920s and 1930s that most cities looked like Chicago gave way to a realization in the 1950s that many of them were still pre-industrial. However, modernization theory in the 1960s suggested that even these would soon industrialize, a belief confounded by the 1970s discussions of the world system, with its pockets of poverty, dependency, and underdevelopment. Early in his career, Castells (1976) even argued that urban sociology did not really exist at all, and what we should be studying was collective consumption and urban social movements. Be that as it may, he and others did continue to study cities within the developing world capitalist system, until the "cultural turn" of the 1980s persuaded some of them to concentrate almost solely on the ideological superstructure instead. It was only in the 1990s that discussions of theories of globalization began to suggest ways in which the Humpty Dumpty of urban theory might be put back together again, even though these ways increasingly led away from traditional conceptualizations of "the city."

As in the late 1960s the most promising line of argument seems to be derived from Marxism, though this time from the world-system variant as developed by Manuel Castells, Saskia Sassen, and others, together with urban geography and planning via Peter Hall. In his book on the "informational city," Castells (1989) showed how the new information technology had reshaped the location and layout of American cities, in a way comparable with the impact of the automobile in the early twentieth century. Sassen followed this with her discussion of the "global cities" (Sassen 1991). This was based on research on urban and economic restructuring during the 1980s which showed the economic impact that the rise of the global corporations and financial service industries had had on the social structures of New York, London, and Tokyo. Later in the decade, Castells extended this kind of argument even further in his ambitious trilogy, *The Information Age*, which succeeded in linking once more many of the kinds of rather disparate social phenomena of the city discussed above to a "grand narrative" of global economic development (Castells 1996, 1997, 1998).

His basic position in his most recent work can be summarized briefly as follows: advanced industrial countries are moving from economies based on manufacturing and industry to economies based on the production, manipulation, and dissemination of information. However, not all regions have access to this new technology, and the excluded areas (the "fourth world," in his terminology) are thereby disadvantaged in the new world economy, leading to increasing polarization. These excluded areas are to be found not only in such obvious locations as Africa and the poorer regions of the former Soviet Union, but also in the ghettos and depressed areas of the larger cities in the core industrial countries. Like Sassen, he sees the growth of the financial services industry in the global cities as leading to the collapse of more traditional forms of production, coupled with the casualization of labor, with full-time predominantly male workers being replaced by part-time predominantly female ones. These changes are in turn having a knock-on social effect on the family, with the breakdown of the traditional "patriarchal family" and its replacement by other kinds of structures and lifestyles.

Meanwhile, the enterprise itself is becoming networked, its constituent parts coupled not by geographical proximity but by information technology. Perceptions of time and space thus become warped, and the boundaries between the real and virtual worlds become increasingly fuzzy. The nation-state itself loses much of its power as it becomes increasingly unable to control the economic activity within its borders, thanks to the multinationals and the currency markets. Politicians who rely on the mass media, particularly television, to get their message across find themselves the stars in virtual reality political soap operas, as in the Clinton impeachment saga and the 2000 American presidential election. While the fortunes of nation-states and their leaders decline, those of regional organizations are on the rise, as nation-states trade a degree of autonomy for longer-term stability. And as the economic and political structures of the twentieth-century world break down, religious, ethnic, and social movements provide place and meaning for people trying to organize their lives in this new post-industrial globalized environment.

This general model of the informational economy and the social and cultural effects that it produces certainly resonates well with many processes and phenomena to be seen in present-day Japan (Eades 2000), but its ramifications go way beyond the boundaries of the city. It is a model of the way in which social processes take place in highly developed informational societies, which may or may not mean that they take place in cities. In Japan these days around 90 percent of the population live in the towns and cities into which much of the country is divided. Administrative boundaries do not necessarily coincide with geographical boundaries. "Greater Tokyo" as a single geographical entity actually extends over several different prefectures of the country in addition to Tokyo prefecture itself. In the south it merges into the cities of Kawasaki and Yokohama, both very large cities in their own right (Cybriwsky 1998: 13–19; Eades 1999a: xviii–xxii). Tokyo prefecture technically includes a national park to the west, where the population density is very low, as well as a number of small Pacific islands a considerable distance to the south which have been made part of the capital for administrative convenience. The whole land area of the country is similarly divided between cities, towns, and villages, and many of the cities and towns contain extensive rural areas, including mountains, forest, and farmland. Cities are fiscal and administrative units, within which many people may in fact live in the countryside. In other words, the more advanced and informational a society becomes, the more the divisions between town and country become blurred, and the more the concept of what constitutes a city begins to disappear. Just as the city disappears as a theoretical object, except for discussions of physically built-up areas or administrative boundaries, so the separation of "city life" from other types of social life and behavior also becomes increasingly indistinct.

Similarly, the boundaries of academic disciplines also become less and less distinct, with material derived from urban sociology, geography, planning, and government in addition to anthropology all becoming grist to the mill. Discussions of urban culture need to be grounded in the processes of the political economy rather more than has been the case with the "cultural studies turn" of the last few years, while culture and lifestyles have obvious impacts in relation to the environment. And finding solutions to urban problems depends not only on the available technology but also on mobilizing people using whatever social and cultural resources are available. So, members of school parent–teachers' associations become agencies for community recycling; groups of housewives living in the same apartment blocks become a distribution network for organic farm produce (Clammer 1997: 41); and new forms of urban employment are created under the banner of "remaking the town" by "restoring" its "traditional" culture and landscape, and attracting tourists to newly organized "traditional" festivals (Bestor 1989: 224–55; Wazaki 1993). The city therefore becomes something which is not *sui generis* or distinct, but the site where a variety of processes common to all capitalist industrial societies increasingly intersect: physical planning and construction, economic activity, residential concentration and the formation of social groups, certain types of political mobilization, and a variety of cultural events, all reflecting in some way or other the dialectic between local historical peculiarities and the forces of globalization and the world economy.

The Relevance of Japanese Urbanism for East and Southeast Asia

Looked at in this way, there is no such thing as the "Pacific Asian city," though the kinds of processes which have been described for Japan may also be observed in relation to other cities within the region as well (Ginsburg et al. 1991; Lo and Yeung 1996, 1998; Watters and McGee 1997). In this final section I will consider some of the most important of these, which together form the focus of much of the most interesting research currently taking place in the region and which are likely to remain important issues for the urban future of the region as well.

High-speed growth and the developmental state

First, there is the underlying economic growth which has made much of the urbanization possible. Many countries of course experience urbanization without economic growth, suffering from the typical environmental and social problems that accompany inadequate service provision and the shortage of formal sector employment. Among the Pacific Asian megacities, Manila and Jakarta are probably closest to this model. However, in Beijing-Tianjin, Hong Kong-Canton, Shanghai, Taipei, and Seoul, on the other hand, rapid urbanization has in many instances been accompanied by more rapid economic growth, resulting in a pattern which is closer to that of Japan. Other parts of the region are also developing their own versions of the Tôkaidô megalopolis: the geographical literature on the region is full of descriptions of urban corridors and regions of various shapes and sizes, and the connections between them (Sit 1985, 1995; Pannell and Veeck 1991; Yeh and Xu 1996; Zhou 1991; Auty 1997; Tang and Parrish 2000).

Underlying these similarities are long periods of extremely rapid economic growth, typically measuring between 8 and 12 percent per annum, and extending over more than a decade. In the case of Japan, high-speed growth lasted from the early 1950s to the early 1970s and resulted not only in the reconstruction of the country but also its emergence as an economic superpower (Tabb 1995). This was followed by similar periods of growth in Taiwan, Korea, Singapore, and Hong Kong, and, more recently, in Thailand, Malaysia, and the coastal regions of China (Aberbach et al. 1994; Bedeski 1994; Chiu et al. 1997).

The reasons for this growth are much debated, and scholars have variously pointed to cultural factors such as the Confucian ethic, the quality of the education system, or the involvement of the state. Discussions of the role of the state can be traced back to the work of Chalmers Johnson (1982) on Japanese development during the prewar and postwar periods. He focused on the role of the Ministry of International Trade and Industry (MITI, or Tsûsanshô in Japanese) and its predecessors during both periods: basically, many of the people who orchestrated Japanese growth in the prewar period were still around to organize its resurgence twenty years later. The state's control of key raw materials and foreign exchange, coupled with direct and indirect administrative "guidance" using networks of former ministry officials who had retired to take up positions in major companies, was responsible for the development of key sectors of the economy, following the basic decision to go for high-tech development rather than low-tech labor-intensive industries such as textile production. Economic growth, in other words, can be traced back to the intervention of the "developmental state" (Johnson 1993; Chan 1993: 58–62), a paternalistic state, in alliance with Japanese big business.

Variations on similar themes can be found in the literatures on other countries of the region. The next generation of miracle economies included Hong Kong, while still under colonial rule, and Singapore, Korea, and Taiwan, all run for long periods by paternalistic autocrats. Economic growth came first: democratization, in the cases of Korea and Taiwan, followed only later. As in Japan, there was an alliance between manufacturing capital and a strongly developmental state. Overholt (1993) has suggested that a broadly similar pattern can be found in China during the period of high-speed growth presided over by Deng Xiaoping, triggered by the economic reforms of 1978 and continuing up to the present.

The Asiatic mode of pollution

Unfortunately, this economic growth also brought with it similar environmental problems in most of these cases, though as wealthy city-states, Singapore and Hong Kong have been rather more successful in keeping these problems at bay. I have summarized these trends in detail elsewhere (Eades 1999b), so a cursory sketch will have to suffice here. As in Japan, the development of heavy industry in Korea, Taiwan, and many areas of mainland China has led to increasing pollution, especially in industrial areas and the associated river basins (Whitney 1991; Williams 1994; Kim et al. 1999). The emission of atmospheric pollutants, thanks to the growth of industry and the increasing number of motor vehicles, and the output of industrial wastewater and solid wastes have also grown rapidly, resulting in air and water pollution. More recently, thanks to the high-speed growth there, there have been similar trends in Malaysia, Thailand, and parts of Indonesia, as the economies have moved from the primary production of agricultural and mineral commodities to industry.

The forests of Taiwan and Korea largely disappeared during the colonial period, but in these southern countries deforestation is currently a major problem. In Malaysia, forests now cover less than half the land area, compared with over two-thirds in the 1960s. The main culprits have been conversion of land to agriculture, dam construction resulting in flooding, mining, logging, and shifting cultivation. The timber industry in many parts of Indonesia also remains environmentally unsustainable, thanks to illegal logging, collusion between villagers, officials, and logging companies, and the flouting of environmental regulations. They are not the only ones to blame:

much of the wood ends up as wood pulp for shipment to Japan, which has financed the pulp mills through its international development program. In Thailand, half the country's forests were cleared between 1960 and 1993. Many of these areas were converted to agricultural land, but illegal logging continues and there are worries that the forest will disappear completely in the next generation. Even so, there are worries about the supply of agricultural land, about half of which is affected by soil erosion, salinity, and acidity. Much of the most fertile land has been affected by urbanization, with building for residential, commercial, and industrial purposes, especially around the major cities, and pollution has also increased as a result of urban waste (Manopimoke 1999). China suffers from similar problems, given that its "rural areas" are often the site of substantial settlements and local industries. With rising economic prosperity, other elements of the Japanese experience have been replicated, such as the construction of golf courses and leisure resorts.

Governments are, of course, not unaware of these problems and are trying to cope with them through planning and legislation. In Japan during the 1970s and 1980s, a realization of the problems led to a policy shift away from the growth of heavy industry to mitigation of its environmental impact. The Malaysian government has responded with an impressive list of environmental control legislation, and environmental concerns have been increasingly integrated into development plans (Sani 1999). This is in addition to support for environmental monitoring, education, research, cooperation, and project coordination by government agencies, and initiatives at the regional level. In Thailand, the government has increased the area of the national parks and has incorporated the need for protection and rehabilitation into development planning since the early 1980s. Taiwan established an environmental protection agency in the 1970s. Public debate about environmental issues has grown along with the process of democratization in countries like Korea and Taiwan (Williams 1994; Kim et al. 1999). But there are still worries about how far these measures can be implemented given that this is usually dependent on small numbers of officials with limited resources, and it has been argued that this makes the role of education, public awareness, and the activities of NGOs that much more important throughout the region. Even in China, which has the worst problems due to its huge population, which is still expanding, Smil detects more willingness to talk about the issues – his own work has been translated into Chinese and circulated among government officials (Smil 1993: xviii).

In most of the countries that have experienced economic growth, the first priority was delivering a higher standard of living to the majority of people rather than environmental protection as a way of establishing government legitimacy in response to people's aspirations. However, in most cases prevention of environmental problems at the planning stage is much more cost-effective than dealing with the problems only when they have become serious later on, assuming that this is possible. As an example, Taiwan in the early 1990s faced the daunting task of trying to deal with thirty years' worth of problems with a staff of 318 in the environmental protection agency monitoring 70,000 factories, over 8 million vehicles, and a population of 20 million (Williams 1994: 252–3). Negotiating the necessary proactive measures is complex, as government has to negotiate with industries to invest in costly technology. They may only be willing to do so if public awareness and pressure through NGOs and so on make it clear that it is in their interests to do so. Public education and awareness therefore become a vital component of any long-term environmental strategy.

Environment, political processes, and the state

This highlights the complex relationship between the state, the economy, political processes, and the environment. In my earlier article (Eades 1999b), I suggested a model of political development in the region which can be summarized as follows: in most of the countries of the region, the postwar period was marked first by a drive for economic growth, followed by a realization of the environmental problems that this growth was causing. In most cases, development plans and guidelines under the pressures of environmental and social movements have begun to reflect environmental concerns, and environmental protection agencies have been set up, though there is considerable variation in the degree to which this process has progressed.

In China, for instance, large parts of the country are still waiting for the early benefits of high-speed growth to appear, in the form of better roads, communications, and electrification. Even in the wealthier cities, the main political problems faced by the government have been the fallout from unemployment due to the closure of inefficient state industries, or from inflation in a situation where the wages and salaries of many people are fixed by the government. In this climate, some of the more obvious environmental policies such as raising the price of energy to private consumers and industry have been difficult to implement. While Smil (1993) takes the pessimistic line that China's environmental problems are so serious that they will act as a severe brake on economic development in the near future, Overholt (1993) argues that economic growth will lead to the development of a wealthy middle class demanding increased political representation and a pluralistic political system. Their demands might well also include quality of life issues such as the urban environment. In Indonesia, Thailand, and Malaysia, the major question is how far environmental demands from the population make headway in the face of the interests of capital in alliance with the political elite.

Environmental concerns seem to be higher on the agenda in Korea and Taiwan, perhaps because the environmental problems are more serious due to their histories and the high level of industrial development. Judging from Williams's account (1994), the Taiwanese environmental movement does seem to have been able to extract concessions from local capitalists and politicians, and Taiwan also seems to have realized that prevention is much cheaper than cure when it comes to dealing with environmental issues. In countries like Taiwan, where basic problems of housing and employment have been largely solved, environmental issues move to the top of the agenda for an increasing section of the population, and this may also be helped by the provision of environmental education in schools.

Even if the public and NGOs take the environmental issue on board, however, there is no guarantee that environmental problems will recede into the background, as a glance at Japan, still the most developed country in the region, shows. The Japanese state represents a balance between the various political players and fractions of capital within Japanese society, one of the most powerful of which is the construction lobby and its political and bureaucratic supporters (McCormack 1996; Woodall 1996). The government provides a steady stream of work at comfortably high prices to the industries, which in turn provide support for the ruling politicians and sinecures for the retiring bureaucrats (the *amakudari*, or "Buddah descending from Heaven" system). There is also a degree of *Yakuza* (gangster) involvement as well, with dummy construction companies which are mob fronts siphoning off money from large contracts (Gill 2000). In the 1950s and 1960s the main construction projects were industrial. In the 1970s and 1980s, when state policy turned to the enhancement of lifestyles, construction followed suit, with an emphasis on airports, golf courses, and so on. Many of them also have long-term consequences for the environment, even if this is less obviously harmful than the integrated industrial projects of the earlier period. In the case of the various projects around Tokyo and Osaka bays, these more recent projects have been very large and very expensive, even if the economic rationale for some of them (e.g., an airport at Kobe, following the opening of the Kansai airport between Osaka and Wakayama) is not entirely clear. In many cases the protests of environmental groups against these projects continue to be ignored, but the limits to their implementation may not be political but fiscal, as the budget deficit rises in the government's attempts to generate employment through laying down more and more concrete. In any case, construction capital is itself highly innovative, with entrepreneurs like the Tsutsumis mentioned above not only providing what the public wants to consume, but even defining what the public wants to consume. Many others have followed their lead, and the results can be seen in the resorts, golf courses, department stores, and theme parks proliferating throughout the rest of the region. They have their own agendas, as have the politicians whom they support.

Ultimately therefore, the future of the Asian environment and its associated cities will depend on whether capital and politicians can strike a deal through which the environment also wins. But even in Japan, the political discourse is still one of addressing economic problems through the traditional measures of financing public works, whether or not they are needed, and at continued risk to the environment. The journey required for most other cities and countries of the region is even longer, so that it is difficult to be optimistic about the region's urban future.

Conclusion

To summarize, at the start of the twenty-first century we are clearly in an era of globalization. Even if we cannot always agree exactly what this process entails, it nevertheless does involve more rapid flows of people, capital, information, and technology around the world, and this has had considerable impact, not only on cities but also on the ways in which we look at them. In the case of Japan, as I have argued, the result has been not only the development of large cities but of a new megalopolis linked together by the high-speed railways. This is not just an aberration but is becoming something of a norm among the cities and urban corridors of East and Southeast Asia, as in other highly developed regions of the world. As the boundaries between cities and between cities and the rest of the country have broken down, so have the boundaries of urban studies, so that much of the best work in the last decade has been on subjects like consumption and environmental problems, which are concentrated in, but not confined to, the city. The city therefore becomes the site where these processes intersect in often interesting ways, rather than an object of study in itself.

In the case of Pacific Asia, the dominant fact of the postwar era has been that of high-speed economic growth. It can be argued that not only are the causes of this broadly similar in a number of different countries, but that the fallout in terms of urban life has also been broadly similar. But rather than types of city, it makes more sense to look at types of development process, with Japan often playing the role of the precursor over the last fifty years, and the other countries following in its footsteps, giving some observers a sense of *déjà vu*.

For urban studies in general, and anthropology in particular, this means a shift of focus, of subject matter, and of methodologies. Third World urban studies since the postwar period were dominated by studies of migration, ethnicity, housing, poverty, the informal sector, and so forth. To some extent these are still there, even if they are presented in a slightly different guise. In the case of Japan, migration is no longer the movement of people to the city but of international migrants into the labor market. The study of ethnicity includes not only these new migrants, but also long-established and rapidly assimilating minorities such as the resident Korean population and (if they can be considered an ethnic minority at all) the *Burakumin*. Housing studies no longer center on squatter settlements but on high-rise apartments and the construction of three-generation homes to cope with the problems of the elderly and the land market. Poverty has been to a large extent marginalized in the new middle-class Japan, as represented by the casual laborers and the cardboard cities in the stations and parks around the major cities, but it is not the all-pervasive problem that it is, for instance, in the cities of the United States. The "informal sector" is represented by a small clutch of ethnographies of the *Yakuza* (Kaplan and Dubro 1986; Herbert, 2000), but otherwise the main split in the labor market is between the small businesses and the large corporations, both of which continue to attract substantial research. But the dominant strand in urban-based research now in Japan focuses on subjects such as consumption, mainstream and alternative lifestyles, tourism and the media, fantasy and theme parks. This strand of research will no doubt remain popular in the years to come, maintaining strong links with cultural studies. At the other end of the spectrum, the urban environment will also remain a major concern, providing the focus not only for environmental activism but for a whole range of voluntary sector activities, political groupings, and NGOs. And as the other cities of the region approach Japan in terms of their maturity and prosperity, similar concerns will gradually take over there as well. An anthropology of cybercultures is just beginning, linking people within the region and beyond. This also promises to be a major area of interest, given the novel methodological possibilities which it opens up, as well as being a further logical step in the shift away from conventional geographical and disciplinary boundaries. This shift, as I have tried to suggest in this chapter, is characteristic of the study of urban life in general in this region against the background of unprecedented high-speed growth.

Bibliography

Aberbach, J. D. et al. (eds.) 1994: *The Role of the State in Taiwan's Development*. Armonk, NY: M. E. Sharpe.

Allison, A. 1994: *Nightwork: Sexuality, Pleasure, and Corporate Masculinity in a Tokyo Hostess Club*. Chicago: Chicago University Press.

—— 1996: *Permitted and Prohibited Desires: Mothers, Comics and Censorship in Japan*. Boulder, CO: Westview.

Appadurai, A. 1990: Disjuncture and difference in the global cultural economy. In M. Featherstone (ed.), *Global Culture: Nationalism, Globalization and Modernity*. London: Sage, 295–310.

Apter, D. E. and Sawa, N. 1984: *Against the State: Politics and Social Protest in Japan.* Cambridge, MA: Harvard University Press.

Auty, R. M. 1997: The East Asian growth model: South Korean experience. In R. F. Watters and T. G. McGee (eds.), *Asia Pacific: New Geographies of the Pacific Rim.* Bathurst, Australia: Crawford, 161–9.

Bedeski, R. E. 1994: *The Transformation of South Korea: Reform and Reconstitution in the Sixth Republic under Roh Tae Woo, 1987–1992.* London and New York: Routledge.

Bestor, T. 1989: *Neighborhood Tokyo.* Stanford, CA: Stanford University Press.

Broadbent, J. 1998: *Environmental Politics in Japan: Networks of Power and Protest.* Cambridge: Cambridge University Press.

Brown, N. 1996: The *nisetai jûtaku* phenomenon: the prefabricated housing industry and changing family patterns in contemporary Japan. D. Phil. dissertation, Oxford University.

Campbell, J. C. 1992: *How Policies Change: The Japanese Government and the Aging Society.* Princeton, NJ: Princeton University Press.

Castells, M. 1976: Is there an urban sociology? In C. G. Pickvance (ed.), *Urban Sociology: Critical Essays.* London: Tavistock, 33–59.

—— 1989: *The Informational City.* Oxford: Blackwell.

—— 1996: *The Information Age: Economy, Society and Culture.* Volume 1: *The Rise of the Network Society.* Oxford: Blackwell.

—— 1997: *The Information Age: Economy, Society and Culture.* Volume 2: *The Power of Identity.* Oxford: Blackwell.

—— 1998: *The Information Age: Economy, Society and Culture.* Volume 3: *End of Millennium.* Oxford: Blackwell.

Cervero, R. 1998: *The Transit Metropolis: A Global Enquiry.* Washington, DC: Island Press.

Chan, S. 1993: *East Asian Economic Dynamism.* Boulder, CO: Westview.

Chiu, S. W. K. et al. 1997: *City-States in the Global Economy: Industrial Restructuring in Hong Kong and Singapore.* Boulder, CO: Westview.

Clammer, J. 1997: *Contemporary Urban Japan: A Sociology of Consumption.* Oxford: Blackwell.

Clifford, J. 1992: Traveling cultures. In L. Grossberg et al. (eds.), *Cultural Studies.* New York: Routledge, 96–116.

Cybriwsky, R. 1998: *Tokyo: The Shogun's City at the Twenty-first Century.* Chichester: John Wiley.

Downer, L. 1995: *The Brothers: The Saga of the Richest Family in Japan.* London: Vintage Books.

Eades, J. S. 1998: Cities of sludge: the politics of waste disposal in New York and Tokyo. In K. Aoyagi et al. (eds.), *Toward Sustainable Cities.* Leiden: Institute of Cultural and Social Studies, University of Leiden, 85–106.

—— 1999a: *Tokyo.* Oxford: ABC-CLIO.

—— 1999b: High-speed growth, politics, and the environment in East and Southeast Asia. In Y. Itakura et al. (eds.), *Integrated Environmental Management: Development, Information, and Education in the Asian-Pacific Region.* Boca Raton and London: Lewis Publishers, 1–18.

—— 2000: Introduction: globalization and social change in contemporary Japan. In J. S. Eades et al. (eds.), *Globalization and Social Change in Contemporary Japan.* Melbourne: Trans-Pacific Press, 1–16.

Edwards, W. 1989: *Modern Japan through its Weddings*. Stanford, CA: Stanford University Press.

Formanek, S. and Linhart, S. (eds.) 1997: *Ageing: Asian Concepts and Experiences, Past and Present*. Vienna: Verlag der Osterreichischen Akademie der Wissenschaften.

Fowler, E. 1996: *San'ya Blues: Laboring Life in Contemporary Tokyo*. Ithaca, NY: Cornell University Press.

Freed, A. O. 1993: *The Changing World of Older Women in Japan*. Manchester, CT: Knowledge, Ideas and Trends.

Frühstück, S. 1998: Then science took over: sex, leisure, and medicine at the beginning of the twentieth century. In S. Linhart and S. Frühstück (eds.), *The Culture of Japan as Seen through its Leisure*. Albany: State University of New York Press, 59–82.

Fujita, K. and Hill, R. C. (eds.) 1993: *Japanese Cities in the World Economy*. Philadelphia: Temple University Press.

Gill, T. 2000: *Yoseba* and *ninpudashi*: changing patterns of employment on the fringes of the Japanese economy. In J. S. Eades et al. (eds.), *Globalization and Social Change in Contemporary Japan*. Melbourne: Trans-Pacific Press, 123–43.

—— 2001: *Men of Uncertainty*. Albany: State University of New York Press.

Ginsburg, N. et al. (eds.) 1991: *The Extended Metropolis: Settlement Transition in Asia*. Honolulu: University of Hawaii Press.

Goldstein-Gidoni, O. 1997: *Packaged Japaneseness: Weddings, Business and Brides*. Honolulu: University of Hawaii Press.

Graburn, N. 1998: Work and play in the Japanese countryside. In S. Linhart and S. Frühstück (eds.), *The Culture of Japan as Seen through its Leisure*. Albany: State University of New York Press, 195–212.

Hannerz, U. 1987: The world in creolisation. *Africa*: 546–59.

—— 1992: *Cultural Complexity: Studies in the Social Organization of Meaning*. New York: Columbia University Press.

Havens, T. R. H. 1994: *Architects of Affluence: The Tsutsumi Family and the Seibu-Saison Enterprises in Twentieth-century Japan*. Cambridge, MA: Council on East Asian Studies, Harvard University.

Herbert, W. 2000: The *Yakuza* and the law. In J. S. Eades et al. (eds.), *Globalization and Social Change in Contemporary Japan*. Melbourne: Trans-Pacific Press, 143–58.

Hirsch, P. and Warren, C. (eds.) 1998: *The Politics of Environment in Southeast Asia: Resources and Resistance*. London: Routledge.

Ivy, M. 1995: *Discourses of the Vanishing: Modernity, Phantasm, Japan*. Chicago: University of Chicago Press.

Johnson, C. 1982: *MITI and the Japanese Miracle*. Stanford, CA: Stanford University Press.

—— 1993: *Who Governs? The Rise of the Developmental State*. New York: W. W. Norton.

Kaplan, D. E. and Dubro, A. 1986: *Yakuza: The Explosive Account of Japan's Criminal Underworld*. Reading, MA: Addison-Wesley.

Karan, P. P. and Stapleton, K. (eds.) 1997: *The Japanese City*. Lexington: University of Kentucky Press.

Kelly, W. 1991: Directions in the anthropology of contemporary Japan. *Annual Review of Anthropology* 20: 395–431.

—— 1993: Finding a place in metropolitan Japan: ideologies, institutions and everyday life. In A. Gordon (ed.), *Postwar Japan as History*. Berkeley: University of California Press, 189–296.

Kim, J. W. et al. 1999: Environmental problems and public awareness in the Republic of Korea. In Y. Itakura et al. (eds.), *Integrated Environmental Management: Development, Information, and Education in the Asian-Pacific Region*. Boca Raton and London: Lewis Publishers, 77–92.

Kinsella, S. 2000: *Adult Manga: Culture and Power in Contemporary Japan*. Honolulu: University of Hawaii Press.

Kondo, D. K. 1990: *Crafting Selves: Power, Gender, and Discourses of Identity in a Japanese Workplace*. Chicago: University of Chicago Press.

Lo, F. and Yeung, Y. (eds.) 1996: *Emerging World Cities in Pacific Asia*. Tokyo: United Nations University Press.

—— 1998: *Globalization and the World of Large Cities*. Tokyo: United Nations University Press.

Lunsing, W. 1998: *Beyond Commonsense: Negotiating Constructions of Sexuality and Gender in Japan*. London: Kegan Paul International.

McCormack, G. 1996: *The Emptiness of Japanese Affluence*. Armonk, NY: M. E. Sharpe.

McCreery, J. 2000: *Japanese Consumer Behavior*. Honolulu: University of Hawaii Press.

McKean, M. A. 1981: *Environmental Protest and Citizen Politics in Japan*. Berkeley: California University Press.

MacPherson, K. (ed.) 1998: *Asian Department Stores*. London: Curzon.

McVeigh, B. J. 1997: *Life in a Japanese Women's College: Learning to be Ladylike*. London: Routledge.

—— 1998: *The Nature of the Japanese State: Rationality and Rituality*. London: Routledge.

—— 2000: Education reform in Japan: fixing education or fostering economic nation-statism? In J. S. Eades et al. (eds.), *Globalization and Social Change in Contemporary Japan*. Melbourne: Trans-Pacific Press, 76–92.

Manopimoke, S. 1999: Economic development and the environment in Thailand: the current situation and the role of environmental education and NGOs. In Y. Itakura et al. (eds.), *Integrated Environmental Management: Development, Information, and Education in the Asian-Pacific Region*. Boca Raton and London: Lewis Publishers, 93–130.

Manzenreiter, W. 1998: Time, space, and money: cultural dimensions of the *pachinko* game. In S. Linhart and S. Frühstück (eds.), *The Culture of Japan as Seen through its Leisure*. Albany: State University of New York Press, 359–81.

Mitsui, T. and Hosokawa, S. (eds.) 1998: *Karaoke around the World: Global Technology, Local Singing*. London: Routledge.

Moeran, B. 1996: *A Japanese Advertising Agency: An Anthropology of Media and Markets*. Honolulu: University of Hawaii Press.

Nakamura, M. 1999: Lake Biwa and the Asian environmental agenda: issues and prospects. In Y. Itakura et al. (eds.), *Integrated Environmental Management: Development, Information, and Education in the Asian-Pacific Region*. Boca Raton and London: Lewis Publishers, 19–28.

Overholt, W. 1993: *China: The Next Economic Superpower?* London: Weidenfeld and Nicolson.

Pannell, C. W. and Veeck, G. 1991: China's urbanization in an Asian context: forces for metropolitanization. In N. Ginsburg et al. (eds.), *The Extended Metropolis: Settlement Transition in Asia.* Honolulu: University of Hawaii Press, 113–36.

Roberson, J. 1998: *Japanese Working Class Lives: An Ethnographic Study of Factory Workers.* London: Routledge.

Rohlen, T. and LeTendre, G. (eds.) 1998: *Teaching and Learning in Japan.* Cambridge: Cambridge University Press.

Sani, S. 1999: Beyond environmental legislation: environmental education in Malaysia. In Y. Itakura et al. (eds.), *Integrated Environmental Management: Development, Information, and Education in the Asian-Pacific Region.* Boca Raton and London: Lewis Publishers, 29–48.

Sassen, S. 1991: *The Global City: New York, London, Tokyo.* Princeton, NJ: Princeton University Press.

Sit, V. F. S. 1985: *Chinese Cities: The Growth of the Metropolis since 1949.* Oxford: Oxford University Press.

—— 1995: *Beijing: The Nature and Planning of a Chinese Capital City.* Chichester: Wiley.

Skov, L. and Moeran, B. (eds.) 1995: *Women, Media and Consumption in Japan.* London: Curzon.

Smil, V. 1993: *China's Environmental Crisis: An Inquiry into the Limits of National Development.* Armonk, NY: M. E. Sharpe.

Smith, R. S. 1978: *Kurusu: The Price of Progress in a Japanese Village, 1951–1975.* Stanford, CA: Stanford University Press.

Stevens, C. 1997: *On the Margins of Japanese Society.* London: Routledge.

Tabb, W. K. 1995: *The Postwar Japanese System: Cultural Economy and Economic Transformation.* New York: Oxford University Press.

Tang, W. and Parish, W. L. 2000: *Chinese Urban Life under Reform: The Changing Social Contract.* Cambridge: Cambridge University Press.

Thompson, G. (ed.) 1998: *East Asian Economic Dynamism.* London: Routledge.

Tipton, F. B. 1998: *The Rise of Asia: Economics, Society and Politics in Contemporary Asia.* Honolulu: University of Hawaii Press.

Traphagen, J. 2000: *Taming Oblivion: Aging Bodies and the Fear of Senility in Japan.* Albany: State University of New York Press.

Treat, J. S. (ed.) 1996: *Contemporary Japan and Popular Culture.* London: Curzon.

Vosse, W. M. 2000: The domestic environmental movement in contemporary Japan: structure, activities, problems, and its significance for the broadening of political participation. Ph.D. thesis, University of Hanover.

Waley, P. 2000: Tokyo: patterns of familiarity and partitions of difference. In P. Marcuse and R. van Kempen (eds.), *Globalizing Cities: A New Spatial Order?* Oxford: Blackwell, 127–57.

Watters, R. F. and McGee, T. G. (eds.) 1997: *Asia Pacific: New Geographies of the Pacific Rim.* Bathurst, Australia: Crawford.

Wazaki, H. 1993: The urban festival and social identity. In A. Cohen and K. Fukui (eds.), *Humanising the City?* Edinburgh: Edinburgh University Press, 127–46.

Whitney, J. B. R. 1991: The waste economy and the dispersed metropolis in China. In N. Ginsburg et al. (eds.), *The Extended Metropolis: Settlement Transition in Asia.* Honolulu: University of Hawaii Press, 177–92.

Williams, J. F. 1994: Paying the price of economic development in Taiwan: environmental degradation. In M. A. Rubenstein (ed.), *The Other Taiwan: 1945 to the Present.* Armonk, NY: M. E. Sharpe, 237–56.

Woodall, B. 1996: *Japan under Construction: Corruption, Politics, and Public Works.* Berkeley: University of California Press.

Yeh, A. G. and Xu, X. 1996: Globalization and the urban system in China. In F. Lo and Y. Yeung (eds.), *Emerging World Cities in Pacific Asia.* Tokyo: United Nations University Press, 219–67.

Zhou, Y. 1991: The metropolitan interlocking region in China: a preliminary hypothesis. In N. Ginsburg et al. (eds.), *The Extended Metropolis: Settlement Transition in Asia.* Honolulu: University of Hawaii Press, 89–112.

Part V
Urban Processes and City Contexts: India and the Middle East

12
Cities of the Past and Cities of the Future: Theorizing the Indian Metropolis of Bangalore

Smriti Srinivas

There is a widely held consensus that urban studies emerging in Western Europe or North America in the 1970s added a critical edge to the vocabulary of urban sociology by the 1980s, stressing the role of spatial conjunctures and disjunction and embedding the city within global structures of capital or labor. Against this stage, the narrative of the 1990s "cultural turn" seems to interrogate or add value to critical urban studies using theoretical frameworks that stress postcolonial, sexual, and other cultural identities. Often occulted through both narratives are other histories of the sociological discipline, national and urban, that reorient both the sociologist and subject-object, or produce an alternative language for understanding the cultures of space and memory. This chapter seeks to foreground these issues by theorizing the city of Bangalore, a site that has been inappropriately baptized as the "Silicon Valley" of India (see figure 12.1).[1] I am less confident of my hermeneutic skills in this enterprise than I am of the necessity for recovering encrypted memories, historical and cultural mediations, and their spaces. At best, this chapter is a suggestion of intertwining trajectories – my own, and those of other urban actors, institutions, and several cities.

Urban Sociology in India/Sociology of the Indian City

In the mid-1980s, Delhi was a city recovering from several wounds. In 1984, Prime Minister Indira Gandhi had been assassinated by her Sikh guards after she ordered the storming of the Golden Temple in Amritsar, Sikhism's most sacred shrine, to repress Sikh separatists who were using the temple as a base for their operations. Both events unleashed a spiral of violence, including the killing of many Sikhs in Delhi and the destruction of their property, followed by months of anguish and terror. Indira Gandhi's son, Rajiv Gandhi, the com-

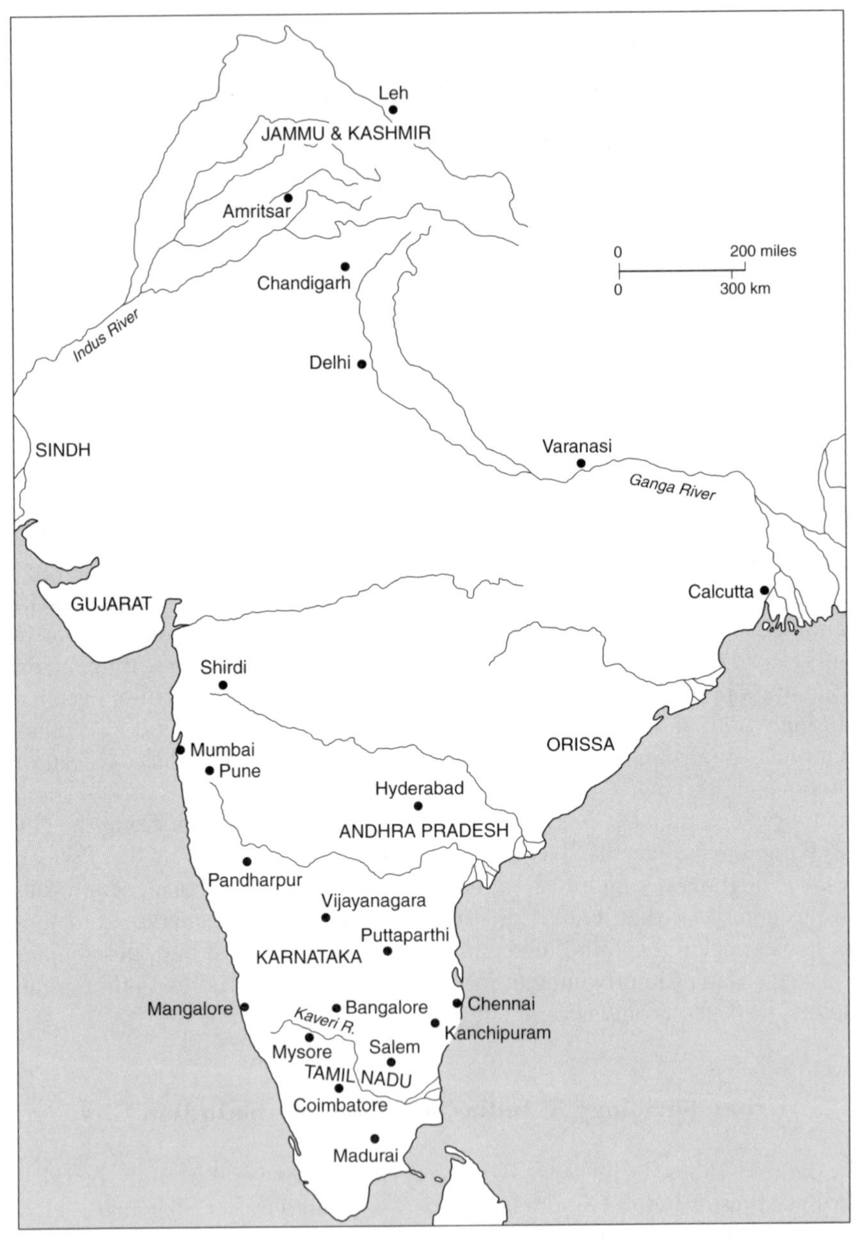

Figure 12.1 Map of South Asian urban sites and places associated with the Sai Baba movement

mercial pilot and reluctant Prime Minister of the country, succeeded his mother in office and in the years to come would usher in India's economic "liberalization." By the mid-1980s, Delhi had also announced its claim to be a "world city" by hosting the Asian Games which resulted, among other things, in the construction of huge overpasses and stadia, and the displacement of large numbers of the urban poor and slums to the city's fringes.

Signs of these altered times were apparent in the city, including the proliferation of police booths on Delhi University campus. Its School of Economics, housing the Department of Sociology, began in 1949 soon after Indian independence and was associated with such august intellectuals as the economist V. K. R. V. Rao and sociologist M. N. Srinivas.[2] The "D-School" stood on the northern side of the city in the old British Civil Lines just outside the ramparts of the Red Fort and the Old City of the Mughal rulers of Delhi. It was largely a social mirror image of New Delhi, on the southern side of the Old City, which bore the signs of national bureaucratic classes, corporate headquarters, and grid-patterned housing colonies for the middle classes. There was something about the location of the D-School that was symptomatic of the graduate training I received in sociology, poised between the trials and agendas of the colonial and the national state. In the interests of decolonization, my department steadfastly refused to make the choice between anthropology and sociology, in part because the classificatory apparatus of colonial knowledge girded the distinction. In any case, if the social complexity of India ranged from tribal groups to "modern" industrial strata, what intellectual sense did the separation make? The ambidextrous training that we received was liberating, although physical anthropology was never a part of the curriculum and quantitative techniques were better taught in the Department of Economics building within the same compound. If anything represents the strengths of sociology of that period, it was the possibility of simultaneously having as one's doctoral peers a student examining shifting cultivation among the tribal peoples of Bastar in Central India, and another whose work focused on the medical discourse of menstruation with fieldwork done at Harvard Medical School. The critique of modernity and its systems of knowledge (whether its defining moment could be traced to sixteenth-century Europe or to the colonial presence in India especially after 1800) were primary impulses driving the structure of courses and reading.

The theoretical and empirical lacunae in the study of the urban, however, were signs of wider cultural and institutional processes. My experience in the 1980s introduced me to three models of the city. The city as sacred space was embodied in the temple town of Madurai in south India and Varanasi in north India; then there was the colonial city, with its cantonment and civil lines overshadowing the older sites of regional rulers such as Delhi, or transforming fishing villages and smaller urban sites into the East India Company's port-fort and then the site of the Raj's bureaucracy such as Chennai (Madras). In both cases, a frozen history seemed to inhabit the space of the urban. Finally, after the abdication of history by sociology and acceptance of the disciplinary regimes of economists, planners, and managers to cities, there was the developmental-managerial city, rooted only in the national and global present and embodied in the Indian Institutes of Management of the nation-state.

The only time that the boundaries between these models blurred was when walking through the streets of Delhi and stumbling upon forgotten enclaves and architectural anomalies: for instance, a medieval hydraulic structure frequented largely by doves and overshadowed by the Soviet embassy building in New Delhi; or a police station built in Tibetan style (someone said by Francis Younghusband) in Old Delhi's crowded markets. The models of the city were usually, however, positioned in epistemologies that seldom intersected, creating a sense of disorientation and discomfort for me. It was hardly surprising that I chose dissertation work in a Himalayan frontier region in Jammu and Kashmir state. In Ladakh, once the cultural "crossroads of Asia" before it was transformed into a battleground between nations, I examined the implications of nation-state formation in this area for the symbolic and material remaking of Buddhist and Muslim identities (Srinivas 1998). Although Ladakh's primary city, Leh, had been a critical entrepot in Himalayan and Central Asian trade for several centuries, I left it for Nubra valley located near the ceasefire line between India and Pakistan, conscious that I did not have the language to study the city.

Urban sociology in (and of) India is a field that is still defining and constituting itself. The first reason for this is that much of the early energies in Indian sociology had been directed to rural India, especially in the years after independence when concerns about the economic and cultural transformation of the rural and tribal landscape permeated social science research. The second reason is a definitional one that has haunted many scholars: D. F. Pocock alluded to this in an early paper where he claimed that the distinction between urban and rural sociologies was superfluous since the city and the village in South Asia demonstrated a continuity of form (Pocock 1960). The third reason is a chronological one: the preoccupation with the colonial city and its physical and imaginative presence in the postcolonial period made it almost impossible to move beyond the four Presidency cities of Mumbai (Bombay), Chennai, Calcutta, and Delhi, key sites of the British Raj. The fourth reason is that even when the postcolonial city appeared as an object of study, most urban research until the latter half of the 1980s proceeded in the shadow of the developmental state concerned with demographic and socio-ecological parameters, industrialization, migration and caste, and the three "Ps" – planning, political change, and poverty.[3]

By far the most serious problem in the study of the city was (and is) the disciplinary hiatus between sociology and history contributing to a collective amnesia at the heart of social science. Some of the most critical work on cities, crucial to any theorizing of the urban past or present, has come from history and archaeology, not exactly the staple fare of sociology in India or indeed in many other parts of the world. Writings by historians, or those with historical lenses, have steadily uncovered the complexity of older "walled" cities, medieval centers, central places and site hierarchies, and sites in the Indus valley, plains of the Ganga River and central and southern India such as Vijayanagara and Kanchipuram.[4] These testify to thriving urban cultures and a diversity of urban models ranging from ports to courts, textile centers, pilgrimage sites, military enclaves, and entrepots. They add to more sociologically focused works dealing directly with single cities, focusing on *ex-nihilo* state capitals such as Chandigarh, or cities in India interpenetrated by colonial contact such as Surat, Chennai or Mumbai.[5] Many of the discussions remind us that the "peasantization" of the Indian sociological imagination may indeed be a colonial and early national product. The historical research also demonstrates that cities in India were part of a world system at different points in time, linked to Africa, the Mediterranean world, South west Asia, China, and Southeast Asia through trade routes over land and sea.[6] Studying the complex relationships between trade, ideological exchanges, diasporas, and early states through the recovery of these histories and flows makes obvious the limitations of economistic arguments about the globalization process as a frictionless, disorienting motion of persons, processes, and products accompanied by a disappearance of a sense of place. For many theorists of the twentieth-century urban experience, the "global" city holds a special place, read as a stage of late capitalism with culture serving the processes of technological innovation and capital accumulation. South Asian cities are never theorized within these frameworks, except as "nodes" in these processes, but are crucial for a more historical urban sociology. Minimally, it is necessary that collective memories are restored both within the city and within the social scientist and this project seems to be finally coming of age.[7]

There is cause to take urban sociology forward if only because of sheer significance of urban centers in India today. While fifteen years ago less than one-third of the gross domestic product of the country was produced in cities, today this figure is almost 60 percent. At the beginning of the twentieth century, India's urban population was less than 11 percent; in the year 2001, with India's population over 1 billion, the proportion of the population living in urban areas is estimated at about 35 percent. In 1901, according to the Census of India, there were 1,811 urban areas in India with only one "metro" city (with a population of over 1 million), Calcutta, which was also the second largest city in the British Empire after London. In 2001, there are about forty metros with a population of 1 million or more (see Shafi 1996).

Discourses of Return

In the mid-1990s, having completed my doctorate from the D-School, I returned to Bangalore, a city in which I had spent a few years as a teenager in the late 1970s and early 1980s, and began working at the Institute for Social and Economic Change. There were few sociologists there, most economists did serious quantitative and demographic work, and those concerned with the city tended to study issues of urban poverty and rural–urban migration. Through several projects on urban religiosity, I was forced to critically engage with the complex realities of Bangalore, which was neither a sacred city nor a colonial city, and seemed to escape in some subtle ways the categories that emerged from demography or concerns about social justice.

Bangalore originated with the activities of a local warlord, Kempe Gowda I (ca. 1510–70), who established an oval-shaped mud-brick wall fronted by a moat protecting a series of bazaars and habitation areas. The choice of the location for the commercial centers and fort rested on the availability of water through an array of artificial lakes or tanks that Kempe Gowda constructed and augmented, bounding the city on various sides. Outside the fort and the commercial centers were smaller settlements linked to the fort and bazaars through a variety of economic and cultural transactions, forests, gardens, and fields. The urban, therefore, included all these elements – fort, bazaars, settlements, tanks, and green spaces.

By the seventeenth century, Bangalore was part of the expanding kingdom of the Wodeyar kings from Mysore, later falling under the authority of General Haider Ali after he assumed control of the kingdom in 1766. He embellished the city by creating the Persian-style Lal Bagh ("Red Garden") and rebuilt the fort in stone. His military adventures, and those of his son Tippu Sultan, led to the formation of an opposing coalition by the expansive British East India Company, which eventually overran Bangalore in 1799. The East India Company reinstalled the Wodeyar kings and made an agreement that allowed the British to maintain a military cantonment northeast of the Old City, thus establishing the familiar dual pattern of urbanization under colonialism. The period of the first Sole Commissioner of Bangalore, Sir Mark Cubbon, from 1834 to 1861 is associated with the opening of the first railway line in Bangalore and a large number of roads and telegraph lines. Toward the end of the nineteenth century, a number of "extensions" based on a grid-plan were laid out, in part because of the growth of the population, the problems of water and sanitation in the Old City, and the plague epidemic of 1899–1900.

Ushered in by the twentieth century, Bangalore was conceptualized as a garden city for its numerous horticultural gardens, the eighteenth-century Lal Bagh, the nineteenth-century Cubbon Park, and hundreds of lakes girding the city. The model of the modern city, based on engineering, scientific research, and development, however, soon overshadowed this model. Bangalore was the site of the Indian Institute of Science, the aeronautics industry, and several other well-known engineering, medical, and scientific institutions. In part, this was because an industrial base was established early as Bangalore was the first city in India to be electrified (about 1902–3), because of British investment, and because of the enlightened policies of the "Diwans" (minister-administrators under the Mysore kings). However, it achieved centrality in scientific production before World War II through its promotion by the "industrialize or perish" slogans of the Diwan, Sir M. Visveswaraya, and as the nationalist utopia of a technopolis. The modern city was augmented by a factory system: while the production base of Bangalore in the early twentieth century comprised glass, porcelain, brick, and tobacco factories, the period from 1900 to 1950 was one of textile hegemony. The economy of the city relied heavily on the textile industry, including state-owned plants, private concerns, thousands of smaller looms owned by individuals, and an entire range of castes associated with different stages of production and marketing of textiles.

Under the aegis of the new nation-state, the model of the modern city was transformed into the model of the developmental city. The rise and the dominance of the public sector (1950–80) through the establishment of engineering works and, later, electronic goods, set the tone of development for nearly three decades when a number of concerns, chiefly public, came into existence. This period also saw intensification of employment in government bureaucracy, the administrations of state-run enterprises, and other parastate organizations. These processes not only caused the city to expand through new industrial estates, but also created some of the largest in-migrations in its history by drawing workers and their families from neighboring regions. In 1901, the population of the metropolitan area was 228,000; in 1951, the figure had risen to 991,000; and in 1981, the population comprised 2,913,000 persons (Bangalore Development Authority 1995: 16). The model of the developmental city spelled disaster for the garden city, as its green, hydraulic basis was engorged by city bus stations, state-run enterprises, and industrial effluents, even while bureaucratic classes retired to what they perceived as a pensioner's paradise.

While, by the mid-1980s, the stage was set for global linkages because of the pool of technical, scientific, and professional strata, it was also set for the establishment and development of local microelectronics, information-based, and software industries in Bangalore such as Infosys Consultants. By the end of the decade, with the liberalization of the Indian economy and the removal of certain restrictions on imports and licensing, the microcomputer revolution occurred in Bangalore. The concept of Bangalore as the "new Silicon Valley" developed through these changes as well as the concessions announced for technology parks by the government in 1985. Symbiotic relationships, such as with Texas Instruments, became more frequent with the high-technology private sector providing software outsourcing for multinational companies. By the 1990s, Bangalore seemed to be poised to renew its promise as the city of the future with a projected increase in its population to 5,800,000 persons by 2001 (Bangalore Development Authority 1995: 16).[8] The metropolitan area today includes three zones: the Bangalore City Corporation containing the Old City and the Cantonment, the area proposed for further conurbation, and the green belt, which is supposed to be free from further urbanization (see figure 12.2). It is constructed as the informational city of India, the Electronic City built on its outskirts with an "informational corridor" stretching along the metropolitan periphery advertised simultaneously by high-technology boosters as well as bureaucrats who claim that it is time to rethink the model of the developmental city.

There is another model that emerges periodically: the "Kannada" city, capital of Karnataka state, invoked as a source of pride for local Kannada-speakers. Already in the sixteenth century, Bangalore had Marathi-, Telugu-, and Tamil-speakers besides those who spoke Kannada, its location between four linguistic regions a contributing factor to multilingualism. While about two-thirds of the population of Karnataka state spoke Kannada as their mother tongue, in Bangalore District's urban areas including Bangalore, however, Kannada-speakers comprised only about a third of the population; there were also Tamil-speakers, Telugu-speakers, and Urdu-speakers. The district also comprises a number of religious groups such as Christians, Muslims, and a variety of Hindu sectarian groups, whose intersections with these languages are complex (Karnataka State Gazetteer 1990: 140–1).[9] Within the model of the Kannada city, these linguistic and religious intersections are often suppressed in favor of a more monolithic cultural history, and various issues – such as over the division of water from the Kaveri River with neighboring Tamil Nadu – have led to linguistic identities clashing, sometimes very violently. This is symptomatic of the ways in which culture often returns to Indian cities in other regions, seen in discourses of violence and secularism, riots, migrants, elections, or linguistic and religious fundamentalism.[10]

To read these five models of Bangalore – the garden city, the modern city, the developmental city, the informational city, and the Kannada city – and ask what they say for an understanding of the urban in India leads us to discourses of return, "quest" stories that tie institutional and personal biographies together. The late nineteenth century and the early twentieth century, for example, seem to have produced several travelers-cum-national heroes such as Mohandas Karamchand Gandhi, better known after his return to

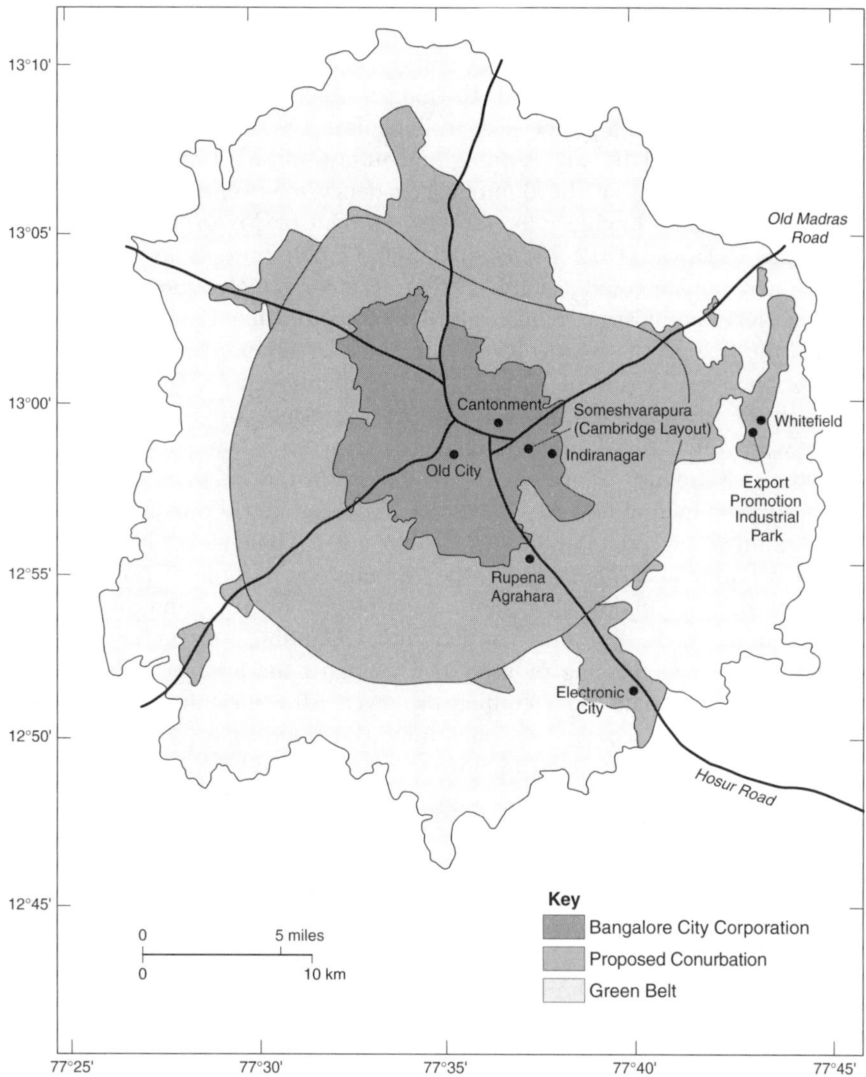

Figure 12.2 Map of the Bangalore metropolitan area in 1995

India from South Africa as "Mahatma" Gandhi. The theme of the quest, which involves the individual leaving in search of knowledge, gaining a vision, and then returning as a hero to build (or destroy) the city, or add to its material and ideological infrastructure in some novel way, is a very old one in South Asian literature. Epic literature, Tamil *Sangam* poetry, and the *Hitopadesha*, for example, mention or depict various quests by businessmen, princes, and ordinary people. In the case of Bangalore, it appears that neither the garden city model nor the model of the Kannada city required leaving and returning, while each of the other models was tied up with an idiosyncratic quest.

One of the quests involved Karnataka's hero, Sir M. Visveswaraya (1860–1962), born in a village close to Bangalore, who was to become one of the great figures in Indian planning and industrialization. After serving as a hydraulic engineer in the Bombay Presidency for twenty-three years, he returned as Chief Engineer for the Government of Mysore in 1909, later becoming its Diwan (1912–18). He had toured Japan, Europe, and the United States, and implemented a number of projects for state-led industrialization such as Krishnarajasagar dam near Mysore (completed 1931), which controlled the flow of the Kaveri River to provide irrigation water. The "industrialize or perish" vision of Visveswaraya, as mentioned previously, was tied up with the model of the modern city. To honor him, the state created the Visveswaraya Industrial and Technological Museum in Bangalore.

Other less august "returnees" to Bangalore in the 1970s were attracted to the developmental city. My father, for instance, after a diplomatic career that spanned several cities in Asia, returned to Bangalore from Beijing with the family in 1977. In India, the "Emergency," a time of political uncertainties for the nation-state, suppression of civil liberties, and the famous urban "makeovers" by Prime Minister Indira Gandhi's son, Sanjay Gandhi – including the bulldozing of the old Turkman Gate area in Delhi – had ended with the Janata Party coming to power. After the tumult, Bangalore seemed an idyllic refuge. Not only were the middle-class "Indian Independence Families" attracted to this cosmopolitan city, which promised to fulfill their many dreams; so were students from several states, as well as professionals from Germany and Britain. Within a decade, the inflow included Jordanian, Iranian, and Nigerian students, Indian families returning from East Africa and Malaysia because of less salubrious political conditions in these countries, and *nouveaux riches* strata that had made fortunes in sites like Dubai.

The narrative of quest and return continued in the 1980s: the Centre for the Development of Telematics (C-DOT), for instance, was closely connected to another returning native, Sam Pitroda, whose career was linked with the model of the information city/society. Pitroda, born in a poor family in Orissa, completed his M.S. degree at the Illinois Institute of Technology in 1964. He built a company in telecom equipment, the sale of which to Rockwell International made Pitroda's fortune. During the early 1980s he gained an introduction to Rajiv Gandhi who, as the new Prime Minister in 1984, made Pitroda a technology adviser in programs as diverse as drinking water, immunization, and adult literacy. C-DOT, a separately managed society, was also a product, meant to transfer technology to rural areas, with an office in Bangalore.

The discourses of return, along with the opportunities created by the modern city, the developmental city, and the informational city, added new social groups to Bangalore. They also generated pressure on the garden city's ecology, and a sense of crisis that was registered periodically by invoking the Kannada city model. The cultural dramas occurring in Bangalore are comparable to the developments occurring in Mexico City, Nairobi, or Kuala Lumpur. This is not only because of the sheer magnitude of the populations involved, but also because the creation of new metropolitan fringes appears to defy all labels: should we call the product the noncentric city, the edge city, exurb, post-suburban region, or simply, urban sprawl? Apart from issues of terminology and management, which are concerns for urban theorists and planners, sociologists and anthropologists have registered the expansion of new ritual forms and religious movements in these cities. A major methodological challenge lies in the interweaving of these two regimes of spatial and ideological production. Examining the expanding frontiers of Bangalore, including public sector industries, new residential colonies, and the "information technology corridor," leads one to realize that they do not occur within "empty spaces" but in sites abundant with spatial and ritual memories. Girding these developments are a number of lakes, older settlements surrounding temples, village farming communities from the sixteenth century, Anglo-Indian exurbs from the nineteenth century, and other autonomous towns which are linked to the new urban terrain in novel geographies. Faced with the richness of Bangalore's urban experience, there are several interrelated propositions that I will extend in this context. First, given the rapid transformation of urban locations and the growing mobility of persons and resources, there has emerged a heightened sense of affirmation of religious sites for different urban communities, not all of which lead to discourses of violence surrounding the construction of cultural identities. Second, routes and sites created by the contemporary city such as highways can become pathways for the reenchantment of the city. Third, and this is the direction I wish to pursue for the rest of this chapter, constructions of the city emerge from a mnemonics of space allied to several ideological histories; in many cases these histories are embedded in discourses of return that employ languages of a sacred quest. These languages, however, do not separate the sacred from the civic, the political, or the affective, and, therefore, redefine the urban in their image.

The Mnemonics of Space

The Sai Baba movement owes its origin to a nineteenth-century saint, Shirdi Sai Baba, closely identified with Sufi genealogies and other mendicant orders in the Deccan region of South Asia. According to various accounts, Sai Baba serendipitously arrived at Shirdi in 1854, a little village in Maharashtra, about sixteen years of age (*Shri Sai Satcharita* 1972).[11] Shirdi had a few hundred houses: 90 percent of the population were Hindu peasants and 10 percent were Muslims, who worked mainly as artisans or agricultural laborers. Baba began to reside in a dilapidated mosque and had few personal belongings besides the robe he wore. While others called him "Sai Baba," he referred to himself and God as the mendicant (*fakir*).

At first, only a few people came to him for medicines that he would make. The incident that altered his presence in the village was a miracle in which he apparently converted water to oil, and almost overnight he seems to have been transformed from a mad mendicant into a holy saint. Worship was at first individual, with sandal paste and flowers, though at times Sai Baba and his Muslim devotees resisted it. Later, about 1908, the transformation from individual to congregational worship began at Shirdi where Baba was worshipped with all kinds of regal paraphernalia along the lines of worship at Pandharpur, an important focus of Vaishnava devotion since the thirteenth century. In addition, a festival commemorating the death of a Muslim saint was celebrated alongside "Rama Navami," the birthday of the Hindu deity, Rama. In 1918, Baba had an attack of fever and passed away.

After the saint died without nominating a spiritual successor, the transmission of his charisma took innovative routes through several contemporary religious leaders. Apart from the development of Shirdi into a huge pilgrimage site attracting devotees from different religious and class backgrounds, there were several holy persons who aligned themselves with Shirdi Sai Baba, creating the basis for the spread of Sai devotion in India and overseas. The All-India Sai Samaj, for instance, created by the efforts of Narasimha Swami, has about a thousand centers in India today. Sathya Sai Baba, the most famous successor of Shirdi Sai Baba, has devotees across the world and is consulted by several heads of state. Meher Baba, described by many as the "avatar of love," has devotional centers in Pune, Mumbai, and Virginia Beach, USA, among others, and it is within his philosophy that Shirdi Sai Baba's Sufi character is preserved. At least three highly popular films on Shirdi Sai Baba's life have been produced and his charisma can also be encountered daily in India as one travels in the three-wheeled "autorickshaw," many of which carry small pictures of Shirdi Sai Baba alongside other deities, prophets, and movie stars.

The mendicant-saint paradigm in the case of Shirdi Sai Baba took shape against a rural background; for his successors, the city and its frontiers have become the most important field for recruitment of devotees. Three sites in Bangalore, lying southeast and east of the city, presenting distinct styles of urban religiosity and devotion to Sai Baba, are the focus of this chapter (see figure 12.2). The first is Rupena Agrahara, a village settlement that today lies on Hosur Road (National Highway 7) within the area proposed for conurbation. The second is Someshvarapura (more generally known as Cambridge Layout), a housing colony east of the Cantonment but within the Bangalore Corporation area, established around the 1950s for personnel from the defense industry and the public sector. The third is Indiranagar, a housing colony between the Old Madras Road (National Highway 4) and the road leading to Bangalore's airport, lying on the edge of the Bangalore City Corporation and expanding in the direction of the proposed conurbation area. The highways themselves were part of a radial system of roads that, up until the late 1990s, led away from the city to others like Chennai, Hyderabad, Mangalore, Salem, or Pune. Today, a new beltway being constructed around the city is connecting these roads as well as the sites of Sai Baba devotion, the materiality of the city keeping pace with its devotional network. While the logic of the city's spatial development proceeds from Someshvarapura to Indiranagar and then onto Rupena Agrahara, the temporal logic of these sites demands a somewhat different presentation: Rupena Agrahara evokes the most resonance with the garden city model, while Someshvarapura is associated with a constituency tied to the model of the modern and the developmental city; Indiranagar bears the signs simultaneously of the developmental and the information city.

Encrypted Spaces, Multiple Bodies

The road to Rupena Agrahara, where Shivamma Thayee lived, is reached via the intermediate ring road. The road is very wide and busy and traveling on it, we pass places like a Hyundai car dealer, Datacons computer company, and a mosque. Once we take the turnoff to Rupena Agrahara, the road becomes bumpy, the straight lines break down, and the area rapidly takes on the character of a village swallowed by the metropolis. We finally reach an enclosed area in which trees and graves abound: going by the name (*agrahara*), this used to be a Brahmin settlement at one point but was taken over by a cemetery and numerous graves marked by representations of Shiva (*linga*) stand like megaliths inside. Within the compound we encounter a Sai Baba school and rented houses.

The person who performs the rituals at the Sai Baba temples is a Tamil-speaker, Mr. Muthuswamy. He is going for lunch but is persuaded to open the temples and show us around. "Who was Shivamma Thayee?" I ask. "Her story is recorded in a book by a professor," replies Muthuswamy. This record is largely written as first-person reminiscence and begins: "I am Shivamma Thayee. This name was given to me by my Guru Sri Shirdi Sai Baba himself during his lifetime. My earlier name was Rajamma" (Ruhela 1992: 1).[12] Shivamma Thayee was born to an agriculturist family in Tamil Nadu. The eldest of four children, she was married in 1904 at age thirteen to a supervisor in a

Coimbatore mill, Subramaniam Gounder; within a year she had a son. Her first meeting with Shirdi Sai Baba occurred in 1906 when he was about seventy years of age; he visited a village close to Coimbatore town with Shivamma Thayee's uncle, who had become a renouncer himself. While it is widely believed that Shirdi Sai Baba never left the environs of Shirdi during the later years of his life, Shivamma Thayee claims that he stayed in the village for two days. He also initiated her with a sacred formula, writing it down in Tamil, and predicted that she would be a great soul. Shivamma Thayee came to be convinced that Shirdi Sai Baba was her real guru and, sometime after her first meeting with him, decided to visit Shirdi.

Her entire family arrived in Shirdi in 1908, her husband somewhat reluctantly, and visited Shirdi Sai Baba in his mosque. She describes Shirdi Sai Baba as about six feet tall, with long hands, fair in color, with a sharp nose and deep blue eyes that shone penetratingly. After her first visit, which lasted about five or six days, she would travel alone to Shirdi about three or four times a year. Shivamma Thayee's continued absorption in her teacher finally led to her husband abandoning her, so she returned to her natal family from Bangalore where she and her husband had been living. Her son grew up to join the police department, but on one unfortunate day he and his wife were both killed in a motor accident. Shivamma Thayee felt that it was Baba who had freed her from all family attachments.

One day in 1917, Baba gave her the name by which she is known today and ordered her to go to Bangalore and found a hermitage (*ashram*) in his name. Thus, she returned to Bangalore and lived for several years in a remote corner of the city begging for alms. Eventually about 1944, one Narayana Reddy donated some land to her in Rupena Agrahara, then an isolated tract, where she did penance for about twelve years. She ate and drank nothing during that time, an ant-hill covered her entire body, and a cobra would come and sit on the matted locks of hair on her head. Eventually she was persuaded by devotees from Bangalore to end her long penance. Shivamma Thayee then turned her attention to the *ashram*, starting a primary school in its premises, founding temples, and extending her blessings to the many devotees who began to gather around her for the worship of Shirdi Sai Baba. Toward the end of her life, she stated: "I am now 102 years old . . . For these last eighty-six years (since I first saw Baba as a fifteen-year-old girl in 1906) I have been attached to Baba heart and soul . . . Each breath taken by me is due to his Kripa (kindness) alone" (Ruhela 1992: 16).

Muthuswamy, now in charge of carrying out the rituals at the temples she built, takes us to the first site, which is Shivamma Thayee's house (see figure 12.3). On one wall of the bare house is a photograph taken in 1963 showing her sitting under a tree in white clothing looking very much the female renouncer. There is also a foot-high silver image of a seated Shirdi Sai Baba that was installed recently. There is nothing else to see and Muthuswamy takes

Figure 12.3 Shivamma Thayee's house and temple constructed by her in Rupena Agrahara

us to the next building, a temple built about 1970, approximately 10 meters on a side and surrounded by coconut trees, the focus of local festivals every year. In the main altar space, flanked by green and white pillars, is a black stone image of a seated Shirdi Sai Baba (see figure 12.4). This has large white painted eyes and looks like a village deity. On either side of it are images of Shiva's sons, and behind it pictures of Shivamma Thayee, as well as a sign that asks: "Why fear when I am here?" Muthuswamy takes us downstairs to the subterranean tomb of Shivamma Thayee; she got the site constructed in preparation for her passing away. This is a black cube on which stands a Shiva *linga*; as you walk around it, you find writing on one side giving Shivamma Thayee's dates: 1889–1994. The space around is limited and dark with only a lamp hanging from the ceiling, which is about 2 meters up. The third temple is a sunny room about 4 meters on a side with a white marble image of Shirdi Sai Baba, about 2 feet high, depicting Baba as a mendicant holding a begging bowl.

On the way back to the main road we meet a descendant of Narayana Reddy, Mr. N. Gopal Reddy, a city councilor and a member of the Congress Party. He is a well-fed man wearing white clothes and lots of gold jewelry. He does not seem to be particularly devoted to Shivamma Thayee; instead of building more temples or graves, he wants to evict the rentiers and use the

Figure 12.4 The black stone image of Shirdi Sai Baba in Rupena Agrahara

land for various social causes such as an old people's home. He speaks enthusiastically about the Shirdi Sai Baba school where about 600 children are fed daily. Fragments of other memories of this area emerge in the course of our conversation: the land where Shivamma Thayee came to live was gifted by one of his ancestors about 140 years ago to be a refuge for renouncers. The area was mainly under paddy cultivation and a tank nearby watered about 640 acres of land. The Wodeyar rulers of Mysore constructed this tank in 1772 in the name of Venkoji Rao and his brother, Baoji Rao, who were their cooks. Now this tank has fallen into disrepair and the government has sanctioned funding for its restoration. The paddy has also disappeared and today the region is on the main route to Electronic City.

The *ashram* of Shivamma Thayee presents a space both encrypted and abundant. The image of Shirdi Sai Baba at the main temple absorbs into its sacral field the worship of dark village deities who are propitiated for a variety of afflictions, their festivals celebrated throughout the night even today in many rural settlements. However, these practices are also true of settlements within Bangalore associated with the model of the garden city whose ritual links to the old central fort and market are sustained by the worship of dark, boundary goddesses whose shrines lie in the vicinity of tanks (see Srinivas 2001). Even though the tank in Rupena Agrahara has disappeared today, the garden city is invoked by the presence of this ritual center. In addition, Shaiva ritual practices, the burial of the dead, non-Brahmin castes, and the bodies of mendicants and renouncers are intertwined with the worship of Shirdi Sai Baba in ways that are quite distinct from the practices at Shirdi. Yet, like Shirdi Sai Baba, Shivamma Thayee continues to "speak from the tomb": despite the current peripheralization of Rupena Agrahara by Electronic City, the *ashram* encapsulates the memory of several other regional, spatial, and charismatic skeins.

Divided Spaces, Ethereal Bodies

Between 1918 and 1950, small gatherings of devotees who had visited Shirdi, usually through their connections with Maharashtra as businessmen or through their employment in the army or bureaucracy, were found in many urban centers of South India. After 1950, some of these groups, usually devotional song and prayer communities in people's homes, grew into large temples. A typical case is Bangalore, where there are four temples dedicated to Shirdi Sai Baba affiliated to the All-India Sai Samaj. The Shirdi Sai Baba temple in Someshvarapura evolved from the efforts of six persons, most of them Tamil-speakers, and all from the Defence Accounts head office in Pune city. After their retirement, they settled in Bangalore and held a prayer session every Thursday. In 1980, they joined forces with a group of three businessmen and their efforts led to the construction of a temple in 1985.[14]

The temple, which is about 30 square meters, has two portions: almost basement-like, below the level of the road, lies the portion of the temple that has some historical continuity with Shirdi (see figure 12.5). At the far end of a largely empty room is a niche in the wall, almost like the prayer niche of a mosque, holding a picture of Shirdi Sai Baba in white clothes with a pipe on his right side. The Sufi or mendicant-like connotation of the picture is, however, interpenetrated with some Hindu aspects: for instance, betel leaves, coconuts, and a lamp stand in front of him; he wears a garland of flowers and various ritual spots on his body are marked with vermilion. At the time that the lower portion of the temple was being constructed, a devotee, Mrs. Vimala Rai, made a pilgrimage to Shirdi where the priest told her that he had been instructed in a dream to give the aforesaid picture to the Bangalore temple.

The portion that most people typically visit first, however, lies a floor above the road and has a life-sized, white marble image of Shirdi Sai Baba. Priests daily decorate the white image with clothes and garlands. The image sits on a silver throne with lions on either side (acquired in 1995) depicting the mendicant as king; silver feet are kept in front of the image for devotees to touch, altogether a very Buddhist set of representations. The rituals, however,

Figure 12.5 The Shirdi Sai Baba temple in Someshvarapura

include Shaiva elements (for example, a statue of Ganesha and symbols of Shiva) and Vaishnava ones (for instance, recitation of the thousand names of Vishnu). Thursday is considered particularly sacred and hundreds of devotees can be seen visiting the temple, touching the silver feet and taking consecrated foods. Of the four important festivals that are celebrated, Rama Navami has become increasingly elaborate over the years and the temple managers see it as the "birthday" of Shirdi Sai Baba.

The temple is actively engaged in social work such as running a charitable dispensary, classes for children, poor feeding on Sundays, and a library containing literature on Baba in several languages. A hospital providing free medical care was inaugurated in 1995. In 1995, the trust of the temple had about 400–450 life members and about 600 ordinary members. The number of devotees at any point in time is certainly far greater than this number; on Thursdays, for instance, over 6,000 rupees (US$142) worth of flowers are sold outside the temple by pavement flower-sellers.

The neighborhood of the temple contains a heterogeneous population in terms of language and regional and sectarian origin, but there is an economic convergence for most of the households are engaged in occupations in the government, in industry, or in private enterprise. The devotees who visit from other neighborhoods also share a middle-level managerial, commercial, and bureaucratic class background with these households. They are mostly Tamil-speakers or businessmen from the regions of Gujarat and Sindh. The men in the former group are employed largely in public sector establishments such as Hindustan Aeronautics, Bharat Earth Movers Ltd., Indian Telephone Industries, the army, or the Public Works Department. The latter group has close links with Shirdi and with family members in Maharashtra, Sindh, and Gujarat. The temple rites certainly mobilize all these groups but do not explain how it is that the mad mendicant with his multiple heritage has come to be imagined in a way that resembles a Hindu guru, even a Hindu deity, with alternative elements being pushed underground. To understand this trajectory, we must examine the efforts of B. V. Narasimha Iyer (later known as Narasimha Swami), regarded by hundreds as the "apostle" of Shirdi Sai Baba.

Like Shivamma Thayee, Narasimha Swami was born in Coimbatore District in 1874. After acquiring a law degree in Chennai, he began to practice as a civil lawyer in Salem town in 1895. He was apparently quite active in public life, serving the municipality and the cooperative bank, activities that elected him to the Legislative Council (1914–20). He was also involved with Annie Besant's Home Rule movement and although he was reelected to the Legislative Council, he refused the position as he had joined the Non-Cooperation Movement by this time. In 1925, after a personal tragedy, he decided to give up his career and search for a supreme teacher (*sadguru*). He wandered in spiritual wilderness for a number of years, from one holy site to another, one saint to another, till the devotional network created by these figures directed him to Shirdi in 1936. There he is said to have had a vision of Shirdi Sai Baba and for many years occupied himself by meeting the saint's devotees and publishing articles on him. In 1939, he returned to Chennai and opened the All-India Sai Samaj as well as the first Shirdi Sai Baba temple in 1952–3.

Narasimha Swami cast himself into the role of an educator on Shirdi Sai Baba and evolved certain methods of "mass contact" – touring different parts of the country, lecturing in schools, devotional groups, and even political meetings, building up a band of volunteers, and producing lockets and calendars for distribution. Like so many other nationalists, he was concerned with defining the framework of a new social order for India that did not make a separation between the civic, the political, and the spiritual. C. R. Rajagopalachari, for instance, one of the premier members of the Indian National Congress and a childhood friend of Narasimha Swami, combined two different discourses – those of national progress and individual duty – whereby a citizen's moral actions were linked to the progress of the state. Just as he saw in Gandhi a messenger for the new state, Narasimha Swami saw in Shirdi Sai Baba a universal guru and emblem of Hindu–Muslim unity.

The casting of Baba as guru was a multilayered construction. At the primary level were Baba's life circumstances and practices at Shirdi. At the secondary level, the regimen of worship, especially joint worship for different communities, formed an important part of the message. Narasimha Swami privileged this feature in a specific way: he stated that the main mass of worshippers at Shirdi were Hindu, carrying on a Pandharpur style of worship while others carried on their own particular devotions. However, Sai worship had to be strengthened through regular and customary forms of worship in new sites of devotion. Narasimha Swami constructed the form of this new worship in scriptural terms with frequent references to the "Great Tradition" of Hinduism. In practice, then, while there is joint worship by Vaishnava and Shaiva believers in the temples created by the All-India Sai Samaj, non-Hindu devotees are an exception and religious practice is constructed in pan-Hindu, nonlocal terms. Writing on the significance of Baba's passing away, Narasimha Swami alludes to the effect of spatial and temporal displacements for a new body of worship:

> The *Mahasamadhi* [passing away] is an event of unique importance. While it took away the physical body so well known and dear to the thousands that had flocked to His Feet, it was the means of refining and sublimating their love to Him, and at the same time starting a new era in Sai Bhakti [devotion] and providing a special *ethereal* entity or Body that the entire people of India if not the world can be drawn to. When He was in the flesh, some were repelled by the limitations and peculiarities of His physical body and surroundings. But now happily, *there is no physical body, its place being taken by an ethereal body or better still, a perfect spiritual phenomenon* that may be treated as a body or not a body according to the ideology, convenience and pleasure of the devotee; *it has furnished a basis for a highly refined religious or spiritual group to gather and work under His Name.* (Narasimha Swami 1965: 21, emphasis mine)

The "ethereal body" of Baba after his passing away is conceptualized as partaking of a larger body of "Hinduism" and given authority by reference to the canons of the Vedic corpus and the *Bhagavad Gita* that have become a source for collective identity. Baba's Islamic heritage has passed into a zone of cultural amnesia in the urban topos of believers. This splitting of Baba's identity acquired a particular force within Narasimha Swami's imaginative world, which was largely nationalist. After 1950, however, the split achieved its objective form in cities like Bangalore through the All-India Sai Samaj, an isomorph of the new metropolitan communities. What is particularly significant is that in the Bangalore temple, the qualities of a corporeal Shirdi Sai Baba were stripped away to produce a bourgeois incarnation unlimited by historical features and cast in marble. The mendicant disappeared in the basement, as the strata associated with the modern city and the developmental city became increasingly visible in Bangalore.

Figure 12.6 Sathya Sai Baba (*left*) and Shirdi Sai Baba (*right*)

Utopian Spaces, Cosmic Bodies

Sometime between Shivamma Thayee's return to Bangalore after 1917 and Narasimha Swami's epiphany at Shirdi in 1936, another figure emerged within the charismatic tradition of Shirdi Sai Baba who was to have an even more significant impact on Bangalore. Sathya Sai Baba was born in 1926 as Sathya Narayana Raju in Puttaparthi village in Andhra Pradesh.[15] Sathya seems to have had a fairly normal childhood, although biographers and oral accounts claim a number of mysterious events at the time of his birth and during his school years. At the age of fourteen, after a prolonged period of "illness" when he exhibited erratic behavior that was read as a sign of possession, Sathya cast off his schoolbooks. He declared that he was no longer the Sathya they knew but Sai Baba of Shirdi who had returned in this new body and that his devotees were calling him (see figure 12.6). Until 1950, when a separate *ashram* was completed in Puttaparthi, he had lived mainly in the house of a Brahmin woman. During that time, and later on, he performed a number of miracles, granted boons, gave visions to devotees who were beginning to pour in, and visited some towns and cities in south India.

In 1957, Sathya Sai Baba left on a north Indian tour to visit temples and urban sites; this marks a watershed in his career for after this year, his public role came to be voiced more explicitly. The year 1968 signaled a movement to the pan-Indian, and even international, role of Sathya Sai Baba. At the First World Conference of Sathya Sai Service Organizations at Mumbai in 1968, he announced that he was the avatar or reincarnation of Sai and he had come to establish righteousness. In June the same year, he left for a tour of East Africa, his only foreign visit so far. In the years that followed, a number of civic institutions such as schools, colleges, and a university were established. The more recent institutions include the Sri Sathya Sai Institute of Higher Medical Sciences in Puttaparthi (1990–1) and a drinking water project covering 750 villages and 900,000 persons (1995–6) in Andhra Pradesh.[16]

The architectural symbol of Sathya Sai Baba as avatar is the "Sarva Dharma Stupa," a thick pillar about two stories high at the Puttaparthi *ashram* designed to hold a lotus on its peak. Its base is made up of five sides with symbols from five "world" religions – Hinduism, Christianity, Islam, Buddhism, and Zoroastrianism. However, certain other institutions and programs make his global role even more evident. The Old Madras Road that runs by Indiranagar links Bangalore with the city of Chennai. On the route lies Whitefield, an exurbia for Anglo-Indian families during the nineteenth century that by the 1960s included chemical industries and other enterprises. Most important of these new institutions at Whitefield is an *ashram* of Sathya Sai Baba attracting thousands of Indian and foreign devotees. The *ashram* also includes a college for male students, hostels, and a home where Sathya Sai Baba resides when he visits Bangalore. Today, an Export Promotion Industrial Park lies between Indiranagar and the *ashram* including land held by companies like General Electric and Texas Instruments. This region, known previously as the village settlement of Pattandur Agrahara, is fast dominating the eastern edge of the city. Next to the highrise Information Technology Park stands the Sathya Sai Institute of Higher Medical Sciences, inaugurated in January 2001 after only fifteen months of planning by the Indian Prime Minister. The institute is free of charge and has diagnostic, pre-operative, post-operative, and surgical facilities chiefly in cardiology and neurology. Its approximate built-up area is 354,000 square feet, the lower floor made of sandstone, the upper floor broken by white pillars, and crowned by a central dome resembling a palace or temple rather than a hospital. In the lush garden in front of the hospital is a central fountain jetting around an image of Dhanvantri, the god of medicine. The growth of Bangalore as the premier information city of South Asia, thus, is matched by this new project of Sathya Sai Baba which occupies a space that is both global and utopian.

The earliest institutions established by Sathya Sai Baba are the Sathya Sai Service Organizations, sometimes just called "*samiti*," in various states and districts in India and also in other countries. The first Sai Organization was registered in 1965 in Mumbai; today there are over 1,200 Sathya Sai Baba Organizations in 137 countries (http://www.sathyasai.org/). Bangalore has a total of about seventy *samiti*, a figure that excludes devotional singing groups. The Indiranagar *samiti*, begun in 1973, stands in an upper-class neighborhood. Most of the area's residents are Hindus but there are also several pockets of non-Brahmin castes and lower-income households belonging to older settlements that were engulfed by the metropolis.

The Indiranagar *samiti* has a convenor selected by other members and normally holds office for about two years. The convenor then chooses three coordinators, each to oversee the educational, spiritual, and service wings. The activities of the educational wing involve a child development program; daily tuition for about 140–160 school students from poor families; yoga and art classes; distribution of scholarships and books to meritorious students; sewing classes for poor mothers and working women; and an adult literacy program. The spiritual wing includes morning and evening rituals, regular rites performed by female devotees, and devotional sessions in people's homes every Monday. Study circles for devotees that focus on Sai literature and other scriptures also take place. There are regular lectures given by speakers on spiritual subjects about once a month. The service wing includes a weekly medical camp on Sunday attended by about sixty to eighty patients that offers both allopathic and homeopathic medicine; periodic vision and dental camps also take place for the benefit of the economically disadvantaged. The devotees have also funded a number of eye, heart, and other surgeries. There is a monthly free-meal scheme called the Narayana Seva (service for Vishnu) where about 400 poor people are given lunch. The service wing also undertakes regular visits to a Red Cross home, an orphanage, and a leprosy home in other parts of the city.

Volunteers carry out most of the educational and service activities in the Indiranagar *samiti*. In 1999, these comprised 103 persons, thirty-seven males and sixty-six females, and excluded the much larger group of devotees who mainly attended the devotional activities. Most of the active workers are distributed fairly equally among the four linguistic groups in South India and also include a large number of Punjabi-speakers. They come from a range of castes, although there seem to be no scheduled castes, Muslims, or Christians among them. There are relatively few from the lower middle class, and most of the workers are housewives or men and women formerly or currently employed in the army, police, or public sector companies, as chartered accountants, scientists, doctors, engineers, computer scientists, teachers, private company employees, and bank employees. In this, the core of the *samiti* is fairly representative of the neighborhood in which it exists. The manager-

Figure 12.7 Sai Darshan in Indiranagar

ial core of the Service Organization have included a retired senior Karnataka police officer, an army brigadier, a housewife from a plantation family, a retired senior officer from Bharat Petroleum, and a senior officer in a nationalized bank.

The Indiranagar *samiti* is part of the East Zone of the Sai Organization in the city. The *samiti* in Bangalore are grouped into four zones named after the directions of the compass; these then form part of a district organization and are further grouped into a state structure with a president for the Sri Sathya Sai Service Organizations. While the activities of the Indiranagar *samiti* are common to those carried out by other *samiti*, it also has a temple associated with it called "Sai Darshan" ("vision of Sai") inaugurated by Sathya Sai Baba in 1989 (see figure 12.7). The temple area is about 40 meters across; the temple is double-storied, painted bright blue with pink pillars, and over the entrance is an image of Ganesha. It is the first temple of its kind in Bangalore where regular rituals are performed to Sathya Sai Baba in the form of a giant photograph with an empty chair alongside on which Baba sits when he visits the temple.[17]

The code of conduct laid down for members of the service organization involves individual, family, and community activities through the institutional framework of three wings. The organizations in the city try to link different spheres – private and public, the individual, family and the neighborhood –

through service work and spiritual exercises. The mediation between spheres, however, occurs through a different kind of logic than simply the outward act of "service": the daily life of a devotee is constructed in terms of miraculous events and coincidences. A female devotee reflects this in her account:

> The first time that Sai Darshan was inaugurated, we needed money for Narayana Seva [free meals for the poor]. Mr. Kushalappa and I were sitting on the steps wondering what we could do. As I was saying that we could all contribute to this amount, Neelu came with 750 rupees, which is exactly what was needed. It seems that one lady had brought money to Swami [Sathya Sai Baba] for service purposes. He took it and gave it to Neelu and said, "give it to Sai Darshan." Swami sent it to us through Neelu. If you start a good program, Swami provides. (Interview, September 22, 1999)

The synchronicity suggested in this account alludes to a "gift economy" that works parallel to the economy of the city. For instance, in 1999, the Indiranagar *samiti* had a corpus fund of Rs. 1.2 million (US$28,500), raised largely by gifts from devotees and active workers. This figure excludes about Rs. 1.5 million (US$36,000) that have gone into the construction of the temple at various stages, of which Sathya Sai Baba contributed probably less than half. The gift economy creates a virtual city that is different from the information city envisaged by the planners of Bangalore. This virtual city has as much to do with the construction of Sathya Sai Baba as a cosmic avatar with a world mission as with an accessible magus. The appearance of Sathya Sai Baba in dreams for guidance, the outpouring of sacred ash and honey on photographs in homes, stories of healing, and other miracles form an ever-growing fund of folklore within the *samiti*. These events are emphasized by Sathya Sai Baba himself, who has referred to these as his "calling cards." In this magus role, Sathya Sai Baba is a part of the devotee's everyday life and affairs. The localization of his charisma is also a feature of neighborhood devotion and is, indeed, heightened through the structure of worship at the *samiti*. The return of the magical in these domains, however, undermines the vast spaces of the developmental and informational city. Behind the wheels of the metropolis, the public and the professional, stands the figure of Sathya Sai Baba who, in his other role as avatar, transcends time, space, and context. The cosmic body of the *avatar* renders the functioning of the city transparent and its corporeality evanescent.

Conclusion

Urban studies have generated different languages for understanding the city, including those emerging from the localization of global capital, the globalization of labor, or cultural identities of various kinds. Within the urban sociology of India, the city defined according to the models of the sacred city, the colonial city, or the developmental-managerial city has tended to freeze history in increasingly archaic vocabularies. Simultaneously, cities like Bangalore have developed within a spatialized chronology including models of the garden city, the modern city, the developmental city, the informational city, and the Kannada city, each manifested in specific features of the built environment and still commanding the loyalty of diverse constituencies. The goal of this chapter, and the cases described in it, is to emphasize that these languages are by themselves historically incomplete unless the cultures of space and memory are brought into a meaningful relationship with each other through discourses of return.

The careers of Shivamma Thayee, Narasimha Swami, and Sathya Sai Baba and their intersections with Bangalore reveal constructions of both the urban and transurban that emerge from existing cultural milieus and older histories. The fashioning of ideological links to Shirdi Sai Baba through journeys of quest and return – as renouncer or village deity, universal guru, or avatar of Sai – signal the emergence of new manifestos about urban space in which memories for the city and its communities are crafted anew. Urban spaces, whether new residential colonies or erstwhile villages, come to encode a cultural aesthetics and ethics embodying several experiences and agendas. Shivamma Thayee's *ashram* recreates Shirdi Sai Baba in the memory of older village deities and as part of a Shaiva history, while affirming his role (and hers) as renouncer rather than as priest. The *ashram* also brings monastic seclusion into the city, an extra-urban refuge within the driving expansion toward the Electronic City. The temple associated with Narasimha Swami is architecturally split, as is Shirdi Sai Baba's body, and tends to exclude non-Hindu devotees while uniting several Hindu sectarian groups. The constituencies of the modern and developmental city, then, exhibit a quiet discomfort with Shirdi Sai Baba's Sufi aspects while forging links to a pan-Indian construction of Hindu tradition. The virtual city created by the Sathya Sai Organizations renders illusory and incomplete the hegemonic claims of the informational city while returning Shirdi Sai Baba in the form of an avatar rather than as mendicant. Located in the Export Promotion Industrial Park, the medical institute seems to create anomalous meanings for ideas of export and technology by channeling these practices through the vocabulary of healing. In each case, they point us to formulations of the urban and being citizens that are deeply embedded in ritual, emotional, and somatic practices of groups within the city even if they exist within the shadows of the developmental state or its software inheritors.

The mnemonics of space, with which this chapter is concerned, can be formulated as an active mode whereby cultural materials, historical events, persons, or places are "recollected" or gathered up into a novel configuration.[18] It consists of devices that rework the relations between these historical and cultural materials in various locales through several processes, what Maurice Halbwachs calls "laws governing the memory of groups." They rewrite cultural resources by changing their position in time and space; they renew them by unusual parallels, by unexpected oppositions, and by combinations; there can be a concentration of events in a single place and a duality of locations across regions (see Halbwachs 1992: 219–22).

These processes are also embodied: memory is part of material reality and its operations occur through forms that share the nature of other parts of a locality such as physical bodies, buildings, or instruments of production. Certain places within the cityscape such as temples or highways and the pathways between and beyond them created through figures such as Shivamma Thayee and others allow memory to be activated or brought into the open. The mnemonic swirls ensuing through these operations and processes are also kinetic moments as these resources are sedimented on and stored in the bodies of citizens through movements, rituals, service activities, coincidences, or dreams. The mnemonics of space create a reorientation within the city, recovering spatially peripheral tracts and older axes of the city from a zone of urban amnesia, and also using contemporaneous axes and institutional sites in other patterns of meaning. The reorientation occurs within a discursive arena that is occupied by academic institutions, multinational capital, or the nation-state, all of which struggle with models of the city, whether "cities of the past" or "cities of the future." The mnemonics of space described in this chapter draw attention to social and discursive lacunae in these models of the city, staging other possibilities for the understanding of the urban tied to the inner, affective, cultural, and spiritual worlds of the subjects of the metropolis.

Notes

1 I would like to thank James Heitzman for creating the maps for this chapter and for his extensive comments.

2 For an account of the Delhi School of Economics that weaves together the personal and the institutional, see Kumar and Mookherjee (1995).

3 A representative but not exhaustive list of works on these themes includes Dahiwale (1988); De Souza (1978); Fox (1969); Mahadev (1975); Majumdar ([1960] 1975); Pantham (1976); Pethe (1964); Ramu (1988); Rao (1974); Rosenthal (1976); Samaj (1958); Vidyarthi (1969).

4 See, for example, Allchin (1995); Bakker (1986); Banga (1991); Blake (1991); Chakrabarti (1995); Champakalakshmi (1996); Gollings (1991); Heitzman (1997); Lutgendorf (1997); Michell and Eaton (1992); Sinopoli and Morrison (1995); Stein (1993).

5 See, for instance, Bhatnagar (1996); Haynes (1991); Kalia (1987, 1994); Llewellyn-Jones (1985); Mines (1994); Patel and Thorner (1995); Ray (1979).
6 See Abu-Lughod (1989); Arasaratnam (1989); Broeze (1997); Chaudhuri (1990); Liu (1988); Penrad (2000).
7 See, for example, Cohen (1998); Ghosh (1994); Joseph (2000); Waghorne (1999).
8 Some recent works on Bangalore include Hasan (1970); Heitzman (1999a, 1999b); Holmstrom (1994); Jayapal (1997); Manor (1993); Sundara Rao (1985); Vyasulu and Reddy (1985).
9 To my knowledge there are no recent census figures for linguistic or religious affiliation in the district.
10 Works on these themes are too numerous to cite here. See, for instance, Das (1996); Engineer (1988); Jaffrelot (1995); Juergensmeyer (2000).
11 See also Rigopoulos (1993) and Shepherd (1985) for detailed studies of the life of Shirdi Sai Baba.
12 In 1992, S. P. Ruhela, Professor of Education at Jamia Millia Islamia University, interviewed Shivamma Thayee for a number of hours via an interpreter, K. S. Jaya Raman, a stores officer at Hindustan Aeronautics Ltd. in Bangalore. After the interview, Ruhela asked her if he might publish the record of her life and experiences with Sai Baba, to which she agreed.
13 The interviewer, Ruhela, states that this was a miraculous instance of Shirdi Sai Baba manifesting himself in another body in a distant place and a proof that he even knew other languages besides Marathi, Urdu, or Arabic.
14 The Shirdi Sai Baba temple in Bangalore and the nature of its urban devotion has been explored in greater depth in Srinivas (1999a), which is an earlier version of this section.
15 Various biographies of Sathya Sai Baba exist, of which the authoritative one is Kasturi (1968). The devotional literature on Sathya Sai Baba is extensive, as are his speeches and writings. Some of the more critical and sociological writings on him include Babb (1986); Srinivas (1999b); Swallow (1982); White (1972).
16 More details about these institutions can be found at http://www.sathyasai.org, the official website of the Sathya Sai organization.
17 In recent years another such temple called "Sai Gitanjali" was opened in a suburb on the south side of Bangalore called J. P. Nagar. One might speculate that in years to come many more temples could become the nucleus of various *samiti* in different parts of the city.
18 These arguments about urban memory are elaborated in Srinivas (2001).

Bibliography

Abu-Lughod, J. 1989: *Before European Hegemony: The World System A.D. 1250–1350*. New York: Oxford University Press.

Allchin, F. R. 1995: *The Archaeology of Early Historic South Asia: The Emergence of Cities and States*. Cambridge: Cambridge University Press.

Arasaratnam, S. 1989: European port settlements in the Coramandel commercial system, 1650–1740. In F. Broeze (ed.), *Brides of the Sea: Port Cities of Asia from the 16th–20th Centuries*. Honolulu: University of Hawaii Press, 76–96.
Babb, L. A. 1986: *Redemptive Encounters: Three Modern Styles in the Hindu Tradition*. Berkeley: University of California Press.
Bakker, H. 1986: *Ayodhya*. Groningen: E. Forsten.
Banga, I. (ed.) 1991: *The City in Indian History: Urban Demography, Society and Politics*. Delhi: Manohar Publications.
Bangalore Development Authority 1995: *Comprehensive Development Plan (Revised) Bangalore Report*. Bangalore: Bangalore Development Authority.
Bhatnagar, V. S. 1996: *Chandigarh, the City Beautiful: Environmental Profile of a Modern Indian City*. New Delhi: A. P. H. Publishing.
Blake, S. P. 1991: *Shahjahanabad: The Sovereign City of Mughal India, 1639–1739*. New York: Cambridge University Press.
Broeze, F. (ed.) 1997: *Gateways of Asia: Port Cities of Asia in the 13th–20th Centuries*. London and New York: Kegan Paul International.
Chakrabarti, D. K. 1995: *The Archaeology of Ancient Indian Cities*. Delhi: Oxford University Press.
Champakalakshmi, R. 1996: *Trade, Ideology and Urbanization: South India 300 BC to AD 1300*. Delhi: Oxford University Press.
Chaudhuri, K. N. 1990: *Asia Before Europe: Economy and Civilisation of the Indian Ocean from the Rise of Islam to 1750*. Cambridge: Cambridge University Press.
Cohen, L. 1998: *No Aging in India: Alzheimer's, the Bad Family, and Other Modern Things*. Berkeley: University of California Press.
Dahiwale, S. M. 1988: *Emerging Entrepreneurship Among Scheduled Castes of Contemporary India: A Study of Kolhapur City*. New Delhi: Concept Publishing.
Das, V. 1996: *Critical Events: An Anthropological Perspective on Contemporary India*. Delhi: Oxford University Press.
de Souza, A. (ed.) 1978: *The Indian City: Poverty, Ecology, and Urban Development*. New Delhi: Manohar.
Engineer, A. A. 1988: *Delhi-Meerut Riots: Analysis, Compilation and Documentation*. South Asia Books.
Fox, R. G. 1969: *From Zamindar to Ballot Box: Community Change in a North Indian Market Town*. Ithaca, NY: Cornell University Press.
Ghosh, A. 1994: *In an Antique Land*. New York: Vintage Books.
Gollings, J. 1991: *City of Victory, Vijayanagara: The Medieval Hindu Capital of Southern India*. New York: Aperture.
Halbwachs, M. 1992: *On Collective Memory*. Chicago and London: University of Chicago Press.
Hasan, M. F. 1970: *Bangalore Through the Centuries*. Bangalore: Historical Publications.
Haynes, D. E. 1991: *Rhetoric and Ritual in Colonial India: The Shaping of a Public Culture in Surat City, 1852–1928*. Berkeley: University of California Press.
Heitzman, J. 1997: *Gifts of Power: Lordship in an Early Indian State*. Delhi: Oxford University Press.
—— 1999a: Corporate strategy and planning in the Science City: Bangalore as "Silicon Valley." *Economic and Political Weekly*, January 30: PE-2–11.

——1999b: Sports and conflict in urban planning: the Indian National Games in Bangalore. *Journal of Sports and Social Issues* 23/1 (February): 5–23.

Holmstrom, M. 1994: *Bangalore as an Industrial District: Flexible Specialisation in a Labour-surplus Economy?* Pondicherry: Institut Français de Pondicherry.

Jaffrelot, C. 1995: *The Hindu Nationalist Movement in India.* New York: Columbia University Press.

Jayapal, M. 1997: *Bangalore: The Story of a City*. Chennai: EastwestBooks.

Joseph, M. 2000: Old routes, mnemonic traces. *UTS Review: Cultural Studies and New Writing* 6 (2): 44–56.

Juergensmeyer, M. 2000: *Terror in the Mind of God: The Global Rise of Religious Violence.* Berkeley: University of California Press.

Kalia, R. 1987: *Chandigarh: In Search of an Identity*. Carbondale, IL: Southern Illinois University Press.

——1994: *Bhubaneswar: From Temple Town to a Capital City.* Carbondale: Southern Illinois University Press.

Karnataka State Gazetteer 1990: *Bangalore District: 1990.* Bangalore: Government of Karnataka Publication.

Kasturi, N. 1968: *Sathyam Sivam Sundaram*, 3 vols. Prasanthi Nilayam: Sanathana Sarathi.

Kumar, D. and Mookherjee, D. (eds.) 1995: *D. School: Reflections on the Delhi School of Economics*. Delhi: Oxford University Press.

Liu, X. 1988: *Ancient India and Ancient China*. Delhi: Oxford University Press.

Llewellyn-Jones, R. 1985: *A Fatal Friendship: The Nawabs, the British, and the City of Lucknow.* Delhi and New York: Oxford University Press.

Lombard, D. and Aubin, J. (eds.) 2000: *Asian Merchants and Businessmen in the Indian Ocean and the China Sea*. Delhi: Oxford University Press.

Lutgendorf, P. 1997: Imagining Ayodhya: utopia and its shadows in a Hindu landscape. *International Journal of Hindu Studies* 1/1 (April): 19–54.

Mahadev, P. D. 1975: *People, Space and Economy of an Indian City: An Urban Morphology of Mysore City.* Mysore: Institute of Development Studies, University of Mysore.

Majumdar, D. N. [1960] 1975: *Social Contours of an Industrial City: Social Survey of Kanpur, 1954–56*. Westport, CT: Greenwood Press.

Manor, J. 1993: *Power, Poverty and Poison: Disaster and Response in an Indian City*. Delhi: Sage.

Michell, G. and Eaton, R. 1992: *Firuzabad: A Palace City of the Deccan*. London and New York: Oxford University Press.

Mines, M. 1994: *Public Faces, Private Voices: Community and Individuality in South India.* Berkeley and Los Angeles: University of California Press.

Narasimha Swami, B. V. 1965: *Significance of Baba's Mahasamadhi.* Madras: All-India Sai Samaj.

Pantham, T. 1976: *Political Parties and Democratic Census: A Study of Party Organizations in an Indian City.* Delhi: Macmillan.

Patel, S. and Thorner, A. (eds.) 1995: *Bombay: Metaphor for Modern India*. Bombay: Oxford University Press.

Penrad, J.-C. 2000: The Ismaili presence in East Africa: a note on its commercial history and community organization. In D. Lombard and J. Aubin (eds.), *Asian*

Merchants and Businessmen in the Indian Ocean and the China Sea. Delhi: Oxford University Press, 222–38.

Pethe, V. P. 1964: *Demographic Profiles of an Urban Population*. Bombay: Popular Prakashan.

Pocock, D. F. 1960: Sociologies: urban and rural. *Contributions to Indian Sociology* 4: 63–81.

Ramu, G. N. 1988: *Family Structure and Fertility: Emerging Patterns in an Indian City*. New Delhi and Newbury Park, CA: Sage.

Rao, M. S. A. (ed.) 1974: *Urban Sociology in India*. Hyderabad: Orient Longman.

Ray, R. K. 1979: *Urban Roots of Indian Nationalism: Pressure Groups and Conflict of Interests in Calcutta City Politics, 1875–1939*. New Delhi: Vikas.

Rigopoulos, A. 1993: *The Life and Teachings of Sai Baba of Shirdi*. Delhi: Sri Satguru Publications.

Rosenthal, D. B. (ed.) 1976: *The City in Indian Politics*. Faridabad: Thomson Press.

Ruhela, S. P. 1992: *My Life with Sri Shirdi Sai Baba*. Faridabad: Sai Age Publications.

Samaj, B. S. 1958: *Slums of Old Delhi: Report of the Socio-economic Survey of the Slum Dwellers of Old Delhi City*. Delhi: A. Ram.

Shafi, S. S. 1996: The "Third Wave" Option. *Seminar* 445 (September): 20–4.

Shepherd, K. 1985: *Gurus Rediscovered: Biographies of Sai Baba of Shirdi and Upasni Maharaj of Sakori*. Cambridge: Anthropographia Publications.

Sinopoli, C. M. and Morrison, K. D. 1995: Dimensions of imperial control: the Vijayanagara capital. *American Anthropologist* 97 (1): 83–96.

Shri Sai Satcharita 1972 (6th edition): Shirdi: Shri Sai Baba Sanstan.

Srinivas, S. 1998: *The Mouths of People, The Voice of God: Buddhists and Muslims in a Frontier Community of Ladakh*. Delhi: Oxford University Press.

—— 1999a: The Brahmin and the fakir: suburban religiosity in the cult of Shirdi Sai Baba. *Journal of Contemporary Religion* 14 (2): 245–61.

—— 1999b: Sai Baba: la double utilisation de l'écriture et de l'oralité dans un mouvement religieux moderne en Asie du Sud. *Diogène* 187: 114–29.

—— 2001: *Landscapes of Urban Memory: The Sacred and the Civic in India's High-tech City*. Minneapolis: University of Minnesota Press.

Stein, B. 1993: *Vijayanagara*. Cambridge: Cambridge University Press.

Sundara Rao, B. N. 1985: *Bengalurina Ithihasa* [*A History of Bangalore*]. Bangalore: Vasanta Sahitya Granthamala.

Swallow, D. A. 1982: Ashes and powers: myth, rite and miracle in an Indian god-man's cult. *Modern Asian Studies* 16: 123–58.

Vidyarthi, L. P. 1969: *Cultural Configuration of Ranchi: Survey of an Emerging Industrial City of Tribal India, 1960–62*. Calcutta: J. N. Basu.

Vyasulu, V. and Kumar N. Reddy, A. (convenors) 1985: *Essays on Bangalore*, 4 vols. Bangalore: Karnataka State Council for Science and Technology, Indian Institute of Science.

Waghorne, J. P. 1999: The diaspora of the gods: Hindu temples in the new world system, 1640–1800. *Journal of Asian Studies* 58 (3): 648–86.

White, C. S. J. 1972: The Sai Baba movement: approaches to the study of Indian saints. *Journal of Asian Studies* 31: 863–78.

13

The Syntax of Jerusalem: Urban Morphology, Culture, and Power

Shlomo Hasson

The city, however, does not tell its past, but contains it like the lines of the hand, written in the corners of the streets, the gratings of the window, the banisters of the steps, the antennae of the lightening rods, the poles of the flags, every segment marked in turn with scratches, indentations, scrolls.

(Calvino 1974: 11)

Introduction: Questions and Major Arguments

There are few cities in the world on which history has left as deep an impact as it has on Jerusalem. Throughout the city's history, each cultural group and every single ruler have attempted to leave their mark on the city's landscape. This has been achieved by establishing temples, churches and mosques, castles and marketplaces, neighborhoods and schools, hospitals and hostels, fortresses, walls, roads, and tombs (Werblowsky 1997; Levine 1999).

Historical research on Jerusalem has conventionally focused on the culture encoded in the landscape of the Old City. Only very few studies have investigated the culture engraved in the urban landscape formed outside the Old City's walls since the 1860s. The reason for this is clear. For centuries the Old City served as the religious and governmental center, and every aspect of city life was contained within the city walls. At present, however, the Old City makes up less than 1 percent of Jerusalem's surface area, and most of the political, economic, and social activity takes place outside the Old City's boundaries. The spirit of the period is no longer confined to the Old City, and certain aspects of it are to be found in the early modern and late modern sections built outside the walls.

The aim of this chapter is to decipher Jerusalem's landscape as it took shape during the premodern, early modern, and late modern eras. Three main questions addressed here are:

1 Which cultures etched their mark on Jerusalem's landscape over time, and how do they express themselves in the urban landscape?
2 What are the relationships between the landscapes created by the various cultures? Do newly formed landscapes recognize earlier ones or perhaps ignore and even obliterate them?
3 What factors explain the nature of the relationships between the various landscapes?

My principal arguments are:

1 Jerusalem's urban landscape embodies three main cultures: a culture of religion and tradition mainly encoded in the Old City's landscape; a culture of nationalism and modernity expressed in the inner city's landscape; and a culture of national conflict, consumerism, and globalism engraved in the outer city's landscape. Each of these cities has its own specific morphological characteristics which, from a historical and geographical point of view, create three distinct cities: the premodern city (the Old City), the early modern city (the inner city); and the late modern city (the outer city). The premodern period lasted until the 1860s. It began to fade – although it never disappeared completely from the urban culture and landscape – with the Great Powers' involvement in the life of the city, the introduction of modern technology, the establishment of modern schools, and the beginning of the exodus from the walled-in city (Shavit 1998). The early modern period began in the early 1860s and ended during the late 1960s, with the uniting of the city and the building of new neighborhoods at a considerable distance from the built-up city. The late modern period began after the city's unification in 1967 and is still in effect as this chapter is written. (See figure 13.1.)
2 At the time of writing, the discourse characterizing the relationships between the three cities is hegemonic, dismissive, and violent. This discourse is oblivious of the traditions, values, and cultures embodied in the various cities' landscapes, and tends to treat them with blatant disdain.
3 The hegemonic discourse is deeply rooted in the prevailing cultural and power systems. These perceive the city as a national and cultural living space to be used for national and cultural expansion, and as a commercial asset intended to derive maximum profit.

This chapter dwells on urban morphology and design, cultural landscapes, political relationships between landscapes, and the factors that shape these relationships. I have chosen to address these issues by investigating them in Jerusalem. In many respects, Jerusalem is similar to other historical cities throughout the world. It encompasses various landscapes that were formed in different periods, and encounters the symptomatic tension between urban

Figure 13.1 Map of the cities of Jerusalem

development and economic growth on the one hand, and preservation of urban landscapes on the other. Nevertheless, Jerusalem differs from other historical cities by virtue of being, since 1967, the focus of national conflict between the Israelis and the Palestinians. This conflict is part of the cultural reality that shapes the city's landscape.

The first section of this chapter reviews the relevant literature. The second interprets the urban landscape. The third explores the relationships between the city's cultural landscapes. The fourth analyzes the factors responsible for these relationships. The summary raises some ideas as to the future development of Jerusalem.

Review of the Literature

Historical cities present fascinating challenges for landscape researchers and for planners who wish to pursue urban development while remaining sensitive to its character and historical values. Much like a detective following clues left behind, both the researcher and planner must expose and extricate values, traditions, concepts, and identities that were encoded in the landscape during earlier periods. The historical city does not render their task any easier because, as Italo Calvino writes, the city "does not tell its past, but it contains it." As such, the question is how to make the city speak and decipher its meaning. To attain this goal, the codes revealing the urban character and values must be ascertained, and the urban components in which they are concealed must be identified.

Landscape and cultural codes

The urban heartbeat. One of the places which contains in a condensed form many of the urban codes is the city center, which is the "urban heartbeat." The nature of the urban heartbeat changes over time in accordance with changes in technological conditions, cultural perceptions, and sociopolitical systems. Religious and governmental structures are part of the urban heartbeat in historic European and Islamic cities as well as in Confucian and Shinto cultures (Wheatley 1971; Lapidus 1973; Braunfels 1988; Benevolo 1993; Grabar [1978] 1995). Up to the present day, these city centers have functioned as the theater of monuments, attracting tourists, commerce, and recreation (Ellin 1996).

The heart of the modern city is the commercial civic avenue, which is also the city's representative boulevard. In Europe the first boulevard of this type was linked with the activities of the prefect of Paris, Baron Haussmann, and the idea was then duplicated in other cities: the Ringstrasse in Vienna, the Grand Via in Madrid, and the Istiklal Caddesi in Istanbul, formerly known as the Grand' Rue de Pera. This commercial avenue, the heart of the modern city, has been occasionally built as an exit route from the old city. In structure and function it embodies the bourgeois experience by accommodating such buildings as the Parliament, City Hall, commercial structures, theaters, museums, and universities (Sumner-Boyd and Freely 1972; Schorske 1980; Hall 1998).

The late modern or postmodern city, defined by Sudjic as "the 100-mile city" (1993), extends over an immense expanse with its components linked by expressways. The expressways branch out to neighborhoods, satellite cities, shopping centers, office complexes, and industrial areas which, in turn, are linked with the global economic system. Today the city's economic heart beats in these centers. They are the focus of development, the centers of economic power. This city tends to duplicate itself endlessly, and is devoid of clear boundaries (Nijman 2000).

Deciphering the city. One of the outstanding researchers of the heart of the modern city is historian Carl Schorske. He decoded the culture encoded in

Vienna's Ringstrasse landscape in the late nineteenth century, a period marked by the industrial revolution, the ascent of the constitutional monarchy, and the rise of the bourgeoisie to political power. He demonstrated that, in contrast to the old city's landscape, which bears the stamp of the crown (palace) and the cross (cathedral), the bourgeois elite strove to engrave its values of law and culture into the urban landscape. A series of structures was thus built along the Ringstrasse to express these values: the neoclassical House of Parliament; the gothic-style City Hall; the Renaissance-style university, and the baroque theater (Schorske 1980).

The critics of the Ringstrasse, however, read the culture engraved in its landscape differently from those who wrote it. For example, architects Otto Wagner and Camilo Sitte criticized the disregard of the problems of the period and exposed the escape of the bourgeoisie to foreign districts far from nineteenth-century Vienna. Wagner called for economic modernization, manifested by fast movement and metallic construction; Sitte sought a return to the Middle Ages, when community life centered around intimate public spaces such as the plaza and the square.

The city heartbeat, namely the urban center, by no means exhausts the urban culture. Values and concepts pertaining to time and culture are scattered across other parts of the city. The question is how to read the entire city and extricate its cultural meaning and significance. Urban planner Kevin Lynch (1960) addressed the task of deciphering the city as a whole. He claimed that the city is not a taken-for-granted phenomenon. It is a mental construct – "the image of the city" – formed throughout an interaction between the city and its observer. Lynch argues that this image consists of five components: nodes, monuments, paths, districts, and edges. In this chapter, I will make use of Lynch's city image but with the addition of other elements, such as scale and the relations between private and public space, which, I believe, mold the perception of the city.

The relations between the city's components

The task of interpreting a city does not end with extracting the meanings of cultures from the landscape. Since historical cities contain cultural landscapes of different periods, the question remains as to the interrelationship between the city's various landscapes. Is there recognition and dialogue between the various cultural landscapes, or disregard and alienation? How does the new city treat its predecessors? What sort of discourse does it maintain with them? Does it acknowledge previous landscapes and preserve the values, traditions, and culture embodied in them, or perhaps it ignores and rejects them?

Specific research studies and evidence from different cities show varied attitudes toward urban structures created in the past. Beijing illustrates the attitude of blatant disregard (Carrel 2000: 125). New avenues, tourist centers, expensive residential areas, and shopping centers for tourists and affluent people are replacing the ancient urban fabric. In an earlier time, a similar fate befell Tokyo's ancient nucleus Edo (Hidenobu 1995).

On a wider scale, Beijing and Tokyo embody what has occurred in many traditional cities. The process of modernization and waves of development have ignored, sometimes even destroyed, a cultural heritage molded over centuries. In Tunisia, for example, the rise of the modern city caused the waning of the old, as it led to commercial and cultural functions being transferred from the old city to the new (Lapidus 1973). In Tehran the Shah built new marketplaces and in the process destroyed old ones; there are those who claim that this alienated the merchants from the Shah and his ways (Galntay 1987). Ancient city centers in Europe have often been diminished by megalomanic construction in their midst. Morphological sensitivity of modern city components toward historical sites can be found in Siena, Florence, Lucca, Munich, and Vienna, where fascinating interrelationships join the modern city with the medieval, Renaissance, and Baroque cities. Relationships of this kind are not to be found in Milan, Genoa, or Brussels, where major sections of the historical cities were abruptly destroyed.

Factors shaping the relationship between the city's components

What are the social, cultural, economic, and political forces that shape the relationships between the city's various components? To answer this question one has to delve into the specific context in which the city's components were formed. For example, the development of Paris's transportation system, initiated by Baron Haussmann in the 1880s and largely spurred by economic considerations, led to the destruction of large sections of the medieval city. Wide boulevards and train stations replaced historical neighborhoods that had flourished since the Middle Ages (Hall 1998). The inhabitants of Beijing, likewise, pointed out the greed demonstrated by a former mayor when he handed over to a Hong Kong tycoon the rights to develop a central area of ancient Beijing (Carrel 2000).

A special case involves cities that have changed hands on which the new ruler wanted to leave his mark. These might be colonial cities whose landscape the new government sought to modify according to its values, or capital cities such as Constantinople [Istanbul] or Jerusalem where the new government sought to leave its mark on the landscape, thus asserting its political control over the city.

Vryonis, who researched the city of Constantinople-Istanbul, discovered a strong parallel between the actions of the Roman Emperor Constantine, who in the fourth century founded Constantinople, a capital equivalent to Rome for the eastern portion of the empire, and the actions of the Ottoman Sultan Mehmet II, who conquered Constantinople in 1453. Both rulers used the urban landscape to strengthen their position and establish their rule, and they relied on similar strategies: sanctifying the city and exalting it as a ruling center, ensuring its defense, spreading the existing culture, establishing a demographic stronghold, and glorifying the city. The city was sanctified through the building of churches and monasteries on the one hand, and mosques and religious schools on the other. It was exalted as a ruling center through the establishment of bureaucratic headquarters and government archives. Schools were built in order to ensure dissemination of the new culture. Setting up military camps and surrounding the city with walls ensured internal and external defenses. Setting up and populating new residential neighborhoods was a way to achieve a demographic stronghold and enhance the city's grandeur. Public buildings, such as hospitals, schools, and mosques, were built with tax money collected throughout the empire in order to add to the city's glory (Vryonis 1991: 16–22). Despite a gap of more than one thousand years between the two rulers, the strategies they employed in order to leave their marks on the city's landscape were remarkably similar.

Reading the Urban Landscape of Jerusalem

Each of the three cities of Jerusalem (the premodern, modern, and late modern) has its own specific morphology. It is revealed in the relations with nature, the character of focal points, the nature of traffic and roads, the residential areas, the land-use system, the nature of public and private spaces, and the nature of the city's edges and attitudes toward nature.

Urban morphology and relation to nature

The premodern city is located very near the meeting point between the desert and the Mediterranean climate. The level of technological development at the time of its creation was poor, and the city was highly dependent upon nature. The natural tendency was to adapt and adjust to nature. This was vividly reflected in the city's morphological structure, that is low, two- to three-story buildings, closed-off courtyards in some houses to provide protection from the summer heat, collection pools for rainwater both within and outside of the city, square roofs with round domes from which rainwater flowed into gutters to be collected into pits (Har El 1970; Ben-Arieh 1977). It is true that during the premodern period some impressive water-engineering enterprises were laid, such as the Shiloah tunnel and the water enterprise from Solomon's Pools and the Ein el-A'ruv spring to the city. However, for a long time most water came from the collection of rainwater, which brought on disease, especially malaria, that dealt severe blows to the city's inhabitants (Amiran 1973). In the early modern period, humans defeated nature by means of technology, bringing water from far away, overcoming diseases like malaria, and laying down the foundations of modern infrastructure (Amiran 1973). Moreover, modern technology enabled the establishment of multistory buildings and the construction of modern roads and consequently massive urban growth. The late modern city largely disregards nature by virtue of advanced technology, air conditioning, and artificial climates. Modern infrastructures spread out over extensive areas enabled massive spread of the late modern city, thus blurring the distinction between city and countryside.

Nodes – focal points

The three cities' nodes reflect the spirit of their times. The main focal point of the premodern city is religious: the Temple Mount/Haram Al-Sharif with the al-Aqsa mosque and Dome of the Rock shrine, the Western Wall, the Church of the Holy Sepulchre, and other churches and synagogues. Alongside these focal points is a commercial node concentrated along the bazaar streets. A third focal point in the premodern city is made up of archeological and historical sites: holy sites, schools for religious studies, palaces, remains of ancient walls and marketplaces, some of which were preserved and some buried under the Old City or in its vicinity. All three focal points, religious, commercial, and archeological, define the "theater of monuments" of the premodern city and serve as a magnet for tourists visiting the city.

The early modern city's nodes are civic and commercial, including the national compound and the commercial center. National revival and the emergence of a nation-state characterized this period. In the period preceding the establishment of the State, national aspirations and values were expressed in the National Institutes Compound. Once the State was established, the National Planning Authority of the Prime Minister's Office prepared a master plan for the city. To symbolize the city functions as a capital of Israel and spiritual center, the planners had to reproduce the religious and cultural symbolic landscapes located in the Old City now outside Israel's jurisdiction. For that purpose a new city image was created: a modern reflection of the old city's nodes within the newly formed city (Sharon 1973). The master plan thus placed institutions reflecting national and cultural revival – the government buildings and the new campus of the Hebrew University – at the central visual basin of the new city. The Israel Museum, the cemetery for national leaders, the military cemetery on Mount Herzl, and Yad Vashem were planned to be built adjacent to this center. These were the main national symbols associated with the Holocaust, Israel's wars, its sovereignty, and

Jewish cultural revival. For a long time East Jerusalem lacked a national center because of Jordan's decision to shift it to Amman. Under Israeli rule, the Haram al-Sharif area became the national center and, to a lesser degree, the Orient House building became the symbol of civic rule.

An additional center in the early modern city is the main commercial center spreading over the Jaffa–Ben Yehuda–King George Streets triangle. Although additional commercial centers developed over time – the ultra-orthodox center in the north, the German Colony center, Gaza Street, and the Giv'at Shaul area – the veteran commercial center is still the main area of attraction for the consumer and leisure-seeking population. In the east of the city, the area around Nablus Gate, Salah-al-Din Street, and adjacent streets has become the commercial center.

The centers of the late modern city are the shopping mall, the stadium, and highrise corporate buildings in Malcha, the technology centers in Malcha and Har Ha-Hotzvim – some already completed and others in the planning stages. These centers are cosmopolitan in nature. The high-tech firms are affiliated with similar groups worldwide. The design of the Malcha shopping mall resembles that of shopping centers throughout the world and the brand names it sells are no different from those found in the West. This may explain why the shopping center is popular not only among Jewish consumers but also among the Arabs who live in the city and its environs.

Paths – roads and circulation

The complex, branched road system of the premodern city developed over a long period of time, in part as an outcome of planning and in part as a result of organic development. The crossroads model of the Cardo and Decumanus, which originated in the imperial Roman city of Aelia Capitolina, is the foundation for the road system in the premodern city (Avi-Yonah 1973). Some roads follow the Roman model whereas others developed over the years based on building constraints. This is a city of pedestrians, and in the past camels and donkeys roamed the streets as well. The main streets are commercial ones: David Street descending from west to east, and the bazaar streets going north–south, which were designed during the Crusader period as a network of commercial routes. Below the commercial streets are narrower ones branching out to alleys that lead to the residential areas (Planning Team for the Old City and Surroundings 1970).

In the early modern city, the main streets and commercial avenues, which are designed in a concentric and radial pattern, replaced the bazaar streets. The first commercial route designed in a linear fashion was Jaffa Street (Holliday plan, 1934). Later, linear routes developed along King George and Ben Yehuda Streets. The early modern city is a city of public and private transportation and pedestrian circulation. On many streets, particularly in the center, all three forms of movement are prominent. The dominant commercial area of the early modern city is the triangle formed by Jaffa, Ben Yehuda, and King George Streets. Other commercial routes developed along Emek Refayim Street and Salah-al-Din. Over the years, some streets were closed off to vehicle traffic.

The late modern city extended the radial route pattern into the metropolitan region. It is also noticeable for its expressways, which are nonexistent in the early modern city. These expressways cross and dissect the city from north to south (Highway No. 1 and Highway No. 4), with traffic consisting primarily of private vehicles. The city's widespread expansion and the heavy reliance on private vehicles led to ring roads being planned, to enable traffic to branch out before it reaches the entrance to the city.

Districts – residential areas

The premodern city had a wide variety of neighborhoods, which were frequently ignored due to the customary division of the Old City into quarters. In its heyday, the premodern city had nearly sixty neighborhoods, the great majority of them independently managed by mukhtars appointed by the authorities (Kark and Oren-Nordheim 1995). The residential areas housing the various religious groups were usually concentrated around sacred sites – mosques, churches, and synagogues. Over time, however, these population concentrations lessened, leading to a significant mixing of religious groups in the various neighborhoods. Furthermore, groups of varying social status lived in the same neighborhood. The Old City neighborhoods were usually dense, with long, joined structures that were closed off from the street to protect the residents. Today, these neighborhoods are experiencing physical and social deterioration. The old families have vacated them in favor of new urban dwellings, and poor families, largely from the Mount Hebron area, have come to live in the Old City in their stead (Zilberman 1992).

The residential neighborhoods are a central element of the early modern city. These were built on hilltops with the valleys between preserved as green areas. They were self-contained and separated from each other. The houses were built to low density, and the building style was modest and plain. Even neighborhoods built as middle- to high-class quarters, such as Baka'a, Talbiya, Rehavia, and Sheikh Jarrakh, usually maintained an unpretentious style. The urban concept consisted of an open, horizontal city which preserved panoramic views, and the neighborhoods possessed a social, economic, or ethnic significance (Kroyanker 1989). This is a compact city whose boundaries are usually identical to those of the inner city. The exception are several neighborhoods built at a considerable distance from the inner city, such as Bet

Ha-Kerem, Neve Shanan, Bayit va-Gan, and, later, Qiryat Ha-Yovel, and the new public housing estates of Gonen (Qatamon) and Ir Ganim. Over the past decade, the population in most of these neighborhoods – especially those located in the city's center – has aged, and many residents have left.

The late modern city has experienced urban expansion and regional dispersion in its residential areas, and later in the land used for commerce and services. In the wake of the 1967 War, new neighborhoods were built in the city outskirts to secure a strategic hold over the city and to affect the demographic balance between Jews and Arabs. The new neighborhoods were built far from the inner city and were connected with it by long roads. Nonetheless, they continued the principle of occupying hilltops and leaving the valleys as green areas. The building style changed in these neighborhoods. Instead of modest, plain structures, the city landscape took on a variety of pseudo-traditional forms, including a blaze of domes, arcs, enclosed courtyards, staircases reaching up to arcs – all drawn, more or less, from the Old City's lexicon of structural shapes (Kroyanker 1988).

During the 1990s, urban sprawl intensified and led to the creation of suburbs around Jerusalem. Suburbanization within the Jewish population has become inextricably linked with cultural (the extent of religious commitment) and socioeconomic segregation. Similar trends were identified among the Arab population, which created a ribbon-like suburb extending across Shu'afat and Bet Hanina, on the way to Ramallah. The ensuing spatial outcome has been the formation of discrete, isolated enclaves. There has been a steady population increase in these areas since the 1970s, among both the Jewish and Arab populations. Today nearly half of the city's Jewish population lives in the late modern outer ring built around the early modern (inner) city.

From a social point of view, the premodern city is characterized by segregation based on religion and, to a lesser extent, ethnic origin. Neighborhoods and quarters that housed different religious groups exemplified this. Segregation based on ethnicity, culture (the extent of religious commitment), and socioeconomic status was quite prevalent in the early modern city. Ethnic neighborhoods were prominent among the poorer population segments, whereas the more affluent population groups tended to live in mixed neighborhoods. The late modern city is a mosaic in which segregation takes myriad forms: religious (Jewish and Arab), cultural (ultra-orthodox and non-ultra-orthodox), and socioeconomic (affluent and less affluent areas).

Land-use pattern

A mixture of land uses largely characterizes the premodern city. Marketplaces, inns, places of worship, and residential areas border on each other. In the early modern city, there is a considerable degree of separation among the various land uses in order to achieve specialization and economic efficiency. In the late modern city specialization and separation of land uses have been significantly reduced in order to produce a less sterile and more convivial city. Thus, for example, areas such as Talpiyyot and Giv'at Shaul display a far-reaching mixture of different land uses.

Public and private space

The premodern city emphasized the importance of privacy, which took form in secluded residential areas. Accordingly, urban development progressed from private to public space – in other words, public space was the residual left over once the private space had been allocated. Places of worship and marketplaces are semi-public spaces, subjected to surveillance, where gender separation is customary and rules of behavior are strictly adhered to and monitored. These spaces do not in the least resemble such public spaces as the urban squares and gardens in old European cities.

The early modern city presents a different set of spatial priorities. The city's design had usually progressed from public to private space. Special attention was given to transportation and there was a vertical separation between the public space – the street and the square – and the residential private space. The late modern city is distinctive in the broad splitting of public from private spaces, although they are often combined in the form of neighborhood parks and gardens.

Edges – the city's outskirts

Each of the three cities relates differently to the city's outskirts. In the premodern city, the wall delimited the city and clearly marked the city's edge. Consequently, the transition from rural landscape and open space to cityscape was sharp and clear. The British Mandate government attempted to maintain this distinction by separating through a special zone the Old City from the surrounding areas, and especially from the newly formed city. It achieved a fair amount of success, although toward the end of British rule numerous buildings were added in the special zone, especially in the northwestern and southwestern areas near Jaffa Gate. After the city was unified in 1967, the large houses next to the wall were demolished and a public park was laid out around the city wall, separating the Old City from the rest of the city.

The principle of sharply defined urban edges and a clear separation between built-up and open lands were also characteristic of the early modern city. This was expressed in all of the outline plans prepared for the city during the British Mandate and the first decade of the State. The first outline plan prepared after the establishment of the State strictly maintained this separation. Within the city, open valleys that were not to be built up separated the neighborhoods, leaving the edges of the built-up area clearly defined. Thus, the early modern city was given visual and functional coherency.

The early modern city developed on the mountainous platform. Its area was clearly marked off by the steep inclines of streams flowing into the Kidron valley in the southeast and the Refayim valley in the southwest, and by the eastern escarpments of the Mount of Olives and Mount Scopus (Master Plan for Jerusalem 1968: 25). The various plans also ensured that the streams would penetrate the city, thus creating landscaped corridors to define the entrance to the city, delimit neighborhoods, and create parks and green areas within the city. In both the premodern and early modern cities, the built-up area spread over the mountainous platform, thus avoiding any sliding toward the steep slopes descending toward the east, west, and south.

The late modern city, on the other hand, is a spread-out city with a growing trend of building in the valleys, which turn westward and eastward. The city itself lacks clear human-created or natural boundaries and the distinction between built-up and open spaces is blurred. Some of the post-1967 neighborhoods, such as Ramot Allon and Gilo, were built beyond the valleys that delimited the early modern city. The Pisgat Ze'ev neighborhood spilled over into the desert, and in its wake the ultra-orthodox neighborhoods of Kochav Ya'akov and Tel Zion (which are outside the municipal boundaries). The Har Nof neighborhood descended into the Soreq valley delimiting the city. Continuous construction drew surrounding suburbs nearer to the city. Moreover, because of massive urban development, especially the construction of roads, the landscaped corridors that penetrate the city and separate its neighborhoods are increasingly eliminated from the city landscape.

The expansion into the open spaces within and outside the city marks the end of the planning concept that characterized the early modern city – that is, well-defined outskirts and a clear distinction between built-up and open areas.

The Urban Discourse: Cross-temporal Relations

The meaning of urban discourse

How do the three cities of Jerusalem relate to one another? This question is a loaded one. It dwells on the relationships between East and West, between a religious, traditional culture and a modern culture of consumerism and industrialization, and between economic regimes formed under different technological conditions. In addition, it seeks to explore the relations between different urban scales and different morphological and architectural patterns. From a social and geographical point of view, the premodern city of tradition and religion is exposed to the aspirations and demands of the early modern national society. Moreover, the late modern city's economic and technological might and its global aspirations encounter these two cities.

These encounters are loaded with tensions, occasionally leading to fundamental conflicts with regard to planning, preservation, and development. Should the city be approached in the spirit of the values of religion and tradition, or should it be viewed as a regenerating entity adapting to new economic, technological, cultural, and social challenges? On the one hand, one finds the claim that urban form is a living, regenerating entity and that each generation reserves the right to mold it according to its values and perceptions. On the other hand is the approach that perceives urban form as a unique entity worthy of esteem and preservation. A middle ground attempts to combine these two approaches, proposing development and renewal while not ignoring urban preservation and restoration. This approach attempts to meet changing social requirements, adapt to technological and economic innovations, and, at the same time, protect the values of nature, landscapes, and historical heritage (Kutcher 1975; Touqan 2000).

Two options: closed-hegemonic discourse and open dialogue

From a contemporary point of view, the crucial question is how the late modern city, which is currently the city under construction, relates to the premodern and early modern cities. Another question is why the late modern city relates to the cities that preceded it the way it does. The responses to these questions reflect the economic-political power structure, attitudes toward history, aesthetic considerations, norms and values, as well as the prevailing fashion in planning and design. Theoretically, one can distinguish between two radically different approaches: a closed-hegemonic discourse and an open dialogue. What characterizes a closed-hegemonic discourse is development and building during a later period, which disregards or rejects the values and traditions of earlier periods. In an open dialogue, on the other hand, building and development during a later period take into consideration, recognize, and appreciate the unique assets of culture, values, and traditions pertaining to earlier periods.

The nature of urban discourse: a cross-temporal analysis

Given the various options the question remains, what type of discourse characterizes the relationship between Jerusalem's three cities? Is it a closed-hegemonic discourse or an open-dialogical one? It appears that the nature of urban discourse has changed over time. Modern urban planning, which began as soon as the British forces entered Jerusalem in 1917, respected the Old City's fabric. Subsequently, the British authorities sent for the City Engineer of Alexandria, Mr. W. McLean, to advise on the planning of the city. McLean's report outlined two delimitation strips between the premodern and modern cities. In the inner strip surrounding the walls, building was forbidden within a range of 300 meters. In the outer strip, which consisted of a 2,000- to 3,000-meter semicircle, extending from the Temple Mount, building was restricted and all structures required a special permit, which was only granted after an additional stringent architectural inspection (Shapiro 1973). The principles of the McLean scheme were approved in 1918 and were preserved in subsequent schemes prepared by British planners: among them Patrick Geddes (1919), Geddes and Ashbee (1922), Holliday (1930), and Kendall (1944). The Kendall plan, however, reduced the inner strip's dimensions by authorizing commercial land use within a 50-meter range from the Old City walls (Kutcher 1975: 50). The principle of a dividing strip between the modern and Old City was also maintained in plans prepared during the first decade of the State of Israel's existence. The 1948/9 Rau's master plan included the entire Old City in the green strip surrounding the city. The outline plan prepared by Shaviv between 1954 and 1959 and approved as a statutory scheme in 1959 stated that the maximum height of city buildings would be five stories, thus protecting the skyline and the panoramic views of the city. The Jordanians, however, relied on the 1944 Kendall plan, though they changed it considerably. The 1964 Jordanian plan reduced the green space around the Old City and marked most of the areas surrounding the Old City as residential ones (Shapiro 1973; Sharon 1973).

When the city was unified in 1967, the Israeli authorities were quite aware of the special opportunity they had been granted. They strove for a sensitive and harmonious blend between the Old City and its surroundings and Jerusalem's new sections. Accordingly, the city's leaders initiated several plans geared toward preserving and restoring the Old City and its surroundings. Hashimshoni and Shweid's 1968 Master Plan revealed a great deal of sensitivity toward the Old City, delimiting it within a broad-scale open public space defined as a nature reserve. This overrode the instructions of the 1964 Kendall plan, which had reserved that space for residential purposes (Master Plan for Jerusalem 1968). Still, according to expert opinion, the 1968 Master Plan already demonstrated a lack of sensitivity toward the urban fabric of the early modern city. The political considerations behind the creation of a united city led to the proposal to build a large commercial center in the heart of the city, linked to a network of wide traffic arteries, lengthwise and crosswise. The new road network was not compatible with the early modern city's narrow road system, and it even impinged on the Old City (Kutcher 1975: 54). The plan for the Old City and its surroundings, prepared in 1973, aimed to create harmony along the interface between the Old City and the early modern city. Accordingly, it set numerous restrictions on tall buildings in the areas around the wall and the Old City's visual basin, and also designated open areas, observatories, and a promenade in the visual basin area (Sharon 1973).

Notwithstanding the criticism leveled against the 1968 Master Plan, it was the only initiative for a comprehensive, long-term plan for Jerusalem. It showed sensitivity toward the Old City's historical character and assets. However, the plan had no sequel statutory scheme for a city in dire need of one. After the first impressive wave of comprehensive planning, restoration, and preservation in the late 1960s and 1970s, the planning enterprise in Jerusalem faded. There was no follow-up to the planning and development of the Old City and no efforts were invested into preparing a comprehensive plan for the city. On the contrary, the construction of the Plaza Hotel in the 1970s was a clear deviation from the principles outlined by previous city plans. The Plaza, located adjacent to the watershed along King George Street, eliminates the open view of the Mount of Olives from the modern city. In the 1980s and 1990s, the construction of the City Center Tower and the Hilton Hotel at the vicinity of the Jaffa Gate perpetuated the trend of obstructing the skylines, landscapes, and views. The new plans to build a highrise hotel and lookout tower on the Armon Ha-Natziv ridge as well as highrise buildings along the French Hill mountain range will exacerbate the trend of dwarfing the Old City's landscape.

During the 1980s and 1990s, the nature of the urban discourse had changed and become distinctly closed-hegemonic. An examination of the urban landscape and, especially, of the relationship between the late modern city and the cities of previous periods reveals a high level of disregard for historical heritage. The premodern city's centers were abandoned. The entrances to the Temple Mount consist of neglected alleyways lined with garbage. The immense buildings of the Hebrew University on Mount Scopus and the Jewish religious colleges and yeshivas of the Jewish Quarter lend them a flavor of being locked fortresses, rising above their surroundings and overshadowing the modest architecture typical of the Old City. The massive building and tall structures in the visual basin of the Old City diminish its key monuments, almost reducing them to naught.

The Israeli government has neither nurtured nor restored the Old City's neighborhoods. There were, however, several widespread restoration and renovation projects, primarily during the 1970s. The highlight was the Jewish Quarter renovation project. Some renovation was also carried out around the gates into the city, and several efforts were invested in improving the physical infrastructure. The characteristic trend since the 1980s, however, has been one of disregard and neglect. Sections of the Muslim quarter and of the Christian quarter have become the desired targets of right-wing groups who wish to acquire property in these sections. With the direct or indirect support of the Israeli government, these groups locate sellers among the Arab population and try to acquire apartments and buildings (Klugman report).

In an attempt to reduce the number of Palestinian residents in Jerusalem, in 1994 the Ministry of the Interior began to confiscate the identity cards of Palestinians who could not prove they lived in Jerusalem on a permanent basis. The results of this policy were counter-productive: many Palestinians with Jerusalem residence IDs who were then living outside the city moved back in. The wave of homecoming accelerated the crowding in the Old City, whose ancient, neglected structures already housed many poor residents, and this has led to the further deterioration of older buildings. Meanwhile, Islamic studies schools and monumental buildings became residential apartments and storage rooms (Touqan 2000: 17). Like other places infiltrated by poorer populations, these neighborhoods have gone through a process of uncontrolled renewal that is not in keeping with the character of the Old City. New rooms are constructed on roofs without any license, domed roofs – a quintessential ingredient of the Jerusalem landscape – are disappearing, and new balconies are being built that deviate from the buildings' lines.

The centers of the early modern period are gradually deteriorating. Jerusalem's civic center, which includes the government office buildings, has been cut off from the other parts of the city. To begin with, the civic center was located at a great distance from residential areas, meaning that after office hours it is largely deserted. Over the years, no attempt was made to incorporate it within flourishing residential areas, which would breathe life into it for most of the day. The heart of the commercial center, in the triangle formed by the Jaffa–Ben Yehuda–King George Streets, thinned and faded, becoming worn out and neglected over the years. Even in the year 2000, when record tourism was anticipated, no efforts at all were invested in enhancing the triangle's appearance or restoring the city center. The liveliness that characterized it during the 1950s and 1960s has vanished. Jaffa Street is startling in its physical squalor and its old, low buildings. Recently it has even become an ecological hazard, because of the amount of pollution it generates. Even Ha-Neviyim Street, which was one of the most charming streets in the city, is now congested with traffic and polluted for most of the day. Ben Yehuda Street looks like a neglected bazaar and the affluent population groups maintain a distance from the triangle, once the city's main attraction. Currently, several tall buildings are being planned for the early modern city without any thought to the functional limitations of the existing network of roads – their capacity to support the inevitable traffic load once the tall buildings are occupied – and without taking the city's visual aspect into account.

One reason for the failing commercial center is the lack of a comprehensive economic planning design. Without a comprehensive development plan based on appropriate reasoning, some activities traditionally held in the center

– such as office, commercial, and service-oriented activities – have relocated to areas not originally designated as commercial and service centers. Unexpectedly, commercial centers, offices, and services have developed along the city's outskirts in the Giv'at Sha'ul and Talpiyyot areas. In the southwest of the city, a postmodern center has sprung up in the Malcha basin. It is made up of a series of completely unrelated buildings and services: a shopping mall, high-tech park, stadium, residential neighborhood, a zoo, a bus terminal, a school for the gifted, and – in the planning stages – a hotel complex, arena, a power station, and wholesale market. The new center consists of modern buildings that spell functionality, and most of them can be accessed comfortably, but they ignore each other and do not take their surroundings into consideration or interrelate with it. They are devoid of any local flavor or identity. They make up a meaningless collage and resemble similar ensembles on the outskirts of any post-industrial modern city. The beating hearts that still convey a sense of identity and locality typical of Jerusalem are few. They are to be found inside the Old City, along the old commercial triangle that, notwithstanding, has survived and still serves as the main venue for consumers and pleasure-seekers and along the commercial street of Salah-al-Din. Secondary heartbeats may be found in the German Colony's commercial center, along Gaza Street and within the ultra-orthodox commercial center at Malchei Israel Street.

The variety of architectural styles that characterized the neighborhoods of the early modern city has ceded its place to the depressing uniformity of public housing in the new neighborhoods. The syncopation that characterized Jerusalem is gradually disappearing. Due to construction in its valleys, a continuous landscape has replaced the pattern of isolated, hilltop neighborhoods. The early modern city's neighborhoods and particularly the beautiful old neighborhoods are threatened by new development projects. Thus, for example, an immense threat hovers over the picturesque Ein Kerem neighborhood. Ha-Neviyim Street is also threatened, with a highrise tower being planned above it that is liable to stunt the street's uniqueness. The Rehavya neighborhood has become part of the city's center; offices occupy the neighborhood's homes, and its streets are congested with traffic. No less disturbing is the damaged topography, as exemplified by the erection of a highrise structure in the Malcha basin, reflecting the might of the technology center. This construction is clearly antithetical to the natural topography, and contradicts the concept that had gained a foothold in several of the city's sites that tall buildings should be reserved for hilltops, not valleys.

Through growth and expansion, the outskirts that once marked off built-up areas and separated them from open areas have gradually disappeared. An expressway was built on the outskirts of the Old City, thus transforming the city's wall into a bank of an incessant river of traffic. Paradoxically, this highway draws a partition between the premodern and early modern cities and bears witness to the clear separation between them. Uncontrolled urban expansion has blurred the formerly clear separation between the late modern city and the green, rustic area. This expansion is prominent at the city's western entrance points, especially along the Jerusalem Forest, which is supposed to be the main green area on the city's outskirts.

Highrise building is a current threat to the city, including in the Old City's visual basin. The absence of any policy in this sphere is one of the characteristics of the hegemonic discourse. When Ehud Olmert was elected mayor in 1993, the Union of Jerusalem Architects was promised a tender for an overall plan for highrise building. The promise was shelved. Consequently, numerous plans for highrise building have reached the various stages of approval, even though the city has no overall plan concerning this issue. After residents of the city's southwestern section fought against construction in the Holyland hill, the Appeals Committee of the National Planning Council recommended to the District Planning Committee that a policy be set on the subject of highrise construction (decision by the Appeals Committee of the National Council, 1998). The chairman of the District Committee did initiate several discussions on the subject, but to date no policy has been consolidated. The attitude of disregard, lack of decision-making, and construction authorizations devoid of policy have all been inherent characteristics of the municipal conduct since the 1970s, and continue to be so at the time of writing.

Factors Shaping the Urban Discourse

How can one explain the prevailing urban discourse, namely the closed-hegemonic discourse that has developed between the various cities of Jerusalem? Presumably the ensuing urban discourse is the result of the balance of political and economic power and the cultural systems underlying it. Jerusalem's landscape has been subordinated to power struggles on the geopolitical, economic, and cultural levels. It is true that planning in Jerusalem has always reflected the power systems and interests of the political and economic powers, but most of the time it was carried out with sensitivity. This is no longer the case. The rules of the game have been broken and the power-holders are those who shape the landscape.

In the absence of democratic principles and long-term rules such as tolerance, recognition of the other, citizen participation in planning, vision, and a comprehensive plan, Jerusalem's character has been subordinated to three power systems: geopolitical, cultural, and economic. The geopolitical power system perceives Jerusalem as a national-ethnic living space being fought over by Jews and Arabs. The cultural power system sees the city as a cultural living space being fought over by secular and ultra-orthodox groups. Finally, the economic power system treats the city as a commercial asset and a source of profit for entrepreneurs and developers.

The geopolitical power system

On the geopolitical level, the government of Israel fought hard to gain control over the city. The main tools used in this battle were expanding Israeli law and the judicial and administrative systems with regard to East Jerusalem in 1967. In addition, the Israeli government expanded the city's boundaries and jurisdiction to include territories formerly under Jordanian rule. Within the expanded area 23,000 *dunams* (about 5,500 acres) were confiscated and used to build Jewish neighborhoods, but not a single Arab neighborhood. Furthermore, a policy of building restriction was adopted to reduce the Arab population growth in the city. For that purpose extensive areas were declared green zones on which building is strictly forbidden, and few building permits were granted to Arabs. In an effort to draw the Old City closer to the new one, some government offices were transferred to the seamline area of Sheikh Jarrakh. The government also supported, both directly and indirectly, the settler associations who were trying to acquire buildings in the Muslim and Christian quarters (Hasson 1996).

The economic power system

On the economic level, a coalition of real estate developers, politicians, and architects currently shapes the urban landscape. From the point of view of this coalition, Jerusalem's special landscape, along with its spiritual and aesthetic values, is an economic resource and an inexhaustible source of real estate profits. Urban planning, which had been under public, professional jurisdiction for generations, underwent a privatization process. The result is a series of disjointed, unrelated projects, which are not inspired by an overall concept and do not communicate with an overall, meaningful urban entity.

With no comprehensive statutory scheme, it is impossible to hold informed discussions on the repercussions of proposed projects, or to ascertain their impact on the city's character and image. Politicians try to develop the city by collecting as much betterment tax as possible, developers are looking for maximum profit, and designers express both these parties' interests by wrapping them in various ideological mantles. This leads to decisions that are biased in favor of developers, while cultural and environmental considerations are swept under the carpet. Thus, many plans for highrise building in sensitive locations, such as the Old City's visual basin, the Armon Ha-Naziv ridge, and the French Hill ridge, have been authorized. Similarly, it was decided to deviate from planning outlines that sought to preserve historic and heritage sites and scenic areas. A case in point is a recently prepared plan for dense construction in the heritage and scenic area of Ein Kerem neighborhood. Similarly, authorization has been granted to land uses that constantly erode green areas, particularly at the edges of the Jerusalem Forest. The permission to build new, luxury apartment towers and complexes reflects the preference being accorded to market power over social and aesthetic considerations. These apartments will mostly be occupied by rich inhabitants (see the case of the David's Village in the Mamila complex), some of whom permanently reside abroad, whose bond with the city can be summed up by way of a brief stay in their luxury apartment.

The current lack of planning is convenient to the city's leaders because they believe that granting concessions to developers is the way to attract investment to the city, to increase tax revenues, and even create jobs. In so doing, architects and policy-makers strive to imitate the North American skyscraper style. Architects and planners in Jerusalem have, for the most part, joined the economic-political forces and those few among them who have voiced objections have had to face retaliation by the authorities, namely, no jobs and a web of slander and mud-slinging.

In contrast to the intense real estate activity, there has been no development of social policy founded on principles of justice in the distribution of public goods, that is, physical and social infrastructures. The immense inequality between Jews and Arabs, between affluent and less affluent groups, between veteran citizens and new immigrants, is paid no attention. A survey conducted by the Municipality of Jerusalem exposed huge discrepancies in public infrastructure and services between the Arab residents in the eastern section of the city and the Jewish residents in the city's west. Despite repeated requests from the municipality, the central government, which has made a point of its commitment to the unity of Jerusalem, has not made available the resources required to address the problem. Socially, immigration absorption has failed miserably, as have the efforts to attract young couples to the city. In the absence of programs in this area, new immigrants avoid coming to the city and many of those who do come leave shortly thereafter. Young couples who are not able to buy an apartment leave the city, and the more affluent leave because of feelings of cultural suffocation and a diminished quality of life. The result has been a negative migration balance since the early 1990s, to the level of 6,000 to 7,000 residents per year (Choshen and Shahar 2000). Many of the out-migrants are secular residents and, as a result, the proportion of the city's secular population is diminishing. Findings from the late 1990s also point to an exodus of the ultra-orthodox population from the city, and census records of Jerusalem's schoolchildren indicate that since 1996 the growth of the city's ultra-orthodox population has also come to a halt.

The cultural power system

The ultra-orthodox politicians who currently hold the key power positions in the Jerusalem municipality serve by and large the interests of their constituency and tend to ignore the needs and aspirations of the secular community. The planning and construction committee, headed by an ultra-orthodox person, allocates land for religious uses (ritual baths, synagogues, and religious schools) all over the city, including secular neighborhoods. Following these allocations ultra-orthodox population moves into the non-orthodox neighborhoods, occasionally displacing the non-orthodox population (Hasson 2001).

The counter-response

The counter-response to the authorities' urban policy (and lack thereof) has been a series of spatial and political conflicts rocking the city. These conflicts are a manifestation of the larger geopolitical, cultural, and economic divisions characterizing the city. In response to the Israeli government geopolitical policy, the Arabs adopted myriad resistance strategies. They refused to recognize the Israeli government, and subsequently refrained from participation in municipal elections or from appealing to the Israeli judicial system. Another resistance measure has been holding onto the land and undertaking large-scale illegal construction. In the absence of a recognized government, the Arabs set up an active civic society characterized by a widespread network of voluntary organizations. Finally, to express their discontent with the geopolitical situation, they have embarked on a national uprising, the intifada. One result of the counter-struggle is the steady growth, in both absolute and relative terms, of the Arabs in Jerusalem. Between 1967 and 1997 the growth rate of the Arab population was 180 percent, but only 117 percent for the Jewish population. As a result, the city's Jewish population shrank from 74 percent of the total in 1967 to 69 percent in 1997 (Choshen and Shahar 1998). The Arab population is currently active in the preservation and restoration of the Old City. In 1981 Jerusalem was recognized as a World Heritage Site, and in 1982 as an Endangered World Heritage Site.

Within the Jewish population, the secular and the ultra-orthodox groups have collided with each other. The most prominent case concerned the Ramot Allon neighborhood where the secular population has waged a continuing battle against the ultra-orthodox takeover of schools, kindergartens, and youth movement facilities within the secular sections of the neighborhood. This opposition was even put to the test in court, which sympathized with the secular population, leaving the ultra-orthodox population with a sense of cultural discrimination. The secular populations in Qiryat Ha-Yovel, Abu-Tor, Ramat Denia, and the new Malcha suburb have all fought against any changes to the cultural image of their neighborhoods brought about by the construction of ritual baths, large synagogues, and yeshivas.

The coalition of real estate developers, architects, and politicians has found itself facing counter-reactions by the city's residents, who have often rallied against projects they perceived as threatening. The residents of the southwestern section of the city attempted to modify the Holyland plan and to thwart the building of an amphitheater in their area. The residents of Ha-Neviyim Street opposed the erection of a highrise building in their vicinity. Ein Kerem residents opposed the plans for dense construction in their neighborhood. Bet Ha-Kerem and Har Nof residents protested the ongoing erosion of the Jerusalem Forest. In the late 1990s, an urban coalition of local and environmental organizations was formed to protect and maintain the city's character. This coalition, "Sustainable Jerusalem," operates on two levels: reactively by opposing plans perceived as jeopardizing sustainable development, and proactively by preparing a comprehensive plan for sustainable development (Forum for the Future of Jerusalem and Society for the Protection of Nature 1999). The planning method and counter-reactions bear witness to a basic flaw in the overall planning system: the lack of any public discussion forum, and the failure to involve the public in decision-making. The result is an urban system filled with conflicts and power struggles in which might decides.

A heavy ideological shroud clothes all of these conflicts: the integrity of Jerusalem as a unified city under Israeli sovereignty, the rectification of past wrongs toward the ultra-orthodox, and beautification of the city. Camouflaging the tensions and converting the conflicts into meaningful aesthetic action is a salient characteristic of the city's urban politics. As far back as when Teddy Kollek was mayor, a committee was set up to discuss ways of involving the public in planning processes. The mayor rejected the committee's conclusions. At the time of writing, the municipality is exploring new ways, such as public hearing and mediation, to involve the residents in the decision-making before the stage of submitting objections. However, mediation processes have usually resulted in minimal benefit to neighborhood residents. Within the scope of the aesthetic act of involving the public, several seminars and public hearings have been held but with no impact whatsoever. The developers presented their plans and the residents criticized them, but the criticism was never recorded in any document. Presumably, public hearing has the capacity to influence. In reality, however, it has not. It acts as an aesthetic front that masks conflicts and tensions and neutralizes social activity. This is part of the aesthetic camouflage process typical of the power and control system.

Conclusions

Jerusalem is a complex city whose various components display tensions and dependence. The urban morphology bears the values of a society of religion and tradition, a society of modernity and nationalism, and a society of modern consumerism and globalism. Each of these societies has left its mark on the urban landscape. Perhaps the ultimate expression of the different societal forms is revealed in the city's nodes. The religious node in the premodern city is embodied in the Temple Mount, the Wailing Wall, the Haram al-Sharif area housing the al-Aqsa mosque and the shrine of the Dome of the Rock, and the Church of the Holy Sepulchre. The Jewish national node, expressed in the civic center, is located in the early modern city. Perhaps the Palestinian equivalent to this node is the Orient House structure, which may be replaced in the future by the Palestinian Parliament building in the city. The consumer and high-tech node, which has global aspirations, is located in the late modern city.

There may be no greater tension than that between the globally oriented modern consumer society and the ethnically oriented society of tradition and religion. No less acute is the tension latent in the relationship between the global economy and the consumerism embodied in the late modern city sections, and the nationalism and particularism embedded in the early modern city. The premodern and early modern cities have clear identities and a powerful bond to their place. The late modern city, which is an outer city, is amorphous and culturally disorganized. It accommodates Arab villages, fortress-like Jewish neighborhoods built out of geopolitical considerations, ultra-orthodox neighborhoods, and prestigious suburbs. It presents a sociocultural mixture of multiple identities, yet it lacks a clear cultural identity. If one were to pinpoint its culture and identity, it would perhaps be a mixture of tribalism, cosmopolitanism, and global orientation.

The question is, which power will get the upper hand within the three cities that make up Jerusalem. Are the identity clashes unavoidable or can a variety of cultures perhaps coexist within this urban entity in an atmosphere of mutual respect and tolerance? Will the power of the globally oriented shopping centers and high-tech firms of the outer city counterbalance the local-ethnic orientation of the premodern and early modern cities? In this respect, Jerusalem's late modern, outer city provides a unique opportunity to avoid religious and national conflict by creating a common ground based on late capitalist production and consumerism. As such, the outer city is the complete opposite of the religious segregation and national polarization of the two other cities.

The late modern city is actually the one currently setting the tone for Jerusalem's design. The rules of the late modern city – efficiency, rapid pace, dependency on private vehicles, and the move to suburbia, urban expansion, and ignoring the landscape in favor of real estate development – are what dictate the character of urban development.

It is not my intention to dwell on nostalgia and blind adoration of the city's ancient structures. Many sections in the premodern and early modern cities are worthy of renovation and rebuilding. Furthermore, development of the late modern city has the potential to reduce tensions and create a city that is less clannish, less fanatical, less steeped in ceaseless conflict. All I wish to propose is that attention be paid to the rules of the other cities in Jerusalem since it is their unity which lends the city its unique character and image. The decision-makers must understand that each of the three cities has syntax of its own, founded on rules and resources, which crystallized during the course of history. To achieve any meaningful urban development, one must be acquainted with these rules and resources and treat them with respect.

Bibliography

Amiran, D. H. K. 1973: The development of Jerusalem. In D. H. K. Amiran et al. (eds.), *Urban Geography of Jerusalem: A Companion Volume to the Atlas of Jerusalem*. Jerusalem: Israel Academy of Sciences and Humanities, Israel Exploration Society, 20–52.

Avi-Yonah, M. 1973: Building history from earliest times to the nineteenth century. In D. H. K. Amiran et al. (eds.), *Urban Geography of Jerusalem: A Companion Volume to the Atlas of Jerusalem*. Jerusalem: Israel Academy of Sciences and Humanities, Israel Exploration Society, 13–19.

Ben-Arieh, Y. 1977: *A City Reflected in its Times: Jerusalem in the Nineteenth Century, The Old City*. Jerusalem: Yad Izhak Ben-Zvi Publications.

Benevolo, L. 1993: *The European City*. Oxford: Blackwell.

Braunfels, W. 1988: *Urban Design in Western Europe: Regime and Architecture, 900–1900*. Chicago and London: University of Chicago Press.

Carrel, T. 2000: Beijing: new face for the ancient capital. *National Geographic Magazine*, March.

Calvino, I. 1974: *Invisible Cities*. Orlando, FL: Harcourt and Brace.

Choshen, M. and Shahar, N. 1998: *Statistical Yearbook of Jerusalem*. Jerusalem: Jerusalem Institute for Israel Studies.

——2000: *Statistical Yearbook of Jerusalem*. Jerusalem: Jerusalem Institute for Israel Studies.

Ellin, N. 1996: *Postmodern Urbanism*. Cambridge, MA: Blackwell.

Forum for the Future of Jerusalem and Society for the Protection of Nature 1999: *The Sustainable Jerusalem Charter.* Jerusalem.

Galntay, E. Y. 1987: Islamic identity and the metropolis: continuity and conflict. In A. Y. Saqqaf (ed.), *The Middle East City: Ancient Traditions Confront a Modern World*. New York: Paragon House, 5–24.

Grabar, O. [1978] 1995: The architecture of power: palaces, citadels and fortifications. In G. Michell (ed.), *Architecture of the Islamic World: Its History and Social Meaning*. London: Thames and Hudson, 48–79.

Hall, P. 1998: *Cities in Civilization*. New York: Pantheon.

Har El, M. 1970: *This is Jerusalem*. Tel Aviv: Am Oved Publishers.

Hasson, S. 1996: Local politics and split citizenship in Jerusalem. *International Journal of Urban and Regional Research* 20 (1): 116–33.

—— 2001: *The Struggle for Hegemony in Jerusalem: Secular and Ultra-Orthodox Urban Politics*. Jerusalem: Floershiemer Institute for Policy Studies.

Hidenobu, J. 1995: *Tokyo: A Spatial Anthropology*. Berkeley: University of California Press.

Kark, R. and Oren-Nordheim, M. 1995: *Jerusalem and its Environs: Quarters, Neighborhoods, Villages, 1800–1948*. Jerusalem: Academon.

Kroyanker, D. 1988: *Jerusalem: Conflicts Over the City's Physical and Visual Form*. Jerusalem: Jerusalem Institute for Israel Studies; Zmora: Bitan Publishers.

—— 1989: *Jerusalem Architecture: Periods and Styles. The Period of the British Mandate, 1918–1948*. Jerusalem: Keter Publishing.

Kutcher, A. 1975. *The New Jerusalem: Planning and Politics*. Cambridge, MA: MIT Press.

Lapidus, I. P. 1973: Traditional Muslim cities: structure and change. In L. C. Brown (ed.), *From Madina to Metropolis: Heritage and Change in Near Eastern City*. Princeton, NJ: Darwin Press.

Levine, I. L. 1999: Introduction. In I. L. Levine (ed.), *Jerusalem: Its Sanctity and Centrality to Judaism, Christianity and Islam*. New York: Continuum, xi–xxiv.

Lynch, K. 1960: *The Image of the City*. Cambridge, MA: MIT Press and Harvard University Press.

Master Plan for Jerusalem 1968: *Jerusalem: The Municipality of Jerusalem*.

Nijman, J. 2000: The paradigmatic city. *Annals of the Association of American Geographers* 90: 135–45.

Planning Team for the Old City and Surroundings 1970: *Old City of Jerusalem*. Jerusalem: Municipality of Jerusalem.

Schorske, C. E. 1980: *Fin-de-siècle Vienna: Politics and Culture*. New York: A. A. Knopf.

Shapiro, S. 1973: Planning Jerusalem: the first generation. In D. H. K. Amiran et al. (eds.), *Urban Geography of Jerusalem: A Companion Volume to the Atlas of Jerusalem*. Jerusalem: Israel Academy of Sciences and Humanities, Israel Exploration Society, 139–53.

Sharon, A. 1973: *Planning Jerusalem: The Master Plan for the Old City of Jerusalem and its Environs*. New York: McGraw-Hill.

Shavit, Y. (ed.) 1998: *Jerusalem: A Biography*. Tel Aviv: Am Oved Publishers.

Sudjic, D. 1993: *The 100 Mile City*. London: Flamingo.

Sumner-Boyd, H. and Freely, J. 1972: *Strolling Through Istanbul: A Guide to the City.* Istanbul: Redhouse Press.

Touqan, S. 2000: Revitalizing the Old City. Jerusalem Quarterly File. *Institute of Jerusalem Studies* 8: 14–18.

Vryonis, Jr., S. 1991: Byzantine Constantinople and Ottoman Istanbul: evolution in a millennial imperial iconography. In I. A. Bierman et al. (eds.), *The Ottoman City and Its Parts: Urban Structure and Social Order.* New York: Aristide D. Caratzas.

Werblowsky, R. J. Z. 1997: The meaning of Jerusalem to Jews, Christians, and Muslims. In Y. Ben-Arieh and M. Davis (eds.), *Jerusalem in the Mind of the Western World, 1800–1948.* Westport, CT, and London: Praeger, 7–24.

Wheatley, P. 1971: *Pivot of the Four Quarters.* Edinburgh: Edinburgh University Press.

Zilberman, I. 1992: The Hebronite migration and the development of suburbs in the metropolitan area of Jerusalem. In A. Layish (ed.), *The Arabs in Jerusalem: From the Ottoman Period to the Beginning of the 1990s – Religious, Social and Cultural Distinctiveness.* Jerusalem: Magnes Press, Hebrew University.

14
Muslim Civil Society in Urban Public Spaces: Globalization, Discursive Shifts, and Social Movements

Paul M. Lubeck and Bryana Britts

> Cities are processes, not products. The three Islamic elements that set in motion the processes that give rise to Islamic cities were: a distinction between the members of the Umma and the outsiders, which led to juridical and spatial distinction by neighborhoods; the segregation of the sexes which gave rise to a particular solution to the question of spatial organization; and a legal system which, rather than imposing general regulations over land uses of various types in various places, left to the litigation of the neighbors the detailed adjudication of mutual rights over space and use. (Janet Abu-Lughod 1987: 173)

Framing: Muslim Movements in Urban Situations

We live in an intellectual moment when the complexity of the global Islamic revival renders it difficult to generalize about Muslim institutions, social movements, and discursive practices. While diversity and locality remain paramount features of Muslim cities, globalization has inadvertently nurtured transnational Muslim networks from the homeland of Islam and extended them into the web of interconnected world cities. Quite opportunistically, urban-based Muslim networks and insurrectionist movements now thrive in the interstitial spaces created by the new global communication and transportation infrastructures. What, then, are the long-term patterns for Muslims in cities?

Since the last millennium, as Janet Abu-Lughod reminds us, "the Islamic city" has been the primary site for: defining power relations between ruler and subject, specifying the rights and identities of spatial communities, and regulating urban social relations between genders. Today's Muslim city remains the epicenter of a burgeoning public sphere in which informed publics debate highly contested Islamic discourses regarding social justice,

Table 14.1 Population trends of major Muslim cities (population in millions)

	Algeria	*Egypt*	*Indonesia*	*Iran*	*Jordan*	*Malaysia*	*Morocco*	*Nigeria*	*Pakistan*	*Syria*
Country 1997	29.4	64.7	203.4	64.6	6.1	21.0	26.9	103.9	144.0	14.9
Largest city[a]	Algiers	Cairo	Jakarta	Tehran	Amman	Kuala Lumpur	Casablanca	Lagos	Karachi	Damascus
Population 1995[a]	3.7	9.7	8.6	6.8	1.2	1.2	3.1	10.3	9.7	2.0
Trend: % urban										
1975	40.3	43.5	19.4	45.8	55.3	37.7	37.7	23.4	26.4	45.1
1980[b]	43.0	44.0	22.0	50.0	60.0	42.0	41.0	27.0	28.0	47.0
1997[b]	57.0	45.0	37.0	60.0	73.0	55.0	53.0	41.0	35.0	53.0
2015	67.5	53.5	52.4	68.8	79.8	66.2	64.3	55.4	46.7	62.1

[a] Source is the United Nations website.
[b] Source is the World Bank, *Development Report 1999/2000*.
Source: Data from the United Nations, *Human Development Report 1999*, unless otherwise noted.

urban public space, legitimate government, political action, and gender relations (Eickelman and Anderson 1999). Muslim urban civil society is dense, diverse, and ubiquitous, encompassing Muslim-inspired charitable organizations, professional groups, insurrectional activists, and cultural associations involving members of all social classes (Norton 1995; Sullivan and Abed-Kotob 1999). The Muslim city, therefore, creates the ambience in which Muslim discourses and civil society groups coalesce to launch a diverse stream of urban social movements divided by tactic and strategy but united in their opposition to what they view as an illegitimate and failed postcolonial political order.

Just how urbanized Muslims are becoming is affirmed in table 14.1. By 2015, at least half and up to two-thirds of the populations of Muslim-majority states will be living in cities with polarized income distributions and miserable living conditions (UNDP 1999). Although increasingly integrated into a Western-dominated urban network, these urban centers stretch across a contiguous, geographical cultural zone – Islamdom – in which most states have Muslim majorities or very large minorities (Hodgson 1974). This growing diamond-shaped zone, which Gellner calls the "Qur'an Belt," stretches from Morocco to Indonesia on the east–west axis and from Kazakhstan to Tanzania on the north–south axis. Herein live the overwhelming majority of the 1.2 billion estimated Muslims, the majority of whom reside in South and Southeast Asia, i.e., at least 650 million.

Urban Structural Processes, Discourses, and Movements

Our objective is to historicize and analyze the meaning and consequences of the unexpected shift from secular national to Islamic discourses, civil society groups, and social movements in Muslim-majority cities since the 1970s. We focus on *Islamism* and *Islamists* as distinguished from the broader and less politicized term, *Islamic*; Islamist refers to the the modern, Western-educated, and highly urbanized groups rather than on traditional scholars, the ulama, or mystical brotherhoods, i.e., Sufi orders (tariqa). In brief, Islamism or political Islam is a modern, male-dominated political movement seeking to reinstitutionalize its conception of Islamic laws (Sharia), institutions (zakat or tithe), and other imagined practices of the first Muslim communities living under the authority of the Prophet and the four successor Caliphs (Esposito 1992; Guazzone 1995). Not unlike sixteenth-century Protestantism and like any other modernist, urban movement, Islamist strategies can be differentiated along a tactical spectrum: armed insurrection (Afghanistan, Algeria, Acheh, and Israel-Palestine), building a parallel civil society (everywhere), popular demonstrations (Nigeria, Morocco, and Iran), or the voting booth (Malaysia, Indonesia, Turkey, Egypt, and Jordan). Among insurrectionary

Islamists, Osama bin Laden's network al-Qaida is noteworthy because it recruits from many nationalities, speaks to a universal Muslim nationalism, and innovates by using the infrastructures of global capitalism to launch its terrorist attacks.

Our central argument is that Islamism is a modern urban movement empowered by a profound discursive shift involving virtually all social classes, genders, and status groups. Ironically strongest in cities most integrated into the global system, the energy driving Islamism is concentrated among educated urban youth caught in the miasmic web of multiple postcolonial crises. Islamism is a palpable force manifested everywhere in urban space: cultural and media productions, daily consumption, urban civil society groups, educational institutions, and social movements. Viewed from the micro-level perspective of urban neighborhoods, Islamism creates a diverse network of civil society groups delivering goods and services, each sharing an appealing cultural narrative claiming "authenticity," yet one that corresponds to the meaningful everyday life discursive practices of Muslim urban communities (Denoeux 1993; Lubeck 1998). As Burke (1998) shows, this change constitutes a truly global discursive shift in popular consciousness from a secular nationalist to an Islamic narrative. Islamism operates at multiple levels: it simultaneously envisions itself as a force for the revival of global Islamic unity, a movement to reform the territorially defined national state, a global insurrectionary movement, and a creator of a moral economy in urban neighborhoods.

At a moment when the postcolonial national state has lost innumerable sovereign powers to US-driven, neoliberal global restructuring, Islamism has seized the popular imagination by seizing from incumbent authorities the most important ideological resource possessed by the postcolonial state: that is, the power to define the meaning of anti-imperialist, populist nationalism for subjects living in most Muslim-majority states (Lubeck 2000). Due to the decline of rival alternative visions, Islamism has emerged as the most powerful anti-systemic political force opposing Western-led globalization especially since the collapse of the Soviet model (1989). Like its predecessor, "Third Worldist," anti-imperialist Marxism, Islamist movements practice open recruitment and universalist appeals to the excluded and oppressed, both Muslim and non-Muslim, whom they target as potential converts. Like Marxism, Islamism is divided tactically into violent insurrectionists and non-violent gradualists. Many observers, appalled by the barbarity of the terrorist attacks on the World Trade Center and the American embassies in East Africa, label the insurrectionist faction as "fascist." However, this is a misleading analogy from Western history for, unlike fascism, Islamist insurrectionists like al-Qaida do not base their appeal on exclusive nationalism, racial superiority, or the mystique of charismatic leaders. Rather, they appeal to all Muslims in the world who feel excluded from the benefits of the neoliberal world economy and oppressed by Western political hegemony. Indeed, while sharing authoritarianism, the insurrectionist Islamist call to arms is much more universalistic; for they practice open multiracial recruitment, advocate governance based upon their interpretation of Islamic law, and, most importantly, declare themselves to be a *vanguard* representing the interests of a transnational Muslim nation (umma). Accordingly, because of their ideology of universalism and internationalism as well as their disciplined organizational structure, insurrectionist Islamists are actually much closer to extreme terrorist sects of the Leninist variety than to Western fascism.

Organizationally in order to explain the discursive shift toward urban Islamism, we briefly review the significance of structural factors – the petroleum boom–bust cycle and the crisis of the postcolonial state – and then evaluate the "demonstration effect" exerted by the Iranian Revolution on urban popular consciousness. Then we dissect Islamism as discourse, civil society group, and social movement in the Egyptian case in comparative perspective. And finally, we conclude with an explanation of the contradictory positions expressed by women representing themselves in urban public space and the novel discursive practices of Muslim feminist groups.

Global Restructuring: Petrodollars and the Rise of Neoliberal Regulation

Because nine of fourteen original OPEC states were Muslim-majority states, the relative equilibrium associated with secular nationalism and state regulation of economy and society fractured considerably during the petroleum boom. Rather than reviving national economic autonomy, however, the petroleum boom of 1973–4 proved to be the last gasp of state-centered economic development and the midwife of greater regulation by global markets and multilateral institutions, i.e., the International Monetary Fund (IMF) and the World Bank (Lipietz 1987).

Three major structural changes occurred as a result of the petroleum boom–bust cycle. First, the boom created an autonomous, corrupt, rentier state elite distributing contracts among clients without an accompanying disciplined social structure of accumulation. State elites invested in noncompetitive construction projects and state capitalist industries (refineries, steel, autos, agro-schemes), allowed inflation and inequality to destroy the preexisting urban moral economy, and, most importantly, disrupted the structure of rural food and labor markets, thus encouraging rural to urban migration in response to the urban construction boom (Richards 1987).

Second, the petro-boom shifted vast financial resources to the Saudi and Gulf states, thereby exposing immigrant labor to conservative and insurrectionist (Wahabbi-Hanabali) doctrines. In turn, the Gulf states funded a global network of Islamic associations, schools, charities, and mosques, all occurring at the expense of the more populated and poorer secular states. Al-Azmeh, speaking for Muslim modernists, asserts that "Petro-Islam . . . has broken the secularist and nationalist cultural, mediatic and, to a lesser extent, the educational monopoly of the modern Arab state" (1993: 32).

Third, with the collapse of oil prices from a high of $41/barrel in 1981 to less than $8/barrel in 1986, the swollen cities of Islamdom, increasingly filled with new immigrants and recent graduates, descended into the austerity phase of the petro-bust (Lubeck 1998). Global neoliberalism forced states to implement structural adjustment policies, i.e., devaluation, privatization of industry, lowering deficits, eliminating subsidies for basic needs, and state withdrawal, all of which increased urban inequality and unemployment among graduates (UNDP 1999).

The Legitimacy Crisis of the Postcolonial Secular State

To be sure, the petro-boom–bust cycle and global restructuring undermined the legitimacy of the secular nationalist state even before the Iranian Revolution made Islamism a viable political option. Historically, ever since the rise of Ataturk's Turkey, Pahlavi's Iran, and Nasser's Egypt, the secular ethnonationalist project spread very shallow roots in Muslim civil society. Indeed, secular nationalism never originated from below: it was almost always a top-down, authoritarian project articulated from above by national, mostly military, elites who assumed control over the authoritarian colonial state apparatus. For military, intellectual, and bureaucratic elites, therefore, the state was an instrument to transform society in the direction of a given Western model of modernity. Interestingly, Muslim royalist regimes (Gulf states, Saudi Arabia, Jordan, and Morocco) in addition to Pakistan are exceptions, oftentimes adjusting more readily to the Islamist discursive shift.

The combined effect of disasters like the 1967 Arab–Israeli war, the generalized stagnation of the development model, and state implementation of neoliberal structural adjustment programs (SAPs) destroyed the social contract between state elites and urban dwellers. Liberalization and austerity reduced state subsidies to the most vulnerable populations and diminished employment opportunities in state industries and bureaucracies for graduates. Not only do SAPs violate Muslim prohibitions against paying interest on debt as well as the obligation for Muslim states to distribute alms or subsidies to the poor (zakat); the transparently foreign management of the SAPs rapidly evaporated any residual fig leaf of legitimacy possessed by secular political elites.

All forces funneled social tension toward cities. The crisis severely impacted the students and graduates of state-sponsored, Western-origin universities, not the traditional Muslim *medersa* training traditional scholars for the ulama. Economic stagnation, widespread corruption, and bureaucratic incompetence dashed the mobility and security aspirations of secondary schools and universities. Hence they constitute a "lumpen intelligentsia" poised for recruitment (Roy 1994). Others paint a grim picture of the Middle East and North Africa (MENA) region. MENA is second only to Africa in rates of population growth; the region's population is expected to double in twenty-seven years, most are less than twenty years old; and Islam and fertility are positively correlated universally (Richards and Waterbury 1996: 80–5). Typically, state educational budgets are biased toward tertiary and secondary education, geared to the state employment of males for jobs that no longer exist. These policies generate a steady stream of recruits – from the countryside, informal economy, and educational institutions – readily absorbed into a network of urban Islamist movements and civil society groups (Sullivan 1994; Wickham 1997).

Discursive Shift: The Iranian Revolution as "Demonstration Effect"

Despite their universality, structural factors alone fail to explain the tectonic discursive shift toward Islamism in the popular consciousness of Muslims living in cities. The pivotal event was the Iranian Revolution (1978–9) and its successful institutionalization as the Islamic Republic of Iran. Clearly, a classic urban insurrection directed against a corrupt, secular authoritarian regime, the revolution depended upon a multi-class coalition of nationalist, Marxist, and Muslim groups led by the charismatic Khomeini, with Shi'ite clergy acting as a disciplined corporate group. Most importantly, advances in global (Western) communication media televised the revolution to millions of Muslims living outside of Iran. Later, as structural adjustment penetrated Muslim cities, the Iranian Revolution demonstrated to the excluded generations facing austerity and misery that the Islamist alternative was a rational, feasible, alternative political project. Not only did the revolution exert a "demonstration effect" on urban Muslim activists, it thoroughly transformed the global Muslim community's vision of what was politically possible to imagine, just as globalization and structural adjustment were emasculating the postcolonial state. Zubaida captures its impact well: "For some . . . Islam in its political and progressive form is more accessible to the people springing as it does from their historical cultural roots . . . acquir[ing] many recruits, a respectability and viability . . . firmly established in the mainstream" (1989: 40). For urban activists who failed to apply Western models of social transformation, the revolution constituted a unique rupture with the past. For unlike other movements, revolutionary Iran survived the onslaughts of powerful antagonists: isolation and destabilization by the United States, Saudi-funded efforts to delegitimize the revolution as an Islamic discourse, and the Iraqi invasion.

We ignore for space reasons questions whether the role of "Twelver" Shi'ite doctrines, clerical institutions, and Khomeini's concept of "rule by jurists" are uniquely Iranian or partially applicable to Sunni urban contexts. To summarize what is applicable: the revolution mobilized formerly excluded groups such as women and recent urban migrants into a mass-based movement that organized demonstrations in cities like Tehran whose population increased from 3 to 9 million between 1970 and 1990 (Roy 1994: 53). Urban civil society and the public sphere mushroomed as new committees, foundations, civil associations, and publications extended into all aspects of urban life. Constitutional innovation created an Islamic Republic with universal suffrage for women who, once mobilized by the revolution, soon demanded equal access to education, work, political office, and gender rights such as a prenuptial contract excluding polygamy and even wages for housework when divorced (Hoodfar 1998). Indeed, Khomeini reinforced the Islamist demand for reinterpretation (*ijtihad*). His final statement (1988) asserted the principle of revolutionary necessity: "the Islamic state had absolute power . . . to adopt such measures as it deemed necessary for the interests of the Islamic state even when these might conflict with Islamic law or a fundamental religious obligation like the pilgrimage to Mecca" (Mayer 1993: 120). Many of these discursive innovations have diffused into Shi'ite communities like Lebanon and even into the Sunni mainstream.

Islamic Reform: The Origins of Modern Islamist Urban Movements

Historians have traced Islamic reform (*islah*) to seventeenth-century reactions to imperialism and Hindu–Muslim syncretism. By the eighteenth century, Wahabbism, a radical, puritanical doctrine opposing rational reinterpretation of the Sharia as well as Sufi brotherhoods, unified Arabia under the Saudi family. In the twentieth century the latter used petroleum revenues, their control over pilgrimage sites (1924–5), and patronage of Muslim pilgrim-scholars to spread a Wahabbi ulama vision of Islamic reform (Lapidus 1988). Alarmed by the technical and organizational power of the European colonial state, modernist urban intellectuals tried to theorize a modern Islamic state capable of reviving or replacing the Caliphate. Islamic modernists – Al-Afgani, Mohammed Abduh, and Rashid Rida – called for returning to "original" Islam (*salaf*), reviving *ijtihad*, and embracing Islam's historical expertise in science, technology, and reason, while denouncing the ulama's passive imitation of the Islamic canon, the corruption of Sufi magical practices, and the collaboration of Muslim rulers with colonialism. Intellectually and practically, however, they failed to realize their project. For, despite considerable influence among the urban intelligentsia, Islamic modernists remained intellectuals, never developing a modern organizational structure capable of mobilizing Muslim civil society toward an Islamist project.

The necessary discursive shift to a modern, civil society-based, urban organization occurred in 1928 when Hasan al-Banna, an Egyptian elementary schoolteacher, practicing Sufi, and devoted reader of Rashid Rida's newspaper, *al-Manar*, founded the Muslim Brotherhood. Beginning as an association for Islamic reform, serving workers in the British-controlled Suez Canal Zone, and soon Cairo (1934), the Brotherhood emerged as the first modern organized, mass-based, multifunctional Islamist organization to speak to the needs of the new urban classes now sprouting in colonial cities. Al-Banna's program proposed: a "return" to purified, Islamic principles and practices, the rejection of the corrupting influence of Western culture, recognizing Islam as a comprehensive way of life for modern urbanites, and, for the first time, a strategy for seizing political power so as to establish a modern Islamic state as an alternative to the then dominant liberal, secular nationalist movement (Abu-Rabi' 1996).

What, then, explains the success of al-Banna's Muslim Brotherhood in Muslim cities? Most important was its modernity: innovative recruitment and membership registration strategies, disciplined organizational techniques, and comprehensive social services for new migrant workers flooding into Egyptian cities. Initially, however, al-Banna required Brotherhood members to follow ritual practices derived from Sufi orders (tariqa) such as swearing an oath, regular devotional exercises, and daily recitations from the Qur'an (Voll 1991). In global terms, while demanding an Islamic state, the Brotherhood vision is pan-Islamic and internationalist, currently claiming branches in over seventy countries (www.ummah.org/ikhwan). With branches in Syria, Sudan, Jordan, and the Maghreb, the Brotherhood also benefited from funding from the Saudi and Gulf states during the petro-boom. Their objective is the Islamization of civil society: schools, mosques, clubs, associations, and social welfare services for those employed as laborers, clerks, and professionals in the Western-oriented, modern urban sector. Ramadan summarizes the organizational shift of Islamic activism:

> The Brotherhood shifted the responsibility for establishing Islamic government from the religiously educated class to the Western incultured class, from the shaykhs to the lawyers, doctors, engineers, pharmacists and army and police officers . . . link[ing] pan-Islamic Egypt before World War I to nationalist Egypt after the war, just as it linked religion to modern science. (1993: 155)

Organizationally similar to communist and fascist mass movements of the 1930s, the Brotherhood instituted a modern, bureaucratically disciplined organizational apparatus into Muslim cities, one led by a Supreme Guide, with membership lists, specialized departments, secret units, modern media, and local branches. The original organization had four types of members: "assistant member, affiliated member, working member and *mujahid*, or combatant member" (Auda 1994: 381). At times quasi-military athletic training and a secret militia were used to pursue objectives. At the local level, cell structures consisted of five and later ten members, bound by personal ties and an elected chief who represented the cell at branch meetings (Mitchell 1969; Denoeux 1993). Mitchell estimated that the Egyptian Brotherhood had 500 branches and 500,000 members by 1949. Banned a year earlier for threatening the state and later for assassinating the Egyptian Prime Minister, the organization went underground yet it supported Nasser and the Free Officers' coup against the monarchy until it became disillusioned with his state socialist policies and his refusal to establish an Islamic state. The Brotherhood then split into radical and moderate factions. After surviving Nasser's suppression, the moderate branch eventually consolidated itself as a middle-class movement committed to gradualism and nonviolence.

Radical Islamist Discourses: Sayyid Qutb as Insurrectionary Theorist

Most Islamists pursue moderate, gradualist, and noninsurrectionary strategies. Sayyid Qutb (1906–66), however, became the theoretician of the radical, insurrectionist, zealous tendency in Islamism. Born in Assiut, southern Egypt, to a prosperous family and educated in Cairo, he worked as an inspector of education. In 1949, courtesy of American aid, he received a scholarship to study in Washington and California. Alienated by America's liberalism, alliance with Israel, and racism toward Arabs, upon his return to Egypt he joined the Brotherhood, acting as a publicist and militant activist. Imprisoned for conspiracy and tortured several times, Qutb was executed for treason in 1966, but not before making his case for an uncompromising Islamic state at his trial (Haddad 1983). Qutb was prolific. His writings include a thirty-volume commentary on the Qur'an, written in a clear, didactic style making it popular among Islamists, the Nation of Islam, and even the revolutionary Iranian students (Haddad 1983: 68). The canonical text of insurrectionary Islamism, *Milestones*, was written while he was being tortured prior to his execution.

Qutb's theoretical arguments mark a radical rupture with the Brotherhood's mainstream Islamist ideas. Because he inspires and justifies vanguardist, insurrectionist movements committed to overthrowing states ruled by practicing Muslims, Qutb is to Islamism what Lenin was for Marxism. To summarize: synthesizing ideas ranging from medievalist Ibn Taymiyya and the Pakistani Islamist Maududi, Qutb defined the contemporary situation as equivalent to the pre-Islamic condition of *jahiliyya*, a state of ignorance similar to Hobbes's "state of nature," the same social conditions that forced Mohammed to withdraw to Medina (Abu-Rabi' 1996). Therefore, merely observing the five pillars of Islam is insufficient if a Muslim cooperates with existing authorities; rather, only an uncompromising implementation of the absolute authority of God (*hakimiyya*) as defined in the Sharia allows one to be defined as an observant Muslim. Hence, true Muslims are obligated to practice holy flight (hijrah) by withdrawing with the "elect" from corrupted Muslims who do not heed the call (da'wa). Corrupted Muslims are branded as atheists or apostates (kafir), thus subject to suppression and holy war (jihad) and, most important for Qutb, "a vanguard must resolve to set it in motion" (Voll 1991: 371). According to Qutb:

> This religion is a universal declaration of human liberation on earth from the bondage to other men or to human desires. . . . To declare God's sovereignty means: the comprehensive revolution against human governance in all its perceptions, forms, systems and conditions. . . . Jihad works to realize the idea of universal revolution not aimed at rule, control or booty. (Haddad, quoting Qutb, 1983: 82–3)

Islam, moreover, is universal and global, not limited to the Arab man. "Its object is the world, the whole world. . . . Whenever there is oppression, Islam is commissioned to eradicate it, to combat it, whether this oppression is against Muslims, against protected peoples or others with whom Muslims have no treaties" (Haddad 1983: 83).

It is easy to see how Qutb's torture, martyrdom, and call for global liberation provide the canonical discourse for urban insurrectionist sects defining themselves as revolutionary vanguards struggling against the inequality and misery engulfing the Muslim cities. A legion of secretive, insurrectionist groups, organized into cells like their Leninist counterparts, have drawn inspiration from Qutb's writings. Islamic Jihad assassinated Sadat; Al-Juma'a al-Islamiyya wages war against tourists while its leader, al-Rahman, was convicted of the World Trade Center bombing. Other groups such as Takfir wa Hijra, Islamic Jihad, and the Armed Islamic Group wage insurrections in Egypt, Afghanistan, Algeria, and Israel-Palestine, respectively (Esposito 1992; Ramadan 1993; Sullivan and Abed-Kotob 1999). Bin Laden's global network draws upon the successors to Qutb. Operating from Afghanistan, insurrectionist groups are trained and funded for operations against Western interests such as the American embassies in Kenya and Tanzania and the destroyer *Cole*.

Clearly modernist in organization and strategy, both moderate and insurrectionary Islamist groups have adopted organizational forms and borrowed mobilizing concepts like vanguardism, human liberation, anti-imperialism, and urban revolution from the Marxist playbook. Studies now confirm the

Marxist background of many of the leading Islamists. For instance, a survey of Hamas activists in Gaza found that 60 percent acknowledge prior membership in Marxist organizations (Eickelman 1997: 34). Burgat and Dowell's study of Islamists in North Africa records their former memberships and dialogue with the left: "part of the secular intelligencia has already begun to reposition itself in a way that brings it much closer to the cultural preoccupations of the Islamist approach" (1993: 83). Willis notes Ben Bella's shift from a socialist ally of the Communist Party to an enthusiastic supporter of the Iranian Revolution and the Algerian Islamists (1996: 90). And finally, Roy is more explicit: Islamists "received their political education not in religious schools but on colleges and universities' campuses where they rubbed shoulders with militant Marxists whose concepts they borrowed . . . and injected with Quranic terminology" (1994: 3).

Urban Egypt: A Case Study of Islamism within Civil Society

Nowhere is the discursive shift from secular nationalism to one or another iteration of the Islamic narrative more complete or more ubiquitous than among the cities of Egypt. Ubiquity, however, comes at the cost of discursive coherence. Fragmentation of authority generates: a multitude of small, violent takfir sects, the "normalization" of the Muslim Brotherhood within the urban middle classes, a new alliance between the authoritarian state and the ulama-based Islamic establishment, and, of course, the efflorescence of informal Muslim associations, mosques, clubs, charities, study groups, and social services (Sullivan 1994). By the end of the 1990s, the discursive practices expressed in the urban public sphere were overwhelmingly Islamic, including those sponsored by state ministries and their clients from the traditional ulama. Parliamentary politics changed further in 2000. Despite persecution, intimidation, denial of legal status, and widespread vote fraud, the Muslim Brotherhood won seventeen seats as independent candidates, thus constituting the largest bloc of opposition members in parliament (Howeidy 2000).

Nasser's premature death in 1970 marked the apogee of Egypt's state-centered development, ended populist redistribution policies, and, effectively, terminated the secular, Arab nationalist developmental project. Sadat (1970–81) adjusted to global restructuring, economic stagnation, and declining popular legitimacy in contradictory ways: by repositioning Egypt as an ally of the United States, by negotiating a peace treaty with Israel, by cautiously liberalizing the economy (*infitah*), by suppressing the Nasserites and leftists, and, most importantly, by allying his regime with the conservative ulama at Al-Azhar University as well as the Saudis. Symbolized by the slogans "Science and Faith" and the "Believer President," he also released from prison the leadership of radical Islamist takfir groups and the Muslim Brotherhood. By the time of his assassination by a takfir group in 1981, Sadat was pressed to juggle contradictory foreign policies while balancing the conflicting demands of domestic groups.

Despite liberalization, structural adjustment, and an opening to new capitalist classes, the state remained bloated, inefficient, and authoritarian. "Public expenditure as a percentage of GNP climbed . . . from 34.4 percent in 1975 to 43 percent in 1984" (Richards 1991; Springborg 1992, cited in Zubaida 1997). Nor, sadly, did Sadat mitigate Egypt's egregious record of human rights abuses. Egypt under Sadat and Mubarak is an unreconstructed, authoritarian state ruled by emergency laws that permit the banning of any association, detention without trial, widespread torture, and "disappearances" of suspects without any accountability whatsoever (Human Rights Watch, http://www.hrw.org/press/2000/egypt). The 1994 torturing to death of Abdel Harith Madani, a lawyer for the Egyptian Organization for Human Rights, by state security has been documented by Amnesty International, Human Rights Watch, and the US embassy (Weaver 1999: 150–2). Finally, rising income inequality, new forms of ostentatious consumption among the privileged, and a burgeoning foreign tourist industry fostered new social cleavages, increased cultural tension, and raised popular resentment toward the beneficiaries of liberalization (Weaver 1995).

Education Policy, Urban Networks, and Civil Society

Let us turn to explaining the structural source of Egypt's flourishing Muslim civil societies and urban social movements. According to Richards and Waterbury (1996), a principal cause is the oversupply of graduates – secondary, post-secondary, and university – relative to the demand for their skills. Between 1970 and 1991, secondary school enrollments more than doubled from 35 percent to 80 percent (1996: 124), averaging 14 percent annual increases between 1971 and 1984. Since the era of Nasser, graduates, usually as a last resort, expected to be absorbed into the poorly paid, stagnant state sector, i.e., between 1976 and 1986, 90 percent of new jobs came from either the government or from emigration abroad (1996: 119). The class and gender bias of educational expenditure also plays a role. In a society where roughly half of the population is illiterate, i.e., 60 percent of the women and 34 percent of the men (1997), Egypt's thirteen universities consumed 38 percent of the education budget in 1984–5. Thus university enrollments roughly doubled between 1971 and 1976 and increased another 50 percent by 1984 to over 660,000 students. Not surprisingly, pay, morale, and working conditions are very low in the educational sector, especially if compared to Saudi Arabia, where Egyptian teachers make ten times an Egyptian salary (1996:

121). Finally, decades of populist educational policy and austerity budgets diminished the standard of graduates so that few have skills demanded by the emerging private sector.

Public Education: Incubator of the Discursive Shift to Islamism

Ironically, a key factor explaining the discursive shift to Islamism originated in the state's tolerance for the Muslim Brotherhood and its Islamization of educational policy. Sadat and later Mubarak shifted toward supporting Al-Azhar and the Ministry of Religious Endowments, thus Islamizing policies affecting women's rights, family law, education, and culture (Ramadan 1993; Auda 1994). Initially, in order to undermine the left and Nasserites, Sadat pursued a "divide and rule" policy by sponsoring Islamist groups in the universities and supporting the publications (i.e. *Al-Da'wa*, *Al-I'tisam*) of the Brotherhood. Note that the Egyptian constitution was amended to require religious education in schools as well as declaring that "Islam is the religion of the state" and that "Sharia was the main source of legislation" (Esposito 1992: 96). According to Starrett, new educational initiatives pumped resources into Al-Azhar's primary school network, increasing enrollment by 70 percent between 1976/7 and 1980/8 (1998: 80–1) and by 125 percent under Mubarak (1998: 105). When structural adjustment policies triggered a food riot in 1977 spearheaded by Islamist groups, Sadat not only retreated from cutting food subsidies but called for greater Islamic educational content and more authority for Al-Azhar and the Ministry of Religious Endowments.

Observe the discursive shift. By 1992 Mubarak's political party, the National Democratic Party, feeling the heat from the Brotherhood's criticism of Egypt's support of the Americans in the Gulf war, declared that "Egypt was not a secular state but an Islamic one." According to Auda, by "[e]xploiting the Ikhwan's strategy, the state began to color its official state ideology with Islamic terminology and pose as the representative of the correct understanding of the Islamic religion" (1994: 394). Alarmed by the rising power of Islamist-controlled civil society located in a network of independent mosques, Muslim Brotherhood media and missionary societies, the Mubarak government created the Higher Committee for Islamic Da'wa under the grand shaykh of Al-Azhar. To counter the Islamist hold on da'wa, the Ministry of Religious Endowments launched "da'wa" caravans to dialogue with youths at local mosques. Seventy-two caravans were reported by the end of 1988 (Auda 1994: 390).

In a crude effort to silence the independent voice of Muslim civil society, the Ministry attempted to license independent mosques by incorporating salaried imams (prayer leaders) and seeking to dictate the content of their

Friday sermons. Besides abusing a longstanding Muslim urban spatial practice regarding community control of neighborhood mosques, the Ministry strategy violated a widely held norm of Muslim civil society that the imam of a neighborhood mosque remain sufficiently independent of the state so as to guide the moral life of the community. Wickham (1997) reports that this policy failed because of the uncanny ability of Islamist activists to obtain licenses for prayer rooms from municipal authorities, even receiving the cooperation of minor religious officials from the Ministry. The fiscal crisis of the state plays a role here, too, for the Ministry administered only 30,000 of Egypt's 170,000 mosques in 1993. Hence, the Ministry cannot afford to pay, or probably recruit, enough compliant religious officials. Indeed, the government already suffered from a shortage of 40,000 imams since Al-Azhar only graduated "5,000 . . . in 1992 of whom only 3,000 showed up for work" (Wickham 1997: 125).

Starrett's invaluable study, *Putting Islam to Work* (1998), assiduously documents the impact the Islamists have had on educational institutions, textbooks, and, ultimately, on the spirit of popular Islamic culture transmitted through universal popular education. Ironically, as the modern state extends and deepens its bureaucratic reach, it simultaneously strengthens the discursive shift to the Islamic narrative. Starrett points out that while enrollments in arts and humanities faculties of universities increased by 8.2 percent between 1981 and 1987, that of Al-Azhar increased by 70 percent. Meanwhile, the circulation of monthly public sector religious periodicals more than tripled from 181,000 to 558,000 between 1983 and 1986 (1998: 90–1). Electronic media programming also became increasingly Islamic. Elsewhere Weaver reports that the Minister of Education disclosed in an interview that "the Islamists had successfully infiltrated primary, preparatory and secondary schools all over Egypt" and then confided, "I could not believe how many fundamentalist teachers we had in the schools" (Weaver 1999: 154). Public schools, therefore, have become discursive agents, contested sites where Islamists, the ulama, and the state struggle over lessons and textbooks, thus inscribing their interpretive narrative into the conscious and unconscious memory of the next generation of Muslim Egyptians.

Discounting the media attention devoted to the spectacular fringe takfir sects, Starrett stresses how the Islamist narrative is inscribed onto the deeper conscious and unconscious discursive practices regulating everyday life. "Egypt's Islamic trend, far from being a . . . fringe movement, . . . is pervasive, persistent and normal, whose effects on individuals and society do not remain confined to . . . political movements and organizations." What is more important are the "changes it has created in the way Egyptians practice, apprehend and represent their religious heritage" and a key institution is "compulsory popular schooling" because it "has encouraged rather than discouraged attachment to Islamic culture. . . . One of the results of mass religious instruction is thus to prepare students just enough to question the authorities of the keepers of the Muslim tradition, and to question their own exclusion from its manipulation" (1998: 187).

Globalization, liberalization, and modernity, moreover, have converged so as to create a decentralized and portable array of mass media products (audio-cassettes, videotapes, satellite dishes) which are impossible for Egyptian state security (SSI) to monitor effectively, let alone control (Eickelman and Anderson 1999). In addition, the fragmentation of Islamic authority coupled with the diversity of sources have reduced the authoritative religious intermediaries leading to greater individual or sectarian interpretation of the Islamic discourse. Starrett captures the dilemma of a corrupt, authoritarian state chasing the discursive shift to Islam:

> it is not the paucity of Islamic culture that accounts for the growth of the oppositional tendencies of the Islamic Trend, but rather its bounty. Each new attempt to correct mistaken ideas by furthering the penetration of Islamic discourse in public space creates an intensification of the conflict between parties seeking to control the discourse. In becoming hegemonic, Islam . . . is forced by necessity not only to provoke limited counterlanguages, but to become itself the language in which cultural and political battles are fought by the vast majority of interested parties. (1998: 219)

Urban Civil Society: Islamist Charities and Networks

The discursive shift to Islamism, of course, is not suspended above urban civil society; rather, it is deeply rooted in a diverse web of informal and formal Islamic organizations: private voluntary and charitable organizations, informal social networks, neighborhood mosques, and especially, the initiatives sponsored by the Muslim Brotherhood. Global neoliberalism abrogated the pact between the citizen and the state whereby citizens "relinquished their claims to basic human and civil rights in exchange for the state undertaking to provide them with education and healthcare, employment and subsidies for such necessities as staples, cooking gas and transportation" (Sivan 1998: 2). Accordingly, these changes allowed Muslim charitable and civil society groups to fill urban social spaces with a parallel social service sector. Rugh's observations illustrate how Islamic civil society operates in Cairo's neighborhoods:

> Many private mosques have expanded into services that compete directly with less efficient and lower quality public services. Services may include the provision of subsidized clothing and food, healthcare, regular educational programs (usually at the preprimary or primary level), after-school tutoring for children, religious instruction, subsidies for students, evening courses, social group activ-

> ities . . . In poor areas mosque representatives hand out free food, clothing, and money in exchange, as one women put it, "for wearing our Islamic dress." Money can also be borrowed through Islamic banks in the approved "profit sharing" way where a fixed interest is not required. (1993: 164)

Others emphasize the higher quality of Islamist social services for nominal fees where the customers are treated with respect. "Islamist medical clinics, well-staffed and outfitted with the latest medical equipment, contrast sharply with state-run hospitals with their low sanitation standards and long delays" (Sadowski 1987: 45). A 1997 newspaper report, quoting a statistical study by Amani Qandil, estimates that Islamic charity organizations provided 14 percent of Egypt's healthcare (Negus 1997: 2). And finally, when compared to government responses to the Cairo earthquake (1992) and floods (1994), observers noted the superior performance of the Islamic charities.

Of course, subsidies cost money and high-quality medical care requires committed professionals. New Islamic banks as well as contributions by Islamist businessmen paying their obligatory Islamic tithe (zakat) through Islamist charities supply the financial support for Islamist social services. Islamic banks, funded originally by Saudi and other Gulf states, have become significant players in the wider Muslim world (i.e., Malaysia, Pakistan, Indonesia). From a tiny number a quarter century ago, Islamic financial institutions have grown to 170 with assets exceeding US$150 billion, including Citibank, Dow Jones, and HSBC (*The Economist*, February 17, 2001, p. 76; *Islamic Index*: http://indexes.dowjones.com/djimi/imhome.html).

Professional Associations and the Muslim Brothers: A State within the State?

Seventy years of Brotherhood activity has clear patterns. One is a cycle of alliance and rupture with the established regime. A second is generational tension followed by renewal through generational succession. A third is the constant formation of splinter groups, typically more radical (i.e., Jama'a, Islamic Jihad, al-Samawiyya), but recently more pragmatic and pluralist such as al-Wasat, which recently received a license to establish an NGO called the Egypt Society for Culture and Dialogue (*Cairo Times*, April 13–19, 2000). A fourth is a gradual incorporation of global liberalism into its rhetoric and organizational forms, if not always in its practices (Esposito and Piscatori 1991; Esposito and Voll 1996; Sivan 1990, 1998).

Officially, of course, the banned Muslim Brotherhood does not exist in Egypt. Once the Sadat–Mubarak governments shifted toward the Islamic current to gain legitimacy, however, the regime has exhibited a cyclical policy toward the Brotherhood; one characterized by a cautious acknowledgment, followed by an effort to incorporate the Brotherhood's program into state institutions and then suppression, using arrests, murder, torture, and detention without trial. Yet the Brotherhood has only deepened and extended its associations and networks into urban civil society. Because of the sympathy it garnered from the public, it now represents the only credible civil opposition in spite of the regime's use of military courts to imprison the leadership in 1995, 1999, and 2000. Local human rights organizations, according to the State Department, "indicate that there are approximately 15,000–16,000 political detainees; it is not clear how many among them are charged and awaiting trial, convicted and serving sentences, or detained without charge" (http://www.state.gov/www/global/human_rights/1999_hrp_report/egypt/html).

Constant suppression and imprisonment of leaders has forced the Brotherhood to develop a multipronged political strategy. Though banned, the Brotherhood's first strategy seeks parliamentary representation via alliances with legal political parties, first with the Wakf, subsequently Socialist Labor. The latter alliance gave them control of a muckraking newspaper, *Al-Shaab*, and thirty-six seats in the 1987 parliamentary election. Parliamentary experience, moreover, has broadened the Brotherhood's understanding of the complexity of the modern state and the need for a legislative check on executive authority. Notwithstanding their commitment to the full implementation of the Sharia in an Islamic state and their support for persecution of intellectuals for apostasy, a capital offense under Sharia, the Brotherhood's parliamentary leaders like Ma'mun al-Hudaybi and Al-Tilmisani have advocated shura (consultation) as a legislative institution where legislators and public can debate applications of Sharia (Auda 1994: 386).

In the late 1980s, the Brotherhood pursued a new electoral strategy, that of contesting for leadership posts in modern educational and professional associations (syndicates), typically regarded as bastions of the educated middle class and urban civil society. The Brotherhood has always been strong in the educational sector. In the 1970s it established Islamic associations (*al-Jama'a al-Islamiyya*) for university students, soon controlling most university student associations. These associations dispensed valuable educational services to students, i.e., notes, photocopied textbooks, and transportation for female students "who felt their integrity endangered in packed, mixed-sex lecture halls" (Denoeux 1993: 151). To be sure, the subsequent move to control professional associations follows logically as the age cohort of the 1970s graduated from universities and entered professional life. Aided by small numbers of voters, the Brotherhood's control of leadership posts of professional associations was systematic and thorough: engineers, 1987; physicians, 1988; pharmacists, 1989; Commerce Graduates' Association, 1989; the Cairo University faculty club, 1990; and lawyers, 1992 (Wickham 1997; Starrett 1998).

Austerity and liberalization explain to some degree the Brotherhood's electoral victories. Wickham cites a 1994 government survey concluding that unemployed graduates numbered 1.4 million, of whom 200,000 held a university degree (1997: 122). Ismail's study of Cairo's informal sector describes university graduates in engineering and law working as day laborers and construction workers, i.e., painters, plasterers, and tile layers (2000: 377). In addition, under the Brotherhood's leadership, the professional associations "have begun to provide employment and income to young doctors, teachers and other professionals, thereby reducing the share of their earnings derived from the state" (Wickham 1997: 123).

Furthermore, the leadership of the medical and engineering associations "have initiated projects in the areas of housing, healthcare, and insurance, established training programs and pilot small business ventures for new graduates"(Wickham 1997: 123). Note the relationship to globalization. As the twin forces of structural adjustment and state withdrawal take their toll on urban living standards, the Islamists have seized the opportunity handed to them by global restructuring so as to employ graduates and professionals in their parallel social and economic social service sector. Quite paradoxically, neoliberalism's privatization policy has buttressed the role of Islamist networks as providers of urban social services and charity while, at the same time, sounding the alarm against the "Islamist threat."

Cairo: Islamism and Survival Strategies among the Popular Classes

To be sure, the quality of urban life for migrants and the poor in Cairo, now approaching 14 million, generates objective conditions encouraging radical protest movements. Islamism, however, is the beneficiary. Richards and Waterbury cite a national housing deficit of over 2 million units. They describe vast districts of Cairo as "slums" where a half million live on rooftops and where "levels of lead in the air may cause brain damage and mental retardation in small children" (1996: 258). Bayat (1997) estimates that 6 million live in Cairo's illegal "spontaneous communities," often squatting in tent cities and shantytowns in cemeteries and other public lands. Liberalization and SAPs explain the widening gap: the income share of the top 10 percent of Egypt's urbanites increased from 26 percent in 1981 to 32.6 percent in 1991. Bayat then concludes that because more than half of Cairo and Giza are classified as "poor" or "ultra-poor" (i.e., ca. 7 million), the charity of religious NGOs fails to sustain a minimal living standard for the poor.

Ismail's (2000) excellent study of militant Islamist groups living in popular quarters of Cairo documents the diffusion of militant and radical Islamist support among the migrant poor, squatters, and the informal sector. For Ismail, "Islamism . . . is not a marginal religious or political movement" but rather "a form of contestation that finds ground in spaces where oppositional positioning develops" (2000: 379). Instead of assuming social pathology and marginality, Ismail portrays radical Islamists as regionally rooted actors who organize specific neighborhood spaces by provisioning parallel economic, political, and welfare services to their constituents. Nor is this phenomenon new to Cairo. By drawing upon historian Edmund Burke's seminal analysis of historic repertoires of urban collective action, Ismail brilliantly explains why the protest movements rooted in neighborhoods, local leadership, and dissatisfaction with the state's local representatives are deeply structural, not novel. Rather, they are continuous movements within a historically legitimated tradition of urban popular protest (Lubeck 1987; Burke 1989). Subverting essentializing explanations which assume social pathology, (i.e., anomie, moral breakdown, and marginality), Ismail documents how radical Islamists like Jihad, Juma'a, and Samawiyya negotiate with neighborhood residents in order to construct a social and spatial moral order for "in order to expand their popular support they [Islamists] must operate within the socio-spatial framework of the communities" (2000: 393).

Therefore, the need to solve rational and objective urban problems is what explains popular support for radical Islamist movements. These include: opposition to police corruption and brutality, the regulation of craft, trade, and labor activities, tensions arising from overcrowded housing where women must share common facilities with nonkin, the migrant need for morally acceptable marriage partners and attraction of Islamist educational and welfare services described above (Ismail 2000). A pragmatic ability to negotiate a meaningful moral and social order in impoverished, immigrant slums explains the triumph of Islamism as the dominant populist, anti-imperialist nationalist discourse in Muslim cities.

Comparative Perspectives: Islamism, Democracy and Urban Insurrection

The Egyptian Brothers' gradualist, pragmatic strategy, based upon mobilizing the cautious middle class, is widely replicated in the cities of Islamdom: the Muslim Brotherhood in Jordan, PAS in Malaysia, Hamas in Algeria, Ghannoussi's MTI/Nahda movement in Tunisia, Virtue/Welfare in Turkey, and Wahid's NI in Indonesia (Kramer 1993, 1995; Salame 1994; Guazzone 1995; Hefner 2000). There is a crude correlation between the success of moderate Islamism and the national level of development and degree of urban social cohesion. Those committed to pragmatism, moderation, and shura (consultation) are dominant in more developed countries and with social groups that are older, better educated, and more secure economically, i.e., the urban middle classes. Conversely, countries experiencing economic and political collapse and/or social disintegration – Algeria, Afghanistan, and Nigeria – are dominated by radical Islamist movements fueled by a vast reservoir of young, impoverished, and disillusioned recruits (Kramer 1995; Lubeck 1998). In urban situations like petro-busted Nigeria, where crime, ethnic conflict, and devastating poverty are normalized, Muslims disillusioned with Western models are rationally choosing a system that they know and hope will bring security, law, and order, i.e., Sharia.

Algiers, of course, is the prime example of an urban tinderbox in a petro-state whose policies secured the triumph of a radical Islamist movement. Here is an ideal-typical case where structural factors – global restructuring, the petro-bust, structural adjustment's austerity, high youth unemployment, brutal military repression, cautious liberalization, and a state legitimacy crisis – converged to generate a powerful social base that resulted in electoral victories for the Islamic Salvation Front (FIS) in 1991. Consider Algiers under neoliberal restructuring, now the apotheosis of urban Islamist insurrection and civil war. A survey found that 75 percent of youth aged between sixteen and twenty-nine were seeking work while, at the same time, "the educational system produced 270,000 unemployed diploma holders. Some 80% of this age group continued to live with their families, often eight persons to a room" (Eickelman and Piscatori 1996: 116). The authoritarian petro-state introduced structural adjustment, followed by political liberalization, at a time of high unemployment when state revenues from oil and gas exports decreased by 40 percent in a year (1985–6), thereby raising the foreign debt from $14.8 billion to $24.6 billion (Willis 1996: 99–100).

Earlier, like Egypt, the regime tried incorporating the Islamist current by implementing a new family law, allowing Afghani-Arab and other radicals to operate openly, and pursuing an Arabization policy that strengthened the Islamists. In October 1988, however, security forces lit the match when they fired on demonstrators and rioters protesting austerity, killing hundreds in Algiers, ending any shred of legitimacy for the FLN. Led by a schoolteacher, Abassi Madani, and a mosque preacher, Ali Belhadj, the FIS mobilized a network of over 900 mosques to become the voice for a generation of disillusioned and miserable urban protestors. Correctly fearing an Islamist electoral victory in 1991, the army bumbled into a brutal civil war when they seized power, canceled elections, and imprisoned the FIS leadership. By eliminating the electoral option for change, moreover, the military also eliminated even the possibility of a peaceful transition to a Muslim democratic order (Roberts 1994; Willis 1996). Hypocritical American prevarication and French support, of course, only increased Muslim disillusionment with the pretentious claims of global neoliberalism.

Kuala Lumpur, in contrast to Algiers, represents the opposite pattern. Malaysia is an exception. It redistributed income while reorienting its economy away from dependence on oil and other commodities and toward

Table 14.2 Gender, education, and labor force participation

	Algeria	*Egypt*	*Indonesia*	*Iran*	*Jordan*	*Malaysia*	*Morocco*	*Nigeria*	*Pakistan*	*Syria*
Adult literacy (% 1997)										
Female	47.7	40.5	79.5	65.8	81.8	81.0	32.7	50.8	25.4	56.5
Male	72.7	64.7	90.6	80.7	92.2	90.2	59.3	68.5	55.2	86.5
Education										
Female primary enrollment[a] (1997)	92.6	90.6	98.6	89.2	N/A	99.9	67.2	N/A	N/A	90.6
Female secondary enrollment[a] (1997)	64.0	70.1	53.4	75.8	N/A	68.5	31.9	N/A	N/A	39.4
Labor force										
Female % labor force[b]										
1980	21.0	27.0	35.0	20.0	15.0	34.0	34.0	36.0	23.0	24.0
1998	26.0	30.0	40.0	26.0	23.0	37.0	35.0	36.0	28.0	26.0
Female % professional and technical	27.6[c]	28.4	40.8[c]	32.6[c]	28.7[d]	43.2	31.3[e]	N/A	21.0	37.0

N/A: not available.
[a] Ratio as % of relative age group.
[b] As percent of total; source is the World Bank, *Development Report 1999/2000*.
[c] Calculated on the basis of data from UN 1994 and ILO, *Yearbook of Labor Statistics*, 1993 and 1994.
[d] Calculated on the basis of data from UN 1995 and ILO, *Yearbook of Labor Statistics*, 1997.
[e] Calculated on the basis of data from UN 1994 and ILO, *Yearbook of Labor Statistics*, 1994 and 1995.
Source: Data assembled from the United Nations, *Human Development Report 1999*, unless otherwise noted.

electronics-based, export-oriented industrialization since the 1980s (Lubeck 1992). In 1969 ethnic rioting between the Muslim Malays and the Chinese forced the ruling coalition to implement a New Economic Policy (NEP). The NEP attempted to: abolish absolute poverty, create an indigenous Malay business and professional class, eliminate the ethnic division of labor, and redistribute corporate equity among all ethnic groups. Most of these goals were achieved by the end of the 1990s: poverty among Muslim Malays declined from 65 percent (1970) to around 13 percent, and a diverse Muslim middle class flowered in cities.

Until recently, when Prime Minister Mahathir moved against his younger rival and designated heir, Anwar Ibrahim, Malaysia was touted as a case where the ethnonationalist party, UMNO, had successfully incorporated the youthful Islamist challenge represented by Anwar Ibrahim and the Islamist student movement ABIM. Table 14.2 presents some evidence for the positive effect exerted by the NEP and electronics-based, export-oriented industrialization on the opportunity structure for young Muslims in Malaysia. By 1998 Anwar's supporters were leading demonstrations protesting Mahathir's abuse of their leader at the Friday mosque in Kuala Lumpur. Influenced by Muslim social movements in Indonesia, Islamists formed coalitions with non-Muslims for political reform (*reformasi*). The election of 1999 confirmed that many Malays had deserted Mahathir and UMNO in favor of Anwar's Justice Party and the ulama-led Islamist party, PAS. The latter emerged as the leading opposition party in a wider democratic alliance with broad multiethnic urban support (*Aliran Monthly*, various). The Kuala Lumpur example illustrates just how income redistribution and export-oriented industrialization policies support civil Islam rather than authoritarian Islamism as the dominant discourse.

Muslim Women in Cities: Gender Relations and New Islamic Dress

Thus far we have argued that "rupturing" events like the Iranian Revolution, the rise of political Islam, and the infusion of pragmatic Islamist institutions into civil society constitute a repositioning of Islamic discourses in the moral imagination of urban Muslims. Yet no issue is more significant than the impact of Islamism on gender relations in the public and domestic spheres. Regardless of Islamism's discursive fragmentation and obvious borrowing from Western-modernist narratives, no issue has aroused more controversy than the bodily representation of women wearing Islamic dress (hijab) in urban public space.

Of course, wearing hijab is structurally rooted in the spatial relocation of increasing proportions of Muslim women from rural to urban situations:

that is, from patriarchal, rural households, policed by extended families, into crowded, impoverished urban neighborhoods, impersonal modern educational institutions, and the enumerated labor force. Tables 14.1 and 14.2 summarize some of these structural changes of location and activity. By 2015 half to two-thirds of Muslim women will live in cities. Rising rates of migration and urbanization have profound consequences for Muslim women: more rural-born women are living in single rooms in densely packed buildings inhabited by unrelated males; more risk being shamed and groped in crowded public transport; more must compete for access to urban education and work; and, in general, more must adjust to a barrage of global-origin commodities and consumption styles. At the same time, rising literacy and primary school attendance are exposing Muslim women to Islamist discourses and even to a new Islamist genre of popular literature (novels, romances, biographies, and pamphlets) (Eickelman and Anderson 1999; Huq 1999). Even more significant is the rise of female secondary school enrollments, reaching 75 percent in Iran, 70 percent in Egypt, and 68 percent in Malaysia. Furthermore, as a consequence of rising secondary and post-secondary education, the female share of professional and technical workers has increased in rough proportion to their participation in the enumerated labor force.

In a superb ethnographic article on "downveiling," that is, the modern styling and relaxation of veiling standards among Cairene women, Herrera describes hijab well "as a form of both resistance and submission to patriarchy, an assertion of cultural authenticity, a reaction against Western imperialism and local secular regimes, a genuine desire by women to live more piously and a practice borne out of economic necessity" (2000: 1). While no one denies involuntary veiling due to the coercive power of Islamist men, and even violence (i.e., Algeria, Afghanistan) against women refusing to wear Islamic dress, a number of more nuanced studies show that veiling represents women's initiative that differs from passive conformity to Islamist patriarchy. A core motivation is political: the search for "authenticity" expressed as a dress performance oftentimes signifying resistance to oppressive secular regimes and/or disillusionment with Westernized global culture. Practically, wearing hijab generates greater respectability, economically affordable dignity, and greater freedom to circulate unmolested in dense urban centers like Cairo. However counter-intuitive to Westerners, hijab actually facilitates the freedom of women, permitting entry into urban employment and educational situations, which, unlike the home or the village, involve same-sex mixing (MacLeod 1991; Hoffman 1995; Gole 1996).

From the perspective of Muslim cultural nationalism, veiling reverses the hegemonic Western discourse: it affirms as authentic and socially powerful that which Western imperialists defined as evidence of Muslim backwardness. Others see it as generational resistance to parental authority and Westernization among the daughters of middle-class families; still others argue veiling indicates class resentment toward elite privilege by working women economically excluded from globalized consumption styles (Taraki 1992).

Taraki's superb study of Jordanian women deftly shows how structural factors – rising rates of urbanization, post-secondary education, and nondomestic labor force participation – are correlated with a rising number of educated women, many with post-secondary degrees, mostly working in the public sector. She points out that 65 percent of working women are employed there, constituting nearly a third of the sector, and that women with more than twelve years of education constituted 74.1 percent of all women employed there in 1987 (Taraki 1992). Hence, because these newly educated women are also new entrants to the urban labor force, often struggling with the dilemmas surrounding new morality and consumption styles, they are attracted to the moral order provided by Islamist discourses and civil society groups. Similarly, Hammani (1997), writing on the use of the hijab by Palestinians during the intifada (uprising), argues that wearing the hijab was redefined as a nationalist symbol of resistance, conveying female nationalist solidarity and respect for the martyrs, while protecting women from assaults from soldiers.

More poststructuralist studies emphasize the blurring of categorical boundaries between modern–traditional, veiled–unveiled. In Turkey, Gole focuses on the "agency of women," arguing that Muslim women's embrace of the hijab and Islamist discourses disrupts conventional distinctions between tradition and modernity by "carving out new public spaces, affirming new public visibilities, and inventing new Muslim lifestyles and subjectivities. . . . In a paradoxical way, radical Islamism instigates democratization of religious knowledge . . . Islamic politics enables Muslim women to participate in public life . . . [and] provides ideological legitimacy for women's newly acquired public roles" (Gole 2000: 94–9).

Leila Ahmed, viewing the hijab as a form of accommodation to modern, urban lifestyles, cites a survey by Radwan comparing attitudes of veiled and unveiled students attending Cairo University. Not surprisingly, veiled women respond more conservatively than unveiled on modern gender issues: on the importance of education for women, 88 to 93 percent; on a women's right to pursue education to the highest levels, 92 to 98 percent; or acceptability of women working outside the home, 88 to 95 percent veiled to unveiled, respectively (Ahmed 1992: 226–7). What is remarkable, however, is how high the percentages are, and how small the differences are between veiled and unveiled women. Modern urban living attenuates differences, according to Lila Abu-Lughod: "most of the women who have taken on the veil are in fact working or expect to work. Most families aspiring to achieve or maintain middle-class status cannot do so without a second income" (1998: 252). Veiling, like Islamism in general, thrives in the urban, modern, and globalized situation.

Discursive Struggle: The Emergence of Muslim Feminists

Despite the deep patriarchy of many Islamist discourses, structural transformations – literacy, education, media, participation in urban public space – have stimulated new gender discourses and new civil society groups. The discursive shift, together with the participation of Muslim women in urban public life (i.e., demonstrations in Iran), have, unintentionally to be sure, disrupted the male monopoly over interpreting the Islamist discourse. Leila Ahmed stresses how Muslim women hear a different voice, one moving away from the legalistic to the "ethical, egalitarian voice of Islam . . . because Muslim women hear this egalitarian voice . . . they often declare (to the astonishment of non-Muslims) that Islam is nonsexist" (1992: 238). Middle-class, educated Muslim feminist activists have entered the discursive struggle over the meaning of Islam for gender relations. Their mantra is that the Qur'an guarantees them equality or, at the very least, separate but equal rights to marriage contracts, child support, marital sexual fulfillment, and even wages for housework after divorce (Hoodfar 1998). Surprisingly, by cultivating the educated women's self-capacity to read and interpret the Qur'an, the Islamist movement has created spaces for discursive contestation by urbanized, Muslim feminist intellectuals. In summary, Muslim feminists promote the egalitarian message (i.e., equality before God, one law, individual interpretation), while eloquently arguing that the ulamas' patriarchal interpretations of women's status, derived from *Hadith* (i.e., sayings of the Prophet Mohammed), were institutionalized in Sharia due to the premodern (tribal) historical context, the influence of non-Muslims (Christians and Persians), and the exigencies of ruling Islamic empires.

In Iran the revolutionary legacy and high female educational standards have created a powerful voting bloc. Women's overwhelming electoral support for Khatami's vision for civil society reinforced gender consciousness and sharpened the debate in the public sphere. Mir-Hosseini's (1999) ethnography on Muslim intellectuals documents the diversity of public positions asserted on gender questions, the increasing number of female public officials (parliamentary deputies, judges, jurist-scholars, police, educators, and bureaucrats), and increasing discursive convergence between Muslim feminists and Western-oriented feminists. In addition, she documents the growing respect for Muslim feminism by feminist intellectuals like Mernissi and Afshar, who now are prepared "to listen to them, to take them seriously, to borrow something of their arguments and approaches" (1999: 6). Nor are the clerics monolithic. She represents Hojjat ol-Eslam Sa'idzadeh as a modernist interpreter of Islam, one clearly influenced by hermeneutical reasoning and social constructionism, who "sees gender inequality in the shari'a not as a manifestation of divine justice, but as a mistaken construction by male jurists" (1999: 272).

Diverse arrays of Muslim female voices now speak on gender issues in educational institutions, the media, and civil society. In Iran, five seminaries have been founded to train women to become mujtahids (interpreter-jurists) and, in 1996, 16 percent (9,995) of enrollment in Iran's religious seminaries were women (Kian-Thiebaut 2000). The oldest and most prestigious, al-Zahra, has all-female instructors, attracting students from all over the Shi'ite world (Mir-Hosseini 1999: 6). While all factions on the discursive spectrum publish journals, the women editors of *Zanan* openly embrace feminism, as does the newspaper *Zan*. Elsewhere in the Sunni tradition Amina Wadud-Muhsin has written a hermeneutical and linguistic reinterpretation of the representation of women in the Qur'an, and Riffat Hasan describes herself as a Muslim feminist theologian who writes on women's rights and Islam. In the realm of civil society the global network, *Women Living under Muslim Laws*, like *Sisters in Islam* in Malaysia, are advocates for justice for Muslim women. Both publish information on issues affecting women (violence, divorce, rights, personal status), lobby governments and multilateral agencies, and organize conferences in order to promote human rights for Muslim women (Othman 1999).

Concluding Reprise

What, then, does the future portend for Muslims in cities? Islamism will remain ubiquitous in everyday urban life because globalization, state withdrawal, and rising urban inequality create a social milieu ideally suited for the efflorescence of both moderate Islamist civil society groups and violent insurrectionary groups using terrorist tactics. Does irony not turn into the theater of the absurd when President "W" Bush advocates "faith-based" initiatives as a solution to state withdrawal from urban social services? Islamism could hardly ask for a better midwife than the policy of global neoliberalism. Far more flexible and pragmatic than imagined, Islamism became normalized by its success in meeting the moral and material needs of urban Muslims.

Nevertheless, given the record of Iran, Sudan, Afghanistan, Pakistan, and other Islamist experiments, what remains problematic is the practice of Islamist democracy upon assuming power. Will Islamists tolerate difference, acknowledge the human rights of women and non-Muslims, accept pragmatic compromises, and relinquish power through fair elections? If one searches for innovative responses to this question, then An-Naim's (1990) seminal work defines one view of the reform agenda for democratic, civil Islam. The brutality of the Algerian civil war constitutes the price of simplistic exclusion of Islamists from the democratic process. Recognizing the popular base of urban

Islamists, civil society theorist Richard Norton draws on the democratic behavior of Turkish Islamists to argue for a policy of inclusion: "a policy of exclusion that attempts to keep people outside of the game is a destructive policy by definition. And a policy of inclusion, structured with intelligence, is a way to stabilize and consolidate a political system" (Mahoney 1998: 32). Urban theorists and policy-makers, therefore, must become far more realistic about the complex, contradictory tendencies contained within Muslim discourses. In practice, this means distinguishing the violent insurrectionists like bin Laden's al-Qaida from the moderate and then entering into a dialogue with modern, civil society-based Islamist movements. The latter must be included in policy and planning agendas. For, like it or not, Islamism will constitute a powerful social force shaping Muslim-majority cities in the twenty-first century.

Bibliography

Abdel-Latif, O. 2000: Islamists come into the fold of civil society. *Al-Ahram Weekly Online*, April 20–6, No. 478.

Abu-Lughod, J. 1987: The Islamic city-historic myth, Islamic essence and contemporary relevance. *International Journal of Middle East Studies* 19: 155–76.

Abu-Lughod, L. 1998: The marriage of feminism and Islamism in Egypt. In L. Abu-Lughod (ed.), *Remaking Women: Feminism and Modernity in the Middle East.* Princeton, NJ: Princeton University Press.

Abu-Rabi', I. 1996: *Intellectual Origins of the Islamic Resurgence in the Modern Arab World.* Albany: State University of New York Press.

Ahmed, L. 1992: *Women and Gender in Islam.* New Haven, CT: Yale University Press.

Al-Azmeh, A. 1993: *Islams and Modernities.* London: Verso.

An-Naim, A. 1990: *Towards an Islamic Reformation: Civil Liberties, Human Rights and an International Law.* Syracuse, NY: Syracuse University Press.

Aliran Monthly (various) http://www.malaysia.net/aliran/monthly/index.html.

Asad, T. 1993: *Genealogies of Religion.* Baltimore: Johns Hopkins University Press.

Auda, G. 1994: The "normalization" of the Islamic movement in Egypt from the 1970s to the early 1990s. In M. Marty and S. Appleby (eds.), *Accounting for Fundamentalisms.* Chicago: University of Chicago Press, 374–412.

Bayat, A. 1997: Cairo's poor: dilemmas of survival and solidarity. *Middle East Report* (Winter), No. 202.

Burgat, F. and Dowell, W. 1993: *The Islamic Movement in North Africa.* Austin: University of Texas Press.

Burke, III, E. 1989: Towards a history of collective action in the Middle East: continuities and change, 1750–1980. In K. Brown et al. (eds.), *Etat, ville et mouvements sociaux au Maghreb et du Moyen-Orient.* Paris: Harmattan.

—— 1998: Orientalism and world history: representing nationalism and Islamism in the twentieth century. *Theory and Society* 27/4 (August): 489–507.

Denoeux, G. 1993: *Urban Unrest in the Middle East: A Comparative Study of Informal Networks in Egypt, Iran, and Lebanon.* Albany: State University of New York Press.

Eickelman, D. F. 1997: Trans-state Islam and security. In S. H. Rudolph and J. Piscatori (eds.), *Transnational Religion and Fading States.* Boulder, CO: Westview, 27–46.

——and Anderson, J. 1999: *New Media in the Muslim World.* Bloomington: Indiana University Press.

——and Piscatori, J. 1996: *Muslim Politics.* Princeton, NJ: Princeton University Press.

Esposito, J. 1992: *The Islamic Threat: Myth or Reality.* Oxford and New York: Oxford University Press.

——and Piscatori, J. 1991: Democratization and Islam. *Middle East Journal* 45 (3): 427–40.

——and Voll, J. 1996: *Islam and Democracy.* New York: Oxford University Press.

Gole, N. 1996: *The Forbidden Modern: Civilization and Veiling.* Ann Arbor: University of Michigan Press.

——2000: Snapshots of Islamic modernities. *Daedalus* 129 (1): 91–118.

Guazzone, L. (ed.) 1995: *The Islamist Dilemma: The Political Role of Islamist Movements in the Arab World.* Reading, MA: Ithaca Press.

Haddad, Y. 1983: Sayyid Qutb: ideologue of the Islamic Revival. In J. Esposito (ed.), *Voices of Resurgent Islam.* New York: Oxford University Press.

Hammani, R. 1997: From immodesty to collaboration: Hamas, the women's movement in the Intifada. In J. Beinin and J. Stork (eds.), *Political Islam: Essays from Middle East Report.* Berkeley: University of California Press, 194–211.

Hefner, R. 2000: *Civil Islam: Muslims and Democratization in Indonesia.* Princeton, NJ: Princeton University Press.

Herrera, L. 2000: Downveiling: shifting socio-religious practices. *ISIM Newsletter*, Leiden, No. 6, October.

Hodgson, M. 1974: *The Venture of Islam.* Chicago: Chicago University Press.

Hoffman, V. 1995: Muslim fundamentalists: psychosocial profiles. In M. Marty and S. Appleby (eds.), *Fundamentalisms Comprehended.* Chicago: University of Chicago Press, 199–230.

Hoodfar, H. 1998: Muslim women on the threshold of the twenty-first century. In *Women Living Under Muslim Laws, Dossier 21*, September, pp. 112–23.

Howeidy, A. 2000: Watch this space. *Al-Ahram Weekly Online*, November 23–9, No. 509.

Huq, M. 1999: From piety to romance: Islam-oriented texts in Bangladesh. In D. Eickelman and J. Anderson (eds.), *New Media in the Muslim World.* Bloomington: Indiana University Press.

Ismail, S. 2000: The popular movement dimensions of contemporary militant Islamism: socio-spatial determinants in the Cairo urban setting. *Comparative Studies in Society and History* 42 (2): 363–93.

Kian-Thiebaut, A. 2000: Women's religious seminaries in Iran. *ISIM Newsletter*, Leiden, No. 6, October.

Kramer, G. 1993: Islamist notions of democracy. *Middle East Report* 23/4 (July–August): 2–8.

——1995: Cross-links and double talk? Islamist movements in the political process. In L. Guazzone (ed.), *The Islamist Dilemma: The Political Role of Islamist Movements in the Arab World.* Reading, MA: Ithaca Press.

Lapidus, I. 1988: *A History of Islamic Societies.* Cambridge: Cambridge University Press.

Lipietz, A. 1987: *Mirages and Miracles: The Crisis in Global Fordism.* Trans. D. Macey. London: Verso.

Lubeck, P. 1987: *Islam and Urban Labor: The Making of a Muslim Working Class in Northern Nigeria.* Cambridge: Cambridge University Press.

—— 1992: Malaysian industrialization, ethnic divisions and the NIC model: the limits to replication. In J. Henderson and R. Appelbaum (eds.), *States and Development in the Pacific Rim.* Newbury Park, CA: Sage, 176–98.

—— 1998: Islamist responses to globalization: cultural conflict in Egypt, Algeria and Malaysia. In B. Crawford and R. Lipschutz (eds.), *The Causes of Cultural Conflict.* Berkeley, CA: International and Area Studies, 293–319.

—— 2000: The Islamic Revival: antinomies of Islamic movements under globalization. In R. Cohen and S. Rai (eds.), *Global Social Movements.* London: Athlone, 141–62.

MacLeod, A. 1991: *Accommodating Protest: Working Women, New Veiling and Change in Cairo.* New York: Columbia University Press.

Mahoney, L. 1998: AUC Forum tackles Islamist movements. *Washington Report*, March.

Mayer, E. 1993: The Fundamentalist impact on law, politics, and constitutions in Iran, Pakistan, and the Sudan. In M. Marty and S. Appleby (eds.), *Fundamentalisms and the State.* Chicago: University of Chicago Press, 110–51.

Mir-Hosseini, Z. 1999: *Islam and Gender.* Princeton, NJ: Princeton University Press.

Mitchell, R. 1969: *The Society of the Muslim Brothers.* London: Oxford University Press.

Mutalib, H. 1990: *Islam and Ethnicity in Malay Politics.* Singapore: Oxford University Press.

Negus, S. 1997: Down, but not out. *Cairo Times*, April 3, pp. 1, 3.

Norton, A. R. (ed.) 1995: *Civil Society in the Middle East.* Volume 1. Leiden: E. J. Brill.

Othman, N. 1999: Grounding human rights arguments in non-Western culture: Shari'a and citizenship rights of women in a modern Islamic state. In D. Bell and J. Bauer (eds.), *The East Asian Challenge for Human Rights.* Cambridge: Cambridge University Press.

Ramadan, A. 1993: Fundamentalist influence in Egypt: the strategies of the Muslim Brotherhood and the Takfir groups. In M. Marty and S. Appleby (eds.), *Fundamentalisms and the State.* Chicago: University of Chicago Press, 152–83.

Richards, A. 1987: Oil booms and agricultural development: Nigeria in comparative perspective. In M. Watts (ed.), *State, Oil, and Agriculture in Nigeria.* Berkeley, CA: International and Area Studies, 85–109.

—— 1991: The political economy of dilatory reform: Egypt in the 1980s. *World Development* 19 (12): 1721–30.

—— and Waterbury, J. 1996: *A Political Economy of the Middle East*, 2nd ed. Boulder, CO: Westview.

Roberts, H. 1994: Doctrinaire economics and political opportunism in the strategy of Algerian Islamism. In J. Ruedy (ed.), *Islam and Secularism in North Africa.* Washington, DC: Georgetown University, Center for Contemporary Arab Studies, 83–118.

Roy, O. 1994: *The Failure of Political Islam.* Cambridge, MA: Harvard University Press.

Ruedy, J. (ed.) 1994: *Islam and Secularism in North Africa.* Washington, DC: Georgetown University, Center for Contemporary Arab Studies.

Rugh, A. 1993: Reshaping personal relations in Egypt. In M. Marty and S. Appleby (eds.), *Fundamentalisms and Society*. Chicago: University of Chicago Press, 151–80.

Sadowski, Y. 1987: Egypt's Islamist movement: a new political and economic force. *Middle East Insight* (September): 37–45.

—— 1993: The new Orientalism and the democracy debate. *Middle East Report* 23/4 (July–August): 14–21, 40.

Salame, G. (ed.) 1994: *Democracy without Democrats? The Renewal of Politics in the Muslim World*. New York: I. B. Tauris.

Sivan, E. 1990: The Islamic resurgence: civil society strikes back. *Journal of Contemporary History* 25/3 (May–June): 353–64.

—— 1998: Why radical Muslims aren't taking over governments. *Middle East Review of International Affairs* 2/2 (May).

Starrett, G. 1998: *Putting Islam to Work*. Berkeley: University of California Press.

Sullivan, D. 1994: *Private Voluntary Organizations in Egypt: Islamic Development, Private Initiative, and State Control*. Gainesville: University Press of Florida.

—— and Abed-Kotob, S. 1999: *Islam in Contemporary Egypt: Civil Society vs. the State*. Boulder, CO: Lynne Rienner.

Taraki, L. 1992: Islam is the solution: Jordanian Islamists and the dilemma of the "modern women." *British Journal of Sociology* 46 (2): 643–61.

United Nations Development Program (UNDP) 1999: *Human Development Report: Globalization with a Human Face*. New York: Oxford University Press. United Nations http://www.un.org/pubs/cyberschoolbus//e_infonation.htm

US Department of State 2000: *1999 Country Reports on Human Rights Practices: Egypt*. http://www.state.gov/www/global/human_rights/1999_hrp_report/egypt.html).

Voll, J. 1991: Fundamentalism in the Sunni Arab world: Egypt and Sudan. In M. Marty and S. Appleby (eds.), *Fundamentalisms Observed*. Chicago: University of Chicago Press, 345–402.

Weaver, M. 1995: The novelist and the sheikh. *New Yorker*, January 30, pp. 52–69.

—— 1999: *A Portrait of Egypt*. New York: Farrar, Straus, and Giroux.

Wickham, C. R. 1997: Islamic mobilization and political change: the Islamic trend in Egypt's professional associations. In J. Beinin and J. Stork (eds.), *Political Islam: Essays from Middle East Report*. Berkeley: University of California Press, 120–35.

Willis, M. 1996: *The Islamist Challenge in Algeria: A Political History*. Reading, MA: Ithaca Press.

Zubaida, S. 1989: *Islam, the People and the State*. London: Routledge.

—— 1997: Religion, the state and democracy: contrasting conceptions of society in Egypt. In J. Beinin and J. Stork (eds.), *Political Islam: Essays from Middle East Report*. Berkeley: University of California Press, 51–63.

Part VI
Urban Processes and City Contexts: The United States

15

The Bullriders of Silicon Alley: New Media Circuits of Innovation, Speculation, and Urban Development

Michael Indergaard

Manhattan is morphing. A new coupling of culture and capital, fueled by efforts to commercialize the Internet, is changing the city. Dreams, schemes, and money grounded in emerging Internet sectors have touched a wide range of actors and places. The nexus of activity has been Silicon Alley, a new media district, which has captured the imagination with its edgy web designs and billions of dollars with its stock offerings. Even as a historic bull market reached its peak many notables declared that the new media was replacing Wall Street as New York's economic engine. Moreover, the city's new role *vis-à-vis* cyberspace is fueling a profound transformation of "real" spaces. New place names and boundaries are replacing old ones as the business district expands to new corners of Manhattan and the other boroughs. Silicon Alley has inspired a "melting pot" architectural style that evokes a blurring of industries. Yet, the melting pot metaphor belies the fact that an array of businesses is being displaced, eroding districts that provide the city with distinctive streets and less affluent New Yorkers with jobs. And in the wake of the dot-com crash Silicon Alley's own future is unclear. Can a just and coherent city emerge amidst a swirl of financial, cultural, and technological forces? A question for the twenty-first-century city is the kind of power relations that will prevail in "heterarchic" spaces formed at the nexus of urban and digital spaces (Crang 2000). Previous work draws attention to the interaction of networks, cultures, and space. I examine the roles that Silicon Alley networks and cultural frameworks are playing in the commercialization of the Internet. This topic touches on key issues that intrigue critical urban theory, especially the problem of reconciling material and cultural analyses.

Networks and the Remaking of Space

Theories of globalization, growth coalitions, and innovation districts use some version of network theory to explain how new systems of symbolic production and information processing are transforming cities. However, they disagree on how much influence local social relations and cultures have *vis-à-vis* these systems.

Global flows or local circuits?

Some authors (Sassen 1991, 1997; Castells 1996) cite global flows of capital, culture, and information as forces that are segmenting, if not overwhelming, cities. Harvey, for example, notes the role of cities such as New York in processing fictitious capital and in producing "images, knowledge, and cultural and aesthetic forms" (1989: 331) but then argues that the logic of the larger system precludes coherent local action. Castells (1996) contends that action is limited by a network "morphology" that links up social segments and territories that possess functional value while discarding those that do not. Urry (2000: 194) claims that corrosive flows of "people, information, objects, money, images and risks" are eroding and making irrelevant human capacities for meaningful action. Moreover, the meaning of local actions is pirated away, "captured, represented, marketed, circulated and generalized elsewhere" (Urry 2000: 197–8).

Growth coalition theories (Zukin 1995; Mele 2000) also depict commercial appropriation of local culture. But in contrast to the local incoherence and powerlessness portrayed in globalization models, this approach stresses the role of local actors in weaving together "circuits" of capital and culture within the city (Zukin 1991). The basic claim in the growth coalition model is that local groups mediate external investment into cities (Logan and Molotch 1987). Recent revisions propose that assorted interests with a stake in the city's "symbolic economy" (real estate, cultural industries, financial industries, and local government) support cultural development strategies, such as museums, that organize local consumption activities and reframe devalued areas. Zukin observes that such actions replace cultural complexity with "a coherent visual representation" (1997: 226); importantly, she adds that imposing "a vision on space" requires the kind of material supports that these coalitions can muster.

Of special interest are accounts of Lower Manhattan's cultural industries and creative "rebels," a group now including "technobohemians" (Hall 1998) who also populate new media districts in London and San Francisco. The ability of cultural and real estate industries to co-opt artists and usurp images of artistic places means that they, in essence, mediate "cultural practices and cultural categories" (Zukin 1997: 241). Mele notes that the avant-garde gains recognition by finding "hidden" cultures for the culture industry (2000: 29). Their enclaves provide not only living sites, but also cultural content to be commodified and new images for real estate interests to exploit. Thus, the "representations" of such places that are in "circulation" often exaggerate the creative subversive element, ignoring less affluent residents who may be displaced by hip gentrifiers.

Innovation districts and digital cities

Theories of innovation districts also stress the role of local networks and cultural processes in shaping a locality's ties with larger systems. Work on computer and cultural industry enclaves (Saxenian 1994; Graham and Marvin 2000; Pratt 2000; Scott 2000; Indergaard 2001) argues that proximity and face-to-face contact provide "relational assets" (Storper 1997) (conventions, ties, and customs) that support collaboration. Local ties grant access to specialized workers, suppliers, and financing. Especially important are financing networks that improve the odds of high-risk ventures (Saxenian 1994; Zook 1999) and allow venture capitalists to act as district power brokers (Castilla et al. 2000).

A number of analysts stress the role of districts in managing and making sensible the intersections of local and translocal networks (Amin and Thrift 1992; Storper 1997; Saxenian 2000). Graham and Marvin (2000) argue that cities possess "cultural and social advantages" for processing "symbolic and representation flows and outputs," while other writers (Pratt 2000; Scott 2000; Indergaard 2001) propose that district networks help innovators gain credibility with external sets of partners, customers, and investors.

It follows that sites for managing and making sensible the intersections of real and virtual business spaces will be new centers of power. The question then is what kind of relationships will such sites have with the rest of the city? Graham and Marvin call for scrutiny of digital city experiments and policies: are they creating "privileged niches, spaces, and corridors" (2000: 92) or are they real efforts "to develop a more inclusive and sustainable urban future" (2000: 90)?

Rethinking the Economy/Culture Divide

Zukin's 1989 postscript to *Loft Living*, her 1982 synthesis of cultural and materialist analysis, recalls being inspired by insights in *Social Justice and the City* that suggested "the city was a spatial and economic, material and symbolic matrix of struggle over capital accumulation" (1989: 206). Zukin (1991) later revised Harvey's theory of capital circuits, proposing that with the rise of a symbolic economy, circuits of capital now interact with circuits of culture. More than ever, the advance of critical urban theory depends on reconciling materialist and culturalist emphases. In fact, the culture/economy divide hampers the analysis of inequality. Indeed, the struggle for inclusiveness in the digital city may pivot on efforts by material interests to exploit the "symbolic power" of technology (Graham and Marvin 2000).

I argue that economic sociology can help here. Beginning with Harvey (1973), critical urban theory has fruitfully, if fitfully, drawn on economic sociology to explain how markets are constructed. The insights of a "new" economic sociology (Smelser and Swedberg 1994) are even more valuable in the wake of the cultural turn. Economic sociology (Fligstein 1996; Carruthers and Uzzi 2000) proposes that markets are held together by cognitive frameworks and conventions that help consumers decide which products are comparable and firms identify who their competitors are, and by networks that facilitate the making of shared meanings. Both the relational and cultural aspects of power come into play during economic restructuring: firms compete for domination by using networks to reach across unconnected sectors (Granovetter 2000), while trying to offer definitions of new products and markets (Carruthers and Uzzi 2000) that are compelling to customers, business partners, and investors.

Importantly, Carruthers and Uzzi propose that a destabilization of firm boundaries ignited by restructuring is likely to accelerate as businesses use information technology to build "two-way relationships" catering to "specialized consumer tastes" (2000: 488). This may result in a "refiguration and recombination" of roles and identities, producing "new modes of exchange, allocations, and valuation" (2000: 492) that change how wealth is accumulated and distributed.

Circuits as socioeconomic networks

Critical urban theorists often use structural conceptions of networks that downplay their relational and cultural features. Castells's stark depiction of networks governed by a functional logic (1996) resembles structuralist accounts of cities that cite the logic of capital. In contrast economic sociologists (Castilla et al. 2000: 219) argue that "a tie or relation between two actors has both strength and content. The content might include information, advice, or friendship, shared interest or membership and typically some level of trust."

In particular, urbanists need to rethink the assumption that financial flows are divorced from, and antagonistic to, culture and social relations – an image originating in utilitarian assumptions about the asocial nature of money (Zelizer 1994). Alternatively, Zelizer argues there are distinctive networks or "circuits" of restricted exchange that incorporate "different understandings, practices, information, obligations, symbols, and media of exchange" (Zelizer 2000: 3). Even in the case of legal tender, people distinguish – in language and in practice – bribes, donations, wages, honorariums, salary, bonus, tips, damages, premiums, and pin money. They typically make distinctive use of money when undertaking "delicate or difficult" matters (1994: 25), such as creating ties, controlling others, dealing with risk, establishing inequality, or constructing identity.

Collins (2000) draws out the implications of these circuits for inequality. He notes different social strata tend to stay within particular circuits of exchange and that the realizable value of a "currency" is problematic outside its circuit. For example, as "fences" and money launderers know, it is difficult to exchange fine art or immense sums of financial capital outside of their own circuits. A key issue, then, is the circumstances in which a currency in one circuit can be "converted" in another circuit. I propose that being able to link circuits or convert currencies are key forms of power in a time of restructuring.

This can be seen in Silicon Alley where deregulation and new technologies have created openings for linking up sectors (media, computers, telecommunications) once kept separate by regulations and delivery systems. In order to do this, new media firms have to construct new ties and stories of markets and products that are credible to potential customers, collaborators, and investors. Thus it is that Silicon Alley has served as an institutional nexus for weaving together circuits and a matrix of power for making relationships, identities, and spaces.

Silicon Alley: The Institutional Nexus

Silicon Alley originally referred to a corridor in Lower Manhattan that followed Broadway south from the Flatiron District through Greenwich Village and into SoHo – the environs of artistic types drawn to old factory lofts and New York University. As of 1995 some 2,350 new media firms in New York City employed 18,300 workers (Indergaard and McInerney 1998). By 1999 the numbers had exploded to some 4,000 firms employing over 138,000 workers (PricewaterhouseCoopers 2000).

Given Lower Manhattan's long association with the cultural industries (Zukin 1989, 1995; Mele 2000), one might ask of the new media, "how new is it?" Even its involvement with information technology has apparent precedents. Fitch (1993) reports that an "Info City trope" devised by Manhattan real estate promoters in the early 1970s had resurfaced a decade later and that an "experimental ferment" on Wall Street was fueling loft conversions. However, this growth ensemble was stalled by the Wall Street collapse in 1987 and the ensuing recession, which plagued the Financial district with vacancy rates exceeding 20 percent – and the city with jobless rates exceeding 8 percent – well into the mid-1990s. Silicon Alley incorporated elements of the previous ensemble but its character was shaped by very different social segments and cultural visions. It became a nexus for a more extensive connection of circuits, some of which had never been imagined.

Party circuit

The defining trait of Silicon Alley is an interest in breaking barriers between the virtual and real worlds. Its story begins with a technobohemian community whose formation was, in part, accidental, but also the result of attempts to provide pioneering Internet users and artists with real-world venues where they could meet face-to-face. The ties and ethos of these web pioneers co-evolved with localized exchange networks – the original "circuits" of Silicon Alley.

The identity of the enclave drew from the rebel imagery of Lower Manhattan's artistic communities and from idealistic visions spawned by the rise of computer networks. This cyberculture had intellectual roots in the School of Arts and Interactive Telecommunication (IT) program at New York University. The IT program turned out a cadre of computer-literate young people who thought computers could facilitate free communication and expression. Many, disdainful of the media giants, believed that anyone could become an online publisher. Even as many creative types remade themselves into entrepreneurs they often did so with a sense that they were going to change society (Indergaard and McInerney 1998).

Graduates of the IT program were prominent in building Silicon Alley's early culture, institutions, and firms. In 1990 one disciple started Echo (East Coast Hang Out), an electronic bulletin board, which she nurtured into a virtual community of 3,500 members. At the same time she also helped organize face-to-face meetings and events for Echo members. She recalled in a 1996 interview that she had wanted it "to be a community, a social space where people would be able to tell the stories of their lives" (Chervokas 1996: 2). An editor of an online newsletter noted that "Echoids" seemed to be on "the staffs of every important Silicon Alley venture" (1996: 1). A similar interest in face-to-face interaction led to the founding of Webgirls in 1995, an association for women in the new media. Its director (interview, July 1998) notes the group's guiding "rule" is that "you need to say what you need and what you can give back. . . . This sets up an exchange." Indeed, such exchanges defined the enclave: web pioneers made sites for friends and freelanced for small firms; "financiers" were usually friends and family.

Silicon Alley's notorious party circuit also helped weave together local ties and sensibilities into distinctive networks. The parties were occasions for one to reaffirm their identity as someone who "got it" – meaning that they believed the Internet would change the world, at a time when few people knew what it was. At these parties they also shared a fascination with the idea that breaking the barriers between the real and virtual worlds created new forms of expression. A prime example is Pseudo, which was both something of a party and a company. It began by operating a "chat community" for Prodigy and evolved into an Internet TV studio. An insider remarks that Pseudo gave its first party in 1994, an epic SoHo affair filled with "club kids, techno-music, drugs, models, cross-dressers, computers" and "the geeks who would eventually become the CEOs of Silicon Alley" (Calacanis 1998: 38). Although many entrepreneurs later exited the party scene, the focus for many groups is still the idea that they are exploring the boundaries between the online and real worlds. The Silicon Alley Jewish Center, for example, bills itself as a nonprofit entity "dedicated to the interpretation of traditional Jewish culture and our evolving Internet-enabled lifestyle."

As web pioneers ventured into the business world they supported organizations and institutions that were more commercial in nature. The most important is the New York New Media Association (NYNMA), a group that now has over 8,000 members representing some 4,000 firms. The district also has its own media circuit – a collection of trade magazines that include paper magazines (*Silicon Alley Reporter*, *AlleyCat News*) and offline newsletters (*@NY* and *Silicon Alley Daily*). These magazines, along with NYNMA, have played a major role in helping firms develop business models and in forging a commercial identity for the district.

All that is solid morphs

Observers note that Silicon Alley firms engage in endless organizational shifts (Indergaard and McInerney 1998; Pratt 2000; Stark forthcoming). Participation in the district often involves reinvention on the part of individuals as well. For example, the founder of a computer services firm who was a music major observes that she hires through an "MIT network" and her "own network of arts, theatre and music people." She remarks (interview, July 1998):

> I have a Columbia grad who is a bassoonist. He does sales for me but I will see if I can train him up. My senior tech person is an MIT grad with degrees in chemistry and theatre. She came to New York and realized she wouldn't get a theatre job . . . I trained her . . . and bill her work out at $120 an hour.

And the co-owner of a web services firm reports (interview, July 1998) that one of his partners "is an adjunct at the Fashion Institute of Technology. A lot of our workers started as his students . . . graphic artists who became programmers." Also recasting themselves as new media participants are corporate veterans who have come to help manage firms and computer-literate lawyers and accountants.

Firms have often changed their names and lines of business but there are also continuities. Although the recent focus has been on Silicon Alley's "national contenders" – the dot-coms who raised and spent large sums of money without making profits – most firms are still small subcontractors and service firms that earn modest profits (PricewaterhouseCoopers 2000). Moreover, the desire to do "cool" creative work still motivates many (Pratt 2000; Neff et al. 2000). Most firms also still rely on their own financing sources. According to a recent survey of firms (PricewaterhouseCoopers 2001: 6) 50 percent are self-financed while 22 percent received private financing; only 12 percent received venture capital and a mere 4 percent were publicly traded.

One big change is that fewer start-ups expect to create an alternative to the corporate media anymore. Many insiders had once claimed that the ability of small firms to "morph" and serve customers "in real time" would be a decisive advantage over corporations (Watson 1997: 3). Moreover, it seemed edgy online publications ("webzines") possessed more compelling content and cost advantages. Ironically, it was the web pioneers who, with missionary zeal, drew resistant corporations to the Internet. Big firms began to throw large amounts of money at web designers as they raced to get their magazines online or to set up glitzy marketing sites. Start-ups sprang up as small fortunes were unloaded (Indergaard and McInerney 1998). Yet, the web shops, which had hoped to be embraced as strategic partners, found themselves treated as disposable subcontractors. Recently, leading web shops have tried to change this circuit by remaking themselves into comprehensive corporate services or consultants. One executive notes (interview, July 1998) that his firm, which started as "five guys in a room," is now "building long-term relationships with Fortune 500 companies." To do this, a firm has "to morph into a business with a global strategy and growth." A partner in a web shop that has "morphed itself" observes (interview, July 1998) that the "new media is being redefined, not by artists or graphics but by how you solve business problems."

Circuits of venture capital and real estate

Silicon Alley's venture capitalists and real estate developers have, like other actors, altered their own identities as they have enmeshed themselves in the district. But the distinctive "relational assets" of these two interests have allowed them to exercise much more power than the web pioneers in making Silicon Alley's commercial circuits and institutions. While the web pioneers struggled to convert cultural creativity into business power, venture capitalists and real estate developers have organized various networks and associations that have translated the enclave's sense of cultural vitality into images of economic vitality.

Previously, New York was a place that supplied venture capital to places such as Silicon Valley but lacked locally oriented funds. A cohort of Silicon Alley venture capitalists formed as individuals left jobs in established financial firms in order to become brokers for Silicon Alley. What is distinctive about venture capital as a circuit of exchange is that venture capitalists provide information, connections, and advice as well as capital, in exchange for equity stakes and managerial influence in firms. The case of Silicon Alley reveals the leverage these networks give venture capitalists in organizing district circuits. Most noteworthy was the role of venture capitalists in organizing a "cybersalon," a gathering of new media and financial types that, with corporate and state funds they solicited, grew into the New York New Media Association (Pratt 2000). The same venture capitalists also served as NYNMA directors and executives.

The existence of an organized new media community spurred the formation of other venture capital firms. Most notable is Flatiron Partners, which has invested $400 million in the new media since 1996 (*Silicon Alley Reporter* 2001). Moreover, the district's venture capitalists have helped create networks of "angel" investors and worked with NYNMA to recruit investors for special projects. NYNMA has backed efforts to promote the district's commercial image, including surveys that have documented the economic importance of the new media sector for the New York area.

In 1995 NYNMA, along with several corporate groups, began to push for the development of a new media hub in Midtown Manhattan – the domain of old media and advertising giants. However, it was a real estate coalition that allowed the New York Information Technology Center to materialize – in the Financial district. Backed by the Alliance for Downtown (a quasi-public authority), Rudin Management Co. provided a vacant office building for the project. City Hall, which hoped to revitalize downtown real estate, offered tax subsidies. Rudin wired the building with high-speed Internet links and launched a PR campaign. The success of this project led the coalition to create a "Plug 'N' Go" program, which subsidized the wiring of thirteen more downtown buildings for new media start-ups (Block 1997). Over 250 firms are now lodged in the Plug 'N' Go buildings (Indergaard 2001).

Online Consumer Circuits

Silicon Alley provides real spaces, grounded in a matrix of material and symbolic resources, for working out Internet business models. A challenge, which few start-ups or corporate units have solved, is creating ties with online consumers that will bring in enough revenue to sustain the endeavor. Experiences of Silicon Alley's "national contenders" suggest that the creation of online "circuits" hinges on issues of user identity, interaction, and information. Of particular importance for power relations is the question of how information – for consumers and about them – is turned into a currency for online consumer circuits.

Online firms may charge an online user directly for a product or service (a subscription for an online magazine or game) – or they may generate revenue from advertisers or retailers. The vintage Silicon Alley model focused on providing alternative content, which, in practice, consisted of a sample of cyberculture or a slice of life from environs of Lower Manhattan. A number of "webzines" that remained true to the alternative spirit won critical acclaim but struggled to draw in enough advertising revenue to sustain themselves. Many firms subsequently develop niche strategies so as to tap advertisers interested in particular demographic segments. For example, Virtual Melanin hosted a website ("Cafe los Negroes") for blacks and Latinos (Bunn 1997). Of special interest was Pseudo's foray into Internet TV. Webcasting live-music parties, Pseudo explored the idea that a group of people interacting face-to-face could create new cultural forms by interacting live with other people through an electronic medium. In exchange for exposing users to youth-oriented ads (cars, soft drinks, clothing) Pseudo offered them a unique experience – hinted at by an executive's remarks (interview, July 1998) that, "We are underground, hip, capture a vibe." Users could participate in the show via chat, message boards, and live call-ins.

Online community

Another model for building online relationship is the community portal, which are networks of sites organized according to some theme. They offer users a sense of community and identity in exchange for exposing them to targeted ads and commercial links. For example, BET.com, an affiliate of Black Entertainment Television, is the leading portal for African American sites. Community Connect offers three "ethnic" sites: AsianAvenue.com, BlackPlanet, and MiGente.

One of Silicon Alley's leading examples is StarMedia, a portal to Latin America. Its founder claims it aims to "capture a unique part of the Latin cyber experience in one place" and to "reconnect this community" (Calacanis 1999: 130). His story of what StarMedia offers suggests a blend of Simon Bolivar and George Gilder: "our historical mission . . . is to break a five hundred year pattern of monopolies in Latin America . . . of political, information, social, economic power by giving individuals the ultimate ability to share information and communication" (1999: 128). Another example is iVillage, a "Woman's Network." Its founder proposes that by "pulling together different sites and categories" in "an environment that is comfortable to women," iVillage can assist women in getting "stuff done and solving problems" (Gould 1998: 24) – especially by providing "information" about shopping. In exchange users are exposed to targeted ads and retail links.

Personal (transaction) space

Leading Silicon Alley dot-coms attracted large numbers of users but almost none made a profit. For example, StarMedia, which led its category by attracting 17 million "unique" visitors a month, lost $115 million during the first nine months of 2000; iVillage, which led its category by attracting 8.4 million visitors a month, lost $37 million in the second quarter of 2000 (*Silicon Alley Reporter* 2001). Hoping to create a "brand" that would set them apart from rivals, firms spent huge sums of money on promotions, advertising, and positioning. Competing to aggregate "eyeballs," not profits, they charged users little or nothing.

Theorists (Carruthers and Uzzi 2000; Scott 2000) propose that consumption may be organized to give consumers a more active role. The question of how Internet users will exercise "choice" looms as a defining issue – one that may be difficult to reconcile with the profit motive. Many firms hope to make e-commerce, ads, and content commercially viable by finding mechanisms to match user segments with the right spaces. The founder of About.com aims to alter "transaction environments":

> The transaction environments on the Internet are not very good right now . . . . With TV people watch one ad after another. On the Internet we get them in the front door and then send them right out. . . . We need audiences that really want to see the ads – in the right area. (Kurnit 2001)

"Personalization" is one strategy firms are now using for "customer relationship management." A consultant (Peppers 2000) counsels firms to add value to the "relationship" through interaction: "If you tell me what you want, I can change how I serve you. With every interaction I can change the product a little bit better to fit you." An executive of SonicNet, a start-up now owned by MTV, favors "personalization with community": "Users can vote at our website on the selection they want and then we play the winner. You can feel like you are part of a group . . . people like to share tastes with others" (Greenberg 2000).

Whether firms, as part of the "relationship," will be gathering information on users is a major issue. The president of DoubleClick, an advertising network that records user "clicking" behavior so as to be able to offer targeted delivery of ads, argues that when consumers are online they are "making a rational choice – they are willing to give up info in exchange for value" (Salzman 2000). A storm of protest resulted when the firm announced plans to match a user's online data with offline databases. DoubleClick retreated in the wake of a FTC investigation into whether it violated privacy rights. However, one commissioner's "warning" shows that little was settled: DoubleClick has "to establish with customers that for giving up information, they get something of value" (Schwartz 2001: 5). So far, DoubleClick's answer is that users get a "free" Internet – thanks to ad dollars.

Thus, the critical issue is how information exchange is structured, and who has the power to organize it. The founder of an online financial service claims, "the virtual world will always follow the real world" (Lessin 2001). Since observers foresee a consolidation that will result in a small number of large firms, one wonders how much power users will have once oligopolistic profits are at stake.

Connecting with the Bull Market

Before Silicon Alley's national contenders had resolved the relationship–revenue problem their attention was diverted to the market for initial public offerings (IPOs) of stock – a circuit that offered new media entrepreneurs the possibilities of gaining windfall amounts of resources, publicity, and/or riches. In 1998 IPOs of stock by a handful of leading Internet firms and a rise in their stock values propelled the Internet to international prominence. The value of Amazon.com increased 638 percent (to $18.9 billion), Yahoo rose 452 per cent (to $11.7 billion), and AOL increased 294 per cent (to $40.9 billion) (Gimein 1998: 40).

Instead of viewing this episode as proof that global capital flows determine local fortunes, I stress the role of Silicon Alley actors in connecting the dot-com segment to the bull market. The first to connect was Earthweb, an online service for "techies." Its value peaked at $89 a share, a market capitalization that exceeded $400 million (Chervokas 1998). Soon thereafter theglobe.com held an IPO that peaked at $97 a share, each share having changed hands five times on average (Gimein 1998: 40). Dozens of Silicon Alley firms began to focus on IPOs. There were multiple motives. The publicity would help a firm to stand out. Cash reserves would enable firms to make acquisitions – thus, gaining new capacities or eliminating rivals. Firms could use stock options to attract or retain skilled workers. Finally, some (if not most) hoped to get rich.

A look at the IPO process shows how venture capitalists and entrepreneurs use their ties and stories to complete a circuit that depends on "serial vouching" (Indergaard 2001). The ties of venture capitalists shepherd firms to the

IPO stage and oftentimes provide links with the investment banks that underwrite IPOs: venture capitalists give firms credibility with both pre-IPO investors and IPO underwriters. The underwriting banks then work with venture capitalists to give a firm credibility with stock buyers. Buyers are stratified into preferred customers – institutional investors – for whom banks reserve stock orders at a set opening price and a mass of unconnected buyers who may pay four or five times as much during the first day of trading. Most of the risk is borne by the latter group, which joins the circuit in the later stages. Those who join early in the process due to privileged positions (venture capitalists, investment banks, institutional investors) are the ones most likely to receive huge returns.

A run of IPOs (there were thirty-four IPOs in all) in the spring of 1999 boosted the standing of Silicon Alley and of firms such as DoubleClick, iVillage, and StarMedia. At the start of 2000 the combined market value of twenty-nine Silicon Alley firms was $29.5 billion (Watson 2000: 1). Executives and founders had hundreds of millions of dollars in stock. New venture capital and nontraditional venture capitalists flooded in. The surfeit of venture capitalists a start-up could choose from, and the stock market's support of IPOs from young firms, led venture capitalists to relax their standards and accelerated the process leading to IPOs.

Circuits and Currencies of Urban Development

As the twenty-first century drew near the local media claimed that the new media was replacing Wall Street as the "engine" of the New York economy (Kanter and Messina 1999). The results of a NYNMA survey (PricewaterhouseCoopers 2000) were impressive; one estimate showed that the number of new media workers in the city grew from 55,973 in 1997 to 138,258 in 1999, an increase of 82,285 (147 percent) (2000: 29). A more conservative estimate (+63,048 jobs) still impresses, since other media sectors (publishing, advertising, motion picture, and TV) only accounted for a gain of about 8,000 jobs while traditional leaders (retail trade, business services, and securities) added 50,000 jobs (2000: 34). In addition, the local media claimed that Silicon Alley's growth helped create "tens of thousands" of service jobs, including business and professional services (e.g., lawyers, accountants) that were "once dependent on Wall Street" (Kanter and Messina 1999: 30).

The new media, along with the city's surging financial and business service sectors, fueled a boom in a revived Manhattan real estate market. The entry of new media start-ups into the real estate market was spearheaded by the IPO stars who were willing and able to pay premium rents for relatively large spaces; a wave of venture capital that followed the IPO run sent many more firms into the market. A January 2000 report claimed that some 100 new media firms were looking for large blocs of office space in Manhattan (Jakobson 2000: 70). During the first half of 2000 the new media and other technology firms leased over 5 million square feet of space, bypassing the financial sector (3 million square feet) as the top leaser of commercial space in the city (Chiu 2000: 1, 54).

As commercial spaces in the original center of Silicon Alley became rented up, new media firms led the way into new territories that included not only Downtown but also, increasingly, parts of Midtown such as Chelsea and the Garment district.

New media stock options

In the wake of the IPOs, new media stock options became a form of currency, used to purchase stakes in other firms and to compensate employees, landlords, and other service providers. Some firms made charitable donations in stock. Along with the IPOs, Silicon Valley models of compensation for employees and business services helped establish the "liquidity" or exchangeability of these options.

When Wall Street and corporations began to use large salaries to woo technical workers, many new media firms turned to stock options, a Silicon Valley tactic, to recruit or retain "talent." It was thought that IPOs would be critical for establishing the value of the new "currency," as is graphically illustrated in comments made by iVillage's founder the year before it enjoyed a spectacular IPO:

> A series of successful IPOs would be good for Silicon Alley . . . no one here has a next-door neighbor who hit it big . . . New York needs the kind of culture Silicon Valley has . . . that believes that options and upsides and incentives are really worth taking as a big part of your package. . . . Initially, a lot of the people we hired were still very hung up on salary . . . We're like, 'Hello? Excuse me? Your salary is to pay your rent. That's all it is. You should take as little as possible' . . . Well, I've been glad to see people around here . . . say, 'Can we take it all in options?' Which is a really great change, where they're beginning to believe that options are the best form of currency. (Gould 1998: 52)

On the first day of trading iVillage's new currency was good as gold: its stock price rose to over $113 a share. The firm was hardly alone in its good fortune. A benefit plan administrator estimated that IPOs created more than 1,000 millionaires among the founders and executives of Silicon Alley firms; another 2,000 have amassed between $500,000 and $1 million (Kanter and Messina 1999).

Many business services began to accept (or actively seek out) stock options as compensation – a common practice among Silicon Valley law firms and accounting firms. For example, a headhunter, which usually asked for a third of the first year's salary that an executive received, now asked for a third of their first year's stock options (Baer 2000). Similar tactics became common in the interior design and remodeling sector where dozens of firms (architects, contractors, project coordinators, furniture dealers, and lighting designers) reorganized, or started up, to renovate offices for new media firms (Croghan 2000b: 58).

Some landlords were wary of the risk of leasing to new media firms, especially compared to corporate clients. As demand exploded some landlords, in the manner of venture capitalists, began to assess the credibility of would-be tenants. They demanded to see business plans and ask "about a company's backers, the size and shape of the funding, its 'burn rate' and 'exit strategy'" (Anderson 2000: 2). Landlords began to accept equity in new media tenants to seal the deals (Aron 2000a; Anderson 2000). Some real estate developers and brokers actively promoted the equity model. Interestingly, Rudin Management led the way in accepting options (Baer 2000), while some brokers advised new media clients who were struggling to find space to entice landlords with options.

New media images

A second currency also spread the effects of the new media to other circuits: new media images. Real estate interests and public sector allies appropriated the images of the new media industry to reimagine how other areas in the city could be transformed. Once again, Rudin Management led the way. Besides wiring the downtown building for the NYITC, Rudin also converted a former Grumman facility into the Long Island Technology Center and is wiring a new headquarters building for Reuters in Times Square. Rudin has also used Internet sites to promote its network of wired buildings, proposing that the electronic links between them (and affiliated buildings in Europe) could facilitate virtual business communities.

Two major public–private initiatives are using the imagery of the new media to transform space. First is the "Digital NYC: Wired to the World" program, which the Giuliani Administration started in 1999 with the goal of creating new media districts across the city. Using the Plug 'N' Go program as a template, Digital NYC offers subsidies to local development corporations, universities, real estate interests, and telecoms that set up wired enclaves outside Lower Manhattan. Interest has been expressed by over a dozen entities in Brooklyn, Long Island City (Queens), Chinatown, the Bronx, and Staten Island. Some projects are packaging new media firms with telecom firms. For example, a telecom "hotel" anchors a site at Brooklyn's Bush Terminal, a twelve-building complex with 5 million square feet of space. The

Digital NYC program has important implications for place identity. At the opening of a site in Long Island City – one of the few industrial centers left in New York – the city's head of economic development announced that "Silicon Alley's boundaries are now extending beyond Manhattan" (Gordon 2000: 2).

New York Senator Charles Schumer launched the second initiative, proposing that a space crisis threatened New York's status as "the world capital of the ideas economy" (Jakobson 2000: 70). To this end he put together the "Group of 35," a high-powered growth coalition that included not only real estate interests but also representatives from entities such as Time Warner and Goldman Sachs – and the CEOs of Agency.com, DoubleClick, and StarMedia. The Group of 35 is considering three neighborhoods as possible high-tech zones, including the "far-West Side" of Manhattan. The West Side location suggests that the new media space crisis might be used to free up space for a new sports stadium desired by Mayor Giuliani, the New York Jets, and a group preparing a bid for the 2012 Olympics (Jakobson 2000).

Circuit Disconnects and Decay

The restructuring of real estate into high-value circuits reserved for dot-coms and corporations incorporated diverse places while displacing their commercial residents. In the wake of the market crash, many new media firms are themselves finding it difficult to remain connected with the new real estate circuits.

Disconnects and expulsions

Initially, the new media were lauded for recycling property abandoned by other industries. However, as their expansion accelerated the new media began to displace clusters of firms from their traditional districts in Lower Manhattan, Chelsea, the Garment district, Chinatown, and other areas. A notable example in Chelsea is the Starrett-Lehigh Building, a 2.3-million-square-foot former railroad terminus. New media firms, paying $30 a square foot in rent, displaced mattress firms and warehousers who had been paying rents in single digits (Aron 2000b: 26). Displacement is taking place in the Garment district even though much of it is supposed to be protected by zoning (Flamm 2000: 24). In the Hudson Square area Trinity Real Estate – owner of twenty-four buildings (50 percent of the area) – refused to renew the leases of dozens of printers, who had paid as little as $7 a square foot in rent; new media and telecom firms are paying up to $38 (Aron 2000b: 26). The new media push into Chinatown, the Flower district, and industrial areas in Queens and Brooklyn has extended the zone displacement. The Digital NYC initiative is contributing as it targets industrial areas in Brooklyn and Queens. For example, manufacturers who moved to Bush Terminal after being displaced from Manhattan are being displaced again as the rent is raised from $5 to $20 a square foot (Boss 2000).

The new media expansion is threatening not just individual firms but entire sectors. Most obvious is the threat to the nexus of specialized resources in the Manhattan garment industry – the designers, producers, materials, showrooms, marketing, and press (Boss 2000). The nonprofit sector, the city's sixth largest employer, is also being threatened by the rise in real estate prices. This is a double blow since not only are jobs at risk but so is the ability of agencies to remain in the neighborhoods they serve. Like the garment firms, many nonprofits are looking to move to Brooklyn and Queens (Croghan 2000a). Individual sectors have tried to organize to protect their districts, for example, in the Garment district and the Flower district. And the New York Industrial Retention Networks is seeking state funds for a "Trust for Industrial Space" – modeled on programs that protect farmland. Other groups are seeking zoning of industrial areas so as to create "industrial sanctuaries." However, restrictions on development are opposed by developers, landowners, and the Giuliani administration (Lentz 2000).

New media circuit decay

After the spring 2000 crash of the NASDAQ index many of Silicon Alley's "national contenders" found themselves facing disconnection, expulsion, and extinction. The "Alley Fund" (a composite of forty-six Silicon Alley firms that were publicly traded) fell over 80 percent – from $1,519 at the start of 2000 to only $276 at the end of October 2000 (Indergaard 2001). Losses in value were remarkable for many well-known firms: Razorfish (–96.4 percent), StarMedia (–95.2 percent), and DoubleClick (–91.8 percent) (Gandel 2001: 1). The results were grim for iVillage employees, who accepted the advice that they take their compensation in stock: its stock value fell 95 percent and the firm, along with many others, was threatened with delisting when its stock value temporarily fell below $1 a share.

For a fair number of prominent firms who have high expenses and low revenues the end is near or has already come. Among those that disappeared was Pseudo, which was not publicly traded but had burned through $35 million in investors' money without coming close to a profit; some 240 employees lost jobs. Another leading provider of alternative content, Urban Box Office, also fell victim to its unrestrained spending, resulting in the loss of over 300 jobs. Earthweb, the firm whose spectacular IPO helped ignite Silicon Alley's bull run, has almost faded from sight. It has sold most of its assets (fourteen websites and eighteen e-mail newsletters), laid off 100 of its 350 employees, and narrowed the scope of its business to recruitment (Blair 2000: 3). Many public firms have cut workforces by 10 to 20 percent in a race to show movement toward profitability. Razorfish, a leading web services firm, has laid off 600 of its 2,000 employees worldwide.

The crash had a multiplier effect due to the fact that the dot-coms had themselves expended enormous amounts of money for online advertising and web services. Besides hurting start-ups that provided advertising or web services to dot-coms, this has also led big media corporations to rethink their commitments to new media units that depend on ad revenue. News Corp closed its digit unit, which was headquartered in Chelsea, a move that will cost several hundred jobs. NBCi cut 320 jobs from a workforce of nearly 700. CNN laid off 130 of 750 workers in its interactive division (*Silicon Alley Daily* 2001).

Over the second half of 2000 new media firms stopped leasing space and returned 3 million square feet of space to the market as sublets (Croghan 2001). Landlords became more restrictive, demanding higher rents and up to three years' rent in advance. Some have set up "temporary" facilities so they can periodically reevaluate new media tenants. Others simply reject new media firms as tenants.

Embracing the e-ville empire

The bursting of the market bubble was a watershed but it does not signal the end of Silicon Alley. Small subcontractors have done relatively well; only 26 percent of firms reported operating losses in 2000 (PricewaterhouseCoopers 2001: 4). Some public firms emerged with large cash reserves, a good reputation, and a credible business foundation. A larger number possess at least one of those virtues. Some firms might survive as independent entities if they desire; however, given a new interest in developing linkages across different media markets, many firms may try to parley their assets into a favorable merger or acquisition deal. An example is the acquisition of About.com for $690 million by publishing giant Primedia. iVillage has acquired its main rival, a San Francisco firm (Women.com), but it and other community portals may also end up as internal units within large corporations. For example, some think StarMedia will be acquired by a media giant from either Mexico or Spain. Web service firms such as Agency.com, Razorfish, and RareMedium have viable businesses but may merge with one another or one of the big five consulting firms that now provide interactive services.

Assessments given in a recent NYNMA forum ("The State of the New York New Media 2001") assume corporations will drive the Internet's commercialization. Silicon Alley notables touted AOL-Time Warner as a local champion: its decision to locate its headquarters in New York meant that "Silicon Alley's upper border is now the Rockefeller Center" (*Silicon Alley Reporter* 2001: 29). They proposed that Silicon Alley will continue to have a strategic role because corporations contending to influence the Internet are dependent on New York's business ensembles. Some entrepreneurs who once aspired to lead the revolution against corporations have morphed into "intrapreneurs" who want to take the revolution within corporations.

Morphing Manhattan: From Silicon Alley to Times Square

Forces of development that the new media helped set in motion remain at work. Speculators are investing in "chic" areas in old industrial areas now associated with "new media lifestyles" (Holusha 2000). Some brokers say they are changing their maps, claiming that new "submarkets" are emerging while old place identities, such as the Garment district, are now "anachronisms." The expanding Midtown and Downtown business districts seem to be on the verge of linking up with emerging centers in Brooklyn and Queens (Goff 2000). And the city is backing development of "Midtown East" – a new business district in Long Island City (Holusha 2001).

Imagine me watching you watching me

Admirers often lament that Pseudo was ahead of its time. In fact, when Pseudo hosted its first SoHo spectacle exploring the intersections of media space and real space (1994), NBC Today created the first TV studio open to the sidewalks of Manhattan: a ground-level glass box in the Rockefeller Center. In the same year Bertelsmann became the first media giant to locate in Times Square – an event that marked a turning point for its redevelopment strategy (Zukin 1997). Now big media firms are flocking to Times Square to set up broadcast studios exposed to the street. The latest is Reuters whose new American headquarters, an executive contends, will "build public awareness" about the firm because Times Square has "become the media capital of the world" (Hughes 2001: 5). The area hosts the Time Squares Studios of ABC (a Disney subsidiary), Viacom's MTV studios, and NASDAQ's MarketSite Tower. Just down the street (in the Garment district) are Condé Net (the digital arm of Condé Nast) and About.com – its presence here confirming its status as a Silicon Alley success story. To round out the ensemble, Cisco, the computer network powerhouse, is negotiating a lease in the area.

Media firms hope to exploit the "branding potential" of having a live broadcast audience. In NASDAQ's case, MarketSite gives a "public face" to a market that lacks a trading floor. Inside CNBC and CNNfn broadcast market reports. Outside is an eight-story-tall video screen that provides LID-illuminated financial news to passersby. NASDAQ's chairman claims the MarketSite Tower stands "for NASDAQ's ideals to be digital, global, and investor-focused" (Hughes 2001: 5).

Real estate interests continue to use images of Silicon Alley even as the focus shifts to Times Square. Max Capital, the landlord for Condé Net and About.com, is remaking properties according to a "New Economy" aesthetic that features a "Silicon Alley" design sensibility. Its president claims the "best thing to come out of the dot-com revolution is style," noting that financial firms, a group he targets, "have taken a lot from Internet companies in terms of style, like casual dress, open layouts, and sleek spaces" (Hughes 2000: 5). He claims that Silicon Alley inspired "the new Times Square style, which is a hip mix of financial, entertainment, and publishing businesses . . . a melting pot of New York industries" (2000: 5). A local media observer interprets this to mean that "New York is no longer made up of individual neighborhoods dedicated to specific industries" (2000: 6).

City of Circuits

Proposing that "places comprise an ensemble of forces," Molotch, Freudenberg, and Paulsen (2001: 792) recently asked, "how do unlike elements conjoin" and what encourages the resulting "combinings to persist"? Harvey and Zukin draw our attention to the role of circuits of capital and culture in a spatialized nexus of power. Using economic sociology I show Silicon Alley to be an institutional nexus for building and conjoining "restricted circuits" (Zelizer 2000) of capital and culture. In a burst of hyperdevelopment, this matrix of power extended far into the rest of the city, transforming space, social relations, and identities.

Some might tell the story of Silicon Alley in terms of the anarchy of markets (for stocks and real estate) and how this results in local incoherence. However, it is because neither capital nor cultural images circulate freely in cities that some "embedded" actors have exercised power in making new media spaces. Venture capitalists and real estate interests have mobilized power through their ability to create and link circuits and convert "currencies." Silicon Alley venture capitalists connected external circuits of capital with localized new media circuits, and then with an IPO circuit in the stock market. Their currency was "smart money" – capital with a reputation due to its linkages with insider networks and information. Real estate interests have linked new media industry circuits with a new circuit of revalorized commercial property through using "wired space" as a currency. The value of these infrastructural upgrades is boosted by subsidies that signal public support and promote new media images. Real estate interests have been able to generate a new currency – images of a cross-sectoral technocultural ensemble – that they are using to connect with a new real estate circuit for corporations (e.g., media giants) that are seeking to remake themselves – and virtual consumers – into symbols of the digital age.

While web pioneers originally sought to enroll corporations in their Internet exploits, it is now likely that Silicon Alley will persist as a real space enrolled in corporate efforts to create online circuits of exchange; the kind of power that online users will wield may be far less than the web pioneers imagined, given that oligopolistic actors and agendas are likely to become dominant. The commercial coherence of online circuits may well hinge on the development of exchange conventions that mesh with oligopolistic webs. Coherence is no guarantee of social justice, as can be seen in the role that imagined cyberspace has had in transforming real space and in creating new forms of inequality. Through both its active involvement and studied inaction, city government has played an important role here, supporting development that is neither inclusive nor sustainable. Despite the high-tech imagery the development strategy is essentially "slash and burn": the clearing away of modest forms of growth spurs hypergrowth of a new monoculture in the short term, but depletes the city's rich milieu.

Bibliography

Amin, A. 2000: The economic base of contemporary cities. In G. Bridge and S. Watson (eds.), *A Companion to the City*. Oxford: Blackwell, 115–29.

—— and Thrift, N. 1992: Neo-Marshallian nodes in global networks. *International Journal of Urban and Regional Research* 16 (4): 571–87.

Anderson, D. 2000: The race for office space. *TheStandard.Com*, January 11, pp. 1–3.

Aron, L. J. 2000a: Web, retail surge earns full house for Midtown South. *Crain's New York Business*, January 17.

—— 2000b: Downtown re-emerges as office mecca. *Crain's New York Business*, January 17.

Baer, M. 2000: The new economy's currency is stock. *New York Times*, March 29.

Blair, J. 2000: EarthWeb selling most of its web sites and news services. *New York Times*, December 27.

Block, V. 1997: Rising firm tally expands geography of Silicon Alley. *Crain's New York Business*, November 24.

Boss, S. 2000: Free trade, high rents hang garment makers out to dry. *Crain's New York Business*, March 13.

Bunn, A. 1997: Upstart startups. *Village Voice*, November 11.

Calacanis, J. M. 1998: The story of Pseudo. *Silicon Alley Reporter* 2 (11): 36–48.

—— 1999: Star gazing. *Silicon Alley Reporter* 3 (8): 126–51.

Carruthers, B. and Uzzi, B. 2000: Economic sociology in the new millennium. *Contemporary Sociology* 29: 486–94.
Castilla, E. J. et al. 2000: Social networks in Silicon Valley. In C. Lee et al. (eds.), *The Silicon Valley Edge*. Stanford, CA: Stanford University Press, 218–47.
Castells, M. 1996: *The Rise of the Network Society*. Oxford: Blackwell.
Chervokas, J. 1996: New York's new media's ground zero. *@NY*, April 12.
—— 1998: Looking beyond the madness. *@NY*, November 13.
Chiu, J. 2000: Space grabbers. *Crain's New York Business*, August 7.
Collins, R. 2000: Situational stratification. *Sociological Theory* 18: 17–43.
Crang, M. 2000: Public space, urban space and electronic space. *Urban Studies* 37: 301–17.
Croghan, L. 2000a: Nonprofits feel the pain of the city's office crunch. *Crain's New York Business*, December 4.
—— 2000b: Silicon Alley style. *Crain's New York Business*, February 3.
—— 2001: Distressed NY dot-coms revitalize parched market. *Crain's New York Business*, January 1.
Fitch, R. 1993: *The Assassination of New York*. London: Verso.
Flamm, M. 2000: A booming economy remakes Manhattan. *Crain's New York Business*, January 17.
Fligstein, N. 1996: Markets as politics. *American Sociological Review* 61: 656–73.
Gandel, S. 2001: NY sidesteps meltdown. *Crain's New York Business*, January 1.
Gimein, M. 1998: Around the globe, new media stock market mania. *The Industry Standard*, December 28, pp. 40–2, 44.
Goff, L. 2000: Tenants' tastes remap Manhattan. *Crain's New York Business*, October 16.
Gordon, C. 2000: You take Manhattan. *@NY*, February 21, pp. 1–3.
Gould, G. 1998: Alley girl. *Silicon Alley Reporter* (September): 20–2, 24, 52, 56.
Graham, S. and Marvin, S. 2000: Urban planning and the technological future of cities. In J. O. Wheeler et al. (eds.), *Cities in the Telecommunications Age*. New York: Routledge, 71–96.
Granovetter, M. 2000: A theoretical agenda for economic sociology. Paper presented at the Second Annual Conference on Economic Sociology, University of Pennsylvania, Philadelphia, March 4.
Greenberg, P. 2000: Comments at Personalization on the Web panel, Silicon Alley Uptown conference, Columbia University Business School, November 17, New York.
Hall, P. 1998: *Cities in Civilization*. New York: Pantheon.
Harvey, D. 1973: *Social Justice and the City*. Baltimore: Johns Hopkins University Press.
—— 1989: *The Condition of Postmodernity*. Oxford and Malden, MA: Blackwell.
Holusha, J. 2000: A developer puts a bet on the meatpacking district. *New York Times*, July 16.
—— 2001: A plan for high-rise offices in Long Island City. *New York Times*, January 28.
Hughes, C. J. 2000: Lobbying for change. *Silicon Alley Daily*, November 30, pp. 4–7.
—— 2001: Convergence converges. *Silicon Alley Daily*, January 11, pp. 3–6.
Indergaard, M. 2001: Innovation, speculation, and urban development: the new media market brokers of New York City. In K. Graham (ed.), *Research in Urban*

Sociology. Volume 7: *Critical Perspectives on Urban Redevelopment*. Oxford: Elsevier Science.
——and McInerney, P. 1998: Making Silicon Alley, remaking cyberspace. Paper presented at the annual meetings of the American Sociological Association, San Francisco.
Jakobson, L. 2000: Back to the garage: Sen Chuck Schumer and his Group of 35 tackle the city's space crunch. *Silicon Alley Reporter* 4 (7): 70, 148.
Kanter, L. and Messina, J. 1999: Unexpected riches remake the city. *Crain's New York Business*, November 29, pp. 28, 30, 32.
Kurnit, S. 2001. Comments. The state of the New York new media 2001. Panel sponsored by the New York New Media Association, January 30, New York.
Lentz, P. 2000: Industrial backers try manufacturing safe haven in city. *Crain's New York Business*, December 4.
Lessin, R. 2001: Comments. The state of the New York new media 2001. Panel sponsored by the New York New Media Association, January 30, New York.
Logan, J. and Molotch, H. 1987: *Urban Fortunes*. Berkeley and Los Angeles: University of California Press.
Mele, C. 2000: *Selling the Lower East Side: Culture, Real Estate, and Resistance in New York City*. Minneapolis: University of Minnesota Press.
Molotch, H. et al. 2001: History repeats itself, but how? City character, urban tradition, and the accomplishment of place. *American Sociological Review* 65: 791–83.
Neff, G. et al. 2000: "Cool" jobs in "hot" industries. Unpublished MS. New York: Graduate Center of the City University of New York.
Peppers, D. 2000: Comments at Personalization on the Web panel, Silicon Alley Uptown conference, Columbia University Business School, November 17, New York.
Pratt, A. 2000: New media, the new economy and new spaces. *Geoforum* 31: 425–36.
PricewaterhouseCoopers 2000: *3rd New York New Media Industry Survey*. New York.
——2001: *New York New Media Industry Survey*. New York.
Salzman, B. 2000: The web as global medium. Address at the Silicon Alley Uptown conference, Columbia University Business School, New York, November 17.
Sassen, S. 1991: *The Global City*. Princeton, NJ: Princeton University Press.
——1997: Electronic space and power. *Journal of Urban Technology* 4: 1–17.
Saxenian, A. 1994: *Regional Advantage*. Cambridge, MA: Harvard University Press.
——2000: Networks of immigrant entrepreneurs. In C. Lee et al. (eds.), *The Silicon Valley Edge*. Stanford, CA: Stanford University Press, 248–75.
Schwartz, J. 2001: Trade commission drops inquiry of DoubleClick. *New York Times*, January 23.
Scott, A. 2000: *The Cultural Economy of Cities*. London: Sage.
Silicon Alley Daily 2001: Media roll-ups. January 18.
Silicon Alley Reporter 2001: The Silicon Alley 100. January.
Smelser, N. and Swedberg, R. (eds.) 1994: *The Handbook of Economic Sociology*. Princeton, NJ: Princeton University Press.
Stark, D. forthcoming: Ambiguous assets for uncertain environments. In P. DiMaggio et al. (eds.), *The 21st Century Firm*. Princeton, NJ: Princeton University Press.
Storper, M. 1997: *The Regional World*. New York: Guilford Press.
Urry, J. 2000: Mobile sociology. *British Journal of Sociology* 51: 185–203.

Watson, T. 1997: It's services stupid. Realtime replaces branding. *@NY*, November, pp. 1–2.
——2000: Billions flowed into Silicon Alley, as Internet industry grew up in 1999. *@NY*, January 6, pp. 1–4.
Zelizer, V. 1994: *The Social Meaning of Money*. New York: Basic Books.
——2000: How and why do we care about circuits? *Accounts* 1: 3–5.
Zook, M. 1999: Regional systems of financing. Paper presented at the Global Networks, Innovation, and Development Strategy conference, University of California, at Santa Cruz, Santa Cruz, CA, November 11–13.
Zukin, S. 1989: *Loft Living*. New Brunswick, NJ: Rutgers University Press.
——1991: *Landscapes of Power*. Berkeley: University of California Press.
——1995: *The Cultures of Cities*. Oxford: Blackwell.
——1997: Cultural strategies of economic development and the hegemony of vision. In A. Merrifield and E. Swyngedouw (eds.), *The Urbanization of Injustice*. New York: New York University Press, 223–43.

16

Fear and Lusting in Las Vegas and New York: Sex, Political Economy, and Public Space

Alexander J. Reichl

Given the recent preoccupation in urban studies with "the cultures of cities" (Zukin 1995), one might be forgiven for concluding that urban culture is a discovery of the late twentieth century – or, at the least, that culture has just reappeared in cities after a long period of dormancy. There is a grain of truth here, in the sense that the renewed attention to the cultural realm reflects important transformations in the urban landscape over recent decades. The spectacular theme-park places, *à la* Disney, that have emerged as defining features of contemporary cities represent a dramatic cultural break from the stark modern forms typical of city-building efforts during the preceding decades. Urban modernism itself was a cultural project, but its aesthetic of rationality dictated a universal form of architecture and planning that promised/threatened to homogenize – physically and socially – cities across the globe. By the 1960s, growing bourgeois disaffection with the monotony of modernism (Wolfe 1981), together with a prevailing public discourse of urban decline (Beauregard 1993), made the notion of urban culture an oxymoron.

The spectacular appearance of postmodern urban places is striking against this backdrop of cultural decline and thus draws attention back to the cultural realm. Of course, it may be that we are witnessing no more than a superficial change in "scenery" that masks "the same purifying separations" of city life sought by modernists (Bender forthcoming). But even if we grant this critique of new urban places as "modernism in costume," we are still left with fundamental unanswered questions: Why dress cities in costumes in the first place? Who designs the costume, and to what purpose? For urbanists who ground their theorizing in the direct experience of city life the existence of the costume itself demands investigation. In this respect, the cultural turn follows a long tradition of drawing on the urban landscape as a blueprint to the circuitry of power (Engels [1845] 1958; Mumford 1938; Benjamin 1999).

Much of the recent work on urban culture has sought to build upon, rather than replace, the critical insights of the new urban sociology. Concerns about processes of capital accumulation and their class consequences remain at the forefront of this new scholarship. This is apparent, for example, in the work of David Harvey (1989), who situated the rise of spectacular urban places in a new political economic order of flexible production; in the work of Sharon Zukin, whose analyses of the "symbolic economy" (1995) and the "urban imaginary" have illuminated the path to a "'new, new urban sociology' that joins political economy and cultural analysis" (Zukin et al. 1998); and in the work of Michael Sorkin (1992) and others concerned about the impact of postmodern urban development on public life in cities. Culture is also, inevitably, at the core of critical scholarship on urban tourism (Judd and Fainstein 1999).

As these and other cultural analyses demonstrate, the cultural realm is not simply an epiphenomenon of economic processes that provides an ideological support for the capitalist order; rather, culture has become an important factor in the production of wealth. This is certainly evident in the industries of tourism and real estate development, where value may be conferred upon a place through the symbolism and imagery that circulate in public discourse. What remains less clear, though, is how new cultural forms of urban development might serve as an instrument of political power. The idea that the nature of the built environment can affect the possibilities of political action appears far removed from structuralist political economy. But the issue is particularly relevant today, as we seek to make democracy work for historically disadvantaged groups while recognizing the limitations of formal political processes – a reality made painfully clear in the 2000 US presidential election. In this context, understanding the impact of spatial practices on democratic political life takes on greater urgency.

This chapter investigates the relationship among culture, political economy, and spatial practices by analyzing the place of sex-related adult entertainment in Las Vegas and New York. Sex may seem an inauspicious subject for an analysis of urban political economy because it appears to fall within a sphere of "moral politics" that involves "passionate conviction" about right and wrong rather than calculated interests (Hunt 1999: ix). In fact, in the field of urban politics, conflicts over adult entertainment are relegated to a distinct arena of "culture wars" that are said to fall outside the explanatory range of dominant political economy approaches (Sharp 1996). But it is precisely because sexual practices are a contested cultural terrain that they promise new insight into the interaction of culture and urban political economy. Commercial sex is significant on a range of overlapping levels, from the economic to the cultural. Sex-related establishments are often visible features of the urban landscape, and they can be profitable components of urban economies; witness, for example, the proliferation of upscale gentlemen's clubs in convention cities. These economic enterprises also interact closely with the symbolic realm of meanings and representations about cities; topless stage shows in Las Vegas signify one thing, and porn shops in Times Square signify another. These meanings then circulate back into the material realm, shaping what is possible and profitable in the form of economic activity.

It is precisely this interaction between the material and symbolic realms that is the focus of much recent work in urban studies. Yet most studies of economic development find a high degree of congruence between dominant material interests and prevailing discursive representations. In New York, for example, gentrification of the Lower East Side was facilitated by the imagery of "urban pioneers" civilizing the "wild west" (Smith 1992; also Mele 1996), and the redevelopment of Times Square was represented as an effort to restore the lost glamor of a historic theater district to a place of urban decline (Reichl 1999). But sex-related businesses often undermine more desirable forms of economic investment due to their negative symbolic baggage. When it comes to commercial sex, therefore, the relationship between the material and symbolic realms is more complex, a site of struggle and contestation.

Las Vegas and New York offer valuable insight into this process. The two cities share a common sin-city legacy from their adolescent days, when prostitution and other forms of commercial sex were rampant. But, at least superficially, they have since followed different historical trajectories. In Las Vegas, an extensive menu of sex-related attractions complements the casino-based economy, and city elites have done little to limit their availability. In fact, sex-related entertainment contributes to a marketable sin-city image that has proven to be more profitable than the family-friendly alternative pursued briefly in the 1990s (Parker 1999). Conversely, in New York Mayor Rudolph Giuliani unleashed his prosecutorial fury on smut peddlers, vowing to close down adult businesses and force them out of the city's central areas. This fits into the mayor's larger crusade against quality-of-life criminals, an effort not only to make the city safer but also to make it appear safer. As these two cases illustrate, the place of commercial sex in a city's economy is closely tied to symbolic representations of the city itself.

In the following analyses of Las Vegas and New York, however, one factor emerges as preeminent, and that is a desire to control public space. In both cities, certain forms of commercial sex are tolerated and others repudiated depending on their relationship to public space. The crackdown on visible sex-related businesses in New York reflects a perception of disorder in the city's central public spaces and a concern about its economic and political consequences. In contrast, the lively sexual commerce that forms an important part of the Las Vegas image and economy is possible because the city, lacking in genuinely public spaces, eludes similar fears of public disorder. The concern about public space is therefore a mediating factor in the interaction between material economic activities and their cultural representations.

Most importantly, these cases demonstrate that the problem of space is a problem of order, and so inherently political. This chapter concludes, therefore, by offering a way to conceptualize public space as a political resource essential to democracy.

Las Vegas

Given its long association with various forms of vice, it is ironic that "[f]ederal spending, and lots of it, triggered the rise of modern Las Vegas" (Moehring 1989: 13). In the early 1900s Las Vegas was a fledgling railroad and mining town and a nascent resort city, with a small but boisterous red-light district that formed on the two blocks of Fremont Street where the sale of liquor was allowed. In the 1930s and 1940s, federal spending on public works and defense projects pumped millions of dollars into the economy of southern Nevada and brought thousands of workers and soldiers eager for entertainment. In 1931, Nevada reinstated legalized gambling (following a brief and failed experiment with Progressive reform), and from that point on Las Vegas began to develop as a resort city catering to adult pleasures.

It was not until the 1940s, however, that Las Vegas began to shed its dusty frontier image for the flashy modern resort image that persists today. The transformation was initiated by mobster Benjamin "Bugsy" Siegal, who brought a Miami Beach-style resort to the Mojave Desert with his lavish Flamingo casino and hotel. Although the Flamingo struggled financially at first and Bugsy was whacked, the formula was replicated in elaborate new casinos/hotels built with Teamster pension funds and controlled by Mafia families. This was a city of pleasures contrived by and for the common man (Wolfe 1965), and each new casino offered the fantasy of an exotic time and place in the explicit semiotics of its "pleasure-zone architecture" (Venturi, Scott Brown, and Izenour 1972). Sex was an integral part of this world of pleasures.

Gambling and prostitution are longtime companions in Las Vegas. Prostitution is legal in rural counties of Nevada, so the conscientious john might legally obtain the services of an "independent contractor" in one of the brothels that operate on the fringes of Clark County (Spanier 1992). But casino operators have long recognized the value of sex to their businesses and have conspired in its availability. In the past, it was understood that the complete Las Vegas experience, termed the "Las Vegas total," included food, lodging, gambling, shows, and a woman for sex (Gottdiener et al. 1999: 78). As one insider described the situation: "A good casino had an arsenal of stunning showgirls, stunning call girls, and stunning classy dames it could call on to grease the high-roller action, and it was a good host's job to match weaponry with circumstance" (quoted in Martinez 1999: 201). Today's corporately controlled casinos keep prostitution at arm's length, fitting with their cleaner image, but it hardly matters; the city has a vast reserve army of escorts, advertised everywhere, who will "come right to your room" with a simple phone call (Gottdiener et al. 1999: 79).

The success of Las Vegas depends, however, on the ability to manufacture desire itself. Therefore, in the creation of modern Las Vegas sexuality had to move from beyond base carnality and into the realm of fantasy. This is the function of the Las Vegas showgirl. Decorated in a costume studded with rhinestones and topped with baroque plumage, revealing bare breasts and long bare legs, the showgirl represents an untouchable object of desire (Schiff and Leibovitz 1996). Showgirls emerged during the 1950s, when casinos competed by offering exotic stage shows imported from Paris. These Parisian-style revues are now a dying breed, falling victim to a proliferation of nude and topless jiggle shows that abandon any pretext of a "classy" presentation of female nudity. Nevertheless, the showgirl still figures prominently in the city's marketing material and remains a powerful icon in the symbolic construction of Las Vegas. Her image establishes Las Vegas as a sexualized place, and one that is safely heterosexual. And, by introducing aestheticized sexuality into the city's image, this endangered creature serves the material interests of the casinos, attracting visitors and fueling the condition of desire that is at the heart of sex and gambling.

Because sexuality remains an important ingredient in the casino economy, themes of sexuality permeate representations of Las Vegas disseminated by the city's local image-makers. Las Vegas is legendary for the power of its marketing machine (Gottdiener et al. 1999). Today it is the Las Vegas Convention and Visitors Authority (LVCVA) – together with the advertising by individual casinos – that serves as the primary image-making device for the city's casino-dominated growth machine. The LVCVA is awarded the lion's share of the 9 percent hotel room tax, and in a metropolitan area with a phenomenal stock of over 120,000 hotel rooms (more than double the supply of New York) averaging 80–90 percent occupancy rates, this translates into an annual budget in excess of $120 million (ten times that of its counterpart organization in New York) (www.lasvegas24hours.com; personal interview with Ruth Nadler, Vice President of Research, NYC & Co., October 12, 2000). The enormous resources of the LVCVA reflect the remarkable degree to which the city's economy is built upon the symbolic realm of images.

Sexuality is a subtle but unambiguous theme in the LVCVA's marketing strategy. The 2000 marketing campaign was built around the theme of "freedom," as in "freedom to do what you want, when you want" (www.vegasfreedom.com). This furthers the image of Las Vegas as an All-American city (Andersen 1994) by linking the Las Vegas experience to the fundamental American values of life, liberty, and the pursuit of happiness. But the sexual suggestiveness is unmistakable in the promised "freedom from inhibitions," "freedom to indulge," "freedom to go nuts," etc. Significantly, the first image on the website is not dice or cards, but a showgirl. Sexuality operates less discreetly on another marketing website, Las Vegas On Line (www.lvol.com), which includes a guide to the city's adult entertainment. This site even offers direct links to hard-core pornography, making explicit the sexuality that operates as a veiled subtext in the official marketing of Las Vegas.

The association of Las Vegas with sexual license is reinforced by the Hollywood dream factory. Hollywood celebrities have frequented Las Vegas to entertain and be entertained since the quickie celebrity divorces of the 1930s (Moehring 1989: 29). In return, Las Vegas has been a favorite subject of Hollywood movies, from *The Las Vegas Story* (1952) and *Viva Las Vegas* (1964) to *Honeymoon in Vegas* (1992) and *Vegas Vacation* (1997) (see Gottdiener et al. 1999: 69–76). Sexuality is a recurring theme in Hollywood representations of the city, whether glamorous, romantic, comic, or decadent. But the stock Hollywood image remains that of the attractive bombshell in a sleek evening gown, dripping jewels, who will blow on some lucky man's dice.

The symbolic construction of Las Vegas is not simply a product of casino interests. Even with a massive marketing effort the production of images eludes tight control, as the grim *Leaving Las Vegas* (1995) illustrates. Moreover, sexuality circulates back into the material realm in the form of activities opposed by the dominant casinos. This is the case with street prostitution and the distribution of graphic fliers advertising sex-related businesses on the sidewalks of the Strip, where the major casinos are located. The casinos mobilized local lawmakers to crack down on both types of activities, the former involving social practices that emerge from below, and the latter involving investment practices of other economic elites. What distinguishes both activities from other forms of commercial sex is their occurrence in public space. And the common response has been to assert control over these spaces.

Las Vegas combats street prostitution by means of a zoning ordinance that designates certain geographic areas as "order-out corridors" (Kalil 2000a, 2000b). Anyone arrested for prostitution in the designated zone is given a suspended sentence provided he or she agrees not to return to the area for a period of six months to a year; those violating the agreement receive mandatory jail time. The zones were first created in 1996, and they have since been expanded twice to complete a buffer around the casino areas of Fremont Street and the Strip. It is a spatial strategy that serves the interests of casinos by sweeping visible prostitution from adjacent public spaces and into surrounding areas.

The casinos have had greater difficulty controlling the distribution of handbills advertising adult entertainment. (Tellingly, the casinos have paid little attention to the ubiquitous ads on taxis and billboards that are of greater concern to families living in Las Vegas, but target people in automobiles rather than pedestrians in the public spaces around the casinos.) Although the Clark County Commission has adopted several ordinances banning the distribution of handbills along the casino corridors, these have been repeatedly struck down in court as an infringement on free speech (Steinhauer 1997; Friess 1998). Consequently, the casinos moved to evade the First Amendment issue by privatizing adjacent public spaces. This was accomplished most dramatically on Fremont Street, an area of older casinos that suffered from a seedy reputation. In 1995, a $70-million makeover transformed the street into a covered pedestrian space featuring a spectacular sound and light show. The new Fremont Street Experience was developed and operated by a casino-led corporation "established in part to put the downtown casino corridor in private hands" (Steinhauer 1997). In 1998 a federal judge ruled that the Fremont Street Experience was no longer a public street (Martinez 1999: 229). On the Strip, the process of privatizing public space has proceeded in a piecemeal fashion as new megaresorts absorb sidewalks into increasingly spectacular, theatrical facades.

New York City

Commercial sex has long been a visible feature of the New York City landscape. From the mid-nineteenth century on, a parallel economy of sexual entertainment has operated symbiotically with the city's premier theater and entertainment district. The relationship was forged downtown by the 1850s and, as legitimate theater migrated uptown in pursuit of cheaper land, so too did the various forms of adult entertainment, from burlesque theater to prostitution. In the 1880s, the theater district had settled around 34th Street and Broadway, as did a notorious red-light district known as the "Tenderloin," where "one-half of all the buildings were reputed to cater to vice" (Federal Writers' Project [1939] 1982: 147). By the turn of the century the entertainment district was stalled in the area of Broadway and 42nd Street, now Times Square, due to the rapid development of real estate farther uptown.

Although sex-related businesses have been associated with the decline of Times Square in the 1960s and 1970s, "prostitutes were a prominent and visible part of the 42nd Street community" by 1885 (Gilfoyle 1991: 301). Just prior to the official birth of Times Square in 1904, outraged citizens found prostitutes operating from 130 separate addresses on thirty neighboring blocks. At the same time, a "two-mile parade of prurient commerce" was reportedly on view along Broadway, with as many as ten to twenty prostitutes trolling each block from 27th to 68th Street (1991: 300). This thriving sex industry was an essential component of the city's economy. Its sex workers were drawn from the ranks of lower-class young women with few career options (Sante 1991) to serve the "sporting men" of the "leisured" and business classes who formed the audience for the legitimate theater (Buckley 1991: 291).

During the 1910s the sex market in Times Square was driven into hiding, largely through the efforts of crusading citizens' organizations that bypassed corrupt politicians (Buckley 1991: 288). But sex soon worked its way back into the economy of Times Square, where it remained for much of the twentieth century. During the Depression, burlesque shows breathed new life into failing Broadway theaters. After Reform Mayor Fiorella LaGuardia rid the city of burlesque in the early 1940s, those seeking erotic entertainment in Times Square might take in a sex education exhibit at a dime museum, or select from the sun-bathing magazines or marriage manuals offered in area bookstores (Buder 1978). World War II brought soldiers and sailors to Times Square and revived the market for prostitution, now often served by male hustlers (Chauncey 1991) whose presence defined the area as a homosexual space well into the 1990s. Following the greater legal and social permissiveness of the 1960s, Times Square became the site of increasingly brazen sex entertainment; soon one could choose from a veritable smorgasbord of hardcore books and magazines, video or live peep shows, topless and nude dancing, massage parlors, and even live sex acts performed on dingy mattresses (Friedman 1993). Prostitution operated within this network of establishments, as well as spilling out into neighboring parks and streets.

Over the course of a century the nature of the sex economy in Times Square changed, but the fact of its existence did not. And it remained an economy built on the demand of white-collar males (New York State Urban Development Corporation [UDC] 1984: 2–132). Nevertheless, Times Square was a very different place in the 1980s than the 1880s as a result of fundamental changes in the city itself. The out-migration of whites and the influx of people of color significantly altered the city's complexion after 1950. Young African Americans and Latinos, whose own neighborhoods were decimated by abandonment, began flocking to Times Square for its easy accessibility and cheap attractions, including bargain movies, fast-food outlets, game arcades, and a relatively safe public space in which to hang out. Consequently, Times Square became not only a sexualized space, but a racialized one as well.

As Beauregard (1993) has illustrated, racial transition fed into the theme of decline that dominated public discourse on US cities for much of the twentieth century. As the nation's premier urban place, Times Square became the ultimate symbol of urban decline. The uneasy mixture of race and sex in representations of Times Square added new urgency to efforts aimed at eradicating the area's sex markets. Public and private elites, backed by the authoritative voice of the *New York Times*, portrayed sex-related businesses as an active ingredient in an explosive formula for public disorder. This theme was evident in the 1969 film *Midnight Cowboy*, which added homosexual prostitution to the blend of troubling images. But it was depicted most vividly in Martin Scorsese's 1976 film *Taxi Driver*, in which a psychologically disturbed cab driver is propelled to an explosion of violence by the depravity of New York. The streets of Times Square, pocked with glaring porn theaters, form the backdrop for this drama; and the recipient of the "hero's" violent rage is a shameless pimp who sells adolescent girls. The movie affirmed Times Square as the physical manifestation of civic decline.

The material effect of this representation of Times Square compelled, and enabled, city leaders to pursue publicly sponsored redevelopment of the area (Reichl 1999). The perception of public disorder in Times Square created a barrier to the westward expansion of the midtown office district, obstructing the post-industrial transformation of Manhattan. Business and civic leaders sponsored sociological studies of the area to document a relationship between adult entertainment and crime, but they were never able to do so; in fact, the crime rate in Times Square was found to be relatively low (Hunt 1978). And the greatest fears of Times Square seemed to have more to do with the visible presence of young African American and Latino males (UDC 1984). Nonetheless, as the *New York Times* declared, "serious investors were discouraged by West 42d Street's mix of fast food and instant sex" (*New York Times* 1980: A18).

By mobilizing these negative cultural images in public discourse, local elites rallied political support for the heavily subsidized redevelopment of 13 acres in Times Square. Public officials condemned scores of properties and displaced hundreds of businesses, including many sex-related businesses, thereby clearing the way for the transformation of 42nd Street into a themed and controlled environment of family-friendly entertainment. The final obstacle was the existence of sex-related businesses elsewhere in Times Square, and Mayor Giuliani moved aggressively against these establishments. His primary weapon was a zoning law, enacted in 1995, prohibiting adult businesses from operating within 500 feet of schools, churches, residences, or other adult businesses. The law sought to disperse sex-related businesses from Times Square and relegate them to remote industrial zones. Although a legal loophole allowed sex shops to continue operating if no more than 40 percent of the establishment was devoted to adult entertainment – yielding such unlikely alliances as sex and sushi – the combined impact of redevelopment and legal pressure significantly diminished the visible presence of adult entertainment in Times Square. And, in a 1998 marketing video produced by the city's tourism bureau, Mayor Giuliani addressed the world proudly from a sanitized Times Square (New York Convention and Visitors Bureau, *New York City . . . Come Visit the World*, 1998).

This does not mean that sex entertainment was being purged from New York's economy. One need only turn to the back pages of the *Village Voice* to find a united nations of women and men in provocative poses advertising their adult body work services. With fees in the hundreds of dollars, this is pricey sex entertainment for those riding high on the city's economy. Graphic depictions of sexuality appear frequently in the many art galleries of Manhattan, and Mayor Giuliani's vindictive response to a work combining graphic sexuality with a dung-covered Madonna suggested that his usual hands-off approach was less a commitment to artistic freedom than a commitment to the economically valuable arts industry. Nor is it too much of a stretch to say that Times Square remains a place where sex sells, albeit in new corporate packaging. Sexuality oozes from giant Calvin Klein billboards, from the pages of Condé Nast publications, and from the MTV videos (strikingly similar to the jiggle shows of Las Vegas) that are disseminated worldwide from a Times Square studio. Giuliani's New York even has room for a new Museum of Sex, which will go by the pathetic nickname MoSex.

Sexuality and Public Space

One might argue that the different approaches to sex-related entertainment in Las Vegas and New York reflect no more than fundamental economic imperatives rooted in each city's economic base. City builders in Las Vegas had to overcome serious natural disadvantages – from a remote location, to scorching desert heat, to an inadequate water supply – in order to establish a thriving economy. Against these odds they built a major city around a tourism-based economy that offered forms of adult-oriented entertainment largely unavailable elsewhere. Commercial sex fits neatly into this formula; in fact, the lower level of spending by families reveals the risk of deviating from it (LVCVA 2000). In contrast, New York developed a diversified economy over a period of centuries and matured into a global headquarters for corporate and financial activity. As such, the city could forego the economic benefits of profitable, but morally suspect, sex industries.

The logic here is sound, but the analysis does not go far enough. It is possible to construct a tourism-based economy that does not depend on sex-related attractions. And there is no *a priori* reason why adult entertainment is unacceptable in a global city. Given the enormous popularity of pornography and the growing corporate involvement, we might as easily conclude the opposite. To understand how certain sex-related businesses came to be embraced in Las Vegas and repudiated in New York one must look to the cultural realm. Adult entertainment circulated differently into the symbolic representations of each city, reinforcing the seductive appeal of Las Vegas and the perceptions of disorder and decline in New York. These contrasting patterns reflect, in turn, the different nature of public space in each city.

Las Vegas has matured into a city almost totally lacking in traditional forms of urban public space (Sorkin 1999). In 1972, the architects Robert Venturi, Denise Scott Brown, and Steven Izenour described an auto-centered city where main street was devoid of pedestrians and the agora was found in the vast spaces of the casinos. It is no coincidence that Hunter Thompson's (1971) "savage journey to the heart of the American Dream" in Las Vegas was conducted from behind the wheel of the "great red shark." The phenomenal city growth of the 1980s and 1990s only reinforced this pattern, producing a vast sprawl of gated residential enclaves (Gottdiener et al. 1999; Sorkin 1999). Although the theatrical architecture of the new casinos has drawn a flow of pedestrians along the Strip, this can hardly be viewed as meaningful public space (Parker 2000). Park space is woefully lacking (Parker 1999), and the city's strategic plan calls for less rather than more, proposing to "link public open space to commercial and residential projects" (City of Las Vegas 2000: 27).

Conversely, public space is woven into the fabric of New York. New York is a walking city, and many of its neighborhoods feature the type of lively, pedestrian-oriented street life described by Jane Jacobs (1961). Open spaces of all sizes, from Central Park to Valmont's playground on West 113th Street, provide places for public interaction, as does the heavily traveled subway system. Even the densely built areas of Downtown and Midtown include a patchwork of public spaces in the form of plazas, atriums, and the like. Times Square has long served as the city's central public space, where large crowds converge to welcome the New Year, commemorate major events, engage in demonstrations and protests, and seek entertainment. In recent years the city's public spaces have come under an increasingly tight web of control: business improvement districts monitor public spaces with private security forces; parks are redeveloped, their green spaces fenced in, and their curfews enforced; plazas are padlocked or absorbed by neighboring shops and restaurants; and so on. But the fact of public-oriented city life survives. Indeed, it is arguably a willingness to trade private space for public space that defines many New Yorkers.

The cultural representations of each city reflect these different levels of publicness, and adult entertainment is especially salient in this respect. There are powerful social norms that seek to confine sexuality to the private sphere of the home, and its entry into the public realm evokes fears of social disorder. As Elizabeth Wilson (1991) has argued, female sexuality has been viewed historically as a moral and political threat to public order in the city. This is a recurring theme today in the pages of the *City Journal*, a mouthpiece for the conservative Manhattan Institute whose contributors are still fighting a revanchist battle against the sexual revolution. One target of criticism is New York's "'sex shops,' where people take off their clothes, gyrate, and reveal body parts usually kept covered in civilized society" (Morgan 1999: 80). Mayor Giuliani receives high praise for recognizing that commercial sex is among the low-level disorders that contribute to a perception that no one is in charge and fuel a spiral of urban decline. Because sexuality is read as a sign of disorder in public space it is problematic in New York. But sexuality operates through less public and more secure spaces of Las Vegas, from its casinos, to its roadways, to its cyber sites.

Theorizing the Political Value of Public Space

The issue of public space is prominent in poststructuralist urban studies, which view the built form as a causal force shaping social relations. Those who argue the value of public space fall into two general camps (see Kilian 1998). The first, following Jane Jacobs (1961), maintains that a sense of trust and security in a city neighborhood is built on the casual, routine contact that occurs naturally on the sidewalks and in the shops of multi-use areas. Problems of crime and disorder arise when people are pulled off the street and put into cars, enclosed turf, and single-use neighborhoods. The second camp, associated with Michael Sorkin (1992), views public space as essential to democracy because it enables diverse groups to represent themselves to themselves and to others. From this perspective, public space is a tool for achieving social justice, its absence a tool of repression. The problem is found in new theme-park forms of urban development that segregate social classes through a mix of semiotic codes and security mechanisms.

Most urbanists share a visceral appreciation for public space (or at least the idea of it), but the practical benefits of a "public city" remain difficult to nail down (Beauregard 1999). Because Jacobs documented city life so brilliantly, the argument regarding the social benefits of public space enjoys wider acceptance; indeed, the influential new urbanism movement draws heavily on Jacobs's principles of public life. The view of public space as a political resource is less widely accepted, in part because it appears at odds with prevailing structuralist approaches to understanding urban power. As this study has demonstrated, however, the politics of public space is implicated in material processes of capital accumulation through the realm of cultural representations.

Because adult entertainment is recognized as a form of speech protected by the First Amendment to the US Constitution, this study reveals an explicit link between efforts to control public space and the desire to limit forms of political expression. In a relatively uncontrolled public space, the mere presence of adult businesses makes a political statement and introduces an element of political conflict. This is directly at odds with the prevailing Disney model of public space (Zukin 1995), which requires a carefully orchestrated package of reassuring images. In Las Vegas, the political impact of adult entertainment is minimized because it is either packaged into privately controlled spaces or it is encountered from the secure space of the private automobile. But the perception remains that the production of marketable public spaces involves cleansing them of discordant political messages.

If we take seriously this issue of political speech and public space, it might be useful to conceptualize public space much as we do other forums for free speech, such as the media. To put a particularly American spin on it, we might think of an ideal public space as *First Amendment space* that provides an avenue for open political expression (verbal and symbolic). In effect, such public space would serve as a spatial grounding for the marketplace of ideas. Conceptualizing public space in this way enables us to recognize its value more clearly. For example, no one would argue that our democracy would fail to function if a particular alternative radio station (such as one of the Pacifica networks) ceased to broadcast. It would be difficult to document precisely its impact on politics, or to demonstrate that its voices could not find other outlets for expression. And yet, we might fight vigorously to save such a station on the grounds that its existence is important to democracy as a matter of principle. And we would be even more alarmed to learn that the fate of this station was being repeated with similar stations across the country. We would require no proof of whether, or how, these stations benefited democracy, individually or collectively, only the conviction that democracy depends on many and varied outlets for expression.

We should think of public space in much the same way. We cannot necessarily say if or when or how a particular public space serves any important political function. Many, even most, may serve no identifiable political purpose at all – just as most media outlets fall short as meaningful contributors to democracy. But we can still hold to the conviction that public space is a valuable forum for political life. There are dramatic examples of this, such as the Mall in Washington, DC, and Times Square (spatial equivalents of the *Washington Post* and the *New York Times*?). And there are local examples such as Tompkins Square on New York's Lower East Side, a traditional arena for working-class mobilization that became ground zero for an anti-gentrification struggle in the 1980s. The political function of public space may also operate more subtly in the form of symbolic speech; for example, through the mere presence of racial or ethnic minorities, or through patterns of dress and behavior. It is difficult to imagine the social and political revolution of the 1960s occurring without the spaces where hippies could present themselves and their alternative lifestyles. Indeed, Hunter Thompson's assault on Las Vegas (as opposed to his assault on mainstream sensibilities) rings hollow because, lacking a public forum, it is spent on a few hapless maids, drivers, and conventioneers.

Arguing that public space should provide a forum for open political expression does not mean that sex-related businesses must be allowed to operate unchecked in any neighborhood. Just as there are boundaries of acceptability governing other forums of First Amendment speech, there should be standards governing public spaces. But these standards should not be imposed in the form of zoning laws. Such regulations merely tighten the noose of disciplinary power over city life, while failing to acknowledge that adult establishments in the West Village have a different value than those in residential areas of Queens. Instead, these arrangements should be resolved through local political action in the form of grassroots movements of support and opposition. As Richard Sennett has argued in *The Uses of Disorder* (1970), potentially disruptive neighborhood influences can be a trigger for community mobilization in the absence of bureaucratic control. Whereas Sennett emphasized the benefit of this collective action for individual psychological development, there is also a distinct value to participatory democracy itself. Unregulated public space can be both a focus of, and a mechanism for, healthy democratic debate and action. The primary role for government is to protect public space as a democratic forum; for example, by preventing harmful forms of expression or dislodging enforced monopoly control (e.g., by drug dealers).

Public spaces controlled locally and democratically have the benefit of being best suited to local needs. Although many people are skeptical of the notion that pornography should enjoy First Amendment protection, two recent books have defended sex-related businesses as important, socially and politically, to public life in New York City. In *Times Square Red, Times Square Blue* (1999), Samuel Delaney draws on his own experiences to argue that the sexual encounters among men in the porn theaters of Times Square were a meaningful form of cross-class contact, and so of value to the social life of the city. In *The Trouble With Normal* (1999), Michael Warner argues that the gay porn shops in the West Village were an integral part of a "public sexual culture" through which the gay community constructed a group identity and accomplished collective action, such as combating the AIDS pandemic. As such, their elimination under the new zoning law is a form of political disempowerment.

In sum, the ideal of First Amendment space suggests that we evaluate public space as we do other democratic forums. This means that the most valuable public spaces are those that are accessible to a range of diverse voices and provide a healthy forum for open political expression. This presupposes nothing about who should be present or what they should be saying; but it does presuppose a limited degree of corporate or state control, such as that exercised by the casinos of Las Vegas or the public–private authorities in charge of Times Square. Above all, a valuable public space must be a place of possibility.

Bibliography

Andersen, K. 1994: Las Vegas, U.S.A. *Time*, January 10, pp. 42–52.

Beauregard, R. A. 1993: *Voices of Decline*. Oxford: Blackwell.

—— 1999: The public city. Published in Finnish as: Julkinen kaupunki. *Janus* 7: 214–23.

Bender, T. forthcoming: The new metropolitanism and a pluralized public. *Harvard Design Magazine*.

Benjamin, W. 1999: *The Arcades Project*. Cambridge, MA: Belknap/Harvard University Press.

Buckley, P. G. 1991: Boundaries of respectability: introductory essay. In W. R. Taylor (ed.), *Inventing Times Square*. New York: Russell Sage Foundation, 286–96.

Buder, S. 1978: 42nd Street at the crossroads: a history of Broadway to Eighth Avenue. In W. Kornblum (ed.), *West 42nd Street: The Bright Light Zone*. Unpublished study, City University of New York, 52–80.

Chauncey, G. 1991: The policed: gay men's strategies of everyday resistance. In W. R. Taylor (ed.), *Inventing Times Square*. New York: Russell Sage Foundation, 315–28.

City of Las Vegas 2000: *Strategic Plan 2005*. http://www.ci.las-vegas.nv.us.

Delaney, S. R. 1999: *Times Square Red, Times Square Blue*. New York: New York University Press.

Engels, F. [1845] 1958: *The Condition of the Working Class in England in 1844*. Ed. and trans. W. O. Henderson and W. H. Chaloner. Rpt. Oxford: Blackwell.

Federal Writers' Project [1939] 1982: *The WPA Guide to New York City*. Rpt. New York: Random House.

Friedman, J. A. 1993: *Tales of Times Square*. Portland: Feral House.

Friess, S. 1998: Handbill ordinance overturned. *Las Vegas Review-Journal*, August 17, p. 1A.

Gilfoyle, T. J. 1991: Policing of sexuality. In W. R. Taylor (ed.), *Inventing Times Square*. New York: Russell Sage Foundation, 297–314.

Gottdiener, M. et al. 1999: *Las Vegas: The Social Production of an All-American City*. Oxford and Malden, MA: Blackwell.

Harvey, D. 1989: *The Condition of Postmodernity*. Oxford: Blackwell.

Hunt, A. 1999: *Governing Morals*. Cambridge: Cambridge University Press.

Hunt, J. 1978: Crime and law enforcement in the bright light district. In W. Kornblum (ed.), *West 42nd Street: The Bright Light Zone*. Unpublished study, City University of New York, 164–216.

Jacobs, J. 1961: *The Death and Life of Great American Cities*. New York: Vintage Books.

Judd, D. R. and Fainstein, S. S. (eds.) 1999: *The Tourist City*. New Haven, CT: Yale University Press.

Kalil, J. M. 2000a: Order-out corridor: city's anti-crime zone may expand. *Las Vegas Review-Journal*, November 15, http://www.lvrj.com.

—— 2000b: "Order-out" law redrafted: city council ok's expanded corridor. *Las Vegas Review-Journal*, November 16, http://www.lvrj.com.

Kilian, T. 1998: Public and private, power and space. In A. Light and J. M. Smith (eds.), *The Production of Public Space*. Lanham, MD: Rowman and Littlefield, 115–34.

Las Vegas Convention and Visitors Authority (LVCVA) 2000: *Visitor Profile Study*. Prepared for LVCVA by GLS Research. Las Vegas: LVCVA.

Martinez, A. 1999: *24/7: Living It Up and Doubling Down in the New Las Vegas*. New York: Villard.

Mele, C. 1996: Globalization, culture, and neighborhood change: reinventing the Lower East Side of New York. *Urban Affairs Review* 32: 3–22.

Moehring, E. P. 1989: *Resort City in the Sunbelt*. Reno, NV: University of Nevada Press.

Morgan, R. E. 1999: Free to strip. *City Journal* 9 (2): 80–7.

Mumford, L. 1938: *The Culture of Cities*. New York: Harcourt, Brace.

New York State Urban Development Corporation (UDC) 1984: *42nd Street Development Project: Draft Environmental Impact Statement*. New York: UDC.

New York Times 1980: A new opening for Times Square. *New York Times*, July 15, p. A18.

Parker, R. E. 1999: Las Vegas: casino gambling and local culture. In D. R. Judd and S. S. Fainstein (eds.), *The Tourist City*. New Haven, CT: Yale University Press, 107–23.

——2000: Las Vegas: an all-American city (book review essay). *Urban Affairs Review* 35: 856–9.

Reichl, A. J. 1999: *Reconstructing Times Square*. Lawrence, KS: University Press of Kansas.

Sante, L. 1991: *Low Life*. New York: Vintage.

Schiff, S. and Leibovitz, A. 1996: Showgirls. *New Yorker*, January 29, pp. 69–77.

Senelick, L. 1991: Private parts in public places. In W. R. Taylor (ed.), *Inventing Times Square*. New York: Russell Sage Foundation, 329–53.

Sennett, R. 1970: *The Uses of Disorder*. New York: Vintage.

Sharp, E. 1996: Culture wars and city politics: local government's role in social conflict. *Urban Affairs Review* 31: 738–58.

Smith, N. 1992: New city, new frontier: the Lower East Side as Wild, Wild West. In M. Sorkin (ed.), *Variations on a Theme Park*. New York: Noonday, 60–93.

Sorkin, M. (ed.) 1992: *Variations on a Theme Park*. New York: Noonday.

——1999: Gambling on the triumph of "taste" in Las Vegas. *Metropolis*, April, http://www.metropolismag.com.

Spanier, D. 1992: *All Right, Okay, You Win*. London: Secker and Warburg.

Steinhauer, A. 1997: Board endorses anti-handbill rule. *Las Vegas Review-Journal*, January 15, p. 1B.

Thompson, H. S. 1971: *Fear and Loathing in Las Vegas*. New York: Vintage.

Venturi, R., Scott Brown, D., and Izenour, S. 1972: *Learning from Las Vegas: The Forgotten Symbolism of Architectural Form*. Cambridge, MA: MIT Press.

Warner, M. 1999: *The Trouble with Normal*. New York: Free Press.

Wilson, E. 1991: *The Sphinx in the City*. Berkeley: University of California Press.

Wolfe, T. 1965: *The Kandy-Kolored Tangerine-Flake Streamline Baby*. New York: Farrar, Straus, and Giroux.

——1981: *From Bauhaus to Our House*. New York: Pocket Books.

Zukin, S. 1995: *The Cultures of Cities*. Cambridge, MA: Blackwell.

——et al. 1998: From Coney Island to Las Vegas in the urban imaginary: discursive practices of growth and decline. *Urban Affairs Review* 33: 627–54.

17

Efficacy or Legitimacy of Community Power? A Reassessment of Corporate Elites in Urban Studies

Leonard Nevarez

In this chapter, I engage the poststructural turn as an urban political economist to reassess one of urban studies' venerable topics, the "urban elite." Older understandings of urban elites have not necessarily outlived their theoretical value, since urban economies and governance continue to be shaped as urban political economy has theorized, by individuals whose power derives from their relations to dominant social institutions. However, urban elites must be reevaluated in light of two developments. First, the sociospatial and poststructural perspectives have challenged important assumptions of the urban elite concept and shifted its analytical focus from efficacy in community power to the legitimacy that urban elites articulate in local politics. Second, recent changes in corporate organization associated with the "new economy" have destabilized the traditional constitution of urban elites. In certain kinds of places, the interests of urban elites, the texture of their power, and the local politics they mobilize raise new questions for research that the poststructural turn frames usefully. I will sketch a new analytical framework using a case study of urban elites in Southern California cities with growing technology-based economies.

Within the social sciences, an elite, urban or otherwise, refers generically to an individual or group ranked highly within any social hierarchy. The concept has often been narrowed to a political one, characterizing a particular answer to the question, "Who governs?" Following Weber, individuals derive legitimate authority and therefore govern most stably through institutions, be they traditional or formal rational. In the neo-Weberian sense, an

I thank several people for their input on this chapter. Krista Paulsen, Rich Appelbaum, and Dick Flacks offered incisive questions and comments on prior drafts. An early discussion with Christopher Mele helped me understand how the issue of legitimacy is central to the new turn in urban studies. I assume responsibility for all the remaining errors and shortcomings.

elite refers to an institutionally derived position with a greater concentration of power than the rest of a social collectivity. Since Weber submerged his normative concerns about elites to a value-free science, scholars have taken contrasting value positions regarding elites, from *a priori* acceptance (e.g., structural functionalism) to moral critique (e.g., C. Wright Mills's power elite), and from ambivalent assertions of modern impersonality (e.g., William Whyte's organization man) to revisionary claims about residual privacy (e.g., G. William Domhoff's ruling class).

A more fundamental issue for the neo-Weberian approach to elites is how amenable institutions are to human will. An instrumental view posits that elites can successfully mobilize the institutions that empower them toward their conscious goals. The current scholarly wisdom about bureaucracy, by contrast, holds that institutional governance is not always transparent to or manipulable by elites. In either case, these and other neo-Weberian approaches to elites foreground a paradigmatic concern for *efficacy*, or elite capacity to effect outcomes that advance the interests of governing institutions. They presume a mechanistic view of social order, which can be analyzed or "read off" from governing institutions, organization and process, even as they leave open empirical questions of which social spheres yield governing institutions (political bodies, governmental bureaucracies, private corporations, etc.) and what level of social order constitutes institutional interest (individual human actors or social collectivities).

Elites of Urban Governance

The elite concept moved onto the urban studies agenda with the community power debates of the 1950s and 1960s. Specifically, the "elitist" school (e.g., Hunter 1953) claimed a core group of business and political actors regularly and successfully promoted their interests through city government. The "pluralist" school (e.g., Dahl 1961) countered there were no urban elites, only interest groups who prevailed on certain issues but neutralized each other in the policy aggregate. Their debate highlighted the question of efficacy yet eventually reached an impasse over paradigmatic differences over which institutions governed cities. Following political science's tenets, pluralists presumed that urban governments were *prima facie* institutions of authority. Elitists found that urban governance lay beyond government in the hands of public–private coalitions, but they failed to theorize the collective interests shared by these coalitions (Alford and Friedland 1985).

In the 1970s, urban political economists transcended the community power debate by shifting the primary question from "Who governs?" to "How do cities generate wealth in capitalism?" Whereas structuralists like David Harvey (1985) theorized macro-level logics of capitalism, humanists revived the urban elite concept by asking, "How do cities generate wealth for capitalists?" Like the earlier elitists, urban political economists gathered robust evidence for hegemony over city affairs by local businessmen and their political allies, but they also developed theories of urban governance by extending neo-Weberian premises to a neo-Marxian problematic. The social production of urban space, that is, *city building*, was now the institution through which urban elites exercised power. Probably the most notable theory of urban elites was Molotch's growth machine, a mutually reinforcing complex of urban actors with common interests in intensifying land-based exchange values through urban growth: higher rents for rentiers, increasing tax revenues for local governments, increased circulation for local newspapers, more jobs for local trade unions, and so on (Molotch 1976).

Interestingly, growth machine theory's appearance roughly coincided with the end of an era when urban capitalist economies were locally centered. During its initial formulations, urban political economy presumed this centrality by pointing to parochial elites promoting the growth of cities. However, not all capitalists were parochial; for one, industrial "big business" often had markets of national or larger scope. Still, they were generally tied to particular localities for at least the Fordist era through sunk capital costs (in factory plants, headquarter offices, etc.), dependence on local labor relations (skilled, nonunionized, etc.), and civic sentiment (capitalists as local "first families"). Such parochial interests created social relations of "local dependence" (Cox and Mair 1988) that bound urban elites together during this early era. What was "good for the city" (local exchange values) was also good for locally based industrial capital. Big business, parochial capital, and their civic and political allies cohered as urban elites with mutually reinforcing interests in urban governance.

Disarticulations of urban economies and elites

As family capitalism declined, the multinational corporation emerged, and a one-world economy absorbed global labor and consumer markets, the era of cohesive urban elites passed irrevocably. Transportation and communication advances now give big businesses more choices about where and how to locate capital. To boost profits, they can exploit geographical differences in wage levels, labor unionization and unrest, taxation, regulation, and other local costs of doing business. The rootless nature of capital and its management have caused urban scholars to ponder for at least fifteen years whether urban agency, urban politics, and, implicitly, urban elites matter anymore (e.g., Gottdiener 1987; Lauria 1996).

Yet because city building still dictates the terms of urban governance, urban elites have not disappeared theoretically. Instead, as the local interests of big businesses diverge from their parochial counterparts, urban elites have disarticulated into two tiers (as even Molotch acknowledged a decade later [Logan and Molotch 1987]). By commanding the capital investment that sets local economies in motion, big business comprises the first tier of urban elites, although its power is increasingly exercised remotely and impersonally. With economic and social investments fixed to particular localities, growth coalitions comprise the second tier, exercising active hegemony over urban affairs as the agents for the first.

Despite this theoretical refinement, the urban elite concept has maintained continuity with its earlier neo-Weberian formulations. Mechanistic and instrumentalist assumptions are upheld by a view of corporations as rational actors that discern economic and political differences across cities and regions and make capital investment decisions based on bottom-line cost–benefit considerations. These assumptions appear, for example, in the recent field of urban regime research, which examines how coalitions of private and public actors coordinate different local agendas, different capacities for power, and different degrees of local dependence to exercise urban governance. In short, efficacy still frames the urban political economy approach to urban elites.

Critiques of the urban elite concept

While mainstream scholars sustained the pluralist denial of urban elites, on the left the urban elite concept's neo-Weberian premises were first undermined in the 1980s by the sociospatial critique of urban political economy. Gottdiener (1985) especially argued that city building does not reflect a mechanistic logic of capitalism or even capitalists; instead, it involves complex dynamics of social conflict and dysfunction beyond the rationale of any institution, much less its human agents. At the microlevel of urban governance, for example, urban elites do not necessarily cohere into a single growth coalition but often fragment into rival growth networks. Their intraurban competition for increasing rents generates uncontrolled growth and other social costs (congestion, pollution, crime, etc.) that are externalized onto residents, thus reflecting an essential contradiction in the social production of urban space (Gottdiener 1985: 214).

Although corporate elites may exploit this contradiction, its logic and process cannot be read off from their instrumental goals. Ultimately, the sociospatial critique has not so much rejected as refined the urban political economy analysis of urban space and governance by reviving a dialectical framework employed by the latter school's intellectual predecessors, Marx and Lefebvre. It challenges the idea that urban elites *effectively* command urban governance, but it retains a theoretical voluntarism by acknowledging that the will of urban elites in both tiers still matters, if not in ways they necessarily anticipate.

By contrast, the more recent poststructuralist turn in urban studies transcends the urban elite problematic by shifting the urban studies agenda from the mechanisms to the meanings of urban space and power. Following Foucault, urban poststructuralism asserts the local discursive construction of domination and resistance, which theoretically precedes and empirically informs (some would say constitutes) actors, culture, and structure. Consequently, the logic of power and resistance cannot be analyzed or read off from the workings of dominant institutions alone. Urban poststructuralism challenges the validity of universal knowledge projects and validates place-specific analyses of dominance, transgression, and their representation on the margins (Shields 1991). For these and other reasons, urban poststructuralists have to date shown little interest in theorizing the general logic and contradictions of the center, be it urban capitalism or its structural agents, urban elites. The poststructural turn has compelled urban political economy and sociospatial scholars to recognize their paradigmatic questions reveal only so much.

Parallel with or responding to urban poststructuralism, many scholars have begun examining a heretofore analytical silence: the local meanings and cultures that inform urban production and governance. Most have not specifically invoked the poststructural turn but addressed its concerns through neo-Weberian political economy vocabularies with their mechanistic and voluntaristic assumptions. Urban regime researchers, for example, arguably espouse a poststructural insight in their collective premise that although growth may be a generic interest of growth coalitions, its form and execution require shared understandings among coalition members that are locally constructed (Stone 1993). These may be accomplished through practices of political cooperation that are charged with local racial relations (Whelan et al. 1994). Additionally, urban experts and consultants may peddle growth tactics and goals that gain advocates through local discourses of political "doability" and persuasive representations of "success" in other places (Molotch 1993: 36).

A smaller group of political economy and sociospatial scholars has explicitly employed a poststructural vocabulary to describe the legitimacy of certain forms of urban development and power that make some urban futures likely and others not. Urban conflict, competitiveness, and decline are not self-evident to business decision-makers, politicians, and residential migrants but are instead understood through historical discourses of ambivalence about cities (Beauregard 1993; Mele 2000). By contextualizing urban power and *legitimacy* within larger discourses of urbanism and domination, these scholars expand the sociospatial critique of elite efficacy in urban governance to the realm of representation. That is, if governance is beyond the grasp of urban elites, is the same not also true for representations of the city or urban capital (Gottdiener et al. 1999: 22)? Although this critique appears to undermine the theoretical value of the urban elite concept as constructed by urban political economy, it also opens up a theoretical space to examine urban elites as *objects*, not subjects, of representation. Before I show how this can be done, I first describe recent changes in corporate organization under the new economy that make such an analysis urgent.

Reconstructing Urban Elites in the New Economy

By "new economy" I refer to the recent ascendance of software design, the production of cultural content (for the entertainment industry, the World Wide Web, etc.), e-commerce, and the advanced professional services that facilitate these and more conventional sectors. Most growth coalitions view these sectors as desirable engines of economic development because their employees earn higher than average wages that trickle down into local economies, and because their "virtual" work creates relatively few hazardous byproducts or land uses. Consequently, growth coalitions target software chief executive officers (CEOs), entertainment executives, professionals, and others in the executive class of new economy sectors as the new tier of urban elites to replace yesteryear "captains of industry."

Industrial reconstruction in the new economy

However, new economy executives are institutionally constituted differently than their industrial predecessors in at least three ways that I now characterize with broad strokes. First, new economy executives preside over relatively more amorphous and impermanent corporations. They increasingly view competitive advantage less as material assets to be owned and amortized and more as organizational competencies that are transient or even accidental to the firm. In this setting, production is organized around fluid constellations of human capital. For example, a small software firm may create a successful product, license or sell it to a larger company through a merger agreement, then retain and reconstitute its original employees in a new firm that designs a new product. One consequence is that most new economy firms are smaller than their big business predecessors. The visibility of corporate giants like Oracle or Disney obscures how 81 percent of Silicon Valley (Santa Clara County) software firms and 91 percent of Hollywood (Los Angeles County) entertainment firms have fewer than twenty employees (US Department of Commerce, Bureau of the Census: *County Business Patterns 1997*). While a small core of large firms provides financing, distribution, marketing, and other essential activities in the commercialization of a product, the highest "value-added" stages of industrial production are often performed by small and impermanent companies (Collins 2000).

Second, new economy firms assume this diminished and mercurial form because cities and regions do much of their organizational work. In industrial districts like Wall Street, Silicon Valley, and Hollywood, firms can avail themselves of the specialized production niches, skilled labor pools, creative milieu, and other external economies that emerge as a critical mass of firms and employees agglomerate (Christopherson and Storper 1989; Sassen 1991; Saxenian 1994). This lets corporations forego many costly activities like workforce training, basic research, and component production that traditional industrials produce in-house, an advantage when responding to uncertainty in product demand and regulatory environments. What they lose in workplace control, corporations gain in flexibility and speed. The shift from corporate to geographical organization imbues firms with new kinds of local dependence on specialized labor markets, information, and other forms of human capital.

Third, industrial deconstruction occurs within the corporate workforce, where occupational categories and status distinctions are increasingly fuzzy. For example, a software designer can work at one firm, consult for a second, become a director on a third firm executive board, and then leave the first to start up a fourth firm. An important condition here is the shortage of skilled labor in expanding new economy sectors, which makes attracting human talent a priority for firms. Whereas industries have addressed talent shortages collectively (e.g., lobbying for increased immigration of skilled foreign workers), firms accommodate them individually by refashioning the corporation to suit labor market demands. After competitive salaries and stock options, these entail lifestyle preferences that explain much of the hip environment characteristic of the dot-com workplaces, for example: casual clothing, nontraditional architecture, game rooms, etc.

Of course, such workplace amenities also serve corporate needs (motivating employees to work long hours, facilitating nonhierarchical "team" collaboration, etc.) and reflect a labor market premium for younger employees. Nevertheless, they represent unprecedented concessions of hierarchical control and "professional" ethos to a tight labor market. For example, most top Wall Street investment banks have recently phased out formal dress codes in order to keep younger employees away from enticing dot-com opportunities (Jakobson 2000). New economy firms also satisfy employee lifestyle preferences through firm location. Especially for software and Internet firms that have a degree of mobility from industrial districts, firms may locate in amenity-rich locations to attract employees and satisfy corporate executives (Florida 2000).

Uncertainty for growth coalitions

These changes disrupt the usual relationship between corporations that control capital investment and growth coalitions who seek it. In place of conventional pro-business overtures, growth coalitions are left with three quandaries. First, what constitutes a "pro-business" environment in the new economy? When it meant minimizing material cost-factors, growth coalitions could offer fiscal incentives, expedite developments, force quiescence on local workers, and alter local land use and regulation to suit corporate demands. Yet as extraordinarily high rents and wage levels in Silicon Valley and Hollywood show, material cost-factors rarely make or break the bottom line in a firm's locational decision. The new economy is talent- not capital-intensive, and virtual work rarely entails sinking major investments into particular physical plants or land uses.

Second, what can growth coalitions do to promote regional specialization and other new forms of corporate local dependence? They often try to provide vital industrial infrastructure like telecommunications capacities, business incubators, or seed capital. However, few have the technical expertise or connections to insular business networks that make these useful. Furthermore, demand for this infrastructure rarely precedes local critical mass, belying the growth machine credo that "if you build it, they will come." These new dynamics of regional specialization deprive growth coalitions of their usual discourses of urban possibilism.

Third, and perhaps most importantly for my purposes, who are the new economy decision-makers that growth coalitions must now address? Whether heard by corporate CEOs, vice-presidents, or real estate divisions, traditional pitches for capital investment appealed to "corporate" rationales for minimizing material cost-factors out of the corporate bottom line. However, although corporate executives still ultimately green light where and how resources flow within and without the firm, they increasingly follow the dictates of human talent further down the corporate hierarchy. The power to control production and thus capital investment in the new economy is shifting from firm executives to what I call "elite workers": firm executives still, but also would-be entrepreneurs, project-based freelance workers, and other workers with commercial ideas and marketable skills.

I contend that changing corporate relations to regions and elite workers in the new economy have left growth coalitions with two crises. The first is a structural crisis of economic development: if minimizing material cost-factors no longer serves corporate interest at the highest value-added stages, then traditional "pro-business" growth coalitions may be handicapped. Underlying this is a second crisis of representation. When growth coalitions bring jobs and other apparent goods of capital investment, they represent to other growth coalitions and their own communities that they know and have successfully negotiated around corporations' local interests. These representations are often a crucial source of legitimacy in conflicts over local growth. However, these representations are threatened when executives control capital investment on behalf of elite workers, not the corporation. What are elite workers' locational interests? Are they a group which growth coalitions understand?

Reframing the problematic of the elite

Urban studies can regard the uncertainties facing growth coalitions as an opportunity to rethink the role of corporate elites in urban governance. Is a screenwriter who locates his small production company in a metropolitan exurb a member of a corporate elite? Does a software designer who locates her small start-up firm to a suburb really exercise elite power? The increment of her investment is dramatically smaller than the industrialists of old, and her locational rationale resembles lifestyle decisions more than a corporate concern for a "pro-business" environment. In short, she appears to be exercising *market* power as a consumer of lifestyle, not elite power.

Should urban studies abandon the urban elite concept when referring to new economy executives' ambiguous location decisions? I believe not, for two reasons. First, capital investment still drives urban economies and mobilizes growth coalitions, thereby giving even freelancers a theoretical increment of economic and political power, so long as they localize capital generated elsewhere. Second, the elite concept also invokes normative claims about the (il)legitimacy and accountability of power that I do not want to abandon. Nor have growth coalitions and their opponents in urban movements abandoned them; when they *believe* new economy executives are conventional urban elites, they hold them accountable to competing standards of elite behavior. These points suggest an analytical framework for urban studies that infuses the urban political economy problematic of urban elites with the poststructural focus on local meaning. I illustrate this analytical framework with a case study of discourses about "urban elites" in the new economy, to examine how locals perceive the nature, motives, and legitimacy of the power exercised by elite workers.

Elite Discourses in the Quality-of-life District

My setting is the coastal California communities of Santa Monica, Santa Barbara, and San Luis Obispo. My data come from roughly a hundred interviews conducted between 1996 and 2000 with new economy executives, local business leaders, and political activists in these three places as well as secondary sources. These places share two aspects that make them useful sites to examine discourses about new economy urban elites. First, they have witnessed recent growth in new economy sectors like software design, high-technology, and entertainment production at levels ranging from critical mass (in Santa Monica) to quite modest (in San Luis Obispo). They also have small to middling populations and territories and lack the fiscal resources or infrastructures that make metropolises and large cities more enticing places to do business. They thus exemplify the suburban and exurban landscape of the new economy where quality-of-life amenities are paramount. To narrow my analytical focus, I will concentrate on their local software, computer design, and Internet sectors (henceforth, "software"). Second, their growth coalitions have historically been checked by sophisticated citizen movements that advocate environmental preservation, slow growth, and (in Santa Monica) rent control. These liberal movements frequently wrest urban governance from growth coalitions long enough to implement policies promoting growth limits, development linkages, and social services. These local controversies offer useful sites to study contesting local interpretations over new economy growth and urban elites.

Quality-of-life migrants

The basis of Santa Monica, Santa Barbara, and San Luis Obispo's place in the new economy begins to varying degrees with how residents and visitors generally equate their beaches, wilderness, architectural distinctions, cultural institutions, and village environs with a "high quality of life." These amenities are not intrinsically desirable but rather have been socially constructed as such through the heavy place-mythmaking of Southern California, as Hollywood films and television have promulgated images of coastal landscapes, outdoor recreational opportunities, and a socially "freer" lifestyle than most places for much of the twentieth century. More regional distinction comes from their contrast to the sprawl, congestion, and suburban homogeneity that characterize much of metropolitan California, out of which a great number of residents have migrated.

Software firms from Silicon Valley and other industrial districts are only the latest to participate in this migration, their numbers growing through a patterned course of events. In the 1980s and 1990s, a first generation of software entrepreneurs and CEOs started up or relocated firms in these places, which were then relatively uncharted territory for software. The industry's affinity for telecommunication and telecommuting, and local infrastructure like regional airlinks to Silicon Valley and research universities, were necessary but insufficient factors in those early location decisions. These pioneer migrants also needed sufficient status in the industry (usually having previously run one or more Silicon Valley firms) to be assured they would remain "connected" to industry centers at remote distances. Their subsequent prosperity in the industry would bring jobs and publicity to the three localities.

Like the elite workers and firms who followed them, pioneer migrants did not view their location decisions in terms of satisfying corporate needs for proximity to external economies of subcontractors, workers, or creativity. Instead, they saw themselves as affluent downshifters (Schnor 1998) taking a lifestyle reward for years in the better-paying but more hectic trenches of Silicon Valley. They also gambled that their personal decision made corporate sense in the context of a tight labor market. As a Santa Barbara software executive told me:

> When I talk to Santa Barbara-based entrepreneurs, I think virtually all of them have made a decision that they want to be in a place with a high quality of life for their family. Basically they make the decision for their family, and then subsequent to that, they say: "Gee whiz, if it appeals to me on this level, it will probably appeal to employees on this level."

Subsequent decisions by elite workers made Santa Monica, Santa Barbara, and San Luis Obispo what I call "quality-of-life districts": new economy enclaves where firms are locally dependent not on agglomeration economies but on quality-of-life amenities that suit labor market demands (Nevarez 1999). There are two variations on the sequence of events that creates quality-of-life districts. First, some migrants to Santa Monica, Santa Barbara, and San Luis Obispo are local. Although spin-offs and entry-level graduates from local universities never leave and thereby never directly experience quality-of-life pushes out of metropolitan industrial districts, they migrate theoretically via the global labor markets that are clustered in Silicon Valley. Second, Santa Monica represents a mixed quality-of-life/industrial district. Given its central location within Southern California's "Digital Coast," locating there makes corporate business sense, since software firms can access external economies made possible by the specialized critical masses in technology, entertainment, and their overlaps in Internet content. Still, with many potential metropolitan neighborhoods where relocating and start-up firms could potentially locate, Santa Monica's regional distinction was set in motion partly by quality-of-life concerns. In the early 1990s entertainment studios and large firms left "blighted" Los Angeles neighborhoods like Hollywood proper for metropolitan edge cities like Santa Monica. Its more recent popularity as a residence for software and entertainment workers reflects the work–lifestyle synergy characteristic of the quality-of-life district.

Contesting claims about "software elites"

Many residents claim to understand and share elite workers' personal desire to find a way to work and live out of Santa Monica, Santa Barbara, or San Luis Obispo. They recognize themselves socioeconomically in these newcomers, since lifestyle migrants to these places have long had privileged levels of education, home ownership, and income derived from education, research, government, arts and culture, high-end business services, retirement, and even inheritances – all livelihoods outside growth-dependent urban economies.

In the research sites, the demographic proclivity to prioritize postmaterial concerns (Abramson and Inglehart 1995) intersects with the local construction of quality of life to sustain a level of political awareness and activism that empowers environmentalist and slow-growth movements in the street and at the ballot box – a familiar outcome in places with such demographic patterns (cf. Protash and Baldassare 1983; Clark and Goetz 1994). I do not want to overstate this correlation between privileged socioeconomic background and liberal activism in part because the new software migrants destabilize it, as I will later show. Yet in my research sites, it is a prevailing belief in the worldview of local citizen movements, a bit of "common sense" reinforced by high-profile role models (for example, the celebrity and retired executive spokespersons for various left-to-liberal campaigns), and the genteel tone of many local nonprofits. This perceived association gives many local liberals reason to believe they understand the new economy dynamics of capital investment better than their pro-growth adversaries. Even more, it builds an expectation that the newcomers will share their political viewpoint and support the preservation and integrity of local amenities, services, and environment.

Although liberal activists claim to get such personal reasons for migration, some of the newcomers' roles as corporate executives make them less comfortable. Used to hearing corporate executives and spokespersons lambaste their local policies, these activists find software executives' intentions rather ambiguous. They want to know whether the "software elites" will support or attack the policies that protect local quality of life. To paraphrase using my theoretical vocabulary, will "software elites" act upon personal or corporate interests?

For their part, growth coalitions have historically claimed that "anti-business" land-use regulations, development linkages, and activism threaten their localities' chances in attracting capital investment. In their lexicon, "quality of life" often means office and residential developments with palm trees and commanding views. Like growth opponents, they are used to negotiating with corporate executives over developments, jobs, and politics and so do not fully understand the new role that amenities play in stimulating new economy investment.

Thus, growth coalitions look to the new software executives for "pro-business" articulations of corporate interest, whereas liberal activists hope they exemplify a new breed of enlightened elites. These conflicting claims embody two kinds of contestation: the first over the politics of growth and economic development, the second over the meaning of corporate elites. In a telling anecdote, a Santa Barbara politico recalled an instance when growth opponents seized the political high ground from under the local Chamber of Commerce:

> [The Chamber of Commerce] did their surveys, which we used a lot in [our] fights, that showed them that . . . the main reason they came here was the quality of life, [but] the main thing they hated was the regulatory structure. Well, come on, folks! Put two and two together!

It is not clear, to me at least, how "two and two" unambiguously add up in favor of growth opponents, as this politico claims they do. His statement suggests another view, that software executives may articulate both conventional corporate interests while remaining personally committed to pursuing personal lifestyle preferences. Nevertheless, in *claiming* that growth opponents understand what new economy executives want from the locality better than growth coalitions, he enlists elite legitimacy to the slow-growth side.

On more systematic fronts, growth coalitions and their opponents scrutinize corporate and executive behavior for signals about which side the newcomers are on. Both sides fail to comprehend fully the new roles for regions and elite workers in capital investment – a discursive silence that fuels their contestation over "software elites." On the pro-growth side, chambers of commerce establish new subcommittees to create value for software firms and steer them around the local "anti-business" waters of land-use zoning and linkage policies. In return, the chambers hope to acquire new members and revenues, broaden their local business networks and scan, and raise their status *vis-à-vis* competing growth coalitions. Yet with few exceptions, the new software firms generally fail to respond to these chamber overtures.

On the slow-growth side, environmental groups look to the new firms for philanthropy and endorsements of the alternative "pro-business" rhetoric that sells the virtues of environmental amenities and growth limits. Instead, their solicitations yield insignificant money, voluntary service, or political support (Nevarez 2000). Both sides also look at local campaign contributions to see which vision of local politics the new firms endorse: a conservative government that gets out of businesses' way, or an activist government that limits growth and preserves the environment. Again, what they find instead is almost no interest by the newcomers. The most visible corporate responses follow "old economy" controversies attributed to software firms, such as real estate proposals that I describe below.

Inarticulate urban elites

Significant support for either political side fails to arise because the new software firms have few forms of local dependence that would lead them to cast their lot one way or the other. The reasons usually reflect the absence of prior industrial and urban development, which attracted software firms to begin with. The land-use needs of software firms in the quality-of-life district are sufficiently routine (e.g., commercially zoned, not extensive, devoid of environmental regulations) to be met on the local real estate market without governmental intervention. They do not find the vital networks of talent and specialized services in local business groups like they might in industrial districts. Their overall lack of corporate concern for "pro-business" social relations in Santa Monica, Santa Barbara, and San Luis Obispo does not mean software firms are devoid of local dependence whatsoever; their attraction to local amenities distinguishes them from the truly mobile, bottom-line-fixated corporation familiar to globalization. However, this local dependence is organized through the labor market, not the corporation. Thus, software executives, whose own authority comes from their labor market status, have difficulty in articulating "corporate" interests in anything local, much less in "pro-business" social relations.

The characteristic exception occurs with corporate real estate projects. These are rather infrequent in the quality-of-life district, where most software firms are too small, too routine in their land uses, and too short-term-oriented to want to develop particular land parcels and expend money, time, and political energy into the development process. However, during my research period a few executives from larger firms unveiled proposals for design studios, R&D campuses, and other real estate projects with architectural distinctions and commanding views of undeveloped coasts, hillsides, and downtowns. Their projects mobilized allies in growth coalitions and galvanized heated local protest, thereby illustrating a very conventional capacity of corporate elites.

Whether the projects eventually got built or not (examples were too few to discern regular outcomes), these software executives made some concessions to the slow-growth camp, such as making campaign donations to liberal politicians, placing an executive on environmental nonprofit directorates, or directly mitigating some project aspect. Executives also faced dissension within their local ranks, from which a few added their voices to the opposition. Furthermore, the (very few) software executives who participated in growth coalitions contradicted some of their parochial counterparts by contending that opposition to real estate projects was not an ominous "bellwether" for the local industry. One executive observed that a Santa Barbara controversy over an extensive R&D campus proposal (which was eventually shelved):

> helped us determine who's the target we're trying to go for [when marketing the area to new software firms]. Are we trying to attract one-thousand-person companies or not? We decided we're not. One-thousand-person companies need more resources, more square footage, more housing than we have to offer here. I think the twenty- to two-hundred-person company is more the size that all of the infrastructure here can support: transportation, the housing, the facilities where you can live or work. If you take an airplane and go over [suburban parts of Santa Barbara], there's a lot of open land there that's perfect for industrial parks, but now we're starting to build a place that says: "How does Santa Barbara make a difference if you're in a big box?"

Do these real estate projects support either growth proponents' or opponents' claims that they can represent the "software elites"? Few came away with such confidence; even fewer recognized that software executives can adopt conventional elite behavior while remaining personally committed to appreciating quality-of-life amenities. The latter insight was also lost on many software executives, who were often befuddled by local expectations that they should conform to either corporate or personal standards of behavior. In so doing, they failed to clear up the ambiguity of their behavior, thereby fueling the contest to represent the local interests of new economy executives.

Conclusion

To contextualize the analytical framework I have sketched, I quote one of the first urban political economists to address the poststructural turn:

> [C]ities are narrative objects. That is, a city is not like a person or a business corporation; it is not a subject that can represent itself. Rather, cities are objects of representation. *People* have to describe their nature, document their past, and predict their future. (Beauregard 1993: 188, emphasis added)

Beauregard is right about cities' inability to represent themselves, but in this chapter I have questioned the certainty with which people and corporations know and represent their own interests. By investigating the local discursive construction of urban production, governance, and legitimacy, urban poststructuralism asks a theoretical question that urban political economy alone cannot answer. The quality-of-life district suggests how far this question reaches. Not just urban landscapes and local cultures but actors' own structural interests can be objects of representation. That the impetus for representation has a structural basis does not overshadow this poststructural insight.

Specifically, new economy executives in the quality-of-life district make for ambiguous and inarticulate urban elites because their local interests are illegible to themselves and others. The labor market pursuits that explain to them why they and their firms appear in the quality-of-life district obscure their understanding of how they set urban economies in motion. Their local independence from "pro-business" social relations separates them from, and makes them unaware of, the parochial allies and discourses that corporate elites traditionally exploit. Still, new economy executives' privileged role in locating capital investment establishes their structural position as urban elites. Furthermore, some executives at certain times do behave as urban elites, flexing political muscles and mobilizing growth coalitions and "pro-business" discourses to advocate corporate real estate projects and other local goals. That they do so with little coordination and inconsistent results might indicate they are simply less powerful, that is, less effective urban elites than the big business of yesteryear. Although perhaps valid from an urban political economy perspective, this conclusion misses the mark if it assumes that new economy elite workers perceive their own interests in city building and urban governance.

What I have tried to show here is that a new structural mechanism, the capacities of labor markets to organize production and capital investment in new economy sectors, gives elite workers a political economic stake in the quality-of-life district different from the conventional corporate interest in "pro-business" social relations. This is not necessarily apparent to many locals, who hold software executives to urban elite standards of behavior and legitimacy. The roots of this discursive problem are structural, since elite workers' independence from "pro-business" social relations allows them discretion in responding to the political controversies they engender (Nevarez forthcoming). This makes for a crisis of representing elite workers' local interests to themselves and others. Beauregard's narrating subjects of capitalism have lost their certainty, at least in the quality-of-life district.

The political futures that these new urban elites open are unclear. For one reason, my case study research design cannot determine what caused software executives to make concessions to growth opponents: effective agency by local opponents, political pragmatism by firms with exceptional local dependence (i.e., vulnerability to opposition), or other factors. However, what is clear is that the very problem of indeterminacy – here, the local contest over the meaning and legitimacy of "software elites" – framed the executives' action. Because the executives' elite workers were uncertain how they should respond as urban elites, it is possible their local interests were inscribed to some degree by one of either competing local interpretations: value-free development versus defense of quality-of-life amenities. How this informs subsequent representations of urban elites remains to be seen, since the future of my research sites is still being written. For this reason, I urge urban studies not to discard the urban elite concept, even as structural trends destabilize its mechanistic premises in settings like the quality-of-life district.

The elite concept has always been normative as well as scientific, and this former sense is shared by the social actors that social scientists examine. When elite workers are thought to be urban elites and are held to certain normative standards by locals in conflict, locals weave their contested interpretations into their own legitimacy conflicts over urban development. It is because people believe in and advance competing understandings of urban elites that the concept shapes the social realities studied by urban scholars.

Bibliography

Abramson, P. R. and Inglehart. R. 1995: *Value Change in Global Perspective.* Ann Arbor: University of Michigan Press.

Alford, R. and Friedland, R. 1985: *Powers of Theory.* New York: Cambridge University Press.

Beauregard, R. A. 1993: Representing urban decline. *Urban Affairs Quarterly* 29: 187–202.

Christopherson, S. and Storper, M. 1989: The effects of flexible specialization on industrial politics and the labor market. *Industrial and Labor Relations Review* 42: 331–47.

Clark, T. N. and Goetz, E. 1994: The antigrowth machine. In T. N. Clark (ed.), *Urban Innovations.* Thousand Oaks, CA: Sage, 104–45.

Collins, J. 2000: Built to flip. *Fast Company* 32 (March): 131.

Cox, K. R. and Mair, A. 1988: Locality and community in the politics of local economic development. *Annals of the Association of American Geographers* 78: 307–25.

Dahl, R. A. 1961: *Who Governs?* New Haven, CT: Yale University Press.

Florida, R. 2000: *Competing in the Age of Talent.* Report prepared for the R. K. Mellon Foundation, Heinz Endowments, and Sustainable Pittsburgh, http://www.heinz.cmu.edu/~florida/talent.pdf.

Gottdiener, M. 1985: *The Social Production of Urban Space.* Austin: University of Texas Press.

—— 1987: *The Decline of Urban Politics.* Newbury Park, CA: Sage.

—— et al. 1999: *Las Vegas: The Social Production of an All-American City.* Oxford: Blackwell.

Harvey, D. 1985: *The Urbanization of Capital.* Baltimore: Johns Hopkins University Press.

Hunter, F. 1953: *Community Power Structure.* Chapel Hill: University of North Carolina Press.

Jakobson, L. 2000: With investment bank brain drain on the rise, Salomon Smith Barney sucks up its pride and doles out cash. *Silicon Alley Daily*, May 24, http://www.siliconalleydaily.com.

Lauria, M. (ed.) 1996: *Reconstructing Urban Regime Theory*. London: Sage.

Logan, J. R. and Molotch, H. L. 1987: *Urban Fortunes*. Berkeley: University of California Press.

Mele, C. 2000: *Selling the Lower East Side: Culture, Real Estate and Resistance in New York City*. Minneapolis: University of Minnesota Press.

Molotch, H. 1976: The city as a growth machine. *American Journal of Sociology* 82: 309–30.

—— 1993: The political economy of growth machines. *Journal of Urban Affairs* 15: 29–53.

Nevarez, L. 1999: Working and living in the quality-of-life district. *Research in Community Sociology* 9: 185–215.

—— 2000: Corporate philanthropy in the new urban economy. *Urban Affairs Review* 36: 197–227.

—— forthcoming: *The New Guys on Main Street*. New York: Routledge.

Protash, W. and Baldassare, M. 1983: Growth policies and community status. *Urban Affairs Quarterly* 18: 397–412.

Sassen, S. 1991: *The Global City*. Princeton, NJ: Princeton University Press.

Saxenian, A. 1994: *Regional Advantage*. Cambridge, MA: Harvard University Press.

Schnor, J. B. 1998: *The Overspent American*. New York: Harper Perennial.

Scott, A. J. 1993: *Technopolis*. Berkeley: University of California Press.

Shields, R. 1991: *Places on the Margin*. London: Routledge.

Stone, C. N. 1993: Urban regimes and the capacity to govern. *Journal of Urban Affairs* 15: 1–28.

Whelan, R. K. et al. 1994: Urban regimes and racial politics in New Orleans. *Journal of Urban Affairs* 16: 1–21.

18

Dream Factory Redux: Mass Culture, Symbolic Sites, and Redevelopment in Hollywood

Jan Lin

Hollywood inhabits a seminal place in Los Angeles as well as the broader geography of American enterprise, cities, and popular culture. Hollywood carries a multiple valence as an economic, spatial, and symbolic site. Hollywood comprises an industry, place, and a "community." By industry I mean a factory complex, a dream machinery of cultural production comprising studios, actors, writers, and producers who control and represent some defining features of our collective life. By place I mean a spatial location, a "bright-light" district which is demarcated by buildings, boulevards, and symbol-laden sites. Communal sentiments are furthermore situated and enacted in the location of Hollywood through place-based rituals such as parades, premieres, and awards ceremonies. By "community" I mean a state of mind or an imagined community, a collective representation of dominant images, icons, and stories of American mass popular culture.[1] There are motion picture colonies and bright-light districts across America and the globe, but in few other places (save perhaps Hong Kong and Bombay's "Bollywood") does the machinery of mass culture so centrally typify the economy and identity of a metropolis, an ideology of collective life, and a particular landscape of global capitalism.

Following the "sociocultural" or symbolic interactionist school of urban sociology (Firey 1945; Wohl and Strauss 1958; Suttles 1984; Lofland 1991), the symbolic Hollywood persists in our urban collective consciousness through the cumulative durability of a number of mawkish seasonal rituals and suggestive sites. These include the Academy Awards, blockbuster film premieres at marvelous movie palaces such as the Grauman's Chinese Theater, celebrity hand and foot ceremonies in the Chinese Theater courtyard, sidewalk inscriptions on the Hollywood Walk of Fame, the Santa Claus Lane parade, and the penultimate iconographic landmark – the Hollywood sign – which fabulously advertises the metropolis from Mount Lee. Cultural spectacles and civic place history did not spring or evolve naturalistically out of Hollywood but were created and perpetuated by impresarios, showmen, entrepreneurs, and boosters, intent on serving private capitalist interest as much as public or community purpose. A study of Hollywood can thus be informed by the political economic perspective of the "new urban sociology" (Gottdiener and Feagin 1988; Logan and Molotch 1988), especially what I dub the "critical cultural school" (Zukin 1995; Gottdiener 1997), as we discern how metropolitan fortunes and identities under postindustrialism are increasingly derived from the fabrication of thematic sites and symbols. This chapter is meant to be a contribution to the critical cultural school.

From a critical cultural studies vantage point, a perspective on Hollywood is not necessarily place-based, being also represented through the semiotic cuisinart of supermarket tabloids and gushing television gossip serials such as "Access Hollywood" and "Entertainment Tonight." The international theme restaurant franchise, Planet Hollywood, invites association with cinema stars as part and parcel of an exclusive culinary and entertainment experience. This celebrity venture capitalizes upon the hegemonic position of Hollywood stars and film exports in the global cultural economy. The power of the Hollywood studios as a machinery of mass culture informs a number of trends associated with globalization discourse: (1) that culture industries are integral features of the new global economy, (2) that the culture industries and consumption-driven capitalism are dominated by a cadre of giant corporate players, and (3) that American cultural products dominate the global landscape of consumer capitalism (Sklair 1991; Barber 1995).

Hollywood is also politically and ideologically contested. As an industry and cultural representation, it is implicated in broader structures and discourses of capitalism, politics, and morality. Conservatives have derided Hollywood for its immorality (evangelicals in the 1920s), its radicalism (McCarthy in the 1950s), its liberal "cultural elitism" (Dan Quayle vs. "Murphy Brown" in the 1980s), and its permissive employment policies (Southern Baptist Convention vs. Disney Corporation in the 1990s). Artists and leftists have denounced Hollywood for its tendencies toward conglomeration and oligopolistic corporate control, its triviality, its tendency to quell artistic creativity in favor of mass profitability, and its lack of attention to, or misrepresentation of, racial and cultural minorities. Strikes and other labor struggles have periodically wreaked havoc on the industry (Clark 1995).

Like America's other major "bright-light" district, Times Square, Hollywood has recurrently attracted its antipodal mephisto, the raffish "red-light" district of tattoo parlors, cheap amusement arcades, and the sex industries, which are attracted by the high density of nocturnal urban sojourners. There is a marked disjuncture between the historic image of Hollywood as a glamorous celluloid "dream factory" and the reality of its human ecology as a rather seedy zone in transition, marked by infrastructural deterioration, commercial decline, and a motley "community" of residentially overcrowded immigrants, homeless youth, and urban transients. The tawdry underside to Tinseltown as a place populated by vacuous starlets and spectators, underemployed screenwriters, and megalomaniacal or tragically heroic studio moguls, has moreover been a recurring literary and cinematic representation such as in Nathaniel West's *The Day of the Locust* (1933), F. Scott Fitzgerald's *The Last Tycoon* (1941), and the more recent Coen Brothers' *Barton Fink* (1991). Californian historian Carey McWilliams described Hollywood as a "terrifying town . . . a place of opportunists and confidence men, petty chiselers and racketeers . . . of people desperately on the make" ([1946] 1973: 334). Another intellectual critique of Hollywood was perpetrated by the Frankfurt School of social theory, precursor to the "mass culture" critique of American capitalism and society.

The growing galaxy of literature on Los Angeles has until now emphasized urban planning (Dear et al. 1996; Scott and Soja 1996; Soja 1996), economic globalization (Sassen 1991; Keil 1998), social control in the "fortress city" (Friedmann and Wolff 1982; Davis 1990, 1998), or the simulated theme park character of the city (Baudrillard 1988; Sorkin 1992). Within urban studies, only Susan Ruddick's study (1996) of homeless youth and subcultural spaces has given sustained attention to Hollywood as a place, while Michael Storper (1989) has informed our understanding of the film industry. Through this analytical window on Hollywood, I intend to augment our understanding of Los Angeles as a world city while contributing to our theoretical and empirical understanding of the connections between globalization, culture, and urban sociology.

The Dream Factory: Mass Culture, Media Conglomerates, and Labor Struggles

Walter Benjamin, in his seminal essay, "The Work of Art in the Age of Mechanical Reproduction" (1936) (Benjamin [1955] 1968), critically reflected upon the emergence of the mass reproduction media (such as lithography, photography, and film), which had promoted the contemporary decay of what he perceived as the original "aura" of art and artistic experience. He stated:

> This image makes it easy to comprehend the social bases of the contemporary decay of the aura. It rests on two circumstances, both of which are related to the increasing significance of the masses in contemporary life. Namely, the desire of contemporary masses to bring things "closer" spatially and humanly, which is just as ardent as their bent toward overcoming the uniqueness of every reality by accepting its reproduction. Every day the urge grows stronger to get

> hold of an object at very close range by way of its likeness, its reproduction. Unmistakably, reproduction as offered by picture magazines and newsreels differs from the image seen by the unarmed eye. Uniqueness and permanence are as closely linked in the latter as are transitoriness and reproducibility in the former. To pry an object from its shell, to destroy its aura, is the mark of a perception whose "sense of the universal equality of things" has increased to such a degree that it extracts it even from a unique object by means of reproduction. ([1955] 1968: 223)

Where Benjamin saw the possibilities of a certain emancipatory potential deriving from the machineries of mass cultural reproduction, he also saw these freedoms as threatened by the emergence of fascism, which deployed mass aesthetics for military mobilization and ideological purpose. Fascist critics and social theorists of the Frankfurt School, Max Horkheimer and Theodor Adorno ([1944] 1988), who spent the war years as political refugees in Los Angeles, launched a harsher invective against what they called the American "culture industry" (defined as a system composed of film, radio, and television). This apparatus of "mass deception" was seen to be oligopolistically controlled by a cadre of studios such as Metro Goldwyn Mayer or Warner Brothers (as Ford and General Motors in the mass production of automobiles), and stunted powers of imagination and critical thought among its consumer audience.

The European critique of Hollywood has been historically matched by the assessments of American writers and intellectuals from the East Coast (such as John Dos Passos, William Faulkner, Aldous Huxley, and Dorothy Parker), who were drawn to the studios by the lucrative salaries offered for formulaic screen writing in the 1920s and 1930s, but often appalled at the corrupting effects on their artistic creativity.[2] The controversial "Hollywood as destroyer" legend is best personified by the experience of F. Scott Fitzgerald (Fine 1993: 3–6), who advantageously worked with the studios at the height of his career, but ended his life in indebted despair and drunkenness as an underemployed Hollywood screenwriter with his half-completed final manuscript, *(The Love of) The Last Tycoon*, which was posthumously published in 1941.

The work at which these writers labored was mundane, hackneyed screenwriting and adaptations for the kind of production conventions that typified early Hollywood, such as screwball comedies, musicals, gangster films, and detective *noir*. These genres persist, but were subsequently supplemented by family melodrama, westerns, and war films, up to the current predilection for blockbuster disasters, science fiction, teen films, and animation (Schatz 1983). The inclination in Hollywood (and its stepchild, network television) to serialize, sequelize, and routinize its production repertoires illustrates the fundamental nature of cinema (and other media such as print journalism, television, and radio) as a mass production machinery of icons, stories, and fantasies, a meaning implicit in the moniker, "dream factory."

This axiomatic tension between artistic creativity and industrial routinization relates to another fundamental problematic of the motion picture industry, the recurring tendency for a cadre of central players to dominate the production, distribution, and exhibitionary apparatus of the cultural production system. The US Justice Department has periodically brought antitrust legislation against the motion picture industry and related mass media, to reduce the concentration of power in an oligopoly of companies, a structure which impedes free enterprise in the marketplace of ideas, thus violating the Sherman and Clayton Antitrust Act and eroding the vitality of the First Amendment. Two landmark cases are relevant.

The first case, Motion Picture Patents Company, was taken against a cartel or trust led by Thomas Edison, Biograph Pictures, and fourteen other inventors who exploited their patents on cameras, projectors, film, and other integrated components, and completely dominated the nascent film industry. William Fox, an independent operator, filed an antitrust suit later joined by the Department of Justice that eventually reached the Supreme Court, which ruled against the Trust in 1918. Concurrently, a number of maverick independent companies armed with bootlegged equipment were emerging, some through the collusion of disgruntled Trust members. Seeking to evade Trust-ordered court injunctions, US marshals, and privately hired Pinkerton detectives, these independents gravitated to the hospitable climate of Los Angeles for their filming, a location which also afforded easy escape to the Mexican border if discovered and prosecuted.

The dismantling of the Trust paved the way for the emergence of the classic "Big Five" studios of the "golden age of Hollywood," a group which included Twentieth Century-Fox, Metro Goldwyn Mayer (MGM), Warner Brothers, RKO, and Paramount. Adolph Zukor of Paramount pioneered a system vertically integrating the three major stages of filmmaking – production, distribution, and exhibition – under one company, a structure which began to be emulated by the others. He established the "star system" with lucrative contracts to talent such as Mary Pickford, Douglas Fairbanks, and Gloria Swanson, fostering simultaneously both the studio's reputation and consumer loyalty. These stars of the silent film era, along with Charlie Chaplin, through the power of pantomime, christened the modern film industry as a universal language of mass culture which transgressed boundaries of cultural and linguistic difference in the polyglot immigrant working classes of America, the cinema's main audience.

Zukor, like other early studio entrepreneurs such as Harry Cohn, William Fox, Samuel Goldfish (later Goldwyn), Carl Laemmle, Marcus Loew, Louis B. Mayer, and the Warner Brothers, were all Jewish. Among the founding studio bosses, only Walt Disney was not Jewish. They typically came from East Coast careers in garments and haberdashery (Goldwyn had been a glove salesman, Zukor and Loew had been furriers [Hall 1998: 529]), where they learned tenacity and hard-sell techniques, or vaudeville, where they defined showmanship and were attuned to the dreams and aspirations of the immigrant masses. Neal Gabler (1988) presents the provocative thesis that the Jews, finding themselves impeded from mobility into the Eastern aristocracy, migrated westward and "invented Hollywood" as an "empire of their own" complete with their own palatial estates and conspicuous rituals of a *nouveau riche* society.[3]

The WASP public and cultural elite was both fascinated and threatened by the rapid rise of the enterprising, showy, movie "moguls," viewing them as "part splendid emperors, part barbarian invaders" (Sklar 1994: 46), thus labeling them with a cultural patina of megalomania, Jewish foreignness, immigrant coarseness, and non-Gentile permissiveness in the kind of morality they condoned. Hollywood was being nationally publicized through the scandalous behavior of personalities such as the film comedian Roscoe ("Fatty") Arbuckle, charged in 1921 with the murder of an actress at a raucous party abundant with bootleg liquor. Forming the Motion Picture Producers' Association, the studios retained the Postmaster Will "Deacon" Hays to litigate a clean-up campaign, which he obliged through a morals clause written into all acting contracts.

By 1925, the "Big Five" or the "majors" dominated in the production of "A" quality films, while an associated "Little Three" (Universal, Columbia, and United Artists) produced lower-budget "B" grade films. Acting in collusion, the Big Five controlled enough first-run theaters to maintain a profitable nationwide exhibition showcase for their shared production output (including the output of the Little Three, which were charged stiff distribution and exhibition fees). Control came through the use of contracted exhibitors or cinema chains in which the studios had partial investments or controlling interests. First-run movie houses, which got films first and charged higher prices, predominated in downtown bright-light districts, while second-runs went to neighborhood houses. The "formula picture" (of standardized genres such as dramas, romances, action pictures, westerns, shockers, and comedies) and the star system were central features of an effective mass manufacturing system that provided a total output of 400–500 feature-length films a year, which through sequential release fulfilled their block bookings in the retailing stage (Hall 1998; Litman 1998).[4]

This pattern of monopolization and price fixing in the film industry again incurred the intervention of the Antitrust Division of the US Justice Department beginning in 1938, which opened litigation against Paramount. An initial consent decree was decided, then the case reinstated in district court, followed by appeal to the Supreme Court, then a remand back to the district court, which in its climactic 1949 ruling ordered the studios to divest themselves of their cinema chains, thus severing the system of vertical integration. A competitive bidding system for motion picture licensing was suggested, but not mandated. The arrival of television at almost precisely the same point as the final Paramount ruling sealed the end of Hollywood's golden era. Suburbanization also wrought major changes in urban geography and the character of consumer demand for motion pictures. Hollywood the location and the industry suffered a major decline in the 1950s and 1960s of these combined trends. Hollywood's locational decline continued until the 1990s, but the industry has been through some complex and intriguing changes that defy facile categorization.

After divestiture of their exhibition complexes, Hollywood began a gradual move into network television programming. Profitability continued to decline in the 1970s, however, and studios began to divest themselves of property such as sound stages, back-lots, and film libraries.[5] This vertical disintegration (now occurring in the production rather than exhibition stage) spread through the industry as location (versus studio and back-lot) shooting began to proliferate. By the 1980s, independent studios such as Lucasfilm became powerful players, while in the 1990s, Miramax demonstrated an ability to produce award-winning films. The major studios, meanwhile, settled into a new system of subcontracting out most functions to a shifting terrain of specialist companies in preproduction, film processing, and postproduction activities. Storper (1989) finds this transition to "flexible specialization" in the film industry to be a paradigm of "post-Fordism" in the advanced capitalist economies.

There is evidence of continuing concentration of power, however, particularly on the distribution level. As table 18.1 reports, the top six film distributors maintained a major share of the market, from 80.4 percent in 1994 to 74.9 percent in 1999. It is significant to observe that the Disney Corporation (not among the major studios in the earlier era of Hollywood) has now become the most productive studio. Disney now owns the formerly independent Miramax, while Time Warner owns New Line Cinema. Ostensibly an independent studio, Dreamworks was actually founded by powerful players in the entertainment industry, including director Stephen Spielberg, ex-Disney chief Jeff Katzenberg, and record producer David Geffen.

Many observers recognize a growing recomposition of the motion picture industry into an entertainment industrial complex wherein the original studios have diversified through merger, acquisition, and sale into related markets such as network and cable television, publishing, recorded music, theme parks, professional sports, multimedia, and telecommunications (Storper 1989; Wasko 1994; Barber 1995; Litman 1998). This kind of interindustry linkage between both the "hardware" technologies of the mass media with the "software" programming content of related culture and entertainment industries is commonly known as "synergy" in management practice (Barnet 1994; Negus 1997). Single cultural products, such as films and television programs, are effectively marketed in multiple formats and effectively advertised through

Table 18.1 Domestic box-office market shares

Distributor	*1994*	*1995*	*1996*	*1997*	*1998*	*1999*	*1999 Revenues ($ millions)*
Disney	19.3	19.0	20.9	14.3	16.0	17.0	1,263.0
Warner	16.1	16.3	15.7	10.9	10.9	14.2	1,061.0
Universal[a]	12.5	12.5	8.4	9.9	5.5	12.7	943.0
Paramount	13.9	10.0	12.6	11.8	15.8	11.6	860.0
Fox[b]	9.4	7.6	12.5	11.2	10.6	10.8	802.0
Sony	9.2	12.8	11.1	20.4	10.9	8.6	637.0
Dreamworks	–	–	–	N/A	6.9	4.4	328.0
Miramax[c]	3.8	3.5	4.3	6.7	5.9	4.4	324.0
New Line[d]	6.2	6.6	5.0	6.2	7.8	4.2	313.0
MGM/UA	2.8	6.2	5.1	2.5	2.9	4.0	310.0
TOTAL	**93.2**	**94.5**	**95.6**	**93.9**	**93.2**	**91.9**	**6,841.0**

N/A: not available.
[a] Currently owned by Vivendi Seagram.
[b] Currently owned by News Corp.
[c] Currently owned by Disney.
[d] Currently owned by Time Warner.
Source: Standard and Poor, *Industry Surveys: Movies and Home Entertainment*, November 16, 2000.

linked promotional campaigns. This trend toward synergy has been accompanied by the increasing conglomeration of entertainment and media companies under the ownership of large diversified supercorporations.

Table 18.2 reports on the diversified activities of some of the largest entertainment and media conglomerates. Some examples include: (1) the 1966 purchase of Paramount by Gulf and Western (in 1994, Viacom bought both Paramount and Blockbuster Video); (2) the 1985 purchase of Fox Broadcasting by Rupert Murdoch's News Corporation; (3) Turner Broadcasting's 1985 purchase of MGM/United Artists; (4) Sony's 1989 purchase of Columbia Pictures; (5) Time Inc.'s purchase of Warner Communications in 1989 to create Time Warner; (6) the merger of Time Warner and America Online (AOL) in 2000, along with Time Warner and EMI Music Group; (7) the merger of Viacom and CBS TV in 2000; and (8) the acquisition of Seagram (which owns Universal Studios) by the French publishing company Vivendi in 2000.

The growing size of American media conglomerates threatens the global cultural endowment. American films, television programming, and recorded music dominate in overseas markets. The global reach of American media corporations has provoked the ire of nations such as China, France, and Iran, fostering allegations of media imperialism and fears of cultural hegemony, and practices of censorship, protectionism, or economic blockade. The global critique of Hollywood's domination in the world market is not new, having been voiced in the 1920s during the earlier phase of US motion picture indus-

Table 18.2 Diverse media and entertainment conglomerates

Industry	*AT & T*	*Cable Vision*	*Disney*	*General Electric*	*News Corp.*	*Sony Corp.*	*Seagram Corp.*	*Tribune Corp.*	*Time Warner*	*Viacom*
New movies			◆		◆	◆	◆		◆	◆
Film library			◆		◆	◆	◆		◆	◆
Theaters		◆				◆	◆			◆
TV shows			◆	◆	◆	◆	◆	◆	◆	◆
Broadcast TV stations			◆	◆	◆			◆	◆	◆
Broadcast TV networks			◆	◆	◆				◆	◆
Basic cable networks	◆	◆	◆	◆	◆		◆		◆	◆
Pay cable networks	◆	◆	◆		◆				◆	◆
Cable/satellite systems	◆	◆			◆				◆	
Radio stations/networks			◆							◆
Recorded music						◆	◆		◆	
Theme parks			◆				◆			◆
Pro sports		◆	◆					◆	◆	
Publishing			◆		◆			◆	◆	◆
Audio players						◆				
Video players						◆				
Retailing		◆	◆						◆	◆

Reflects assets as of October 2000. Mergers of AOL with Time Warner and Vivendi with Seagram Corp. were pending as of October 2000.
Source: Standard and Poor, *Industry Surveys: Movies and Home Entertainment*, November 16, 2000.

try growth. The American media conglomerates have grown bigger and more diversified, however, and the proliferation of their products abroad has been accelerated by ongoing revolutions in technologies of cultural reproduction, and the compression of time and space through innovations in telecommunications and transcontinental transport. As the mass culture critique has met globalization discourse in the 1990s, the critique of Hollywood has become both renewed and amplified.

Globalization also affects the film and television industry through the growing trend of "runaway production" to countries such as Canada, Australia, the United Kingdom, and Mexico, which have become attractive sites for location shooting, production, and postproduction because of lower labor and production costs, preferential exchange rates, subsidies, and tax incentives. A study commissioned by the Screen Actors' Guild and the Directors' Guild of America in 1999 found that $10.3 billion was lost to runaway production in 1998, with some 60,000 jobs lost in the three previous years (Screen Actors' Guild 2000).

Hollywood labor interests have not been quiescent as they are confronted by economic restructuring in the media and entertainment industries. There is a widespread feeling among Hollywood rank-and-file actors and writers of being bypassed by the economic boom of the 1990s at a time when corporate revenues were increasing sharply from new markets such as cable television, overseas markets, and the commercialization of the Internet. The Screen Actors' Guild (SAG) and the American Federation of Television and Radio Artists (AFTRA) staged a six-month strike in 2000 seeking to win "jurisdiction" for writers, actors, and directors over advertising revenue "residuals" for film and television programs and commercials that extend into cable, overseas, and Internet markets. Labor actions included pickets in Hollywood street locations and at headquarters offices of major advertising companies, as well as congressional lobbying in Washington, DC. Celebrity actors and actresses have joined rank-and-file actors and writers.

Symbols and Culture in Urban Theory

Milla Alihan (1938) is sometimes credited with initiating the "sociocultural critique" of human ecology theory. Walter Firey (1945) subsequently offered a codification of this perspective, through his attention to the way that certain places in central Boston (e.g., historic parks such as the "Commons," ancestral cemeteries, aristocratic quarters, and ethnic districts), withstood competitive real estate pressures in the central business district, through the strength of sentimental attachments and symbolic meanings ascribed to these sites by the populace. Richard Wohl and Anselm Strauss (1958) followed with an article that observed how the vast size and complexity of the metropolis could be reduced or simplified through certain iconographic landmarks (evoked also through verse, song, and literature) which symbolically represented the identity or "biography" of a city. To illustrate, the Hollywood sign and the Grauman's Chinese Theater are two major storied sites which personify the character of Los Angeles.

Gerald Suttles (1984) refined the sociocultural position by more systematically clarifying how urban culture is marked in the spatial quotidian (through statuary, place names, commemorated buildings, and bumper stickers) and generalized as collective belief (through journalism and popular cultural catchphrases, folklore, and sports legends). Urban boosters create the myths and artifacts which celebrate the memories of the founders, entrepreneurs, and heroes of the city, while authors, artists, and journalists (especially critics, columnists, and experts) formulate and qualify the tastes, aesthetics, and reputations of local culture.[6] Suttles blasts Firey for interpreting local urban culture retrospectively. Suttles sees culture not just serving a "residual" or "restorative" (1984: 283–6) function that gradually acquires the patina of antique or artifact, but something that is actively promoted, created, and interpreted by boosters, artists, and journalists in the "shock cities" of the American urban frontier.

The notion of "shock cities," which Suttles borrows from Asa Briggs, draws us close to the characterization that John Logan and Harvey Molotch (1988) offer of American cities as "growth machines," wherein place entrepreneurs and developmental elites promote public consent and sanction through the joining of civic boosterism with a rhetoric of value-free economic development. The sociocultural school could be strengthened by the kind of critique of capitalism offered by the "new urban sociology" (Zukin 1980; Gottdiener and Feagin 1988), which debunks human ecology for disregarding the centrality of political and economic interests in the process of urbanization and the discourses of urbanism. Critical cultural studies is increasingly part and parcel of the new urban sociology, as we discern the growing deployment of thematic and symbolic metaphors in urban development under postindustrialism (Zukin 1995; Gottdiener and Feagin 1988). More often the cities under advanced capitalism do not grow from the production of manufactured goods, but instead from their ability to competitively orchestrate the mass production and consumption of culture (through devices such as festival marketplaces, heritage tourism and urban theme parking, sports and convention complexes, and entertainment functions). A study of Hollywood as both a seminal apparatus and a location of mass cultural production can be a highly instructive case for analysis.

Hollywood the Place and Icon

Hollywood originated in 1887 as a subdivision developed by a Kansas prohibitionist named Horace Henderson (Harvey) Wilcox. The name was suggested by his wife Daieda, purportedly inspired through conversation with a woman passenger on a train bound for the East, who described her suburban Chicago summer home as Hollywood (Torrence 1979: 25). Driven by the need for water, the development was annexed to the City of Los Angeles in 1910, which was then relatively water flush with arterial wells and in the process of building the Owens River Aqueduct. The association with the movie industry became regularized during the 1910s, as the emergent independent studios began to locate there, fleeing the court injunctions issued by Edison's Trust.

The Hollywood Chamber of Commerce was formed in 1921, with its first major activity the formation of a special committee which convinced Hollywood Boulevard merchants to leave their lights on after 9 p.m., to stem the air of desolation that descended on the street each night and enhance the boulevard's image as the Great White Way of the West. Department stores, boutiques, and hotels were lured to the district. In 1924, the Retail Merchants' Bureau, a division of the Chamber of Commerce, instituted the Santa Claus Lane Parade, led by a movie celebrity in a sleigh drawn by reindeer. The pageant broadened to include marching bands, equestrian teams, public officials, and more film personalities, and began drawing larger crowds in the 1930s. It remains an important device of the Hollywood Chamber of Commerce to this very day, purportedly attracting 1 million spectators each year. Beginning about 1925, guides began sprouting along Hollywood Boulevard offering tours to the studios and the homes of the stars.

The Hollywood sign was originally erected in 1923 as a means of advertising Hollywoodland, a prestigious real estate subdivision financed by a syndicate that included Harry Chandler of the *Los Angeles Times*, a development which still rests below Mount Lee. The 50-foot-high and 30-foot-wide letters were initially conceived as an advertising gimmick that would only last a year, but carried on because of its popularity as a Los Angeles icon. Four thousand lightbulbs originally studded the border of each letter to brilliantly emblazon the Los Angeles night until 1939, when maintenance of the sign was discontinued. By 1949, serious dilapidation had set in (symbolizing also the film industry's uncertain fortunes with the Paramount antitrust case of 1948 and the growing impact of television). The Hollywood Chamber of Commerce stepped in and restored the sign without the last four letters to read just "Hollywood," but continuing deterioration led to recurring fund-raising campaigns in the 1960s and 1970s. The sign was designated a historic-cultural monument by the Los Angeles Cultural Heritage Board in 1973, and in 1978, a new campaign kicked off by a fund-raising dinner hosted by Hugh Hefner at the Playboy Mansion West ultimately brought in over $300,000 to finance demolition and erection of a modernized sign.

The Hollywood Walk of Fame is another iconographic device which is literally inscribed upon the sidewalks of Hollywood Boulevard and Vine Street.

It was conceived and patented by the Hollywood Chamber of Commerce in the 1950s as a promotional device specifically aimed at reglamorizing the fading luster of the district. The commemorative sidewalk is comprised of a sequence of charcoal terrazzo squares embedded with coral terrazzo stars outlined in brass, with each star's name also imprinted in brass inside the stars. A Hollywood Improvement Association was formed, which raised $1.25 million for the sidewalk and streetlight improvements through a special assessment on property owners. The first eight stars to be commemorated in the 1960 groundbreaking included Preston Foster, Joanne Woodward, Ernest Torrence, Olive Borden, Edward Sedgwick, Louise Fazenda, Ronald Coleman, and Burt Lancaster (Torrence 1979: 240). By the time that construction was completed sixteen months later, nearly 1,600 stars had been dedicated to personalities in five major artistic categories, including motion pictures, television, radio, recorded music, and live theater. Since then, a new star has been added each month to bring the current total to over 2,000.

Dream Palaces and Mass Spectacles

The prosperity of the 1920s had stimulated moviegoing, which in turn spurred film production and the construction of motion picture exhibition places. A succession of ostentatious Hollywood movie palaces were built in this era, including Sid Grauman's Million Dollar, Metropolitan, Egyptian, and Chinese Theaters, the Warner Brothers Theater, and the Hollywood Pantages. These spectacular pleasure palaces built upon a formula that theater manager Samuel "Roxy" Rothafel (formerly Rothapfel) had pioneered in New York City, at the Strand and Roxy Theaters, and penultimately, at Radio City Music Hall. Extravagant architecture, opulent interiors, and impeccable service were joined to create sensuous and refined environments that would elevate the moviegoing experience from its vaudeville and nickelodeon roots. Neal Gabler attributes this quote to Roxy: "The theatre is the thing, that is, the psychology of the theatre, its effect on the audience . . . The best pictures ever produced will never succeed in an unattractive environment" (1988: 96).

In Chicago, the Balaban brothers and Samuel Katz built a series of ornate movie palaces, including the Valencia, the Oriental, the Tivoli, the Riviera, and the Granada. The opening of the Riviera in 1924 near a streetcar transfer point in the prosperous north-side neighborhood of Uptown around an area of dance halls, cabarets, and arcades created a sensation, and Uptown became one of the definitive "bright-light" areas of Chicago during the Roaring Twenties (Gomery 1992: 45).

Back in Los Angeles, theater impresario Sid Grauman introduced the red-carpet "Hollywood Premiere" in 1922 at the Egyptian Theater, complete with searchlights and celebrities arriving in limousines. The Chinese Theater, which also showcased premieres, eventually became an American landmark when Grauman began promoting hand and footprint ceremonies to forever memorialize Hollywood stars in the cement of the front courtyard, with the opening honors going to Mary Pickford and Douglas Fairbanks in 1927. Considerable debate surrounds the original inspiration for this extravagant device,[7] but the ritual has endured to become a central spectacle which ensures the continued imprimatur of Hollywood as both focal location and collective representation in American popular life.[8]

The annual awards ceremony for the Academy of Motion Picture Arts and Sciences is perhaps Hollywood's most distinct seasonal spectacle, but has never been associated with a consistent location. The Roosevelt Hotel, across the street from the Grauman's Chinese Theater, was the site of the first Academy Awards ceremony in 1929. The event was then moved out of Hollywood except for two periods, 1944–6, when it was held at the Grauman's Chinese Theater, and 1951–60, when the Pantages Theater was employed. For the past three decades, the ceremonies have alternated between the Shrine Auditorium and the Dorothy Chandler Pavilion, which are both downtown.

Like sporting events, festivals, and performances, which occur seasonally throughout the urban milieu, Hollywood premieres, rituals, and award ceremonies generate Durkheimian moments of effervescence, when the spirit of our collective consciousness and group life percolates to the surface and insinuates itself. As cultural events, these rites also testify to the current fashion by which our urban culture is enacted, exhibited, and consumed through regularized procedures of entertainment, spectatorship, and tourism, as a break from the mundane realities of routinized labor processes. In a capitalist society increasingly marked by massification in commodity production as well as consumption, the mass media promote the possibilities for universal accessibility through reproductive technologies like film, cable television, videotape, and the Internet. While the act of cultural consumption has been hypothetically democratized, control over the production and distribution of cultural products is still threatened by the hegemony of some dominant corporate players. Our role as active participants has, moreover, been diminished relative to our growing status as passive spectators. The writing of the Situationist critic of commodity fetishism, Guy Debord, is here relevant:

> The agent of the spectacle placed on stage as a star is the opposite of the individual, the enemy of the individual in himself as well as in others. Passing into the spectacle as a model for identification, the agent renounces all autonomous qualities in order to identify himself with the general law of obedience to the course of things. ([1967] 1983: paragraph 61)

Set and costume designer Tod Hackett, at the climax of Nathaniel West's apocalyptic *The Day of the Locust*,[9] contemptuously observes the plague of mob behavior during a movie premiere at a fictitious Hollywood dream palace called "Kahn's Pleasure Dome" (a veiled reference to a fusion of the pleasure dome in Coleridge's "Kubla Khan" and Sid Grauman's Chinese Theater):

> At the sight of their heroes and heroines, the crowd would turn demoniac. Some little gesture, either too pleasing or too offensive, would start it moving and then nothing but machine guns would stop it. Individually the purpose of its members might simply be to get a souvenir, but collectively it would grab and rend. ([1939] 1962: 176)

Some have presumptuously interpreted the apocalyptic and orgiastic crowd at the conclusion of West's novel as a premonition of the urban disorder, racial disturbances, and spectacular celebrity scandals that characterize contemporary Los Angeles. Los Angeles has perennially bred a double-sided mythology of Edenic sunshine and dystopic *noir*. Similarly, at its metropolitan heart inhabits Hollywood, the dream factory which generates stories about the beautiful as well as the damned, a bright-light spectacle which inevitably attracts its devilish red-light antithesis, an economic and symbolic apparatus as praised for its profitability as it is politically denounced.

Redevelopment and the Reclaiming of Hollywood

Dramatic change is underway in Hollywood, the location. Promotion and improvement schemes have been endemic since the 1920s, and wholesale redevelopment scenarios have been floated since the 1950s. In the 1980s, competing proposals were offered, one emphasizing the inventory of sites along the Hollywood Boulevard (this urban theme-parking scheme was promoted by the Community Redevelopment Agency), the other proposing a shopping mall at the intersection of Hollywood and Vine (Ruddick 1996: 169–72). These projects both died, victim to the regional recession and public controversy over the use of city subsidies. By the 1990s, however, different versions of the mall and theme-park scheme had metamorphosed and fused into a new, larger plan.

The beginnings of the recent turnaround are often attributed to the Walt Disney Corporation, which spent $6 million on a refurbishment of the El Capitan Theater for a 1991 reopening. The theater, a flagship venue for Disney's family- and children-oriented films, is now one of the top per-screen grossers in the nation. In September 1996, the Los Angeles City Council approved the formation of a Hollywood Business Improvement District (BID). The forty-one members of the BID have agreed to a special assessment totaling $600,000 a year for street cleaning and armed security patrols (the BID is still one-tenth the size of its Times Square counterpart). The Warner Hollywood Theater was refurbished and reopened in late 1997 as a new home for live musicals, followed by the reopening of the Egyptian Theater in early 1998. The Egyptian Theater, renovated by the City of Los Angeles, has been leased to American Cinematheque, a nonprofit organization that features international films, classic and art-house films, and retrospectives on American filmmakers and actors, often in festival format.

The centerpiece of the redevelopment effort is the Trizec-Hahn Corporation's monstrous plan for a $388 million "urban destination entertainment" center that includes a twelve-screen multiplex theater operated by Mann Theaters Corporation, interactive entertainment, exhibition space, and a shopping mall. The site covers eight and a half acres behind the Grauman's Chinese Theater at the intersection of Hollywood Boulevard and Highland Avenue. To make the location a transportation nexus, the City of Los Angeles is also constructing a new subway station at the site.

The project will address what one Hollywood Chamber of Commerce representative has identified as the problem of the "fifteen-minute tourist" who arrives on Hollywood Boulevard primarily to see the Grauman's Chinese Theater courtyard, but after viewing the urban decline that besets the Boulevard, departs subsequently for more sanitized locations such as the Universal Studios theme park and its associated open-air shopping arcade (the CityWalk), or Disneyland. The redevelopment effort seeks to "create satisfaction and meet expectations" of the tourists.[10] Tourists have a vision of Hollywood as a Tinseltown populated by glamorous celebrities, and the various rituals and iconographic sites offer tourists the tantalizing possibility of proximity to the stars, which is a primary motivation for the journey to Hollywood.[11] Tourists are lured on board Hollywood sightseeing trolleys with the titillating, incessant reminder that "You May Even See A Star! You May Even See A Star! You May Even See A Star!"

The Trizec-Hahn project is the brainchild of David Malmuth, a developer whose reputation stems from his successful renovation of the New Amsterdam Theater in New York's Times Square for the Disney Corporation, a project widely regarded as a keystone of the recent revival of the district. Malmuth then unsuccessfully lobbied with Disney's head, Michael Eisner, to submit a bid for the Hollywood and Highland site. When Disney balked, Malmuth moved on to the San Diego-based Trizec-Hahn, and directed their winning proposal. Key to Malmuth's pitch to the Los Angeles Community Redevelopment Agency (CRA) were his deft negotiations to bring the Academy Awards back to Hollywood (scheduled for March 2002) from their present venue at the Dorothy Chandler Pavilion downtown (Goldin 1998). A 3,500-seat auditorium specially wired for live broadcast is being built at the back of the site. Visitors entering from Hollywood Boulevard through a giant curtained 70-foot-high portal will have to walk through a series of grand arches in the shopping arcade to the Academy Theater.

Considerable controversy swirled around the project from the inception of planning, especially given the planned $90 million subsidy the City of Los Angeles will incur through tax abatements and financial contributions toward construction of the Academy Theater and the giant underground parking garage. Small businesses and middle-class residents were concerned about the monstrous scale of the project, and implications such as noise, traffic congestion and parking problems, rising property taxes, and primary and secondary displacement of businesses and residents. Other critics drew attention to the host of social problems besetting the low-income immigrant population of Hollywood that could be addressed with equivalent public expenditure.

Hollywood has in fact emerged in the past three decades as a reception center for a cross-section of new immigrant flows to Los Angeles, who are drawn to the district's availability of affordable multi-unit rental housing and proximity to employment opportunities in the urban core and the affluent Westside. Many of these apartment complexes and manor houses (some grandiose but many cheaply constructed) were built initially to house the corps of aspiring actors, screenwriters, and other personnel that converged upon the district in the early days of the film industry. Today, the district houses populations of newly arrived immigrants of considerable race and ethnic diversity, including Russian Jews and Armenians, Central Americans (including Guatemalans and Salvadorans), and Asians (Filipino and Thai). Much of this new population is experiencing poverty and residential overcrowding.

There is indeed a glaring disjuncture between the boosterish fantasy of reduplicating a "boulevard of dreams" that recalls the glamorous Hollywood of yore when the majority of present-day Hollywood lives a separate reality. A linkage plan negotiated by City Councilor Jackie Goldberg offers public subsidy in return for a "living wage" agreement by Trizec-Hahn ($7.50/hr plus benefits) to be applied to salaries of security and service personnel hired at the finished site. A "first source" agreement stipulates that personnel hired will be primarily drawn from the Hollywood Community Redevelopment Agency zone, or from Los Angeles census tracts with high poverty levels. Hires from these two categories are expected to be 30 percent of all personnel. The language for this agreement was derived from a similar compact negotiated in Oakland. Goldberg is trying to pressure the CRA board to accept first source hiring agreements in all CRA project areas.[12]

Conclusion

The sociocultural school drew initial urban sociological attention to the defining salience of symbolic representations and culture in metropolitan life and geography decades before the recent "cultural turn" in urban studies. The sociocultural school, however, is overdue for reinvigoration through a strong dose of political economy, as we recognize that the production of urban symbolic sites is shot through with issues of political and capitalistic interest. The critical cultural school of the new urban sociology provides an instructive window on the historical emergence and current status of symbolic sites in Hollywood. A critical perspective on urban culture recognizes that many of the defining symbols, rituals, and meanings of urban places are produced through direct capitalistic intent. This perspective is revealing as we witness how the fabrication of thematic sites and symbolic references is currently proliferating as a strategy of postindustrial profit-making in American cities. The critical cultural school is sensitive to the issues raised by the mass culture critique of consumption-based capitalism, raising fundamental questions about the nature of aesthetics, the prospects for artistic freedom and public discourse, and issues of power and control, as our cultural production systems grow increasingly massified (Zukin 1995: 1–47; Gottdiener 1997: 143–59).

As the industrial machinery of Hollywood recomposes and horizontally integrates into the growing repertoire of culture industries in the new global economy, the mass culture critique has acquired revived relevance. As the machinery of mass culture attains a truly global reach, the production studios of Hollywood are increasingly just another link in the programming and marketing portfolios of the diversified media and entertainment conglomerates. A similar trend is apparent in the original location of Hollywood itself, where media interests are reclaiming territory through redevelopmental projects with fused characteristics of theater, theme park, and shopping mall. The linkage agreement negotiated by representatives of City Councilor Jackie Goldberg's office addresses the labor but not the housing needs of the poor and immigrant population that proliferates in the district surrounding the Hollywood redevelopment district. Like a blockbuster urban "space invader," the Trizec-Hahn mega-project will revivify the bright-light district and gentrify surrounding neighborhoods, displacing many local businesses, residents, and operations associated with alternative lifestyle activities.

Larger social justice issues absorb the industry side, the dream factory, which has recently been beset by labor disputes. The artistic, directorial, and studio production personnel of Hollywood seek just compensation from the media and advertising companies through strikes, pickets, and political lobbying. Related labor issues include runaway production, race and ethnic diversity in staffing as well as programming, and age discrimination in the media and advertising industries. This study of Hollywood as factory town as well as boulevard suggests that social justice issues resound across both economy and territory, with the "cultural turn" in urban studies and the new economy of American cities.

Notes

1 What Hollywood is not is a Tonniesian *Gemeinschaft* community, a network of primary affiliations, obligations, or bonds.

2 Dorothy Parker once quipped (in a coy reference to the general lack of political activity) that the only "ism" that Hollywood embraces is plagiarism (Kotkin 1996).

3 Gabler psychoanalytically interprets their aim as a kind of "ruthless" assimilation which involved the "patricide" of their paternal endowment of Eastern European accent, custom, language, and religion (1988: 4). A similar thesis has been promoted by Michael Rogin (1996), who centrally situates the first feature-length sound film, *The Jazz Singer* (1927), in his analysis. This film features Al Jolson (born Jakie Rabinowitz) as an aspiring entertainer who rejects parental expectations to become a synagogue cantor, in favor of life on the stage as a blackface performer, for the love of a Gentile girlfriend and the promise of the modernity of American mass culture versus Old World traditionalism. David Roediger (1991) offers a more economic interpretation of blackface minstrelsy in the Reconstruction era, when Irish Americans sought both economic mobility and assimilation into "whiteness." The racial and ethnic perspective on Hollywood and American mass culture is an intriguing topic that easily deserves a separate essay for sufficient development.

4 Studio success in dominating industrial linkages from production forward to exhibition contrasted with a more tenuous system in finance and control. A dependence on East Coast financing meant that while production was based in Los Angeles, decisions on investment and financing were made in New York. Louis B. Mayer and Irving Thalberg (the tragic "prince" or "boy-wonder" of the studios) perfected the model at MGM whereby the producer shuttled regularly between the coasts in order to negotiate between finance and production, conception and execution. Fitzgerald's *The Last Tycoon* (in the uncompleted climax, which exists only in note form), whose protagonist Monroe Stahr is based on Irving Thalberg, has the producer's plane crash en route to New York, though Thalberg in reality died of a heart attack at the age of thirty-seven.

5 Twentieth Century-Fox, for instance, divested itself of back-lots on the land which is now called Century City on the Westside of Los Angeles, a highrise complex of offices and commercial and residential buildings.

6 See Lyn Lofland (1991) for a valuable review of the intellectual genealogy of socioculturalism or "interactionist urbanism" which argues for the central influence of Anselm Strauss. Aside from Lyn Lofland, David Hummon (1988) and David Maines and Jeffrey Bridger (1992) have made additional contributions to the development of an urban perspective on cultural life and collective representation.

7 Some say Grauman was inspired when actress Norma Talmadge accidentally stepped on fresh cement while visiting the theater. Another report is that Grauman himself slipped off a builder's plank into wet cement, and hit upon the idea. Mary Pickford's husband, Buddy Rogers, claimed that the concept arose when her pet dog walked over fresh cement (Gabler 1988: 102; Torrence 1979: 128).

8 The celebratory dropping of the ball in New York City's Times Square every New Year's Eve is an analogous mass spectacle which attracts the throngs to the crossroads of the world. This event was also a promotional gimmick, in this case for the *New York Times* newspaper, whose move to the location in the early 1900s gave the bright-light district its modern name.

9 Nathaniel West wrote the book during a sweltering summer at the Parva-Sed Apta, one of numerous shabby Hollywood boarding houses, suffering from gonorrhea and a recurring prostate problem. Born Nathan Weinstein, West was comrade to fellow screenwriters F. Scott Fitzgerald and Dashiell Hammett, and known for ribald nocturnal forays to brothels, cockfights, Filipino taxi-dance halls, and secret sorties with police-beat reporters to view the sites of obscene domestic murders. Like characters out of the paintings of the damned, the novel is populated with sycophants, pariahs, deceivers, and loiterers (Rolfe 1991: 100–8).

10 Expressed by Ron Merckling of the Hollywood Chamber of Commerce in an April 1999 interview.

11 Observed by Bill Welsh of the Hollywood Chamber of Commerce in an April 1999 interview.

12 Reported by Roxsana Tynan of the Office of City Councilor Jackie Goldberg in an April 1999 interview.

Bibliography

Alihan, M. 1938: *Social Ecology*. New York: Columbia University Press.

Barber, B. 1995: *Jihad vs. McWorld*. New York: Ballantine Books.

Barnet, R. 1994: *Global Dreams: Imperial Corporations and the New World Order*. New York: Simon and Schuster.

Baudrillard, J. 1988: *Selected Writings*. Ed. Mark Poster. Cambridge: Polity Press.

Benjamin, W. [1955] 1968: *Illuminations (Essays and Reflections)*. Ed. and Intro. H. Arendt. Trans. H. Zohn. New York: Schocken Books.

Clark, D. 1995: *Negotiating Hollywood: The Cultural Politics of Actors' Labor*. Minneapolis: University of Minnesota Press.

Davis, M. 1990: *City of Quartz: Excavating the Future in Los Angeles*. London: Verso.

—— 1998: *Ecology of Fear: Los Angeles and the Imagination of Disaster*. New York: Metropolitan Books.

Dear, M. J. et al. (eds.) 1996: *Rethinking Los Angeles*. Thousand Oaks, CA: Sage.

Debord, G. [1967] 1983: *The Society of the Spectacle*. Detroit: Black and Red.

Fine, R. 1993: *West of Eden: Writers in Hollywood, 1928–1940*. Washington, DC: Smithsonian Institution Press.

Firey, W. 1945: Sentiment and symbolism as ecological variables. *American Sociological Review* 10: 140–8.

Fitzgerald, F. S. [1941] 1993: *(The Love of) The Last Tycoon*. New York: Simon and Schuster.

Friedmann, J. and Wolff, G. 1982: World city formation: an agenda for research and action. *International Journal of Urban and Regional Research* 6 (3): 309–44.

Gabler, N. 1988: *An Empire of Their Own: How the Jews Invented Hollywood.* New York: Crown Publishers.
—— 1998: *Life the Movie: How Entertainment Conquered Reality.* New York: Alfred A. Knopf.
Goldin, G. 1998: Mall-ywood: can David Malmuth's "urban destination entertainment center" save the Boulevard? *L.A. Weekly* 21 (4): 26–42.
Gomery, D. 1992: *Shared Pleasures: A History of Movie Presentation in the United States.* Madison: University of Wisconsin Press.
Gottdiener, M. 1997: *The Theming of America: Dreams, Visions, and Commercial Spaces.* Boulder, CO: Westview.
—— and Feagin, J. R. 1988: The paradigm shift in urban sociology. *Urban Affairs Quarterly* 24 (2): 163–87.
Hall, Sir P. 1998: *Cities in Civilization.* New York: Pantheon Books.
Horkheimer, M. and Adorno, T. W. [1944] 1988: *The Dialectic of Enlightenment.* Trans. J. Cumming. New York: Continuum.
Hummon, D. 1988: Tourist worlds: tourist advertising, ritual and American culture. *Sociological Quarterly* 29: 279–302.
Keil, R. 1998. *Los Angeles: Globalization, Urbanization and Social Struggles.* Chichester: Wiley.
Kotkin, J. 1996: Mass media wars: L.A. versus N.Y.C. *American Enterprise* (March/April): 39–42.
Litman, B. R. 1998: *The Motion Picture Mega-Industry.* Boston: Allyn and Bacon.
Lofland, L. 1991: History, the city, and the interactionist: Anselm Strauss, city imagery, and urban sociology. *Symbolic Interaction* 14 (2): 205–23.
Logan, J. and Molotch, H. 1988: *Urban Fortunes: The Political Economy of Place.* Berkeley: University of California Press.
McWilliams, C. [1946] 1973: *Southern California: An Island on the Land.* Salt Lake City: Peregrine Smith Books.
Maines, D. and Bridger, J. 1992: Narratives, community and land use decisions. *Social Science Journal* 29 (4): 363–80.
Negus, K. 1997: The production of culture. In P. Du Gay (ed.), *Production of Culture/Cultures of Production.* London: Sage, 67–118.
Roediger, D. 1991: *The Wages of Whiteness: Race and the Making of the American Working Class.* London: Verso.
Rogin, M. 1996: *Blackface, White Noise: Jewish Immigrants in the Hollywood Melting Pot.* Berkeley: University of California Press.
Rolfe, L. 1991: *In Search of Literary L.A.* Los Angeles: California Classics Books.
Ruddick, S. M. 1996: *Young and Homeless in Hollywood: Mapping Social Identities.* New York: Routledge.
Sassen, S. 1991. *The Global City: New York, London, Tokyo.* Princeton, NJ: Princeton University Press.
Scott, A. J. and Soja, E. W. 1996. *The City: Los Angeles and Urban Theory at the End of the Twentieth Century.* Berkeley: University of California Press.
Schatz, T. 1983: *Old Hollywood/New Hollywood: Ritual, Art, and Industry.* Ann Arbor, MI: UMI Research Press.
Screen Actors' Guild 2000: U.S. runaway film and television production study report. http://www.sag.org/runaway/monitorreportrelease.

Sklair, L. 1991: *Sociology of the Global System*. Baltimore: Johns Hopkins University Press.
Sklar, R. 1994: *Movie-Made America: A Cultural History of American Movies*. New York: Random House.
Soja, E. W. 1996: *Thirdspace: Journeys to Los Angeles and Other Real-And-Imagined Places*. Cambridge, MA: Blackwell.
Sorkin, M. (ed.) 1992: *Variations on a Theme Park: The New American City and the End of Public Space*. New York: Hill and Wang.
Standard and Poor 2000: *Industry Surveys: Movies and Home Entertainment*. New York: McGraw-Hill.
Storper, M. 1989: The transition to flexible specialisation in the U.S. film industry: external economies, the division of labour, and the crossing of industrial divides. *Cambridge Journal of Economics* 13: 273–305.
Suttles, G. 1984: The cumulative texture of local urban culture. *American Journal of Sociology* 90: 283–304.
Torrence, B. T. 1979: *Hollywood: The First 100 Years*. Hollywood, CA: Hollywood Chamber of Commerce.
Wasko, J. 1994: *Hollywood in the Information Age*. Austin: University of Texas Press.
West, N. [1939] 1962: *The Day of the Locust*. New York: New Directions Books.
Wohl, R. R. and Strauss, A. L. 1958: Symbolic representation and the urban milieu. *American Journal of Sociology* 63: 523–32.
Zukin, S. 1980: A decade of the new urban sociology. *Theory, Culture and Society* 5: 431–46.
—— 1995: *The Cultures of Cities*. Cambridge, MA: Blackwell.

Index